ACTIVE MEASURES

ACTIVE MEASURES

The Secret History
of Disinformation
and Political Warfare

THOMAS RID

FARRAR, STRAUS AND GIROUX | NEW YORK

Farrar, Straus and Giroux
120 Broadway, New York 10271

Copyright © 2020 by Thomas Rid
Printed in the United States of America
First edition, 2020

Library of Congress Cataloging-in-Publication Data
ISBN: 978-0-374-28726-9

Designed by Richard Oriolo

Our books may be purchased in bulk for promotional, educational, or business
use. Please contact your local bookseller or the Macmillan Corporate and
Premium Sales Department at 1-800-221-7945, extension 5442, or by e-mail
at MacmillanSpecialMarkets@macmillan.com.

www.fsgbooks.com
www.twitter.com/fsgbooks · www.facebook.com/fsgbooks

10 9 8 7 6 5 4 3 2 1

CONTENTS

What Is Disinformation?   3

1921–1945: Deceive

1. The Trust   17
2. Japan's *Mein Kampf*   33
3. The Whalen Forgeries   47

1945–1960: Forge

4. American Disinformation   61
5. The Kampfgruppe   74
6. LC–Cassock, Inc.   85
7. Faking Back   101
8. Kampfverband   116
9. Red Swastikas   123
10. Racial Engineering   134

1961–1975: Compete

11. *Dezinformatsiya* Rising   145
12. The Book War   167
13. Operations Plan 10-1   180
14. The X   194
15. The Fifth Estate   215

1975–1989: Escalate

16. Field Manual 30-31B   231
17. Service A   243
18. The Neutron Bomb   255
19. Peacewar   263
20. Nuclear Freeze   278
21. Nuclear Winter   288
22. AIDS Made in the USA   298
23. The Philosophy of "AM"   312

1990–2014: Hack

24. Digital Measures   329
25. First Digital Leaks   336
26. Anonymous   351
27. Sofacy   360

2015–2017: Leak

28. Election Leaks   377
29. Guccifer Two   387
30. Trolled   397
31. The Shadow Brokers   410

A Century of Disinformation   423

NOTES   437
ACKNOWLEDGMENTS   493
INDEX   495

ACTIVE MEASURES

What Is Disinformation?

N MARCH 2017, THE U.S. SENATE SELECT COMMITTEE ON INTEL-
ligence invited me to testify in the first open expert hearing on
Russian interference in the 2016 presidential election. Committee staffers from both parties wanted me to help present to the American
public the available forensic evidence that implicated Russia, evidence that
at the time was still hotly contested among the wider public, and that, of
course, the Russian government denied—as did the president of the United
States. The situation was unprecedented.

The other two witnesses were Keith Alexander, former head of the National Security Agency, and Kevin Mandia, CEO of FireEye, a leading information security firm. Just before the hearing began, a staffer brought us
from the greenroom to the witness table. Everybody else was seated already.
As we walked in, I looked at the row of senators in front of us. Most of the

committee members were present. Their faces looked familiar. The room was crowded; press photographers, lying on the floor with cameras slung around their necks, were soon ushered out. I envied them for a moment.

The senators sat behind a giant semicircular, heavy wooden table that seemed to encroach on the witnesses. Early on in the hearing, soon after our opening statements, Senator Mark Warner, D-VA, asked if we had "any doubt" that Russian agents had perpetrated the hack of the Democratic National Committee and the disinformation operation that took place during the campaign. He wanted a short answer. I considered my response as Mandia and Alexander spoke. The digital forensic evidence that I had seen was strong: a range of artifacts—not unlike fingerprints, bullet casings, and license plates of getaway cars at a crime scene—clearly pointed to Russian military intelligence. But despite the evidence, the offense seemed abstract, hypothetical, unreal. Then I thought of a conversation I'd had just two days earlier with an old Soviet bloc intelligence officer and disinformation engineer.

On the way to the Senate hearing in Washington, I had stopped in Boston. It was biting cold. I drove out to Rockport, a small town at the tip of Cape Ann, surrounded on three sides by the Atlantic Ocean. Ladislav Bittman had agreed to meet me at his studio there. Bittman, who died a year and a half later, was perhaps the single most important Soviet bloc defector to ever testify and write about the intelligence discipline of disinformation. A former head of the KGB's mighty disinformation unit once praised Bittman's 1972 book, *The Deception Game*, as one of the two best books on the subject.[1] Bittman had defected in 1968, before an experimental prototype of the internet was even invented, and seven years before I was born.

We spoke the entire afternoon in a calm, wood-paneled room. Bittman was bald, his face wizened, with youthful eyes. He listened carefully, paused to think, and spoke with deliberation. Indeed, Bittman's memory and his attention to detail were intimidating, and he would not answer my questions if he didn't know how. I was impressed. Bittman explained how entire bureaucracies were created in the Eastern bloc in the 1960s for the purpose of bending the facts, and how these projects were proposed, authorized, and evaluated. He outlined how he learned to mix accurate details with forged ones; that for disinformation to be successful, it must "at least partially respond to reality, or at least accepted views." He explained how leaking stolen documents had been "a standard procedure in disinformation activities" for more than half a century. He estimated that individual disinformation operations during the Cold War numbered more than ten thousand. And he brought the examples to life with stories: of a make-believe German neo-Fascist group with an oak-leaf logo, of forged Nazi documents hidden in a forest lake in Bohemia, of U.S. nuclear war plans leaked again and again all over Europe, of a Soviet master-forger flustered in a strip club in Prague. This careful and thoughtful old man taught me more about the subject of my forthcoming testimony than any technical intelligence report I had read or any digital forensic connections I could make. He made it real.[2]

IN EARLY 2016, I WAS IN THE MIDDLE OF AN EXTENSIVE TWO-YEAR TECHNI-cal investigation into MOONLIGHT MAZE, the first known state-on-state digital espionage campaign in history, a prolific, high-end Russian spying spree that began in the mid-1990s and never stopped. With luck and persistence, I was able to track down one of the actual servers used by Russian operators in 1998 to engineer a sprawling breach of hundreds of U.S. military and government networks. A retired systems administrator had kept the server, an old, clunky machine, under his desk at his home outside London, complete with original log files and Russian hacking tools. It was like finding a time machine. The digital artifacts from London told the story of a vast hacking campaign that could even be forensically linked to recent espionage activity. Our investigation showed the persistence and skill that large spy agencies bring to the table when they hack computer networks. Those big spy agencies that had invested in expensive technical signals intelligence collection during the Cold War seemed to be especially good at hacking—and good at watching others hack.

Then, on June 14, news of the Democratic National Committee computer network break-in hit. Among the small community of people who research high-end computer network breaches, there was little doubt, from that day forward, that we were looking at another Russian intelligence operation. The digital artifacts supported no other conclusion.

The following day, the leaking started, and the lying. A hastily created online account suddenly popped up, claiming that a "lone hacker" had stolen files from Democrats in Washington. The account published a few pilfered files as proof—indeed offering evidence that the leak was real, but not that the leaker was who they claimed. It was clear then, on June 16, that some of the world's most experienced and aggressive intelligence operators were escalating a covert attack on the United States.[3]

Over the next days and weeks, I watched the election interference as it unfolded, carefully collecting some of the digital breadcrumbs that Russian operators were leaving behind. In early July, I decided to write up a first draft of this remarkable story. I published two investigative pieces on the ongoing disinformation campaign, the first in late July 2016, on the day of the Democratic Convention, and the second three weeks before the general election. But I noticed that I was not adequately prepared for the task. I had a good grasp of digital espionage and its history, but not of disinformation—what intelligence professionals used to call "active measures."

WE LIVE IN AN AGE OF DISINFORMATION. PRIVATE CORRESPONDENCE GETS stolen and leaked to the press for malicious effect; political passions are inflamed online in order to drive wedges into existing cracks in liberal democracies; perpetrators sow doubt and deny malicious activity in public, while covertly ramping it up behind the scenes.

This modern era of disinformation began in the early 1920s, and the art and science of what the CIA once called "political warfare" grew and changed in four big waves, each a generation apart. As the theory and practice of disinformation evolved, so did the terms that described what was going on. The first wave of disinformation started forming in the interwar years, during the Great Depression, in an era of journalism transformed by the radio, newly cutthroat and fast-paced. Influence operations in the 1920s and early 1930s were innovative, conspiratorial, twisted—and nameless for now. The forgeries of this period were often a weapon of the weak, and some targeted both the Soviet Union and the United States at the same time.

In the second wave, after World War II, disinformation became professionalized, with American intelligence agencies leading the way in aggressive and unscrupulous operations, compounded by the lingering violence of global war. The CIA now called its blend of covert truthful revelations, forgeries, and outright subversion of the adversary "political warfare," a sprawling and ambitious term. Political warfare was deadliest in 1950s Berlin, just before the Wall went up. The Eastern bloc, by contrast, then preferred the more honest and precise name "disinformation." Whatever the phrase, the goals were the same: to exacerbate existing tensions and contradictions within the adversary's body politic, by leveraging facts, fakes, and ideally a disorienting mix of both.

The third wave arrived in the late 1970s, when disinformation became well-resourced and fine-tuned, honed and managed, lifted to an operational science of global proportions, administered by a vast, well-oiled bureaucratic machine. By then the term "active measures" was widely used in the Soviet intelligence establishment and among its Eastern bloc satellite agencies. The name stuck, and indeed was quite elegant, because it helped capture a larger conceptual and historical trend at play: after 1960, the measures were becoming progressively more active, with the East gaining an upper hand. Then the Soviet Union collapsed, and any remaining sense of ideological superiority retreated.

The fourth wave of disinformation slowly built and crested in the mid-2010s, with disinformation reborn and reshaped by new technologies and internet culture. The old art of slow-moving, highly skilled, close-range, labor-intensive psychological influence had turned high-tempo, low-skilled, remote, and disjointed. Active measures were now not only more active than ever before but less measured—so much so that the term itself became contested and unsettled.

Surviving our age of organized, professional deception requires a return to history. The stakes are enormous—for disinformation corrodes the foundation of liberal democracy, our ability to assess facts on their merits and to self-correct accordingly. That risk is old. Yet the crush of a relentless news cycle means that everything feels new, breaking, headlong; established orders appear fleeting, with views veering to the fringes, and new fissures cracking open. The crisis of our Western democracies has too often been referred to as unprecedented. This sense of novelty is a fallacy, a trap. The election interference of 2016 and the renewed crisis of the factual has a century-long prelude, and yet, unprepared and unaware, most Democrats before the 2016 election and most Republicans after the election *underestimated* and played down the risks of disinformation. Conversely, many close observers of the highly contested Special Counsel investigation of 2017 to 2019, still not fully risk-aware after the 2016 election, ended up *overestimating* and playing up the effects of an adversarial campaign that was, although poorly executed, designed to be overestimated. The best, and indeed the only, potent antidote against such pitfalls is studying the rich history of political warfare. Only by taking careful and accurate measure of the fantastic past of disinformation can we comprehend the present, and fix the future. A historical inquiry into the rise of active measures reveals a quintessentially modern story, one closely tied to the major cultural and technical trends of the past hundred years.

The twentieth century was a vast test lab of disinformation and professional, organized lying, especially during the interwar years and the Cold War, and yet Western scholars and the wider public have largely chosen to ignore the history of organized deception. Historians usually prefer telling true stories to retelling fakes. There are exceptions; several episodes have recently been well documented, for example, the tale of the Zinoviev letter,[4] a 1924 forgery that turned into a major British political scandal, or the persistent 1980s hoax that AIDS was a weapon developed by the United States Army.[5] The CIA's less aggressive cultural covert action campaign in the early Cold War is well explored, most famously the Congress of Cultural Freedom.[6] Military deception at war is also well researched.[7] But most twentieth-century disinformation operations have simply been forgotten, including some of the most extensive and successful. Twenty-first-century liberal democracies can no longer afford to neglect this past. Ignoring the rich and disturbing lessons of industrial-scale Cold War disinformation campaigns risks repeating mid-century errors that are already weakening liberal democracy in the digital age.

Recognizing an active measure can be difficult. Disinformation, when done well, is hard to spot, especially when it first becomes public. It will therefore be helpful to clarify what an active measure is, and what it is not.

First, and most important, active measures are not spontaneous lies by politicians, but the methodical output of large bureaucracies. Disinformation was, and in many ways continues to be, the domain of intelligence agencies—professionally run, continually improved, and usually employed against foreign adversaries. Second, all active measures contain an element of disinformation: content may be forged, sourcing doctored, the method of acquisition covert; influence agents and cutouts may pretend to be something they are not, and online accounts involved in the surfacing or amplification of an operation may be inauthentic. Third, an active measure is always directed toward an end, usually to weaken the targeted adversary. The means may vary: creating divisions between allied nations, driving wedges between ethnic groups, creating friction between individuals in a group or party, undermining the trust specific groups in a society have in its institutions. Active measures may also be directed toward a single, narrow objective—to erode the legitimacy of a government, for example, or the reputation of an individual, or the deployment of a weapon system. Sometimes projects are designed to facilitate a specific political decision.

These features, easily misunderstood, give rise to three widespread misconceptions about the nature of disinformation, which is generally seen as sophisticated, based on propagating false news, and occurring in the public sphere.

Almost all disinformation operations are, in fact, imperfect by design, run not by perfectionists but pragmatists. Active measures are contradictory: they are covert operations designed to achieve overt influence, secret devices deployed in public debates, carefully hidden yet visible in plain sight. This inherent tension has operational consequences. Over the decades, dirty tricksters in various intelligence agencies, Western and Eastern, have discovered that tight operational security is neither cost-effective nor desirable, for both partial and delayed exposure may actually serve the interests of the attacker. It is not an accident that disinformation played out in shifting shadows, not in pitch-black darkness. Often, at least since the 1950s, the covert aspect of a given disinformation campaign was only a veneer, imperfect and temporary by design.

Also, disinformation is not simply fake information—at least, not necessarily. Some of the most vicious and effective active measures in the history of covert action were designed to deliver entirely accurate information. In 1960, for example, Soviet intelligence produced a pamphlet that recounted actual lynchings and other gruesome acts of racial violence against African Americans from Tennessee to Texas; the KGB then distributed English and French versions of the pamphlet in more than a dozen African countries, under the cover of a fake African American activist group. In more recent memory, intelligence agencies have passed on genuine, hacked-and-leaked data to WikiLeaks. Even if no forgery was produced and no content altered, larger truths were often flanked by little lies, whether about the provenance of the data or the identity of the publisher.

Finally, disinformation operations do not always take place in public. Some highly successful active measures reached their target audience without ever being publicized in a newspaper, radio broadcast, or pamphlet, and sometimes they were more effective for that very reason. The KGB called such operations "silent" measures.[8] One of the most spectacular operations of all time was a silent measure—the Stasi-engineered outcome of West Germany's first parliamentary vote of no confidence in April 1972, which kept the chancellor in power against the odds. Private victims will find it harder to dismiss a rumor or a forgery that is never subjected to public scrutiny and criticism.

This book will extract three main arguments from the history of disinformation over the past century. The first argument is conceptual. At-scale disinformation campaigns are attacks against a liberal epistemic order, or a political system that places its trust in essential custodians of factual authority. These institutions—law enforcement and the criminal justice system, public administration, empirical science, investigative journalism, democratically controlled intelligence agencies—prize facts over feelings, evidence over emotion, observations over opinion. They embody an open epistemic order, which enables an open and liberal political order; one cannot exist without the other. A peaceful transition of power after a contested vote, for example, requires trusting an election's setup, infrastructure, counting procedures, and press coverage, all in a moment of high uncertainty and political fragility. Active measures erode that order. But they do so slowly, subtly, like ice melting. This slowness makes disinformation that much more insidious, because when the authority of evidence is eroded, emotions fill the gap. As distinguishing between facts and non-facts becomes harder, distinguishing between friend and foe becomes easier. The line between fact and lie is a continuation of the line between peace and war, domestically as well as internationally.

Disinformation operations, in essence, erode the very foundation of open societies—not only for the victim but also for the perpetrator. When vast, secretive bureaucracies engage in systematic deception, at large scale and over a long time, they will optimize their own organizational culture for this purpose, and undermine the legitimacy of public administration at home. A society's approach to active measures is a litmus test for its republican institutions. For liberal democracies in particular, disinformation represents a double threat: being at the receiving end of active measures will undermine democratic institutions—and giving in to the temptation to design and deploy them will have the same result. It is impossible to excel at disinformation and at democracy at the same time. The stronger and the more robust a democratic body politic, the more resistant to disinformation it will be—and the more reluctant to deploy and optimize disinformation. Weakened democracies, in turn, succumb more easily to the temptations of active measures.

The second argument is historical. When it comes to covert active measures, moral and operational equivalence between West and East, between democracies and non-democracies, only existed for a single decade after

World War II. The CIA's skill at political warfare was significant in the 1950s, especially in Berlin, and was, in practice, on par with, or even more effective than, Soviet *dezinformatsiya*. Western intelligence agencies shunned few risks, using cutouts, front organizations, leaks, and forgeries, as well as a shrewd balance of denials and semi-denials. But just when the CIA had honed its political warfare skills in Berlin, U.S. intelligence retreated from the disinformation battlefield almost completely. When the Berlin Wall went up in 1961, it did more than block physical movement between the West and the East; it also came to symbolize an ever-sharper division: the West deescalated as the East escalated.

The third argument of this book is that the digital revolution fundamentally altered the disinformation game. The internet didn't just make active measures cheaper, quicker, more reactive, and less risky; it also, to put it simply, made active measures more active and less measured. The development of new forms of activism, and new forms of covert action, have made operations more scalable, harder to control, and harder to assess once they have been launched.

The rise of networked computers gave rise to a wider culture of hacking and leaking. A diffuse group of pro-technology, anti-intelligence activists emerged in the late 1970s, gathered momentum in the late 1990s, and would unleash torrents of raw political energy another decade after that. Early hippie activists tapped into the power of First Amendment activism in the United States, later incorporating strains of techno-utopianism, hacker subculture, cyberpunk, anarchism with a libertarian bent, anti-authoritarianism, and an obsession with encryption and anonymity. Many early crypto and anonymity activists became known as the "cypherpunks," after a famous email list by that name. The second issue of *Wired* magazine, issued in May 1993, featured three of these "crypto rebels," faces covered by white plastic masks with keys printed on their foreheads, bodies wrapped in the American flag. Ten years later, the Anonymous movement, which embodied many of the same rebellious values, would embrace nearly identical Guy Fawkes masks as its trademark. Another decade after that, Edward Snowden, the iconic intelligence leaker who likewise combined a belief in the power of encryption with far-out libertarian ideas, also appeared wrapped in the American flag on the cover of *Wired*. The movement's breathless optimism expressed itself in slogans and themes: that information wanted to be free, sources open, anonymity protected, and personal secrets encrypted by default, yet government secrets could be exposed by whistle-blowers, preferably anonymously, on peer-to-peer networks. Much of this idealism was and is positive, and in many ways, activist projects have helped strengthen information security and internet freedom.

And yet, at the fringes, this emerging subculture embraced a combination of radical transparency and radical anonymity, along with hacking-and-leaking, stealing-and-publishing—and thus created what had existed only temporarily before: the perfect cover for active measures, and not only thanks to the white noise of anonymous publication activity, from torrents to Twitter. What made the cover perfect was the veritable celebrity culture that surrounded first Julian Assange, then Chelsea Manning, and finally Edward Snowden. These self-described whistle-blowers were widely idolized as heroes, seen by their supporters as unflinching and principled in the face of oppression.

The situation was a dream come true for old-school disinformation professionals. The internet first disempowered journalism and then empowered activism. By the early 2010s, it was easier than ever to test, amplify, sustain, and deny active measures, and harder than ever to counter or suppress rumors, lies, and conspiracy theories. The internet has made open societies more open to disinformation, and foreign spies started to disguise themselves in Guy Fawkes masks. Activist internet culture shrouded what used to be a shadowy intelligence tactic in a new, star-spangled cloak of crypto-libertarianism.

The other feature that made active measures more active was a major operational innovation: by the 2010s, active measures seamlessly overlapped with covert action. Networked computers, their vulnerabilities baked in, meant that information no longer targeted only minds; it could also now target machines. It had long been possible to convince, deceive, or even buy publishers, but now their platforms could also be hacked, altered, or defaced. Machines, moreover, put up less resistance than human minds did. Active measures could even be technically amplified, by using semi-automated accounts and fully automated bots, for example. The machines created the online equivalent of the laugh track in a studio-taped TV show. Moreover, computer networks could now be breached in order to achieve effects that once required a human hand, such as manipulating or incapacitating infrastructure, logistics, or supply chains. Automation and hacking, in short, became natural extensions of the active measures playbook: exercised remotely, denied at little cost, and falling short of physical violence. The line between subversion and sabotage became blurrier, operations more easily scalable, and harder to deter. The internet, with its very own culture, created a vast new human-machine interface that appeared to be optimized for mass disinformation.

Yet it wasn't all sunshine and rainbows for aggressive intelligence agencies. Yes, manipulating malcontents and malware made measures more active. But the internet exacerbated an old problem for spies. Like all bureaucracies, secret organizations crave metrics and data, to demonstrate how well they perform in the never-ending governmental competition for resources. Naturally this show-me-the-data dynamic has long applied to disinformation as well. "The desire for speedy, easily visible, and audible success sometimes makes the intelligence service the victim of its own propaganda and disinformation," observed Bittman, the Czech defector, in the early 1970s.[9] Forty years later, by the 2010s, data had become big, engagement numbers soared, and the hunger for metrics was more ferocious than ever. Yet disinformation, by design, still resisted metrics. If more data generally meant more reliable metrics, then the internet had the reverse effect on the old art of political warfare: the metrics produced by digital disinformation were, to a significant degree, themselves disinformation. The internet didn't bring more precision to the art and science of disinformation—it made active measures less measured: harder to control, harder to steer, and harder to isolate engineered effects. Disinformation, as a result, became even more dangerous.

1921–1945: Deceive

The Trust

N MARCH 1988, ROBERT GATES, THE DEPUTY DIRECTOR OF THE
Central Intelligence Agency, was scheduled to have breakfast
with a writer from the Hoover Institution, Stanford University's
conservative research center. The writer, a friend of Gates's, had recently
spotted a curious footnote deep in the thick book he was reading. The footnote mentioned an obscure, never-published CIA study on "The Trust," a
mysterious Soviet organization that existed, or was believed to exist, for a
period of five years in the 1920s. Walter Pforzheimer, the curator and pioneer
of the Agency's Historical Intelligence Collection, had assigned the study
to two seasoned CIA operatives specialized in Russian intelligence; it was
completed in March 1967. The CIA's history staff prepared a careful letter in
response. The Trust, Gates told his friend from Stanford, had served "a mildly

Feliks Dzherzinski,
legendary Soviet
spymaster, founder
and head of the Cheka,
then of the GPU and
OGPU; pictured here
in September 1918
(Ria Novosti)

useful role in educating a number of Agency employees on certain Soviet intelligence techniques." This was a wily understatement.

Operation Trust is one of the most dramatic and daring conspiracies in intelligence history. The story involves revolutionary Communist spies, exiled royal insurgents, love, extortion, kidnappings, mock and real executions, a fake book, and most of Europe's intelligence agencies extant in the interwar period. Most significantly, the campaign, which ran over half a dozen years, triggered the creation of the first dedicated disinformation unit. It was so successful that even its beginning and end remain hotly contested.

The most authoritative and detailed source on the Trust is the superb analysis released in 1988 by the CIA, which did not exist in the 1920s and therefore had no axe to grind. In 1997, Russia's foreign intelligence agency—the direct descendant of the Cheka masterminds of *Operatsiya Trest*—published its own, somewhat less detailed, less balanced account of the campaign, reportedly derived from thirty-eight volumes of files in the Russian state security archives.[1] The stories told by the two adversarial spy agencies overlap in many important details.

By 1921, the civil war had triggered a mass emigration of conservative and anti-Communist Russians. More than one million people left the motherland behind and took with them a romanticized view of life in Imperial Russia. The "Whites," as they were often called, retained many of their leaders, their military and intelligence organizations, and even some of their weapons, along with, most important, a counterrevolutionary vision for Russia's future. Many of the most aggressive émigré groups wanted to reinstate the monarchy. The new Soviet government estimated that the Russian émigrés scattered across Europe and Asia numbered one and a half to two million. The émigrés published their own periodicals, of which there were more than a dozen worldwide by 1921 (and more than forty over the course of the 1920s, in Paris alone).[2]

In July 1921, Lenin warned the Third Congress of the Communist International that the émigrés were publishing their own newspapers, were well organized and plotting, and that "the enemy [had] learned." Lenin warned his fellow Communists that they would "make every possible attempt and skilfully take advantage of every opportunity to attack Soviet Russia in one way or another, and to destroy it."[3] In reality, life in exile was harsh. The monarchist émigrés were in a dire position, living in constant fear of betrayal, arrest, execution, and poverty. Even the grand duke of Russia, heir to the throne, was able to pay the rent on a small castle outside Paris only by removing and selling individual stones from his wife's diamond necklace.[4]

Heading the legendary Bolshevik secret police under Lenin was an iconic personality, "Iron" Feliks Edmundovich Dzerzhinsky. Dzerzhinsky's organization became known as the Cheka. Later, throughout the Cold War, intelligence officers across the entire Eastern bloc would proudly refer to their "Chekist" heritage. Dzerzhinsky, tall and rail thin, was a pugnacious revolutionary. He had spent years in tsarist prisons, where guards had beaten him so brutally that he later hid his permanently disfigured jaw under a bushy goatee. From his office in the red-brick Lubyanka, the iconic Cheka headquarters, the irritable Dzerzhinsky ruthlessly crushed counterrevolutionary activities within Russia and abroad.

Dzerzhinsky committed his best officers to subverting the White political leaders. Artur Artuzov, head of the counterintelligence department, was in charge of the offensive. A trained metal engineer and the son of an Italian-Swiss cheesemaker, Artuzov was a hardened, burly Bolshevik with an acute ability to sense the weaknesses of his enemies.[5]

Finding an opening wasn't easy, but in November 1921, Bolshevik spies intercepted a fateful letter in Estonia (not yet under Soviet control). The letter, sent from a would-be insurgent officer in Tallinn to the Supreme Monarchist Council in Berlin, contained a report of a conspiratorial meeting held in the Estonian capital, where local Russian monarchists had met with a Moscow-based activist. Alexander Yakushev, forty-five years old, was the son of a professor and looked like one himself, with a monocle over his nose, a receding hairline, and a small goatee.[6] He was an aristocrat, a famously efficient administrator, charming, and a ladies' man—indeed, the CIA noted that his trip from Moscow to Tallinn was related to a love affair. Yakushev had worked as a civil servant for the tsar, and carried on under the Bolsheviks as a senior official responsible for waterways in the Ministry of Railroads. Now Artuzov held a letter in which the White insurgents praised Yakushev. "He thinks just as we do," the insurgents wrote. "He is what we need. He asserts that his opinion is the opinion of the best people in Russia."[7]

The missive went on to recount Yakushev's view about the coming counterrevolution: "The government will be created *not from émigrés* but from those *who are in Russia*," it said, with emphasis. Yakushev had also told the Whites in Estonia that active counterrevolutionary organizations already existed in Russia, and that they had even infiltrated the Bolshevik administration. The aristocratic Yakushev then dismissed the significance of the émigrés in Europe, saying, as the letter quotes him: "In the future they are welcome in Russia, but to import a government from abroad is out of the question. The émigrés do not know Russia. They need to come and stay and adapt to the new conditions."[8]

He went on: "The monarchical organization in Moscow will give directives to organizations in the West, not vice versa." He even threw in the thought of a "Soviet" monarchy.

The intercepted letter inspired Artuzov. The remarkable letter exposed "contradictions," to use the language later favored by active measures specialists, within the monarchist cause. He explained to Dzerzhinsky that the White Russian activists themselves had practically provided a game plan to the Cheka of how to subvert the White Russian movement, and it was signaled by the underscored line: "The government will be created *not from émigrés* but from those *who are in Russia*." Artuzov then drew Dzerzhinsky's attention to the second part of the letter, in which the Estonia-based writer praised Yakushev's intellect, connections, and supreme insight. With all his credibility and charm, Yakushev would be the perfect asset.

"Yakushev is a very interesting person," said Dzerzhinsky, "we need to learn as much as possible about him, how deep his monarchical convictions are." Dzerzhinsky had a personal connection to Yakushev; they had worked together on a transportation issue in 1920, the previous year, and Dzerzhinsky thought it might be possible to convince him to switch sides. He suggested setting up a faux-monarchist organization to engage in "operational play"[9] with the Supreme Monarchist Council in Berlin and other émigré organizations. But first, the Cheka needed to arrest Yakushev, turn him, and use his credibility to lure the White Russian insurgents either into complacency abroad or into returning to Russia, where they could be apprehended.

Artuzov quickly came up with a cunning plan for interrogating Yakushev. (In their report, CIA analysts appeared to be very impressed with this plan, and discussed it at length.) Soon, the unsuspecting Yakushev returned to Moscow, where the Cheka had arranged for a temporary duty assignment in Irkutsk, Siberia. The train ride alone, one way, would take nearly a week. But the trip was only a cover.[10] As Yakushev made his way to the train station to depart for Irkutsk, secret police seized him and took him to the Lubyanka. He was told to get ready for extensive questioning and not to worry about his family, who would be told by telegram that he had contracted typhoid in Siberia and would have to wait it out there.

Artuzov personally led the interrogation. For the first three weeks,

Artuzov questioned Yakushev about his career under the tsar. Artuzov cleverly increased the pressure through this line of questioning, all the while keeping Yakushev from learning what it all was about. The interrogation soon turned to Yakushev's extramarital affairs and his questionable morals. Artuzov then interrupted the questioning for a week, to let Yakushev simmer in doubt and regret. In the next session, Artuzov wanted to startle Yakushev. The Cheka knew, he told his victim, that Yakushev had met with an infamous British spy, Sydney Reilly, back in 1917. The Cheka knew that he had discussed the future of Russia with Reilly, and that Yakushev had signaled his willingness to sell Russia to the British. Artuzov even revealed that the conspiratorial meeting took place in the dressing room of a female dancer. What kind of patriotism was this?, Artuzov asked. How could such betrayal of the motherland be defended?

Artuzov left Yakushev alone for another week, to simmer this time in mortal fear. When he returned, Yakushev was led into a more pleasant, well-furnished office. Artuzov asked a few easy, casual questions to set the worn-out Yakushev a little more at ease. Then came the coup de grâce: What did Yakushev discuss with the White émigré in Tallinn? Yakushev denied having visited anyone in Tallinn. The moment was tense. Artuzov then opened the door and into the room came one of Yakushev's lovers, the cousin of the monarchist he had met in Estonia, who confirmed that he had made the trip. After she was led out of the room, Artuzov handed him the original intercepted letter describing, in detail, the conspiratorial conversations he had held in Tallinn. At this point, Yakushev fainted.

Pulling himself together, Yakushev realized that execution could come at any minute. He began to write down everything he knew about the monarchist resistance. After a few days, he was again called to see Artuzov, his interrogator. Artuzov told him that the Cheka had carefully considered his case, and had come to the conclusion that he was not a complete traitor; after all, he had counseled the émigrés against using terrorism. He was sent home and told to resume his work—but first, in his final meeting with Artuzov and Dzerzhinsky, the spy chief made him an offer. The secret police would support the creation of a false Moscow-based monarchist organization, and

Yakushev would be its leader. "You will have deputies for military and political units, you will be headquartered in St. Petersburg and Moscow, and you will travel to Europe to meet 'like-minded people,'" said Dzerzhinsky.[11] He assumed that Yakushev knew what was going on, but nevertheless spelled it out for him, for the idea was so daring: "All this will be a game, our game with your participation, under the code-name 'Trust.'"[12]

Dzerzhinsky now began to treat Yakushev with respect. "I don't expect from you, Alexander Alexandrovich, an immediate answer," he said, using an endearing yet formal way of address common in Russia. "Go home and consider this carefully."

Soon, with Yakushev's cooperation, the Cheka set up its faux-monarchist organization, with 400 nonexistent members. It was officially called the Monarchist Organization of Central Russia, or MOTsR, in its Russian acronym. The historical record is inconclusive on the question of whether the core of MOTsR already existed in Moscow (as the CIA study assumed),[13] or if Dzerzhinsky created the fake organization from scratch (as the SVR, Russia's post–Cold War foreign intelligence agency, claimed in an official history).[14] Either way, the Cheka now worked to build the mirage of a monarchist insurgency in the USSR. Dzerzhinsky's operational play was on.

On November 14, 1922, Yakushev departed for his first trip to Berlin in his new role, aiming to make contact with the Supreme Monarchist Council. Per his instructions, Yakushev was to make clear to the Russian monarchists in Berlin that he considered the Paris-based grand duke, Nikolai Nikolayevich, grandson of Tsar Nikolai I, the only acceptable leader of post-Soviet Russia. The new monarchy was supposed to restore the old monarchy without a single change. One of Yakushev's main tasks was to make contact with the grand duke himself, in order to gain prestige and credibility among the wider émigré community.

Yakushev's meeting with representatives of the Supreme Council was a remarkable success. Charming, eloquent, and poised, Yakushev spoke with authority. His Cheka handlers had told him that the émigré Supreme Council did not have good intelligence on actual conditions in Russia, so Yakushev told the émigrés that Russia was beginning to awaken from the horrific nightmare that was the Bolshevik revolution. He told them that anti-Communist forces were reasserting themselves even inside the administration, that the Trust was best positioned to collect intelligence and to report to the émigrés about the future of the monarchist restoration from Moscow, and that it would be prudent not to jeopardize their efforts by interfering from abroad. His sangfroid was uncanny. The Supreme Council appeared convinced.

The Berlin trip boosted Yakushev's self-confidence. He was not very impressed with the émigré leaders he had met, and considered himself more than a match for them. None of them, he thought, had the charisma to foment counterrevolution and lead a new government in the USSR. Yakushev's Berlin visit, as the CIA historians concluded in a shrewd psychological analysis, "left him with the heartfelt conviction that Russia's future was in the hands of the Bolsheviks for better or worse." The former tsarist official was now ready to devote himself to the Chekist "operational play," and would no longer even feel guilty for playing along.

In the summer of 1923, Yakushev returned to Berlin, which was one of the hotbeds of émigré activity. He had scheduled a meeting with a more hawkish and hardened group of émigrés, centered around the charismatic and visionary General Pyotr Wrangel, a Baltic German nobleman and one of the last commanders of the White Army in the final stages of the civil war.[15] Wrangel, combat-experienced, surrounded himself with professional military officers. When Yakushev sat down with Wrangel's men, he made an impeccable impression on the monarchists: a decent gentleman was sitting on the sofa in front of them, not the Bolshevik brute some of them had expected. Yakushev was calm, he spoke neither quietly nor loudly, perhaps even with a hint of indifference, and he did not use gestures. He exuded a calm self-confidence.[16]

Yakushev told the monarchists in Berlin that they should move slowly, that they should conserve their strength for the day of restoration and wait until the Bolsheviks were ready to collapse from within, rather than risking everything with premature attacks or acts of terror. The future Russian government, he added, would be made up of those who fought for it from within.

But Wrangel's chief of intelligence was skeptical, and began needling Yaku-shev with sharp questions: How could all this monarchist activity take place among Cheka agents? Yakushev said that the émigrés had been away for too long, and were no longer well informed about conditions in the USSR. The meeting was over quickly, and not everybody was convinced. But one person in particular was taken in by Yakushev, and seeds were planted that would come to fruition two and a half years later.

The Trust had another main goal, besides deceiving the monarchists: de-ceiving Western intelligence agencies, specifically about the military strength of the still young and fragile USSR. This military active measure was of par-ticular urgency, as the reorganized Cheka—by now called the GPU, which stood for State Political Directorate—reportedly had learned from its foreign spies that preparations were under way for a new intervention against the So-viet Union.[17] After Yakushev returned from Berlin, he was tasked with estab-lishing contacts in a number of foreign intelligence services.[18]

One of the first on the target list was Estonia's small but well-connected service. Yakushev would send letters from MOTsR to the Supreme Monarchist Council through the Estonian mission in Moscow. The GPU suspected that Estonian spies were intercepting and reading these letters, which were sent in their own diplomatic pouches. Dzerzhinsky's men thought that once the Es-tonians had steamed open and perused the planted missives, they would try to make contact with MOTsR, provided of course that the letters contained details of intelligence interest. So Yakushev, with a little help from the GPU, included in his letters carefully doctored material on the Red Army. The Es-tonians took the bait. "From that moment the transfer of disinformation ma-terial to the Estonian intelligence service began," recalled the official history of Russian foreign intelligence.[19]

On January 11, 1923, a remarkable institutional innovation saw the light of day:[20] Artuzov created an office for *dezinformatsiya*, or disinforma-tion.[21] The sheer volume of deceptive material that passed through these in-telligence channels was large enough to trigger bureaucratic innovation in Russian foreign intelligence. The GPU reportedly coordinated with the Rev-olutionary Military Council, Russia's highest military authority, to set up a special bureau to "prepare disinformation for Western military intelligence services."[22] The goal, according to a GPU participant, was "to deter military intervention by the Western powers."[23] The GPU *deza* office would produce fake Politburo minutes, memoranda, and misleading military reports to exaggerate Soviet strength. The new office was authorized by the party's Central Committee, and initially placed forged stories in the official Soviet press.[24] One of Artuzov's assistants later boasted in a report about the effectiveness of military disinformation, which gave the Red Army an awesome phantom capability: he claimed to have "provided the staff of every state in Central Europe" with forged statistics about military strength.[25]

Trust business would take Yakushev to Tallinn, Riga, Helsingfors, Warsaw, Berlin, and Paris. In August 1923, Yakushev made his most significant trip: to meet Nikolai Nikolayevich Romanov, the grand duke of Russia, in Paris. Nikolai was an ascetic and devout man of imperial bearing, toweringly tall at six feet six and the embodiment of military virtues. He lived in near isolation at Choigny, the castle he rented twenty miles outside Paris. Traveling with Yakushev was a former monarchist general, Nikolai Potapov (who was now a loyal Bolshevik general and, in fact, one of the founders of the Red Army). The meeting lasted three hours. By that time, Yakushev had his spiel down: communism, even socialism, had lost face in Russia; the eternal Russia was resurrecting itself; and MOTsR, back home, was the agent of change. The émigrés faced a dangerous situation now: if they helped foreign powers to intervene in Russia and prey on her, then Russian patriots—who hated intervention—would rally and unite around the Bolshevik government. It was best to sit and wait and support the monarchists on the ground in Moscow. Yakushev reported that the grand duke was fully convinced, saying, "Not only do I agree, but will not stop consulting you, or will make a step without you, not only now, but in the future will always seek your advice."[26]

By mid-1924, the Trust had established relations with Finnish intelligence. To make the transfer of documents and people more credible, the Trust operated a "window" on the Soviet-Finnish border. These "windows" were remote border crossings manned by ostensibly loyal border guards who would let Trust agents and messengers (in reality, Soviet intelligence officers) in and out of the Soviet Union. By this time, the faux monarchists in Moscow had also established working relationships with Estonian, Polish, and British intelligence services.[27] The Russian masterminds understood that these smaller intelligence agencies, self-interested and eager to establish good working relationships, were keen to pass on what they considered valuable intelligence to their much more formidable Western counterparts. One Polish intelligence officer who analyzed the Trust later spelled out the logic at work in the spy agencies that cooperated so willingly with MOTsR: "Why run new chains, why engage in dangerous clandestine activities, why use up large sums of money," the Polish officer asked, "when almost weekly there arrived from Moscow diplomatic pouches with prettily sealed envelopes containing the answers to almost all their questions?"[28]

One of Dzerzhinsky's special projects, in particular, made the Trust famous in popular culture: the killing of Sydney Reilly, an eccentric former British intelligence officer and a particularly ardent anti-Bolshevik. By the spring of 1925, Dzerzhinsky had a plan to use the Trust to lure Reilly to Russia to be executed.

In May, Reilly received a cryptic letter from a trusted MOTsR contact, relayed to him through an MI6 officer in Tallinn. The message alluded to "big business possibilities in Russia which, in all probability, would have a big influence on European markets." The whimsically coded note was designed to convince Reilly that the counterrevolution was imminent, and he took the bait. Reilly arranged with White émigrés in Paris to go to Russia via Helsinki in September 1925. Yakushev himself came to Helsinki to meet Reilly there, via one of the faux-illegal "windows" on the Finnish-Russian border. Reilly, after some initial hesitation, agreed to travel to Russia for a three-day trip, to Leningrad and then by train to Moscow, to meet the Trust leadership. Soviet state security arrested Reilly in Moscow on his way back to the station.

Dzerzhinsky's men knew that news of Reilly's arrest would damage the credibility of the Trust among the émigrés, perhaps irrevocably so. Therefore, in order to protect MOTsR's reputation abroad, Artuzov came up with another cover story. Instead of Reilly, one of Artuzov's most trusted assistants traveled back to the "window" at the Finnish-Soviet border. There, late in the night of September 28 or early the next morning, Soviet intelligence staged a sham shooting incident at the border. The following morning a truck arrived and removed the three "corpses." All this was carefully staged to convey the impression to the Finnish guards that Reilly and two MOTsR operators had been killed in an attempt to cross the border. A Leningrad party paper, *Krasnaya Gazeta*, announced Reilly's death. But Soviet newspapers lacked credibility. Rumors flamed up that MOTsR was, indeed, a Communist front.

Almost immediately, the Trust implemented another plan to repair this damage to its reputation. An opportunity presented itself in the person of Vasily Shulgin. Shulgin was a former conservative member of the Duma and a prominent political figure under the tsar, a staunch monarchist, wealthy landowner, and now a respected and popular émigré writer. Shulgin had curious, youthful eyes and a bushy mustache that seemed to smile, its tips pointed upward. His son, a young soldier, had disappeared in the chaos of the civil war in the Crimea in the summer of 1920; Yakushev knew that the writer was consumed by the desire to find his lost son.[29] The two had met in Berlin in 1923. Now Yakushev invited the journalist to come to the USSR, promising that the Trust would make every effort to find his lost son. Shulgin, against better advice, accepted.

In the fall of 1925, he left Paris for Warsaw. Just before Christmas Eve, on the night of December 22, Shulgin "illegally" entered the USSR.[30] The journalist moved through one of the false windows near Stolbtsy on the Soviet-Polish border. He toured first Minsk, then Kiev, Moscow, and the new Leningrad (the city had been renamed the previous year). The entire time, Shulgin was accompanied by ostensible monarchists who were carefully curating his travel experience.

In Moscow, Yakushev greeted him, and introduced him to MOTsR's leadership. The OGPU front—the GPU had been reorganized again in the meantime—enacted a conspiratorial atmosphere for their visitor. Shulgin was so well known in Russia, they told him, that he had to disguise himself.[31] All this "made a big impression on him," as Russia's official intelligence history recalled. The OGPU's rationale for the charade was elaborate: Dzerzhinsky wanted to impress on Shulgin that real life in Russia was vibrant again, that

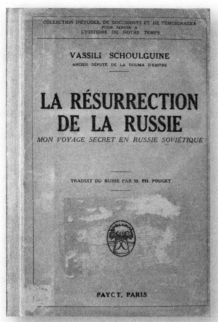

COLLECTION D'ÉTUDES, DE DOCUMENTS ET DE TÉMOIGNAGES
POUR SERVIR A
L'HISTOIRE DE NOTRE TEMPS

VASSILI SCHOULGUINE
ANCIEN DÉPUTÉ DE LA DOUMA D'EMPIRE

LA RÉSURRECTION DE LA RUSSIE
MON VOYAGE SECRET EN RUSSIE SOVIÉTIQUE

TRADUIT DU RUSSE PAR M. PH. POUGET

PAYOT, PARIS

Dzerzhinsky's fake counterrevolutionary council, the Trust, lured one of the most articulate White Russian authors back to the new Soviet Union, staged a trip for him, and encouraged him to write a travelogue—in order to quell anti-Soviet resistance abroad. Shulgin sent his manuscript back to his hosts for review, to make sure he did not imperil the nonexistent rebels; instead, Dzerzhinsky approved the draft.

the émigrés were out of touch with what was really going on in the USSR, and that Bolshevism was being hollowed out from within. The attempts to locate his son, genuine or not, were unsuccessful. Shulgin now had closure. When the curators of his trip noticed that their ruse was working, and that Shulgin was positively impressed by what he saw in Soviet Russia, they decided to escalate. Shulgin's literary talent was well known. Would he want to write a book-length travelogue about his trip, Yakushev suggested?

Initially Shulgin had no plans to write a book on his journey to Russia, a trip that he thought had been "illegal," arranged by insurgent monarchists at great risk to their personal safety and to the wider cause. "Initially I categorically refused to describe my illegal journey," Shulgin later recalled. "I feared that I would let my 'friends' in the Trust down."[32] But Yakushev argued that it was important to spread the truth about Russia. The Russia-based monarchists suggested that he could freely write a first draft of the book manuscript abroad, and then have the draft censored by MOTsR in Moscow for security reasons, so he would not have to be concerned about damaging the insurgency. Shulgin agreed again. In February 1926, Shulgin left Russia for Paris, got down to work, and soon relayed a manuscript to Moscow. "Dzerzhinsky and Artuzov," notes the official SVR history, "were the first readers of Shulgin's book manuscript."

His book, *Three Capitals: Journey to Red Russia*, was published in early 1927, first in Russian with a Berlin-based émigré press,[33] then in French in Paris.[34] The publication "created a sensation," the head of the Russia desk in Polish intelligence at the time recalled.[35] Shulgin remained critical of Lenin, but portrayed Russia as rejuvenating and energetic. Forty years later, as a very old man, Shulgin reflected on the episode. Next to his own signature, he said, there was "an invisible, but indelible remark: 'I authorize printing, F. Dzerzhinsky.'"[36] Shulgin's secret journey illustrated the levels of deception at play. The OGPU did not just lure its opponents to Russia under false pretenses to have them removed from the scene; Soviet spymasters, with derring-do and ingenuity, had devised an artful and elaborate active measures campaign.

MOTsR had grown so large that the OGPU had compartmentalized it into separate projects, known as "legends." By 1927, the sham monarchist insurgency reportedly comprised fifty "legends."[37] The Trust was at the peak of its success. But around the time Shulgin's book came out that year, the organization began to unravel. In April its finance officer, Edward Opperput, defected and fled to Finland. Opperput broke cover and revealed the various layers of deception that MOTsR had been running for more than half a decade. The Opperput revelations themselves, however, were devastating for White Russian emigration. Nothing and nobody, it suddenly appeared, was trustworthy—not even Opperput's defection. It was impossible to say whether he genuinely defected and broke cover, or if OGPU dispatched him to terminate the project with maximum effect. Opperput reportedly continued to work as a Soviet agent until he was shot by the Germans in 1943.

The actions of the Trust, more than any other event in the 1920s, would shape the future of disinformation. It was spectacularly successful. Polish intelligence later declared that—"without exaggeration"—Operation Trust had inflicted "incalculable damage" on the Russian émigrés, undercutting their political and military capabilities to the point of rendering the counterrevolutionaries insignificant.[38] This success gave the Chekists great self-confidence. Their project had illustrated that their tradecraft was sufficiently daring yet fine-tuned to be more than a match for the world's finest intelligence agencies. "From this point on," the CIA concluded in its study, "Russian intelligence became a force to be reckoned with."[39]

The project also served as an inspiration for future active measures. In 1953, the main historical display in the study room at Soviet intelligence headquarters showed Feliks Dzerzhinsky, and the inscription under his portrait was devoted to the Trust.[40] *Operatsiya Trest*, as one prominent Soviet defector reported, figured prominently in the active measures training at the Andropov Red Banner Institute, the First Chief Directorate's academy of foreign intelligence.[41] As late as 1997, the official Russian foreign intelligence history celebrated the disinformation operation as a towering success story. "The disinformation work carried out by MOTsR played a distinctly positive role," the SVR's official history recounted, and added that Soviet spies were able to confirm the effectiveness of the two-step ruse that fed disinformation to Polish, Estonian, and Finnish services, who in turn passed on the deceptive material to their partner agencies in France, Britain, Japan, Italy, and "in some measure" the United States. The adversaries of the USSR, taking the disinformation at face value, arrived at an "exaggerated notion of the Red Army's military power," the SVR concluded, which in turn led them to reject intervention against the USSR.

But the Trust foreshadowed the future in a third, unexpected way. Over time, the project became more and more like a Russian matryoshka doll, with several layers of disinformation nested and stacked into one another. Even the most cautious and best-informed analysts had great difficulty determining when they had reached the innermost shell of the nesting deception game, and the end of the deception. The Polish General Staff, especially one of its longtime staff officers, is one of the best sources on the Trust. These analysts, when evaluating the Trust at the time, seriously considered the possibility that Dzerzhinsky was not fooling Russians abroad but Russians at home. Himself Polish by origin, Dzerzhinsky had managed to convince other once fiercely anti-Bolshevik Polish intelligence officers to join the Cheka. One of

the arguments that he reportedly used to turn these Poles was that by joining and serving in the Cheka, they would be in an ideal position to "wreak a
bloody vengeance on the Russians" for all that Russia had done to Poland.
"The idea occurred to us," recalled the influential Polish military intelligence
officer Jerzy Niezbrzycki (better known as Wraga), "that he himself remained
an enemy of Russia."[42]

Dzerzhinsky was not an enemy of Russia. Yet the influence of the innovative Trust did not stop abroad: a prime example is Shulgin's book, *Three
Capitals*. It was available in the Soviet Union only with permission from the
censor, called Glavlit. Nevertheless, the available copies were highly sought
after and oversubscribed in libraries popular with Bolshevik intellectuals.[43]
Shulgin's travelogue was a popular read among the Soviet elite—yet very few
knew that it was disinformation.[44]

The fake White Russian counterrevolutionary organization would serve,
throughout the entire Cold War, as a towering example of an intelligence
tactic with a bright future: a way to subvert, support, and exploit political
activists, "like a sticky fly strip attracting insects," as the official SVR history put it.[45]

2.

Japan's *Mein Kampf*

I N 1926, THE CHINESE, JAPANESE, AND RUSSIAN SPHERES OF influence collided in Manchuria, a large region of China that lies north of Korea, which was then a Japanese colony. The period was chaotic in the Far East. China was descending into a cataclysmic civil war that pitched the Communist Party against the Nationalist Party. With China weakened, both Japan and Russia were eyeing up the fertile territory sandwiched between them, over which the two countries had clashed in 1905. This Northeast Asian great game was the context in which the most mysterious and momentous forgery of the twentieth century emerged: the so-called Tanaka Memorial, better known in the United States, after Pearl Harbor, as Japan's *Mein Kampf*.

Imperial Japan was a high-profile target of Russian spying efforts in the early twentieth century; "Iron" Feliks Dzerzhinsky boasted in the mid-1920s

Tanaka Giichi, prime minister of Imperial Japan from 1927 until his resignation on July 2, 1929. Tanaka's fake grand strategic plan, which first surfaced in Nanking, China, predicted Japan's invasion of Manchuria and attack on Pearl Harbor. (National Diet Library)

of his excellent sources there. The OGPU had particularly productive residencies in Seoul and Harbin, a Manchurian city with a sizable Russian minority. At one point, reportedly in late 1925, Dzerzhinsky spoke to Politburo members about the impending arrival of an extremely important document from Japan. He "ecstatically" told Leon Trotsky, a fellow early revolutionary, that the document could provoke international crises, possibly even war between Japan and the United States.

"Wars are not provoked by documents," Trotsky objected.

"You have no conception of the importance of this document," responded Dzerzhinsky. "It embraces the seizure of China, the destruction of the United States, world domination."

Trotsky was not convinced. "Mightn't your agent be duped?" he asked, indicating his disbelief that anybody would put such a plan on paper.

Trotsky sensed that Dzerzhinsky wasn't completely sure himself that the document was genuine, and that, "as if to dispel the doubts in his own mind," Iron Feliks began to outline more details. He claimed that the OGPU had paid around $3,000 for the photographic copies of the original Japanese document. But problems with the camera gear made it difficult to capture the war plan in one go, so the delivery of the full document was significantly delayed as it traveled from Japan in several separate shipments of undeveloped film.

"The document has arrived," announced Dzerzhinsky one day. The memo was hastily translated and analyzed. As the draft and intelligence reports were passed on by the OGPU to the Kremlin, Politburo members were "all staggered" by the contents of even the first pages. But other prominent Bolsheviks shared Trotsky's skepticism of Dzerzhinsky's bold claims.

"Isn't this perhaps a poem, a forgery?" asked in flowery language Nikolai Bukharin, another famous Marxist writer, Politburo member, and editor of *Pravda*. Dzerzhinsky exploded.

"I have already explained to you," said Dzerzhinsky, his Polish accent growing stronger with his agitation, "that this document is supplied by our agent, who has proved his complete trustworthiness." Dzerzhinsky reiterated that the original text was first photographed in Tokyo, in the archives of the Japanese Naval Ministry. "Our agent introduced our photographer into the premises. He himself didn't know how to operate a camera," said the OGPU spymaster, adding defensively: "Is it perhaps your opinion that the Japanese admirals themselves placed a forged document in their secret archives?"

Still, Dzerzhinsky and his advisors agreed on one thing: that the sensational contents should be published, and that the best place for publication was the United States. But it was hard to come up with a credible cover story of how the document had been obtained from Tokyo. Trotsky recalled, "Any reference to the real source, i.e., the GPU, would arouse additional mistrust." It was 1926, and the odds of blowback were considerable: "In America the suspicion would naturally arise that the GPU itself had simply manufactured the document in order to poison relations between Japan and the United States." It turned out to be even more difficult to covertly surface the document in the United States than the OGPU expected. Dzerzhinsky died in July 1926; Trotsky was expelled from the Communist Party in the fall of

1927, and left Russia in 1929—all before the Tanaka Memorial was published for the first time.

There is only one account of these remarkable dialogues between Trotsky and Dzerzhinsky: a most extraordinary memoir written by Trotsky a dozen years after these conversations allegedly took place. Trotsky then lived in Mexican exile, where he wrote prolifically while living among artists. A Soviet secret agent famously killed Trotsky at his home in Mexico City by striking his head with a mountaineering ice axe. One of the last articles he worked on—but was unable to finish before his killer struck—was titled "The Tanaka Memorial." It remains unclear why Trotsky was so invested in attempting to claim that this forgery was, in fact, not a forgery.

Tanaka Giichi was born into a samurai family, and was himself a highly decorated general. He had a thin gray mustache, a short-trimmed crew cut even as a civilian, and piercing, unsmiling eyes, and was usually formally dressed in uniform or a suit. From 1927 to mid-1929, Tanaka was the prime minister of Japan. He had served in Moscow as a military attaché of the Imperial Japanese Army for three years, and later had a planning role in the Russo-Japanese War of 1905; he was known for his expansionist policies toward Manchuria, and for arresting Communists at home. This hawkish martial leader made for a convincing author of the document that would soon be known as Japan's *Mein Kampf.*

The first (non-Soviet) account of the text that later became known as the Tanaka Memorial dates back to September 9, 1929. That day, a Manchurian Railway Company employee reportedly sent a note to Japanese consular authorities in Mukden, later Shenyang, the capital of Manchuria. Railway lines were a strategic asset in military and economic terms, especially in the vast plains of northeast Asia. The note said that Chinese delegates, en route to a conference in Kyoto, had purchased an inflammatory Japanese policy document "from a friend in Tokyo," and that they paid 50,000 yen for it, a steep price (approximately $23,000 in 1929).[1] In a separate report, the governor of Manchuria told an American delegation, which was also in Mukden on its way to the same conference, that the document had been purchased from an anonymous Japanese source.[2] Tanaka, who had just retired as Japanese prime minister, died later that month. So far, the mysterious memo was only a rumor.

The first known printed copy surfaced in an obscure Chinese weekly in Nanking, the relocated capital and seat of China's nationalist government, two months after Tanaka's death. The magazine, *Current Affairs Monthly*, had links to the Kuomintang, the nationalist ruling party.[3] "Recently we found this secret document in Tokyo," the editor noted. The magazine printed the nearly 20,000-character document in Traditional Chinese in December. The Japanese government swiftly intervened and requested only weeks later that Chinese authorities suppress further dissemination of the document, "on the ground that it was a fabrication," as a senior Japanese diplomat recalled. The Chinese authorities reportedly agreed. Later in 1930, a Japanese retranslation (of what was, after all, a purported "translation" from an original Japanese document) appeared in Tokyo.[4] This initial publication in Nanking, and the Sino-Japanese hiccup it caused, was entirely ignored in the English-speaking world.

Then, the following year, Japan began to posture more aggressively toward China. On September 17, 1931, *The China Critic*, an English-language newspaper from Shanghai with offices in New York and London, again quoted from the mysterious Tanaka memo that articulated Japan's imperial ambitions in such seductive simplicity: "In order to conquer China, we must first of all conquer Manchuria and Mongolia; and in order to conquer the world, we must first of all conquer China."[5] The quote was striking, and would be repeated many times; its timing was even more striking. The following day, the Japanese invasion of Manchuria began. *1931*

Suddenly, the mysterious document appeared prescient, if not prophetic. Six days later, *The China Critic*, amid a barrage of articles criticizing the ongoing Japanese invasion of Manchuria, published the full 17,000 words of the soon-to-be-infamous Tanaka Memorial. The text was a verbatim translation of the original Chinese version that surfaced in Nanking, with only minor edits.[6]

Once it had been published, OGPU officers in China sent the document back to Moscow. Just two months later, in December 1931, the official journal

The Comintern pushed the Tanaka forgery out in five languages in the December 1931 issue of *Communist International*, only months after it first surfaced in English, editing out—revealingly—two key paragraphs in the process.

of the Moscow-based Communist International, known as the Comintern, reprinted the Tanaka memo in its entirety and in five languages.

In March 1932, the Comintern in Moscow—unaware that the Tanaka Memorial had already been published in Japan—ordered the San Francisco bureau of a Soviet front organization, the Pan-Pacific Trade Union Secretariat, to smuggle the Memorial from the United States into Japan, and to try to publish it there in the third antiwar issue of *Pan-Pacific Worker*, a Communist magazine. The Comintern archives show that the Tanaka Memorial had to be translated: "In view of the time required," the protocol says, it was decided "to at once begin translating the Tanaka Memorandum (from the English to Japanese)."[7] Nowhere did the Comintern archives refer to the document as a forgery.

The Comintern and KGB's predecessor organizations had learned how to construct a disinformation operation in such a way that the victim's denials, even when credible, would strengthen rather than weaken the effect of an operation. The goal of the publicity in Japan may have been to provoke Tokyo into proclaiming more and louder denials.

Over the next months, the memo "stirred unusual interest in the capitals of the world," as *The New York Times* reported in May 1932. A long investigative piece in the *Times* carefully traced the emergence of the document, and weighed the evidence for and against its authenticity. The main argument in favor of the Memorial's authenticity was that it had accurately predicted Japan's aggression against Manchuria, including the construction of two strategic railway lines connecting Manchuria to Mongolia that Japan was actually building.

Nevertheless, despite its merits, the evidence that revealed the document to be a forgery was overwhelming at closer inspection. First, no Japanese original could be found. The memo further claimed that the emperor had called a conference seven years earlier, when in fact he was an invalid at the time and could not have done so, and that a Japanese prince had been instructed to oppose said conference when in fact that prince was seriously ill and had died before the supposed meeting took place. The memo also got a number of simple facts wildly wrong, such as Japanese investments in Manchuria or the geographical area of Mongolia. A well-staffed Imperial Japanese prime minister simply would not pass a draft so riddled with errors to the emperor. The *Times* also reported that other forged strategy documents with similar names had been circulating in China at the time. The *Times*, in short, thoroughly debunked the hoax that was the Tanaka Memorial.

But to little avail. The Tanaka war plan was too simple, too convincing, too seductive for details and evidence to get in the way. The more aggressive Japan became, the more emotionally charged became the debate, and the more credible the forged war plan. Japan occupied Manchuria throughout the 1930s, as the Chinese civil war continued. Many Communist publishing houses—along with independent ones—republished the document in pocket-book form around the world, in around four dozen editions, including in English, French, German, Spanish, Portuguese, Russian, and even Esperanto.[8] One version, published in 1936 in San Francisco's Chinatown, bore a yellow cover with an ominous subtitle: *A Prediction of a Japanese-American War.*[9] Pearl Harbor was still five years in the future.

In April 1940, Joseph Taussig, a rear admiral in the U.S. Navy and commander of the Fifth Naval District in Norfolk, Virginia, was called to testify in front of Congress on the continued crisis in East Asia, and on Japanese foreign policy more specifically. Taussig started out by quoting from the Tanaka war plan, and told the Senate that the Navy had a copy of the Memorial in its archives. Some senators were already familiar with the document, and queried the admiral on its merits.

"I am convinced it is a paper that was written with the idea of being carried out," Taussig responded, brimming with confidence, even doubling down while under questioning on his assessment that the text was real.[10]

Meanwhile, in Mexico City, Leon Trotsky read about the admiral's testimony. He decided to wade into a controversy that would help shape how many Americans saw World War II. Trotsky began his paper on Tanaka by quoting Taussig's congressional testimony, and then came to the support of the U.S. Navy admiral by claiming to be able to verify the authenticity of the controversial Japanese document, "completely and incontrovertibly."[11] The mysterious pamphlet, claimed Trotsky, was first photographed in Tokyo in the Ministry of Naval Affairs, and brought to Moscow as undeveloped film. "I was perhaps the very first person to become acquainted with the document in English and Russian translations of the Japanese text," Trotsky wrote.[12]

Just a few months after Trotsky's piece on Tanaka was published, *Click* magazine released its November 1941 issue. *Click*, published in Philadelphia, was a glossy gossip magazine, its covers usually adorned with women in bathing suits. That November, the cover featured Jane Russell in a red romper, seemingly looking at a front-page announcement of what *Click* called "Japan's *Mein Kampf.*"[13]

The story cut right to the chase: "America is next on Japan's list of victims!" It was November. On December 7, a Sunday morning, more than 350 Japanese bombers raided Pearl Harbor, killing more than 2,400 Americans

	PAGE
J. Franklin: Total Defense	3
Kids Learn About Life	6
Japan's Mein Kampf	10
Bike Cycle?	14
Hawes on Hats and War	12
Click's Guide & Cartoons	21
Complete Superman Story	26
Short, Short Story	28
Bill Stern on Football	30
Warden Lawes on Crime	43

JACK BEUTEL MEETS THE REAL JANE RUSSELL—See page 22

In November 1941, *Click* magazine covered the Tanaka plan, dubbed "Japan's *Mein Kampf*," and announced a forthcoming attack on the United States. The attack on Pearl Harbor came on December 7.

and inflicting punishing military losses on the U.S. naval base in Hawaii. The day would be seared forever into America's collective memory.

The following Sunday night, NBC reported that "the famous Tanaka Plan" was "widely quoted in Washington today" as an explanation for Tokyo's military aggression.[14] Another week later, the author of the *Click* article appeared on New York Public Radio. "That story," said the announcer, "was an amazing prophecy."[15] A month after Pearl Harbor, one prominent[16] China correspondent reflected in *The Washington Post* on "those amazingly ambitious plans of Japan's military clique" that had been laid out so accurately in the Tanaka Memorial twelve years prior.[17] "The fury with which the Japanese denounced this memorial as a forgery appeared at the time to be considerable confirmation of its authenticity," the *Post* concluded, effectively interpreting a denial as a confirmation. The treacherous attack on Hawaii had now removed any lingering doubt; "the baron's words have been acted upon," said the *Post*. America's elected representatives took note. Three days later, on

January 13, the U.S. House of Representatives passed a five-line resolution in order to make sure that the secret plans for Japanese military expansion—a document that had already been credibly debunked as a forgery—would be made available to a wider American public. The resolution demanded that the pamphlet entitled "The Memorial of Premier Tanaka," a Japanese secret design for the conquest of China as well as the United States and the world, published by World Peace Movement, 108 Park Row, New York, New York, in 1932, be printed as a public document.[18]

Out of dozens of available editions, Congress named in its resolution the one slim bound booklet by the World Peace Movement in New York. About a decade later, the CIA would identify this group as an early Soviet international front organization.[19]

Soon, in 1942, Harper and Brothers published the edition of the document that would become the best known, titled "Japan's Dream of World Empire" and dubbed Japan's *Mein Kampf* on the jacket. Hitler was in power, the Third Reich an ally of Imperial Japan, and now at war against America. Anti-Japanese sentiment was at its apex in the United States, with more than one hundred thousand Japanese Americans incarcerated in concentration camps. In 1944, Frank Capra, a highly influential Hollywood director, used the Tanaka document to explain Japan's aggressive actions against Manchuria and Pearl Harbor in a widely watched, U.S. War Department–supported, six-part movie called *Why We Fight*.[20]

The war ended with two era-defining nuclear blasts, in Hiroshima and Nagasaki. Japan's imperial army was crushed, along with Tokyo's imperial ambitions. At the same time, in an odd historic twist, a badly burned copy of the Tanaka Memorial was found in a folder of military documents in the smoldering, bombed-out Japanese Embassy in Berlin's Tiergarten. That document, mysteriously, was in the German language.[21] World War II itself had established the Tanaka plan as perhaps the single most iconic forgery of the twentieth century.

The trajectory of the Tanaka Memorial had reached a peak, but over the decades that followed, the text had an obscure afterlife in Cold War disinformation operations. In February 1960, Nikita Khrushchev visited Indonesia.

The KGB had just established its own organizational unit for disinformation the previous year. At a press conference in Jakarta, Khrushchev condemned U.S.-Japanese security cooperation and warned that the Japanese ruling classes were again reviving the Tanaka blueprint for subjugating the rest of Asia, with American aid.[22] The last operational use of the Tanaka Memorial came in a two-page spread on "ethnic weapons" that ran in the Kuwaiti daily *Al-Qabas* in 1987. The piece accused the United States of developing a "germ bomb" that would target only brown-skinned humans. The Arabic-language story was spread over two pages and illustrated with pictures of military units in gas masks and schematic petri dishes.[23] The United States, the story in *Al-Qabas* claimed, had taken over biological weapons research from the Japanese, who were simply carrying out Tanaka's sinister plans for imperial world domination.

By then, however, an increasing number of historians had thoroughly debunked the perennial hoax.[24] Forty years of searching in Japanese archives had uncovered no Japanese original.[25] But many historians who focused their scholarly attention on the Tanaka memo limited their investigations to assessing the document's authenticity, and ignored the question of its authorship.

Then, in 1989, Stanislav Levchenko—a KGB defector who had served as an active measures officer in Tokyo—co-authored with an eminent U.S. Information Agency disinformation specialist an ambitious history of Russian covert action against the United States. Levchenko claimed that the Tanaka Memorial was in fact a Soviet forgery, although he and his co-author provided no fresh documentary evidence.[26]

However, a curious set of new details emerged in Moscow after the turn of the new millennium. In 2003, Sergei Kondrashev, the former head of the KGB's disinformation shop, Service "A," sat with an official newspaper in Moscow[27] for an interview about his father-in-law, a legendary KGB officer who had served in Harbin, China. Kondrashev explained that the single main goal of Russian intelligence in China in the late 1920s was to reveal Japan's militaristic plans. "And here our spies have achieved tremendous success," said Kondrashev. "And now"—he smiled at his interviewer—"get ready to hear a sensation." Kondrashev began recapitulating known elements of the story.[28] But the old man didn't get to the point quickly enough, so his eager and impatient interviewer interrupted him with another question. Whatever sensation Kondrashev had in mind remained unclear. He died in 2007.

Eventually, in 2006, something remarkable happened: the SVR, the successor organization to the KGB's First Chief Directorate, finished the first official history of Russian foreign intelligence, published in six volumes. Its nine authors were a team of intelligence veterans and current SVR officers who described a range of operations on the basis of archival material.[29] The team of nine had worked on the official, "truthful" history for fourteen years. The director of the SVR not only awarded them a prize in recognition of their work for Russia but also published the tome under his name, Yevgeny Primakov.[30]

Volume Two features an entire chapter on the Tanaka Memorial.[31] In 1927, the official history recounts, Soviet operatives in two residencies, one in Seoul and one in Harbin, China, succeeded in obtaining the Tanaka Memorial. A young Soviet illegal in Seoul managed to recruit an agent in the Japanese political police, and "The result of one of the operations, brilliantly conducted by the spy, was the receipt of a secret document entitled 'Tanaka Memorandum.'"[32] The capture of the document—still treated, in the official history, as genuine and accurate—was praised as one of the "biggest achievements" in the work of Soviet foreign intelligence in the Far East. Never in its six volumes does the history engage with the authoritative archival research that had been done in the meantime, especially in Japan; its authors even ignored that, for decades, the Tanaka Memorial had played a starring role in active measures.

The fantastic saga of the Tanaka Memorial illustrates the power of events and emotion. The credibility of the debunked Japanese war plan was boosted, again and again, by the raw emotions unleashed by Japanese military action, first the invasion of Manchuria, then the raid on Pearl Harbor. As late as 2015, a governmental Sino-Japanese research commission, with ten historians from each country, was unable to agree that the Tanaka Memorial was indeed a forgery,[33] for the Chinese researchers feared admitting that a key document about the Japanese invasion was inauthentic. This potent psycho-logical resonance made the Tanaka Memorial one of the most spectacular of all active measures of the past century.

Debunking a forgery in sober, fact-based analysis has limited effect if its emotive appeal is high. The Tanaka episode therefore offered a valuable case study to disinformation specialists in the Cold War: the forgery showed how to craft an organized lie so that neither denials nor details could dent its momentum. The recipe so successfully tested in Nanking was to shield a forgery under the armor of a larger truth—that of Japan's militarism and Tokyo's aggressive foreign policy.

Finally, and most important, the episode shows how the KGB and its successor organizations thoroughly disinformed themselves, their own archives, their own officers, their own leaders, their own history, and their own public—and indeed forever blurred the line between historical fact and fiction. It will likely remain impossible to identify, with high confidence, the forgers of the Tanaka Memorial. The best available accounts, from Japanese historians, conclude that the initial forgery was crafted by local Nationalist Chinese groups.[34] A curious Comintern slipup appears to confirm that the forgery was indeed Chinese, and not Russian. When the Memorial first surfaced in English in 1931 in Shanghai, Moscow was very quick to have the document translated and republished in five languages—Russian, French, German, Chinese, and English—all in the Comintern's international journal, *Communist International*.[35] But during this first push, the editors in Moscow *removed* two key paragraphs.

"Although the power of Soviet Russia is declining," read the cut text, "her ambition in Manchuria and Mongolia has not diminished for a minute." The faux Tanaka, in short, accused Soviet Russia of imperialism and then suggested that Japan ought to "secretly befriend Russia in order to hamper the growth of Chinese influence." It is highly unlikely that Chekist forgers would have included such a statement, only to remove it later—it is, however, highly likely that local Chinese forgers would have put into Tanaka's mouth the plan for a Russian-Japanese conspiracy against Manchuria. Just weeks before the initial Chinese forgery surfaced in Nanking, protesters in Mukden accused

Japan and the Soviet Union of plotting to detach Manchuria from China (although there was no substance to this concern).[36]

The question, thus, is when the OGPU appropriated the document for its own purposes. Trotsky's account provides a glimpse into what these discussions could have looked like. Yet Dzerzhinsky, shrewd and cunning to an extreme, may simply have started building his deceptive nesting game by deceiving the Politburo first. Trotsky as well as the SVR historians probably worked with the best available inevidence they had. The intelligence archives of the Eastern bloc, however, are tainted by a century-long history of disinformation. The more an intelligence agency engages in organized and persistent disinformation operations, the more disinformation is likely to have been deposited in official archives and the memories of former officers. The only way to attempt to distinguish between the two is by studying the whole history of disinformation.

The Whalen Forgeries

GROVER A. WHALEN, NEW YORK'S COMMISSIONER OF POLICE from 1928 to 1930, was tough yet pompous. He was a burly man, usually fashionably dressed, who wore a neatly trimmed mustache and his dark hair styled back. Known as a ruthless enforcer of the law, he modernized and grew the NYPD, adding men and arms, and deployed squads to stamp out organized crime, to thrash speakeasies instead of just closing them, and to break up Communist demonstrations by force. "There is plenty of law at the end of a nightstick,"[1] runs one of Whalen's infamous lines.

Whalen's term spanned a moment in history when peace was already fragile. In October 1929, the New York Stock Exchange crashed, and industrialized nations spiraled into the Great Depression. In the United States, 3.7 million people and counting were out of work by the early spring.[2] On

Members of the Fish Committee, which investigated Communist activities in the United States, meeting to discuss communism on May 9, 1930. Grover Whalen, the NYPD commissioner, is in the middle. Whalen became the victim of the first major disinformation operation targeting the United States. The active measure was anti-Soviet in nature.

(Library of Congress / Corbis / VCG via Getty Images)

March 6, 1930, a worldwide "Unemployment Day" saw workers clash with authorities across the Western world.[3] The police used tear gas in front of the White House, but nowhere was the police reaction as brutal as in Manhattan—where a crowd of 75,000 had gathered in Union Square—and Whalen led the charge. At one point the police commissioner "saw a roughly dressed fellow give a woman a push and grabbed the man by his coat collar, shook him, and handed him over to a plainclothes man," one eyewitness reported, adding that the plainclothes detective then proceeded to "make a casualty out of Mr. Whalen's capture."[4] The use of force, as Whalen understood, was always a show of force. But the NYPD took things too far that day, with mounted police driving their horses to trample over demonstrators who had fallen to the ground, and Whalen came under pressure. Rumors started circulating in the city that the commissioner was going to step down.[5]

He denied the rumors, and on April 26, he led a police parade of 6,000 men down Fifth Avenue, to strains of martial music and the clattering hooves of mounted units. Whalen, wearing his trademark top hat, saluted the on-lookers.[6] Four days later, Whalen again marshaled an immense police force to counter the May Day demonstration of some 25,000 Communists.[7]

Then, on May 2, the police commissioner revealed a bombshell to the papers. The NYPD's "radical squad," led by Inspector John Lyons, had investigated the hidden hand behind the Communist riots. Lyons and his men were hard-liners who believed that communism simply represented organized violence and should be outlawed as an insurgent force.[8] "After strenuous and painstaking investigation," Whalen told reporters on May 2, the NYPD had come to the conclusion "that the Communist International of Moscow was directly operating in the United States through certain agencies having head-quarters in the city of New York, fomenting strikes and riots."[9] Whalen also charged that the official Soviet trading organization, known as Amtorg, was a den of spies that cultivated revolution in the United States on Moscow's behalf.

TRUE

The finding was bold, if not unprecedented. Three years earlier, London's Scotland Yard had uncovered similar subversive activity by raiding Arcos Ltd., a Soviet commercial entity similar to Amtorg.[10] And just seven weeks before Whalen made his allegation, authorities in Berlin had confronted the Soviet envoy over subversive activity whipped up by the Comintern. After all, the Comintern advocated world revolution.

Still, Whalen had to provide solid evidence for such an explosive allegation. The NYPD's undercover radical squad had seized six letters, but it remained unclear how they found the documents. Five of the documents were from A. Fedorov, a Comintern leader; the sixth, also in Russian, was a response from Amtorg, printed on company letterhead and signed by T. G. Grapfen, Amtorg's secretary and treasurer. The thrust of the documents was that Moscow was exploiting "the approaching economic crisis"—the Great Depression—by kindling strikes and riots in the United States. Grapfen's letter listed thirty agents, men and women, allegedly dispatched from Moscow to New York. The documents, presented in triumph by the NYPD commissioner, were a picture-perfect smoking gun. "It will be noted that these documents reach this country by courier from the Soviet embassies of Berlin or Paris," Whalen told the press.[11] Under political pressure as he was, the commissioner failed to see that it was too good to be true.

That same day, Amtorg countered that the documents were forgeries. The chairman of the board, Peter Bogdanov, at once wrote a letter to Whalen demanding a "thorough investigation" and shrewdly pointing out that the Soviet trade group facilitated $150 million in trade. *The New York Times*, in its first story on the affair, cited a list of inconsistencies in the six revealed documents, for instance, the misuse of a Russian official title, a misspelling of the unofficial Soviet ambassador's name, and an inaccurate address. The *Times* quoted several critics who called out Whalen's "fantastic fraud."[12]

Whalen stood firm. "I am afraid the documents will have to speak for themselves," he responded when confronted with the denials. "They are very definite and complete."[13]

Three days later, *Izvestia*, the official outlet of the Central Committee in Moscow, commented on the affair. An editorial accused Whalen of being an "adventurer" and his activities a "public scandal." The paper implied that Whalen and the NYPD had manufactured the fraudulent documents. "This tactical step of Whalen's is extremely awkward and is thus destined to fail."[14]

Eventually, what would later be called metadata gave away the backstory of how the forgeries were made.

That story began four months earlier, in a cluttered, narrow printshop in a five-story brick building in Manhattan's East Village. Max Wagner, a Russian-born immigrant, ran the shop. He had been in the typesetting business for twenty-five years, eighteen of them in New York, where he served the small market for Russian work. Nobody in the city had a better selection of Cyrillic type. That January day in 1930, a man entered Wagner's printshop. He also was Russian, light-complexioned, forty years old, about five feet tall, and balding. The stranger wanted to order three different types of stationery in two stages: first, he wanted to see three different proofs, and then, after inspecting them, he would order one thousand copies of each. He gave Wagner a handwritten text and showed the printer his plans for the layout and

The front page of *The Forward*, May 3, 1930. Max Wagner, an East Village Russian-language printshop owner, saw his own work, a forgery, reproduced in *The Forward* that day. *(The Forward)*

form of the stationery. One of the samples the man ordered was an improvised letterhead for the Comintern. In the top-left corner it was supposed to say "Workers of the world, unite!"[15] On the bottom, the words **EXECUTIVE COMMITTEE** were to be set in large, bold print. The man also wanted Wagner to include the dateline "Moscow, _____ 19__" so that the letter writer could fill in the blanks with the day and the year, and to list the Comintern's street address in Moscow and a local Moscow phone number, 3 20 29. The mysterious man told Wagner he could use whatever type he considered appropriate. The whole interaction took a couple of minutes.

Wagner got to work. The next day the man came back and looked at the proofs with satisfaction. He did not notice, or did not care, that some of Wagner's type had been slightly damaged, and that the small print that said "Secretariat of the American Department" on the Comintern letterhead had smeared and was barely legible.[16] He gave Wagner a small deposit, took back his own improvised layout sample as well as six of the proofs—two each of three different letterheads—and left the shop, promising to return. Wagner kept one sample of each proof, but he never saw the man again.

But he would see the documents again. Four months after the stranger's visit, *The Forward*, a Yiddish New York daily, ran a front-page story on Whalen's showy announcement. When Wagner saw images of the incriminating letters on the front page, he immediately recognized his own proofs.[17]

A few days after Wagner spotted the reprints, an enterprising investigative journalist from the *Evening Graphic* named John Spivak turned up in his shop, and Wagner relayed the story of how he made the unique Comintern stationery. The *Graphic* ran the story on the twelfth, giving advance notice to Fiorello La Guardia, future mayor of New York, then a member of the House of Representatives for New York's 20th District. La Guardia, standing in Congress, held up a copy of Wagner's letterhead. "There is no question," La Guardia said, that the letters "were printed in New York City and not in Moscow."[18]

The Whalen forgeries soon helped trigger a congressional investigation. In early June, the House opened the Special Committee to Investigate Communist Activities in the United States, better known as the Fish Committee—named after Congressman Hamilton Fish, Jr., an unflinching anti-Communist. The Fish Committee, which advertised its bias in its very name, inadvertently helped to illuminate the story of the Whalen forgeries.

The committee held some of its hearings in New York. One day, when questioning the *Evening Graphic*'s Spivak, the committee learned of the existence of the printer's East Village shop. Before lunch, Fish dashed off a handwritten subpoena for the printer. Without any time to prepare, Wagner rushed to the hearing in time to be the first witness of the afternoon session. In garbled, Russian-Yiddish-accented English, he told Congress his story.

One congressman asked the printer how he was able to spot his own work. "I can recognize work I do," responded Wagner with confidence, and pointed to the form of the type.

"Is that the only way you can tell?" said the congressman.

"That is the only way to tell," Wagner said.

"Are there no particular marks on the copies?"

"I got certain types, and nobody got those types. I got lots of types." In disarming detail, Wagner described the mechanics of his work: the Moscow dateline to be left blank, the Moscow street address and phone number, the workers-of-the-world banner. Then Wagner added that some cases of his small type were broken, and pointed the committee to the third line of the forgery: "The small type on the third and fourth line is not distributed yet," Wagner said, referring to the smeared ink that had escaped his mysterious client's attention. He even returned to his shop—during his testimony—in order to get the receipt from the German vendor of this particular type.

"I guarantee this is my work," he said.

Amtorg's legal defense had prepared an extensive list of errors that also revealed the documents to be forgeries. The corporation's counsel listed twenty-three errors over eleven typewritten pages, including a mention of a nonexistent institution, the erroneous use of official titles, incorrectly named senior officials, consistent misspellings, and wrong addresses.[19] The evidence was overwhelming. There could be no doubt: the documents were forgeries, and the forgeries were made in New York.

Yet ninety years later, despite all the evidence, the question of who made the Whalen forgeries remains unanswered. No historian has ever uncovered what happened in America's first great disinformation scandal.[20] Just before the Soviet Union collapsed, Stanislav Levchenko, the KGB defector, and his American co-author speculated that Grover Whalen became the first U.S. victim of a shrewd Soviet intelligence operation designed to remove a particularly fierce anti-Communist voice. But they were wrong, led astray by their own professional biases. In fact, the Soviets were the victim, and Whalen merely an unexpected pawn in a bigger game.

By early 1930, most European countries had recognized the Soviet Union, which was founded in 1922, and yet the United States had still not reestablished diplomatic relations with Russia since the Bolshevik seizure of power in 1917. The United States' anti-Communist leanings were stronger than Europe's. Even much of organized labor was sharply anti-Communist. The American Federation of Labor (AFL) purged "Reds" from its ranks[21] and regularly warned of Soviets stirring trouble. One of the AFL's most aggressive voices was its vice president Matthew Woll, who had, in 1928, alleged that Amtorg was an intelligence front. "The charge is made that it is through Amtorg that all the money for communist activity in this country is handled," he declared in October 1928, more than a year before the Whalen affair.[22] He drew parallels with "the case of Arcos, the 'Amtorg' of London and Peking."[23] America had no Scotland Yard, Woll complained, so no one was getting to the bottom of Russian activities in the United States.

Yet Woll had no compelling evidence for Amtorg's supposed subversive activities. Woll was part of an influential and well-connected group of anti-Communist industrial leaders in the United States who were lobbying hard against recognizing the Soviet Union. America's highly visible, ideologically motivated opposition to Marxism was practically an open invitation for disinformation and forgery. With his statements against Amtorg, Woll was broadcasting the establishment's readiness to be tricked.

Then, on March 4, about six weeks after Max Wagner produced the forged stationery, Woll predicted a congressional investigation into Amtorg. He had written a letter to five hundred U.S. firms and members of Congress, alerting them to the "subversive activities" of the Third International in the United States. Woll charged that these activities were directed through Amtorg by Moscow, adding that there would be "no difficulty in presenting documentary evidence as to what is going on, including the financing and promotion of communist propaganda and the staging of so-called 'unemployment' demonstration."[24] The AFL, apparently, knew of documents then circulating in New York. The Whalen affair had started to take its course.

Eventually the Fish Committee heard from dozens of witnesses under oath. Among them was a former White Russian army officer who, two American journalists alleged, had offered to sell them documents that proved that the Comintern had staged riots in America. One Hearst reporter recalled that he was offered the documents for $15,000.[25]

Perhaps the most credible witness was Wagner himself. A young father who had seen the workhouse a few years ago, he was easily intimidated by police investigators, and clearly terrified while testifying. The man who commissioned the forged letterheads, Wagner said under oath, called himself "Yasova." This man, a fellow Russian, worked for *Novoe Russkoe Slovo*, a pro-monarchist, New York–based daily.[26] But that wasn't all. During Wagner's testimony, in another dramatic turn, it was revealed that another anti-Communist Russian émigré in New York had visited Wagner's shop, this time pretending to be one of two police officers investigating the forgeries. Wagner mentioned the name of the man who ordered the forgeries—Yasova—to the purported police officers, one of whom was Gregory Bernadsky, a well-known anti-Red activist who also happened to be the interpreter for the Fish Committee at the very moment of Wagner's testimony. Bernadsky ran ads for his gambling nightclub in *Novoe Russkoe Slovo*. Now that police officer, to Wagner's confusion, appeared to be sitting right behind the two congressmen who were interrogating him.

Wagner went on to tell the Fish Committee that the two purported policemen soon returned to tell him that the mysterious Russian who ordered the stationery had left. "They came back and told me he went to Europe," Wagner said, "and I think one of them was that man there." He pointed at Bernadsky.[27]

Bernadsky jumped from his chair, screaming: "It's a lie! It's a lie!"[28]

The reporters in the room perked up at the unexpected drama. "Shut up and sit down!" ordered a representative from West Virginia, around the cigar in his teeth. Yet Bernadsky, white-faced and shaking, continued to cry out "It's a lie" from the translator's bench.

Wagner had revealed too much information about his client, Yasova, who ordered the forged letterheads. "There are some people who know him very well, right in this room right now," added Wagner, under oath. "There are in this room now people who know him."[29] But the Fish Committee ultimately was not interested in getting to the bottom of the Whalen forgeries. The committee, after all, was set up to investigate malicious Communist activities, not malicious anti-Communist activities.

Finally, a month after the affair had died down, Bernadsky, the gambling monarchist translator and police impostor, came forward with new details. Bernadsky stressed that the six Whalen documents were forgeries—but *Soviet* forgeries. Amtorg had been too quick and too detailed in its rebuttal, implying that the same-day denial was planned well ahead of time. Amtorg, he claimed, had forged its own documents. "Their idea in this clever scheme is to make the public believe that all documents are forged," he told *The New York Times*, so that when genuine Soviet documents were discovered, the public would no longer care or trust them. This maneuver would become a classic method of denial and distraction: the conspirator accusing the victim of conspiracy.

In the Whalen episode, the available forensic evidence was remarkably strong, with witnesses testifying under oath and providing a wealth of detail. After the hearing, there could no longer be any doubt that the Whalen documents were forged in New York. The Fish Committee was able to subpoena and interview nearly all of the protagonists; even some of the masterminds of the operation were in the room, likely Russian monarchist émigrés trying to keep the United States from recognizing the Soviet Union. Yet even excellent evidence was not good enough, for the investigation was too ideologically biased, politicized, and ego-driven. Whalen himself tried to smear the witness, Wagner, by citing his criminal record. Six years earlier the printer had been arrested for possessing "indecent pictures," Whalen charged.

The Whalen episode has another timeless lesson in store. The forgeries show that delayed exposure may be in the interest of the attacker. At first, Whalen's pompous press announcement made sure the affair became front-page, international news. But soon it was the cloak-and-dagger story of covert investigations and intrigue that inspired reporters' and readers' imaginations—still more after the politicized congressional investigation.

The initial forgeries were badly done, and it is unlikely that the small group of Russian monarchist émigrés designed their ruse to be discovered so quickly. Yet the exposure itself would offer a second opportunity to exploit the division the first had created. The disinformation operation did not stop on May 3, and continued to escalate as the investigation got under way, probably to the surprise of the perpetrators.

The doctored documents showed how successful forgeries would work for the next century. They articulated a story that the targets of the ruse already believed—in this case, that Amtorg was a den of spies. They stated a basic fact, albeit with embellishments; Amtorg actually did have links with Soviet intelligence, and indeed served the interests of the Soviet revolutionary government. The line between true and false was far easier to blur when true and false were as close together as the fingers of a clenched fist.

1945–1960: Forge

American Disinformation

BERLIN LAY IN RUINS. THREE YEARS AFTER THE END OF THE war, houses were bombed out and rubble lined the streets. The smell of dust was ubiquitous in the summer, burned wood and coal in the winter, and dead bodies in recent memory. Among the ruins, people searched for a new life. Yet violence lingered. Political rallies looked like military parades, posters evoked an epic ideological struggle, even radio voices sounded like sharp-edged tin, especially in East Germany, in the "Soviet occupied zone," which the Germans called the *Sowjetzone*.

The Russian occupying forces continued to operate prison camps called "special camps," filled with German political prisoners, in the *Sowjetzone*. Rumors of abuse made the rounds in the violated city. Just-released political prisoners spoke of harrowing experiences under the inhumane camp

Richard Helms speaks with the actor Robert Redford on Rikers Island, New York City, in 1975. As chief of operations in the Directorate for Plans, Helms signed off on the CIA's most aggressive political warfare operations in the 1950s, many of them designed to blur the line between fact and fiction. (Photograph by Terry O'Neill / Iconic Images / Getty Images)

conditions. A number of youthful, idealistic German activists could not simply look on.

"Inaction Is Murder!" screamed the announcement for one rally, on October 17, 1948, in the Titania-Palast, Berlin-Steglitz. "Berliners! Come hear and see the truth." The placard also announced Rainer Hildebrandt as a speaker and representative of political youth organizations in Berlin. "I have to make a declaration," Hildebrandt said that Sunday afternoon. Berlin youth groups, he said, had decided to found a "Fighting Group against Inhumanity," the *Kampfgruppe gegen Unmenschlichkeit.* Such a martial name was not uncommon in the political vocabulary of the immediate postwar period in Europe. The goal of the new organization was the systematic investigation of crimes against humanity. "Those who are suffering and dying must have at least one certainty," Hildebrandt proclaimed: "that the world will learn about their plight." But telling truth from lies, facts from fiction, and news from propaganda was hard—and Hildebrandt himself was about to make it even harder.

Hildebrandt looked the resistance fighter that he was. Thirty-four years old, tall and handsome, he had dark piercing eyes and wore his curly brown hair combed back, and claimed that he had been a prisoner of the Nazis himself. When Hildebrandt founded what he called, in English, the "Fighters Against Inhumanity," he ran it out of his Grunewald apartment at Höhmannstraße 4. He lived just ten minutes from Gleis 17, a logistics hub for the deportation of Berlin's Jews just six years earlier. Now some of the very same concentration camps in the East were occupied again, with Germans, and Hildebrandt found it hard to take.

Events moved at reckless speed in the first years after the war. On September 2, 1945, weeks after the United States devastated two Japanese cities, World War II formally ended with Japan's surrender. A month later, on October 1, the Truman administration abolished the Office of Strategic Services, America's battlefield-tested proto–intelligence organization. About three weeks after that, the United Nations was formed in a bout of optimism and hope. Yet with every passing month, it became clearer and clearer that the war had marked not only the end of a deadly global ideological clash but the escalation of a different one. On September 18, 1947, the U.S. government formally created the Central Intelligence Agency, a new spy bureaucracy with quickly expanding authority. Two months later, on December 17, 1947, Truman's National Security Council authorized the CIA to perform covert action.

Meanwhile, political tensions in Europe mounted. On April 3, 1948, the Truman administration initiated the Marshall Plan to rebuild the war-ravaged continent. Later that month, George Kennan, a charismatic and strong-willed U.S. diplomat, drafted an influential memo titled "The Inauguration of Organized Political Warfare," in which he suggested the creation of a central office to employ all the means at the nation's disposal, "short of war." Kennan was alarmed by the Soviet Union's aggressive outlook. "Lenin," he wrote, "so synthesized the teachings of Marx and Clausewitz that the Kremlin's conduct of political warfare has become the most refined and effective of any in history."[1] Washington needed to up its game. On June 18, the National Security Council created an office of "special projects" to coordinate secret offensive operations against the expanding Communist powers.[2] Six days later, the Soviet Union accelerated a creeping crisis and put Berlin under siege by blockading rail, road, and water access to Allied-controlled areas of the city. The Allied response was the Berlin Airlift, a gargantuan logistical operation to keep symbolic Berlin free and supplied. It was then, under the steady hum of Allied transport aircraft, that Hildebrandt formed the Kampfgruppe. With Berlin under blockade, the CIA formally established the Office of Policy Coordination to run the aggressive anti-Communist political warfare campaigns called for by Kennan. Frank Wisner, formerly with the OSS and staunchly anti-Soviet, was tasked with running a shadow war against the enemies of Western liberal democracy.

Berlin Operations Base was right at the front in this war. On July 4, 1945, a team of OSS intelligence officers flew to the vast, subdued German capital. As the Americans approached Tempelhof Airport, the entire ravaged city underneath was still under Soviet control. Allen Dulles, who had been appointed the OSS Berlin station chief, chose for its headquarters a curious building in the posh suburb of Dahlem, a part of Zehlendorf that had suffered little bomb damage, on a small, nondescript, and leafy residential street. At first glance, the new base at Föhrenweg 19/21 could have passed for a large family home, one with too few windows—the building had been designed and built in 1936 by Albert Speer, the Nazi master architect. Field Marshal Wilhelm von Keitel, commander of the Oberkommando der Wehrmacht, had used it as a bombproof secret headquarters during the war; it had thirty-three rooms, two underground stories, 18-inch-thick, steel-reinforced concrete floors and walls, and its own escape tunnel.[3]

The entire western part of bombed-out Berlin soon became an outpost in what was, effectively, increasingly hostile enemy territory. The city immediately turned into the battleground of an intelligence war with protagonists from five major countries. BOB, as the CIA abbreviated its Berlin Operations Base, attracted a particularly aggressive breed of operators.

On March 18, 1949, BOB's chief sent a bold memo to CIA headquarters, then still housed in the old OSS building at 2420 E Street in DC's Foggy Bottom. The two-page missive was classified "secret," and the subject line read "Operation GRAVEYARD."[4]

"The group GRAVEYARD," announced the memo, was founded in Berlin about a year earlier by "a small group of young German intellectuals." Their goal was getting ex-inmates of prisons and concentration camps in the Soviet zone to tell their stories in public meetings and in writing—"an extremely difficult undertaking," the CIA case officers in Berlin acknowledged, given the intimidation tactics at play in East Germany. "Nevertheless, several such meetings have already been held, the first of which was already broadcast via RIAS," the U.S. radio station in Berlin. On February 14, 1949, *The New York Times* even picked up one of Hildebrandt's stories. The *Times* reported that Russians had thrown 250,000 Germans into prison camps, and, quoting Hildebrandt, that "more than 100,000" of the prisoners had died.[5] "Considerable publicity ensued," the CIA's Berlin memo concluded. It was unusual for a secretive agency to approve of publicity, but Wisner was on the lookout for aggressive covert action programs. The U.S. operators in their bombproof former Nazi bunker had noticed, with admiration, how fearlessly the young Kampfgruppe tackled the Soviet occupiers. Hildebrandt's outfit then consisted of just fifteen idealistic individuals, yet, despite its idealism and improvised setup, the Kampfgruppe was already handling about sixty visitors daily, all the while interrogating "approx. 8 ex-prisoners or other political refugees from the Soviet Zone." The CIA saw a prime opportunity to achieve two goals at the same time: gathering valuable intelligence and exposing Soviet atrocities. "Operations by this group have already been protested by Soviet authorities," the CIA wrote in its initial project approval memo in March 1949.

On August 3, 1949, Wisner's Office of Policy Coordination authorized an increase of funds for the new covert political warfare front. Less than two months later, on September 23, the United States announced that the Soviet Union had detonated an atomic bomb; a week after that, Mao Tse Tung proclaimed the People's Republic of China. Communism appeared to be innovating and expanding fast. The war in the shadows was escalating just as quickly.

The CIA's Berlin Operations Base gave handsome Hildebrandt the code name Paul V. Boudreau. U.S. officers considered him "a highly motivated intellectual young German who can be fully relied upon to carry out with complete sincerity and zeal the particular activities contemplated under this project."[6] He guarded the organization's first trove of documents under his own bed.[7] But the charismatic Hildebrandt was not a gifted organizer (although much later he would found the famous Checkpoint Charlie Museum on Berlin's Friedrichstraße).[8]

The CIA's Berlin station suggested that, "for the time being," the new front organization should be run without direct contact, but "entirely through a well-qualified American cut-out in Berlin." This shadowy middleman had already been subsidizing GRAVEYARD with U.S. taxpayer money, the CIA memo noted, and could easily explain an increase in funding. The memo suggested a monthly subsidy of DM 1,000 for the front organization, plus $100 for supplies, "mainly cigarettes, coffee and lard." GRAVEYARD was the first of a series of code names, which became increasingly drab as the proposal was passed up the chain of command. The CIA's Berlin station forwarded to the Heidelberg office, where the code name became EARTHENWARE; a few days later, CIA headquarters christened the project DTLINEN, which remained

SECRET

PROJECT OUTLINE

Project Cryptonym or Subject: DTLINEN

    Sub-Project Cryptonym or Identification:

    Amendment No. 2

Originating Division: EE

    a. Division Chief [   ]   Ext. 2062

    b. Branch Chief : [   ]   Ext. 3311

    c. Case Officer : [   ]   Ext. 3303

Target Area: East Germany

Type of Project: Psychological and Political Warfare

Financial Mechanism: Subsidy

Funds requested. [   ] for Fiscal Year 1955

Current Status: Operational since 1949 under authorization of Project
Outline (EARTHENWARE), approved 24 May 1949; Project
Outline (Revised), approved 16 August 1949; and Project
Amendment No. 1, approved 29 August 1950.

SECRET

A CIA Eastern European Division Project Clearance Sheet, dated October 27, 1954, seeking approval of another round of funding for the Kampfgruppe. The stated objective was to "harass and weaken the Soviet administration of East Germany."

the cryptonym for the Kampfgruppe for an entire decade. The declassified files specifically on DTLINEN are extensive: nearly 800 pages, spanning more than ten years, make them one of the two best-documented political warfare fronts in intelligence history.

But DTLINEN was not the only front outfit that the young CIA pioneered in Berlin—in fact, it was one of three. Each had a different goal: to collect incriminating and compromising details on its target; to publish information based on those details, aimed at specific target audiences; and to forge and to deceive the adversary. Such covert operations were inherently risky, and it soon became clear that those in the greatest danger were the CIA's indigenous German activists and assets.

One of the Kampfgruppe's sister outfits became known as the Investigation Committee of Free Jurists, or the *Untersuchungsausschuss freiheitlicher*

Juristen, often shortened to UfJ. The organization became operational in December 1949, and was soon code-named CADROIT. The project, as one memo to CIA headquarters explained, had been "subsidized and guided by CIA since inception in 1949."[9] The American spy agency judged the committee, as it had Hildebrandt's Kampfgruppe, a tool of "psychological and political warfare." The specific objective of CADROIT was to "promote and sustain popular anti-Communist resistance in East Germany (including East Berlin)."[10] It was in the U.S. national interest, according to this argument, to prevent the "complete Sovietization" of East Germany, and to minimize the economic, political, and military help that the GDR would be able to contribute to the Soviet Union. By 1956, the CIA was spending $250,000 per year on the project, which was considered highly effective. "The UfJ has achieved an international reputation as an efficient anti-Communist organization," the CIA case officer boasted in a memo intended to justify an increase in funding for "psychological and political warfare" in Berlin, adding that articles praising the legal society and its activities had appeared in *Time, The New Yorker, New Statesman, Reader's Digest,* and *The Nation,* as well as in leading publications in Switzerland, the Netherlands, Italy, and France.[11]

In the last week of July 1952, the UfJ organized a major, contentious event, the International Congress of Free Jurists, the goal of which was to expose crimes and injustices of all kinds committed in the name of communism.[12] "Congress sponsored by Committee of Jurists, a most reputable anti-Commie organization," U.S. diplomats in Berlin cabled to Washington.[13] They expected that 107 jurists from 43 countries would attend. But East German state security would not simply tolerate such an event.

The Soviets instructed the Ministry of State Security to make an example of Walter Linse, a West Berlin–based UfJ lawyer with a PhD and deep dueling scars on his upper left cheek. As the head of UfJ's economic section, he had been particularly active in exposing Soviet trade links. Three weeks before the Congress, the Stasi hired a group of notorious petty criminals.

At 5:00 a.m. on July 8, 1952, the criminals took a taxi from West to East Berlin. The men paid their fare in advance to make the cabbie less suspicious of the unusual trip at such an early hour. Then, just before they crossed the sector border, one passenger handed a pack of cigarettes to the driver. He took it. The border guards stopped the cab, asked the driver to step out, and arrested him for smuggling cigarettes. Next, the taxi's license plates were removed and installed on a prepared Stasi passenger car, a four-door Opel sedan. The criminals then drove back to West Berlin, rendezvoused with their co-conspirators at a prearranged meeting place, and proceeded to Linse's home.[14] The unsuspecting lawyer left his house at 7:30 a.m. Two of the criminals approached Linse and asked him for a light. Linse looked down, reached into his pocket for a lighter—and a small hard bag filled with sand smashed into his face. The attackers dragged their victim into a car and raced off. A delivery truck driver happened to witness the scene and gave chase, but could not catch up.

The Stasi interrogated Linse in East Berlin, all the while issuing a semi-denial that the kidnapping had even taken place, saying Linse had simply gotten "lost." Yet *Neues Deutschland*, the official East German newspaper, mocked protesters and Linse's supporters: "Not a single agent of war-mongering imperialism will be safe, wherever he hangs out—be it in West Berlin, Bonn, Paris or even Washington."[15] Only two days after Linse's capture, the Stasi arrested twenty-seven active UfJ informers.[16] On instructions from the Ministry of State Security in Moscow (the MGB), the GDR's supreme court staged the first trial of the informers to coincide with the meeting of the Free Jurists.[17] In the MGB's view, the kidnapping and ensuing trial "disorganized the work of the congress to a significant degree and undermined the anti-Soviet propaganda associated with it."[18] Linse was executed in a Moscow prison in 1953.

Meanwhile, a legendary CIA officer named William King Harvey had taken over as chief of Berlin Operations Base. Harvey was gun-toting and foulmouthed, gruff and bitingly sarcastic; Indiana-born, he was profiled—and caricatured—in *Playboy* as "the American James Bond."[19] His preference was for double martinis, and stories of his drinking excesses were legion. Harvey barely spoke a word of German, but he inspired lifelong loyalty in his core staff, dubbed the "Berlin Brotherhood." His deputy was the equally self-confident Henry Hecksher, a German-born ex–U.S. Army intelligence officer who had studied in Berlin.[20] Under Harvey, BOB's staff grew to 250, making Berlin the CIA's largest base worldwide, larger even than most country stations.

Stanley Gaines,[21] a senior intelligence officer and veteran of the Normandy landings, scrutinized almost all of BOB's plans in Frankfurt. "Nobody was Bill's equal," he said later. "Bill Harvey was the best operations executive I've ever seen. Everything that BOB did cleared through Bill, which was a feat in itself."[22] Harvey's office walls were lined with guns, with thermite bombs on top of the safes, ready to destroy documents in the event of a Soviet invasion.

Harvey was, famously, the driving force behind digging the Berlin Tunnel to tap into Soviet landlines under the Soviet sector—perhaps the single most daring intelligence operation of the entire Cold War. The tunnel was exposed in April 1956. At the same time, Harvey also oversaw what is likely the CIA's most aggressive disinformation operation ever, an operation that has not been explored publicly to date.[23] More even than the CIA's efforts with the Kampfgruppe and the UfJ, this third front was covert, prolific, innovative, aggressive, and deceptive.

Harvey's front was initially known as Aktionsgruppe B. Around two years in, the group acquired a public-facing cover identity, Cramer Werbung, or Cramer Advertising Office. Years later, when its publications became more open, the cover became known as Äquator publishing. The internal CIA code name, LCCASSOCK, was so obscure and cryptic that analysts occasionally misspelled their own code name as "LCCOSSACK."[24]

The nascent CIA front was born forging. From August 5 to 19, 1951, the Socialist Party in East Berlin organized the World Youth Festival. Communist parties from around the world sent their delegations to Berlin. The event was a major demonstration of the power of Communist ideology—and therefore a major target for anti-Communist covert operations. The CIA was on high alert and reported on the global preparations in exquisite detail (Saxony, for example, had 518 serviceable buses in 1951, 170 of which were used to ferry attendants to Berlin for the festival).[25] Field reports indicated that the FDJ, the Socialist Party's youth group, was preparing to assemble "one and one half to two million youths" from eighty countries in the Soviet sector.[26]

KI, then the foreign intelligence agency of the Soviet Union, was also watching preparations closely. Russian intelligence reports highlighted the risk presented by the fact that West Berlin was opening its border crossings to participants in the East Berlin festival (and that a leader of the Kampfgruppe was part of the Berlin mayor's coordinating committee). But it appears that KI was not aware of the major disinformation operation that would be launched at the festival.[27]

Meanwhile, some of West Berlin's most hardened liberal political activists were keenly anticipating the Communist youth rally. One of them was thirty-three-year-old Karl-Heinz Marbach. Marbach, lean and blond with an engaging smile, was a remarkable individual. During World War II he commanded a submarine in combat off the Norwegian, North African, and French coasts. Marbach's U-boat, a type-VIIC attack boat, sank one British steam merchant, the *Glendinning*, on July 5, 1944.[28] One of his ships was tasked with testing submarine-borne anti-aircraft artillery as a "first line of defense" against allied bombers. He briefed Admiral Karl Dönitz, head of the German Navy in the war and Hitler's brief successor at its end, advising him against the tactic.

Marbach later surrendered his U-boat to a British commander in Oslo, and spent two and a half years as a prisoner of war in French custody. While he was interned, his young wife, a journalist, was raped by Russian soldiers.[29] His experience during the war, especially his time as a POW, would later turn him into "a seasoned 'Cold Warrior,' strongly independent, freedom-loving, anti-Soviet," as the CIA would assess.[30] Back in Germany after the war, Marbach worked as a freelance journalist for several newspapers; he also worked for the Kampfgruppe for three months in early 1948, but was unaware of U.S. interest in the group.[31] In 1950, when Marbach was producing forgeries for the Ministry of All German Affairs in Bonn, the CIA finally made contact with him.[32]

The CIA's Office of Policy Coordination gave Marbach full operational clearance in July 1951, initially to work on a satirical newspaper, the *Tarantel*, which the CIA was funding.[33] (Marbach's first contracted forgery had been a small, onetime production of a falsified newspaper commemorating Stalin's birthday in December 1950.)[34] Then, as the 1951 youth rally approached,

Marbach and a few friends calling themselves Aktionsgruppe B prepared their resistance. Marbach produced three forged editions of the GDR's flagship youth newspaper, *Junge Welt*, in order to subvert the socialist spirit of the mass rally. Aktionsgruppe B printed and distributed a total of 180,000 copies of their forgery, supported by a onetime grant from BOB.[35]

One year later, when the larger project known as LCCASSOCK got under way, Marbach's clearance was expanded.[36] Berlin Operations Base authorized LCCASSOCK objectives in August 1952: to "produce and distribute one phony edition of a E. Ger. Magazine in 20,000 copies."[37] In the beginning, the operation alternated phony editions of their magazine with party bulletins and issues of the magazine *Die Volkspolizei*. The forging operation would drastically expand from there over the course of nearly a decade.

The CIA had discovered that disinformation worked best when factual content was carried by phony outlets—when the source was fake, but the content accurate. "The effectiveness of the LCCASSOCK effort depends in great part on the authenticity and the factualness of its materials," one secret memo reported.[38] Consequently, when the CIA tasked its front with falsifying specific issues of official East German magazines, the BOB case officers facilitated contacts and knowledge transfer from other covert front organizations, such as the Kampfgruppe or the UfJ, with specific expertise. In exchange, many of LCCASSOCK's falsified editions printed the return addresses of the less-covert sister organizations, in order to facilitate the backflow of intelligence and defections.[39]

To this day, the only reliable source for LCCASSOCK's work is the CIA's own archive. No participant has spoken or written about the outfit in any meaningful detail, yet I was able to locate some of the front's output in German bookshops and libraries. After World War II, the United States took the lead in influence operations—by harnessing the raw energy of the youthful German organizations that emerged from the rubble of West Berlin. Today, these front organizations are among the most revealing disinformation case studies from that time. Recently declassified CIA documents provide a unique perspective on how a large bureaucracy ran a well-resourced, covert, deniable, and persistent campaign of political warfare against a confident adversary.

By the early 1950s, the Kampfgruppe's reporting was so productive that it effectively became West Berlin's own proto–intelligence organization, nearly on a par with the then still unofficial predecessor organization of West German foreign intelligence, then known as "Organization Gehlen."[40] But in contrast to other Western intelligence agencies, the CIA-funded front had its priorities reversed: information operations were the goal, and intelligence collection a means to this end.

The Kampfgruppe

N JUNE 1949, ENABLED BY GENEROUS AND EVER-INCREASING CIA funding, the Kampfgruppe, or KgU, moved into a large villa in Berlin-Nikolassee, at Ernst-Ring-Straße 2–4. The organization grew to ninety employees over a range of subdivisions, complete with unemployment insurance, health benefits, and Christmas bonuses.

The Kampfgruppe's original purpose was servicing its up-to-date registry of arrested individuals. Its documentation claimed that the group had registered 108,058 political prisoners in the East, including 8,966 women and 14,772 adolescents. More than thirty thousand of them were found to be dead. The search service drew a vast number of visitors from the Soviet zone and East Berlin to the KgU's headquarters in West Berlin. These visitors didn't just come seeking information; they were also sources themselves, about recent arrests or even on informants working for the East German

Rainer Hildebrandt,
founder and leader of
the *Kampfgruppe gegen
Unmenschlichkeit*, an anti-
Communist activist outfit
and CIA front in Berlin
(Gerhard Gronefeld, Deutsches
Historisches Museum)

Ministry of State Security (MfS). In 1949, the KgU received 5,000 visitors at its headquarters; in 1950 the number jumped to 26,000, and reached almost 80,000 in 1953.

The KgU logged reports and registered the visitors, among whom were a few individuals of interest for the CIA. In a representative month in the mid-1950s, the KgU debriefed approximately twenty members of the East German People's Police and another twenty-five individuals in relation to the MfS; the organization submitted around two hundred raw intelligence reports to the CIA per month,[1] and even had a covert office. And every month, as now-declassified CIA sources show, the KgU interviewed around thirty-five secret visitors, and screened them for operations potential.

The CIA's relationship with its Berlin front was complex. Secretive, aggressive, ideologically driven groups with outsize ambitions tend to attract leaders with the same qualities, and outsize egos to match. In late 1951, the CIA was pulled into an internal KgU power struggle that culminated in a seven-and-a-half-hour meeting that included Hildebrandt; his deputy, Ernst Tillich; a core staffer, Walter Dethloff; and the American case officer as an arbiter. The result was a successful mutiny against the mercurial Hildebrandt. Five different KgU staff members presented evidence of Hildebrandt's flawed leadership to their CIA case officer. They alleged that their leader had used his contacts to avert police action against him for "several cases of seduction of minors"; that he embezzled funds; that he maintained associations with one man and one woman who were proven MfS agents; and that Hildebrandt's claim of being a concentration camp victim was false. Five members of the KgU's core staff then refused to cooperate with Hildebrandt and tendered their resignations to their CIA handler, who refused them.[2] The meeting ended with a resolution to force Hildebrandt out of the organization that he had founded. "In all fairness to Boudreau," the case officer wrote to the CIA's mission chief in Frankfurt, referring to Hildebrandt by his CIA alias, "never before have I had an opportunity by personal observation to convince myself of the fact that Boudreau is not only a psychopath, but also a very sick person."[3]

After Hildebrandt's removal, Ernst Tillich took over. Tillich, forty-two, dubbed Charles Newham by the CIA, was a religious socialist who had been arrested by the Gestapo for subversive activity and interned in the Sachsenhausen concentration camp for more than two years.[4] At least initially, Tillich seemed to be a more capable administrator and savvy political operator; he corresponded with Ernst Reuter, mayor of Berlin, and even Konrad Adenauer, the chancellor of the Federal Republic.

"KgU" didn't just sound like a Russian three-letter agency; it pioneered a unique blend of skills and capabilities that the KGB would begin to optimize only a decade later. The Kampfgruppe had established itself with a clear mission, to expose the inhuman conditions in Soviet zone concentration camps,[5] but soon expanded its operations to compiling lists of Germans working as Soviet informers and broadcasting their names on RIAS, the three-year-old U.S. radio station in Berlin. The group also researched and publicized data on abuse inflicted by the People's Police in East Berlin.

Before the KgU, political warfare and information operations had long been a by-product, a side activity, a risk. Disinformation required publicity, and publicity ran counter to the organizational culture of self-respecting intelligence agencies. The KgU—conceived to reveal, to publicize, and to influence—reversed this logic.

At first, the CIA was unprepared to take advantage of the opportunities offered by this new kind of front organization. To old-school intelligence officers, collection and influence didn't pair; intelligence work was to be kept separate from political warfare. In one memo from late 1952, just before Bill Harvey arrived, officers at Berlin Operations Base articulated their recommendations accordingly: "In our opposition to the interlocking of intelligence and psychological warfare interests, we should be unyielding," wrote the outgoing head of BOB. "As far as KGruppe activities outside the strict purview of psychological warfare are concerned, we shall strive if possible to eliminate them altogether." Yet Harvey's predecessor acknowledged the tension, and admitted that the KgU's intelligence work might be "indispensable," and that stopping it could "seriously harm U.S. coverage of the Eastern Zone of Germany."[6] The aggressive and risk-taking Harvey, it appears, saw not a problem but an opportunity. Project DTLINEN, under his leadership, was set to become a lean and aggressive political warfare outfit.

Among the KgU's first operations was a graffiti campaign. On July 20, 1949, in commemoration of a failed assassination attempt against Hitler five years earlier, youth groups swarmed out to paint large Fs—for freedom (*Freiheit*) as well as adversity (*Feindschaft*)—on streets, shop windows, and walls throughout Berlin, and distributed flyers to propagate the message. The GDR regime reacted by hiring contractors to turn the F into FDJ, the acronym of the regime's own youth organization. But the Stasi also punished KgU sympathizers with long prison terms and, in a few cases, even with the death penalty.

Another core activity was organizing lectures and presentations, in order to reach their target audience face to face. The group was officially recognized in Germany as a public entity, one whose stated goal was to offer the "support of science for the systematic discovery of crimes against humanity and the scientific exposure of their underlying ideologies."[7] The KgU, with U.S.

support, grew from 147 lectures in 1952 to 780 in 1955; in 1956, the KgU claimed that it hosted 1,339 talks and workshops that reached an audience of 146,000 attendants.[8] The KgU would even establish a West German office with four more staff members dedicated to organizing events and lectures.

The Kampfgruppe had already demonstrated a manipulative, deceptive, and risk-taking approach. Hildebrandt, for example, knew that spreading blatant and open anti-Russian sentiments was counterproductive. His tactical goal was to recruit informants and attract defectors. In one 1951 text about the Red Army, Hildebrandt went out of his way to highlight the humanity of occupation, employing disinformation tactics in the process. Many East Germans, he recalled, "have stories to tell of Russian friendliness." One such story was that of an old, sick German woman in a cottage in the countryside. One day a Russian woman stopped by the cottage and asked the old German lady for a glass of water. The Russian woman explained that she worked in a Russian Army canteen and her long way to work made her thirsty. The next day she came again, asked for water, and left. The German woman then saw a portion of butter the Russian woman had left behind. Day after day, the Russian woman took a glass of water, and left some food item, neither woman commenting on the exchange. "I have to go back to Russia," said the Russian woman one day. When the German woman thanked her, she said, "Don't thank me, thank Him," adding: "You live so close to freedom. Maybe the East Zone will be free soon. But when will we be free . . . ?"[9] Countless such stories could be told, Hildebrandt noted, and the spirit of resistance and even revolution was ripe within the Red Army. He even co-chaired an association to promote Russian-German friendship.

At the height of its activities, the KgU would produce six monthly brochures. *Die Wahrheit*, or "The Truth," was a general interest mini-magazine with a subheading that indicated that it was published by the Kampfgruppe in 100,000 copies per month, with the CIA footing the bill of DM 4,500.[10] *Der Kämpfer* was a monthly newsletter for the GDR armed forces, providing news from the ground forces, naval, and air force "with a western twist." *Der Parteiarbeiter*, "The Party Worker," targeted Communist functionaries; *Geist und Leben* was a cultural news outlet with a focus on suppression of the church and spiritual life in East Germany; *Elternhaus und Schule* targeted parents and students; and the *KgU-Archiv* was intended for an exclusively Western audience. Subtitled *Reports from the Soviet Occupied Zone*, the monthly 12-page publication ran articles such as "Students in the Soviet Zone" or "Suffocating Small Companies."

Distributing the brochures across the border was a challenge. By late 1951, the KgU was dispatching 15,000 neoprene balloons of material per month. The KgU even had its own chemical laboratory, run by the twenty-six-year-old activist and chemistry student Wolfgang Kaiser. His most important achievement was manufacturing a drop mechanism that was used to tie leaflets to balloons and then jettison the propaganda material slowly over its target area as the fuse burned down. The government in East Berlin falsely claimed the balloons were rigged with explosive charges to release their payload of papers.[11] The KgU budget request for 1957, for example, contained an order for 16,000 uncolored meteorological DAREX balloons from Dewey & Almy Co. of Cambridge, Massachusetts. The KgU maintained three ballooning bases until 1960.[12]

Meanwhile the fighters did fight, through sabotage and acts of what the CIA referred to as "administrative harassment." In early 1955, the KgU forged a letter purportedly from the mining division of DIA, a large state-owned trade enterprise in the GDR, and sent it to an East German mining company, Fabian & Co., in Senftenberg. The letter instructed the mining company to "immediately cease" its exports of siliceous quartz sand to its present export partners. The notice was professionally produced, with the proper letterhead, logo, serial numbers, a stamp, signature, footer, and stiff bureaucratic greetings—and it worked. In another operation, KgU sent a batch of forged letters to state retail stores in a town in Saxony, allegedly from the government in East Berlin. The fake letters instructed the stores to drastically reduce all prices for subsidized goods. The shops had sold out before the forgery was discovered.[13]

Throughout the year 1954, the KgU carried out 157 such administrative harassment operations, mostly forgeries. The CIA counted 70 false instructions and invitations; 41 items of "false information"; 16 instances of sending "true anti-Communist information under false letterheads"; plus a dozen false orders and forged postage stamps and documents.

Balloons were one delivery platform used by the Kampfgruppe to post messages and leaflets into East Germany. (BStU, via Enrico Heitzer)

Some had an international dimension, and affected U.S. allies and neutral countries along with enemies. One of the "most successful" operations, according to the CIA, involved "a falsified letter, purportedly originating" with the East German trade ministry. The fake note, sent to GDR recipients in Switzerland, Sweden, the Netherlands, Spain, Czechoslovakia, Hungary, Finland, and China, instructed international firms that the GDR could not accept orders for several years in light of its deteriorating economic and financial situation. The doctored letter also deliberately confused the West European companies by saying that the trade "had not resulted in the propaganda value which the GDR had expected."[14]

The CIA, learning through its various Berlin fronts, was getting better at the art of forging. The Agency had laid a clever trap for the GDR government in Berlin-Pankow, for its reaction would make the problem worse. Three East German newspapers swiftly called out the "vicious falsifications." The trade ministry, unsure which international customers had received the forgeries, mailed out a correction and explanation to all its international customers. The KgU, through well-placed collaborators, managed to intercept some of these genuine letters and replace them with another round of forgeries. The CIA's assessment concluded that the GDR's prestige abroad had taken a hit, and that, "as a by-product, the operation produced a list of firms engaged in West-East trade."

The KgU also engaged in hardware sabotage, engineering stink bombs to obstruct demonstrations and experimenting with the use of acids to damage machinery. On February 26, 1952, the KgU allegedly used acid—dubbed "Schnapps"—to mess with a sixty-ton hydraulic press at a logistics company in Oberspree, which led to an interruption of work for the duration of three shifts.[15] The KgU called sabotage S-Aktionen, which stood for disturbance actions, or Störaktionen. In March 1952, for example, an activist on a motorcycle scattered about one hundred so-called tire killers and incapacitated three Soviet vehicles.

The CIA even used the Kampfgruppe to interfere in East German elections. The KgU's Section VII, the "Propaganda and Covert Section," was responsible for ballooning and distribution logistics throughout East Germany. Section VII was also in charge of all of DTLINEN's political leaflets, targeted forgeries, and "confusion operations."[16] The election interference was timed for the GDR's communal vote in 1957, on June 23. Section VII planned to produce four separate leaflets, with a total distribution—by

mail and balloon—of 9.5 million copies over a seven-week period, exposing the farcical nature of the East German elections. The election interference was "highly effective," Bill Harvey told CIA headquarters immediately
after the vote. "Depending upon election results and reactions, we may put
out a follow-up leaflet in two to three million copies in July."[17] The Kampfgruppe's productivity was "at peak of effectiveness," as Berlin Operations Base
assessed[18]—so much so that the CIA's Berlin base needed to throttle leaflet
production over the GDR vacation cycle in 1957.

An in-depth look at CIA political warfare from the 1950s is revealing in
several ways. First, these early cases show the resourcing and planning that a
large intelligence bureaucracy was pouring into designing, authorizing, shaping, funding, maintaining, securing, evaluating, and eventually liquidating
what would soon become known as active measures. The CIA examples of
the Kampfgruppe and LCCASSOCK also illuminate the difficulty of measuring effects. The CIA worked with Marbach's LCCASSOCK, for example, to
develop techniques to build "various contest, poll, and opinion gimmicks"
into feature items of publications to test reader reactions.[19] The CIA introduced censorship evaluations in April 1956, which meant that 3 percent of all
LCCASSOCK items mailed into "denied areas" were control letters (the control
letter return rate was 20 percent over the next twelve months).[20]

As the KgU's success reached its height, the CIA discovered that its most
aggressive political warfare operations were paradoxically shielded by publicity and humanitarian ethics. The CIA didn't do a particularly thorough job
of camouflaging the fact that the KgU was an American intelligence operation. Hildebrandt and his deputy knew that they were working for a U.S. intelligence agency, and CIA case officers, after some initial caution, stopped
using a cutout when interacting with them. Nominally, the KgU received
donations from individuals and organizations sympathetic to the group's
goals, yet the cover for CIA funding was wafer-thin—the case officer turned
over bags of cash directly to Hildebrandt, and apart from "small gifts" from
German individuals, the KgU received "its entire financial support" from the
Americans. At the KgU, as the CIA noted in August 1956, "covert operations
are conducted behind an overt façade."[21]

Therein lay the paradox: a partially compromised operation was less, not more, at risk than a fully compromised one. "The KgU has frequently in the past been accused by East and West German news media of being an instrument of a United States intelligence service," a CIA internal risk assessment reported in 1957; select individuals in the government in Bonn and West Berlin also knew of the CIA's involvement. "Considering this," one Agency memo concluded, "it is believed that repercussions in the event of a compromise would not be very great in West Germany or Europe." Soviet authorities could gain "only little capital" in the case of a proper public compromise. Even more important, exposing the hand of the U.S. government would not backfire inside the United States, as the German front organization was engaged in a "basically humanitarian" program. The CIA had discovered the odd dynamic that publicity afforded a degree of protection to its secret disinformation operations.

The Agency discovered this sweet spot right in the middle between covert and overt operations just as its Kampfgruppe front was at peak effectiveness. On June 26, 1957, around eight years into the operation, Bill Harvey was more optimistic than ever. "Indications of effectiveness of DTLINEN material infiltrated into the Zone, always encouraging, are currently increasing at an impressive rate," he reported to headquarters.

Amping up political warfare, however, would also amp up political tensions—not just for the victim but also for the attacker. Aggressive and unconventional operations, designed to cause friction for an adversary, also caused friction among allies. By August 1952, the largest source of funds for the Kampfgruppe was the Ford Foundation,[22] and several other private individuals and nongovernmental organizations supported the resistance in West Berlin. A CIA audit shows that Ford provided a grant of DM 31,500 a month, just under half of the Kampfgruppe's budget at the time.[23] The Ford Foundation had asked the CIA "to look after its interests," especially to make sure that the funds were used for their intended purpose: to "create and keep alive resistance in the Eastern Zone."[24] Initially, the Ministry for All-German Affairs in Bonn—informally known as the Kaiser ministry—provided some funding, but the CIA did not appreciate the Kaiser ministry's more timid approach and wanted full control of its own disinformation front. "The Ford grant," Berlin Operations Base observed once, "completely undermined whatever leverage Kaiser thought he had" with the Kampfgruppe.[25] When the Ford Foundation and German authorities discontinued their funding, the CIA stepped into the breach with around $70,000 per month. In May 1953, the CIA recorded a total annual operating expenditure of DM 819,000, a remarkable sum for the early 1950s.[26] The covert section of the budget contained a number of regular line items, such as secretaries and technicians: "Administrator (Harassing Section) 450.00 DM" and "Man who works as part-time balloon filler 100.00 DM."[27]

The CIA exerted operational control in a number of ways that went beyond funding. One was editorial guidance. "The KgU, under CIA guidance, conducts administrative harassment operations in the Soviet Zone, based largely on information received from its East German covert informants and on mail intercepts," one memo explained. Another form of control was selecting targets, or, in the CIA's occasionally dry bureaucratic jargon: "the production and carefully targeted distribution of falsified administrative instructions."[28] The American intelligence apparatus also secretly kept tabs on the phone lines of its own front organization.[29]

However, the CIA's management of the KgU would ultimately lead to its closure. The main reason for the KgU's existence had already disappeared in 1950, when the last "special camps" for political prisoners in East Germany were closed. For nearly a decade, the CIA had "control of the entire organization through complete dependence upon CIA funds for activities."[30] The project's termination document highlights that the Kampfgruppe was "totally dependent" on the CIA and "could not sustain itself."[31] However, the CIA did not staff the project for close oversight and control. Only two case officers were assigned to run the vast Kampfgruppe operation, one in the field and one in headquarters.[32] The CIA liquidated the project in 1960, and the KgU ceased to exist.

LC–Cassock, Inc.

THE DECLINE OF AMERICAN DISINFORMATION IN BERLIN IS linked to its very success, and at the heart of this story is Project LCCASSOCK—the CIA's and Bill Harvey's most prolific, innovative, and aggressive forgery factory, probably of the entire Cold War. For more than ten years, LCCASSOCK produced and distributed a range of high-quality magazines, newspapers, and brochures across Germany, and even in Switzerland and Austria. Its main focus was East Germany. "The principal target area is the GDR," the CIA specified in one of around 300 archived documents, with more than 1,200 pages in total, on LCCASSOCK and its staff. The CIA used its front as an "experimental workshop" for political warfare.

Some inside the CIA began to recognize a basic problem in its approach to the ideological confrontation that was the Cold War, barely a decade after

Karl-Heinz Marbach, a decorated Wehrmacht U-boat commander, became the CIA's principal agent for LCCASSOCK, code name for a West Berlin–based publishing organization first known as Cramer Advertisements, and later as Äquator Publishers.
(Herbert Forst)

fighting had stopped in Europe: focusing on the strengths of the Soviet Union meant neglecting one's own strengths. "Concentration on the enemy's techniques has tended to result in the overlooking of potential psychological weapons which originate in, and are peculiar to, the free world," the CIA wrote in one project outline.[1] The driving force behind the CIA's psychological weaponry was Karl-Heinz Marbach, the former U-boat commander.

A CIA staff officer spotted Marbach in 1950, and contacted him in the fall that year; the CIA-sponsored propaganda production under Marbach got under way in April 1952.[2] By the mid-1950s, LCCASSOCK's objective had become ambitious: to "weaken and/or destroy Communist manifestations in the GDR and the Federal Republic."[3] Large-scale forgeries were the means to this end. The physical cover for the operation was an advertisement and public relations firm, with offices at Kurfürstendamm 136, on West Berlin's bustling main commercial avenue. The firm, Cramer Werbung, was registered with the West Berlin authorities.[4]

Measuring impact and making adjustments was important, so the CIA paid its front organization to "cultivate" mail correspondence with readers of its publications in Eastern Europe. LCCASSOCK included "political action efforts," which included maintaining relationships with political activists, journalists, and academics. The CIA was also testing ongoing mail censorship procedures in East Germany and adjacent countries in the East. Cramer had a mail control office, a "customers office," and a printing shop.

LCCASSOCK used different cover businesses over time, beginning with the ad hoc Aktionsgruppe B, then PR Cramer,[5] and finally the printing house Äquator Verlag GmbH. Over the same period, Marbach's operation evolved, in the words of one secret memo, from "a four-man 'illegal' show" operating from Marbach's home to a "firm" with around thirty-five efficient employees with full tax benefits, end-of-year bonuses, security routines, and several offices.[6]

The falsification operations were highly specific, and required in-depth knowledge of East German affairs. To better falsify Die Volkspolizei, the in-house magazine of the GDR's People's Police, writers received help from the Kampfgruppe or the Free Jurists, who debriefed police defectors. The completely "black," or unattributed, publications could be so convincingly Communist in tone that some resistance-minded distributors took issue with the "Marxist tenor" of the documents they were supposed to relay.[7]

The GDR did not take to disinformation lightly, and attempted to kidnap Marbach in the summer of 1952, a few months after LCCASSOCK ramped up operations. The kidnapping was foiled by Cramer's security officer, but East Berlin authorities kept harassing Marbach. In December 1953, the same month Walter Linse was executed, the main GDR radio station "revealed" (incorrectly) that Marbach was an agent of the Gehlen organization, and even broadcast his home address.[8] Meanwhile two distribution leaders were "lost" to East German security forces. Nevertheless, the CIA considered the risks of the operation low; LCCASSOCK was undeterred, and increased security along with production. LCCASSOCK even had a backup plan in the event of German tax authorities looking into the organization: the CIA disinformation front was using several wealthy former Wehrmacht colleagues of Marbach's "as cover for the source of funds for the project," one memo explained.[9] The CIA also had plans to evacuate Marbach from Berlin in case of a Soviet invasion.

The distribution office was installed in a building separate from the editorial offices. No outsiders were permitted. "All meetings with distribution cut-outs are held outside LCCASSOCK installations," a lengthy CIA review noted.[10] The front firm hired delivery cars, and changed them frequently. Meanwhile, the pace of operations accelerated steadily. Each month the small outfit falsified an average of two different GDR publications. By early 1954, the covert PR agency had produced around thirty falsified issues of official East German publications, at least 20,000 copies in each case, adding up to approximately 600,000 items of what the CIA called "dummy issues."[11] The distribution logistics of such large amounts of paper were significant and visible, and therefore ran in a building separate from the Kurfürstendamm office. LCCASSOCK was even able to handle special debriefings: the security officer would take visitors of high value to a friend's pub, which was equipped with a hidden tape recorder.

The list of forged publications was exhaustive. It included the main outlets with target groups across the whole society: *Die Wochenpost,* a popular GDR weekly; *Neuer Weg,* the official SED organ; *Neue Zeit,* the official Soviet magazine in German; *Der Wegweiser,* the information bulletin of East Germany's nominal liberal party; *Junge Generation,* the FDJ's official outlet; *Die Tribüne,* a trade union journal; *Der Freie Bauer,* a farmers' publication; *Die Frau von Heute,* the GDR's women's magazine; and even *Junge Welt,* a well-known newspaper for a young audience.[12]

The CIA saw the falsified editions as particularly effective. Phony editions of existing publications could be targeted at highly specific audiences that were normally inaccessible to Western propaganda, such as the People's Police or the FDJ, the Socialist Party's youth organization. In addition, releasing forged magazines into the GDR presented only minimal risk to the distributors. The CIA also gleaned from field reports that forgeries, once recognized, had their own unique appeal: "duplicating exactly the format and make-up of legitimate East German publications is in itself an unusual psychological attraction to readers of LCCASSOCK publications even after their true character may have been recognized."[13]

Sometimes minor details would go a long way. On June 29, 1953, just days after a major popular insurrection in East Berlin was suppressed with military force, the CIA took advantage of the general confusion. LCCASSOCK produced an official SED magazine that gave faux-official guidance: telling the workers that GDR residents wanted freedom and free elections, but also warning readers not to fight tanks with bare hands. Berlin Operations Base knew that there might be little interest in an SED booklet just after the riots—and therefore added *Streng Vertraulich!*, or highly confidential, to the cover. "We believe that this will enhance the appeal of the magazine to everyone and remove the stigma of party literature, since all people are interested in reading confidential material," one CIA request for an increased forgery budget explained.[14]

But large-scale forgery came with unexpected repercussions. In March 1956, when distributing forged issues of *Die Wochenpost*, the glossy illustrated weekly, LCCASSOCK ran into problems related to legal liability for copyright and trademark infringements.[15] Marbach simply changed the name to *Das Illustrierte Wochenblatt*.

In early 1954, BOB under Harvey was spending $60,000 per year on the forgery outfit. The organization would soon grow to thirty-two full-time German employees, several of them experienced journalists, not including freelancers who were brought in for specific projects.

By late 1956, CIA headquarters was ready to escalate its Berlin operations. In a memo that went from Germany to the head of the CIA's Psychological and Paramilitary Staff in October of that year, LCCASSOCK's tasks were reemphasized: the unit, just like the KgU, was to begin producing "falsifications of official East German correspondence for the purpose of administrative harassment."[16] LCCASSOCK's tool kit kept expanding, and the front soon ventured into uncharted terrain.

Klatsch means "gossip" in German, and is also the sound of slapping somebody in the face. *Klatsch* is what Marbach and his team called a fake gossip magazine, planned and implemented "as a direct attack on the Nationale Volksarmee (National Peoples' Army) and the GDR security services." Executives in Washington wanted to ensure that *Klatsch* was "entertaining enough" to maintain a decent readership. The CIA was confident in its leaked and outright-invented gossip—so confident, in fact, that it even counted postal censors and "the mailman" among the publication's target audience. *Klatsch* also was meant to showcase liberty itself as a "distinctly *Western* product," one memo emphasized. In the Soviet bloc, BOB explained, trivia and gossip were alien to what was mainly a political and argumentative press landscape: "*Klatsch* is aimed at this contrast and at East German readers who, we think, particularly appreciate it."[17] *Klatsch* made "no claim to veracity," but printed anecdotes in order "to inspire a chuckle, stick in the memory, and to be repeated."[18] *Klatsch* was mailed to 1,500 Communist Party members in East Germany.

The stories in *Klatsch* were wild. One, for example, claimed that Khrushchev had accused Stalin of murdering his second wife. Another claimed that scientists were on the verge of discovering a gas that would divert the continental winds—and that the Soviet Communist Party's 20th Congress had embraced the invention, hoping to prevent balloons containing print material from being swept across the border that divided the two Germanys.[19]

The magazine was a success. Like the KGB and the Stasi and even MI6 before it, the CIA was quick to grasp the time-tested recipe of tabloid success: "many pictures, short texts, features, a touch of sex, and a tendency towards sensationalism."

LCCASSOCK even ventured into prophecy. Astrology, though not particularly fashionable in the West, gained political significance when transplanted into the Soviet bloc. As Harvey's Berlin outpost noted, astrology was much more popular in Germany than in the United States; most major German magazines regularly carried horoscopes, usually printed next to the cross-word puzzle. Yet this high popular demand for astrology was subdued in the East, where seeking truth in the stars was incompatible with "the precision of dialectic materialism," as Berlin Operations Base noted. This created an opening for covert operations. LCCASSOCK published an astrological maga-zine, called *Horizont*, and Berlin Operations Base explained to Washington that the publication was conceived as "a direct attack on advocates of Mos-cow Communism through the vehicle of astrological analysis and prophecy."

Measuring performance was crucial for follow-on funding from the CIA, so the front produced an array of accounting figures to show how valu-able it was. LCCASSOCK, like the KgU, reached peak performance in 1957. The disinformation front produced and published 855,969 media items that year, almost twice the number of items produced in 1956.[20] The front's average monthly output was an impressive 71,300 media items. The boost in operational capacity became possible because LCCASSOCK's own, CIA-funded, low-cost printing plant became operational that year. At the same time, LCCASSOCK expanded its mailing lists. It mailed 651,917 media items to recipients in East Germany in 1957. By September 1958, the list included more than 42,000 addresses. One way to measure effect was by counting the number of correspondents. CIA's disinformation mill had received re-sponses from 2,074 recipients; "at present the ratio is 20:1," BOB wrote in September 1958. About 13 percent of Äquator's 1957 media output, 114,033 items, was distributed in Soviet bloc countries other than the GDR (and Russia)—"satellite countries," in Cold War jargon. By fall 1958, the number of non-GDR correspondents was 721. The most favorable responses came from Polish recipients, followed by Czechs, Romanians, Russians, and Bulgarians.[21]

In early September 1957, just weeks before the USSR's launch of *Sput-nik*, LCCASSOCK prepared a series of letters with personalized horoscopes for officials in the Ministry of State Security. The letters were mailed to pro-regime Berlin residents in the expectation that the collaborators would pass on the odd horoscopes to the actual targets in the MfS. Hans Fruck, the new deputy head of the Stasi's foreign intelligence arm, HVA, was targeted with eerie horoscopes predicting his doom. "These actions were designed to introduce a note of uncertainty within the MfS bureaucracy and, perhaps, to mislead MfS investigative energies," BOB reported back to Washington. The CIA base knew that the phony horoscopes were getting through to their MfS targets, but the results were unclear.[22]

Nevertheless, the CIA stuck to the horoscope tactic, and even upped the ante. In June 1958, LCCASSOCK prepared "400 horoscope harassment letters" for selected Socialist Party (SED) and Stasi personalities. The letters, ostensibly prepared by a nonexistent astrological research institute in West Germany, were designed to exploit an opening rift among members of the SED's central committee, notably between Fritz Selbmann and Walter Ulbricht, two influential Socialists: each letter contained "a carefully written horoscope analysis of the status and future of Fritz Selbmann, particularly in his relationship to Ulbricht." The goal of the operation was to bolster Selbmann's prestige at a time when his internal opposition was at a high point ahead of the SED's fifth major convention, a major, highly choreographed political rally with the motto *Socialism Is Winning*. Even Nikita Khrushchev attended. Russia was leading the space race, and for a brief moment the GDR thought it could compete with—or even outdo—the West German economic miracle of the postwar years. Guided by two case officers, Marbach's team produced 662 copies of a forged "black" letter to party members, printed on original letterhead from an SED-linked anti-Fascist association of political opponents of Nazi Germany.

The goal was to drive a wedge between the Communist old guard and the new and more opportunistic SED factions supporting Ulbricht. A collaborator of Marbach's wrote the forgery "in an appropriate 'anti-fa' tone and with a view to creating a maximum divisive effect," as BOB reported back to headquarters a few months later. The 662 fake letters were sent to Antifa activists, Socialist Party members, to the party's Central Committee, and to editors at East German newspapers just prior to the opening of the GDR Party Congress.[23]

The political warfare planners at Berlin Operations Base were careful to manage expectations at CIA headquarters. The disinformation campaign

(6) In June 1958 LCCASSOCK produced 662 copies of a black letter in an operation directed at the Fifth SED Party Congress. For this action BOB furnished original letterhead stationery from the "Komitee der Antifaschistischen Widerstandskaempfer," the GDR association of German Communist refugees from Naziism. The text of the letter was based on themes discussed with the case officer and was written by a LCCASSOCK collaborator in an appropriate "anti-fa" tone and with a view to creating a maximum divisive effect between the "old guard" and the opportunistic Ulbricht factions within the SED. The letters were prepared for distribution to members of the "Widerstandskaempfer"

| FORM 53c 10:57 (40) | USE PREVIOUS EDITION. REPLACES FORMS 51-28, 51-28A AND 51-29 WHICH ARE OBSOLETE. | CLASSIFICATION SECRET | ☒ CONTINUED | PAGE NO. 3 |

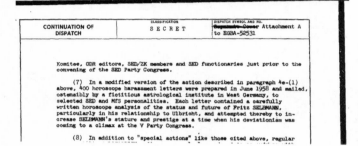

| CONTINUATION OF DISPATCH | CLASSIFICATION SECRET | DISPATCH SYMBOL AND NO. ~~Crusade-Cover~~ Attachment A to EGBA-52531 |

Komitee, GDR editors, SED/ZK members and SED functionaries just prior to the convening of the SED Party Congress.

(7) In a modified version of the action described in paragraph 4e-(1) above, 400 horoscope harassment letters were prepared in June 1958 and mailed, ostensibly by a fictitious astrological institute in West Germany, to selected SED and MfS personalities. Each letter contained a carefully written horoscope analysis of the status and future of Fritz SELBMANN, particularly in his relationship to Ulbricht, and attempted thereby to increase SELBMANN's stature and prestige at a time when his deviationism was coming to a climax at the V Party Congress.

(8) In addition to "special actions" like those cited above, regular

A secret CIA memo from September 1958, from William Harvey at Berlin Operations Base to the Eastern European Division at CIA headquarters, discussing anti-Stasi disinformation operations (CIA)

that Marbach and his team were designing and implementing was counterintuitive, neither wide nor narrow, designed neither for mass influence nor targeting of individuals. Instead, the Berlin base saw LCCASSOCK's operations as "specific influence," which was in theory more concentrated than mass media operations but less concerned with direct individual reactions. This unusual format meant that evaluating operational effectiveness was equally unusual: "The criteria of LCCASSOCK effectiveness should accordingly be more exacting than those employed in mass influence operations and less demanding than those required by singleton actions."

As one officer reported in a secret memo, signed off by Harvey, "I feel that LCCASSOCK, because we have used it as a kind of psychological warfare workshop to test ideas and to experiment, has as a result developed a body of thinking which has already proved useful and will be increasingly so in the future." The CIA's Berlin-based "experimental workshop" attempted to identify and analyze population attitudes and mental responses, the officer went on, and its approach "approximated that of a psychologist with his patients."

Schlagzeug, published by Äquator, was Germany's most significant jazz magazine in the mid-1950s. The CIA first funded the magazine, then attempted to spin it out as a for-profit publication.

The experiments had demonstrated that "an indirect approach," exemplified by the front's forays in astrology, gossip, rumor, and women's magazines, worked best to get into the mind of the target. The approach was tailored to Communist society, where individuals would have a hard time reconciling their past experiences and expectations with the harsh realities of everyday life—hence the temptation to escape from this reality into "superstition and fantasy."

In late 1958, Harvey signed off on a memo to the chief of the Eastern European Division that would hasten the end of LCCASSOCK. Over 15 pages, classified as secret, the memo discussed the commercial viability of a jazz magazine. The first issue of *Schlagzeug* had been published in September 1956. "Along with astrology, we consider [jazz] one of the most potent psychological forces available to the West for an attack on Moscow Communism," Harvey argued.[24] The reader response to the publication of *Schlagzeug*'s first issue was unprecedented. The CIA front received one written reaction, "including a number from FDJ Chapters,"[25] for every 88 copies. The jazz magazine was frequently shared hand-to-hand at FDJ meeting places and dance halls, U.S. intelligence officers believed. Harvey and his propaganda team considered *Schlagzeug* one of their most effective covert publications, and the one "most susceptible to further development and expansion."

The music magazine soon absorbed more than 10 percent of the front firm's time and resources. It was professionally produced, often featuring African American jazz icons like Ella Fitzgerald and Sidney Bechet on the cover, with black-and-white pictures and a new pop-art coloration each month. One or two articles per issue were subtly subversive. One July 1959 piece highlighted the visit of international jazz legends to Berlin despite Soviet resistance—pictures showed Louis Armstrong enjoying a sausage and beer as he chatted with Willy Brandt, then Berlin's mayor, or Art Farmer and Gerry Mulligan, cool bebop stars, visiting the sunny Brandenburg Gate in sports jackets and shades, drab East Berlin at their backs. The magazine wasn't blatantly pro-capitalist; it wanted to be edgy and bohemian. One editorial highlighted the rebellious character of jazz, comparing the music to subversive art like Dadaism.[26] For the most part, however, the magazine was just about jazz, and was mainly distributed in West Germany; only minor quantities went to the GDR.

In May 1956, a "strong *Schlagzeug* delegation" attended a jazz festival in Frankfurt am Main, and the head of LCCASSOCK's distribution operation continued on to Austria and Switzerland to set up outlets through magazine sales agencies and concert halls. The magazine, per BOB's summary, had matured into "an attractive, informative, and technically responsible journal of jazz." *Schlagzeug* represented an all-German approach to jazz, the memo argued, "thereby maintaining, incidentally, its usefulness as a KUCAGE medium for Soviet bloc consumption" (KUCAGE was a cover name for the CIA's psychological and paramilitary operations staff). Never mind its paramilitary backers and its ex-Wehrmacht chief: the jazz magazine had "gradually

Schlagzeug covers, featuring jazz legends from the September, July, and November 1959 issues

come to be recognized by jazz experts and fans alike as the best journal of its kind presently appearing in Germany," the BOB memo boasted, adding that *Schlagzeug* was now fully accredited by the West German Jazz Federation. The Berlin station pointed out to Langley that more than 20,000 fans had paid to hear Benny Goodman in Berlin during a recent show in May,[27] and concluded that the jazz cover for its disinformation front had a bright future: "Our suspicion [is] that the jazz movement in Germany and in Europe generally is not only much more intense, more pervasive and popular, but is more profitable than in the United States."

The problem was that the numbers did not check out. By 1958, LCCAS-SOCK had become a noteworthy cost item. Although financial details are mostly redacted from the files, the figures become clear through careful reading: the average monthly costs of the entire LCCASSOCK operation from March to June 1958 were DM 35,687, plus total monthly salaries of DM 19,516.[28] The budget included a number of perks for the CIA's unwitting German employees at Äquator: union scale increases; promotions; travel, rent, and utilities; a yearly round-trip flight to West Germany; and "operational entertainment for contacts for political action."[29] In 1958, the CIA's covert action objective changed and the Agency significantly cut its support for LCCASSOCK, which then amounted to three-quarters of the front firm's budget. By mid-1959, despite the jazz-generated income, the monthly salary costs covered by the CIA still averaged $5,000.[30] BOB operatives may have dreamed of turning their beloved jazz magazine into a profitable start-up cover for even more aggressive operations, but in reality, their love of jazz helped bring down one of the most aggressive covert ops of the Cold War.

The publication of *Die Frau*, LCCASSOCK's women's magazine, backfired in a similar fashion. Throughout 1956, Marbach's outfit produced three issues of the magazine, printing 20,000 copies each time. The first issue that year had a famous pro-Western Russian ballet dancer on the cover, Tatjana Gsovsky. One story presented modernist mid-century interior design as a form of protest against "attacks against privacy."[31] The spy base, under the gun-toting Harvey, even produced a "pony edition" of *Die Frau*, at a cost of DM 9,470, and mailed almost ten thousand copies with pictures of ponies into the Soviet zone. As of January 1957, the covert editors of *Die Frau* were in active mail correspondence with 185 women in the Soviet bloc.[32]

The covert action specialists in Washington did not appreciate *Die Frau*.[33] One reviewer assessed that it was "an attractive publication which certainly entertained our secretaries here," yet pointed out that it was "in no way different, better, or prettier" than other women's magazines. The reviewer saw it as a "questionable" publication, with unclear tactical benefit. The reviewers were similarly skeptical about LCCASSOCK's dating service, the *Von Herz zu Herz* newsletter, a monthly publication that also peaked in 1956. "We fail to understand the purpose behind the lonely hearts leaflet," one reviewer wrote.[34] *Die Frau* first led CIA reviewers to question the impact and rationale of LCCASSOCK's "marginal" publications. Jazz, fashion, and love, it turned out, were too indirect an approach to winning the Cold War. By mid-1957, the overly experimental political warfare workshop in Berlin was slowly falling out of favor.

The CIA changed its covert action objectives in 1958, cutting back financial support for and reorganizing its Berlin front organizations.[35] On November 29, a Saturday, the BOB case officer went over to Galvanistrasse to

Die Frau was a CIA-funded
women's fashion and
home-decorating magazine
published by Marbach.
(Clint Montgomery)

discuss two upcoming "black letter" operations, one directed against a Chinese commune, the other a local Party chapter. But that afternoon, Marbach objected. He argued that Äquator Verlag had matured into a well-reputed and respectable publishing business, and could no longer afford to indulge in "dirty" spy operations.

"There is some merit in this argument," the CIA case officer conceded. But he pushed back against Marbach, arguing that surely an operation could be compartmentalized and run in a way that would not inflict reputational harm on the publisher. Marbach objected again, arguing that black ops were bad, per se, and "inappropriate to the present Cold War situation." The case officer departed in a rage. "Who in the last analysis is running LCCASSOCK— we or L-1?" he asked in his report, referring to Marbach by his informal cover name. The former Wehrmacht officer, the CIA officer complained, "is the product of a long KUBARK handling policy which led him to believe that he is a completely free agent who happens of his own free will to be cooperating

The CIA front LCCASSOCK pioneered a tactic later frequently adopted by Eastern bloc intelligence: exposing the Nazi past of German politicians in order to compromise or topple them.

with us," he wrote, using one of the CIA's vintage cryptonyms for itself. The case officer found it hard to believe that Marbach would not yield, "despite the money we've poured into the project," and despite "our quite obvious legal ownership" of 76 percent of the Äquator publishing house. "In my opinion this 'alice-in-wonderland' kind of relationship with L-1 cannot go on much longer," he wrote. The case officer was so angry that he confessed a personal antipathy to Marbach, and called him an "intellectually shallow person."[36]

One of Äquator Verlag's most aggressive operations took place after Marbach had articulated his displeasure, and after the CIA had already decided to liquidate. In May 1959, LCCASSOCK published a 32-page booklet entitled "The Great Betrayal. Moscow and Anti-Fascism."[37] The collection of ten articles argued that once the veil of institutional anti-fascism was lifted, communism in fact had been aiding and abetting fascism again and again, in the Hitler-Stalin Pact, for instance. Most notably, the pamphlet leaked the names of 180 prominent politicians, business leaders, and scientists in the GDR who had been members of the National Socialist Party during the Third Reich. The list included titles, full names, NSDAP entry dates, and membership numbers. Fifty-two members of the new East Berlin Parliament had been former Nazis. Three East German MPs had been members of the SS, and one even part of Adolf Hitler's elite personal guard unit. The booklet did not name its editor or authors, and it gave only one source for the list of names: the investigative committee of the Free Jurists, aka CADROIT.

The CIA phased out operations by January 1, 1960, and then legally terminated LCCASSOCK on May 31, 1961, after a lengthy eighteen-month liquidation process.[38] Marbach went on to work for West Germany's still young foreign intelligence service, the Bundesnachrichtendienst, or BND, but quickly fell out of favor for breaching security protocol. He continued his career at the German Ministry of Defense.

Faking Back

MEANWHILE, SOVIET BLOC POLITICAL WARFARE OPERATIONS were ramping up, especially those targeting the United States. CIA analysts noted "a noticeable increase" in the use of active measures between 1957 and the following year, which led to an "intensive investigation of the subject," according to a 1960 classified study. Between January 1, 1957, and July 1, 1959, the study found, thirty-six Soviet forgeries of international significance emerged. What alerted the CIA and prompted the Agency to go public with a study was that they were not simply looking at stand-alone forgeries, but at advanced and persistent campaigns that endured for months and even years, and deployed carefully crafted messages, repeating and improving them over time.

The CIA was gravely concerned about the Soviets' newly aggressive political warfare. The director, Allen Dulles, decided to brief Congress on the

Ladislav Bittman, as he was known in Czechoslovakia, in about 1957.
Bittman defected from Czech intelligence in 1968 and became one of
the most important voices on disinformation. (Elizabeth Spaulding)

secret study, and appointed Richard Helms, perhaps the most experienced
covert action executive and one of Dulles's most trusted aides, to testify in
front of the Senate Judiciary Committee on June 2, 1961.

Helms was urbane, cool, sure-footed, and tight-lipped, in the telling
of friends and colleagues. He was the quintessential career intelligence
officer, who would make it all the way to director of Central Intelligence.
Helms, a veteran of the OSS, the CIA's predecessor, was transferred to Berlin in August 1945. He worked on special operations even before the CIA's
Directorate of Plans was created in 1952. For almost the entire decade,
he oversaw the Agency's most aggressive operations, including its Berlin
fronts.[1]

"Would you rise and raise your right hand?" Senator Keating said to Helms that day. "Do you solemnly swear the evidence you give in this proceeding will be the truth and nothing but the truth, so help you God?"

"I do," Helms responded.

Helms commenced his prepared remarks by pointing out the long history of the Russian art of forgery. "More than sixty years ago, the tsarist intelligence service concocted and peddled a confection called the *Protocols of the Elders of Zion*," he told the Senate. The *Protocols*, the most notorious anti-Semitic tract of modern times, was fabricated around the turn of the century and first appeared in 1903, when the St. Petersburg newspaper *Znamya* serialized portions of the document.[2] In 1921, *The Times* of London conclusively exposed the text as a forgery, but, as Helms pointed out, the Soviets were still spreading the bogus document as late as 1958. The Holocaust was still a fresh and painful memory, and framing his adversaries as anti-Semites was a powerful opening move.

Helms then compared the act of forging—with which he himself was so well versed—with performing a magic trick. The KGB forgers were the magicians; the CIA investigators, watchful bystanders; and the American public was the audience. The bystander's task was to spot minor flaws in the execution of the trick. But the problem, of course, was that calling the forgers out would inadvertently help them. "When Soviet sleight of hand improved, one of our problems was demonstrating that the act was a fake without providing the magician with free tips on how to perfect his performance," Helms told the Senate.[3]

Helms started out confidently, but he was on very thin ice, and he knew it. He had sworn to tell the truth about deception, and yet his own agency was probably even more prolific and brazen in the "art of forgery," as he called it, than the KGB was at the time. But Congress didn't know that, and the White House didn't either.[4] Not even his own CIA analysts studying Russian forgeries knew how deeply their own agency was embedded in the business of large-scale forgeries in Germany. But the Russians knew, and Helms knew that they knew what he was hiding from Congress and the American people—that he was himself playing a magic trick that day on Capitol Hill.

Neues Deutschland, an official East German news outlet, featuring the forged
Rockefeller letter, February 1957

At first the session was closed, but the transcript, a 127-page booklet, was
cleared for publication two weeks later.[5]

The full story of this hearing begins on February 15, 1957. *Neues Deutschland*, East Germany's official daily newspaper, published by the central committee of the Socialist Unity Party of Germany, had extraordinary news.

It presented to the world the "authentic text" of a secret letter from the
chief of America's largest oil trust, the Standard Oil Corporation, to the president of the United States. "Rockefeller Gives Directive for Supercolonial-
ism of the U.S.A.," the headline blared, implying that the White House was
simply a puppet of powerful capitalist interests. The story revealed a cynical
American plan to achieve world domination: Nelson Rockefeller purportedly instructed President Dwight D. Eisenhower to use first economic aid
to make countries dependent on the United States, and then political power

and military alliances to force a repayment in blood. To make the long, personal letter an easier read, *Neues Deutschland* interspersed the text with pull quotes and subheadings, offering instant interpretations:

American Prestige Catastrophically Fallen
"What is Good for Standard Oil is Good for the U.S.A."
"Iranian Foreign Policy under U.S. Control"
"Economic 'Help' Draws Military Pacts After It"
Controlling Political Moves of Neutral States
Bring Colonies of Others Under U.S. Control

The paper boasted that it possessed the English original, in full, and from a "categorically reliable" albeit unnamed source.[6] *Neues Deutschland* printed a translation of the entire letter in German, around 3,500 words in total, as well as excerpts of the English original copy, to establish credibility. An editorial in *Neues Deutschland* referred to an important remark from Lenin: it would be the task of Communists to reveal to the masses the secret origins of wars. "We were guided by this remark when we published the text of the secret letter," one editor wrote. "From the pen of the scion of the blood-stained Rockefeller dynasty the world learns the secret of how people are robbed of their national sovereignty and independence and brought under the sway of the U.S. monopolies in order to help in a U.S.-instigated war for world domination."

The Rockefeller letter appeared at first glance to be shrewdly crafted. The letter mentioned talks at Camp David between President Eisenhower and Nelson Rockefeller, which had in fact taken place and been covered in the press. The letter also contained statements that the purported author, Rockefeller, had actually made: "Although, for instance, economic and technical aid to underdeveloped countries last year amounted to more than one billion dollars, more than half of this sum was actually devoted to three countries in which military and political rather than economic considerations were the determining factors."

The real Rockefeller, then a special assistant to the president and a champion of development assistance, had made a similar argument to Eisenhower two years prior, according to a report in *The New York Times*.[7] KGB forgers had lifted language from the *Times* in order to imitate Rockefeller more credibly. But the letter contained a number of sloppy errors: the typing was slipshod, with several strikethroughs, ragged margins, errors in punctuation, spelling, and grammar, and, as CIA analysts pointed out with horror, "a rather uneven typing touch." Nelson Rockefeller's actual correspondence, by contrast, was always clean, proper, and free of errors, and the oil magnate disliked the pronoun "I," an important detail that the forgers had apparently missed.

Within twenty-four hours of the letter's appearance in East Berlin, Radio Moscow picked up the story, with translated readings of the letter immediately aired in Greece, Vietnam, the Middle East, Iran, Turkey, Yugoslavia, Indonesia, and across Latin America. Portuguese, Japanese, Korean, and Mandarin translations and broadcasts followed three days later, with twenty-one additional broadcasts in the next three days after that. An Indonesian announcer reported that the letter showed that "the imperialist interests of Rockefeller and other U.S. billionaires decide the direction of the foreign policy of the U.S. government, which is the fascistic executor of their wishes."[8]

Neues Deutschland, citing the broad global resonance of its Rockefeller "revelation," including the most recent printing, in the Syrian daily *Al-Qabas*, upped the ante. Again quoting its "absolutely reliable source," still without specifying any details, *Neues Deutschland* published another scandalous and secret American memorandum under the headline "The Enemy of Arab Freedom."[9] Dubbed the "Dulles Memorandum," the document was a letter allegedly written by Secretary of State John Foster Dulles for President Eisenhower. The Dulles Memorandum spelled out the real, hidden objective of U.S. foreign policy in the Middle East: to suppress Arab national independence movements and establish the United States as the colonialist heir to France and Britain, in order to access oil and to open nuclear-capable military bases in the Middle East.

And the new memo circulated the globe just like the Rockefeller letter: first TASS, the Russian News Agency, played the Dulles memo, then Pravda and Radio Moscow, Turkey, Iran, and stations across the Middle East, then China's Radio Peking, and later in India. The global campaign persisted

Members of a Strategic Air Command B-52 combat crew race for their always ready-and-waiting B-52 heavy bomber; 1960s. KGB disinformation targeted the SAC in innovative ways. (U.S. Air Force)

for nine months after the two initial forgeries surfaced in Berlin. The CIA counted more than one hundred replays of the two letters, more than eighty of them through Radio Moscow.

The military tensions between the two superpowers were about to increase. In the first week of October 1957 alone, the U.S. Strategic Air Command initiated a 24/7 nuclear alert in response to the perceived Soviet missile threat—and the USSR launched *Sputnik*, the first satellite. On November 7, the National Security Council sent a grim confidential report to Eisenhower on deterrence and survival in the nuclear age.[10] To lessen the vulnerability of the Strategic Air Command to a surprise attack, the White House experts recommended that the time by which an adequate number, "possibly 500," of nuclear-armed bombers should be under way ought to be reduced to between 7 and 22 minutes. Public fear of atomic war was ripe then, and the Soviets were alarmed.

On November 22, 1957, Khrushchev gave an interview to three prominent American journalists, including William Randolph Hearst, Jr., editor-in-chief of Hearst Corp. and heir to his father's publishing empire. Hearst had won a Pulitzer Prize for an interview with Khrushchev two years prior, so the Soviet leader knew the exchange was a high-profile messaging opportunity.

The key message Khrushchev wanted to get across was on "military psychosis." A significant part of America's active strategic bomber force was airborne twenty-four hours a day, seven days a week, armed with hydrogen and atomic bombs, and, Khrushchev feared, ready to devastate his homeland. "This is very dangerous," Khrushchev told the American journalists. He was particularly concerned about the number of aircraft in the air at all times, and that "many people" would be piloting the armed bombers. "There is always the possibility of a mental blackout when the pilot may take the slightest signal as a signal for action and fly to the target that he had been instructed to fly to," Khrushchev said. Even an isolated nuclear bomb would trigger immediate retaliatory action, so one psychologically unstable pilot could effectively start a nuclear holocaust. "Does this not go to show that in such a case a war may start as a result of sheer misunderstanding, a derangement in the normal psychic state of a person, which may happen to anybody?"

Khrushchev's "military psychosis" argument made intuitive sense, was hard to counter, and made deploying more nuclear weapons appear reckless—in short, it was perfect raw material for disinformation.

By April 1958, the Soviet Union introduced "urgent measures" to the UN Security Council, requesting "an end to flights by United States military aircraft armed with atomic and hydrogen bombs in the direction of the frontiers of the Soviet Union."[11] The Soviets warned that continuing the flights might lead to a "breach" of world peace. Two weeks after the resolution was tabled, and five months after the Khrushchev interview, on May 7, 1958, *Neues Deutschland* published a remarkable letter, allegedly from a U.S. defense official, Frank Berry, to the secretary of defense, Neil McElroy. Berry was America's most senior official in charge of military health and medical issues. That Wednesday, the front page of *Neues Deutschland* read: "Sensational Admission of the American Ministry of War: Certifiably Insane Pilots in Control of U.S.A. Atomic Bombers."[12]

In the letter, which *Neues Deutschland* ran in its entirety, in English, Berry claimed that 67.3 percent of flight personnel in the U.S. Air Force suffered from "psychoneurosis." The document stressed that this was an "impressive" figure that could not fail to cause alarm. The Berry letter then referred to an unnamed expert report that singled out officers and airmen in the Strategic Air Command, claiming that members of these crews were "inadequately controlled by the subject's will," and pilots were prone to hysterical syndromes and "fits of unaccountable animosity." The document named a number of U.S. nuclear bases, and alleged chronic overstrain of the pilots' nervous systems— not just due to intercontinental flight schedules but also as a result of the ample consumption of alcohol, the use of opium and marijuana, sexual excesses and perversions, and "extreme fatigue due to constant card playing."

First Khrushchev had articulated the theory of military psychosis. Then *Neues Deutschland* provided the scientific evidence. Now it was time for examples and case studies.

Five weeks after the Berry letter surfaced, the KGB got lucky. Vernon Morgan, a twenty-one-year-old native of Elizabeth, Indiana, was a mechanic second class at the U.S. Air Force's 86th Bomb Squadron in Alconbury, England. Just after midnight on June 13, Morgan, who was not a trained pilot, climbed into a B-45 twin-jet Tornado, a light bomber. Morgan managed to get the Tornado off the ground in the middle of the night, but shortly after becoming airborne, it tilted to the right and, with a flaming explosion, crashed into the main railroad line between London King's Cross and Edinburgh near the village of Abbots Ripton, just a few minutes before an express train was due. A political firestorm ensued in the UK. "Leftist British leaders have voiced fears that some airman might steal a plane with a hydrogen bomb in it and cause a catastrophe in just such a crash," *The Washington Post* reported.[13] Within three days, Soviet newspapers and Radio Moscow had reported the incident and cited the crash as an illustration of the risks indicated by the Berry letter.

The intense press coverage in Britain showed that the nocturnal Tornado crash, the military psychosis theme, and the fear of accidental nuclear war resonated in Europe. Three weeks later, the Soviets fired their next salvo.

On July 3, 1958, the Russian ambassador in London, Jacob Malik, gave a speech to book publishers and editors at the Paternoster Club on Great Queen Street.[14] Malik spoke about the dangers of nuclear war, and mentioned that American officials had acknowledged that nuclear bombers could be airborne at any moment. The Soviet ambassador then told his audience that he had received a letter from a U.S. Air Force pilot stationed in England. The anonymous pilot allegedly told the Soviet embassy that he intended to drop an atomic bomb in the next few days.

One of the journalists in the room asked whether the letter could be made public. Malik at once said he would have to check with Moscow. Just a few hours later, in the early evening, the embassy handed over copies to an American and a British news agency. Written in awkward English, it was posted from Ipswich, addressed to Malik, and signed by "W." Despite a lack of indications that the letter was authentic, memories of Morgan's crash were still fresh and the letter's contents so sensational that the story could not be ignored. "W," the alleged American Air Force pilot, announced that he and his crew would go rogue and would drop a "deadly load" during a routine flight, in order to show "how horrible an atomic war could be." They had chosen a target in the North Sea, so that "not too many people" would be killed. "D-day," the letter said, would be sometime in the first week of July.[15] The pilot then offered "all the secret information we know" to Soviet intelligence. The crew wished then to enter the USSR's airspace near Leningrad. "W" even requested that the Soviets warn the Red Army's anti-aircraft defenses "not to open fire on us and let us know where we can land."

The letter was intended to lend credibility to the Soviets' insinuation that NATO pilots were mentally unstable. But this time, luck was not on their side. One person who read the press coverage of the mysterious letter was an unemployed farmhand and ex–Royal Air Force pilot who had been discharged for mental instability. William Stanley Whales, of Ipswich, held a grudge against the RAF for discharging him after fifteen years of service. The frustrated Whales decided to claim the letter in order to raise the public profile of his complaints against the RAF. Whales got in touch with the local correspondent of the British Press Association and signed a phony seven-page confession, claiming he had simply looked up the name of the Russian ambassador in the Ipswich public library.

Whales's timing was good, as a wave of anti-nuclear-arms protests was sweeping the UK. His claim generated much publicity itself, and was covered in the major newspapers in the United States and Britain. Without knowing it, the former Royal Air Force crew member was deflating the threat—and countering a Soviet disinformation operation by highly effective means. Suddenly the Soviet embassy found itself in the rather awkward position of having to defend a forged letter, written by a made-up mentally unstable airman, against the false claims of a real mentally unstable airman. When consulted by *The New York Times,* a Soviet embassy spokesperson in London dismissed Whales's claim as "imaginary."[16]

Early the following week, Russian disinformation specialists decided to double down on their operation, and Malik, the Soviet ambassador, released two more letters to British officials and journalists. One of them was allegedly from the same "W" who had written the first letter, reiterating his nuclear threat: "If there is no delay, I will drop the bomb within the next five days." The other was from one of W's crew members: "We have many persons of high rank on our side and will have no real trouble in flying off the bomb."[17]

By July 1958, the Soviet barrage of forgeries directed against the United States was brazen and aggressive—perhaps as much so as the CIA's own operations in Berlin. The CIA therefore decided to fight back against the Soviet forgeries from within the United States. Only weeks after the pilot letters appeared, Dulles, the CIA director, secretly reached out to one of *The Washington Post*'s most influential columnists, Roscoe Drummond. With the Berry campaign in full swing, Drummond wrote several columns about Soviet forgeries. In one column, "Spreading the Poison," Drummond discussed in detail how fake documents could be revealed as such. The columnist highlighted, for example, English-language inconsistencies: the Rockefeller letter, for one, used the phrase "the hooked fish needs no bait," which is British rather than American, as well as the adage "ramming home" (of an idea), which would be "driving home" in American parlance. Drummond revealed secret details, for instance that a clandestine radio transmitter, called "Our Radio," which broadcast in Turkish and claimed to be located in Turkey, was in fact a Soviet device located in Leipzig, East Germany. Drummond also highlighted arcane technical evidence: the typeface of the Rockefeller letter forgery, surfaced in *Neues Deutschland*, could not have been written on an American typewriter, and was in fact typed out on a prewar machine made in East Germany.[18] Drummond obliquely noted that the forged document had been "analyzed by technicians," but he did not say whose, and indeed never mentioned that Dulles had provided him with a classified internal study.

Drummond received the material "enthusiastically," Dulles reported at an internal CIA meeting two days before the first column appeared.[19] Dulles was happy with the result, and thought Drummond's column "succeeded admirably" in revealing the Soviet forgeries[20]—because he had simply reproduced the CIA's secret list of forensic artifacts.[21]

The KGB was undeterred. On October 2, 1958, *Neues Deutschland* ran an article claiming that a U.S. Air Force officer stationed in Kaiserslautern had leaked a secret order from General Thomas Power, head of the Strategic Air Command, that prohibited U.S. crews from flying aircraft carrying atomic or hydrogen bombs over U.S. territory (no such order was issued). TASS reported on the Power order hoax on the same day; so did Radio Moscow, which broadcast the story into Britain, and tied it to the Berry letter. The next day, the clandestine radio station España Independiente—which claimed to be located in Spain, but was actually in Bucharest, Romania; it was the oldest Soviet clandestine radio operation, launched in 1941—spread the fake news story in Spanish without crediting any source.[22] On November 20, Radio Moscow replayed the story, this time in Arabic, Turkish, and Japanese, again tying the Power order to the foresight of Frank Berry, whose purported warning had started the campaign. By then, the joke at the CIA was that in the Soviet mind, Frank Berry's prophetic powers rivaled those of Marx and Lenin.[23]

But it was the KGB who had the last laugh on this matter. Less than a week after Malik surfaced the letter at the Paternoster Club, the CIA's LCCASSOCK front, also at peak performance then, launched its disinformation attack against the Socialist Party's 5th Congress in Berlin, which Khrushchev was attending. The KGB and CIA were watching each other's disinformation operations in real time. And Russian intelligence soon decided to retaliate with an operation right out of a John le Carré novel, which would effectively turn CIA analysts into a disinformation tool to be used on the CIA's leadership. The full effect of this covert, highly targeted effort took several months to filter through the CIA's bureaucracy.

In March 1960, the CIA finished a 200-page report, "Sino-Soviet Bloc Propaganda Forgeries," that had been in the works for years. The report was classified as secret and only released nearly forty years later. The study contained a detailed breakdown of the Berry campaign and several other Communist forgery and propaganda actions. The KGB knew, thanks to Drummond's CIA-informed, detail-dripping columns in *The Washington Post* and other sources, that American intelligence was closely watching Russia's globally expanding disinformation operations. The vast Russian spy station in Karlshorst, in East Berlin, also knew of LCCASSOCK; the KGB even knew of *Schlagzeug*, the CIA-funded jazz magazine that was published on both sides of the Iron Curtain.

So, in December 1958, Karlshorst retaliated. Russian disinformation operators forged the CIA's own forgery: they reproduced an accurate *Schlagzeug* mailing envelope and used it to mail out their own booklet to 4,000 West German addresses. The Russian operators mailed it out "black," and changed only one detail: the return address proved, on CIA investigation, to be an empty lot in West Berlin—a clever way of signaling to the Americans that they knew who was really behind the jazz magazine. The booklet was nominally printed by the real Publishing House for German Youth, the Kulturverlag der Deutschen Jugend, and devoted to a "culture program" that contained songs, skits, and plays to use for an amateur theatrical performance—in other words, the KGB was more or less openly ridiculing LCCASSOCK as an amateur performance. The Russian spymasters even asked a young Socialist author, Werner Bräunig, to compose a song on mentally unstable U.S. Air Force pilots, complete with a score for piano accompaniment:

THE FLYING PSYCHONEUROSIS
BY WERNER BRÄUNIG

There flies Jim from Alabama,
there flies Jack from Tennessee
high above the city
wearing heated pants,
with the bomb aboard
and the psychoneurosis,
and on the automatic pilot is printed: Liberty.
 And what can happen—
 how does that concern us?
 That does not concern us at all!
There flies Jim from Alabama
high over the State of Wisconsin
and there is a city
and people walk in rows,
and there is a (psychoneurotic) crack
and he shoots them up—
there were a few people killed
 And if such a thing can happen—
 doesn't this concern someone?
 Doesn't this concern us at all?
There flies Jim from Alabama
Over you, and over me.
With death in his head,
and then he sees red,
and he pushes the button
and it's over for you and for me!

And because that can happen tomorrow,
it does concern us!
Mankind! It even concerns you!

The Washington CIA analysts who reverse-engineered the campaign saw the song as a "direct tribute to the Berry Letter." But these analysts were unaware of the covert operations run by Berlin Operations Base, and so considered *Schlagzeug* a "bona fide West German periodical" in the secret document that they passed up to the CIA leadership. But the KGB's musical taunt was not lost on the Agency's executives in charge of covert action.

Richard Helms understood. He was Frank Wisner's chief of operations in the Directorate of Plans, which swallowed the Office of Policy Coordination in August 1952. Helms oversaw the CIA's covert actions for the next six years, meaning that he had himself renewed LCCASSOCK's funding and cover many times[24] and was well aware of specific operational details of the various Berlin front organizations in the late 1950s, including *Schlagzeug*.[25] Then, in early 1961, Dulles selected Helms to testify in front of the Senate Judiciary Committee on Soviet-made forgeries.

Helms, in full command of the details of the entire Berry forgery campaign, briefed the Senate on these details, down to the level of grammatical errors in specific forgeries and the fake claim by Whales, the real mentally deranged RAF officer in Ipswich. His entire congressional briefing was based on the same secret CIA study on Soviet forgeries, which relayed many details of the KGB's *Schlagzeug* taunt, including the full text of Bräunig's song. Those CIA officials who knew of LCCASSOCK also would have noticed an ominous absence: Radio Moscow did not report on the *Schlagzeug* jab; it was meant for the CIA's ears only. Helms saw no need to communicate this humiliation to Congress; he dropped any mention of the CIA's own forgery and influence campaigns from the Senate testimony. Helms pulled off his own shell game, and got away with it.

8.

Kampfverband

N THE SUMMER OF 1956, OMINOUS LEAFLETS APPEARED IN SEV-
eral Western countries, often mailed to officials and relatives of
military service personnel in the United States and the United
Kingdom, including diplomats stationed in Germany. One of the American
recipients was Elim O'Shaughnessy, chief of the Political Division of the
American embassy in West Germany. The leaflets seemed to come from an
ominous neo-Nazi group. The group's logo was an iron cross against two
symmetric oak twigs, signed with the group's name in old German gothic
font: Kampfverband für Unabhängiges Deutschland, or "Fighting Group for
Independent Germany."

The group's declared goal: to reinstate the great German Reich by pushing out the new occupiers. In August 1956, the German ambassador to
France, Vollrath von Maltzan, received a leaflet, marking the start of a French

Henriette Trémeaud, wife of the prefect of Strasbourg, circa 1957. She died in a terrorist attack that was designed to be a disinformation operation.

(Photograph by Keystone-France / Gamma-Keystone via Getty Images)

campaign. That winter, more than 150 individuals in the Germany-bordering Bas-Rhin department received the strange, threatening letters.

"French Oppressors!" one such leaflet was titled. The pamphlet was addressed to the authorities and inhabitants of Alsace, a region between France and Germany that had been contested for centuries. "We have looked on long enough as you cheekily spread yourself out in Alsace-Lorraine, a country that you seized in unjust treaties," the supposed neo-Nazi group wrote in awkward German.[1] Indeed, the German was so oddly phrased, stilted and twisted, it was outright laughable. The self-proclaimed Kampfverband wrote, for instance, that Alsace-Lorraine would always sing "our" songs in German, not "your blasphemous chansons!" The leaflet continued in even more bizarre language, rendered into deliberately awkward English here: "Your dirty hands, which are strangulating our people in Alsace-Lorraine, attempting to bring them to their knees with blackmail and threats, we will beat them into

Kampfverband logo, designed by Czechoslovak intelligence. It reads as "Fighting Group for Independent Germany."

two parts."[2] Even the group's full German name was missing a definite article. "Clearly no German could have written this leaflet," *Die Zeit*, a highbrow German weekly, commented: "the spelling and language errors in this fabrication are too numerous!"[3] The Kampfverband mailed the leaflets in both German and French, issuing bilingual hate messages to pitch France against Germany: "*Wir warnen Euch! Prenez garde!*"—*We're warning you*. The group targeted government officials. "Your spies, officials, and teachers," the leaflets concluded, "will not escape their just punishment."

On May 14, 1957, a small parcel arrived in Strasbourg, at the prefecture of the department of Bas-Rhin. The prefecture had its headquarters in a majestic nineteenth-century building on Place de la République. The parcel, nineteen by fourteen centimeters, was wrapped in white paper and addressed to the prefect, André Trémeaud. It had been mailed from a post office at 25 Boulevard Diderot in Paris, opposite the Gare de Lyon. Trémeaud's secretary received the package. Noticing a card from Carlos Garcia Soldevillad, European representative for the cigar maker H. Upmann of Havana, she thought that the cigars were a personal gift for the prefect. Without opening the box, Trémeaud left it on his desk. Only days later would he find out that the box contained not fine Upmann cigars but approximately 250 grams of acetone peroxide—"enough explosive to kill a dozen persons," as investigators later assessed—wired up with an electronic trigger that would set off an explosion when the box was opened.[4] Without realizing it, the prefect had placed a deadly IED right in front of him.

The evening of the delivery, Trémeaud was hosting a reception at the prefecture to celebrate the opening of a session of the European Coal and Steel Community, the organization that ultimately led to the creation of the European Union. René Pleven and René Mayer, both former French prime ministers and key drivers of the still-fragile European integration project, were present at the reception that evening.[5] Less than two months earlier, on March 25, 1957, the Treaty of Rome had been signed, establishing Europe's ambitious attempt to bring peace to a violence-ridden continent. The box of fine cigars would have come in handy for a political after-dinner discussion over wine and spirits, but Trémeaud, preoccupied, forgot to bring the Upmanns downstairs.

Two days later, Trémeaud took the cigar box to his private residence. The next day, on May 17, the prefect met with Pierre Pflimlin, who had also briefly served as France's prime minister. Meanwhile, the prefect's elegant wife, Henriette Trémeaud, was sorting out some household items on the first floor. She noticed the cigar box, placed it on a small round table, and began to open it with a knife. The explosion was violent—it shook the walls, blew out the windows, devastated three rooms—and killed Henriette Trémeaud immediately, ripping open her entire upper body, severing one of her hands and part of her face, as the table deflected the force upward, leaving her high heels unscathed. The salon clock stopped at 12:54.

A police and counterintelligence investigation commenced, run by the Direction de la surveillance du territoire, or DST. The DST soon found that Carlos Garcia Soldevillad, the cigar salesman, didn't exist. The first assumption was that Algerian militants were to blame; the Battle of Algiers, a bloody guerrilla campaign waged by Algeria's National Liberation Front against the French authorities in the North African colonial territory as well as mainland France, was in its late stage by May 1957, and Trémeaud had been the prefect of French Algeria from 1952 to 1955. Trémeaud's domestic staff, an Algerian woman among them, was initially under investigation. But in the following weeks, a more sinister explanation would emerge.

The second wave of the mail campaign hit in mid-May 1957, just two days before Trémeaud received his improvised explosive device. The timing was highly suspicious, and a combined German-French police investigation got to work. It soon discovered that the Kampfverband letters were mailed from the same Paris post office as the deadly cigar box,[6] and there were additional pieces of evidence that seemed to confirm the link between the Kampfverband and the Strasbourg bombing. The German Federal Police in Wiesbaden would soon find that the address label and a note on the lethal cigar package of Strasbourg "were written on the same typewriter that was also used to type out the Kampfverband pamphlets as well as the address information on the corresponding envelopes."[7] The conclusion: the bomb and the pamphlets came from the same perpetrator. By June 1957, the French press reported the growing conviction of the investigating authorities that the Kampfverband für Unabhängiges Deutschland had attempted to kill a group of senior French politicians in Strasbourg.

But who was behind this strange ultranationalist group? The mysterious masterminds had made a few sloppy mistakes.

On July 5, 1957, six weeks after the misdirected operation in Strasbourg, the French ambassador in Bonn received an envelope sent from Munich. It appeared to contain a leaked document,[8] a letter written by Elim O'Shaughnessy, the State Department official who had also received a Kampfverband leaflet. O'Shaughnessy's signature was typewritten. The letter called the attention of "the State Department" to "West German ultranationalist groups." The U.S. diplomat then advised his government to support and take advantage of the reactionary neo-Nazi extremists in Germany. O'Shaughnessy credibly identified the letter as a forgery, and this raised a worrying question: What else was fabricated? Was the Nazi group a ghost?

The O'Shaughnessy letter was also mailed to the British ambassador in Bonn—with the clear intention to drive a wedge not just between Germany and France but also between the United States and Britain and France, its most valuable wartime allies in Europe. The entire operation began to look more and more like a hostile intelligence campaign, and the CIA's counterintelligence specialists started to pay close attention.

On the far side of the Iron Curtain, the Soviet bloc intelligence agencies observed the investigation from a distance. The BKA, the German Federal Police, arrested several West German citizens and interrogated them in connection with Kampfverband activity. This was most curious—the neo-Nazi group was an invention; it didn't have members to be arrested. The still-hidden inventors of the Kampfverband came to the conclusion that some of the leaflets must have accidentally fallen into the hands of real Nazis, who then disseminated them under their own initiative. After all, the operation had received a lot of publicity, and segments of the public were taking the fighting group and its threats seriously, some real Nazi holdovers likely among them. The public discussion of right-wing terrorism in Strasbourg was so widespread that it even provided cover for follow-up active measures: "The U.S.S.R. could openly join the fray without fearing that the French public and investigatory agencies could deduce Soviet involvement in the matter," one Soviet bloc defector later recalled.[9] Indeed, in May 1958, Radio Moscow tried to revive the story with a long French broadcast aired in France, warning listeners about the nefarious Kampfverband—which the broadcast called a "West German neo-fascist organization," implying that it was secretly supported by West Germany's government in Bonn.[10]

The CIA carefully analyzed the 1958 Radio Moscow broadcast and the O'Shaughnessy forgery. In 1957, CIA officers had debriefed a Stasi defector who told his interrogators that the Hauptverwaltung Aufklärung (HVA), the foreign intelligence branch of the Ministry of State Security—the Stasi—had already conducted active measures before 1957. But disinformation and "psychological warfare," the defector said, had been officially announced within the HVA as a "major operational responsibility," just as the cigar box bomb shook Strasbourg and France that spring.

Shortly after debriefing this defector, the CIA tried to use the same individual to help determine the source of the anti-French leaflets. "When the defector [. . .] was shown copies of the leaflets signed Kampfverband fuer Unabhaengiges Deutschland," the CIA recorded in a debriefing report, "he promptly identified them as a product of one of the HVA operations."

The conclusion seemed obvious: bomb, pamphlets, and forgery were all part of the same operation, and the Stasi's HVA was behind it all. "It has been established that the *Kampfverband* is a phantom organization, existing only as a signature placed on letters and leaflets which are prepared by the East

German foreign intelligence service HVA," the CIA concluded.[11] Shortly thereafter, in his testimony before the Senate, Richard Helms brought up this episode and accused the Ministry of State Security in East Berlin of having plotted the terrorist attack under a false flag: "Evidence discovered during police investigation pointed toward the nonexistent West German group as the murderer, precisely as the East German intelligence service had intended," Helms told the Senate Committee of the Judiciary.[12]

But the CIA was wrong. The defector either lied or erred. The HVA didn't do it.

The truth emerged only after ten years had passed.[13] In 1972, Ladislav Bittman published his memoirs, *The Deception Game*. Bittman had defected four years prior from the Czechoslovak Státní bezpečnost, or StB, the state security agency. Bittman, a major, had been the deputy head of the Disinformation Department in Prague's famously aggressive intelligence agency. Bittman confirmed that both the cigar bomb and the leaflets were StB operations, carefully planned from Prague (cooperation between Prague and East Berlin in special operations was only established later). A Czech police investigation after the end of the Cold War would even identify the specific operatives behind the attack that felled Henriette Trémeaud.[14]

The operation had to be approved by the highest members of the Communist Party in both Czechoslovakia and the USSR. "Trémeaud's assassination went beyond the pale of usual intelligence practice," wrote Bittman in 1972. "Every operation of that kind must be approved by the highest party echelons."

The cigar box hit job and its accompanying campaign of hate and intimidation had a strategic objective that went beyond killing a group of public figures. As Bittman described the wider political aim of Operation Strasbourg: "The intent was to prove to the world public that the German Federal Republic was a fascist seedbed; the *Kampfverband für Unabhängiges Deutschland* was created, at least on paper, to produce fascist propaganda on a large scale."[15]

Red Swastikas

N THE WEE HOURS OF CHRISTMAS DAY 1959, A YOUNG STUDENT was walking home from mass in Cologne. Along his route was the synagogue on Roonstraße, a majestic brownstone structure with a large round window over its imposing entry arches. Chancellor Konrad Adenauer had opened the new Jewish house of worship only two months earlier; it stood on the sacred ground of an older synagogue that had been burned during Kristallnacht. But on this holy night, the student noticed fresh graffiti around the entrance, blaring in red and black paint: "Germans demand: Jews out." Swastikas had been smeared on the walls, and Hebrew inscriptions painted over. The student immediately called the police.

Later that day, another member of the public noticed a defacement at the memorial for the victims of the Nazi regime, half an hour's walk north of the synagogue. Somebody had poured black lacquer paint into the inscription,

The KGB had swastikas and anti-Semitic graffiti daubed in red and black paint on the walls of the newly reopened synagogue in Cologne. The incident opened an extensive, global anti-Semitic disinformation campaign designed to harm West Germany. (Hansherbert Wirtz, Kölnische Rundschau)

which read "Seven Gestapo victims rest here. This memorial remembers Germany's most painful time, 1933–1945." But this time the perpetrators made a mistake: they left behind a can of paint that had their fingerprints on it. One day later, a hastily created police task force was able to apprehend two twenty-five-year-old men, Arnold Strunk and Paul Josef Schönen. Strunk, a baker, confessed. Both were members of a small, right-leaning political party.[1]

But the swift arrest of the two initial perpetrators did not stop the anti-Semitic incidents. In fact, Cologne was only the beginning. Over the following few days, a veritable wave of hate crimes started rolling across the Federal Republic: first the slogan "Juden raus" and swastikas and sometimes other epithets

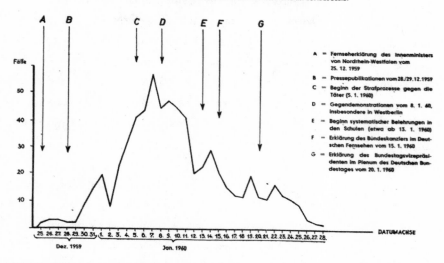

TATZEITEN-STATISTIK
DER SCHMIER- UND STORAKTIONEN VOM 25. 12. 59 BIS 28. 1. 60 IM BUNDESGEBIET

A = Fernseherklärung des Innenministers von Nordrhein-Westfalen vom 25. 12. 1959

B = Pressepublikationen vom 28./29. 12. 1959

C = Beginn der Strafprozesse gegen die Täter (5. 1. 1960)

D = Gegendemonstrationen vom 8. 1. 60, insbesondere in Westberlin

E = Beginn systematischer Belehrungen in den Schulen (etwa ab 13. 1. 1960)

F = Erklärung des Bundeskanzlers im Deutschen Fernsehen vom 15. 1. 1960

G = Erklärung des Bundestagsvizepräsidenten im Plenum des Deutschen Bundestages vom 20. 1. 1960

Timeline of Soviet-engineered anti-Semitic campaigns—telling fake from real anti-Semitism quickly became impossible (German Ministry of the Interior)

appeared on benches, memorials, and walls in Braunschweig and Offenbach, then across the Ruhr, the Rhineland, Lower Saxony, Bavaria, and Hesse.[2] By mid-February, the federal government in Bonn had counted 833 anti-Semitic incidents across all West German states. The interior ministry had identified 321 perpetrators. The hate crimes even leaped across the Iron Curtain into East Germany: during the first six weeks of 1960, the authorities in East Berlin recorded 251 cases of swastika graffiti and 55 other cases of anti-Semitic crimes.[3]

Even worse, the outbreak of anti-Jewish sentiment oddly appeared to be a global phenomenon. On the night of December 30, a synagogue in Notting Hill, London, was defaced with three large white swastikas and "Juden raus."[4] Over the next weeks, more incidents occurred in the United Kingdom, in London but also in towns from Axminster to York. Five Jewish members of Parliament received threats. Anti-Semitic graffiti and other incidents also occurred in Italy, in Rome, Turin, Venice, and Treviso. The Italian police had arrested forty-four members of two neo-Fascist groups by January 6.

Incidents also occurred in Toulouse and Bordeaux; in Brussels, Amsterdam, Vienna, Oslo, Geneva, Tel Aviv, Cape Town, and Montreal, as well as in Mexico, Rhodesia, Chile, even Hong Kong[5]—and a few days later in Argentina, Ecuador, Spain, and Greece. On January 11, in Fontainebleau, close to Paris, even the private home of General Hans Speidel—the supreme commander of NATO ground forces and a former Wehrmacht general—was defaced with several swastikas in tar. At the same time, anti-Jewish slogans appeared across Israel: on mailboxes in Haifa, at a medical building in Zichron Yaacov, and in Petah Tikvah, in Central Israel, on forty slips of paper marked with red crayon swastikas.[6]

Particularly concerning were the events in New York, then still the city with the world's largest Jewish population. At one Jewish cemetery in Staten Island, one hundred headstones were defaced with swastikas, smeared in yellow paint.[7] On January 4, three synagogues were desecrated within twenty-four hours. Red swastikas, six feet high, were painted on the Free Synagogue in Flushing. The Corona Jewish Center and Temple Emanu-El, at Fifth Avenue and Sixty-fifth Street, were similarly defaced, as was a building used by Jewish war veterans.[8] In the following days more acts of vandalism were reported, including at a yeshiva in Brooklyn.[9] At least thirteen cities across the United States were affected, including Washington, Detroit, Cincinnati, and Chicago. At the University of Maryland, two hundred cars were pinned with pamphlets with titles like "Jews Are Thru in '72."[10] Rabbi Max Meyer of the Free Synagogue suspected that the wave of anti-Semitism was inspired by the widely reported events in Cologne on Christmas Day.

The political reaction in Germany was intense. Chancellor Adenauer immediately called his cabinet to an emergency meeting. The government decided to pass a law against *Volksverhetzung*, loosely translated as hate crimes against an ethnic group. Bonn tried to reassure the world that the perpetrators did not represent an important political current in Germany, and would be rooted out. In West Berlin, forty thousand marched against anti-Semitism. Willy Brandt, the mayor, spoke of a "devil's brigade given a holiday from Hell to plague us."[11] Israel's justice minister spoke in the Knesset about the ugly new phenomenon, and sent an official note of concern to Bonn.[12]

The American Jewish Committee issued a sharp statement and warned that the events in West Germany threatened "not only Jews but all free people."[13] Even the White House intervened: "The virus of bigotry," Eisenhower wrote in a telegram to the National Conference of Christians and Jews, should not be allowed to spread "one inch."[14]

As the wave of hate crimes continued in Germany and spread globally, Germany faced more and more pressure. Adenauer soon raised the stakes. In a dramatic radio and TV broadcast, the chancellor called on the German public to react immediately when they spotted a troublemaker "and give him a good thrashing. That is the punishment he merits."[15] The following Sunday, fifty thousand Londoners, stretching for a mile and a half, marched on the German Embassy in protest against the outpouring of anti-Semitic hate. "The Blood of Millions Cries Out," read one of the banners.[16] Reports appeared that some British companies were firing German employees just for their nationality. One large convenience store in London removed German-made typewriters, coats, and shoes from its shop windows.[17]

Yet the swift global spread of events also raised questions. After the events of Christmas 1959, Adenauer was quick to publicly mention the possibility of a Communist conspiracy intended to discredit the Federal Republic in the eyes of its allies. Even the Israeli justice minister, Pinhas Rosen, told the Knesset that there was no other explanation than an international conspiracy, and noted that the German language had been used in many international incidents. Yet *The New York Times* noted that "no evidence of such a plot could be found."[18] *Süddeutsche Zeitung*, one of Germany's main broadsheets, was equally skeptical and suspected the government of trying to use communism as a "scapegoat."[19] West Germany's Social Democrats, the SPD, also did not find the evidence strong enough to implicate Moscow or the East German government.[20] Authorities in East Berlin, predictably, denied the allegations as "new provocations."[21]

A few weeks later, the German federal government published a white paper in response to the anti-Semitic incidents.[22] The report revealed some remarkable intelligence findings: one year earlier, on January 23, 1959, the Central Committee of the Socialist Unity Party (SED) had held a special meeting, chaired by Walter Ulbricht, the East German head of state. The SED's central committee had already recognized that publications about West German anti-Semitic tendencies were highly effective in damaging the reputation of the Federal Republic among allies and neutral countries. This meeting took place only a few months after Ulbricht's own congress had been attacked by LCCASSOCK, an operation of which the MfS and the KGB were likely aware. Now Ulbricht had turned the tables. In the secret January meeting, Ulbricht and his comrades decided "to use action groups to organize Nazi incidents in several cities in the Federal Republic and to deface Jewish places of worship with Nazi symbols," according to the BND, West Germany's external intelligence service.[23]

One week prior to this meeting, on January 15, 1959, the "Caucus for German Unity," a group linked to the East German Politburo, issued a pamphlet called "Witch-hunt on Jews." Its argument: that West German anti-Semitism was rooted in the government itself. On March 9, East Berlin's Ministry of Foreign Affairs reiterated the claim. Immediately after the Christmas attack in Cologne, *Neues Deutschland* was ready with the appropriate headline: "Perpetrators in High Office," and, two days later, "The World Judges Bonn."[24] On January 7–8, the SED's own newspaper claimed that the West German Ministry of Defense, specifically its "Office for Psychological Warfare," had instigated and controlled the ongoing wave of anti-Semitism.

Meanwhile, West German authorities in Hanover arrested two neo-Nazi perpetrators who had taken part in the Communist world youth festival in East Berlin. The ministry also reported that Communist agents had tried to convince West German clerics to declare from their pulpits that the federal government was responsible for the anti-Semitic incidents. Strunk and Schönen, the pair responsible for defacing the synagogue in Cologne, also had traveled to East Germany twice in 1959, and even had repeated contact with Russian civilian personnel on a military base.[25] On January 16, German police announced that they had arrested twenty-two-year-old Bernhard Schlottmann, leader of a banned neo-Nazi student league in Berlin, who had confessed that he had worked as an agent for East German state security for the past fourteen months, reporting to his handler every two weeks.[26] He was later jailed for treason.

One of the strongest pieces of evidence implicating East Berlin, and Moscow to an even greater extent, appeared the following day. Prompted by the publicity and the aggressive targeting of the UK, it appears that, in a highly unusual move, British intelligence officials passed to the press two encrypted messages from Moscow to Berlin.

The first, sent from Moscow in December 1959, spelled out the purpose of the active measure. "In West Germany," the order read, "our comrades have an extremely easy task for they will be able to use the Nazis for discrediting the class enemies." The directive was circulated to Communist Party activists in West Germany, with the help of what Moscow called its "Pankow forgers," a reference to East German authorities. The secret message went on to explain that the operation was deniable: "If any of these people are caught redhanded it can clearly be established that he or she is a Nazi," the message allegedly[27] read. "If necessary, Nazi leaflets can be supplied by the division of practical strategy," it added, possibly referring to a specialized unit at the Ministry of State Security in East Berlin.

The second directive, likely intercepted by British intelligence in January 1960, is even more remarkable. It assessed the success of the global anti-Semitic active measure. The encrypted message highlighted that "undercover comrades have proved to the world that a potential Nazi threat exists not only in Germany but in the whole western world. The socialist [Russian] government's argument that West Germany is a potential bastion of Nazism and that consequently West Germany must under no circumstances be fully re-armed has been considerably strengthened."[28]

The Soviet agitators had "proved" to the world what their own ideologues considered an objective truth. Yet the semi-clandestine Russian masterminds knew they had made a pact with the devil, and that they were indeed risking strengthening an ideology that was hostile to their own. "Our comrades must, however, continue to work amongst Nazis with the greatest skill to prevent them from unwittingly helping to strengthen Nazi movements,"

Moscow telegraphed to East Berlin. The directive closed by warning that effective countermeasures would have to be taken at the "slightest indication" that matters were beginning to get out of hand.

More evidence of a hidden Soviet hand accrued over time. In the ensuing three and a half decades, at least seven defector accounts surfaced confirming that the swastika activity was a joint Soviet bloc active measure executed on KGB orders.[29] Based on these accounts, it is possible to reconstruct parts of the planning phase of this extraordinary active measure.

The bureaucratic setup of disinformation in Moscow moved slowly at first. In late December 1958, Nikita Khrushchev appointed Alexander Shelepin as the second chairman of the KGB. Shelepin, with authorization by the Central Committee, created a new unit in charge of disinformation just a few weeks into his tenure. Department D pulled together various officers from different parts of the KGB's vast First Chief Directorate to coordinate and direct disinformation operations. *1911-1968*

Shelepin's most brilliant appointment was Ivan Ivanovich Agayants, a highly decorated career intelligence officer from Ganja (Gence) in Azerbaijan. Agayants was tall, slender, and balding, with lively eyes and a voice scarred by tuberculosis. A ferocious reader who knew the names of hundreds of his devoted subordinates, he spoke fluent French, Farsi, Turkish, and Spanish, as well as English and Italian.[30] Agayants's intelligence career started in 1930, at the knee of Artur Artuzov, the mastermind of Operation Trust. From 1937 to 1940, he served in France, and later, then in his late thirties, as the resident intelligence officer in Tehran from 1941 to 1943.[31] With his short mustache, impeccable suits, and wry smile, he had the bearing of an aristocrat. Agayants was "charming, highly cultured, courteous, kind," said Evdokia Petrova, a defector who knew him, "an intelligent and able officer."[32] This appealing façade belied a ruthless operator. Agayants had a gift for choosing talented individuals, and was widely respected in the party's Central Committee. Agayants's new department had a staff of around forty to fifty officers, with twenty additional operators serving in the KGB's Karlshorst station in East Berlin.

Berlin and West Germany as a whole were his top targets. The Federal Republic, Agayants knew, was struggling with its dark recent past. As an

Armenian, he also knew the power of national trauma. The memory of the Holocaust was so fresh that historians had not yet begun to use that term. And occasionally anti-Semitism still raised its ugly head. In late 1957, Ludwig Zind, a fifty-one-year-old high school teacher in Offenburg, had made vile anti-Jewish comments during a beer hall argument. ("I am proud that I and my men broke the necks of hundreds of Jews with shovels during the war," he said to a Jewish businessman.)[33] Zind, a former Nazi storm trooper, repeated his outburst of hate in court and was sentenced to one year in prison in April 1958.[34] But he was popular in his community, and not much later, the World Jewish Congress office in Frankfurt started receiving abusive letters ("One day we shall break every bone in the body of the Jewish bastard who denounced Professor Zind," read one). The affair was widely covered in the international press, and Agayants became aware of it.[35]

Germany's recent Nazi past was an open wound that presented a prime opportunity: by portraying West Germany as riddled with neo-Nazis, the Soviets could weaken Bonn, alienate it from its French, British, and American allies and occupying authorities, delay or prevent German rearmament, paralyze the political debate, and drive a wedge into NATO. But before Agayants and his new Department D could execute such an ambitious operation, the KGB needed a test run.

Agayants dispatched a small group of intelligence officers to a Russian village about fifty miles from Moscow. Their instructions: instigate anti-Semitism and gauge the village's reaction. One night the KGB team kicked over tombstones, daubed swastikas, and painted anti-Jewish slogans. Officers reported back to Agayants that most villagers were shocked and frightened by the incident. But among a small number of Russians, they reported, the Nazi symbols and slogans also triggered latent anti-Semitism and inspired them to become anti-Jewish activists on their own.[36] The disinformation specialists in Department D then decided to move forward with the operation on a global scale. It is likely that a driving force behind the operation was Vassily Sitnikov, Agayants's deputy and a KGB colonel with a specialization in German affairs. Sitnikov had served in Potsdam, Berlin, and Vienna, and also appreciated the depth of the trauma that was the Holocaust in Germany. One KGB defector,

Peter Deriabin, later recalled Sitnikov as one of the masterminds behind the idea.[37] Sergei Kondrashev, who later briefly headed the KGB's active measures shop, recalled that Russian intelligence instigated right-wing "hate sessions against Jews" and arranged the desecration of Jewish grave sites.[38] Another former senior KGB officer, Oleg Kalugin, who served in New York in the early 1960s, recalled in his memoirs how his agency executed the operation, and specifically referred to smearing swastikas on three synagogues: "My fellow officers paid American agents to paint swastikas on synagogues in New York and Washington. Our New York station even hired people to desecrate Jewish cemeteries," he wrote, referring to the yellow swastikas on Staten Island. "Attempting to show that America was inhospitable to Jews, we wrote anti-Semitic letters to American Jewish leaders," Kalugin added.[39] In 2017, I met Kalugin for lunch at an upscale restaurant in Washington, D.C. As we got ready to order, with an empty table in front of us, I pushed a large image of the Cologne synagogue Swastika defacement across the starched tablecloth to him. Kalugin looked at it, unsurprised and almost disinterested, "Oh, we did it," he said; "we did it in many places of the world," describing the activity as "maintaining anti-Semitism."[40] Yet another KGB source, Rupert Sigl, who worked in East Berlin during the swastika campaign, told one interviewer that he was ordered to translate hate letters from Russian into German in order to mail them to Jewish families in West Germany.[41]

One of the most noteworthy aspects of this spectacular disinformation campaign is the absence of the Stasi's foreign intelligence arm, the HVA. The HVA was then headed by Markus Wolf, who had a Jewish father, and it appears that he resisted Agayants's request to participate in the campaign. Wolf wrote a short chapter on active measures for his 1997 memoirs, in which he mentions an anti-Semitic operation, expresses doubts about its ethics, and alludes to his resistance, specifically questioning "whether I as the son of a Jewish father would have been the right one to authorize or to initiate the desecration of Jewish cemeteries and other neo-Nazi hate crimes."[42]

The operation helped lift Agayants to legendary status in the history of Soviet foreign intelligence. His name was enshrined in gold at the KGB's modernist headquarters.[43] By the time he retired, his disinformation shop had grown to more than one hundred officers. "It can be said without exaggeration," summarized Russia's 2006 official history of external intelligence, that "the new stage of intelligence activity in the field of 'actions of influence' and other active measures is inextricably linked to the name Igor Agayants." The official history does not include any details of Agayants's most notable successes, but there can be no doubt that the hate campaign that started on Christmas of 1959 was an important part of his legacy. "It was under him," the official KGB history notes, "that the most effective form of active measures was born—integrated actions that took on a proactive, offensive, and long-term character."[44]

10.

Racial Engineering

THE KGB DID NOT SEE ITSELF AS INHERENTLY RACIST. "OUR active measures campaign did not discriminate on the basis of race, creed, or color: we went after everybody," wrote Oleg Kalugin, who coordinated a number of race-baiting disinformation operations in the KGB's New York City station in the early 1960s.[1] The goal was to show that the Western world was plagued by tensions among a number of racial, religious, and ethnic communities. The KGB stations in New York and Washington, Kalugin later recalled in his memoirs, "engaged in numerous 'active measures,' in which we spread disinformation and stirred up trouble in the black and Jewish communities, among others." Kalugin recalled his encounters with black activists in New York City: "I struck up a friendship with an editor from *The Liberator* and went with him on several trips to Harlem, where I was the only white man in many of the clubs we visited."[2] Some

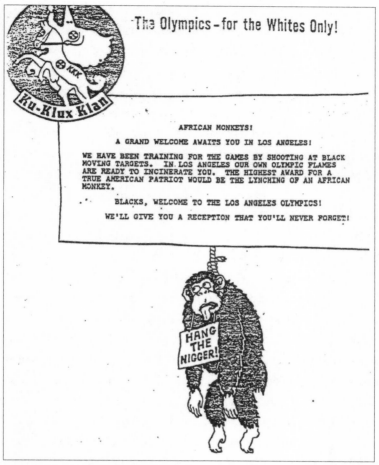

Example of a forged letter, purportedly written by the KKK, to International Olympic Committee members in numerous African and Asian nations in advance of the Los Angeles Olympics (Image from Library of Congress)

KGB officers saw engineering racism as a legitimate way to expose racism. "I knew our propaganda was exaggerating the extent of racism in America, yet I also saw firsthand the blatant discrimination against blacks," Kalugin wrote.[3]

The Ku Klux Klan leaflets came in the mail. Postmarked in New York at 8:00 p.m. on Sunday, November 27, 1960, the short text was titled "White America Rejects A Bastardized United Nations." "A foul stench spreads out from the East River and hangs over New York like a pall—the greasy sweat of the Black Races of Africa and the Yellow Races of Asia which have invaded the United Nations. It is enough to make every White Protestant American vomit." The one-page leaflet was mailed to the UN delegations of Chad, Liberia, Somalia, and Benin, as well as to Indian diplomats.[4] The purported KKK leaflet contained a series of slurs against the "BLACK and YELLOW PERIL," and also attacked Catholics, Jews, and France. The leaflet even called Nikita Khrushchev, then the first secretary of the Communist Party of the Soviet Union, the Antichrist. The forgery ended with a direct threat against the foreign diplomats residing in New York City: "The KU KLUX KLAN warns the Black and Yellow 'delegates' to stay close to the buildings of the United Nations and the brothels of Harlem, and not to defile the hotels and restaurants of the White City." The authors signed off the message with an odd tagline, underlined three times: "THE FIERY CROSSES SHALL BURN!"[5]

The U.S. ambassador to the United Nations, James Wadsworth, asked the FBI to investigate the next morning. The anonymously mailed letter contained a few clues for the investigators—first, inexact usage of American phrases. "These monkeys should have been tanned and feathered," the leaflet said, misusing the American expression "tarred and feathered." Then there was something curious about how the leaflet surfaced. In some cases it was mailed, in envelopes with no return address, to the specific hotel room numbers of traveling African delegates. That information was specific, time-sensitive, and not publicly accessible, which made it less likely that the letter was simply racist hate mail from a deranged civilian, or indeed from the KKK.

The timing was also noteworthy. The letter was sent to the African and Asian delegations just as the UN General Assembly began to debate colonialism, in response to a suggestion from Khrushchev that all colonial people should be given independence—hence also the seemingly out-of-place swipe at France, which was still a colonial power.

The New York Times reported on the FBI's ongoing investigation, but did not mention the possibility that the alleged Klan mail could be a hostile active measure, surely to the delight of its authors across the Iron Curtain. But although the Times didn't report it, FBI investigators did immediately suspect that the leaflet could be the work of "a foreign delegation."[6] The FBI passed the investigation over to the CIA. The Eastern Europe specialists in Langley soon concluded that the purported KKK leaflet had been "manufactured in East Germany," just like the O'Shaughnessy letters and a flood of other active measures at the time.[7] It is more likely that the letters were conceived of in Moscow.

The KGB had developed a fascination with American racial tensions. Soviet disinformation operators understood one thing: although America's unresolved trauma with regard to slavery cut deep, the potential to exploit that wound was small, at least at the time. The African American "distrust of whites was stronger than the ideological fissures dividing this world," one 1960s Cold War defector wrote, reasoning that blacks in the United States would rather turn to Africa than to the USSR.[8] Accordingly, Russian disinformation campaigns would exploit America's race problem by pulling in Africa, as they had with the UN forgery. The KGB's Department D and its subsidiaries could work the racial rift from both sides: they weren't simply posing as the KKK—remarkably, the same Russian operators posed as an African American organization agitating against the KKK.

The 15-page pamphlet started with a one-line, all-caps cover page, inscribed "TO OUR DEAR FRIENDS." "Dear Brethren," the text began, introducing the purported authors as members of the "African Friends Association," based in the United States. "We feel you must be on your guard against the new danger which threatens you," the pamphlet continued in bold print. "The greedy hand of American imperialism is reaching out to grab the riches of your countries." The U.S. government was only pretending to be a friend to the African people, especially to the Republic of Congo, which had just become independent and was not yet aligned with one of the Cold War superpowers. "We, Negroes living in the United States of America, are going to reveal the truth to you about the way the Americans really treat people with dark skin," the pamphlet went on. Four hundred years before, it said, "our forefathers" were forcibly brought from Africa to America, and sold into slavery. Sixty million African Americans, the covert Russian authors told their African readers, were a larger group of people than the whole population of the Congo, and they had experienced "the most unspeakable suffering and torment."[9]

Over several pages, the document reported accurate statistics and real cases of race crimes against African Americans, directly quoting the Civil Rights Congress, the National Council of Churches of Christ, and the National Association for the Advancement of Colored People, as well as respected news organizations such as the Associated Press and *The Washington Post*. The KGB reported, for example—truthfully—that Edward Aaron, thirty-four, had been abducted, beaten, and castrated by Klansmen in Birmingham, Alabama.[10] Russian intelligence also reported, again accurately and actually leaving out some disturbing details, that a police officer, W. B. Cherry, shot three black Americans in Dawson, Georgia, in a period of two weeks, only to be acquitted by white judges in court.[11] The pamphlet contained nine disturbing pictures of graphic lynching violence, such as a black infant bitten by a dog and a body with fingers severed hanging from a tree, and, on its final page, a cartoon of a black corpse dangling from the arm of the Statue of Liberty.

The pamphlet also outlined how African Americans were the targets of legal discrimination in several Southern states, explaining that interracial marriage was off-limits in twenty-nine states; that in fourteen states, "negroes" were forbidden by law to travel in trains together with whites; and that in eight states, the law limited riding buses as well, resulting in the arrest of more than sixty protesters at a bus terminal in Nashville, Tennessee.[12]

The pamphlet did contain several falsehoods, such as the claim that African Americans were forced to "pay for their shanties twice as much as the whites do for their apartments," or the closing all-caps warning: REMEMBER THAT IN THE UNITED STATES OF AMERICA THE KU KLUX KLAN IS ORGANIZING SPECIAL UNITS OF RACIST KILLERS TO BE SENT TO THE CONGO. But by and large, the pamphlet was a disturbingly well-sourced and well-crafted document. "Do not allow the American noose to be tightened around the necks of the African peoples!" it concluded.

The leaflet took what was perhaps America's most debilitating cultural flaw and turned it into a Russian foreign policy boon. The pamphlet first surfaced in Africa in November 1960, and was still being circulated by Russian *rezidenturas* throughout the continent seven months later. It was ultimately published in at least sixteen African countries. A French edition was distrib-

Image of a lynched man
from an inauthentic African
American pamphlet titled
"TO OUR DEAR FRIENDS,"
distributed across Africa
by the KGB
(Image from Library of Congress)

uted in French-speaking countries in Africa. "This poisonous little racist tract is a headache for our diplomatic missions in Africa," Richard Helms told the Senate Judiciary Committee in June 1961—an especial headache because it contained many harsh truths, despite its provenance.

Soviet active measures did not just impersonate organizations and individuals at the fringes of American political culture; they also supported and funded existing groups.

One target was a man named Menachem Arnoni. Born in Poland in 1922, Arnoni was imprisoned in several concentration camps during World War II; he survived and made his way to the United States. In New Jersey he founded *The Minority of One*, a far-left political magazine. His magazine's subheading whimsically stated that it was *dedicated to the elimination of all thought restrictions, except for the truth*. He called it "the publication for the thinking individual."[13]

Image of Klansmen
from the same
pamphlet
(Image from Library of
Congress)

Arnoni was a radical pacifist and a radical individualist, ideologies that were, in Arnoni's view, intricately linked. He rejected "nationalistic prejudice" that would only perpetuate antagonism between camps of nations, with each identifying the other as the villain. Peace, therefore, would hinge on honest self-criticism, and on the individual's ability to resist and reject "the hypnotic influences of a totalitarian mass psychology."[14] In 1965, Arnoni addressed a student audience at Berkeley University in the striped uniform of a concentration camp inmate, telling the students that he ran *The Minority of One* with the fearlessness of a man who had "lived a thousand lives, and . . . died a thousand deaths."[15] The monthly magazine drew a dedicated following and regularly sponsored ads in *The New York Times* and *The Washington Post*.

The magazine, written for a liberal avant-garde audience, tended to publish fierce criticism of U.S. foreign and defense policy. On the last page of each issue, Arnoni penned an editorial printed in a blue box, titled *Of What I Am Ashamed*. Bullet points might include "the U.S. government," or "the State Department," or "the Department of Defense," for not limiting nuclear armament, for example, or for producing biological weapons, or for barring an East German ice-hockey squad from competing in Colorado.[16] Arnoni was among the first pundits to denounce the American military's involvement and moral failure in Vietnam.[17] The combination of independence, including from advertisers, and criticism of the government made Arnoni an attractive influence agent.

Oleg Kalugin was introduced to Arnoni in his capacity as a Radio Moscow correspondent, "and we hit it off immediately," Kalugin recalled.[18] Arnoni was a decade older than the undercover spy, and the Russian was impressed by the publisher's experiences and by his eloquence and exuberance. They struck up a form of friendship. At some point, Arnoni began complaining about the financial difficulty of running his magazine, and Kalugin soon proposed that the still-new Department D fund and support Arnoni. "We decided to use Arnoni and his publication to further the Soviet cause in the United States," he recalls, and soon *The Minority of One* "unwittingly did the bidding of the KGB."[19]

The Soviet backers, however, were not too happy with the narrow and "effete" audience of *The Minority of One*. The KGB thus suggested reaching for a national platform by placing advertisements in *The New York Times*. Arnoni liked Kalugin's idea. The two of them worked on the text of the ad, and agreed on a critique of America's growing involvement in Vietnam. The New York *rezidentura* sent the draft ad to Moscow; the center made a few changes, and authorized a few thousand dollars of funding. Several more KGB-funded *Times* ads followed, some of them signed by American public personalities. In March and April 1963, for example, Arnoni was the signatory of an expensive ad in the *Times* (and in *The Washington Post*) titled "An Open Letter to President John F. Kennedy," which strongly urged the president to end the war and make peace in Vietnam.[20]

The KGB also funded Arnoni directly, with cash, and even aided in the publication of texts ghostwritten by Agayants's disinformation shop. "At some point, I offered to write an article for *Minority of One* and he agreed," wrote Kalugin. "In fact, the article on American militarism was written by the KGB propaganda department in Moscow." The magazine would publish several Soviet-produced articles under a pseudonym.

The information flow went both ways. Kalugin was impressed by the depth of Arnoni's knowledge about Israel and the Middle East. The publisher personally knew David Ben-Gurion and Golda Meir, two of Israel's most prominent prime ministers. "I often sent Moscow his assessment of events in the Middle East," said Kalugin.

By the early 1960s, the United States was shutting down its two most aggressive disinformation fronts in Berlin, the Kampfgruppe and LCCASSOCK. The USSR, however, was only getting started.

1961–1975: Compete

Dezinformatsiya Rising

D ISINFORMATION CAME OF AGE IN THE 1960S. DESPITE SOME remarkable successes in 1960 and 1961, Soviet active measures in general lacked direction and resources—and tilted to the extreme in the early years.

Department D, after its founding in early 1959, had been directly tied to the Presidium of the Communist Party. Agayants had a stellar internal reputation in the Soviet intelligence bureaucracy, and his appointment indicated the importance that Khrushchev assigned to the campaign to erode American supremacy. Department D was then staffed by forty to fifty specialists in Moscow alone, organized by region and function. In 1962, Department D was upgraded to a larger organizational unit, known as Service A,[1] one of only two special sections within the KGB's vast First Chief Directorate, some twenty thousand officers strong.[2] Agayants's unit was remarkably

Igor Agayants, legendary pioneer of KGB disinformation tactics and head of Department D when it expanded to Service A in 1962

productive. Five years after its founding, the unit was running between 350 and 400 operations per year, according to the U.S. intelligence report that first revealed the existence of Department D (two years after the organization had been upgraded to service status, unbeknownst to U.S. intelligence then).[3]

Agayants was especially adept at identifying the right kind of personnel for disinformation, which was no minor achievement: the best disinformation officers required a rare combination of creativity, cultural empathy, and outside-the-box thinking, but also rigor, discipline, and ideological firmness. Under Agayants's deft leadership, active measures became a career-making field. The new unit's responsibility was to identify and analyze enemy fissures and failures, and then to exploit the discovered vulnerabilities in a systematic, worldwide effort.

Moscow's decision to instruct its satellite services to follow the lead of the KGB's First Chief Directorate was a transformative step in the development of this holistic system. Between 1961 and 1964, Soviet bloc intelligence agencies in East Germany, Czechoslovakia, Bulgaria, Poland, and Hungary also founded active measures departments. The CIA's alarm over the increase in activity triggered the 1961 Senate hearing on Soviet bloc forgeries where Richard Helms gave his testimony. But the CIA was catching only a fraction of the overall disinformation production at that time. A significant number of operations targeted developing countries, which made detection harder.[4] The purpose of the KGB's activities, in the view of the CIA, was to "defame and discredit" U.S. government departments and agencies in charge of national security and to "divide" Western allies.

It took many decades for the details of Soviet bloc activities in the 1960s to trickle out, thanks in large part to defectors such as the Czech intelligence officer Ladislav Bittman, who defected in 1968 and published his memoirs shortly thereafter. Bittman was an exceptional officer, sharp, methodical, yet with a strong appetite for risk. A member of the Communist Party since age fifteen, he entered the intelligence community after securing a doctorate in law from Charles University in Prague,[5] where he also later enrolled part-time in the journalism school in order to develop the skills and contacts necessary for a career in disinformation. He worked as an analyst for four years, then for eight as an operative recruiting and running agents, and for two years as the deputy chief of Department 8, which was responsible for disinformation[6]— "an elegant expression for activities called in plain English 'dirty tricks,'" he told Congress decades later, with a smile.[7]

By 1964, special operations were under one roof within the StB, the Czech state security agency, and their production took a sharp upward turn. Previously, different regional departments had handled their own special operations, which meant that resources from other departments could not be put to use for active measures in areas that were particularly important to leadership. Meanwhile, KGB advisors were supervising the development and execution of operations at multiple levels in the bureaucracy.

"This development marked the beginning of a new era of secret games and intrigues against the non-Communist world," said Bittman of the disinformation upgrade in Moscow and its satellite states.[8] A paradigm shift was under way. Eastern intelligence agencies, like their Western counterparts, used to treat disinformation as a task secondary to the primary mission of gathering information. But after 1961, active measures slowly began to rise in internal significance, attracting some of the most ambitious officers, and the quality of special operations further increased.

Bittman tells a story that captures one defining paradox of this bureaucratic innovation. A few weeks after Department 8 was established, a senior official from the Secretariat of the Central Committee of the Czech Communist Party spoke at the StB. Over the 1950s, Soviet ideologues had changed their interpretation of Western activities against communism. Key thinkers in Moscow believed that the United States and the Western alliance had shifted their priority away from using military force toward what they called "ideological subversion" of communism. The threat had widened in scope: now it wasn't simply NATO troops, tanks, and missiles that led to a feeling of siege in Moscow. "Any unsanctioned attempt by Western scholars, students, artists, or journalists to establish close contact with their Eastern counterparts was immediately condemned by the Party," Bittman recalled, and seen as proof of "a carefully planned and directed operation to undermine Socialism in Eastern Europe."[9] The Soviet bloc, true to the theory of ideological subversion, needed to respond in kind.

Bittman, a bright and diligent student, was confused as he heard the Central Committee official lay out this theory of subversion during the lecture at his new place of employment. He spoke up:

"I do not think the very term 'ideological subversion' is correct. It implies that our opponent's ideology has a subversive, explosive power which we should stop with whatever means. But we as Marxists believe in the strength and the superiority of our own ideology, do we not? We consider it a scientific theory, so what are we afraid of? Why should we avoid direct confrontation with our opponents on a free democratic discussion basis? Could you comment on this, please?"

The young and idealistic Bittman had put his finger on a sore spot and a paradox. For a long moment there was complete silence in the lecture hall. Some of Bittman's StB colleagues looked at him tersely, wondering whether their young colleague had just crossed a line by asking such a provocative question. The Party official emptied his glass of water, carefully considering his response, and then proceeded to accuse the imperialists of playing dirty tricks, ignoring Bittman's question. When the event was over, Bittman got up to leave the room. But the StB Party secretary pulled him aside. "I would not recommend that you ask provocative questions next time," he said.[10]

In one question, Bittman had captured two defining paradoxes of active measures: first, that justifying and running disinformation at scale against a foreign adversary required seeing your own ideology as both stronger than the enemy's and more vulnerable; and second, that finding and training the most talented minds for disinformation meant that officers needed to be just like Bittman: creative, questioning nonconformists who would also conform to orders and not question the party line.

The CIA, meanwhile, had no illusions about one of the central goals of the disinformation apparatus. "The objective of the overall program is to achieve the destruction, break-up and neutralization of CIA," one internal report observed in 1965.[11] And indeed, the KGB's new disinformation shop immediately focused its work on the CIA.

One of the most remarkable early episodes in Department D's anti-CIA activity came early in 1961, when a 160-page book appeared under mysterious circumstances. The book was titled *A Study of a Master Spy*, and was a highly critical account of the CIA's director, Allen Dulles. The named authors were Bob Edwards and Kenneth Dunne. Edwards was a maverick member of Parliament in London and a veteran of the International Brigades in the Spanish Civil War. The CIA knew "nothing" about Dunne at the time.[12] The book appeared first in London and was soon translated into Spanish and Arabic, with publishers in Buenos Aires and Cairo.

In March 1964, Dulles, now retired from the CIA, participated in a TV roundtable with Peter Deriabin, then one of the most high-profile KGB defectors living in the United States. The moderator brought up active measures.

"What is disinformation, anyway?" he asked.

"Well, this is it," Dulles said, and held up a copy of *A Study of a Master Spy*. "Here's a booklet that was written about me." Dulles then cryptically alluded to the purported author being a member of a legislature in a friendly country, then turned to the former KGB officer sitting next to him, adding, tongue-in-cheek, "I am the 'master spy'—I have found out recently after certain research had been done, that the real author of the pamphlet is a Colonel Sitnikov, whom I believe you know, or know of. He is the real author."

"Sitnikov?" responded Deriabin. "I used to work with Sitnikov in Vienna." Deriabin explained that after several tours abroad, Sitnikov now was back in Moscow. As the deputy head of Department D, Sitnikov had played a role in the massive global wave of engineered anti-Semitism; one of his next big projects was the anti-Dulles booklet. The colonel had it researched and drafted, and then "served up for final polish and printing in the United Kingdom," as the CIA later explained in an internal study.[13]

Now Dulles was joking with Deriabin about Sitnikov's creative writing. "He has a whole dossier on me," said Dulles. "I've read some things there about myself that even I didn't know."

In 1961, the CIA observed in an internal, classified study that West Germany had been "flooded" with forgeries "for years."[14] The years 1957 and 1958 in particular, one CIA analyst observed, "saw a noticeable increase in internationally distributed propaganda-by-forgery" that sought to promote "division in the West." Langley analysts pointed out that they observed "rather elaborate progressions in prolonged campaigns."[15]

These anti-Western disinformation campaigns were aggressive, fast-paced, and used innovative methods that evolved quickly and in unexpected, frightening ways.

One such measure exploited a military exercise known as FALLEX 62. In September 1962, NATO held the first exercise that acted out the assumption that World War III could start with a major Soviet attack on Western Europe. The Berlin Wall had just gone up the previous year. FALLEX 62 was equally highly classified and disconcerting: in the scenario, a medium-sized nuclear device is said to have exploded over a German army airfield, followed by several nuclear strikes against airfields and missile bases in the United Kingdom, Italy, and Turkey. Within days, 20 to 30 million people in the United Kingdom and Germany have died. Major American cities are incinerated by multiple H-bombs. NATO's counterstrike fails to stop the Soviet advance into Germany. Hamburg falls, defenseless. Even Robert McNamara, the U.S. secretary of defense, came to Germany for the secret exercise—but that secrecy would not last.

"World War III started in the early evening hours on Friday, nearly three weeks ago," reported *Der Spiegel* on October 8, 1962. The then fifteen-year-old magazine was known for its investigative chops, and its cheeky, confrontational tone had lifted its circulation to nearly half a million readers. Now a detailed, sixteen-page story spilled the beans on FALLEX 62. Germany's most senior four-star general appeared on the cover of *Der Spiegel*, smiling uncomfortably, an iron cross around his neck. *Bedingt abwehrbereit*, read the title: "Defense readiness limited." The story attacked Franz-Josef Strauss, Germany's hawkish defense minister, and blamed the dismal state of Germany's conventional defenses on his infatuation with nuclear missiles. Rudolf Augstein, the magazine's publisher, saw himself as in a "fight" with Strauss.[16]

Eighteen days later, the authorities struck back. Germany's Federal Criminal Police and military intelligence troops raided the *Spiegel* offices and the homes of the journalists, first in Hamburg and later in Bonn. The police seized the offices and sealed them off, evicting the magazine's staff, and arrested Augstein along with three editors, charging them with treason. The crackdown on *Der Spiegel* was instantly interpreted as an attack against the freedom of the press. "*Spiegel* dead—liberty dead," thousands of demonstrators chanted in Hamburg. After 103 days of crisis, Augstein was freed, all charges dropped—and Strauss was sacked. The affair became a landmark in Germany's coming-of-age as a mature liberal democracy. And as with the remotely engineered wave of anti-Semitism a couple of years earlier, the KGB's hidden hand in the *Spiegel* affair was fully revealed only decades later.[17]

The revelation started to emerge in 1977, thanks to the Pentagon's own espionage organization, the Defense Intelligence Agency. Earlier that year, Walter Hahn, a hawkish Austrian-born former military intelligence officer who had interrogated German war criminals for the Nuremberg Trials, had named a Czech defector in the journal he edited, *Strategic Review*.[18] A contact

An icon of Bavarian conservatism, Franz-Josef Strauss (right), speaking with the Christian Democratic chairman Rainer Barzel at a party event in 1972. Hostile active measures upended the political careers of both men.
(Photograph by Köhler-Kaeß / ullstein bild via Getty Images)

then invited Hahn to attend a classified briefing given by said defector, Jan Šejna, to a group of Pentagon officials.

Šejna had fled to the West in 1967. As one of the highest-ranking Communist defectors—he had been a general and senior administrator of the StB—he was in high demand with intelligence agencies. At the 1977 DIA briefing, Šejna mentioned Franz-Josef Strauss and *Der Spiegel* as targets successfully struck by Eastern bloc active measures. Hahn, a German-speaker, immediately recognized the explosive potential of this revelation. Later, in the early summer of 1978, Hahn sat down with Šejna. His private notes on the conversation are among the most detailed accounts to date on the planning of the *Spiegel* operation. Hahn wrote:

> According to Sejna, the calculation was that the publication by *Der Spiegel* of NATO documents would have the effect, at the very least, of triggering a scandal which would put Strauss under fire for his failure to prevent leaks from the Defence Ministry. At best, given his volatile nature, Strauss might overreact and thus get himself into

deeper difficulties. Sejna said that he was present when the Czech minister of the interior, Rudolf Barak, presented the plan for the Spiegel operation to the Czech Central Committee. Barak had to get approval at the highest level because it represented a "strategic operation" involving the transfer of documents.[19]

In October 1979, Hahn met Strauss, now the governor of Bavaria, in Munich, and told him about Šejna's revelations. Strauss had been the target of several active measures over the years, and found the story plausible. Hahn then decided that Šejna's revelations needed to be made public. His own *Strategic Review* was not significant enough, so he turned to William F. Buckley, Jr., an icon of American conservatism and the founder of *National Review*. Buckley did some more research and then, on January 15, 1980, published a widely syndicated column, "The Vindication of Strauss."[20] A cunning Soviet plan to discredit Strauss, Buckley explained, was executed through Czech and German agents who encouraged a mole in Strauss's own ministry to leak classified (and accurate) material to *Der Spiegel*. From there, the history-making political scandal ran its course.

Now the story was out, but Buckley's column did not provide enough detail to be fully authoritative on its own. About a year later, speaking at a Conservative Party event, an influential British conservative financier said that the campaign by *Der Spiegel* to discredit Franz-Josef Strauss "was orchestrated by the KGB."[21] Augstein did not take kindly to what he saw as a smear. In March 1981, attorneys acting on behalf of Augstein and *Der Spiegel* issued a writ for libel. The lawsuit that followed, and the defendant's investigative work, brought to light the details that would allow reconstructing the larger operation.

The story began early in 1960, in a high-level meeting of the International Department. The head of the International Department was Boris Ponomarev, a soft-spoken, dangerously good listener, an art he perfected in proximity to Stalin, whose tranquil surface belied the fierce Party ideologue beneath.[22] At the meeting, Ponomarev emphasized the significance of West Germany, the biggest and most important country in Western Europe. The International Department's goal, he said, was to prevent politicians from rising to power. The only name he specifically mentioned was Franz-Josef Strauss. Ponomarev instructed his team, among them Ilya Dzhirkvelov, who later defected, to "improve the situation."[23]

A delegation of around a dozen German editors with links to the Social Democrats was scheduled to visit Moscow in March 1961. A month before the delegation arrived, the KGB's disinformation unit and the German section of the International Department laid the groundwork for their visit. Ponomarev called another meeting in the International Department, making clear West Germany's strategic importance for the USSR and his government's full support of the Social Democrats. The delegation of editors was an opportunity of the first order, Ponomarev explained. "Tell them frankly," he instructed his staff, "that we regard Adenauer as a politician whose days are numbered, and Strauss as a follower of Hitler and as a revanchist who is harming the whole of Europe with his actions."

With these high-level intentions articulated by the Central Committee, the KGB got down to business. Soon Agayants, the master of dirty tricks, and his deputy Sitnikov, the German specialist, sat down with Dzhirkvelov, who was the point man for the incoming German delegation of editors. Agayants wanted to bait them with information on Strauss. "When you talk to the Germans," Agayants told Dzhirkvelov, "you can hint that we have information concerning Strauss's connections with the American intelligence service." The disinformation chief then told his subordinate that the CIA had recruited Strauss when he was a prisoner of war, that the German politician now received large sums of money for his collaboration with U.S. intelligence, and that Strauss was more interested in his personal fortune than in a peaceful future for Germany. The story appeared convincing on its face. "If you are asked what proof you have," said Agayants, "you can say that we even have *documentary* proof, but that you can produce it only on the condition that it will be published in the West German press without the source being revealed."[24] It is unclear whether Agayants even told his own man, Dzhirkvelov, that the story was a lie. Either way, the Social Democrat editors did not take the bait that time.

Nevertheless, Eastern bloc intelligence agencies continued to target Strauss so aggressively that some of the mud they slung would stick. The

KGB even installed a specialized station in Dresden in the late 1950s, the sole purpose of which was to conduct active measures against West Germany and Austria. The Dresden office specialized in planting deceptive stories in respectable German-language outlets. The material prepared in Dresden, with help from Moscow and Berlin, would then be taken to the West by visiting contacts. Colonel Arkady Boiko, then the head of the Dresden *rezidentura*, claimed numerous successes. But the biggest coup, Boiko said, was the successful use of *Der Spiegel* to compromise Franz-Josef Strauss.

Once the *Spiegel* affair had run its course and Adenauer had sacked Strauss, his potential successor, various Soviet officials bragged about the success of their operation. "We successfully used *Der Spiegel* to undermine Strauss,"[25] Ponomarev crowed at another top-secret meeting in 1963. "One of the best jobs ever," said Alexander Yefremov, the deputy secretary-general of the International Organization of Journalists, another Soviet front organization.[26] Dzhirkvelov, the later defector, considered "forcing Strauss to resign after his exposure in *Der Spiegel*" a key success.[27] "There can be no doubt at all," he wrote, "that the anti-Strauss campaign in *Der Spiegel* was launched on the basis of KGB-planted material."[28] Other Soviet officials who mentioned the *Spiegel* affair of 1962 as a successful intelligence operation were Alexei Adzhubei, Khrushchev's son-in-law and then the editor of the government daily *Izvestia*; Pavel Gevorkyan, deputy editor-in-chief of Novosti's North American Department; and Leonid Zavgorodny, an assistant to Khrushchev.[29] Vladimir Koucky, secretary of the Czech Central Committee with the foreign affairs portfolio, bragged at length about the success of the operation against Strauss at a 1965 meeting of Warsaw Pact officials in Prague.[30] Yet another KGB defector, Oleg Gordievsky, later reported that "during my time with the KGB in the 1970s, officers of the German division were openly praised for their deft use of *Der Spiegel* in undermining Strauss."[31]

In hindsight, the KGB's internal assessment of the Strauss takedown is a pivotal moment in the history of active measures. But not for the reasons cited by Soviet operators. Editors at *Der Spiegel* countered their critics—and, without knowing it, the boastful Communists—by pointing out that Strauss's downfall in 1962 was not caused by the initial FALLEX 62 leak but the reaction of the German authorities to the leak, the arrest of editors and journalists, the ensuing public outcry, and the fact that Strauss subsequently entangled himself in contradictions through inept crisis management. The editors were right. The episode illustrates the tendency of intelligence agencies to overstate the effects of active measures, or, to be more precise, it illustrates the difficulty of measuring their effects. The raw material of disinformation is made of existing conflicts and existing divisions, so causal effects are therefore extremely difficult to prove. As Service A scaled up bureaucratically and got better at disinformation, it also scaled up the risk of self-disinformation. This dynamic is, far from case-specific, a structural feature of professional active measures.

Meanwhile, Agayants was perfecting the tactical disinformation game, and one of the game's key strategies is the art of deniability, the art of designing and structuring releases so that the victim's denial will only strengthen an operation. Just three months after Strauss's ouster, a rare Western attempt at driving wedges into the Communist bloc served as a helpful illustration of how *not* to structure an information operation.

On Saturday, March 9, 1963, the Paris newspaper *Le Monde* printed a notable letter, purportedly forwarded for publication from the Chinese embassy in Bern, Switzerland.[32] The letter was written comrade-to-comrade, addressed to the official outlet of the French Communist Party, called *France Nouvelle*. The Chinese Communists were allegedly reprimanding the French for not publicizing a previous letter, related to a disagreement between Communist politicians in Paris and Beijing. The letter quickly was revealed to be a forgery, one printed on the letterhead of a regular newsletter distributed by the Chinese embassy's press service.

A never-identified Western intelligence agency likely designed the letter to drive a wedge between China and the Soviet Union.[33] But whoever produced the forgery, in Langley, London, or Paris, failed to apply a tactic perfected in Moscow: the art of designing a forgery so that it would continue to appear authentic even after the supposed author denied it. About ten days later, *Le Monde* printed the Chinese denial, "solemnly" declaring that "our service has never sent said letter."[34] The correction made the measure useless.

The reason: the forged letter was embarrassing for the recipient, not for the sender, and it was easy for the sender to deny authorship. The Chinese had nothing to hide, and the contents of the letter were not supposed to be kept secret by the Chinese for other reasons. This meant that a Chinese denial of authenticity was immediately credible.

THE EASTERN BLOC, BY NOW, WAS LESS PRONE TO SUCH OBVIOUS MISTAKES in tradecraft, and began to take operations to a new level—even a cinematic level. Later in the winter of 1963, the world was mesmerized by the hunt for mythical Nazi gold, supposedly sunk deep in a cold and remote Alpine lake in Austria's Styria Province.[35] In the end no gold was found in the depths of Lake Toplitz, but a different treasure was lifted: twelve chests of Nazi-counterfeited British pounds, two chests of printing plates for counterfeiting, various fake stamps[36]—and the idea for a daring operation.

Deep in the mountainous Bohemian forest, halfway between Munich and Prague and almost directly on the border between East and West, were two adjacent lakes, Devil's Lake and Black Lake, each ringed by pine trees, with rugged banks that dropped sharply into the dark depth. The lakes, their names a hint, were the subject of local legends, some old, some recent. Wehrmacht and SS units had once occupied a now burned-out cottage overlooking Black Lake during the war, and local lore had it that the bodies of water were hiding a dark secret. In April 1964, the producers of Czechoslovak TV's *Curious Camera*, intrigued by the high-profile Nazi gold hunt in Lake Toplitz, decided to make an investigative documentary feature film to "reveal the secrets" of the two mysterious Bohemian lakes.[37] The TV producers needed government approval, so the Ministry of the Interior was in on the adventure from the beginning, and by extension, Department 8. Bittman, a sports diver, took part in the initial survey of the thick, loose layer of mud on the lake floor—the film crew, of course, did not know that their friendly ministry official was in the business of dirty tricks. The initial survey had already attracted considerable public interest. Filming was swiftly scheduled for later in May. Bittman wrote a memo just two days after the survey, on

May 3, 1964, and spelled out the idea for what would become the most cinematic disinformation operation of the entire Cold War: Operation NEPTUN.

Bittman, during that initial dive, turned up an "important finding," he wrote, namely a soldered metal box stuck in the mud at 12 meters' depth in the Black Lake. His disinformation unit, he suggested, could exploit the coming publicity and simply add a few boxes to what was sitting on the lake floor by dropping two to four chests of authentic Nazi documents—along with "two or three forgeries" to compromise several top officials in West Germany. Bittman reasoned that the dramatic staging in the mysterious Bohemian lake, as the full project proposal suggested two days later, would boost the operation's effectiveness: "The romanticism associated with the Black Lake and Devil's Lake, and the way these materials will be discovered, will be attractive to a wide range of readers," said the proposal, "especially in the West."[38] Department 8 added that the government would always have full control, as state security would seize the sunken materials immediately after the TV crew had lifted them, just as the Austrians had seized the lifted material at Lake Toplitz before journalists could view them. The interior minister swiftly approved, and Department 8 hastily began its own diving survey of the Black Lake and its muddy ground—this one geared not to finding a treasure but to hiding one.

In the middle of the night of May 19–20, 1964, an olive green Soviet GAZ truck made its way from Prague to the Bohemian forest. The GAZ carried four Wehrmacht chests loaded with paper, each about 75 kilos in weight, as well as diving gear and an inflatable military rubber raft. The GAZ was followed by a civilian car with four passengers: the chief of StB's First Directorate, Josef Houska; the head of Department 8, Jiří Stejskal; a KGB active measures advisor detailed to the StB named Shundenko; and Bittman, Stejskal's deputy.[39] At some point during the long nightly drive, Bittman glanced over to his boss's boss, Houska, who looked worried; Bittman knew that if the operation failed, the careers of everybody in the car would end.

The operation had several objectives: first, to remind the world—West Germany in particular—of Nazi war crimes. May 8, 1965, marked the twenty-year anniversary of the Wehrmacht's capitulation, and according to the West

Ladislav Bittman in his neoprene suit during Department 8's Black Lake survey on May 14, 1964. The fellow active measures officer holding the scuba tanks would lose one of his fins on the operational night dive five days later. (Archiv bezpečnostních složek)

German criminal code, liability for murder committed during the war would expire with the statute of limitations on that day.[40] Department 8 was concerned that both genuine and fake accusations of war crimes could lose some of their edge as a result.[41] The second goal was to "support anti-German tendencies in the West." And a third goal was deceiving the BND, West Germany's spy agency: Czech TV would "discover" documents that contained a list of German wartime informants, many of whom, the StB assumed, were still informing the BND.[42] If so, the leak would freeze BND assets.

The StB had carefully planned most parts of the operation, down to taking a chemical probe of the lake water, sampling the rotten wood, purchasing new diving gear with depth meters and compression tables, outlining safety procedures for the lake dump, marking the right spot on the lake bed, pre-corroding antique soldered metal crates, and meticulously planning a timeline of the entire procedure.

Yet Bittman's plan had run into an unexpected snag. The historical documents were surprisingly hard to find. The files needed to meet two criteria:

they needed to be valuable to the press and ideally sensational, and their contents had to be unknown to historians and the wider public. A group of Department 8 officers had frantically searched the Czechoslovak archives, while taking care not to tip off actual archivists—but to little avail. Eventually Bittman consulted with KGB advisors at the StB, asking for help. Soon Moscow came back with an offer to send a sufficient amount of genuine Nazi documents to Prague, but the delivery would take some time.

Department 8 decided to forge ahead in the interim. The Czech officers filled four soldered metal boxes with blank sheets of paper, finished the boxes' surface, coated the crates with asphalt, attached weights, and loaded the bundled crates into the GAZ. The group of three cars left Prague, rendezvoused at midnight with a local border guard, and arrived at Black Lake at two in the morning. The group slipped a black raft onto the quiet surface of the lake. Bittman and another diver checked their gear; put on their wet suits, masks, fins, and Aqua-Lungs; hauled the chests overboard; and glided into the cold, clear water just after three in the morning. Visibility was about 20 meters. On his way down, at about 5 meters of depth, Bittman's partner lost one of his brand-new Bonito Super Fins. Nervous about the floating forensic evidence left behind, they carried on, pointing a lamp toward the lake bottom, quickly identifying the preselected spot where the mud was shallow. Bittman placed the cases there and covered them lightly with mud, so that it would look like the crates had been sitting there for nearly two decades. On the way up, Bittman even spotted the lost fin. He grabbed it. At five they had packed up and left.

Next came the mock discovery of the documents. The TV crew started its search at Devil's Lake, two kilometers to the south. To the StB's surprise, the search team actually found sunken explosives in Devil's Lake. The explosives were detonated with a bang on a nearby meadow. After the large black plume of smoke cleared, a three-man-deep crater appeared. The unexpected drama, assumed Department 8, added credibility to their Black Lake ruse. Eventually, after nearly a week of searching Black Lake, divers found the sunken cases.[43] Meanwhile, Department 8 was still waiting for the actual documents to arrive from Moscow.

The lake was closed off to the public. Photographers took pictures of

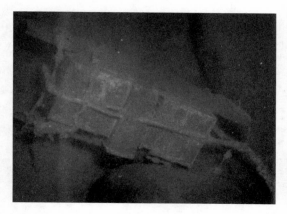

The soldered metal crates were placed at a depth of about 15 meters on the floor of the Black Lake in order to be discovered by a TV investigation a few days later. The boxes contained blank paper because the KGB had not yet delivered the Nazi documents to Prague.
(Archiv bezpečnostních složek)

the recovered crates. They were immediately transported by motorcade to Prague, and handed to a team of government engineers to examine the boxes for explosives and to open them safely. The engineers were not in on the deception, and concluded in their detailed memo that the way the bundles of documents were stored pointed to "quick, improvised work" done by somebody without serious technical means, which would be expected of "a retreating army in disarray."[44] The engineers passed on the documents without opening the innermost envelopes. On July 16, Department 8 published a press release through the Ministry of the Interior:

> The explosive finds from Devil's Lake were rendered harmless near Zelezna Ruda. The cases from Black Lake were carried away to Prague. After a detailed technical examination it was determined that the cases contained no explosives, whereupon they were opened. Within the cases were sealed metal boxes containing Nazi papers from the time of the Second World War. The papers were given over to a group of experts.[45]

The myth of Black Lake was born. The Associated Press and several large European newspapers reported the story the next day,[46] some adding that a secret Luftwaffe unit had been stationed close to the remote lake. The famous Nazi-hunter Simon Wiesenthal, head of a Holocaust documentation center in Vienna, suspected (correctly, as it later turned out) that the nonexistent files

A team of Prague firefighters dive and lift the sunken crates of empty sheets of paper as Czechoslovakia's *Curious Camera* is filming; early July, 1964.
(Archiv bezpečnostních složek)

in the lake could be from Heinrich Himmler's Reichssicherheitshauptamt, the SS's secret security service.[47]

But even the StB did not know which secrets would be revealed—Moscow still hadn't mailed the promised documents to Prague. Nearly two more months passed. The Interior Ministry needed to act, and eventually, in late August, announced that the eagerly anticipated international press conference would be held on September 15. The StB and its disinformation officers were getting nervous. Finally, five days before the press conference, a disinformation officer from Moscow arrived in Prague with several sacks full of Nazi documents—nearly 30,000 pages in total.[48]

Carefully selected intelligence analysts pored over the documents, attempting to find material that they could use. Prague's Department 8 also suspected that Moscow's Service A might have forged all or some of the documents, although the Soviets claimed that they were genuine. Some documents had handwritten Cyrillic annotations on the margins, which made them impossible to use in the Black Lake ruse, as no Nazi would make notes in Cyrillic; but that did help convince the Czech analysts

A government convoy transports the then-nonexistent Nazi secrets back to Prague, July 14, 1964. (Archiv bezpečnostních složek)

that they were authentic, since no Russian forger would use Cyrillic notes either.

The most sensational documents revealed new details on wartime scandals. There was material about an SS historical commission on a failed putsch in Austria in 1934, and on German intelligence operations in then-allied Italy, with reports from SS agents spying on Italian Fascist leaders. The Czechs contributed a few Nazi documents on their own, most notably on the forced expulsion of 300,000 Jews in the Protectorate of Bohemia and Moravia.[49]

On September 15, the Interior Ministry in Prague held its long-awaited press conference. The minister spoke for one hour in numbing detail. Czechoslovak diplomats, trying to malign West Germany, confidentially shared documents related to the Nazi persecution of their citizens with the U.S., British, French, and Dutch embassies, as well as with Jewish community centers. The Czechs also shared some of the documents with Simon Wiesenthal's documentation center, which helped generate international publicity. The French press focused mainly on the evidence of war crimes.[50] The Italian press coverage focused on German spying on Mussolini. Austrian researchers

Cyrillic handwritten notes on a document of the Reichssicherheitshauptamt, the SS's intelligence agency, originally seized by the KGB and delivered to Prague in mid-1964 for the NEPTUN operation
(Archiv bezpečnostních složek)

published several Anschluss-related documents. The *Los Angeles Times*, publishing one of the few U.S. stories about the operation, only mentioned the lack of Nazi gold.

The StB soon concluded that the fake in the lake was a spectacular success. NEPTUN, by March 1965, had spawned more than twenty "submeasures," Houska reported in a self-congratulatory memo to the interior minister. The StB carefully kept track of the press coverage, counting twenty-five Italian stories, eighteen in West Germany, and seven in Austria, as well as coverage in the British, French, Belgian, Swiss, Latin American, African, and U.S. press. All three goals had been achieved, Houska claimed: the West German Parliament would extend the statute of limitations on war crimes as it buckled "under the general public pressure that we caused through the 'NEPTUN' action."[51] Second, the spy chief stressed that "we succeeded in provoking and supporting tendencies and moods against the Federal Republic of Germany, especially in Austria, Italy, Holland, Belgium, France and Great Britain." And finally, "it can be assumed" that the StB "somewhat disrupted" West German intelligence.[52] The KGB seemed to agree. A few months later, the head of the First Chief Directorate himself wrote a letter to Houska, praising the measure, "The implementation of the 'Neptune' action had, in our view, a significant political effect," read the top-secret note from Aleksandr Sakharovsky.[53]

Actual evidence for such breathtaking claims of success, alas, was not available. The Bundestag did indeed extend the statute of limitations for war crimes in March 1965. Nevertheless, Houska's bold claims of NEPTUN's direct impact were a wild exaggeration.[54] Germany's coming-to-terms with its dark past was a gargantuan, decades-long, identity-defining process that was then well under way. Proving any causal effect on Germany's image in the West remains equally difficult, even with the benefit of hindsight—it was easier to see the costs of NEPTUN, at least in retrospect. Very few in the Interior Ministry were in on the deception. Much of the government, the official press agency, and the public, as well as the wider Soviet bloc, were more thoroughly disinformed than was the adversary. Worse, the StB could not even exclude the notion that they themselves had been played. "The theoretical possibility exists," admitted Bittman, "that some of the material had been falsified by Soviet experts."[55]

Ivan Agayants happened to be visiting Prague as the fake hunt for the Nazi documents was under way. According to Bittman, the Czech officers, perhaps a little overconfident at first, misread their stern superior from Moscow.

"What are we going to do with Agayants tonight?" one major asked his colleagues on one of the first days.

"Maybe a few girls would change his mood," the deputy head of the disinformation unit suggested.

Czech state security took the elegant KGB colonel to a Socialist strip show at the Alhambra bar. He did not appreciate the occasion. As the show progressed, the KGB colonel grew visibly uncomfortable. During the break he indicated that he didn't feel well, and wanted to return to the hotel. Agayants apparently preferred to talk about Russian literature. The Czech officers even drove Agayants down to Black Lake for a short visit to witness the filming of the Nazi document dive.[56]

A few days later, sitting in a Department 8 office overlooking the majestic Vltava River, Agayants leafed through a large pile of newspaper clippings. As he finished, pushing the pile back on Bittman's desk, he said, "Sometimes I am amazed how easy it is to play these games. If they did not have press freedom, we would have to invent it for them."[57]

That same year, the KGB initiated and approved direct cooperation on disinformation campaigns between the humongous East German Stasi and the leaner but more agile StB. General Markus Wolf of the Stasi's HVA and Colonel Josef Houska of the StB's First Directorate signed a formal agreement that sought to establish "broad mutual cooperation in the sphere of disinformation" between their agencies.

12.

The Book War

ATE ONE SEPTEMBER AFTERNOON IN 1961, THREE ENGLISH
children were having fun in a playground sandbox off the leafy
Tsvetnoy Boulevard in Central Moscow. Their mother, Janet
Anne Chisholm, sat nearby. A Russian man, strolling by, stopped and then
approached the children, smiling. He handed them a small box of candy, then
disappeared. The children gave the box to their mother. Inside, below the
sweets, were hidden cassettes of exposed film with pictures of secret documents, taken with a tiny Minox camera. The mother was married to the Moscow station chief of MI6; the passerby was a GRU officer; and the children
in the sandbox, props for a carefully planned "brush-pass"—a sleek move to
pass documents from agent to handler.

Oleg Penkovsky was one of the most effective spies of the entire Cold
War. The GRU officer, who was promoted to colonel at the age of thirty-one,

Colonel Oleg
Penkovsky of the
GRU awaiting the
verdict at his trial
for espionage in
May 1963—as
the CIA was busy
planning the release
of his engineered
memoirs
(Photograph by Stuzhin &
Cheredintzev / Keystone /
Hulton Archive / Getty
Images)

passed a wealth of information to his country's enemies, including some 5,000 photographs of documents and sketches and valuable, extensive debriefs during several visits to London and Paris. The CIA logged ten thousand pages of English-language reports based on Penkovsky's material. Most of the secret meetings between the CIA, MI6, and their GRU spy took place at the Mount Royal Hotel, off Oxford Street. Penkovsky's personal requirements on these unusual business trips were dental treatment and "to meet some English ladies." The British spy handlers obliged, as CIA archives revealed many years later: "MI6 (with MI5 help) met the requirements."[1] (They told her he was Alex from Belgrade, she was twenty-three, it took two hours, and £10 changed hands.)[2]

Not all meetings with Penkovsky went so smoothly. At one of the first meetings with his CIA handlers, Penkovsky suggested a plan for "taking Moscow hostage," along with the entire Soviet leadership. "He proposed deploying 29 small nuclear weapons in random fashion throughout Moscow in suitcases or garbage cans," one of the American officers present reported. "We were to provide him the weapons, instruct him in welding them into the bottoms of standard Moscow garbage cans, and provide him with a detonator to be activated at our direction."[3] Only with difficulty did his CIA handlers convince Penkovsky that this plan was impracticable. In the end, the GRU colonel was swayed not by strategic considerations but by the disappointing state of nuclear weapons miniaturization at the time.

Penkovsky, who spoke little English, was a daring spy. He worked for the CIA and MI6 for sixteen months, from April 12, 1961, to September 4, 1962.[4] The Cold War was at its most freezing then; the Berlin Wall went up in June 1961 and the Cuban Missile Crisis escalated in the late summer of 1962, pushing the world to the brink of nuclear annihilation. The GRU spy, ambitious to the point of recklessness, passed detailed plans and descriptions of missile launch sites in Cuba to the CIA. Without Penkovsky's help, the Americans would have struggled to identify Soviet missiles at their launch pads and to track their operational readiness.

The KGB, however, eventually started surveilling Penkovsky. Peeking through his window with a tiny camera in a flowerpot, the KGB found spy gear hidden in the desk of his apartment's private study. He was arrested in September 1962. Eight months later, the Supreme Court of the USSR convicted the forty-four-year-old of high treason and sentenced him to death by shooting in Lubyanka Prison. When the judge read the verdict, the audience in the overcrowded courtroom clapped and cheered for thirty seconds. "The spy Oleg Penkovsky has been executed," reported TASS on May 16, 1963.

Penkovsky's trial triggered the CIA's most aggressive active measure since Berlin's LCCASSOCK was terminated three years earlier. On May 3, before the court proceedings began, the current CIA director had a detailed seven-page memo on his desk, laying out the risks and the CIA's response options. "An article will be placed in Turkey which will cover Penkovskiy's biography as extensively as the ostensible sources will permit," the memo said.

The CIA used the Istanbul newspaper *Cumhuriyet* to tell the world about this remarkable man. The U.S. government wanted it known that Penkovsky was a professional military officer, that he was decorated for valor in World War II, and that he served in military intelligence. To bolster this truthful story, the CIA noted that "a photograph of Penkovskiy in uniform with decorations will be printed"[5] in *Cumhuriyet*. The memo went on to point out, in a similarly confident tone, that the initial Turkish article would "be replayed in major western media to the greatest extent possible."[6]

One week later, the article was in fact printed in *Cumhuriyet*, with the picture, on the front page.[7] And the text was "replayed," as planned, when *The Washington Post* translated and repeated the core facts of the original story. The *Post*'s Stephen Rosenfeld reported that the text in the Istanbul newspaper "had the ring of knowledgeable sources," and that Penkovsky had passed "secret documents pertaining to the Soviet Union's missile strength" to the United States.[8]

This planted Turkish story was only the beginning. The early May CIA memo, written before Penkovsky's trial, effectively planned to send a ghost to haunt the KGB: "As presently foreseen, the major effort will be the preparation of the 'memoirs' of Penkovskiy," the SR division, as the CIA called its team of Soviet-Russia experts, informed the CIA director. The story was to track Penkovsky's own views on the Soviet regime, its history and its prospects, "as carefully as possible." The only forgery explicitly spelled out in that early memo was the planned cover story of how the memoirs and other documents would surface in the West: that the files "had been left in the West in the personal possession of a confidant" charged by Penkovsky with making them public should he be arrested in Russia. Already, by May 3, 1963, the CIA noted that preparatory work on the memoirs had begun.

Around two years after Penkovsky's execution, in late 1965, twenty-nine different newspapers—including *The Washington Post*, the *Los Angeles Times*, and *The Observer* in London—serialized excerpts of a hot new book. It became known as *The Penkovsky Papers*.

The *Papers* starts off with a short personal biography that seeks to explain why Penkovsky became a spy. His father enrolled as an officer in the White

Army and died fighting Communists during the Civil War; he never knew his son. Penkovsky eventually became an ambitious commander himself in the very army that had "chopped White officers to pieces," as Penkovsky once claimed, adopting a Russian army saying.[9] His personal and his professional history were forced to converge. "I feel contempt for myself, because I am part of this system and I live a lie," Penkovsky recounted. "I know the Army and there are many of us in the officer corps who feel the same way."[10]

As a scientific liaison officer, Penkovsky had a wide range of contacts with senior leaders in the Party and Army. The information that he passed on, and consequently also his memoirs, covered technical details of the intelligence trade, the political dynamics of the Communist Party, and even the sexual escapades of Moscow's security establishments.

The book includes a training manual on handling and supervising American agents by the GRU's Anglo-American Affairs Directorate. The section explains how to set up a secure dead drop, how to meet with sources under surveillance, what to wear to a weekend rendezvous with a local agent ("light colors predominate"), and even how an intelligence officer is supposed to order beer properly in an American bar without attracting "undue" attention: "It is not enough to ask, 'Give me a glass of beer'; it is also necessary to name the brand of beer, 'Schlitz,' 'Rheingold,' etc."[11]

Penkovsky airs dirty laundry. He alleges that Ivan Kupin, commander of the artillery and missile troops of the Moscow Military District, lived with his cypher clerk while serving in East Germany as an artillery commander of the 1st Tank Army, concealing the relationship from his wife. After first promising to marry his clerk, he left her pregnant, and she hanged herself. Investigators found photographs of Kupin among her belongings. In Penkovsky's telling, moral decay and abuse of power were rampant.[12]

Penkovsky reserved particular ire for Nikita Khrushchev. He recalls first meeting Khrushchev in 1939, when the future Party chairman was a member of the Kiev District Military Council, wearing a uniform that "fitted him like a saddle fits a cow" (a Gogol reference).[13] The memoirs accuse Khrushchev of heading "a government of adventurers," calling the Politburo "demagogues and liars," who would only pretend to have an interest in peace while in truth risking a nuclear holocaust. "I know that the leaders of our Soviet state are the willing provocateurs of an atomic war," wrote Penkovsky. This allegation in particular roiled Moscow. All these details were published in U.S. newspapers in the first two weeks of November 1965, and the book became one of the Cold War's bestselling spy stories. John le Carré didn't just review it for *Book Week*; it even inspired one of his novels.[14]

On November 13, the Foreign Ministry in Moscow summoned Stephen Rosenfeld, *The Washington Post*'s Moscow correspondent, who had already covered Penkovsky's trial. The *Post* had just published the twelfth installment of its series on Penkovsky. F. M. Simonov, a diplomat working in the ministry's press department, confronted Rosenfeld, reading from a statement: "*The Washington Post* began on 31 October the publication of the so-called *Penkovsky Papers*," he lectured. "The papers are a falsified story, a mixture of anti-Soviet inventions and slander which are put into the mouth of a demasked spy." The publication of the forgery, the Moscow diplomat explained, would poison international relations and make rapprochement more difficult. "Responsibility," Simonov declared, "is shared by anybody who has anything to do with the publication of *The Penkovsky Papers*." Then the Russian diplomat issued a warning: "We expect that measures will be taken so that no articles and materials of such kind will be published in *The Washington Post* in the future."[15]

The *Post* did not budge. The next day, publication of the memoirs went on as planned. The *Post* reported on the Soviets' threatening words, and on Moscow's view of the controversial spy memoir. "In fact," the *Post* quoted a Soviet press release, "the so-called 'Penkovskiy Papers' is nothing but a crude forgery cooked up, two years after Penkovskiy's conviction, by those whom the exposed spy had served."[16] The publication of the American forgery in newspapers across the United States, said the Soviets, was "to be regarded as nothing but a premeditated act in the worst traditions of the 'Cold War.'"

The D.C. newspaper had become a battleground of U.S. versus Soviet disinformation operations. Russia directly accused the CIA of running a disinformation operation against Moscow—or was the KGB by now engaged in a disinformation campaign of its own? It was impossible to judge. The *Post* understood this dilemma, and did something unexpected: it ran two remarkable articles in the following two days, articles that would *agree* with the Soviets, and challenge the authenticity of *The Penkovsky Papers*.

Victor Zorza had devoured an advance copy of Penkovsky's book. Zorza, a Polish-born Briton, was a prolific investigative journalist with a microscopic attention to detail, and one of the world's foremost Kremlinologists. He quickly noticed that something was off.

A small Russian publishing house based in West Germany had noticed the announcements of the memoirs in the international press. The press reached out to Doubleday, the book's U.S. publisher, offered DM 1,000 for the Russian-language rights, and requested the original manuscript in Russian. Doubleday accepted the deal, and Zorza concluded that Doubleday's acceptance in good faith indicated that they actually did want to send the Russian manuscript. But the U.S. publisher could not track it down. Doubleday, Zorza reported, had twice asked the "State Department" about the Russian original, without success. This was suspicious enough. Zorza then embarked on a highly detailed linguistic analysis. The text was not a straightforward translation. There were too many passages and entire sections, Zorza concluded, that betrayed "the alien hand—or tongue."[17]

Early on November 16, the CIA prepared a copy of Zorza's meticulous analysis for the director's daily press clippings. An analyst, Sharpie in hand, underlined the words "Work of CIA" in black for the Agency's leadership. Zorza closed with a sharp critique addressed at his readers in Langley, thickly underlined for the director: "Some of my best friends are in the CIA, but if they want their psychological warfare efforts to remain undiscovered, they must do better than this."[18]

Two days later, the USSR's seasoned ambassador in Washington, Anatoly Dobrynin, met with Llewellyn Thompson, formerly the U.S. ambassador in Moscow, to discuss *The Penkovsky Papers*. The conversation was tense.[19]

"The United States Government was not responsible for their publication," Thompson told Dobrynin. "As the Ambassador is aware, our newspapers and publishing houses are free to print what they please. The responsibility is theirs and theirs alone."

Dobrynin was having none of it. He told his U.S. counterpart that he would inform Moscow, per diplomatic practice. But then he added, "Of course you understand, and I understand, somebody in an American agency was responsible for writing these papers." The Russian ambassador then noted that he had not suggested that the decision for this Penkovsky plot was made by the White House, implying that the CIA may simply not have told the State Department.

Thompson stood his ground. He repeated what he told Dobrynin before: that the State Department had checked with the CIA, and that the Agency had denied any involvement.

Except the CIA was involved, and indeed had not told the State Department. Dobrynin and Zorza were right—the memoirs were fake. But they were also wrong in an important way. The real story had still more surprises in store.

The CIA believed that Penkovsky was arrested on or about September 4, 1962. In the sixteen months leading up to his arrest, the spy had held forty-five secret meetings with personnel of the CIA's Soviet Russia Division in Britain, under the auspices of MI6. All of the conversations were taped. Already, four weeks after Penkovsky's arrest in Moscow, even before he was shot at Lubyanka Prison, the CIA's Russia experts had finished compiling his "memoirs" from the transcribed tapes—and the Soviet Russia Division had also already decided to surface the transcribed, still-secret memoirs as an anti-Communist active measure. "The 'Memoirs' will eventually be surfaced, in some form, in the open press," an internal CIA memo noted on October 4, 1962.[20]

But the operation ran into an unexpected difficulty early on. The CIA had asked Deriabin, one of the Agency's "star Soviet defectors,"[21] to write a first draft of the Penkovsky memoirs in Russian, "assisted by the entire" Soviet Russia Division of the CIA. Deriabin was no stranger to active measures, and would later even publish a newsletter on Soviet dirty tricks, so, officially the translator, he became the ghostwriter. But Deriabin's draft would not survive. It seems that Deriabin couldn't suppress his old KGB forgery habits. He falsified parts of the story in his first Russian draft by simply inventing a twist: that Penkovsky had secretly worked for the KGB for an extended period of time. When the CIA's Russia hands read Deriabin's first draft, they weren't happy with the ex-KGB operative's creative approach. On May 1, 1963, the SR Division voiced concerns: "We believe that to base the story of Penkovskiy's life on the fiction that he was a KGB Agent throughout most of his career is wrong." The allegation, as those most familiar with the case at the CIA pointed out, "would not be accepted as true by those whom we want to impress with the documents—the officers of the Soviet intelligence services." The Agency's internal literary critics also pointed out that Western journalists already had difficulty understanding the Penkovsky narrative, and "to throw in this further twist might confuse them totally."[22] Instead, the CIA wanted to keep the story accurate and reliable. "We think that not only would the story be more valid, but also more dramatic if it sticks closer to the main facts and to Penkovskiy's own words." Deriabin was out as ghostwriter, although he would still be mentioned as the translator of the final book.

The CIA needed a proper ghost. The Soviet Russia Division went to look for a "competent writer who could revise the Memoirs into a form more suitable for publication." They turned to Frank Gibney, an experienced journalist and editor, who agreed to edit and rewrite the entire manuscript.[23] And there was the reason why the SR Division didn't want to share the original Russian manuscript with Doubleday—it didn't match Gibney's final English version. The CIA finally sold the manuscript's publication rights through a front organization created specifically for that purpose, called the Penkovsky Foundation.

It took many years for this backstory to come out. The Church Committee, a landmark investigation into intelligence activities, referred to *The Penkovsky Papers* as a "CIA book" in 1976. "The book was prepared and written by witting agency assets who drew on actual case materials," the committee report stated.[24] The moral of the story was clear for Rosenfeld, who was kicked out of Moscow in retaliation for serializing the book in *The Washington Post*. "The real victims of this operation were American citizens," he wrote. Zorza had observed already in 1965 that intelligence agencies in open democracies "suffer from the grave disadvantage that in attempting to damage the adversary they must also deceive their own public." Rosenfeld agreed: the operation undermined a core pillar of liberal democracy, the free press. Was the deception of the American public, he asked, "a by-product or part of the intent?"[25]

In one important aspect, the CIA's critics erred. The covert operators in Langley did not falsify any content, only the cover story. The Directorate of Plans, which approved covert and clandestine operations, had significantly deescalated its political warfare game; the Penkovsky book was a far cry from the level of ruthless aggression and forgery displayed by its front organizations in Berlin.

On November 6, 1964, David Murphy, chief of the Soviet Russia Division, prepared a memorandum for Richard Helms, then the deputy director of plans. The memo's title: "Request for Approval to Publish the Penkovskiy Memoirs."[26] The memo discusses the work the CIA put into writing the memoirs: SR case officers who had worked with the GRU spy, and knew his personality, made sure the draft preserved Penkovsky's style, "often his exact words," as well as his "Russian flavor." The CIA even secured a copy of the transcript of Penkovsky's trial, translated it, and used the trial material to fill in some blanks, including references to the CIA itself and MI6 (which were technically still classified). Murphy's memo stressed that the CIA should not glorify their spy: "The picture of Penkovskiy-the-man which thus emerges is not only an accurate one, but also one which is interesting and believable."[27] The Agency expected "great" financial income from the book, and even an eventual movie or TV series, which it planned to donate to an unspecified anti-Communist organization. The memo closed by stressing that State Department clearance was not required. Helms approved.

MEANWHILE, THE EAST ESCALATED THE OPERATIONAL PLAY WITH BOOKS.

The little volume felt like a Bible, but smaller than pocket-sized, with a sturdy hard cover in burgundy; the fine cloth spine spilled open to 592 pages of thin, high-quality paper. The book was available in German and English. Its title in both languages: *Who's Who in CIA*.

The publisher was one Julius Mader, simply listed as a private individual at an address in "Berlin W 66, Mauerstr. 69." Even this information was deceptive: "W" did not stand for "West," as the address was in East Berlin, just one block past Checkpoint Charlie. *Who's Who in CIA* claimed to be, according to its rather clunky subtitle, "a biographic encyclopedia of 3,000 members of staff of civilian and military intelligence agencies of the USA in 120 states." The book did not limit itself to the CIA, but merely used the well-known three-letter agency as a placeholder for the entire American intelligence community. It contained six fold-out charts, including one that showed the Pentagon's intelligence structure, one for the National Security Agency, one for various secret CIA front organizations, and an organigram of the FBI. Many of the listed individuals had actually worked for the CIA at some point.

Yet the book was mischievous, almost comical. Mader accused the CIA of engaging in "subversion [. . .] psychological warfare and dirty methods," while employing exactly those methods. The list of agents included numerous prominent individuals whose inclusion was far-fetched to say the least—there was President Lyndon Johnson, Senator Eugene McCarthy, and even George Meany, an iconic labor union leader and the founder of AFL-CIO. The book also included two perforated cards in the back for readers to submit "missing biographies" of U.S. intelligence officials, with the small type assuring potential submitters that their names could be withheld from publication.[28] It was July 9, 1968, and *Who's Who* cost 10.50 East German Marks, or about 25 U.S. cents.

The following day *Neues Deutschland* ran a rave review of Mader's book on that "shadow government of the USA," the largest imperialist secret organization, even more powerful than the rest of the American government combined.[29] The Associated Press and *The Washington Post* had already announced the book uncritically, without noting the possibility that it was a disinformation operation.

"Suddenly the book war became white hot," the *Los Angeles Times* reported, treating Mader's book as the active measure that it was.[30] *Time* magazine also ran a critical review. By November, reported *The Washington Post*, the spy book had sold out in one bookstore in D.C. "Some institutions," the store reported, ordered large numbers of the book, so it ordered 150 extra copies by airmail.[31] The *Who's Who* was likely a must-have object in foreign embassies in the capital.

At second glance, however, the Mader measure was less sophisticated than it looked. The fold-out charts seemed impressive, but were lifted from open sources. The "leaked" names were mostly drawn from the State Department's biographical register. The CIA knew Mader, a real individual, as an agent of influence in Soviet bloc disinformation activities, and even had an agent in place with a direct link to him.[32] One CIA reviewer said of the thousands of listed individuals that "99 percent of them were entirely innocent of any intelligence connection"[33]—that also was an exaggeration. The real number of CIA officers in the book remains unknown. Nevertheless, many outside reviewers immediately recognized the book for what it was.[34]

Julius Mader was notorious, at least in intelligence circles. He had already published seven books in the 1960s, all of them attacking Western spy agencies—but he was not working alone. A dozen years later, Bittman was asked about *Who's Who* before the House Select Committee on Intelligence.

"I am very familiar with the book," responded Bittman, "because I am very sorry to admit that I am one of the co-authors of the book." Bittman went on to explain the genesis and purpose of the operation:

> The book *Who's Who in the CIA* [sic] was prepared by the
> Czechoslovak intelligence service and the East German intelligence
> service in the midsixties. It took a few years to put it together. About
> half of the names listed in that book are real CIA operatives. The
> other half are people who were just American diplomats or various
> officials; and it was prepared with the expectation that naturally
> many, many Americans operating abroad, diplomats and so on,
> would be hurt because their names were exposed as CIA officials.[35]

Some reviewers and even the CIA had criticized the joint KGB-Stasi-StB publication for being inaccurate, and hence a botched operation—but including innocents was not an error; it was part of the action. The purpose of the operation, as Bittman explained, was to "paralyze" not just the CIA but also those innocent diplomats, journalists, and others falsely implicated in spying.[36] In Western countries, the book was more likely to be seen as an obvious fake. In the developing world it would cause more harm, even deadly harm, as it turned out. The CIA's damage assessment has not been declassified, but Mader's little red book was damaging enough to cause the CIA to retaliate in kind. Langley's response was years in the making.

The Stasi's now-open archives have confirmed Bittman's account: the Ministry of State Security in East Berlin listed Mader and his secretary as "officers in special service."[37] He was promoted to major in 1964, and received a salary from the Stasi. He had several code names, including FAINGOLD, HUNTER, and X54. "With our help, Mader has become currently one of the most important writers within our area of work," noted one performance review in the early 1960s.[38] Indeed, as happens with many a successful author, Mader eventually became a little too infatuated with his own prowess. One Ministry of State Security file noted: "He must be reminded now and then that his achievements have been based not only on hard work and much initiative but also on the results of the MfS's work and the varied support which he has received from the Ministry."[39]

Operations Plan 10-1

O NE OF THE KGB'S MOST SENSATIONAL DISINFORMATION OP-
erations came to light for the first time in December 1967,
packed as a present under a Christmas tree in Norway. The
operation was part of a campaign, code-named STORM by the KGB,[1] that would
rage for more than a dozen years, striking all across Europe and causing vast
reputational damage to the United States. The main document in play was a
war plan—outlining America's strategy for a European guerrilla war.

By 1957, American military and intelligence planners anticipated and
began to plan for a "hot war" with the Soviet Union. Europe's forests and
rivers and cities would be the battlefield. U.S. Air Force planners populated
their target list with hundreds of cities and bridges and junctions and airfields, including many targets in West Germany and Austria, complete with
appropriate nuclear yield requirements for each target. The army planned to

The most impactful leak of the Cold War contained U.S. military war plans with a "cosmic" classification level, and began in a Socialist newspaper in Norway at Christmas 1967.
(Sosialistisk Venstreparti)

blow up bridges on the Rhine to slow advancing Warsaw Pact troops. The CIA prepared for action behind enemy lines. The Agency's Clandestine Services division staged a series of "politico-military war games" to understand what would happen in Europe in the case of an all-out Soviet invasion.[2]

The CIA would contribute to European defense through a number of different projects. One early focus was recruiting and training potential resistance fighters and saboteurs in Eastern Europe, including Germany. These projects had various code names, such as LCPROWL, KMHITHER-C, or AE-DEPOT, a U.S.-based clandestine paramilitary training program in irregular warfare techniques, so that assets could recruit and lead indigenous insurgent forces behind enemy lines. The projects were so secret that they had no liaison with allied or other friendly governments and their intelligence services; even U.S. special forces in Europe would be informed on the details only once war broke out.[3]

The Department of Defense, in May 1955, had created a new command for special forces in Paris, the Support Operations Task Force Europe, abbreviated SOTFE. SOTFE was in charge of unconventional warfare, and controlled all special operations forces in Europe, including the U.S. Army's 10th Special Forces Group, a new and secretive Detachment "A," and early Air Force special operations squadrons. Some of these elite U.S. units were effectively guerrilla sleeper cells, trained in urban warfare. The soldiers would usually not wear uniforms but rather fashionable civilian clothes, with shades and beards, even during heavily armed exercises in German cities. The U.S. Army's guerrilla units would, in turn, depend on the CIA's successful recruitment of insurgents. In the event of a hot war, the U.S. commandos, fluent in local languages, would stay behind or deploy forward behind enemy lines, and secretly rendezvous with the CIA-trained indigenous insurgents. The plan foresaw that they would fight in more than one hundred local theaters at once, in twenty-three European countries.[4]

The initial planning was optimistic. Thirty days after the outbreak of war, newly created U.S. special forces units could arm 14,000 European insurgents (2,000 in East Germany alone); after half a year, the number of anti-Communist guerrillas could be as high as 112,500.[5] One American special operator later admitted that those plans were "ambitious and extremely dangerous," even "suicidal."[6] The blueprint for unconventional war had different titles at different agencies. The CIA named it the "Global War Plan for Clandestine Operations." SOTFE called it Operations Plan (OPLAN) 100, with later versions, sections, or annexes designated as 100-1, 100-2, or 10-1.

The American war planners had no illusions about what all-out war would look like: "General war will include tactical and strategic employment of nuclear weapons and can be expected to enhance conditions in which unconventional warfare (UW) will be pursued," the U.S. planners wrote in the Global War Plan, an exceptionally aggressive document. The CIA was also prepared to use a range of "exceptional" measures, including the overthrow of hostile governments through political action and even eyebrow-raising methods such as "counterintelligence, psychological warfare, or political action against allies of the United States." Even worse, once war had broken out and partisan forces were confronting the Soviets, the guerrilla fighters were supposed to be ready to escalate to the most drastic measures: "CIA will be prepared to use nuclear, chemical, and bacteriological weapons in clandestine operations in general war as feasible, subject to approval by the President before actual use is undertaken."[7]

West German and Austrian cities, U.S. war planners foresaw, would be behind enemy lines in this scenario. The plan was a reaction to the United States' worst nightmare at the time.

The top-secret SOTFE document first surfaced in a Norwegian newspaper in late December 1967. "This can happen here," read the headline, over an illustration that depicted the top-secret war plan wrapped like a present, alongside a bomb disguised as a bauble, beneath a Christmas tree crowned with a NATO tree-topper.[8] The leaked document had been sent anonymously to Oslo from a Rome address. About a month later, the war plan appeared in *Paese Sera*, an Italian newspaper with pro-Soviet sympathies.[9] On March 3, 1968, the Hamburg-based far-left politics-and-sex magazine *Konkret*— edited by Ulrike Meinhof, who would soon achieve notoriety as a co-founder of the Red Army Faction terrorist group—published excerpts of a six-page document that, its editors claimed, they found "in Norway."[10] The document and the excerpts appeared to be genuine, apparently without forged content slipped into the file. Two weeks later, the UK periodical *Peace News* noted it also had received the "top-secret" document and quoted from it.[11]

The Department of Defense reacted at once. The U.S. commander-in-chief of Europe immediately proposed briefing allied delegations to NATO on "the authenticity of certain pages" of the operations plan. But on March 8, 1968, the State Department in Washington sent an urgent telegram to U.S. embassies in all NATO capitals, declining the commander's request. The cable, classified as secret and signed by Secretary of State Dean Rusk, bore as its subject line "COMPROMISED USEUCOM OPLANS." Most diplomats who received the telegram themselves did not know what kind of information these operational plans contained. But the message was clear: no U.S.

diplomat was authorized to speak about the document's authenticity. "In event of public or press queries, you should take line that USG neither confirms nor denies authenticity of documents," the telegram concluded.[12]

The story, perhaps as a result of the U.S. government's swift action, did not catch on that March. Ivan Agayants and his busy operators in the KGB had failed, for now. However, the U.S. government anticipated that their highly sensitive documents would surface in other NATO countries in the near future. And indeed they would, under the most dramatic circumstances.

On October 8, 1968, Major General Horst Wendland, the deputy director of West Germany's foreign intelligence service, the BND, was found dead at his desk in Pullach, not far from Munich. The general had shot himself. The German police closed off the cemetery for Wendland's funeral so that nobody could take pictures of Germany's top intelligence officers, almost all of whom were in attendance. Munich's criminal police accepted "incurable depression" as the cause and did not investigate further,[13] yet the intelligence chief's suicide came at a suspicious moment. On the very day of his death, a German Navy rear admiral, Hermann Lüdke, had also killed himself with a gun. Two weeks before that, a microfilm with nine photographs of top-secret NATO documents had been traced to him, and Lüdke was suspected of working for a foreign intelligence agency.[14] Four additional suicides among German military officers and civil servants, in the space of just a few weeks, set alarm bells ringing in Bonn. Chancellor Kurt Georg Kiesinger ordered a high-profile investigation.

The highly publicized suicides sent shock waves through the NATO security establishment. By December, one former French intelligence officer, Philippe de Vosjoli, publicly articulated the fear that the KGB had deeply penetrated the German security establishment, and that recent suicides among military and intelligence officers were the acts of desperate men who feared they would be burned by recent Soviet bloc defectors.[15] But neither the CIA nor MI6 had any reason to suppose that Wendland's suicide was based on more than his known issues with depression.[16] They were right.

Wendland was not, in fact, a mole. But when Service A heard of his suicide and the surrounding theories, they immediately spotted an opening for

TOP SECRET

d. Paragraph 2, page 2, lines 6 and 7, the words "provides US Army atomic weapons support for Allied forces as directed" are deleted.

e. Paragraph 3a, page 2, the letter "B" is changed to "C."

f. Paragraph 3b, page 2, the words "Seventh United States Army" are changed to read "Seventh Army."

g. Paragraph 3b(4), page 2, line 1 is changed to read "On order of CINCUSAREUR, release ground • • •."

h. Paragraph 3b(5), page 3, is superseded as follows:

(5) (Superseded) 32d Artillery Brigade continues present mission.

i. Paragraph 3d, page 3, the words "Berlin Command" are changed to read "US Army, Berlin."

j. Paragraphs 3g(5) and (6), page 4, are rescinded.

k. Paragraph 3h, page 4, is superseded as follows:

h. (Superseded) Northern and Southern Area Commands. USAREUR OPLAN 302, paragraph 3h, applies.

l. Paragraph 3i, page 4, is superseded as follows:

i. (Superseded) Special Ammunition Support Command. USAREUR OPLAN 302, paragraph 3i, applies.

m. Paragraph 3j(3), page 4, is changed by deleting everything after "messages" and substituting the following:

Use of nuclear weapons with yields of 10 KT or less is authorized in friendly and neutral countries provided: R-hour has been declared, and military necessity dictates. The use of nuclear weapons of larger yield than 10 KT requires the specific approval of CINCUSAREUR.

n. Paragraph 3j(5), page 4, is superseded as follows:

(5) (Superseded) Assume operational direction of Allied forces willing to accept US leadership, and provide combat and logistic support to Allies to the extent that the success of US-Allied operations will be enhanced.

Forged page added to OPLAN 10-1. The forgery claimed that low-level military commanders were authorized to use nuclear weapons against European targets.

an actual conspiracy implicating the dead general in relation to the OPLAN. But to pull off such a maneuver, Service A needed some inside knowledge from the time when the OPLAN was stolen. Agayants needed some truth to flank his lie, and he was in luck.

Heinz Felfe was an operative for the BND; a confidant of its legendary founder, Reinhard Gehlen; and one of the most damaging spies in postwar Germany. He passed thousands of documents to Moscow.[17] Felfe, who had also been an SS-Obersturmführer in the Third Reich, was convicted of treason by federal judges in Karlsruhe in 1963 and sentenced to fourteen years in prison. Only six years later, with the BND still roiling from Wendland's recent suicide, Felfe was released, and he immediately slipped through the Iron Curtain into what conservative West Germans called the Soviet Occupied Zone. Soviet intelligence immediately reactivated the former SS officer, probably with the intention to use him for ongoing active measures.[18] "Every day in jail I will pay back," said Felfe.[19]

In 1969, Felfe naturally no longer had access to current documents. But the former mole still knew the inner workings of the BND, and he had known Wendland years before, around the time when the OPLAN was stolen from the Americans. Felfe and the American war plan, in short, had two things in common: neither had much immediate intelligence value, yet both offered very high disinformation value. Agayants's team in the KGB had a brilliant idea—they could use an obsolete German asset to relaunch an obsolete American war plan.

Still, Service A's specialists knew from experience that enhancing the documents with some creative writing would make them even more controversial. Dark truths were even darker when flanked by a dark lie. Therefore the KGB included a confusing single page instructing specific edits to the existing SOTFE plan. The edits page was marked "TOP SECRET." Most of the edits were banal (for example, "page 3, the words 'Berlin Command' are changed to read 'US Army, Berlin'"). Then the forgers snuck in an edit to one longer paragraph, with each sentence underlined for emphasis. The paragraph in question read:

> Paragraph 3j(3), page 4, is changed by deleting everything after "messages" and substituting the following:
>   Use of nuclear weapons with yields of 10 KT or less is authorized in friendly and neutral countries provided: R-hour has been declared, and military necessity dictates. The rise of nuclear weapons of larger yield than 10 KT requires the specific approval of CINCUSAREUR.[20]

The final abbreviation referred to "Commander in Chief of United States Army Europe." To the trained eye, this paragraph stood out as forged for several reasons: the corrections page appears to be slotted into the collection of documents; the font and layout of the classification markings are different; line breaks are not uniformly indented, as was customary then; U.S. Army documents at the time were never underlined for emphasis (only for headlining); finally, and most important, the delegation of nuclear release authority becomes highly suspicious in a "leaked" document when accompanied by a fake cover letter written solely to stress the delegation of nuclear release authority.

It was Felfe, the German double agent who fled to Moscow, who had helped write that well-crafted and convincing cover letter. The thrust of the letter was that Wendland, already depressed, had shared top-secret files with a friend, confided in him, and instructed this anonymous friend to release the documents to the public should something happen to him.

Service A planned to release the letter and the accompanying leaked-and-forged documents in a number of European countries simultaneously, and therefore drafted the cover letter in English. Posing as Wendland's friend, Felfe wrote: "Major General Wendland reached a prominent position in the German intelligence service (BND) and had access to top-secret documents and other information which severely depressed him. Shortly before his untimely death, he entrusted me with copies of several documents and asked me to publish them at an appropriate time."[21]

The cover story implied that the documents contained a secret so dark that it helped push the depressed Wendland over the brink into suicide. The letter went on:

My friend was particularly disturbed by the fact that the Americans could use atomic, chemical, and radiological weapons without prior consent of the U.S. Congress or the President since permission to use them follows automatically when those weapons are supplied to special groups.[22]

The targets to be destroyed are determined by the commanders of these groups . . . In other words, the lives of millions of people depend on the decisions of a handful of American officers . . . It well may be that knowledge of this was one of the reasons that led to my friend's tragic death.[23] He wanted to make these facts known, but could not do anything because of his duty.[24]

The secret documents in the letter were titled O-Plan 10-1.

Next, the KGB softened the ground. In June, the Soviet news agency

ABC, a far-left Italian sex-and-politics magazine, reported on actual U.S. war plans based on a forged KGB cover letter in July 1969.

Newa reported that the Wendland affair was "very serious." Newa implied that the BND general had killed himself not because he was suffering from depression but for a more sinister reason. "In Bonn the rumor is making the rounds that Wendland was involved in an espionage affair," Newa reported, correctly;[25] the *Frankfurter Allgemeine Zeitung* had even covered that rumor.[26] Then came the lie: "Linked to his name is the leak of important secret information from the Bundesnachrichtendienst and NATO intelligence services."[27]

ABC was an Italian far-left illustrated broadsheet not averse to mixing large pictures of nudes with risqué political news.[28] On U.S. Independence Day 1969, the magazine's cover featured a topless model accompanied by the headline "Here Are NATO's Secret Plans." The story, which included menacing pictures of tanks and nuclear missiles, followed the KGB's script to the letter. Opening with Wendland's suicide, *ABC* noted the general's known severe depression, but then added that "a few days before his death, Horst Wendland confided in a friend." *ABC* concluded, "the use of atomic weapons is entrusted to groups of officers engaged in local activities, as can be the American military leaders in Europe. In other words, it may be a temptation for an American to decree the destruction of Milan, Rome, Vienna or Frankfurt, in the hope of preventing the destruction of New York."

The same package that *ABC* received in Milan was also mailed to two British peace journals, *Sanity*, the monthly magazine of the Campaign for Nuclear Disarmament, and again *Peace News*.[29] Their copies also arrived anonymously, postmarked from Rome, with the forged cover letter from Wendland's "friend."[30] Both peace magazines carefully considered the possibility that the aggressive U.S. Army war plan was an Eastern forgery, and both concluded that it wouldn't really make a difference whether the top-secret document was forged or not; "in the end it hardly matters whether it is or not," wrote *Peace News*, "since if COMSOTFE OPLAN NR 10-1 is a fabrication, we can guess there is a document almost exactly like it."[31] *Sanity*'s justification was more eloquent but equally twisted. "If they are forgeries they should not be regarded lightly," wrote *Sanity*, "for the authors must consider them near enough to the truth to be accepted; close enough to be a convincing basis for deception." And that close-enough-to-truth, the magazine's lead article reasoned, was "a dreadful indictment" of where things stood in Europe.[32] One day after the UK peace magazines and *ABC* in Italy revealed the American nuclear war plan, *The Times* of London picked up the story from the excerpts published by the peace magazines and ran it under the headline "U.S. to Hand Out H-bombs," although the piece also acknowledged the possibility of a forgery. One British peace activist then forwarded the full document to *Ramparts*, a far-left Berkeley magazine. The "frightening document," *Ramparts's* editors wrote not long after, had triggered a "tremendous controversy" in the United States and Europe over the last few weeks.[33]

The revived operation was already a stellar success.

In Germany, the weeklies *Der Spiegel* and *Stern* received their copies. The latter magazine, the editor of which, Henri Nannen, had served in a Wehrmacht propaganda unit, was favored as an outlet by the Stasi and the KGB. *Stern* was the embodiment of sensationalism, drawing a circulation of 1.8 million with the combination of pinups and intrigue typical of Germany's sexually and politically liberated 1960s, where voyeurism often masqueraded as liberation. When *Stern's* reporters peeled open the voluptuous Italian envelopes that June, they could not believe their luck. An anonymous leaker had mailed a particularly indecent secret American war plan. The magazine headlined its sensational story "Treason by Mail," and opened by calling Wendland's suicide into question, immediately adopting the KGB's framing and credulously quoting the fake cover letter, but stopping short of reproducing the leaked documents.

U.S. defense policy in Europe and, to an even greater extent, the BND were getting pummeled by this unusually successful active measure. The Wendland affair was an extremely unpleasant situation for German intelligence already, and now a hostile power was taking ruthless advantage of the tragedy, implying that West German intelligence had compromised highly classified U.S. war plans. After multiple news outlets in three countries had blamed the American leak on the BND, *Der Spiegel* revealed the true source of the leak: Robert Lee Johnson, a former U.S. Army sergeant already infamous for stealing documents for the KGB.

Johnson, disappointed by not getting a promotion, had offered his services to the Soviets in Berlin back in 1953. He met with officers from KGB's Karlshorst *rezidentura*, was recruited, and worked as a spy, off and on, until he deserted in 1964 and his wife reported him to the FBI. The KGB trained the sergeant in basic espionage techniques during his honeymoon in the town of Brandenburg (he had told the army he was in Bavaria). Years later, Johnson would become one of the best-placed spies of the entire Cold War.

In 1961, Johnson received a top-secret security clearance, and soon applied to work at the Army Forces Courier Center at Orly Field, Paris, "a sort of post office for top-secret materials," as one receptionist explained to Johnson when he inquired.[34] There the KGB's Paris station invested months in Johnson's painstaking work to breach the high-security vault at Orly Field. The prep work included making imprints of a security key, X-raying a number lock with a miniature radioactive device, and Johnson volunteering to repaint the vault in order to examine the entire building inch by inch. From mid-December 1962 to April 21, 1962,[35] Johnson breached the high-security vault several times, snapping pictures on his miniature camera of some documents with "cosmic" classification levels. The intelligence value of these documents would change when the FBI caught Johnson in late 1964. He pled guilty in the spring of 1965. By 1967, some of the documents were ready for recycling.

"Disinformation," announced Der Spiegel's headline. The magazine delved in remarkable detail into Service A and its use of Felfe to frame the dead Wendland. Der Spiegel's source, most likely, was somebody with links to West German intelligence.[36] A veritable spy-versus-spy game began to play out in the glossy pages of competing Hamburg weeklies.

The exposure of the active measures in Der Spiegel did not end them—it enhanced them. Der Spiegel, likely with help from the BND, solved a problem for the KGB: it proved the leak was real. Service A now also knew that it could count on Stern's anti-American inclinations. Stern had reported that German generals would consider insubordination in the case of nuclear war, for the German generals knew that their own families and communities would be incinerated if they acted in support of the American plans.[37] The KGB rewarded Henri Nannen's magazine with another major story sourced from the American vault at Orly Field.

In early January, Stern received an envelope stuffed with undeveloped film negatives. Reporters took the negatives to the darkroom and discovered an even more extraordinary top-secret document that Johnson had passed on to Russian intelligence: an extensive handbook of European and Middle Eastern targets for American atomic weapons, titled "Nuclear Yield Requirements."

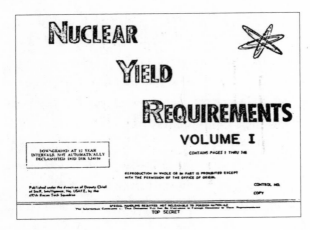

The cover page of a major leak of top-secret U.S. military documents

Stern claimed that "high U.S. officials" had confirmed the "absolute authenticity" of the yield requirements, and proceeded to list a remarkable number of targeting details. Among the numerous West German targets were Kiel (target number 0737E), Flensburg (0740E), Schleswig (0736E), Lübeck (0741E), and many more. The story laid out how large populations would be killed or "slowly and painfully languish and die" in the aftermath of an attack. There were Austrian targets, including Vienna, Linz, and Innsbruck, and targets in Iraq, Egypt, and Syria.[38] Nannen knew well that he was doing the KGB's work. Justifying his use of the leaked files, he wrote, "STERN is only fulfilling its duty to inform the public with facts," adding that not even the German defense minister in Bonn was allowed to see these documents. In response, the German government called the plans "outdated," implicitly confirming their authenticity. Both the State Department and the Pentagon refused to comment.[39]

For Nannen, the material was simply too valuable not to report. The magazine ran one more feature story on the leak,[40] pointing out an angle of particular German interest: it was outrageous that the secret document had been passed to the Russians by an American spy, which meant that even Moscow knew about U.S. war plans that would set "Rhine and Main ablaze," while West Germany, a NATO ally, and its Ministry of Defense in Bonn were kept in the dark.

An excerpt from a thirty-page leak of top-secret U.S. Air Force nuclear yield requirements, here listing West German targets ("GW"). The listing is likely genuine.

In fact, Nannen had the better arguments on his side, and Western intelligence officials indirectly helped him make them. The revelation that the secret plans were actually sourced from an infamous U.S. spy (and not from Wendland) added credibility to the next, even more disturbing batch of documents, the Nuclear Yield Requirements, and both the KGB and *Stern* knew it. But the U.S. government, paralyzed by its own classification restrictions, never identified which sections of the document were authentic and which were not. The OPLAN would reemerge; it was only a matter of time. U.S. authorities would later count at least twenty different surfacings of Robert Lee Johnson's stolen documents, according to the State Department's Bureau of Intelligence and Research.[41] The cache was a disinformation gold mine. In many ways, the leak, enhanced with a dash of forgery, foreshadowed the future of disinformation.

The X

T HE STASI'S MASTER OF DISINFORMATION WAS ROLF WAGEN-
breth. Born in 1929, thin, fit, quick, and disciplined, he carried at all times a leather-bound, carved-out Bible, a pistol
and medication for a chronic kidney illness hidden inside.[1] His unit, Abteilung X, was known as "the X" (pronounced as the number ten). Department X was part of HVA, the foreign intelligence arm of the GDR's Ministry
of State Security. The X was highly secretive, even within the HVA, for the
HVA held to a dictum of active measures then considered self-evident: that
an exposed measure was a dead measure.[2] Only in 1986 did Wagenbreth receive permission to talk about his work with a group of senior Stasi officials
from across the organization. He delivered this still-secret talk in a covert
location in Belzig, a remote area in the serene Brandenburg countryside. The
notes from this lecture are a rare surviving record of Wagenbreth's dark art.

Rolf Wagenbreth was head of the Stasi's disinformation unit, Department X, for almost the entire Cold War. He often carried a hollowed-out Bible with medication and a pistol hidden inside. (BStU)

"One profession is particularly close to my heart, a profession that can get away with nearly anything," Wagenbreth told his colleagues, "and this group are our dear journalists." Journalists with a good reputation, he said, had excellent access to officials with security clearances and business executives, and could even travel through the Iron Curtain without a cover. Intelligence and journalism, in Wagenbreth's view, had "entered a kind of marriage," he said. "They complement each other and can't let go of each other." The Stasi knew that the press was addicted to leaks, and that scoop-hungry reporters would even publish anonymous leaks; they also knew that it was extremely difficult for journalists to tell whether a source was genuine or fake, and even harder to tell if the content of a leak was accurate or forged. And it was another notch harder still to tell whether an anonymous leak contained some shrewd mix of both, handcrafted for maximum impact. This symbiotic relationship found its fullest expression in the active measures field. "What would active measures be without the journalist?"[3] Wagenbreth asked the Stasi leaders. "Revelations are their métier." The X, of course, had the same métier.

For Wagenbreth, more competitive and polarized media outlets presented a major opportunity. "For the man on the street it is getting harder to assess and to judge the written word," Wagenbreth explained. "He is ever more helpless in the face of the monsters that are opinion factories. This is where we come in as an intelligence agency."[4]

Wagenbreth had been a member of the German Communist Party since age sixteen, and became a major in the Ministry of State Security (MfS) by the time he was twenty-four. Shortly after the completion of the Berlin Wall, the MfS opened a new special department, VII/F, already headed by Wagenbreth, which five years later would be expanded into the X.[5] Wagenbreth would thus run disinformation for almost the entire Cold War, until the end of 1989.[6]

The overall idea of disinformation wasn't just recommended by the KGB. Communist parties across the bloc considered active measures an instrument of policy. Within the Stasi, especially its foreign intelligence arm, the HVA, Department X was seen as a particular favorite of Markus Wolf, the HVA's charismatic and respected director.[7] Wolf discussed progress with Wagenbreth in weekly meetings, often considering specific operational methods, potential improvements of ongoing operations, and foreign reactions to current and finished active measures.

Markus Wolf instilled as much awe as respect among his staff. Tall, handsome, vain, and emotionally cold, he was usually dressed in a tailored suit, smoked strong West German cigarettes, and preferred French cognac. The door to his office suite was cushioned on the inside with soundproof leather; the sound of a knock did not get through, but Wolf's secretary reported on visitors who failed to try.

In the spring of 1966, Markus Wolf was called to a meeting in Moscow on short notice, to meet the first deputy chief of the KGB's First Chief Directorate. After speaking about the wider context, the officer deferred to Igor Agayants, the head of Service A.

"Comrades," Agayants intoned, "this strategic assessment requires a new quality of active measures, clear strategies leading into the 70s and effective measures that go beyond merely destructive methods." Agayants rearticulated the strategic objective that had been set by the Central Committee: "The long-term goal is to remove the USA from the so-called Atlantic Alliance."[8]

*1966
STILL
TRUE
2021*

Wolf got the message. On the flight back, he began sketching out plans to upgrade the HVA's own disinformation unit, and the X was born.[9]

West German intelligence was aware of HVA active measures from the beginning. In March 1959, Max Heim, an HVA officer with the rank of captain, fled to West Germany. He had been responsible for running espionage operations against the Christian Democrats in the Federal Republic. Heim, a Wehrmacht veteran, defected before the Stasi formed a specific unit for disinformation, but in his debriefings with West German security services, he was already able to detail what he called "intelligence work of corrosion," or *Zersetzungsarbeit*.[10] *Zersetzung* is a morbid German word for disintegration by malicious external forces—it applies to the disintegration of a body politic, of a community, of an individual's mental stability, or even of human tissue. The nascent peace movement, as the X understood early on, represented an opportunity to corrode the soft tissue of the Western body politic.

The East Berlin Central Committee of the Socialist Party was by then already drafting concepts on "the continued development of peacewar in West Germany." The phrase *peacewar, Friedenskampf* in German, was a particularly Orwellian bit of authoritarian jargon. The Stasi collected intelligence on peace activists, even the minutes from meetings of minor West German peace groups. The early campaigns against budding peace activism foreshadowed by far the largest, longest, and most expensive disinformation campaign in intelligence history: the subversion of the peace movement in the West.

Throughout the 1960s, annual Easter marches became a focal point of the West German peace movement. The events mushroomed along with the fear of nuclear war, growing from about 1,000 demonstrators in 1960 to 150,000 in 1967.[11] Shortly after Easter 1967, the KGB and the Stasi held one of their annual meetings on active measures. The Vietnam War was escalating, and a range of operations was designed to "deepen the contradictions"[12] between West Germany and the United States in intelligence and military matters.

Operation TRIBUNAL, for example, was meant to reveal the "dirty character" of America's war in Vietnam, and would be supported by KGB documentation on chemical warfare in Indochina, as well as West German military participation in Vietnam.[13] Operation SCIENCE was designed to accuse German scientists in the United States of spying by, for example, surfacing "disinforming documents" on the Nazi past of prominent German scientists now working in the fast-advancing U.S. space program.[14] Operation STORM was set up to "sharpen contradictions in NATO" and to shore up opposition to West Germany's military aggression.[15]

The most successful operation authorized by Moscow that April was DEVASTATION, a mission to accuse West Germany of building weapons of mass destruction, including missile technology. Wagenbreth's and Agayants's units planned to reveal "incriminating documents" on West German scientists who were working on the development of weapons of mass destruction.[16] The German and Russian disinformation experts, remarkably, did not clearly delineate where invented "revelations" diverged from genuine ones— the KGB routinely disinformed its own partner agencies. "Both sides agreed that documents realized in international organization contain credible details,"[17] reported the meeting protocol. The two agencies also agreed that the KGB would send an advisor to Berlin, in September 1967, to help plan and execute DEVASTATION.[18]

After about a year of low-level planning, an opportunity arose. Markus Wolf wrote a memo to his superior, Erich Mielke, in August 1968, suggesting that the HVA "deploy a system of coordinated active measures, from the area of the GDR as well as in the operational area, in order to uncover and reveal West Germany's plans, intentions, and progress with A[tomic], B[iological], and C[hemical] weapons armaments. To achieve this goal we could use information from the MfS, and take advantage of recently withdrawn unofficial collaborators."[19]

"Unofficial collaborators" was Stasi jargon for spies. Wolf suggested that two press conferences be held with fake West German defectors, one with a focus on nuclear weapons development, the other on chemical and biological weapons. Wolf then suggested scheduling a press conference with one specific HVA spy, an asset who had worked for "a prolonged period of time" as a scientist for "a West German research institute involved in research on toxic agents."

Weeks later, West German scientists working on sensitive technologies—eight in all, among them nuclear physicists and microbiologists—began to disappear, some without a trace. On September 30, the Associated Press reported that Klaus Breuer, a thirty-three-year-old atomic scientist at the Frankfurt Institute of Nuclear Physics, had left West Germany to move east with his wife and five-year-old son.[20]

Then, on November 23, *1968* Ehrenfried Petras, a thirty-eight-year-old microbiologist working for the Institute for Microbiology in Grafschaft, announced his defection on prime-time East German TV.[21] He said he had applied for asylum in East Germany, so that he could use his skills "in the service of peace."[22] Claiming that he had worked on bacteriological and chemical warfare projects funded by the West German government in Bonn, the scientist said that he felt that his work had been put to ill use, for military ends. *The New York Times* reported the story from Berlin, never calling Petras's account into question. The *Times* quoted him as saying he decided to quit after the defense ministry in Bonn asserted "unlimited control" over research projects.[23] Every major West German wire agency and newspaper covered the spectacular Petras "defection."[24]

Two weeks later, on December 6, Petras held another televised press briefing, this time claiming that the West German Ministry of Defense had recently created a special WMD working group focused on offensive weapons. He said he had worked on VX, a highly lethal chemical warfare agent. Now *The Washington Post* treated him as a credible source.[25] At the end of the month, *Neues Deutschland* printed a full-page interview with Petras.[26] "It became clear to me that the institute was solely concerned with the preparation of WMD warfare," *The New York Times* quoted him.[27]

Next, another scientist, Herbert Patzelt, who worked for the European Atomic Energy Community, told his superiors that he had to leave for West Germany on urgent family business. He soon reemerged in East Germany. "I began more and more to doubt whether my knowledge and work was being put to the right use," Patzelt said on TV. "West German says Bonn works towards A-Weapon," reported Reuters from East Berlin.[28] On January 15, 1969, the GDR's national council topped off the PR blitz with an international press conference in Berlin and the publication of at least two "realized"— HVA jargon for *made-up*—documents, one on Bonn's "Atomic Cartel,"[29] and later a brochure titled "Bonn Preparing Poison War."[30]

In reality, the defense ministry in Bonn had indeed considered the use and production of chemical weapons (although not biological and nuclear weapons).[31] In 1968, however, before DEVASTATION was executed, Bonn explicitly decided not to prepare an active use of chemical weapons.[32] But the faux defections and revelations repeatedly tricked the finest newspapers in West Germany and the United States. After the campaign was completed, in March 1969, Wolf boasted that the public performance of several important unofficial collaborators had made a crucial contribution to active measures against WMD production in West Germany.[33]

Only years later would the truth begin to trickle out. In 1979, the BfV, West Germany's internal intelligence agency, debriefed a recent defector from Wolf's agency by the name of Werner Stiller. Stiller had worked on science and technology for the Stasi and was familiar with the HVA's nuclear espionage activities.[34] He told the BfV that Breuer, Petras, Patzelt, and the other apparent West German defectors were in fact HVA-trained agents who had been spying on their employers. Petras, and likely others, were called back in late 1968 because the HVA was concerned that their cover was at risk. The BfV explained that "one disinformation technique, repeatedly used until recently, is so-called 'revelations' by MfS agents after they have been called back from their assigned area of operations."[35] As with the OPLAN 10-1 and the Nuclear Yield Requirements, already obsolete documents were put to an effective final use.

In 1972, another opportunity arose for East Germany to sabotage the

West: the Olympic Games, which would be held in the country for the first time since Nazi Germany had hosted them in 1936. West Germany's official motto for the Olympics was *Die heiteren Spiele*, or "the cheerful games." East Germany countered with a major propaganda campaign linking the Olympics to National Socialism: "Is two times 36 perhaps 72?"[36]

The games coincided with another infamous political event: the extreme right-wing 1st National-European Youth Congress was scheduled to be held in Planegg, close to Munich, one week after the Olympics concluded, on September 16–17.[37]

Far-right youth groups across the West widely anticipated the festival. A German right-wing youth magazine called *Mut* had published an appeal to meet in Planegg in December 1971, arguing that Western Europe was under attack from within, that it was time "for all young patriots" to prepare for a "counter-attack."[38] Extreme-right groups translated the article into a number of languages and spread it to fringe magazines across the West—*The New American* in the United States, *Nation Europa* in Germany, *CEDADE* in Spain, but also in Italy and France. More than a thousand far-right organizations were expected to attend the Planegg congress, including the Falange from Franco's Spain. The FBI considered the U.S. group a militant white-supremacist organization, and surveilled its activities. Meanwhile, Soviet bloc intelligence was watching the right-wing extremists closely.

The confluence of the youth congress and the Olympics offered a prime opportunity for active measures operators. Wagenbreth and one of his colleagues traveled to Sofia, Bulgaria, in October 1971, and for the first time discussed the possibility of attacking the Olympic Games with a covert operation. The games themselves were not the actual target. The HVA designed what it called Operation ZEUS with three explicit goals: to distract and "occupy" West German intelligence and police agencies during the Olympics; to keep the adversary's ideologues on the back foot; and to implicate German right-wing groups.[39] The Olympics just supplied the platform for this performance.

Next, Wagenbreth's unit forged a leaflet that purported to come from the organizers of the neo-Nazi youth congress. The faux leaflet called for a stronger far-right movement in order to "free Europe," as it approvingly quoted the secretary of the 1936 Olympics Games, and highlighted that the games in 1972 also were not global but European, "reflecting the racist understanding of the superiority of European nations," as the X explained in an internal memo.[40] HVA operatives posed as far-right extremists, even threatening violent action[41] to escalate the confrontation between West German police and the radical right, to "engage their forces in the fight against extremists."[42] The Stasi distributed the pamphlet to the press and various national Olympic committees.

A few months before the games began, the Stasi's acting head of disinformation met with a delegation of the Bulgarian disinformation unit in East Berlin. The X leadership informed the Bulgarians that they were preparing a range of additional measures under the ZEUS code name, including threatening letters sent from supposed right-wing extremists to the federal and state interior ministries in Bonn and Munich. Department X also suggested sending another batch of letters to the same interior ministries, this time purportedly from "emigrant organizations" in Germany, in order to "create compromising materials on the basis of which arrests and liquidations of emigrant organizations could be carried out." Major Hans Knaust of the HVA asked Bulgarian state security for help in distributing the racist leaflets to newspapers in Turkey, Italy, Greece, and Arab countries in order to harm West Germany's image and "strengthen disagreements between NATO countries."[43] Another planned component of ZEUS was the publication of a brochure on "Neo-Nazism and the Olympic Games," in a circulation of 5,000 to 10,000 copies, and under the auspices of "a democratic organization" in West Germany.[44] Four of the planned measures were reportedly realized, according to an annual summary preserved in the archives of Bulgarian state security.[45]

That same spring, in April 1972, Chancellor Willy Brandt of Germany faced an unprecedented vote of no confidence in Parliament. The conservative opposition had hoped to bring this vote for more than a year.[46] The end of his government appeared certain. The conservatives, the party of the opposition, aimed to stop Brandt's *Ostpolitik*, or policy of détente vis-à-vis the

Soviet bloc, and the impending signature of a treaty with Moscow. The republic held its breath on the morning of April 27. At 12:59, conservative MPs began dropping their voting cards. Twenty-three minutes later, the carefully hand-counted result was announced: only 247 votes of no confidence came up, two short of victory. Frantic jubilation broke out among the Social Democrats and the Liberals—and shock among the Christian Democrats. Two conservative MPs had defected. The parliamentary coup had failed. Brandt remained chancellor. The history of West Germany took a different course.

The extraordinary story of what happened in secret would only be revealed more than thirty years later, and some of its most important details have never been reported before.

In early 1972, the West German government slowly teetered toward crisis as more and more members of Parliament defected from Brandt's social-liberal coalition. In early March, *Der Spiegel*, in a cover story, reported that "Bonn is preparing for new elections," likely as a result of an impending vote of no confidence.[47] The MfS in East Berlin had an interest in keeping Brandt in power, as the German chancellor's *Ostpolitik* was economically and politically advantageous for the Soviet bloc. That spring, Wolf ordered Department X to prepare an emergency plan to deflect the predicted challenge to Brandt: the department would prepare to bribe and trick two conservative MPs into abstaining during a vote of no confidence. On April 24, the opposition finally voted to schedule the historic vote for three days in the future.

The first was Julius Steiner. One year after the vote, in June 1973, Steiner admitted that he received DM 50,000 to abstain. Steiner confessed in the same interview that a few months after the vote, he began working as a double agent for West German intelligence, in order to mislead the Stasi[48]—but Steiner claimed that he was bribed by the Social Democrats, not the Stasi. "Watergate in Bonn?" asked *Der Spiegel* (at the time, the American Watergate scandal was in full swing).

Steiner's revelations immediately triggered a parliamentary investigation by the defeated conservatives, launched by another MP, Leo Wagner, the executive officer of the conservatives. Democracy in the Federal Republic of Germany was "under its darkest cloud yet," said Wagner as he pressed for a parliamentary investigation, to applause from his fellow conservatives. Wagner alluded to foreign intelligence agencies secretly pulling strings in Parliament, and pointed out that the decision to keep Brandt in power had been subject to "massive influence."[49] It was important to restore public trust in the high chamber, he said.

Leo Wagner's short speech must count as one of the most cold-blooded acts in parliamentary history. For Wagner himself was the second Stasi influence agent. But nobody suspected him, and indeed, the investigation was inconclusive. But Wagner didn't know the full story. As he stood at the lectern that Friday afternoon in Bonn, deceiving the entire Bundestag, Wagner himself had been deceived by Department X.

The full history of the rigged vote did not emerge until after the Cold War had ended. In 1997, Markus Wolf, the former head of the HVA, confirmed that the MfS had indeed bribed Steiner with DM 50,000, then just under $17,000.[50] Steiner, code-named SIMON, had even visited East Berlin around a dozen times in the early 1970s to meet with his handlers.[51]

The Leo Wagner story took much longer to trickle out, and it reveals the professionalism of Department X better than any other. In 2000, Germany's federal prosecutor revealed that Wagner was a Stasi asset and influence agent; the East Germans had also paid Wagner, who was in financial trouble at the time. "Same tariff," Wagenbreth later boasted internally, DM 50,000.[52] Department X had code-named Leo Wagner LÖWE, or lion.[53] The HVA officer in charge of swaying Wagner's vote was Horst Kopp.

"Shit is hitting the fan again," Wagenbreth had opened the meeting with Kopp in advance of the vote of no confidence. The X chief explained the likely vote distribution to Kopp and his supervisor. "Two hundred and forty-seven," he had told Kopp, "that means we need two votes to hold the chancellor."[54]

"Tell me." Wagenbreth looked directly at Kopp. "Aren't you working with that Georg Fleissmann?"

He was. Fleissmann was a Bavarian journalist from Nuremberg. For six years, since 1966, Fleissmann had been spying for the HVA, motivated partly by his own financial troubles. Fleissmann was a gifted spy. On Kopp's

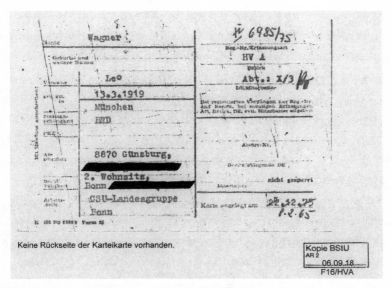

The Stasi foreign intelligence record card of Leo Wagner, a conservative member of Parliament. Wagner was a spy and influence agent run under "foreign flag," meaning he believed he was acting in U.S. interests. (BStU)

instructions, he had, for example, recruited a hawkish, pro-American senior naval intelligence officer in the West German Ministry of Defense. The naval officer was a staunch anti-Communist and psychological warfare specialist, and Fleissmann had managed to recruit him "under foreign flag" to work for the Stasi. "Under foreign flag," in HVA jargon, meant that the naval officer believed he was actually passing on secret material to an American agency—not to his own sworn enemy. Especially as socialism lost its pull as a recruiting tool, HVA more and more wore the mask of foreign entities when recruiting agents, and internally even distinguished three different types of "flags." By the end of the decade, 4 percent of all HVA informants were run "under foreign flag."[55]

"What do you think, could Fleissmann also buy Leo Wagner?" Wagenbreth asked Kopp.

Fleissmann knew Wagner well. The journalist, working for HVA, had recruited Wagner as another Stasi asset "under foreign flag" in 1970. The X, via Fleissmann, had successfully curated the belief in Wagner's mind that by spying on his own party, and ultimately by defecting from his party's vote, he would help, as the X put it, "American commercial circles with an interest in trading in the East," and carefully avoided even mentioning the U.S. government.[56] Fleissmann had even traveled to the United States, to call Wagner from there, in order to make the foreign flag more credible. In anticipation of the vote of no confidence against Brandt, Kopp had to prepare a fine-tuned explanation of these vague U.S. interests for Wagner. "I had to write four drafts," Kopp recalled, "then Wolf and Wagenbreth eventually doped out what to say to him."[57]

Kopp met with Fleissmann at a hotel in Budapest. Kopp and Fleissmann agreed on a deal over coffee, at a quiet table behind some potted plants. Coming up with the right, fine-tuned language took several drafts. Wagner, although he was in debt, was still a conservative Bavarian politician, and working for Communists would have been a bridge too far for him.[58] Wagner took the money and voted for the Americans. Or so he thought. Brandt survived the vote, and *Ostpolitik* was saved.

Two years after the HVA's remarkable election interference, the X launched another timeless disinformation campaign: it manufactured far-right, neo-Fascist sentiments in West Germany in response to the government's guest worker program of the 1970s. The operation, known as RIGAS, was launched with a two-page flyer impersonating a far-right West German party, the Deutsche Volksunion (DVU).[59] The goals were to "aggravate the relations between the Federal Republic, Turkey, and Greece"; to "internationally discredit the right-wingers in the Federal Republic"; and to "provoke action by foreign workers."[60] The pamphlet's two paragraphs, printed under the headline "Deutsche, wehrt euch!" (Germans, defend yourselves!), tapped into the dark undercurrent of white supremacy still present in West Germany:

> 2.5 million "guest workers" enrich themselves and their degenerate people off of Germany. Yet about 600,000 German men and women are unemployed and temporary work is spreading like a pestilence.
>
> It is a brazen lie to claim that foreign workers would raise the economic well-being of the German people. Inflation is rampant

DEUTSCHE , WEHRT EUCH !

2,5 Millionen "Oastarbeiter" bereichern sich und ihre auf
niederer Entwicklungsstufe stehenden Völker an Deutschland.
Aber rund 600.000 deutsche Männer und Frauen sind arbeits-
los und Kurzarbeit breitet sich aus wie die Pest.

Es ist eine unverschämte Lüge, wenn behauptet wird, Fremd-
arbeiter heben den Wohlstand des deutschen Volkes. Trotz
der 2,5 Millionen Türken, Griechen, Jugoslawen, Italiener,
Marokkaner und Tunesier grassiert die Inflation und Fremd-
arbeiter werden immer mehr zur ernsthaften Gefahr für die
Sauberkeit und den Bestand der deutschen Nation.

Tatsachen sprechen für sich:

. Mehr als 20.000 Türken stellten den Antrag auf deutsche
Staatsbürgerschaft; es wurden 60.000 Ehen zwischen Türken
und Deutschen geschlossen.
Das ist Vernichtung des Deutschtums und Zerstörung deutschen Blutes.

RAUS MIT DEN MOHAMMEDS !

. Türken überwiesen im vergangenen Jahr fast für eine Mil-
liarde Devisen in ihr armseliges kleinasiatisches Armen-
haus. Insgesamt waren es um 8 Milliarden Mark, die von
Fremdarbeitern 1973 aus Deutschland verschleppt wurden
- mehr als ein Fünftel des deutschen Außenhandelsüber-
schusses. Mit diesen Geldern gleichen die Bankrottregie-
rungen ihre Zahlungsbilanzen aus.
Das ist Auspowerung Deutschlands durch anatolische Bett-
lerhorden, europäische Hinterwäldlerstaaten und nord-
afrikanische Kameltreiber.

RAUS MIT DIESEM ASOZIALEN GESINDEL !

Stasi-designed anti-Muslim leaflet distributed in West Germany, and also covered in the Turkish national press

(BStU, via Christopher Nehring)

despite the 2.5 million Turks, Greeks, Yugoslavs, Italians, Moroccans, and Tunisians. Foreign workers are quickly becoming a serious danger for the purity and the survival of the German nation.[61]

The X, writing as the DVU, added that twenty thousand Turks had applied for German citizenship, and that sixty thousand marriages between Turks and Germans had been recorded already. "This is the destruction of Germanic identity and the infestation of German blood," Wagenbreth's officers wrote. "Out with the Mohammeds!"

The HVA dispatched a small group of informal collaborators, code-named RACER, to a number of West German cities to distribute the leaflet.

Wagenbreth had personally requested that the Stasi's Department VIII assist with the distribution of the leaflet to "centers of guest workers in Düsseldorf, Cologne, Mainz, Mannheim, Ludwigshafen, Frankfurt, and Heidelberg."[62] This particular active measure had significant international potential, especially since it was immigration-related and naturally involved other countries—NATO countries, best of all.

Both the HVA and their Bulgarian counterparts considered RIGAS a measurable success. In early December 1975, officers in Sofia reported to East Berlin that the Turkish daily *Sabah* had published on its front page a full translation of the fake DVU leaflet, headlined "Leaflets Insulting Turkey Are Being Distributed in Germany."[63] The Bulgarian officers reported that this impressive placement in *Sabah* was the result of a group of Turkish guest workers returning from West Germany handing over a copy of the offensive flyer to the Turkish Telegraph Agency in Konya. "The content of this poster is a matter for all Turks and greatly offends our country and our compatriots working in the FDR," said the *Sabah* report forwarded to the Stasi.[64] A few months later, the HVA reported back to Sofia about another RIGAS success. The fake flyer also prompted the state prosecutor in Cologne, as well as the criminal police in Munich, to initiate investigations into Gerhard Frey, the head of the DVU (the investigations were dropped, as the DVU was able to prove that it was not the author of the leaflet).[65] The measure went on for well over a year. As late as May 1976, the MfS was planning to release forgeries to provoke Turkish and Greek guest workers in Frankfurt, Cologne, Munich, and Stuttgart.[66]

On October 3, 1974, Helmut Kohl was on the phone with Kurt Biedenkopf. Kohl was the head of West Germany's Christian Democratic Union, the CDU (and later chancellor). Biedenkopf was the CDU's general secretary. The party head and his general secretary spoke about disagreements in the party about Kohl's stamina, discipline, and leadership style.[67]

Listening in to the conversation was the Stasi's Main Directorate III, which then passed on the transcript to the X for operational use. The subunit responsible for West German parties was X/2. X/2 was able to get its hands on a so-called agent-report form. The form was used by the U.S. intelligence community, specifically by the Military Intelligence Group, in order to record and archive intercepted phone conversation protocols. The active measures team at X/2 had the idea to transcribe the Kohl-Biedenkopf disagreement on an American intelligence form, and then launch the accurate transcript on the accurate U.S. intelligence form. The Stasi made four copies, packed them in a yellow-brown envelope, and, in early June 1975, had collaborators mail the four packages anonymously to *Stern* and *Der Spiegel*, as well as to two members of the intelligence oversight commission of the West German Parliament in Bonn—that commission would have authorized the surveillance, had it been lawful. The Stasi mailed the letter from Kaiserslautern, where the U.S. Army's 527th Military Intelligence Group was based.

Two weeks later, on June 19, 1975, *Stern* ran the story on its cover, illustrated with a topless model on a beach.[68] The magazine reprinted the full transcript, including the English-language agent-report form, with its official-looking black frames and frame explanations: "4. Report of findings," then "5. Typed name and organization of special agent," and "6. Signature of special agent."[69] The magazine considered various scenarios that could have led to the leak, but considered the most probable one that the Allies continued their long-standing postwar surveillance practices against West German politicians.

The affair went viral and became front-page news across the German-speaking countries. *Stern* was widely criticized for unscrupulously using illegally obtained source material. *Der Spiegel,* the following week, ran a cover story that tried to reframe the "surveillance affair" as a "press scandal."

All the while the question of attribution loomed large. The West German police investigation found that the two anonymous letters had been written with an IBM Selectric typewriter with a German-language typeball. The stamps on the envelope were licked by an individual with blood group O.[70] *Der Spiegel's* investigative reporters also noted that only the first page of the four-page transcript was printed on the American agent-report form, and that it was the incorrect form in the first place (the correct form would have been the "telephone intercept" form). *Der Spiegel* discussed the possibility that either rogue West German intelligence officers with a pro-Bavaria bent leaked the intercepts, or that the Stasi wanted to "inflict more reputational damage on CIA."[71] Nevertheless, even *Der Spiegel* considered a U.S. intercept-and-leak the most plausible explanation. Perceptive reporters pointed to errors in punctuation in the leak's cover letter, and a confusion of German party acronyms (CDU and CSU), an error that nobody with first-rate knowledge of Bonn's political scene would have committed. The implication was that neither West German nor East German intelligence would be so sloppy. A caricature depicted Kohl on the phone under a poster of a spy with the caption: "Psst, friend listening in."

Meanwhile, the MfS noticed, to its surprise, that the debate in West Germany was more interested in the surveillance than in the conflict between Kohl and Biedenkopf. As a result, HVA/X assessed that the operation was a partial failure: "we did not succeed in exacerbating the conflict between the Union parties."[72] Nevertheless, East German intelligence assessed that the surveillance affair of the summer of 1975 succeeded in confusing their West German adversary agencies, and pinning down resources for a considerable amount of time.

Department X forged and made up entire issues of internal newsletters, some public, others not. The practice was not unlike that of the CIA's Kampfgruppe and LCCASSOCK a dozen years earlier, and quite possibly inspired by American political warfare tactics. *Die Mitte*, "The Center," was a forged six-page periodical for Christian Democrats, allegedly edited by a CDU working group in Bonn, Düsseldorf, and Frankfurt, with an anti-Kohl and anti-Strauss slant. X played all sides, and published an equivalent newsletter for the West German Social Democrats, called *SPD Intern*, styled as the voice of the inner-party opposition.

Perhaps the most successful of these internal newsletters was made for the liberal FDP, then the third-largest party. Ironically, Wagenbreth, who personally took interest in this operation, called the fake liberal paper *X-Informationen*. *X-Informationen* appeared every two weeks between October 1964 and fall 1968, in 500 copies.[73] The respected *X-Informationen* carried many genuine articles and often had an anti-American slant.[74] The small magazine was edited and published by a journalist and HVA influence agent code-named KARSTÄDT,[75] in reality Rudolf Schelkmann, a former Waffen SS major and member of Hitler's elite bodyguard.[76]

East German intelligence also published an internal newsletter for the West German armed forces, called *Der Bund*—named after a colloquial nickname for the Bundeswehr, and pithily taglined STRATEGIC—ATLANTIC—EUROPEAN—SOLDIERLY. In order to keep its cover, the fake military paper would even invoke "the Soviet threat," but only to call the reliance of the United States as an ally into question. The actual German army journal *Wehrdienst* quoted the MfS serial forgery several times, and the German military reportedly never uncovered the magazine in their midst as an adversarial disinformation operation.[77]

The HVA reserved its most brazen project for its nemesis, West German foreign intelligence, the BND. The X knew that a group of former members of the legendary Abwehr, the military intelligence department of the Wehrmacht, still kept in touch and met regularly. One of the chief organizers of this group had worked for both the famous Wilhelm Canaris, an admiral and head of the Abwehr until the SS executed him for resisting Hitler, and later for Reinhard Gehlen, the equally famous founder and head of the BND. The former intelligence officers organized and distributed an internal newsletter called *Die Nachhut*, "The Rearguard," which petered out in the mid-1970s. When the HVA learned about the end of *Die Nachhut*, the X got excited: "For us this was worth gold," two operators recalled later.[78] The HVA in Berlin started publishing its own newsletter for current and former BND staff, called *Die Neue Nachhut*, or "The New Rearguard." *Die Neue Nachhut*, like the original, called itself an internal "information organ," appeared quarterly for at least three years, and was mailed anonymously from Munich to current and former members of the BND, including its former and current presidents, Reinhard Gehlen and Gerhard Wessel.[79] The newsletter had a FOR OFFICIAL USE ONLY header, to make it appear more institutional, and identified its publishers as retired employees of the BND. The X forgers used actual internal

BND information to bolster the credibility of their periodical, down to mundane details like parking space and office availability. The Stasi also reportedly included previously unpublished material from the Wehrmacht archives of the BND's predecessor organization.

The newsletter was well done. In March 1980, for example, the West German defense minister, then a Social Democrat, spoke at a party conference and publicly mentioned BND reporting on Soviet troop movements in Central Asia ahead of the invasion of Afghanistan just a few weeks earlier. The press had reported that the minister called out the BND for failing to collect intelligence on Kremlin decision-making.[80] The HVA's disinformation then shrewdly put an insult into the minister's mouth, one he never used: "our people in Pullach [the BND] are under orders to stop analyzing and to start delivering facts," reported *Die Neue Nachhut*, elegantly mixing true and fake reporting.[81] The HVA's goal was to politicize the BND, and to drive a wedge between the famously conservative staff and its social democratic political masters. "We admit we had good fun," two of the X officers recalled.[82]

Whether the fun was effective remains questionable. The BND reportedly was suspicious early on. In a response to a question from a conservative member of Parliament, West German authorities stated that they considered *Die Neue Nachhut* a sabotage attempt, but they could neither confirm nor exclude that they were dealing with "disinformation from an Eastern agency."[83]

In 1976, the Christian Democrats of West Germany were defeated in the general election, prompting the Bavarian branch of the party to break off on its own and form a fourth party. An uproar ensued, and the Bavarians eventually reversed their decision; the conservative party was reunited. But the HVA's West German specialists had been watching closely. By the general election of October 1980, West Germany had been governed by a social-liberal coalition for eleven years. For the occasion, the HVA planned to reawaken the "spirit of Kreuth"—Kreuth referred to the town in which the conservative crisis initially played out.

Wagenbreth turned to a decorated influence agent who was intimately familiar with the West German party landscape and its inherent conflicts.

His brainchild, a thirteen-page paper titled "Return to Kreuth," allegedly written by General Secretary Edmund Stoiber of the CSU,[84] recommended that the conservative party be split in two. The CSU, the Bavarian conservatives, embodied a different brand of conservatism and had always had a very strong regional identity. The paper proposed, in case of a renewed electoral defeat, to spin out a Germany-wide CSU as a fourth political force in the Federal Republic.

Wagenbreth authorized the paper and had it sent to *Der Spiegel* as an anonymous leak. The weekly magazine contacted its alleged author, Stoiber, who denied everything. But the *Spiegel* reporters did not buy the denial, which was made in the heat of an election campaign, and eventually decided to publish the full "Return to Kreuth" paper. "It has been confirmed that the paper is neither a 'forgery' nor a 'falsification,'" *Der Spiegel* wrote on September 29, 1980.

The goal of the Kreuth operation was "influencing the federal elections of October 5, 1980," Germany's federal state prosecutor pointed out in a later indictment.[85] Just days before the election in October 1980, several of Germany's biggest newspapers fell for the ruse. The conservatives finished even weaker than they had in the previous election.

Over the course of the Cold War, nobody bested Wagenbreth's HVA in psychological warfare. The Stasi was aggressive, unafraid of risk, unscrupulous, and highly innovative. But its most significant advantage was that the organization was geographically, linguistically, and culturally so close to its greatest enemy. The HVA was staffed by Germans who shared the same history, culture, preferences for food and drink, experiences of the war, even traumas and fears and sometimes family ties. All of this enabled the Stasi to craft active measures that were far more sophisticated than almost anything that the KGB was able to deploy in the United States or other countries, during the Cold War and since.

"There were few private conversations and even fewer secrets in Bonn," as an in-house CIA journal put it in 1993.[86]

The HVA, in one CIA historian's assessment, "fought primarily a civil war on German territory, where it had the advantage of proximity, common language and culture, area knowledge, and multiple points of access to an open society."[87] It was "one of the best," especially in its shrewd use of influence agents and active measures.

Only one picture of Wagenbreth was ever published, in 1991.[88] Even after the Berlin Wall came down, Wagenbreth would resist publicity, slamming the door shut in front of journalists—that once-beloved tribe.[89] Then, in 1993, the German federal state prosecutor indicted Wagenbreth, along with two other X officers, for deploying "'active measures' to attack the sovereignty and inner stability of the Federal Republic."[90]

The Fifth Estate

B
Y THE EARLY 1970S, MOST AMERICANS HAD FORGOTTEN about *Who's Who in CIA*, that odd little book published a few years earlier. But in Langley, the brazen dump of staff identities was still a fresh and open wound. On August 10, 1970, the body of Daniel A. Mitrione, a USAID advisor to the Uruguayan police, was found in a stolen 1948 Buick convertible in Montevideo, gagged, bound, and shot twice in the head.[1] Mitrione had been—incorrectly—identified as a CIA operative in Mader's directory two years earlier, and the Tupamaro guerrillas who killed Mitrione reportedly cited his listing in the KGB's half-forged CIA directory as a justification.[2] Six days after his assassination, the East Berlin publication *Berliner Zeitung* claimed that Mitrione was "an experienced CIA agent," and reproduced his entire *Who's Who in CIA* entry "from page 361."[3]

Richard Welch, a CIA officer in Athens, was killed by far-left terrorists in December 1975 after his name was exposed by *Counterspy*, a Washington-based anti-intelligence-community activist project. Welch's widow is shown with President Gerald Ford. (Courtesy Gerald R. Ford Presidential Library)

Langley,[4] in turn, pointed out publicly that Mitrione was an actual diplomat, not an intelligence officer.

Anger rose in Washington, leading to what may be described as the CIA's last known aggressive active measure during the Cold War. The retaliation also came in the form of a tell-all book, titled *KGB: The Secret Work of Soviet Secret Agents*, by John Barron, an investigative journalist at *Reader's Digest*. In contrast to Mader's obscure volume, *KGB* would become an international bestseller.

Two months before Barron's book release, the new CIA director, William Colby, received a confidential memo on his desk with the subject line "Publication of Reader's Digest Book 'KGB.'"[5] The memo explained, "This book is not a CIA project but Barron has been in touch with Agency officers [. . .] for consultation and advice ever since 1967 when the idea for the book originated." Barron had worked on the book for six years, supported the entire time by the CIA,

The KGB and later, in retaliation, the CIA—each with the support of allied agencies—
engineered the publication of the names of thousands of intelligence operatives
working for the other side: *Who's Who in CIA* versus *KGB*.

along with the FBI, MI6, and other European intelligence services. The CIA
had provided Barron with material, "carefully proof-read" the final manuscript
"for factual errors," and made "corrections and additions of some substance" to
passages in which Barron was discussing the organization of the KGB.

Yet the section of the released memo that described the CIA's cooperation with Barron is heavily redacted, and the Agency denied a renewed FOIA
request for declassification. David Blee, who signed the memo for the CIA's
Directorate of Operations, had himself been exposed by the KGB in *Who's
Who in CIA*. He pointed out to Colby that Barron carefully cited his "non-
CIA" sources, but that the wealth of detail, accuracy, and currency of his information would mean that knowledgeable readers could "infer that the CIA
and/or the FBI either wrote or were active collaborators in the book."[6] Barron's remarkable book indeed contained a wealth of fresh detail, and I am
treating *KGB* as a highly reliable source precisely because several declassified
CIA memos make clear that the Agency proofread the book for factual errors, helped improve it, and later carefully studied its content. The Agency's

unusual active measure, which the CIA of course never described as such, was explicitly not a form of disinformation.

Yet Barron's book contained a particularly heavy payload, one directed right at the heart of the Soviet Union's intelligence community: a 35-page appendix that listed hundreds of names of KGB and GRU officers working under various covers worldwide. Thirty years after Barron's book came out, the CIA declassified a document that shed more light on his sourcing: in 1975, the CIA prepared a secret analysis of "machine input" from Barron's book (meaning the analysis was done with then-cutting-edge computer technology) that showed that of the 1,557 persons identified in the book, 942 "were identified by classified sources only," from the CIA and other Western agencies.[7] Barron told *The New York Times* two years later that he had received "quite a bit of help" from the CIA when writing the book, but added that he had compiled the list of Russian operatives from a variety of sources.[8] The CIA's secret 1975 machine analysis also noted that "some of the names were pre-selected as RIS [Russian Intelligence Services] when they were furnished to him [Barron] by the various intelligence services."[9]

Anonymous sources also told *The New York Times* in 1977 that the CIA had helped Barron because the book would "serve an operational purpose" in the Agency's delayed response to *Who's Who in CIA*. The 1974 bestseller can therefore be seen as a rare Western joint active measure directed against Soviet intelligence. One year after its publication, the Church Committee commenced an investigation into intelligence abuses that drastically changed intelligence oversight and established the permanent Senate Select Committee on Intelligence. One particularly sore issue was the covert use of journalists and publishers, which led the CIA to change its policy and become even more cautious.

BARRON'S BOOK SUCCEEDED IN ROILING THE KGB, AS THE CIA HAD HOPED. BY 1977, the KGB had produced an up-to-date, highly classified internal directory of U.S. intelligence personnel, one "as thick as a Manhattan phone directory," as Oleg Kalugin later recounted. The KGB tome on American intelligence "contained biographical information on ten thousand current and former CIA agents," according to Kalugin; it is unclear whether he exaggerated this number. He delivered the book as a present for the KGB chairman, Yuri Andropov, on the occasion of the sixtieth anniversary of the Russian Revolution, sometime in 1977. Kalugin was incensed by Barron's book, and his instinct was to retaliate and escalate yet again:

"When John Barron's book *KGB* was published listing the names of hundreds of KGB officers, I told Andropov, 'Give me the appropriate order, and we'll publish the book *CIA* all over the world. Every CIA officer around the world will become known.'"[10]

Andropov did not appreciate the suggestion.

"Don't do that," he said. "Just use it for our work. It will be more valuable to us that way."[11]

The KGB leadership never informed its own officers that they had been exposed by an American operation—an omission that would frustrate Soviet foreign intelligence officers, as one prominent defector recalled decades later, when they discovered that the main enemy had revealed their names publicly.[12] According to a defected archivist, the KGB would write as many as 370 internal reports on the damage caused by Barron's book, and even engage in a range of elaborate disinformation operations to discredit Barron himself.[13]

Barron, a former naval intelligence officer, was an unusually hard-charging investigative journalist, and his interests neatly aligned with those of the CIA. Meanwhile, a similarly unusual and hard-charging group of political activists had formed in Washington, D.C. Their interests would align with the enemies of the West.

Anti–Vietnam War resistance in the United States peaked in the early 1970s. Daniel Ellsberg's Pentagon Papers started to appear in June 1971. One year later, the Watergate affair began to run its course, further undermining public trust in the security establishment in Washington. In February 1973, three young former military intelligence officers gathered in Washington to channel their antiwar energy against a new target: America's spy agencies. One of them was twenty-seven-year-old Perry Fellwock, who also used a pseudonym, Winslow Peck, which sounded slightly more real than his actual name. Fellwock had joined the Air Force in 1966 and then spent four years as an NSA analyst in Turkey and South Vietnam. Fellwock had traveled to Berkeley to sit with *Ramparts* magazine for about fifty hours of interviews on his work for the NSA. In August 1972, *Ramparts* published a 24,000-word feature on Fellwock, using his Peck pseudonym, titled "U.S. Electronic Espionage: A Memoir."[14] The article, mostly accurate in content, was the first detailed public exposé of NSA eavesdropping operations and the so-called Five Eyes technical intelligence alliance among the United States, Britain, Canada, Australia, and New Zealand. The former NSA analyst saw himself as a whistleblower. "Daniel Ellsberg's releasing the Pentagon Papers made me want to talk," Fellwock told *Ramparts*.[15] The CIA, NSA, and GCHQ—the UK's technical intelligence agency—took note of the publication. So did the KGB.

Joining Fellwock were K. Barton Osborn, twenty-nine, who claimed to have worked as an "agent handler" in U.S. Army Intelligence and Security and that he had served as a consultant for the CIA's infamously brutal Phoenix Program in Vietnam, and twenty-six-year-old Timothy Butz, who had served with Air Force reconnaissance in Vietnam and Germany. The three former intelligence officers vehemently opposed the Five Eyes, which they saw as a "white-Anglo-Saxon-protestant nation communications intelligence dictatorship."[16]

The three activists formed the Committee for Action/Research on the Intelligence Community. Fellwock announced CARIC for the first time over Thanksgiving 1972 in Chicago, on a flyer that he distributed at a conference of the People's Coalition for Peace and Justice, an outfit with links to the Communist Party. Four months later, in March 1973, CARIC published its first—soon to be notorious—bulletin, *Counterspy*. Around the same time, the novelist Norman Mailer had also founded a New York–based organization to investigate American intelligence agencies, and his had a better name: the Fifth Estate. In January 1974, CARIC and the Fifth Estate joined forces and formed the Organizing Committee for a Fifth Estate. The Fifth Estate was a volunteer organization, with new headquarters established at 2000 P Street NW, just off Dupont Circle in Washington, D.C.

The Fifth Estate grew out of late-1960s counterculture, and was especially inspired and modeled on the *Whole Earth Catalog*, then a cult publication. Produced in the San Francisco Bay Area by Stewart Brand, an iconic, technology-embracing hippie maven, the *Whole Earth Catalog* was an early techno-utopian vision of back-to-the-land living that embraced cybernetic feedback loops, community, wholeness, flattened hierarchies, and the motto "access to tools." Brand's catalog would become a prototypical social media platform (and later became the first actual social media platform when it was taken online, in 1984, as the Whole Earth 'Lectronic Link, or WELL).

Inspired by Brand's work, Butz, Osborn, and Peck aimed to consolidate their *Counterspy* bulletins into what they planned to call *The Whole Spy Catalog*, an ever-evolving catalog of their own that would be equally focused on tools and community-building. "*The Whole Spy Catalog* will be an essential working tool for the developing Fifth Estate," they wrote in their first annual report.[17] Indeed, the idealistic pioneers envisioned the Fifth Estate not as an organization but as a movement, as an accountable counterpart to the intelligence community itself, this time with a renewed emphasis on both intelligence and *community*: "The Fifth Estate is a non-partisan, non-profit, alternative intelligence community serving the American public," they wrote in an early issue of *Counterspy*. The young activists had no shortage of self-confidence and bravado. "The Fifth Estate spies on Big Brother," they added, in a characteristic Orwell reference. They aimed to build their new movement around "campus and community based action/research groups."[18] *Counterspy*'s first issue, for example, included a questionnaire for readers to fill out, asking potential contributors to list the intelligence agencies they worked for. The CIA assumed this was an attempt to secure sources.[19]

The Fifth Estate, like the *Whole Earth Catalog*, advocated for greater citizen access to advanced technology. Technology, they argued, must enlighten humanity, not hasten a descent into what they dubbed *technofascism*. Their lofty goal, guided by science fiction, was to "restrain further development of technofascism—the societal form described by George Orwell in his prophetic novel *1984*." Computers, in early 1975, were large and prohibitively expensive machines that served powerful corporate, military, and intelligence

Former CIA officer Philip Agee at a press conference on November 29, 1976. The KGB's code name for Agee was PONT. (Getty Images)

interests—yet the beginnings of the age of personal computing were already anticipated by the counterculture avant-garde. "Technology," the Fifth Estate activists wrote, must not be used "to fill dossiers on our friends, families, and neighbors. As long as advanced technology is controlled by an elite few, technofascism is being advanced and promoted."[20] The activists, with Norman Mailer's support, decided to take some of the tools they acquired working for intelligence agencies and turn them against those very intelligence agencies. As they explained to their readers, "Information gathered by the Fifth Estate goes through a traditional intelligence cycle consisting of: collection, production, analysis, dissemination, and operations."[21] America's alternative intelligence community had thus openly announced that it was planning to run operations against the CIA. Naturally, adversarial intelligence agencies took an interest. The KGB's Service A would soon be in on the action.

Philip Agee was a former CIA officer with eleven years of service for the Agency under his belt.[22] In 1968, Agee was stationed in Mexico City, where his drinking habits, poor financial management, and alleged sexual advances on American diplomats' wives came to the attention of his CIA superiors, who reasoned that Agee's behavior threatened public exposure and asked him to resign.[23] Agee quit in November 1968, at the age of thirty-three.[24]

Ironically, Mader's *Who's Who in CIA* had already exposed Agee with biographical details earlier that year, correctly noting his overseas postings in Ecuador and Uruguay.[25] But the red-bound intelligence directory did not receive wider public attention, partly as a result of the significant number of unreliable forged entries. One day Agee approached the KGB *rezidentura* in Mexico City and offered what one senior Soviet intelligence officer later called "reams of information about CIA operations."[26] The KGB Mexico station chief, however, suspected that Agee was a CIA plant, what spies then called a "dangle," an undercover agent posing as a defector in order to inject disinformation into the KGB, and rejected Agee. Agee then went to Cuba's foreign intelligence agency, the Dirección General de Inteligencia, or DGI, which welcomed its first high-profile CIA source with open arms and soon shared Agee's file with the KGB.[27] Oleg Kalugin recalled the disappointment of failing to recruit the American quasi-defector himself: "The Cubans shared Agee's information with us. But as I sat in my office in Moscow, reading reports about the growing list of revelations coming from Agee, I cursed our officers for turning away such a prize."[28]

In December 1971, Agee moved from Mexico to Paris, where he lived hand-to-mouth at different addresses in the Fifth Arrondissement. It was then that he began to entertain the idea of writing a tell-all book on the CIA. From late 1972 to mid-1977, he lived first in London, then in Truro, Cornwall, and finally in Cambridge, maintaining contact with the KGB through the *Literaturnaya Gazeta* correspondent in London. The KGB would later claim, in a self-congratulatory, likely exaggerated memo, that Agee's tell-all on the CIA was "prepared by Service 'A,' together with the Cubans."[29] Agee himself admitted that he cooperated with the Cuban government: "In Havana, the Biblioteca Nacional José Martí and the Casa de las Américas provided special assistance for research and helped find data available only from government documentation," he wrote in a foreword to his book. "Representatives of the Communist Party of Cuba also gave me important encouragement at a time when I doubted that I would be able to find the additional information I needed."[30] These Cuban party representatives, according to Russian intelligence archives, were agents of the DGI. Agee visited Cuba six times while writing the book.[31] "Quite frankly, I don't care whether they're intelligence officers or not," Agee later said about his Cuban interlocutors.[32] KGB files list

Agee as an agent of the DGI, and provide details of Agee's collaboration with the KGB, but the available documents do not formally list the CIA defector as a Russian agent.[33] Agee later insisted that he had never talked to the KGB.

Inside the Company, Agee's first book, was published in January 1975. Agee exposed the true names of 170 CIA personnel, as well as numerous operations and agents in Latin America. The dump forced the removal of more than one hundred active foreign agents. Two years after publication, the CIA estimated the monetary damage caused by Agee's operation at $2 million, but noted that the actual damage was greater and hard to measure: "There have been many instances in which our liaison contacts are less cooperative and frank than in the past because they feel we can no longer keep secrets."[34] The Agency, which relies on the cooperation of in-country sources, noted that it had encountered "numerous cases of current and prospective clandestine agents" who refused to spy for the United States because, citing Agee's book as an example, they felt the CIA was no longer able to protect their identities.[35]

By the time his book was published, Agee was based in Truro, in the picturesque English countryside, and had recently begun writing for *Counterspy*. Agee also joined the newly assembled advisory board of the Fifth Estate. "Freedoms for future generations can only be insured by vigorous monitoring of our government," wrote Agee and Mailer in *Counterspy*.[36] In the same issue, Agee wrote: "The most effective and important systematic efforts to combat CIA that can be undertaken right now are, I think, the identification, exposure, and neutralization of its people working abroad."[37]

Counterspy's call to "neutralize" CIA staff working abroad was about to have consequences.

On December 23, 1975, Richard Welch was mingling at a Christmas party at the American ambassador's residence in Athens, Greece, accompanied by his wife and daughter. The CIA station chief in Greece, Welch was an amiable man, with round glasses, an orderly mustache, and the manner of a tweedy professor.[38] Just after 10:00 p.m., the Welches returned to Psychiko, an Athens suburb.[39] As they got ready to park, a small black car drove up close, and then, as Welch stepped out of his car, three masked assassins opened fire, hitting him three times, then sped away into the night.[40] Welch died in a local hospital shortly thereafter. The gunmen were members of a Marxist revolutionary organization known as 17 November. The editor of a local English-language daily, *The Athens News*, had exposed Welch as a CIA operative about a month earlier, and printed his home address.

Anonymous sources immediately blamed *Counterspy* for Welch's murder. "This is about as close as you can come to fingering a man," one intelligence source told the *Chicago Tribune* hours after the killing: "They set him up for murder."[41] A year earlier, in December 1974, *Counterspy* had published a detailed list of CIA personnel in a feature titled "Chiefs of Station: Who's Who & What They Do." The article identified Welch as the CIA's man in Lima, Peru, with his date of birth and overseas postings.[42] In an internal memo written after the Athens killing, the CIA determined that the list was "fingering Welch for assassination, wittingly or unwittingly."[43] In fact, however, it was again the KGB, not Agee, who first outed the victim: *Who's Who in CIA* first publicly outed the officer as "Welch, Richard Skeffington," and listed his correct date of birth, date of joining the CIA, and several postings.[44] CIA analysts must have been aware of this detail, but chose to blame *Counterspy* and Agee instead.

In a long internal memo written less than a week after Welch's assassination, the CIA argued that the five main activists then running the Fifth Estate were "probably under Marxist control or operation" and that they had close ties with radical groups, "some of them, at least, Communist controlled or infiltrated."[45] The CIA offered no specific evidence for such bold claims—indeed, it appears that some American intelligence analysts, roiled by the killing of one of their own, had trouble grasping that the goals and methods of newly radicalized activists could so smoothly align with, but not be controlled by, Soviet intelligence. No solid evidence of Communist "control" of *Counterspy* has ever surfaced. The best that the CIA memo could offer was calling into question whether the Fifth Estate was really as poorly funded as it claimed, and pointing not only to the extent of its operations but also its nicely furnished offices on P Street. Even the White House appeared to blame *Counterspy* for the escalation in Athens. In a twisted way, Soviet active measures had penetrated the minds of CIA officers, apparently impairing their ability to analyze in a sober, fact-based, and detached manner.

Welch's assassination in Athens drastically raised the profile of anti-intelligence activism in the United States, especially that of the Fifth Estate and Philip Agee. A week later, Welch was buried at Arlington Cemetery. President Gerald Ford escorted Welch's black-veiled widow at the funeral service, walking right behind the eight marines who carried Welch's coffin through the freezing cold and bright sun. Several generations of diplomats and intelligence officers were present at the rare, somber ceremony, including Secretary of State Henry Kissinger and the current CIA director, William Colby, who had signed off a few years earlier on Barron's book, *KGB*. Welch's name was not mentioned once during the ceremony.[46] What was also left unspoken was an assumption that many intelligence officials held at the time, although there was little evidence to support it: that they had come together in Arlington as the result of a successful Soviet active measure.

The confusion would only get worse. On November 17, 1977, the Home Office in the United Kingdom served Agee with a four-page deportation order, alleging that he had maintained contacts with foreign intelligence operatives and disseminated information deemed harmful to Britain's security.[47] British authorities accused Agee of being a Soviet bloc influence agent without offering concrete evidence and in a context that appeared motivated by domestic political divisions.[48] The deportation order was highly publicized, and offered an opportunity for a major follow-up Russian active measure.

Agee had become a cause célèbre on the left. His supporters prepared a legal case, established a "defense committee," and received the support of more than one hundred members of Parliament, several trade unions, and parts of the wider public. *The Guardian* and other newspapers also sided with Agee. On January 9, nearly five hundred demonstrators marched past the modernist U.S. Embassy in Grosvenor Square.[49] Agee was nominated to be the rector of Dundee University in Scotland. "He is a serious candidate," said the Students' Union. "His actions in exposing the CIA have made him very popular with the student body."[50]

Service A naturally tried to exploit the situation—first by attempting to initiate support campaigns for Agee, and then by taking credit for those campaigns. Anti-American feelings were already strong among the European left, and Agee had become a symbol of resistance. Therefore, paradoxically, it became harder for the KGB to prove success and easier to claim it.

Part of Agee's KGB file was later smuggled out of Russia. The documents referred to Agee under his code name, PONT, and claimed that "campaigns of support for PONT were initiated in France, Spain, Portugal, Italy, Holland, Finland, Norway, Mexico and Venezuela,"[51] which was probably an exaggeration. The KGB's London residency, which among insiders had a reputation for inflated claims,[52] announced that it had been able to "direct" prominent Labour politicians to support Agee.

There was, however, some curious evidence that Service A did attempt to exploit the Agee controversy in Britain that summer. In June 1976, Agee, still in the UK, received a purportedly leaked, confidential State Department document in the mail, dated December 1974 and signed by Henry Kissinger. The document listed "economic, financial, and commercial intelligence requirements" for the United States, and allegedly had been sent out to all embassies. The U.S. Embassy in London soon clarified that the document was a partial forgery, designed to intimate that the United States was engaged in economic subversion of its allies. Agee published the document in mid-1977 in a book in London. KGB files later identified the document as the work of Service A.[53]

In hindsight, the fake leak is noteworthy for an unexpected reason: the active measures officers in the First Chief Directorate mailed the file to Agee *anonymously.* "I hope I will be able to send you more before too long," an unnamed writer said in a cover letter addressed to Agee. "The work that you and others like you are doing is very inspiring. I wish you success." The missive vaguely implied that its author worked for the U.S. government, and was signed by "an admirer."[54] By mid-1976, it appears, Service A was keen to maintain Agee's belief that he was occupying the moral high ground, acting not in the interest of an adversarial spy agency but in support of the higher principles of open, transparent, liberal democracy—so the KGB decided not to reveal its hand to a man who had knowingly approached and received support from Soviet intelligence just a few years earlier. Agee, the KGB shrewdly decided, was more effective and convincing if he could claim to be a genuine part of a movement, to others and, perhaps even more important, to himself.

1975–1989: Escalate

16.

Field Manual 30-31B

THE ROMANCE BETWEEN AGEE AND THE *COUNTERSPY* ACTIV-
ists was brief. Before long, personalities clashed and an internal rift opened, as is common in organizations driven by
energetic activists with big egos. In the summer of 1976, Agee's faction split
away from the Fifth Estate and started a new magazine, the *Covert Action Information Bulletin*. "We have felt, since the beginning, that there is an important and vital role to be played by the sort of exposés for which *Counterspy*
had become world-famous," the editors wrote. "We decided the dissemination of such information must resume." First CAIB was also headquartered
at Dupont Circle, but later relocated into a small office in the National Press
Building in Washington, D.C. The activists were publishing, researching,
and collecting compromising intelligence—in short, they were running their
own form of active measures. The line between activism and active measures

In March 1978, the Red Brigades kidnapped and later killed Aldo Moro, the head of Italy's conservative party. The KGB used a forged U.S. Army manual to blame the CIA for the killing.

had begun to blur, and the KGB no longer needed Agee and his co-editors to be witting influence agents—unwitting, they were even more useful.

Nothing illustrates this new dynamic better than *Covert Action Information Bulletin*. The first editorial, published in the summer of 1978, expressed confidence that there was enough subscriber demand "to make this publication a permanent weapon in the fight against the CIA, the FBI, military intelligence, and all the other instruments of U.S. imperialist oppression throughout the world."[1] The editors encouraged readers to submit leads, tips, suggestions, and guest articles. It was another attempt at a *Whole Earth Catalog* of counterintelligence activism, predating the internet yet already beginning to act like a community engagement platform and outlet for user-generated content and anonymous leaks. In its opening editorial, the new magazine vouched to go after the CIA especially: "we will never stop exposing CIA personnel and operations whenever and wherever we find them."

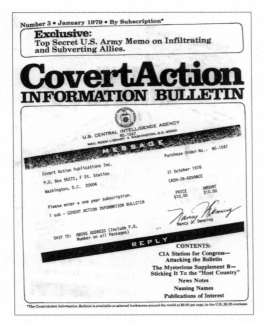

Number 3 • January 1979 • By Subscription*

Exclusive:
Top Secret U.S. Army Memo on Infiltrating and Subverting Allies.

CovertAction
INFORMATION BULLETIN

U.S. CENTRAL INTELLIGENCE AGENCY
NE-1547
MAIL ROOM LIBRARY • WASHINGTON, D.C. 20505

MESSAGE

Purchase Order No.: NE-1547

Covert Action Publications Inc.
P.O. Box 50272, F St. Station
Washington, D.C. 20004

31 October 1978
CASH-IN-ADVANCE

PRICE   AMOUNT
$10.00 $10.00

Please enter a one year subscription.
1 sub - COVERT ACTION INFORMATION BULLETIN

Nancy J. Denning

SHIP TO: ABOVE ADDRESS (Include P.O.
Number on all Packages)

REPLY

CONTENTS:
CIA Station for Congress—
Attacking the Bulletin
The Mysterious Supplement B—
Sticking It To the "Host Country"
News Notes
Naming Names
Publications of Interest

*The CovertAction Information Bulletin is available at selected bookstores around the world at $2.00 per copy, in the U.S.; $2.35 overseas.

Covert Action Information Bulletin, a new anti-intelligence community journal, first published the full English version of the U.S. Army manual FM 30-31B after a self-described Army "whistle-blower" personally delivered the KGB forgery to the activists.

The editors then added a call for submissions, including a post office box address for anonymous mail, emphasizing a particular interest in "copies of US diplomatic lists and US embassy staff and/or telephone directories, from any countries."[2]

The second issue contained a how-to guide for uncovering CIA officers under diplomatic cover, and an "exclusive" column titled "Naming Names" revealed the identities of U.S. intelligence personnel serving under cover in France, Italy, India, Venezuela, and Jordan. In January 1979, in its third issue, the *Bulletin* opened with a bang: "Exclusive: Top Secret U.S. Army Memo on Infiltrating and Subverting Allies." The lead article foreshadowed the future of disinformation. To understand the significance of this extraordinary publication, one must grasp the significance of one of the KGB's most sophisticated and impactful forgeries, known as FM 30-31B.

U.S. Army field manuals are commonly abbreviated as "FM," and usually designated with a number. The 30 series was focused on military intelligence. FM 30-31 was an actual publication on the theory and nature of insurgencies, and the use of military intelligence to crush them, as informed by the Vietnam War. The extensive manual was first issued in 1967, and was updated in 1970 and again in 1972. The document also contained a classified (SECRET NOFORN) supplement, mentioned on its first page, which was designated as FM 30-31A, *Stability Operations—Intelligence Collection*.[3] Doctrinal publications constantly evolve, so in 1981, as the army reconsidered its battlefield approach after defeat in Vietnam, FM 30-31 became obsolete.[4]

The KGB became aware of FM 30-31, including its secret supplement, not long after it was finished in 1970. The disinformation specialists at Service A sensed a triple opening: aggressive U.S. bombing campaigns in Vietnam were fueling anti-Americanism abroad and fracturing the American body politic; Europe was facing a wave of extreme-left activism that veered into militancy and terrorism; and decolonization was sweeping across the developing world, often accompanied by subversion and insurgency. So the Soviet forgers got to work on a document that would exploit all three causes. It would become known as Field Manual 30-31, Supplement B, or FM 30-31B.

The forgery was of very high quality. The document was written in a nearly flawless rendition of the drab, bureaucratic English, sprinkled with abbreviations and jargon, commonly used in U.S. military manuals. FM 30-31B started off with an explanation of why it was a top-secret document with restricted circulation: because the army considered friendly "host nation agencies" a target for U.S. intelligence operations. "The fact that U.S. Army involvement goes deeper can in no circumstances be acknowledged," the document said. It went on:

> U.S. involvement in these less-developed nations threatened by
> insurgency is part of the world-wide U.S. involvement in the struggle
> against Communism. Insurgency may have other than Communist
> origins; in tribal, social, religious, or regional differences. But,
> whatever its source, the fact of insurgency offers opportunities
> for Communist infiltration which, in the absence of effective
> countermeasures, may culminate in successful Communist take-over.

The forgers included sentences designed to antagonize third countries, and bound to cause insult, for example: "Few of the less-developed nations provide fertile soil for democracy in any meaningful sense."[5]

FM 30-31B wasn't designed just to embarrass the United States. The forgery was a stroke of genius—and performed a veritable jujitsu move on the CIA. The disinformation artists of Service A effectively managed to re-define far-left, anti-American militants as American puppets, creating a self-radicalizing, positive feedback loop: violently resisting American power would only prove the strength of American power, and thus trigger more violent resistance. The conceptual trick came on page 11, under the heading "Agents in Special Operations": "There may be times when [host country] governments show passivity or indecision in face of Communist or Communist-inspired subversion, and react with inadequate vigor to intelligence estimates transmitted by U.S. agencies."

In short, the United States wanted its allies to crack down on radical leftists when told to do so. The document continued:

> Such situations are particularly likely to arise when the insurgency seeks to achieve tactical advantage by temporarily refraining from violence, thus lulling [host country] authorities into a state of false security.

Moderate militants were even more dangerous than raging radicals, the faux manual implied. Next came the instruction for U.S. troops:

> In such cases, the U.S. Army intelligence must have the means of launching special operations which will convince [host country] governments and public opinion of the reality of the insurgent danger and of the necessity of counteraction.

The United States needed to convince gullible allies that they were in danger of political violence by *engaging* in political violence:

> To this end, U.S. Army intelligence should seek to penetrate the
> insurgency by means of agents on special assignment, with the task
> of forming special action groups among the core radical elements of
> the insurgency. When the kind of situation envisioned above arises,
> these groups, acting under U.S. Army intelligence control, should be
> used to launch violent or nonviolent actions according to the nature
> of the case.[6]

The fake document concluded "by order of the Secretary of the Army," and was signed by the U.S. Army chief of staff, W. C. Westmoreland.

The KGB's fantastic forgery provided a twisted but appealing rationale for why the CIA would secretly engage in far-left terrorist attacks. In one sweep the forged document would also render American denials incredible, at least among those who were becoming more and more critical of America's global engagement and the spread of military bases overseas. The disinformation masterpiece laid the groundwork for one of the most pernicious and persistent conspiracy theories of the twentieth century.

Supplement B would soon be put to work.

In the summer of 1974, Turkey invaded Cyprus, its neighbor and fellow NATO member. The crisis called the close military cooperation and assistance between Turkey and the United States into question, all as Turkey began to experience a bout of domestic political violence. Then, in late March 1975,[7] a Turkish magazine, *Barış*, carried a major news story about a mysterious U.S. Army manual, titled "Field Manual 30-31, Stability Operations—Intelligence," dated January 1970. *Barış* implied that the U.S. government was secretly using its foreign military bases to orchestrate political violence in friendly countries, and began to serialize the secret "Supplement B" to the insurgency manual. The magazine treated the fake manual as a blueprint for American interference in Turkish affairs, and included a piecemeal translation of the full document in a detailed 46-part series that ran daily. Still, despite the publicity in Turkey, the story soon subsided.

Over the following year, American military assistance in the Philippines increased drastically. The United States had stationed nearly 13,700 military personnel on bases there. On September 14, 1976, the mysterious insurgency manual resurfaced. An anonymous, self-described "concerned citizen" in Thailand left a photocopy of the top-secret supplement to FM 30-31B at the Philippines Embassy in Bangkok, where a janitor found it early in the morning of September 16. The embassy, confused by the sudden appearance of a top-secret American document, passed the document complete with envelope and cover letter to the U.S. embassy in Bangkok. The letter was addressed to Ferdinand Marcos, president of the Philippines, and was supposedly written by an American whistle-blower in Thailand. The letter obliquely referred to "some secret American documents revealing the dangers of the countries concerned of having U.S. troops and advisers stationed on their territories."[8] The alleged source justified the leak of classified material in the last paragraph: "I am doing this as one of an American group opposed to excessive U.S. military involvement in matters beyond the scope of reasonable American interest." The letter did not refer to the earlier surfacing in *Barış*.

Two years later, in the fall of 1978, the document appeared once again, this time in Spain. The country had just overcome the dictatorship of Francisco Franco, and a bitter debate on whether to join NATO was beginning to divide the country. The Soviet Union was gravely concerned that the incorporation of Spain into NATO could alter the balance of power in Europe. A Cuban intelligence officer shopped the full document, and an accompanying article, to news outlets in Madrid. *El Triunfo*, a far-left weekly magazine with links to the Spanish Communist Party, printed the translated FM 30-31B along with an article by Fernando Gonzalez, a member of the Spanish Communist Party in close contact with a KGB-linked officer at the Soviet embassy in Madrid. Gonzalez used the document as evidence that the United States was deeply involved with radical terrorist groups in Western Europe, and specifically named the Italian Red Brigades as an example, including the infamous "Moro affair"—a dramatic incident that began six months before *El Triunfo* printed the KGB forgery.

On March 16, 1978, a dozen members of Italy's most notorious terrorist group, the Red Brigades, blocked the path of two cars, one carrying Aldo

Moro, the head of Italy's main conservative party, the Christian Democrats. The attackers mowed down Moro's five bodyguards with machine guns and kidnapped the politician. The police found 710 bullet casings at the scene. Moro had been on his way to the prime minister in order to request a vote of confidence for Italy's first Communist-supported government in more than thirty years. Italy was immediately seized by crisis.

Radio Moscow pounced. Hours after Moro's kidnapping, the station's English-language shortwave broadcast called the abduction a "crime of reaction," and darkly hinted at many "attempts by a right-wing force to aggravate the situation in Italy." Two days later, in an Italian-language broadcast, Radio Moscow alleged, in contradiction of the established facts, that the kidnapping was "prepared by internal and international reactionary forces." In another broadcast two days later, Radio Moscow quoted L'Humanité, a French Communist Party newspaper, reporting—again without evidence—that the real culprits of the abduction were "secret services whose activity is connected with the NATO military base in Naples." Then, on April 2, with Moro still abducted and alive: "Well, to call a spade a spade, that service behind the kidnapping is called the Central Intelligence Agency."[9]

The prolonged crisis, exacerbated by pictures of Moro appearing in the press and one false claim that he had been killed, offered fertile ground for conspiracy theories. Over time, many Italians came to believe that the Red Brigades weren't actually red, but black—that is, they weren't Communist, but secretly Fascist. TASS, the Soviet Union's official news agency, encouraged this line of thinking by claiming that the Red Brigades were only operating under a mask of leftism, that they had outside help, and that the operation's real goal was to induce a rightward shift. On May 9, Moro's bullet-riddled body was found under a blanket in the trunk of a red Renault R-4 parked halfway between the Christian Democrat and the Communist Party headquarters in Rome.[10]

So, when El Triunfo printed FM 30-31B, Italy held the most important audience.[11] To many Italians, the field manual finally offered documentary evidence of a spy plot. The Milan-based weekly L'Europeo, left-leaning and often sharply critical of the United States, published detailed excerpts and pictures of the forged documents that the magazine's editors considered "absolutely authentic."[12] "In the Moro case we are talking more and more about an international conspiracy," *L'Europeo* reported,[13] arguing that Italy was currently in phase two of an armed insurrection, marked by an expansion of criminal acts and selective terrorism, according to the sequencing of the U.S. manual.

As soon as the piece came out, *L'Europeo*'s publisher, Giovanni Valentini, received a letter from the U.S. embassy in Rome. An American diplomat told him that publishing the document would be "inopportune."[14] Valentini, convinced that the document was genuine, printed a second article, along with the embassy's letter.[15] Attempting to contain the spreading conspiracy theory, the State Department wrote in its letter that the document was fake: "The article published in *Triunfo* assumed the existence of a 'supplement' to U.S. Army Field Manual FM 30-31, an unclassified publication. Such a supplement has never existed," a U.S. Foreign Service officer explained to Valentini, making a mistake that would soon backfire in the United States. Supplement B may not have been genuine, but Supplement A was real.

The conspiracy theory only spread from there. In December 1978, the *World Marxist Review* hinted that the CIA had secretly used the Red Brigades or instigated them to assassinate Moro. "There arises the suspicion that the 'Red Brigades' (or those who manipulate them in Italy) are pro-Fascist organizations skillfully camouflaged as 'reds,'" the Marxists wrote. "A few months later this was confirmed by a secret document which appeared in an October issue of the journal *L'Europeo*." The forgery and subsequent claims were so convincing that several foreign governments made inquiries to the U.S. government, and the Italian Senate launched an investigation. So far, the full forgery had not been published in English.

Then, one day in late 1978, the U.S.-based team of the new *Covert Action Information Bulletin* was approached by a potential source. Three editors, William Schaap, Ellen Ray, and Louis Wolf, met with an unnamed man just outside Washington. The anonymous "whistle-blower," as Wolf termed him, said he worked for the U.S. Army and that he had experience in the area of "destabilization," in counterinsurgency, and that he had seen enough. The man was wearing civilian clothes, but from the manner in which he spoke, Wolf recalled, the editors inferred that their source was "clearly a man of the military." He mentioned Field Manual 30-31, and then offered the full Supplement B to the activists.

Ray, Schaap, and Wolf were intrigued. So far they had published only two issues of the *Covert Action Information Bulletin,* and they were keen to break news to make a name for their journal. The setup was too good to be true. "We were afraid to ask too many questions," Wolf commented later, "because we were concerned not to get the document."[16]

Eventually the mysterious source handed over the document, and the editors busied themselves with trying to confirm the top-secret material at hand. "We read that thing six ways to Sunday and back," Wolf remembered. They decided to publish the full English version in their third issue, albeit transcribed and not in the original layout.

FM 30-31B represents a turning point in the history of disinformation, a moment when active measures became fully activated. Disinformation operations rely upon tactics that exploit technology, political divisions, and tensions between allies. Political fissures and friction are a function of the target. The design of the divisive material and the craftsmanship of disinformation are a function of the attacker. The technological substrate and the available media platforms are a function of the operational environment. The higher the quality of all three, the more active a measure will be—or, put another way, the lesser the political divisions within the target organization, and the more primitive the telecommunications environment, the more value the attacker will have to add at all stages of an operation in order to make and sustain an active measure.

FM 30-31B, therefore, can be seen as an important high-water mark in the history of active measures. The Vietnam War had introduced new and deep divisions into American society specifically and the West more generally. Ellsberg, Fellwock, and even Agee were radicalized by America's conduct on the battlefield in Southeast Asia. The rise of improved printing technology and then the personal computer was starting to make community organization and new media creation easier than ever, as illustrated by the Fifth Estate, *Counterspy*, and the *Covert Action Information Bulletin*. The *Bulletin's* publication of the forgery was accompanied by an equally masterful piece of investigative conspiracy theory.

"Is the document genuine?" William Schaap asked. He then offered the following explanation for why he and the other editors believed it to be so:

> When the document was referred to in Turkey, there was no response from the U.S. When it was published in full in Spain, there was no response. When the [U.S.] Embassy heard that it was to be published in Italy, they informed the publisher of a major magazine [*L'Europeo*] that it would be "inopportune" to do so, and when it appeared that it would nevertheless be published, the Embassy announced that the document was a forgery—in a letter which said there was "no" supplement to FM 30-31, a statement which was itself untrue.[17]

All this was correct. Schaap concluded that it was "hard to imagine" that the document was not genuine, and added that "we believe, as do publishers in several other countries already, that the document is real."[18] The entrepreneurial activists had added real value to an existing active measure, and improved its performance.

Only months after the original FM 30-31B had finally been published in Washington, the KGB continued to put the manual to work abroad. But elsewhere, activism was not yet as helpful as it was in the United States. In the mid-1970s, Portugal had finally overcome dictatorship, and was turning toward the West. In the summer of 1979, Soviet officers prepared Portuguese-language translations of FM 30-31B, and started covertly circulating the manual among military officers in Lisbon.

The impact of the *Covert Action Information Bulletin* did not stop there. Louis Wolf, one of the editors, was a conscientious objector who said that the napalm bombings of the Laotian villages where he labored in the 1960s had pushed him over the edge into activism.[19] A decade later, he focused on researching the names to expose. His work ethic bordered on the obsessive.

Wolf's apartment was a ten-minute walk from the National Archives, where, for the better part of five years, he spent eight to ten hours a day researching names in various diplomatic registers, retracing the careers of American diplomats, devoting a couple of hours to each name. Wolf owned a worn copy of *Who's Who in CIA*, but, he said, "we didn't put too much stock in the Mader book."[20] Instead, Wolf used a methodology laid out in an infamous article published in a Washington magazine, titled "How to Spot a Spook," from 1974.[21]

On July 2, 1980, at a news conference in Kingston, Jamaica, Wolf mentioned some of the names he had researched in the National Archives.[22] Jamaican television rebroadcast the details, including addresses, telephone numbers, license plates, and the names of fourteen alleged CIA officers at the Kingston station, shortly thereafter.

Two days later, three men attacked the home of Richard Kinsman, a U.S. embassy official. The would-be assassins fired twenty .45-caliber bullets from a submachine gun about one hundred feet away, hitting the concrete walls of Kinsman's house. The attackers also detonated a grenade on the front lawn. Kinsman, who was at home, was unhurt.[23] The attack came only forty-eight hours after Wolf's televised press conference. The *Covert Action Information Bulletin* had named Kinsman—likely correctly[24]—as the CIA's Jamaica station chief in its October 1979 issue.

Activism and active measures became harder and harder to tell apart.

Service A

HE KGB'S FOREIGN INTELLIGENCE ARM, THE FIRST CHIEF DI-
rectorate, was still housed at KGB headquarters in the Lubyanka when Department D was upgraded to Service A in the
early 1960s. But the old offices were becoming overcrowded and crammed.
Finally, in June 1972, the First Chief Directorate moved[1] to its new home in
a vast, Y-shaped modernist building complex in the forest southwest of the
capital, near Yasenevo—Moscow's equivalent to Langley. A Finnish architect had created a sleek design with a winged tower, its access ways and parking lots elegantly integrated into the forest landscape, air-conditioned offices
overlooking birches and meadows, and several well-appointed libraries. The
futuristic amphitheater in white marble could seat an audience of eight hundred, and the headquarters further boasted a gym, pool, soccer pitch, tennis
courts, and even a *banya* (sauna bath) for higher-ups.[2] The road sign on the

The modernist building of the KGB's First Chief Directorate, "The Forest," outside Moscow (Marina Lystseva)

approach simply read "Scientific Research Center." The internal KGB nickname for the remote intelligence center was *Les*, or "The Forest," spoken with envy. By 1985, Service A occupied more than half of the space on the third floor.[3]

The head of Service A was Vladimir Petrovich Ivanov. Formerly undercover as a TASS correspondent in Vienna, in 1975 he took over as head of Service A, where he would stay until 1990. In 1979, Ivanov gave two secret briefings, "The Role and Place of Active Measures in Intelligence,"[4] and the other on the use of "influence agents."[5] Among the audience was Colonel Dimo Stankov, head of the Bulgarian disinformation unit. Stankov brought back to Sofia almost thirty pages of notes from his weeklong stay in Moscow.

Stankov's workshop notes, carefully typed up back in Sofia, are the most detailed and reliable glimpse at the doctrine of disinformation as it stood in the spring of 1979. Indeed, these briefing transcripts are the single best primary source on the organization of Soviet active measures. The KGB never opened its most secret archives; the Stasi's HVA destroyed or hastily dispatched to Moscow its most sensitive operational documents and files just after the Berlin Wall came down. But a large number of extraordinary documents survived in the archives of Bulgarian state security, one of the KGB's most aggressive and esteemed foreign partners, including in the business of disinformation.

Ivanov noted that Service A was established in 1959.[6] The Communist Party then consolidated the new service within the KGB's First Chief Directorate. The agency was already running active measures at an impressive tempo by 1960, when the CIA held its first congressional hearings on Soviet forgeries, and its pace only picked up as more resources flowed into Service A. Sergei Kondrashev, who briefly headed the unit in 1968, estimated that he reviewed "three or four new proposals a day," which he recounted added up to "surely hundreds every year."[7] That figure counted only the USSR's operations.

By 1979, active measures had hit a peak. Influence operations had steadily risen in importance within the KGB's foreign intelligence organization, and active measures had become so widespread that different parts of the Soviet intelligence and military establishment wanted to be part of the disinformation game. "Active measures have become too common and too successful," said Ivanov in 1979, just after FM 30-31B came to the end of its life cycle and just before OPLAN 10-1 was recycled yet again. "The divisions of the KGB have acquired a certain taste [for active measures], and many now insist they can prepare and conduct them on their own," he complained, his frustration that Service A had to defend its turf internally thinly veiled.

Nonetheless, the KGB insisted on strict centralization when planning and executing active measures. Vladimir Kryuchkov, head of the First Chief Directorate since 1974, argued that active measures had taken "their rightful place in the overall enterprise of intelligence."[8] Kryuchkov issued a special order that governed the administrative setup of active measures in the KGB. Proposals that originated in the field would have to be authorized by the head of Service A or his deputies, and any active measures to be implemented in field residencies would have to be signed off by the head of the relevant regional unit at the KGB.

In fact, many disinformation operations originated in the field, or with a desk officer at headquarters with country-specific expertise. But Ivanov insisted on signing off on every operation. When particularly sensitive agents were involved, or when the KGB's Operations Department did not want to have their identities disclosed to lower-ranking officers, only the head of Service A was looped in. Only the leadership had high visibility into the entire range of operations, some executed by partner agencies in the Soviet bloc. "Work in this area requires a great deal of precision," Ivanov insisted. "There must be a center, to avoid unwanted failures and blunders."

Ivanov chaired a monthly meeting to discuss overarching disinformation themes for different world regions. The day-to-day work, by contrast, was more in tune with current events, both at the center and to a greater extent in the field. Each December, Ivanov's outfit prepared reports on the past year of active measures work performed by each KGB station; in January, a plan was set with specific actions for the new year. Specific active measures were assigned deadlines and responsibilities. Service A also set an overarching two-to-three-year master plan and prepared a daily bulletin, classified as top secret, on ongoing active measures worldwide.[9]

The "A" in Service A was usually in quotes in internal memos, and measures simply referred to as "AM." Service A also worked with external experts and contractors. Ivanov oversaw a range of covert operators who kept in touch with fifty to sixty scientists, researchers, and specialists, usually not revealing their identity and purpose to these useful outsiders, although some were trusted agents. Not all were Russian. The disinformation division would commission these outside consultants, for a fee, to carry out research on issues of political, economic, historical, or cultural interest to the KGB. Some of these paid disinformation consultants, as the KGB's internal documentation showed, were international journalists.

Ideally, an "AM" would start and end in the field *rezidenturas*. Service A would talent-spot among young, promising officers, who would then be pulled into Service A for one to two years, to familiarize them with the administrative disinformation process, before they were posted abroad. As

The fake memoirs of a Chilean
general, Carlos Prats, drafted
by Service A and polished
by a Chilean writer, Eduardo
Labarca, who was recruited by
the KGB as a consultant for
this project

Ivanov described the setup, "In the service they participate in the development of the actions from the beginning to the end."

Ivanov named as an example of a successful operation the forged diaries of the assassinated Chilean defense minister Carlos Prats. The 137-page
book, titled *Una vida por la legalidad* (A life within the law), appeared in
paperback in 1977 in Mexico.[10] Prats's assassination was a pivotal event in
Augusto Pinochet's 1973 coup, and the unexpected appearance of his memoirs was "arousing more interest than just about anything else written about
Chile's socialist experiment and its bloody consequences," according to an
unsuspecting news article and review that was published in *The Washington
Post* and *The Guardian* that March.[11] Almost certainly, a Service A memo
would have cited the high-profile press coverage as proof of success. "Two
operatives had worked on this document for more than a year," Ivanov said
in his briefing. "The diaries have anti-American content, and were printed in
Mexico."[12]

In the case of Prats's diary, the consultant was Eduardo Labarca, a writer and journalist exiled from Pinochet's Chile who was then working for Radio Moscow. Ivanov's officers approached the Chilean writer through an exiled intermediary in the Chilean Communist Party, not long after Prats's assassination. The undercover officers suggested that he help them write an "improved" memoir.

Labarca, fiercely opposed to the brutal Pinochet dictatorship, did not see any ethical problem at the time and agreed. Labarca's handler was a KGB operative, under TASS cover, who had been friendly with Labarca back in Chile. The handler never mentioned the KGB explicitly, but Labarca understood who his handler was referring to when he used the ominous "we" to refer to a powerful secret organization. "It was one hundred percent clear who they were," Labarca told me, forty years later. "I knew that I was involved in an intelligence operation."[13]

Labarca was already a paid employee of Radio Moscow, and did not receive additional money from his handler—although he was tasked to work exclusively on the fake book for several weeks. He soon received a first draft, which was, he recalled, "badly written."[14] Prats was a cultured man, and the language in the KGB draft of the general's "memoirs" was too plain. The Service A authors also did not appreciate some local Chilean complexities: although Prats had loyally worked for the Allende government, he was not ideologically as committed to communism as the KGB ghostwriters made him out to be. About a month later, Labarca returned a more professional, more credible text, which won him praise from his handlers.

An "AM" such as the Prats forgery, Ivanov explained, would be first authorized by his own signature, as the head of Service A; then by the chief of the operative regional unit; the deputy chief of the responsible directorate in charge of Chile; and then—one level up—by the head of the First Chief Directorate; and finally, in the case of high-impact operations, by the KGB director.

Service A produced three types of plans for day-to-day disinformation activities, each approved by the head of the First Chief Directorate: the "prospective plan," which covered a long-term outlook; a two-to-three-year plan, which articulated basic directions focused on a specific region or country or on an individual problem, such as NATO force modernization; and an annual, department-specific plan. Often the Russian disinformation unit coordinated such annual plans with partner disinformation units, and the East German Department X, for instance, would in turn agree on annual plans with Prague's operatives. These plans contain a detailed list of individual active measures, complete with specific objectives, targets, and assigned responsibilities, and are therefore an invaluable source for the historian of disinformation.

Oral disinformation, as Ivanov outlined in his 1979 lecture, could be highly effective, even deadly, especially in developing countries. On November 20, 1979, a group of several hundred extremist insurgents seized Islam's holiest site, the Grand Mosque in Mecca. It took Saudi special forces nearly two weeks to reclaim the holy compound, with assistance from Pakistani and French commandos. The KGB was not involved in this crisis—not yet.

One day later, though, Service A made its move. One goal of Soviet policy in Pakistan at the time was to weaken Muhammad Zia-ul-Haq, the unflinchingly pro-American president. The KGB instructed Soviet agents, likely through the Press and Information Department at the Soviet embassy in Islamabad, to spread the rumor—by word of mouth—that the U.S. government was behind the seizure of the Grand Mosque. Radio Pakistan first announced the attack in mid-morning on November 21, without specifying that fundamentalists were executing the attack. A high-level U.S. intelligence report later revealed, "Soviet diplomats spread the rumor in late 1979 that the United States was behind the seizure of the Grand Mosque in Mecca."[15]

The false story spread through Pakistan like a fire in dry brush.[16] By midday the effects were apparent. Protesters spontaneously gathered outside the American Embassy, and the armed and angry group of Pakistani youths quickly swelled to more than one thousand. Two marines guarding the embassy tried to disperse the crowd by firing shots in the air, but the situation escalated, and one marine was struck and killed by return rifle fire from the crowd. More than one hundred staff members retreated to a high-security, steel-lined room on the top floor in the red-brick embassy.[17] Then the mob set

A Pakistan Army helicopter flies over the burning American Embassy after it was attacked by anti-American demonstrators in Islamabad on November 20, 1979. Soviet disinformation operators whipped up the deadly protest, and claimed it as their success. (AP Photo)

the embassy on fire. The flames climbed up the building, roasting the floor in the crowded code vault. Hours later, when the floor coating started to bubble from the heat below, and when breathing in the vault became nearly impossible, the embassy staff made a dramatic escape through a roof hatch. Two Americans and two Pakistanis were killed in the frenzy. Similar attacks happened in American cultural centers in Rawalpindi and Lahore, along with demonstrations at consulates in Karachi and Peshawar.

The near-catastrophic events in Islamabad were widely covered in the American and international press. That publicity, in turn, presented another opportunity for an active measure, this time one that could strike directly at President Zia. Amid the chaos of the Islamabad incident, with the Grand Mosque in Saudi Arabia still under siege, Soviet intelligence officers now turned to third countries and spread the rumor that the Pakistan Army was secretly responsible for burning the Islamabad Embassy: "KGB officers and Soviet diplomats in Islamabad tried to convince third-country officials and even U.S. personnel that the Pakistani Army was involved in the burning of the U.S. embassy," a U.S. intelligence study based on clandestine sources noted a year later.[18]

According to Stankov's notes, Ivanov concluded his presentation with a few observations on "the concept of disinformation." Ivanov pointed out that Service A had first been marked by a "D." The name change had a deeper meaning. "After many years of practice and theoretical generalizations, the comrades from Service 'A' have brought some clarity to the concept of disinformation," Ivanov explained, specifically on the "working methods that are widely used are exposing, compromising, and influencing governments, organizations, and individuals." He cautioned against getting "carried away" by the excessive development of forgeries. In the early 1970s, oral disinformation had been a backwater, but by 1979, the power of the spoken word accounted for around one-quarter of his unit's active measures work. "That's why we need people—agents of influence, with confidential ties, who will keep secret our involvement in these measures."

Ivanov explained that it was very important to understand the specific target of a disinformation operation. Diplomats were softer targets than intelligence officers, he said. "An intelligence officer will by default report data to the relevant agency, where serious analysis will reveal the forgery." Not so diplomats. "If the target is a career diplomat, he is required to inform his ambassador, who, without much analysis, will forward the information to his ministry."[19]

Finally, by the time of Ivanov's briefing, Service A was encountering new challenges: technology, computers, and even hacking. The KGB was running such a large number of active measures that merely keeping track of all the operations was a major undertaking, and Russia's well-resourced spy agency had adopted cutting-edge computer technology for that purpose. Office staff readied a punch card for each proposed disinformation operation. The card was prepared for "mathematical processing and perforation, then transferred to the computerized machine," Ivanov explained. The KGB's disinformation machine was called Актив-1, or "Active-1." Demand was so high that Active-2, a second large computer, was already in preparation. Without such "strict accounting," no operations could be executed, or planning for after-action assessment.

Service A had its own cipher clerks and two cipher machines to handle secure, encrypted communications, both outgoing and incoming, on disinformation in the making. The disinformation planners were supported by the KGB's encryption service, which handed key material directly to Ivanov's personal staff.

Technology didn't just improve the execution of active measures, however; it also worked against them. Ivanov noted that, for example, improved satellite reconnaissance and the West's signals intelligence capabilities made active measures about any military movements much more difficult. New technologies created new forensic problems.

Technology also created new targets. Not long after Ivanov's presentation, his unit reportedly engaged in the first disinformation hack of a telecommunication system.

In October 1981, a large Soviet nuclear-armed submarine ran aground near Sweden's Karlskrona Naval Base, violating Swedish territorial waters. The incident was highly embarrassing for the Kremlin. To deflect some political heat, Russian intelligence launched a small active measures campaign that took advantage of a new semi-electronic messaging system called the Mailgram, a 1970s invention of Western Union. A sender could relay a message to Western Union, by phoning it in, for instance, and the firm would then transmit the message electronically to a post office close to the recipient, where the message would be printed out and physically delivered by mail. But the Mailgram setup was easy to exploit.

All of a sudden, on November 8, a dozen Mailgrams started appearing across Washington, offering dirt on Swedish-American relations. The U.S. ambassador to Sweden received one, as did the Swedish mission to the United Nations in New York, and several newspapers in the United States and Europe. Also, perhaps to trip up investigators, one message apiece was sent to a Polish journalist and to a TASS correspondent who had just left the United States.

While the Mailgrams were circulating in the Washington area, on November 10, 1981, TASS alleged that Sweden, a neutral country and not a NATO member, had carried out radio-signal reconnaissance against Russia and its allies on behalf of NATO.

One of the Mailgrams, sent to Albert Bobikov of TASS, was a forged offer of a leak from Fred Iklé, the U.S. undersecretary of defense for policy. The Iklé impersonator offered an "official copy of U.S. Swedish agreement on use of Karlskrona Naval Base Sweden for U.S. satellite reconnaissance monitoring of Poland from relay station which sends up coded signals to satellite giving it commands to photograph Poland from Karlskrona." The message was phoned in and relayed in remarkably bad English: "Please reply if interested in copy of Swedish U.S. agreement of such I found myself completely disgusted with my government and its knowledge of Swedish neutrality."[20]

An agent phoned the Mailgrams to a Western Union office in New Jersey between November 8 and 11, 1981. But the Western Union clerk did not obtain the number from the source, so the FBI was not able to use it as a first lead to identifying who might have prepared the Mailgrams. Instead, the attackers spoofed false senders, and had Western Union send the bill to the impersonated users.[21] Service A had the bill sent to the Swedish ambassador to the United States, Wilhelm Wachtmeister, two senior U.S. State Department officials, and one Pentagon official. All told the FBI that they did not, in fact, send the messages falsely attributed to them.

The Soviets had hacked the system. They called the Western Union toll-free number and exploited an authentication flaw in the architecture of the mailing system. The toll-free calls were routed to a central Western Union facility in New Jersey, where one of many operators took the call. The operator then typed the text of the Mailgram into a computer, read the text back to the caller, and then electronically relayed the message to a Western Union facility closer to the Mailgram's destination (in the case of Washington, that delivery station was Middletown, Virginia). Western Union did not independently confirm the recipient's address or the telephone number to which the unauthenticated caller asked to bill the charges. "Obviously," concluded the FBI, "the true senders of the Mailgrams were aware that they could have the charges billed to the addresses or telephone numbers of the alleged senders without verification."[22]

Whoever wrote the documents, the FBI pointed out, had a solid knowledge of satellite photo reconnaissance operations. The forgers also had nonpublic knowledge of senior officers in the U.S. Department of State and in the Pentagon. "So it was not an amateurish job, to say the least," one FBI investigator told Congress. The language used in the Mailgrams, however, was "substandard," in the FBI's assessment, which suggested to the feds that the messages were drafted by non-native English speakers.

The perpetrators of this operation were not positively identified, according to an FBI report submitted to Congress in 1982. But federal counterintelligence officials considered the evidence and in light of the historical and geopolitical context: "Circumstantial evidence thus suggests that this was a Soviet operation."[23]

The Neutron Bomb

NEUTRON WEAPONS ALWAYS EXUDED AN EERIE FASCINATION. In 1960, when specialists in the U.S. military considered them only a theoretical concept, Senator Thomas Dodd of Connecticut alluded in a talk on the future of war to the possibility of adjusting the energy of an atomic explosion so that "instead of heat and blast its primary product is a burst of neutrons." This burst of neutrons, the senator said, would do negligible physical damage, but it would immediately kill all life in the target area; as *The New York Times* put it, such a weapon "would, in short, operate as a kind of death ray." The U.S. Army developed the new device to better deter Soviet armored divisions—it was less contaminating and caused less collateral damage than tactical nuclear weapons. The Soviet Union immediately opposed the neutron bomb.[1]

In early July 1977, news broke that the United States had successfully

A sign reading "Neutron Bomb NO" at the Cologne airport, awaiting Leonid Brezhnev's 1978 visit. The anti-neutron-bomb campaign was one of the Cold War's best-funded and most successful active measures. (Photograph by Steche / ullstein bild via Getty Images)

detonated the weapon. "Neutron Bomb Tested!" screamed the front page of the *Los Angeles Times*. Protesters immediately mobilized; a small group of determined activists even collected their own blood in vials, which they flung against the stone pillars framing the river entrance to the Department of Defense.[2] With blood dripping from the Pentagon, the Soviet Union's covert action infrastructure began to mobilize as well. Its operational objective was threefold: to prevent the NATO-wide deployment of what the U.S. military called "enhanced radiation weapons"; to divide NATO by pitching European allies against the United States; and to distract from the Soviets' own simultaneous military expansion.

Over the next two weeks, in July 1977, the Soviet Union ramped up the number of press stories on the neutron bomb issue. The CIA monitored more than 3,000 broadcast items weekly. Ten days after the first test, 5 percent of all Soviet bloc news stories were covering the neutron bomb. A week later the level rose to 13 percent, more than any other topic. On August 1, 1977, the official Soviet news agency announced an International Week of Action Against the Neutron Bomb.[3] One commentator in *Izvestia* called the new technology "inhuman." The Patriarch of the Russian Orthodox Church called the weapon "satanic." Indeed, viewed from a Communist perspective, the neutron bomb was the ultimate capitalist weapon: a destroyer of people, not property. The Soviets understood that such an anti-capitalist critique would be even more powerful when it came from blue-collar factory workers. "I will never forget the stern privations that fell to the lot of our people during World War II," a worker from the Motor Repair Factory No. 1 was quoted in *Vechernyaya Moskva*, an evening paper: "Fascist Germany wanted then to wipe off the face of the earth Moscow, Leningrad, Kiev, and other Soviet cities and villages and to turn all of us into obedient slaves. The American imperialists have gone even further, blasphemously declaring that the neutron bomb will only kill people, leaving all material structures intact."[4]

Two days earlier another paper attributed a nearly identical quote to a worker in Uzbekistan, 1,500 miles south of Moscow.

In mid-July, *Der Spiegel* ran a cover story titled "*Neutronen-Bombe*, America's Wonder-Weapon for Europe." The magazine argued that the new radiation weapon would lower the threshold for nuclear use, and thus render more probable an all-out nuclear war that would rage across Germany. Europeans were genuinely concerned about the weapon, and the Soviets worked hard to fan the flames. Various front groups were mobilized for the cause. Peace councils organized protest meetings in a number of Eastern bloc countries in Europe, and the official newspapers of various European Communist parties published anti-neutron-bomb commentaries.[5]

"What had begun as a manifestly Soviet effort now appeared to many as a general public reaction to the alleged horrors of the 'neutron bomb,'" the CIA concluded a year later.[6]

The Carter administration announced in September 1977 that the president would not approve production of so-called enhanced radiation weapons unless America's NATO allies in Europe agreed to deploy them as well. The announcement provided an opening for the Soviets: public opinion in Europe could now shape a U.S. military policy—and active measures, in turn, could shape public opinion in Europe. The anti-neutron-bomb campaign shifted from the United States to Europe. Leonid Brezhnev, Khrushchev's successor and the fifth leader of the USSR, mailed a letter to every Western European head of state, warning them that a NATO deployment of the neutron bomb would threaten détente. These announcements, as the CIA observed, received heavy media coverage worldwide.[7]

The United Nations' first Special Session on Disarmament was held in New York from May 23 to June 28, 1978. The Soviets softened the ground ahead of the summit with a barrage of apparently grassroots peace movement events. By early February, the World Peace Council, through a "sub-front," as the CIA later determined, organized a symposium in Vienna in collaboration with the International Atomic Energy Agency, an official UN body, and put the neutron bomb on the agenda. Twenty-two different country delegations attended. The main event, however, was held in Amsterdam, beginning on March 18, and was organized mainly by the Dutch Communist Party. The Dutch minister of defense, a Christian Democrat named Roelof Kruisinga, had just resigned in protest against his government's refusal to condemn the weapon, triggering a vote in Parliament against deploying the new weapon, ten days ahead of the rally.[8] The condemnation passed with more than a two-thirds majority, making it politically impossible for The Hague to agree to NATO deployment.[9] More than forty thousand peace activists from all over Europe took to the streets in the mass rally called the International Forum Against the Neutron Bomb. Among the many speakers at the rally were the American critic Daniel Ellsberg, of *Pentagon Papers* fame; the Patriarch of the Russian Orthodox Church; and the World Peace Council's Romesh Chandra.[10] Every tenth house in Amsterdam and other cities displayed a Dutch Communist Party–issued poster reading "Stop the Neutron Bomb."

President Carter's doubts grew as a result.[11] He was aware of the events in the Netherlands, and on the day of the Amsterdam rally he told his closest advisors that he would oppose the neutron bomb. When NATO officials

M110 203mm self-propelled Howitzers are staged in a parking area at the port of Antwerp, September 1984. The M110 was capable of firing the W79 Mod 0 shell, a tactical nuclear artillery projectile with an enhanced radiation mode (a "neutron bomb") that could be switched on or off.

(Bram de Jong / Dirk Van Laer / U.S. Department of Defense)

indicated that the KGB could be a force behind the international anti-neutron-bomb movement, many were skeptical. "There is no evidence" of KGB influence, commented *The Guardian* a few weeks after the Dutch vote, as uncertainty about the future of the enhanced radiation weapon lingered.[12] In early April, the news broke that Carter had postponed production of the neutron bomb, alienating some European allies, Germany among them.

The active measures campaign, however, did not end. The covert campaign had been flanked by forgeries along the way. On June 8, 1978, for example, several Belgian newspapers received an anonymous piece of mail that contained a photocopy of a letter from Secretary General Joseph Luns of NATO, purportedly to the U.S. permanent representative to NATO, William Tapley Bennett, Jr. In the letter, Luns informed Bennett that "with the help of [his] friends" in Belgium's defense ministry, "the listing of the journalists showing negative attitude to the neutron bomb" was well under way. Luns implied, ominously and without specifics, that some of his Belgian friends were "overzealous" about taking action against the listed journalists.[13]

When some of the named journalists reached out to NATO, the authorities immediately and publicly stated that the missive was a forgery. Almost two months later, though, the Belgian publications *De Nieuwe* and *De Volkskrant* published articles on the Luns letter, along with the fake documentation, both without any mention that the missive had been officially labeled a forgery.[14]

The CIA agreed with Soviet diplomats and spymasters that the neutron bomb active measures campaign had been an extraordinary success. Anatoly Dobrynin, the longtime Soviet ambassador in Washington, later recalled in his memoirs that "the Soviet campaign had undercut American plans to deploy in Europe a new kind of nuclear weapon." The partly covert campaign, Dobrynin wrote, had successfully redefined a defensive weapon as an offensive one.[15] "That the campaign was successful was confirmed when the Americans finally abandoned their idea," concluded the KGB defector Ilya Dzhirkvelov, adding, "I can state with confidence that we received considerable help in achieving our aim from the foreign correspondents whom we supplied with disinformation."[16] In September 1979, the chief of the International Department of Hungary's Communist Party, János Berecz, wrote, "The political campaign against the neutron bomb was one of the most significant and successful since World War II."[17] The Soviet Union awarded an official decoration to its ambassador to The Hague, recognizing his success in advancing the anti-neutron-bomb campaign through the Dutch Communist Party.

The U.S. intelligence community calculated in 1980 that an operation of the magnitude of the "neutron bomb" campaign "would cost over $100 million," if the U.S. government were to undertake it.[18] Levchenko, who defected from the KGB in 1979, as the neutron bomb campaign was ongoing, estimated the price tag at $200 million (equivalent to more than $600 million in 2018).[19]

U.S. intelligence was likely more reliable in its overall assessment of the effectiveness of a Russian campaign than were the Russian intelligence officers, because the CIA did not have to justify spending hundreds of millions on the active measure. CIA analysts pointed out that accurately measuring the impact of the campaign was difficult, if not impossible, for the Soviets as much as for the Americans, one reason for which was that most voters and activists in Europe genuinely did oppose the mysterious weapon. A significant amount of the opposition was entirely unrelated to Soviet active measures. Yet CIA analysts conceded that "the Soviets made 'neutron bomb' a household scareword in Europe, if not throughout the world."[20]

Congress took note of all of these events. Prompted by new anti-American forgeries such as FM30-31B as well as the neutron bomb campaign, the U.S. House Intelligence Committee held several open hearings that would give an opportunity for the CIA to present details of Soviet active measures to the American public, and to refocus America's attention on disinformation. The CIA's point man for the hearing was John McMahon, the deputy director for operations. McMahon, a burly man with white hair and drooping glasses, brought with him five additional intelligence officers and a wealth of detail. During the hearing, McMahon engaged in a revealing argument about the nature of front organizations with John Ashbrook, a hawkish Republican from Ohio.

"You identified the World Peace Council as the largest of the major Soviet front groups used in propaganda campaigns," said Ashbrook. "Is that correct?"

"Yes," said McMahon.

The World Peace Council was founded in Paris as the World Committee of Partisans for Peace in 1949, the same year the CIA started working the Kampfgruppe in Berlin. In 1951, the French government expelled the organization for alleged fifth column activities. The council then moved to Vienna, but after three years, Austria also banned the group for "activities directed against the Austrian state." The U.S. State Department later described the World Peace Council as an "archetypical front organization."[21] (Soviet diplomats agreed with this assessment. Arkady Shevchenko, the Soviet Union's undersecretary general of the United Nations, witnessed the council's work in New York during the neutron bomb campaign: "Particularly annoying were the ceaseless requests from Moscow to assist the Soviet-controlled World Peace Council," Shevchenko recalled, adding that the nominal peace organization "swarmed with KGB officers.")[22]

Ashbrook was aware of some of the World Peace Council activity, and continued his questioning of McMahon. "All right," he said. "Does it or does it not have an American affiliate?"

"It has an American affiliate," the CIA officer responded.

Ashbrook grew impatient: "The American affiliate is the U.S. Peace Council, is it not?"

"Right," said one of McMahon's staffers.

"The American affiliate of the World Peace Council, the U.S. Peace Council, had their founding convention just last fall. It was November 9 to 11 in Philadelphia," Ashbrook said, turning to the CIA's McMahon. "Do you target that?"[23]

McMahon was confused.

"We would not target it," he said about the U.S. front organization, "nor would we follow it." The CIA's McMahon pointed out that the Peace Council would be the FBI's responsibility, and then added, tersely, "I must point out that the Communist Party is a very legal institution in the United States."

Ashbrook expressed his frustration with letting a known Soviet front group go on its merry way. "I guess that is just a part of the problem we have in the West," he said.

"That is part of an open society, sir," responded McMahon.

The CIA's Directorate of Operations had understood perhaps one of the most insidious threats posed by successful disinformation campaigns: overreacting to active measures risked turning an open society into a more closed one. The more difficult question was how to draw the line between reactions that defended the former and those that encouraged the latter. Only the future would tell.

Peacewar

ONE HOT FRONT OF THE COLD WAR RAN RIGHT ALONG THE West German–East German border. Neither Soviet nor American tanks ever crossed the Fulda Gap, the lowlands between Hesse and Thuringia where a surprise attack would have been most likely. Chemicals were never drained into the Rhine to set the river ablaze as a flame barrier; nor did nuclear-tipped SS-20 missiles rain down on Hamburg and Frankfurt, as leaked U.S. planning documents foresaw. Yet it was the specter of war itself that opened another battlefield in the Cold War, one that stayed open for more than two decades.

Friedenskampf, or "peacewar," was the Stasi name for the systematic and persistent subversion of the West European peace movement. The German composite word sounds just as absurd as the English version—except it didn't, at least not within the Eastern bloc's ideological universe in the

Generals for Peace was a Stasi-initiated and Stasi-funded group of around ten
ex-NATO generals that advocated against nuclear force modernization in Europe.
(Rob Croes / Anefo / Nationaal Archief)

decade before the Cold War came to its abrupt end. The secret Soviet code
name for *Friedenskampf* was more honest: the larger campaign to influence
the global peace movement bore the internal cryptonym MARS—the name
of the ancient Roman god of war.

The KGB's archives remain closed, but original, top-secret Russian
files are not necessarily off-limits: the archives of intelligence agencies that
acted as KGB proxies are now open, including the MfS in East Berlin and
the DS in Sofia. With the help of this archival material, available in German
and Bulgarian, a reconstruction of the overarching MARS campaign is possible, complete with plans, design, and assessment of specific measures. The
campaign was so vast that it left a clear archival footprint even in secondary
archives.

MARS was listed for the first time in late-1970s joint operating plans
between the German and the Bulgarian foreign intelligence agencies, in the

context of anti-neutron-bomb operations.[1] In 1978, Albert Norden, a fierce ideologue and member of the East German Politburo in charge of agitation, wrote to one of his senior executive officials about the need to prop up the peace movement on the other side of the Iron Curtain, in the Federal Republic of Germany. "The FRG's peace movement needs help," Norden wrote. "It is one of the weakest in all of Western Europe."[2] He then told his staff to come up with a proposal to bolster the pacifists on the other side of the Berlin Wall. MARS persisted through the entire Cold War, until 1990[3]—it was one of the longest recorded active measures in history.[4] The campaign's goal was to stitch scattered peace activism into a unified mass movement and a political force that the established powers in Western Europe and the United States would have to reckon with; the means to this end involved creative use of the now time-tested toolbox of dirty tricks.

By the late 1970s, the Soviet Union had brought a new missile system online. Dubbed by NATO the SS-20 Saber, it was a state-of-the-art, intermediate-range ballistic missile with a nuclear warhead and a range of more than three thousand miles. The Warsaw Pact nations could now wipe out all European NATO targets from bases in Ukraine and Belarus. To deter such an attack, in December 1979, in what became known as the "double-track decision," the Atlantic Alliance opted to deploy 108 Pershing II missiles to West Germany, and more than 460 ground-launched cruise missiles, the majority of them to Britain.[5] Thirteen days later, the Soviet Union invaded Afghanistan. Détente was over. The world was on edge.

In late April 1980, the Bertrand Russell Peace Foundation in London launched a wave of protests against nuclear weapons in Paris, London, Berlin, Lisbon, and Oslo. Fears fueled the protest, fears that the world was entering the most dangerous period in history. "We do not wish to apportion guilt between the political and military leaders of East and West," the Russell Foundation wrote. "Guilt lies squarely upon both parties." Peace activists from West and East then called on the United States as well as the Soviet Union to halt their dueling missile deployments.[6]

The KGB and the Stasi saw the Russell Foundation's initiative as a major threat—not because its goal was realistic but because, in the Soviets' view, the pan-European approach made it harder, if not impossible, to unilaterally weaponize the peace movement against NATO. The Warsaw Pact countries did not want a nonaligned peace movement, but the possibility of unilateral criticism that would align with the Soviet policy of opposing NATO's double-track decision while ignoring the SS-20 missiles already deployed in Eastern Europe.

The UK peace campaign was particularly dangerous because of English-language publicity, which could be more easily picked up in the United States as well as across Europe. The KGB decided to interfere with the protests in London.

About a month after the pan-European push for peace, in mid-June 1980, a number of British members of Parliament and newspaper editors received a 125-page booklet in the mail. The packages were posted anonymously from Paddington and Croydon, were marked "top secret," and appeared to contain leaked documents. Among the recipients were nine Labour MPs, including Stan Newens and Stan Orme, who forwarded a copy to the defense secretary, Francis Pym, who passed the booklet to the U.S. embassy and from there to the CIA. The targeted MPs had all had dealings with the World Peace Council.[7] At least five UK news outlets also received the secret U.S. documents, including *The Sunday Telegraph*, *The New Worker*, the *Tribune*, and the *New Statesman*.

The leak was titled *Top Secret Documents on U.S. Forces Headquarters in Europe*. The cover showed the logo of the U.S. Department of Defense in green, and beneath it: "Holocaust Again for Europe." The book's second page, usually reserved for publisher and copyright information, was completely blank. The third page contained only one line, "Information Books No 1." The preface was signed off with "London, October 1980," and a curious "publisher's note": "This booklet is published as a public service and as part of the growing campaigns against nuclear war and for freedom of information on important issues. We hope to extend this service in the future."[8]

The "we" referred to the officers of Ivanov's Service A. Timing the leak had been made "horrifically simple," according to the preface;[9] presidents and prime ministers "of the NATO bloc" had effectively made the decision by increasing missile spending and by stationing "new terror weapons in Europe." The arguments in favor of NATO force modernization were phony, the authors argued. There was no looming Warsaw Pact military superiority in Europe. The United States had already planned the destruction of Europe: "There is no 'Soviet threat,' there is a very real American threat to Europe." The pamphlet then outlined the familiar argument that the American military-industrial complex, especially "electronics interests," stood to make a lot of money from researching and producing modernized weapon systems, such as the new cruise missile.

What followed was a most extraordinary self-reflection. "That view probably looks very much like Soviet propaganda," the KGB wrote in skillfully colloquial English, "and pretty cheap propaganda to boot."[10] It did indeed.

Yet the move was clever. The anonymous authors then countered the anticipated counterarguments: "Our collection of Top Secret paperwork dates from early in the 1960s and last got a major airing in the west European press a decade and more ago," they wrote. "Newspaper legend has it," they added, that an American serviceman photographed the top-secret documents in a NATO vault near Paris, and subsequently passed the documents "to the Russians." These Russians indeed knew by now that hardened activists didn't mind where the secrets came from, so they decided to be honest, or somewhat honest: "True or false, the legend has never been seriously challenged in the west, and neither has the authenticity of the documents."

The authors then singled out OPLAN 10-1, that zombie of a leak which had already made repeated appearances in West European newspapers over the last dozen years. The leaked documents illustrated American plans for Europe, which could be summed up, wrote the KGB, as "better dead than red."

This active measure was a masterful display of disinformation tradecraft, at least at first glance. To further bolster the credibility of the leaked documents and its own analysis, the preface quoted a catalog of authoritative Western voices: the NATO secretary general, the well-respected International Institute of Strategic Studies in London, *Le Monde* and *Le Monde Diplomatique*, the U.S. magazine *Ramparts*, the West German newspapers

Die Welt and *Stern*, and the Italian weekly *ABC*. The leak contained the now old but still clever forgery about U.S. field commanders deciding to use nuclear weapons on their own. Two of the quoted newspapers, *ABC* and *Stern*, had already, helpfully enough, reported this myth as fact, back in 1969 and 1970. The KGB had kept careful tabs on the story, and a decade later quoted both *ABC*[11] and *Stern*'s reporting on the forged nuclear release authority to lend their analysis and their leak more credibility, even though the German and Italian magazines were generally better known for revealing not secrets but the flesh of scantily clad women, a detail that a British audience would not be aware of.

Ivanov's Service A forgers saw themselves as cultured and subtle. They used pop culture, driving home the time-tested fear of a military officer going rogue with a reference to *The Deer Hunter*, an acclaimed Vietnam War movie starring Robert De Niro that came out in 1978. The punch line was written in awkward English, butchering genitives and punctuation: "One 'deer hunter'—one Hiroshima. That's the ghastly equation wrapped up in the document's jargon-laden prose. Now nip down the library and take a look at some Hiroshima or Nagasaki photographs—and think about them in the context of Glasgow, Marseille, Frankfurt or your own home town."[12]

One of the journalists who covered the renewed leak was Duncan Campbell, a young investigative reporter who, four years earlier, had penned the first press story to reveal the existence of GCHQ, the UK's technical intelligence agency and then a highly secretive organization. Writing in the *New Statesman* under the headline "How to Blow Up the World," Campbell had correctly identified that the source of the leaked material was "the Soviet KGB."[13] Campbell did not take the "deer hunter" bait, but his story treated the mysterious top-secret documents as "virtually completely authentic."

Campbell had asked Jim Dobbins, a U.S. embassy spokesperson in London, if the leaks were the authentic product of a 1960s Russian spy in Paris. "Nothing would indicate otherwise," said Dobbins, and he merely hinted to Campbell that the documents could have been altered or tampered with. The U.S. government never publicly substantiated the fact that the document was partially a forgery, and thus helped keep a damaging leak alive.

Months later, in December 1980, the same documents surfaced in the Netherlands; several newspapers and politicians again received anonymous mailings with the same "Information Books No. 1" leak.[14] Then, three years later, in January and May 1983, at least three newspapers in West Germany received a 74-page booklet sourced from the same U.S. war plans. This time the envelopes came from a nonexistent "Society for Reasonable Politics, Inc.," mailed from Ulm and Düsseldorf in West Germany.[15] Editors considered the documents genuine, and informed the authorities accordingly.[16]

In retrospect, the leak seems crude. It played into existing fears in Britain and Europe, but the booklet ultimately received limited attention in the press in the 1980s. Nevertheless, the stunt was only an opening salvo in the MARS campaign.

Only a few official Stasi documents on disinformation planning escaped destruction. One rare exception is a top-secret Stasi memo from the early 1980s on supporting the West German peace movement. The document is known as "Concept for Political Active Measures to Advance the Peace Movement in the Federal Republic of Germany," and is dated August 17, 1981.[17] Its author was Kurt Gailat, head of the HVA's powerful Department II, "Parties and Organizations in the Federal Republic of Germany."[18] Gailat was famous among HVA and KGB insiders for his knowledge of the West German party system.[19] During the 1970s, he handled one of the best-placed agents of all time, Günter Guillaume, personal secretary to Chancellor Willy Brandt. Gailat even wrote a secret PhD thesis on subverting the West German Social Democrats.[20]

Supporting the Western peace movement was of course not a goal in itself for Eastern intelligence agencies. Gailat was clear about the real objective: "thwarting NATO's plans to deploy qualitatively new atomic medium-range ballistic missiles by the year 1983."[21] Strengthening the peace movement was only a tool to weaken NATO, and it wasn't even directly applied. The stronger the West German peace initiative, reasoned Gailat, the stronger the chance that medium-range nuclear missiles would become a central theme in West Germany's parliamentary elections, scheduled for 1984. The peace-supporting active measures, Gailat wrote, aimed "to increase the intelligence influence on the budding peace movement in the Federal Republic of Germany in order to stimulate and to strengthen [the movement]." Shaping grassroots political activists in an adversarial country required high-level insights and informal contacts, and the Stasi officers knew it. "This requires the targeted deployment of a network of IM [unofficial collaborators] and KP [contact persons] as well as the creation of new operative positions," Gailat explained in his request for authorization. He knew that West Germany's Social Democrats would try to integrate and absorb the peace activists, and that his secret service would need to counteract such cooperation. The message that the Stasi prepared for the peace activists and the left wing of the Social Democrats was simple: more missiles in Europe meant less public support for the SPD's governing coalition.

At the time, West Germany was governed by a "social-liberal" coalition, a merger of the social-democratic SPD under Helmut Schmidt and the free-liberal FDP under Hans-Dietrich Genscher. If Bonn's governing coalition was a knotty, unwieldy log of wood, Gailat was carefully studying the log's surface structure and fibers, his axe and wood-splitting wedge at the ready. Gailat, in his programmatic "peacewar" memo, suggested one measure in particular that would prove highly effective: "Bundeswehr officers are to be recruited in order to have them question the justification of the planned rearmament from a military-strategic point-of-view," he wrote.

This recruitment—soon to be known as "Generals for Peace"—was already under way at the HVA. Peter Bach, in the HVA's Department IV, was closely observing Bundeswehr officers who expressed any political view, and the time was ripe to support some of them.

The story of a most unusual military disinformation operation begins in September 1980 at the World Parliament of the Peoples for Peace, in Sofia, Bulgaria, an event sponsored by the World Peace Council. Three former NATO generals, from Italy, France, and Portugal, were present in Sofia. All three had made connections with the World Peace Council after retirement. The Italian, Nino Pasti, had once worked on nuclear affairs in a senior position at NATO. Now Pasti, a left-leaning member of the Italian Parliament, was busily writing pamphlets attacking the neutron bomb and later the proposed Intermediate Nuclear Forces deployments. A book followed in short order.

On May 18, 1981, Generals for Peace issued a volume of interviews in Bonn.[22] The book was titled *Generale für den Frieden*, the group's name in German. "The unthinkable has become thinkable. Atomic war has moved into the realm of the possible," read the solemn book jacket. "The threat of a nuclear holocaust looms over Europe. Humanity's naked survival is at stake." The book's authors argued that the balance of nuclear power in Europe was a "fetish" and an engine for increased defense spending. The culprit was clear, according to the generals: "The key is, again and again, the NATO double-track decision of December 1979."[23] The generals vigorously opposed the deployment of cruise missiles to the UK and of Pershing II missiles to West Germany. They argued that a "missile gap" between the Atlantic Alliance and the Warsaw Pact did not exist, and that the American, British, and French arsenals were more than sufficient for tactical requirements in a potential European theater of war.

This kind of semi-covert publication activity was not rare, especially in 1981. That year alone, the KGB reportedly funded or sponsored 70 monographs, 4,865 news articles, 60 films, 1,500 radio and TV programs, 3,000 conferences or exhibitions, and many thousands of reports.[24] But the work of the ex-NATO generals stands out. At one point, the group boasted more than a dozen officers, with at least one general or admiral each from Canada, France, Greece, Italy, the Netherlands, Norway, Portugal, the United Kingdom, and the United States, and two apiece from Germany and Greece. The two West German generals, Wolf Graf von Baudissin, one of the founding fathers of the new German army, and Gert Bastian, were particularly crucial for the small outfit. Bastian, like his partner Petra Kelly, was an iconic figure in the German peace movement.

The generals represented an extraordinary success for the Stasi in particular. "Several [active] measures against NATO's double-track decision were bundled under the collective term 'MARS.' The founding of the 'Generals for Peace' outfit was one of them," the Stasi Department X colonel Günter Bohnsack later explained.[25] "Out of this rather loose gathering grew a real movement," he said. "People telephoned each other, organized debates, talked to each other. This created a real force that was in line with Moscow's ideas and we always controlled this through our intelligence services in Moscow and East Berlin."[26] One particularly important aspect, as usual, was money. "There was a whole range of expenses which were paid jointly by Moscow and the GDR," Bohnsack recounted, adding that some of the generals did inquire about the origins of the funds.

The publisher and the editor were also secretly funded by the East.[27] The Cologne publisher Pahl-Rugenstein released the book. In 1978, an internal MfS note explained that Pahl-Rugenstein was led by a Communist Party member and that it developed its book lists "in consultation with the leadership of the brother party," which was Socialist jargon for the government of the GDR.[28] One joke at the HVA was to call the subsidized outlet "Paul Rubelschein."[29]

The book was collated and edited by Gerhard Kade, a former officer in the German Navy, a historian, and a vice president at the Vienna-based International Institute of Peace, another pro-Soviet outfit linked to the World Peace Council. Kade worked directly with the HVA and the KGB. The Stasi knew him under the cover name SUPER, a cryptonym that reflected his significance;[30] the KGB had him on file as ROBUST.[31] Kade was "the brains and engine" behind Generals for Peace, in the words of the HVA chief, Markus Wolf: "What Kade's friends and colleagues in and out of Generals for Peace did not know and would have been horrified if they had found out, was that a good deal of Kade's ideas came from Moscow and a substantial amount of money and other help came from East German foreign intelligence."[32]

Wolf himself came to a nuanced conclusion on the status of the group. "The generals were acting out of conviction," he said, noting that most of the officers were entirely unaware of Kade's working relationship with foreign intelligence agencies. This dynamic made it easier for the HVA to run the operation. "The publications of the generals revealed the influence that we exerted over Kade," Wolf wrote in his memoirs.[33] As archival research later revealed, Kade had already published a book in 1979 for which he had received "significant" help from the East German regime.[34]

Despite this shrewd setup, the international press coverage did not immediately take off. In October 1981, the group of officers was profiled in English in *Peace Courier*, the journal of the World Peace Council, with brief statements from some of its members.[35] The U.S. intelligence community was quick to label the generals as what they were, an "ad hoc front group."[36] But it took about a year for the group to receive mainstream press coverage in the United States.

President Ronald Reagan was inaugurated on January 20, 1981. For the first time in history, the inaugural ceremony was held at the West Front of the Capitol, instead of the East. The speech contained several oblique references to the Cold War, the Soviet Union, and the ideological superpower confrontation. "Above all," Reagan told the crowd assembled on the National Mall, "we must realize that no arsenal or no weapon in the arsenals of the world is so formidable as the will and moral courage of free men and women." Throughout the 1980 presidential campaign, the Republican nominee had promised that, if elected, he would rebuild America's military might to better deter the USSR. "Freedom," Reagan thundered in his inaugural speech, "is a weapon our adversaries in today's world do not have. It is a weapon that we as Americans do have." Just days after his speech, the Soviet Union's top spies decided to turn the "weapon" of freedom against itself. Openness, they understood, was a weakness as much as it was a strength.

Meanwhile, the HVA had carefully analyzed attitudes among younger middle-class West Germans and found what Wolf called a "fundamental shift in values."[37] Career success and material wealth had declined in significance for the Baby Boomer generation, and solidarity, community, and individual fulfillment had become more important. Technology had come to stand for war, and capitalism for alienation. "These were important aspects for our work," said Wolf. The Stasi was able to recruit collaborators from the ranks of the peace activists. The agency focused its recruitment effort on West German students whose studies offered a plausible cover for political activism.

A similar dynamic applied in other Western European countries. It is possible to get a sense of scale of the MARS influence campaign by simply listing some of the uncovered activities. In 1981, for example, the Danish government expelled a Soviet diplomat named Vladimir Merkulov, a second secretary of the Russian embassy, who could "with a high degree of certainty" be labeled a KGB major.[38] Merkulov reportedly handled and ran a Danish influence agent, Arne Herløv Petersen, whom Danish authorities considered a particularly productive agent of influence for Moscow. In 1980, Petersen published *True Blues*, a pamphlet attacking the British government and especially Margaret Thatcher, the text of which, authorities maintained, had been supplied by Merkulov. Over the years, they reported, the journalist met Merkulov twenty-three times in clandestine meetings, and was photographed on several occasions. Petersen received considerable quantities of liquor, cigarettes, and other gifts, as well as travel to the Soviet Union. Merkulov, for example, advised his asset not to join Denmark's Communist Party, as he would be more effective as an independent.[39]

Even neutral Switzerland was targeted. Aleksei Dumov was the local bureau chief of the Novosti press agency in Bern, and oversaw a branch in Geneva. On December 5, 1981, Dumov's local staff played "a critical role" in organizing a very large peace demonstration in Bern. The Novosti office also had a leading role in designing and organizing the Swiss Appeal for Peace and Against Nuclear Death, and was even involved in spreading the false report that Swiss intelligence had murdered a Soviet diplomat in a Swiss hotel in 1980. On April 23, 1983, the government closed the Bern bureau of Novosti, and Swiss authorities expelled Dumov for "persistent and grave interference in Swiss internal affairs."[40] A few days later, the Swiss government identified Leonid Ovchinnikov as Dumov's handler and the KGB officer responsible for Novosti.[41] Neither in Denmark nor in Switzerland were the influence agents brought to trial.

A comparable drama played out in the Netherlands at the same time. Amsterdam and The Hague had already been hotly contested ground during the neutron bomb campaign three years earlier. In April 1981, in preparation for a NATO Council meeting in Rome, the Dutch internal security service, the BVD, prepared a confidential report on a "hidden feature" of the nuclear weapons debate.[42] The report laid out, in detail, the interactions between the Dutch Communist Party, the Central Committee in

Moscow, and various front organizations. "It is known that KGB officers in the Netherlands have received instructions from Moscow to promote protests against the neutron bomb," read the report. *De Telegraaf*, the country's largest daily, spoke of "clear proof" of Soviet involvement in the Dutch peace movement.[43]

One curious figure in the Dutch influence campaign was Vadim Leonov, a thirty-one-year-old KGB operative in The Hague, operating under the cover of a TASS correspondent. Leonov was young, handsome, and stylish, with an engaging smile. On April 15, 1981, shortly after the BVD report came out, Dutch authorities expelled him.[44] Leonov later gave a remarkably boastful interview to *Reformatorisch Dagblad*, a conservative newspaper. The anti-neutron-bomb protests were "manipulated" by a small group of hard-core ideologues who followed a "blueprint from Moscow," arranged through him, said Leonov. He added: "If Moscow decides that 50,000 demonstrators must take to the streets in the Netherlands, then they take to the streets. Do you know how you can get 50,000 demonstrators at a certain place within a week? A message through my channels is sufficient."[45]

The self-confident undercover correspondent could not resist making a sardonic comment about the peace activists he had worked with. Once a demonstration would be scheduled, the stylish KGB man said, "then everything is arranged with military precision, under the leadership of principled conscientious objectors."[46] Editors at the *Dagblad* first thought the expelled Russian was pulling their leg, and decided to publish only after a congressional hearing in Washington appeared to confirm the wider story.

MARS was a truly global campaign. The attention to detail on display could be remarkable. One example is the slogan "No New Missiles in Europe," a line pushed aggressively by front organizations in the nuclear freeze campaign. The cynical slogan worked in favor of the Soviet position, especially the little word "new," as it tacitly accepted the recently established presence of Soviet SS-20 medium-range missiles in Europe while condemning U.S. weapons modernization. The slogan reportedly emerged in 1981 at demonstrations in West Germany, on placards distributed by Communist front organizations. The World Peace Council distributed large round pins that

The World Peace Council, a Soviet front, produced and distributed signs, posters, and pins to rally the Western European public against NATO's deployment of more capable nuclear weapons.

depicted two giant missiles pointing at Europe, with a "NO" printed across the button in red, under the banner "NO TO NEW US MISSILES IN EUROPE!"[47]

In May 1983 at a peace rally in Williamsburg, Virginia, during a high-profile summit meeting of industrial nations, particularly shrewd and well-equipped protesters displayed a German-language banner in the background for replay by the German TV networks covering the summit.[48] Of course, that banner could have been the work of genuine peace activists.

In early 1982, Markus Wolf spoke approvingly of the peace movement in front of his East Berlin staff. "We already achieved a lot," he said, yet he saw a need to escalate. An increased effort was necessary "to strengthen through active measures the peace movement in West European states and to defend against attempts of division."[49] These comments were most remarkable. The MfS, and likely also the KGB, projected their own methods onto their adversaries. Stasi officers were so mired in conspiratorial thinking that their internal jargon even had a verb for uncovering a conspiracy: *dekonspirieren*, or "deconspire." So the officers in the East assumed—wrongly—that Western intelligence agencies were themselves using the peace movement to infiltrate and divide the Eastern bloc.

The Stasi therefore both supported and subverted peace activists. When activists on the approved list traveled to East Germany, to visit the official peace council, for example, state security made sure that they received "especially preferred, polite treatment" at immigration checkpoints.[50] Other activists, even in West Germany, would become the target of harassment. The Stasi targeted Jürgen Fuchs, a writer and peace activist in West Berlin, in an operation called OPPONENT; the goal of this *"Zersetzung,"* as the Stasi wrote in one particularly chilling memo, was to

> coerce Fuchs to turn inward, to continuously occupy him with everyday annoyances in order to make him insecure, to discredit him in public, and eventually to incapacitate him with respect to his attacks against the GDR.[51]

The Stasi was particularly concerned about a small West Berlin–based group with an "anti-Communist orientation," known as the Arbeitskreis, or Working Group for a Nuclear-Weapons-Free Europe. The group, founded in 1981, advocated for a united Europe with no nuclear weapons on either side of the border that divided the two Germanys. To Wolf's men, this goal was tantamount to attempted "anti-Communist repurposing" of the peace movement. When the Arbeitskreis prepared a peace conference for May 1983, titled "Second European Conference for a Nuclear-Weapons-Free Europe," East German state security saw the group as persistently attempting to "continue a process of division in the peace movement, to distract from the fight against NATO's missile policy, and to penetrate Socialist countries."[52] The HVA therefore considered the group a threat, classified it as an "enemy object," and ran operations against it.

20.

Nuclear Freeze

THE MARS CAMPAIGN WOULD SOON DEPLOY ITS ENTIRE TOOL kit against the peace movement in the United States. And the United States, more religious than most European countries, offered an even larger target surface: the KGB began attempting to "develop contacts with religious figures in the United States," as the FBI reported to Congress. The Soviet rationale was that the participation of American clergy would add moral legitimacy and political weight to the peace movement. In early 1982, six Russian officials, five of them affiliated with the KGB, regularly participated in the "Christian-Marxist" dialogue workshops held by a Southern Baptist Convention ministry working with the United Nations. The undercover agents stressed the Soviet desire for peace, and encouraged expanding church activity into the disarmament field.[1]

The FBI watched as KGB officers "personally contacted several, major

Protesters outside the 1983 World Economic Summit in Virginia. The central banner reads "No New Nuclear Missiles." The FBI found that distinguishing between genuine and engineered protest became impossible. (AP Photo)

American peace organizations, including the Nuclear Weapons Freeze Campaign."[2] These recruitment and influence methods became evident in the way the KGB approached Alan Wolfe, then a thirty-four-year-old budding public intellectual and a member of the editorial board of the left-leaning *The Nation*. One day in 1976, Wolfe was sitting in his office in Berkeley, working on a manuscript, when an "exceptionally well-dressed man" appeared at his office door. The man introduced himself, revealing a Russian accent, and offered his card, which said that he worked at the Soviet consulate in San Francisco. "Could we get together and chat at some future time?" the Russian officer said politely. "No doubt a man like yourself is very busy."

They met up two weeks later. The purported diplomat then introduced Wolfe to a Moscow-based academic, who invited him to visit and lecture. Wolfe agreed, and visited the Soviet Union in October 1977. The writer found the lack of fruit and the omnipresent minders "most unpleasant," but the formal meetings "enlightening."[3]

The FBI's counterintelligence investigators were paying attention, and quickly determined that Wolfe had been targeted for recruitment by the Soviets. The KGB arranged the young writer's trip to Moscow and Yerevan in order to "cultivate and influence him," as the FBI noted in an internal report.[4] Two federal agents soon visited Wolfe at his house. A terse conversation ensued. "You see, Alan," said one of the FBI officers, "the spy business is a serious affair." The two officers inquired whether Wolfe knew that the Soviet Union was attempting to influence the peace movement in the United States. Wolfe told them that he knew that the president thought so, but that he did not trust *Reader's Digest* on the subject of communism.

"Do you believe *Reader's Digest*?" Wolfe asked, referring to John Barron's then-prominent reporting on the KGB's subversion of the peace movement. The FBI agent responded that, if forced to respond either yes or no, his answer would be "most definitely" yes.[5]

The Communist Party of the Soviet Union provided guidance and money to its U.S. comrades, and, in November 1979, the American Communist Party founded the United States Peace Council as an affiliate of the World Peace Council. In 1981, the FBI learned that Soviet officials had informed the head of the World Peace Council, Romesh Chandra, that the USSR had "big plans" for joint WPC and USPC activities in 1982 and 1983. Moscow, the FBI reported, was "elated" by how easy it was to organize events in the United States, and made clear to Chandra that they would provide funds for WPC activities in the United States.[6]

The FBI's counterintelligence division considered the Communist Party in the United States "one of the most loyal, pro-Soviet communist parties in the world." Its leadership regularly accepted Soviet directives as well as funding. Between the late 1950s and the late 1970s, the American Communist Party received more than $30 million from the Soviet Union. By the early 1980s, the annual funding flowing across the Iron Curtain from east to west reached around $2.75 million per year, the FBI estimated.[7] The G-men also carefully watched as the Soviets targeted perhaps America's most charismatic peace activist.

Born into a family of former plantation owners in Huntsville, Alabama, Randall Forsberg turned to activism at the age of thirty-seven, in 1980. Charismatic, eloquent, with a fresh PhD from MIT under her belt, Forsberg became an anti-arms-race advocate. She played a key role in launching the idea of a "nuclear freeze," a verifiable halt in the testing, production, and deployment of all nuclear weapons—by both the United States and the Soviet Union.[8]

The high point in Forsberg's career was the June 12 rally in New York's Central Park, which she helped organize. It was the largest demonstration in American political history to date, with around 700,000 participants, and it was meant to coincide with the Second Special Session on Disarmament at the United Nations. "We've done it!" Forsberg shouted, as she addressed the sprawling Manhattan rally that day. "The nuclear freeze campaign has mobilized the biggest peacetime peace movement in United States history," she said. "The politicians don't believe it yet. They will. They think it's a fad. It's not."[9]

The giant rally was also a principal target of MARS. The USSR used "nearly every instrument" at hand against the June 12 Committee, the organization that coordinated the landmark political event. Even Forsberg herself was a target: "The KGB has targeted Randall Forsberg [. . .] for active measures purposes," the FBI reported after the event.

One of the first planning conferences for the nuclear freeze campaign in the United States was held in March 1980 at Georgetown University, in Washington, D.C. Two Soviet participants stood out to the FBI: Yuri Kapralov, an undercover KGB officer from the embassy, tasked with penetrating the peace movement, and Oleg Bogdanov, an active measures specialist from the International Department of the Central Committee, which was still headed by an aging Boris Ponomarev, who had targeted Franz-Josef Strauss and Der Spiegel so aggressively twenty years earlier. Kapralov was a panelist at the conference, and his performance was reportedly "very impressive."[10] As the American protest movement gained steam over the next month, Kapralov hit the conference circuit. On Veterans Day 1981, in November, 151 college campuses held a teach-in on disarmament that drew around 100,000 participants.

"It's funny," said Kapralov at Harvard, "when our leaders talk very clearly about their desire for peace, some of your people just discredit it as transparent propaganda. We would prefer that your leaders would talk as clearly and as forcefully for peace and arms control as ours." The audience applauded. *The Boston Globe* reported that Kapralov was "one of the most effective speakers."[11]

The KGB had two assets placed inside the June 12 Committee, according to a secret U.S. government report. The FBI had "reliable sources" indicating that Soviet intermediaries played "a major role" in the June 12 Committee; the influence agents "successfully campaigned" to focus the demonstration on U.S. arms control and disarmament policies, and not include criticism of the USSR's force modernization and missile programs.[12]

In Europe, meanwhile, the HVA-supported Generals for Peace were gearing up for the same UN session. Kade, the cutout, had arranged for more than a dozen ex-NATO officers to meet in Vienna in February 1982, at his World Peace Council–supported institute. A group of thirteen agreed to sign a memorandum, to be launched in Bonn on June 4, 1982.[13] Generals for Peace even registered as an NGO with the United Nations.[14] It was only then that major newspapers in the United States fell for the peace-loving generals. *The New York Times*, in late June, profiled Brigadier Michael Harbottle, one of the group's most prominent and active members. Harbottle, polished and eloquent, was a British World War II veteran and later the chief of staff of the UN Peacekeeping Force in Cyprus. Now the British officer made a politically charged, even subversive suggestion: active-duty NATO officers, he told the *Times*, must "reverse traditional military thinking," in order to show "the same courage, willingness to take decisions and persistence that officers so far have only been asked to prove in hostilities."[15] The British brigadier openly dared his fellow military officers to disobey orders. Three days later, the *Christian Science Monitor* profiled Admiral Hyman Rickover, the U.S. member of the Generals, and praised the admiral's drive and tenacity. "Kudos to a new group of retired NATO officers who are trying to get their active-duty colleagues not to wait until retirement before standing forth against the arms race," the *Monitor* raved, effectively endorsing military insubordination in the United States.[16]

Wolf considered the work of the ex-NATO officers "paramount." The group's "influence over the disarmament debate was huge in comparison to its size," the former HVA chief recalled in his memoirs.[17] The peace movement writ large was fascinated by the supportive warriors. At one photo shoot staged in the run-up to a NATO meeting, the Italian, Pasti, flanked by fellow members of Generals for Peace, cradles a live white dove in both hands, his horn-rimmed eyes sternly pointing ahead into the future. In September 1982, the Stasi claimed credit for the group's success, its typical dry, bureaucratic jargon telegraphing the eerie passive voice of a vast, clandestine bureaucracy: "The movement 'Generals for Peace and Disarmament' was further expanded," said the top-secret two-page memo, and "now operates on an international level (including at the UN), and has become a firm component part of the peace movement." Wolf was more direct. The generals achieved "cult status in the movement," he recalled.[18]

By 1985, the activist generals had published a significant number of papers and articles on nuclear disarmament and arms limitation "that were drafted by the staff of HVA's Department X, Unit 1, sometimes in close cooperation with KGB,"[19] as Germany's general prosecutor confirmed in a detailed hundred-page indictment when the Stasi archives opened after reunification. The Bulgarian archives confirm those details. Also in 1985, for example, the Bulgarian disinformation department sent a request to its Stasi counterpart that the generals incorporate the demand for a nuclear-weapons-free zone in the Balkans into a memorandum that they would present at a peace symposium in Stockholm in 1985.[20] The generals, internally code-named UNION,[21] became such a successful influence operation that Moscow and East Berlin started competing over their use.[22]

The question of whether the generals were witting or unwitting agents of political warfare remains. "Some of them did not want to know," the HVA officer in charge of coordinating the group told me later.[23] In 1986, a team of party-loyal East Berlin producers, Heynowski and Scheumann, finished a prominent documentary production titled *Die Generale*, and dedicated their film to "the political leadership and its peace offensive." In March that year, the Ministry of State Security even facilitated bringing four of the ex-NATO generals, including Harbottle and Bastian, to East Berlin for a screening of a working draft of the two-part film. The Socialist Party authorized exceptional immigration procedures at the highest levels, and made sure that the four generals could all cross at Invalidenstraße without much delay or having to stamp their passports. Without a doubt, the four generals would have noticed the highly unusual arrangements of their semi-covert visit. They were no longer unwitting agents, if they ever were.[24]

All of this, though, was happening in secret. Peace activists across the Western Hemisphere did not know that several well-resourced, highly creative intelligence agencies were trying to subvert, manipulate, and divide the international peace movement—and that these agencies believed their conspiracy was a success.

In late 1982, President Reagan gave a speech about economic policy to a crowd of veterans at the Hyatt Regency Hotel in Columbus, Ohio. After finishing his prepared remarks, the president spontaneously decided to continue. "Coming in here, I passed a lot of your fellow Ohioans out there on the street," the president said. Some were applauding and waving, while others were protesting, he noticed. But Reagan knew something that the demonstrators along his motorcade did not. So Reagan told the veterans what he thought the protesters were actually doing: "They were demonstrating in behalf of a movement that has swept across our country that I think is inspired by, not the sincere, honest people who want peace, but by some who want the weakening of America, and so are manipulating many honest and sincere people."[25]

The next day, Reagan's unscripted statement made the news in papers across the country. The Cold War was on, and the president did not even have to spell out the mysterious foe. Everybody in the audience that day knew which force he was referring to. "Well, I, too, want a nuclear freeze after we have been able to negotiate the Soviet Union into a reduction on both sides of all kinds of weapons," the president said, adding that he would propose a freeze "when we're equal," not with the Russians "in a superiority that would bring closer the chance of nuclear war."[26] The peace movement, Reagan implied, was making nuclear war more likely.

Activists as well as political opponents were aghast. "It was McCarthyism," *The New York Times* responded three days later, "all delivered in the familiar aw-shucks style." After all, eight states were about to vote for nuclear freeze initiatives just a few weeks hence. Tom Wicker, an eminent columnist at the *Times*, wrote that their own president was trying to manipulate these sincere and honest Americans, not some mysterious foe. There was "not a shred of evidence" for such a dark conspiracy against the peace movement, he wrote.[27]

One enraged reader wrote to *The Washington Post* that Reagan's assertion was "myopic and ludicrous," and that his statement smeared "the integrity of the tens of millions of Americans who are legitimately concerned about the omnipresent threat of nuclear war."[28] Soon, peace activists pressed the White House for evidence. On November 12, the White House referred the press to Barron's *Reader's Digest* investigation as a reliable source. Barron told *The Washington Post* that "three intelligence and/or security services" had helped him, but he refused to identify them. "I have reason to believe that the president made very extensive inquiries, before he spoke, on the facts in that article," Barron told the *Post*.[29] In hindsight, however, it was Reagan who, by attempting to counter MARS with his unscripted comments, had given the influence campaign a shot in the arm, raised the public profile of Russian interference, and deepened existing divisions in the process.

"The proof is nonexistent," blasted *Counterspy*. The magazine pointed out, correctly, that Barron had a "history of writing for undercover purposes."[30] *Covert Action Information Bulletin* called Barron a "fraudulent journalist" for working "hand in glove with the CIA."[31] The FBI agreed with *Counterspy*, at least on the evidence, in a secret internal counterintelligence report it had just prepared; FBI counterintelligence investigators found it "extremely difficult" to determine the extent to which the Soviet Union had "influenced or manipulated" the nuclear freeze or anti-neutron-bomb movement. "We do not believe that Soviets have achieved a dominant role in the U.S. peace and nuclear freeze movements or that they directly control or manipulate the movement," the unclassified section of the report concluded.[32] On December 10, 1982, Americans would read in some of the nation's biggest newspapers that there was "no evidence" that any Soviet efforts had significantly influenced policy makers or the turnout to peace demonstrations.[33]

The other side was more confident in its assertions. One month before Reagan spoke out about the subversion of the peace movement, the KGB and the Stasi were internally assessing the MARS campaign and making plans for 1983 and beyond. Their joint operations had made "important contributions for the deepening and widening of the peace movement," one memo assessed on September 3, 1982. Operators in Berlin and Moscow agreed that measures intended to "influence" the reactions to Soviet initiatives had been successfully "realized" in West European countries. The success of the Generals for Peace initiative was singled out: "The Generals for Peace have been further expanded, now operate on an international level (including in a UN framework), and have become a stable component of the peace movement."[34] Service A and Department X further stressed their fruitful joint work in "initiating activities with a mass character (demonstrations, conferences, etc.)" in order to condemn Reagan's hawkish policies and to demand the cancellation of the NATO double-track decision from 1979.[35] One final, specific area of success was the "further continued process of differentiation" within the three established West German parties—this was Eastern bloc jargon for exacerbating tensions, for driving wedges into conflicted political parties in Bonn. The West German coalition government eventually fell, just over three weeks later.

"I think 99.9 percent of the people active in the peace organizations are honest. But they want a leader or two," said Major Stanislav Levchenko, the KGB officer who defected to the United States in 1979.[36] Levchenko had been an active measures officer at the Tokyo *rezidentura*, and had worked on the MARS campaign. The secret of disinformation, he said, was that "the KGB distorts or inverts reality." The trick was to make activists and others support Soviet policy unwittingly, by convincing them they were supporting something else.

"Almost everybody wants peace and fears war," he told one American journalist shortly after he defected. "Therefore, by every conceivable means, the KGB plans and coordinates campaigns to persuade the public that whatever America does endangers peace, and that whatever the Soviet Union proposes furthers peace . . . To be for America is to be for war; to be for the Soviets is to be for peace. That's the art of active measures, a sort of made-in-Moscow black magic. It is tragic to see how well it works."[37] The black magic even worked on Levchenko, and the KGB itself.

Nuclear Winter

NUCLEAR WINTER WAS NOTHING SHORT OF A GLOBAL NIGHT-mare, one that haunted the world in the final years of the Cold War. As simulations and data from volcanic eruptions showed, a major nuclear attack by one of the superpowers would kick up so much dust, and burning cities and forests would produce so much smoke, that Earth would be enveloped in cold darkness "within 1 to 2 weeks," per *Science* magazine.[1]

The attack scenario was grim: with 25,000 square kilometers of built-up urban terrain in flames, 130 million tons of fine particles would be carried into the troposphere, lifted by the updraft created by nuclear fireballs and mushroom clouds.[2] Nuclear detonations at or near the ground could eject soil particles, vaporize earth and rock. The blasts' powerful emissions of light would start vast fires in cities and forests. Smoke would billow into the skies

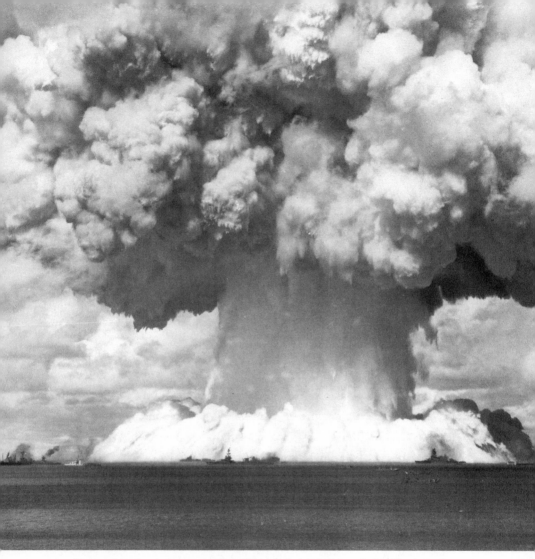

Images of nuclear tests were cruel reminders that global nuclear destruction was only minutes away at any given time. Active measures tapped into this genuine fear.
(U.S. Navy)

for weeks. Atomic war, from a planetary view, was like lighting a bonfire in a small room without any windows to let out the smoke.

The nuclear winter scare had its public debut on Halloween 1983. Five hundred scientists, officials, and environmental activists gathered under the banner "The World after Nuclear War" in Washington, D.C.[3] The group included ambassadors and representatives from more than twenty countries, and its star was Carl Sagan, who had just published the first article on nuclear winter the previous day. Halloween, said Sagan, was originally a Celtic festival named for the Lord of the Dead, marking the beginning of winter with vast bonfires. "The original Halloween," Sagan said, "combines the three essential elements of the TTAPS scenario: fires, winter, and death."[4]

The TTAPS project, an acronym derived from the last names of the five main researchers, had been in the works for months. *Science* published the paper a day before Christmas in 1983. Sagan, one of America's most prominent scientists, was one of the lead authors. The TTAPS study suggested that there was a "threshold" of nuclear detonations, which could be between five hundred and two thousand nuclear warheads. Once a nuclear attack surpassed this threshold, it would trigger global mayhem, thus ensuing the attacker's own self-destruction. The *Science* piece used data and technical language. Nuclear winter wasn't political science; these were hard, cold facts. Sagan also placed a less technical article about nuclear winter in *Foreign Affairs*.

One month earlier, on November 23, the CIA sent a classified memo to the National Intelligence Council. The memo mentioned the nuclear winter theory with concern, referring to "a new analysis and conclusion which apparently throws all previous estimates on recovery out the window."[5] Recovering from a nuclear war might not be possible, the CIA concluded, and the climate effects would have strategically "profound implications." An intelligence estimate of a few months later fretted over how the hypothesis would interfere with the doctrine of nuclear deterrence: "A concept of deterrence that depended on the credibility of launching a retaliatory strike with a large number of nuclear weapons would be meaningless." Devastating climatic effects would change the strategic equation not just for deterrence and retaliation but also for a first strike. A massive preemptive nuclear strike, the CIA wrote, "would literally be suicidal for the Soviets even if U.S. territory bore the brunt of the nuclear detonations."[6]

That wasn't all. U.S. Air Force planners began to worry that flying fine particles could hide ground targets from overhead reconnaissance; that the soot could interfere with aircraft engines; that atmospheric dust and vapor could hamper high-frequency communications as well as satellite down-links; and that the extreme cold and darkness could add even more stress to personnel working in ground command-and-control centers.

Yet something seemed odd. The nuclear winter idea was just too convenient for the Soviet cause. The TTAPS study appeared just when Moscow was doing everything it could to counter NATO's nuclear modernization in Europe. Reagan wanted Pershing II missiles in West Germany, and arms control negotiations on Intermediate-range Nuclear Forces in Geneva had stalled. Could it be that the KGB had infiltrated the climate science community and tricked not just *Science, Foreign Affairs,* and the CIA, but many millions of Americans and Europeans?

Sergei Tretyakov was a career foreign intelligence officer and once one of the youngest colonels in the SVR, the successor organization to the KGB's First Chief Directorate. From 1995 to 2000, Tretyakov was the deputy at Russia's second-largest intelligence outpost, in New York, where he was responsible for all covert operations in the city and the UN. He defected in late 2000 and handed over more than five thousand cables to the CIA.[7] In 2008, he published his memoirs, titled *Comrade J.* In the book, Tretyakov made an extraordinary claim: that the notion of nuclear winter was one of the KGB's most successful disinformation operations.

"I am not a scientist, nor did I ever meet Mr. Sagan or his coauthors," Tretyakov wrote, introducing his revelation. But the former colonel had been well connected in Russian intelligence: "I did have several conversations with the former KGB official responsible for scientific propaganda during this time period," Tretyakov said. "She told me repeatedly the KGB was responsible for creating the entire nuclear winter story to stop the Pershing missiles." Such an operation would certainly fit the KGB's established pattern of disinformation operations. Treyakov continued: "I don't know if Mr. Sagan ever knew the KGB was behind his effort, but inside the KGB, the nuclear winter propaganda was considered the ultimate example of how the KGB had completely alarmed the West with science that no one in Moscow ever believed was true."[8]

Tretyakov appeared credible. He was an experienced and highly successful

Vladimir Alexandrov,
a Soviet climate
researcher, studied
nuclear winter
models on American
supercomputers.
(UCAR)

intelligence officer, with more than sixty case officers under his command in New York. After his defection, he wrote four hundred memos for the CIA, the FBI, the State Department, and even the White House. The U.S. government allegedly compensated him with the highest amount ever paid to a U.S. intelligence source. "This man literally held the keys to a Russian intelligence gold mine," one unnamed FBI source said.[9]

Nuclear winter, it appeared, was a Soviet hoax. The KGB itself saw it as one of the most successful disinformation operations of all time. Yet, on closer examination, the story brings into sharp relief a finding that is even more surprising—and even more dangerous.

At the heart of the tale of nuclear winter is the mysterious death of Vladimir Alexandrov.

In the early 1980s, Alexandrov was one of the USSR's most prominent climate scientists. After 1978, Alexandrov, then in his early forties, had more contact with American colleagues than any other Russian scientist.

Alexandrov was a jovial, gregarious man who was fond of barbecuing spare-ribs and hamburgers. One Christmas, when the Cold War was at its grim-mest, he played a baritone Santa Claus at an Oregon nursery school. He also had more contact with American supercomputers than any other Soviet sci-entist, at two of the three main research centers on the effects of nuclear war: the National Center for Atmospheric Research in Boulder, Colorado, where he worked with a Cray-1A supercomputer, and at Lawrence Livermore Na-tional Laboratory, east of San Francisco, which he visited several times from Oregon State University.

By early 1983, the idea of nuclear winter was beginning to form among a growing number of U.S. climate scientists. In April 1983, Alexandrov was among the approximately one hundred scientists invited by the American Academy of Arts and Sciences to a meeting held in Cambridge, Massachu-setts, in order to assess the climatic effects of thermonuclear war. It was around the time of that conference that some scientists started to use the term "nuclear winter."

Just days earlier, the Reagan administration had escalated the arms race by proposing a fantastically ambitious missile-defense program in a speech to the nation. The president suggested that he would make nuclear missiles "impotent and obsolete" by way of a new strategic doctrine that became known as "Star Wars."[10] At the same time, the existing NATO schedule called for a deployment of modernized weapons to Europe by December 1983.[11] Moscow was concerned that the new weapons had the range and precision to hit command-and-control centers in Russia. Meanwhile, the peace movement across Europe had gathered force, anti-Americanism was on the rise, and civil unrest was brewing.[12] As the 1983 superpower stand-off was intensifying, Moscow's security establishment encouraged Alexan-drov to speak out, and facilitated a global lecture tour in the hope that his exaggerated, more-extreme nuclear winter scenario would further strengthen the political resistance against NATO's nuclear modernization.

By the end of August 1983, a small Soviet delegation, again including Alexandrov, joined an illustrious international security conference on nuclear war at the Centre of Scientific Culture in Erice, a small town and hilltop fort near Sicily's western coast, where Alexandrov gave an "update of climatic impacts of nuclear exchange." About 200 miles from one of Europe's most active volcanoes, Alexandrov presented a grim computer simulation of smoke and dust in the atmosphere, supported by the USSR Academy of Sciences Computing Center in Moscow.

Alexandrov outperformed even Sagan's doomsday prognostication. He presented a three-dimensional climate model that took as its point of departure one of the original TTAPS scenarios. The Soviet scientists predicted a biblical fall in temperatures forty days after nuclear war: a 30°C (54°F) drop in the western United States, a 40°C (72°F) cooling in the U.S. Northeast, and a 50°C (90°F) decrease in Europe.[13] There would be no more rain to wash the sun-blocking dirt from the sky.

On December 8, 1983, the U.S. senators Edward Kennedy and Mark Hatfield invited eight nuclear-freeze-supporting scientists, four from the United States and four from the USSR, to speak in the Senate Caucus Room. "A group of Soviet and American scientists agreed today that a large-scale nuclear exchange could mean the extinction of the human race," *The New York Times* reported the next day.[14]

One of the Russian scientists in the U.S. Senate that day was Sergei Kapitsa, of the Moscow Physico-Technical Institute. Until then, Kapitsa said, nuclear arsenals had worked as a deterrent to nuclear war by providing a "tacit mutual hostage arrangement between the opposing nuclear powers." The new climate science changed this balance of terror. "Now," Kapitsa told the senators, "the whole of the earth and human civilization itself are held hostage." Any growth of nuclear arsenals could only erode security and stability, he said, not only for the nuclear powers but for every country on earth. Alexandrov handed Kennedy a balalaika as a gift.[15]

Two weeks later, *Science* published the TTAPS study. In the accompanying *Foreign Affairs* article, Sagan thanked first his *Science* co-authors, and then named Alexandrov and his "Soviet colleagues" for providing "independent confirmations" of the nuclear winter hypothesis.[16] In January 1984, Alexandrov joined Sagan, Stephen Gold of Harvard, and fifteen other scientists for a three-day workshop at the Vatican, in order to draft a report for the pope.

Alexandrov appeared on U.S. television with Sagan, and the two even testified together in Congress in the fall of 1985. "Vladimir Aleksandrov of the Computing Centre of the Soviet Academy of Sciences, who is here, did the first global circulation model on nuclear winter," Sagan told the House Committee on Science and Technology.[17]

Under scrutiny, however, Alexandrov's role was less significant than Sagan made it appear. Richard Turco, co-author of the original TTAPS study, told *Science* that Alexandrov's paper was "a very weak piece of work, crude and seriously flawed . . . The Soviets have contributed little to the international 'nuclear winter' study effort thus far, and quite a few people are extremely disappointed,"[18] he said. The CIA reiterated this skeptical assessment internally: "Soviet research on Nuclear Winter is not convincing." Russian scholars made only modest conceptual advances when measured against the original TTAPS study. Instead, the scientific work on nuclear winter under way in Russia was not backed up by independent research and was derived "almost entirely from U.S. ideas, data, and models."[19] Soviet science had bad data, limited computer equipment, and a politically fueled appetite for extreme findings, all of which pushed Soviet scientists to make wild exaggerations. One such exaggerated finding, the CIA pointed out in December 1984, was that a nuclear exchange would "signify either the disappearance of the human race or its degradation to a level lower than prehistoric."[20]

The Pentagon agreed with the skeptics at the CIA and elsewhere a few months later. On March 1, 1985, Caspar Weinberger, the secretary of defense, handed the military's nuclear winter study to Congress. "It is hard to tell the difference between scientific workers and propagandists," he wrote. Soviet scientists had uncritically borrowed worst-case scenarios and sometimes "obsolete" mathematical simulations from others, without independently running the numbers; Soviet science was heavily criticized by international scientists as "crude" and "flawed." As an example, Weinberger named a "widely publicized" primary atmospheric circulation model by Alexandrov and his co-author, G. Stenchikov: "Given the sources and inputs and methods for their 'studies,' their findings do not represent independent verifications of the hypothesis." The Pentagon added, in direct reference to Alexandrov, that "in private the Soviets acknowledge the exaggeration."[21]

Alexandrov's American colleagues and friends knew that something was off, and pressured him to raise his scientific standards. "We were working him over pretty hard in private," one American atmospheric scientist later recalled. "His nuclear-winter stuff was at the extreme fringe, but he was beginning to come down."

The Weinberger study must have roiled Alexandrov—and the Kremlin. A few weeks later, Alexandrov was traveling to Spain to attend an international conference when he was intercepted by staff from the Soviet embassy in Madrid. What happened there remains unclear. After leaving the embassy, Alexandrov gave a disoriented talk at the conference, and disappeared from Madrid on April 1. He left behind his passport in a garbage can at the Hotel Habana, and his mother, wife, and daughter in the Soviet Union.[22] The Russian embassy settled the hotel bill. Only after Alexandrov had been missing for 108 days, and one day after *The New York Times* reported on the mystery, did Moscow's Foreign Ministry request that the Spanish police look into the incident. Nothing came of the investigation. One year later, Moscow started pushing a competing narrative: the CIA or MI6 had made the Soviet scientist disappear because militarists in Washington were trying to withhold fresh evidence that nuclear winter was real.[23] Another year later, Senator Edward Kennedy inquired with the CIA, on behalf of Alexandrov's family, about whether the Agency knew if the scientist was alive or not. William Webster, the CIA director, told Kennedy that neither U.S. nor allied intelligence agencies knew anything of "Dr. Aleksandrov's situation."[24]

The episode has a surprising conclusion: the KGB had disinformed itself. The KGB's head of scientific propaganda in the mid-1980s had a professional incentive to exaggerate the success of her work, and therefore claimed that the KGB was "responsible for creating the entire nuclear winter story." Even Soviet defectors shared a certain professional deformation that made themselves and their past work look more significant than it really was. In July 1985, when news of Alexandrov's disappearance had just broken, two KGB defectors listed the nuclear winter tale as an example of disinformation in their newsletter on Soviet active measures. Stanislav Levchenko and Peter Deriabin, both experienced in disinformation, singled out Alexandrov as an agent of influence "chosen to exaggerate both the causes and effects of a nuclear winter for foreign policy purposes."[25] A more careful examination of the trajectory of the idea of nuclear winter, however, reveals its organic origin in the American climate-research community. What really lifted the theorem to worldwide success was not Soviet propaganda in the guise of research but several highly visible U.S. scientists with a knack for branding and publicity, most notably Carl Sagan. The Soviet attempt to hijack this debate largely failed. The nuclear winter theory emerged, evolved, and disappeared in the West.

A similar dynamic applies, in even more dramatic fashion, to the most infamous disinformation story of the entire twentieth century.

RESEARCH STILL ONGOING, 2021
SEE WIKIPEDIA.
— CURRENT VIEW, N.W. NOT LIKELY

22.

AIDS Made in the USA

A VAST DARK CLOUD OF BILLIONS OF BUZZING MOSQUITOES swarms toward a distant city skyline. The lead mosquito's legs are armored with spikes, its eyes and mouth so magnified they appear gigantic. At second glance, the creature's mouth is not that of a normal mosquito, but an engineered, razor-sharp syringe. The swarm is emanating from the dark eye sockets of a human skull, a skull smoking a cigarette.

This bizarre illustration appeared in *Literaturnaya Gazeta* on February 3, 1982, above a long story titled "Incubator of Death." The piece, written in the first person, was a kind of travelogue into a CIA factory for weaponized mosquitoes. The author, Iona Andronov, started his adventure after visiting the editor of "the journal 'Covert Action' in Washington," (a reference to *Covert Action Information Bulletin*). That Washington editor showed Andronov,

An illustration of U.S. biological weapons that did not exist, in *Literaturnaya Gazeta*, Moscow, February 1982 (*Literaturnaya Gazeta*)

he claimed, "leaked documents from the CIA" that led his investigation to Lahore, Pakistan. En route from Moscow to Lahore, Andronov recounted, his luggage was taken away during a layover, then he was followed by Pakistani security, and diplomatic phone numbers appeared to mysteriously stop working. American spies were on his heels. Nevertheless, the intrepid reporter managed to charm his way into the secret mosquito lab.[1]

The story was a poorly executed reaction to a new problem.

About a year earlier, in the summer and fall of 1980, the United States had raised concerns about the Soviet use of chemical weapons in Southeast Asia, especially in Laos and Afghanistan. The USSR invaded Afghanistan in late December 1979, and Soviet forces immediately started using chemical agents against the mujahideen resistance fighters. In December 1980, the United Nations General Assembly passed a resolution that established a technical UN investigation into the use of chemical munitions.

By the fall of 1981, the U.S. government had recorded evidence of forty-seven Soviet chemical attacks in Afghanistan alone. Afghans described gray, blue-black, and yellow chemical clouds wafting from land mines and bombs, rockets fired from fixed-wing aircraft, and gas sprayed from Hind helicopter gunships. In one incident, witnesses described finding three mujahideen dead, their hands still in firing position on their rifles, indicating that the Soviet chemical agent had been extremely rapid-acting and did not cause physiological reactions before death. Other witnesses described abnormal bloating of dead bodies and blackened skin with a dark-reddish tinge, indicative of rapid decay. By early 1982, the U.S. government was making more and more harrowing evidence available to the UN and the wider public.[2] What the State Department did not say was that the United States had been secretly funding the mujahideen, and that the Soviets were gassing America's proxies.

The killer mosquito story was part of a larger, more complex campaign to deflect blame, and to compromise the U.S. and NATO over biological and chemical weapons. The campaign was code-named TARAKANY, "cockroaches" in Russian. Even if the Soviet claim that the CIA was developing chemical weapons in Lahore was revealed as fake, that revelation would make it easier for the USSR to claim that the CIA's reports of Soviet chemical weapons in Afghanistan were equally made-up. Just when the United States was getting ready to publish a major report on Soviet chemical weapons, *Literaturnaya Gazeta* alleged that the Pakistan Malaria Research Center was a CIA-funded laboratory to breed weaponized mosquitoes.

The story was clumsy but creative. Iona Andronov depicted the Americans he met in the "mosquito factory" as cartoonish villains—fat, fiendish, crude, and cunning. The University of Maryland lab in Lahore and its fight against malaria, he claimed, was only a façade; behind it were "poisoners from overseas" who plotted to infect entire cattle herds with viruses and then take advantage of the seasonal migration of the herds from Pakistan to Afghanistan to start an epidemic of encephalitis in Afghanistan. The *Gazeta* story also claimed that a recent outbreak of dengue fever in Cuba had been caused by imported Lahore-bred mosquitoes. TARAKANY replayed similar tales about U.S. killer germs in India, Iran, Bangladesh, Lebanon, and South

Africa. The KGB considered its "cockroaches" campaign a big success, especially after Service A concluded that Pakistan had declared the American head of the University of Maryland lab in Lahore persona non grata as a result of their work. Andropov, the chairman of the KGB, even awarded a testimonial to his resident in Pakistan.[3]

Just a few months later, *Covert Action Information Bulletin* published a special issue on chemical weapons. The *Bulletin* also claimed that the same virulent 1981 outbreak of dengue fever in Cuba had been a CIA operation— it was unclear whether the idea originated at Dupont Circle or Yasenevo.[4] The Soviets launched an entire range of measures in the early 1980s that attempted to blame various diseases on the United States, particularly the Cuban outbreak of dengue fever.[5]

It was against this background of military escalation in Afghanistan and weapons of mass destruction in South Asia that one of the most infamous disinformation campaigns of the entire Cold War emerged: the story that AIDS was an American biological weapon developed at Fort Detrick, Maryland.

"Rare Cancer Seen in 41 Homosexuals," reported *The New York Times* on July 3, 1981. The cancer was said to appear in one or more spots anywhere on the body. Eight of the forty-one known victims had died within two years after noticing the spots; the cause of the outbreak was unknown. It was the first major press story on what would become known as Acquired Immune Deficiency Syndrome (AIDS), also commonly named after its virus, HIV.[6]

The pandemic soon grew into one of the most alarming public health emergencies of all time. "A Disease's Spread Provokes Anxiety," read the headline in *The New York Times* on Sunday, August 8, 1982. The virus suppressed the body's own defenses, setting the stage for secondary infections, including various rare forms of cancer and pneumonia. The pandemic began its global spread among gay men, and New York and San Francisco were its first American epicenters. The Centers for Disease Control in Atlanta counted 505 cases in the United States by August 1982, half of them in New York; 202 of these early patients had already died. Initial reporting also discovered thirty infected immigrants from Haiti, all heterosexual, including women. Early on, researchers suspected that AIDS was transmitted through sexual contact or blood, but clinical research trials into the new disease were only beginning.

"It's unfortunate we don't have anything positive to recommend to people at the present time," said Dr. David Spencer, New York City's health commissioner. "We just don't know."

"It's basically frightening because no one knows what's causing it," one twenty-eight-year-old law student told the *Times* after taking a test in a clinic in Greenwich Village. "Every week a new theory comes out about how you're going to spread it."[7]

In June 1983, gay rights supporters proceeded through Manhattan carrying a banner that read: A.I.D.S.: WE NEED RESEARCH, NOT HYS-TERIA. Not all activists, it soon turned out, shared this sober attitude.

The theory that the U.S. government had funded and weaponized AIDS first emerged in America's gay rights activist community. Charley Shively was the founder and editor of *Fag Rag*, a well-established Boston-based anarchist gay periodical founded in 1970. Shively was angry. "They say our sex is adolescent, compulsive, retarded, irresponsible, sinful and dreadful," he wrote.

Shively knew that AIDS had primarily affected Haitian immigrants, that it was alleged to come from Africa, and that it affected gay men and drug users, and he knew that the U.S. government discriminated against all of these groups. He simply connected the dots. In *Gay Community News*, he claimed that there was "a frightening likelihood that AIDS has been funded all along by the federal government."[8] Alluding to recent reports alleging that the U.S. military researched "ethnic chemical weapons," he observed that "AIDS sounds just like such an ethnic weapon." He claimed that there was evidence "that the CIA itself is responsible for introducing the disease in the western hemisphere." He pointed to the U.S. naval base at Guantánamo as the likely point of origin; the engineered virus had spread from there first to Haiti, he conjectured, and then to the United States.

The moment was ideal for a disinformation campaign, as the marchers' signs in New York made clear: there was yet little research into AIDS, and an abundance of hysteria. The CDC now counted 1,641 infections and 644 deaths in the United States.[9] The cause for the epidemic had still not been identified. Two Stasi disinformation officers observed that the fear of AIDS had spread much faster than the virus itself. "The campaign concept would almost emerge by itself," they recalled.[10] Starting the campaign, however, was harder than expected. In the end, neither the KGB nor the Stasi started the theory that AIDS was U.S.-engineered.

"AIDS may invade India: mystery disease caused by U.S. lab experiments." So read the sensational first-page headline in *Patriot*, an Indian newspaper, on July 16, 1983. *Patriot*, under a picture of five smiling girls, printed an anonymous letter from a "well-known American scientist and anthropologist." There was no name in the byline, only "New York."[11]

The *Patriot* letter was a masterfully executed disinformation operation: comprising about 20 percent forgery and 80 percent fact, truth and lies woven together, it was an eloquent, well-researched piece that gently led the reader, through convincing detail, to his or her own conclusion.

It began: "AIDS, the deadly mysterious disease which has caused havoc in the U.S., is believed to be the result of the Pentagon's experiments to develop new and dangerous biological weapons." The new disease was indeed mysterious and had caused havoc in the United States, especially in New York. The World Health Organization had warned of the dangers of AIDS, the story noted correctly, since it was highly virulent and had no cure. France and the Netherlands, which used American blood donations, had stopped importing the potentially infected U.S. blood, and Britain, Germany, and Denmark were considering similar measures. The story correctly described the recent history of AIDS, from its spread to the United States from Haitian immigrants, then to drug consumers and homosexuals primarily in New York, and then, by February 1983, on to thirty-three more states, with New York still accounting for 49 percent of all recorded cases.[12]

Patriot then quoted from official Pentagon and CIA documents that had in fact been published a few years earlier, after a prolonged Freedom of Information battle.[13] "According to these documents," the *Patriot* letter reported, the Department of Defense as well as the CIA had "tested new types of biological weapons in the densely populated areas of the U.S. and Canada, such as New York, Philadelphia, San Francisco and Winnipeg." The *Patriot* letter echoed many of the reported—and accurate—themes of scandalous medical experiments that the U.S. government actually undertook in the 1960s and early 1970s, perhaps most infamously the MKULTRA experiments, popularly known as the CIA mind-control program: that the U.S. Army and the CIA had conducted research on diseases and psychotropic agents with volunteers, drug users, and prisoners as "guinea pigs"; that the experiments continued despite President Richard Nixon's ban on bioweapons in 1968; and that Fort Detrick, in Maryland, was a center of the secret research.

Patriot, with a circulation of around 35,000, was no ordinary Indian paper. The Soviet Union had helped fund the left-wing outlet when it opened in 1962, for the explicit purpose of circulating Soviet-friendly stories and publishing disinformation, according to a KGB defector.[14] But Ivanov's Service A officers had misjudged the situation in India. The fear of AIDS had not reached the subcontinent yet, the excellent *Patriot* "AM" did not get much pickup in India—and it went entirely unnoticed in Europe and the United States; not even the U.S. State Department was aware of the article when it came out.[15]

The KGB and Service A were in a regional mind-set, and misjudged the potential of the escalating AIDS crisis in the United States and Europe itself. The AIDS article in *Patriot* was a continuation of the bioweapon disinformation campaign of the previous year, designed to distract from U.S. revelations on Soviet chemical warfare in Southeast Asia. *Patriot* noted that the United States was about to transfer its biological experimental setup to military sites in Pakistan, from which vantage the virus would pose a grave threat to India.[16]

The HIV virus, the cause of the deadly syndrome, was then in the process of being identified, and the U.S. government only announced the cause of AIDS almost a year later, in April 1984.[17] More uncertainty and more hysteria meant that AIDS conspiracy theories continued to fester at the far-left fringes of American civil rights activism, still, so far, without meaningful input from Soviet disinformation operators.[18]

American intelligence analysts, meanwhile, were investigating the reverse question: whether AIDS was a Soviet biological weapon. The CIA was aware that the Red Army was engaged in "military-related research on an AIDS-like virus," as one internal study reported in February 1985. The

Совершенно секретно

Справка № 2955

Нами проводится комплекс мероприятий в связи с появлением в последние годы в США нового опасного заболевания т.н. "Синдрома приобретенного иммунодефицита – СПИД" (по английски "*AIDS-AQUIRED IMMUNE DEFICIENCY SYNDROME*"), и последующего его широкого распространения на другие страны, включая западноевропейские. Целью мероприятий является создание за рубежом выгодного нам мнения о том, что это заболевание – результат вышедших из под контроля секретных экспериментов спецслужб США и Пентагона с новым видом биологического оружия.

Было бы желательно, если бы Вы смогли подключиться к осуществлению указанных мероприятий через Ваши возможности в партийных, парламентских, общественно-политических и журналистских кругах западных и развивающихся стран путем продвижения в буржуазную печать следующих тезисов:

I. Впервые появившись в конце 70-х годов в Нью-Йорке, СПИД к 1985 г. стал одним из наиболее опасных заболеваний в мире. Только в США зарегистрировано более 12400 заболевших, из которых около половины умерли. По подсчетам американских медиков, число случаев поражения СПИД удваивается каждые полгода. В настоящее время в США носителями вируса СПИД являются уже около 3 млн. человек. Поскольку болезнь имеет очень длительный инкубационный период (от I года до 5 лет), выявление ее на ранней стадии, когда еще есть надежда вылечить больного, крайне затруднительно. Несмотря на то, что американские и французские ученые смогли в 1983 г. выделить вирус СПИД, эффективных лекарств и методов лечения этого заболевания создать не удалось. К 1985 г. СПИД распространился далеко за пределы США: многочисленные случаи заболеваний СПИД отмечены практически во всех странах-импортерах донорской крови из США. Всемирная организация здравоохранения объявила СПИД одной из самых опасных болезней на земле. При этом отмечалось, что она сильнее всего угрожает развивающимся странам.

A KGB memo instructing Bulgarian intelligence to help spread the myth that AIDS is a U.S. weapon (COMDOS, via Christopher Nehring)

CIA also noted that the disease was introduced into the United States from a single source, Haiti. However, CIA analysts concluded that AIDS was not a Soviet-developed biological warfare agent.[19] The pandemic continued to spread. By the summer of 1985, the CDC had reported more than ten thousand AIDS cases in the United States, with deaths surpassing five thousand. Serologic tests became available, and the U.S. military started testing its personnel for AIDS in September.

That same month, on September 7, the KGB's First Chief Directorate sent a secret memo to some of its satellite services about a new campaign in the planning stage, code-named DENVER.[20] The United States had accused the USSR of noncompliance with the 1972 Biological Weapons Convention, and now DENVER was designed to turn the accusation on its head, and to show that the United States was secretly manufacturing bioweapons.

The KGB memo explained:

> We are executing a complex of measures in connection with a new, dangerous disease that has emerged in the USA in recent years, [...] AIDS, and its subsequent spread to other countries, including West European countries. The goal of these measures is to generate, for us, a beneficial view in other countries that this disease is the result of out-of-control secret experiments by U.S. intelligence agencies and the Pentagon involving new types of biological weapons.[21]

The point of departure of the planned active measures campaign, as the KGB told its Soviet bloc partners, was the "factual" article published in *Patriot*. The KGB then instructed its partners to help spread the theory that AIDS was U.S.-made to "party, parliamentary, social-political, and journalistic circles in Western countries and the developing world." The "facts" published in the Indian press offered the blueprint, as the KGB noted:

> Taking into account this message [in *Patriot*], taking into account the U.S. Army's interests in the AIDS symptoms, and also taking into account the speed and geography of its spread, one assumption

is bound to appear most plausible: that this very dangerous disease is the result of a number of Pentagon experiments with new kinds of biological weapons. This is also confirmed by the disease initially affecting only particular groups of people (homosexuals, drug addicts, Latinos).[22]

Shortly thereafter, on October 2, Rock Hudson, a Hollywood and TV celebrity, became the first major public figure to die of AIDS. Public fear increased.

On October 30, *Literaturnaya Gazeta* ran the headline "Panic in the West: or, What Is Hiding Behind the Sensation Surrounding AIDS."[23] The paper was the KGB's "prime conduit in the Soviet press for propaganda and disinformation," according to Oleg Kalugin.[24] The piece that relaunched the DENVER campaign closely mirrored the earlier measure in the Indian press. Its author, Vitaly Zapevalov, accurately cited details about the new disease and its spread in American cities over the past two years, basing his analysis on authoritative U.S. news reports.

"Why," he asked ominously, would AIDS "appear in the USA and start spreading above all in towns along the East Coast?" Next, the *Gazeta* piece outlined several covert American biological warfare programs, again based on verifiable public sources. Zapevalov also cited accurate details about Fort Detrick. The author then referred to the two-year-old *Patriot* forgery to connect the dots. "All of this information, taken together with the AIDS mystery, leads to serious considerations. The solid newspaper *Patriot*, published in India, for instance, openly expressed an assumption that AIDS is the result of similar inhuman Washington experiments."[25]

The article was a success, although its pivotal role became clear only later on. Radio Moscow's World Service immediately replayed the story, and the U.S. government noted that the text was also replayed in Kuwait, Bahrain, Finland, Sweden, and Peru.[26] But no English-speaking or German news outlet picked up the story, not even in East Germany.

In the United States, the theory continued to spread—still on its own, without any link to Soviet disinformation—that AIDS was likely the creation of an American bacteriological warfare program. "Link AIDS to CIA warfare," cried New York's *Amsterdam News*, a paper popular among African Americans. The story quoted an earlier investigative report on the CIA's attempted assassination of Patrice Lumumba of Zaire. The CIA, *The New York Times* had reported, had been developing biological agents for such targeted assassinations. A former clinical director from Downstate Medical Center in Brooklyn then claimed that "similar experiments are being conducted openly on Western homosexuals, drug addicts, and African-Americans." The doctor from Brooklyn also accused the CDC of refusing to investigate whether the CIA had engineered AIDS.[27]

Meanwhile, in East Berlin, Jakob Segal, the retired director of the Institute of General Biology at Humboldt University, closely studied the October article in the *Literaturnaya Gazeta*.[28] Segal and his wife, Lilli Segal, were members of the Soviet Communist Party and survivors of the Holocaust. The Segals were worldly, cultured, charming, and spoke several languages— and would soon become the prime influence agents of the AIDS myth.

"AIDS: USA—home made evil, NOT Imported from AFRICA" was distributed as a free booklet at a summit in Harare, Zimbabwe, that took place from August 26 to September 6. The booklet contained a detailed 52-page study titled "AIDS—Its Nature and Origin," bylined by Jakob Segal, his wife, and another collaborator.[29] Already two days ahead of the conference, the *Harare Sunday Mail* reported on its cover that arriving attendees were discussing the American role in creating and disseminating AIDS.[30] The story was widely replayed in Africa.

The KGB was running DENVER as a joint campaign with help from partner agencies.[31] Ten days after the conference, the deputy head of the X, Wolfgang Mutz, traveled from Berlin to his partners in Sofia, Bulgaria. Mutz briefed his counterparts on a long list of ongoing active measures. One, code-named MIRROR, also boosted in Harare ten days earlier, was a slim book nominally written by the East Berlin correspondent of *Patriot* and *Blitz*, an investigative Indian weekly. The book, *Devil and His Dart: How the CIA Is Plotting in the Third World*, was dripping with anti-American clichés and CIA conspiracy theories. Mutz told the Bulgarians that it contained a list with the names of 300 CIA officers,[32] again titled, like HVA's earlier volume, *Who's Who in CIA*.[33] The Americans, Mutz added, had already bought 600 copies of "our book" from the publisher.[34] HVA had the book translated and published in German. The Bulgarians agreed to help push the anti-CIA pamphlet into Lebanon and Syria.

Then Mutz told his counterparts that the AIDS campaign, DENVER, occupied "a considerable amount" of the resources in his department, and added that another HVA department had done "a great deal of scientific work." Mutz was referring to the 52-page Segal study that had surfaced in Harare, and to HVA's science and technology department, which listed Segal as a collaborator.[35] The Bulgarians considered it challenging to find a local scientist to "support the German professor's thesis."

Operation DENVER's first major Western breakthrough came on October 26, 1986, in Britain. "AIDS Sensation," announced the *Sunday Express*, a right-wing tabloid: "The killer AIDS virus was artificially created by American scientists during laboratory experiments which went disastrously wrong."[36] The British paper relied heavily on Jakob Segal's narrative on the origins of AIDS; a British reporter called Segal at least three times,[37] and the UK tabloid repeated Segal's claim—that the virus was engineered at Fort Detrick—multiple times. Newspapers in at least thirty countries reported on or reprinted the piece, including *The Australian* and Italy's *La Stampa*.[38]

Tireless repetition would eventually catapult the disinformation into many millions of American households as prime-time evening news. By the end of March 1987, the USSR's global radio stations had covered the hoax more than a dozen times, and Soviet print media had replayed the story another dozen times. In the first three months of 1987 alone, DENVER-related stories had appeared more than forty times worldwide.[39] The piece with by far the biggest impact was unremarkable, one of the many repetitions: on March 30, the Associated Press in Moscow carried a report under the headline "Soviet Bulletin Says AIDS Leaked from U.S. Laboratory."[40] The AP report was a write-up of an eight-paragraph story in TASS, which had in turn reported on a six-paragraph editorial printed in *Novosti*.[41] A producer at *CBS Evening News* saw the AP headline and found it "so extraordinary" that it was slated for discussion on the network's flagship news show. That day, the iconic presenter Dan Rather read the following announcement to the approximately 15 million viewers of CBS Evening News:

> A Soviet military publication claims the virus that causes AIDS leaked from a U.S. Army laboratory conducting experiments in biological warfare. The article offers no hard evidence, but claims to be reporting the conclusions of unnamed scientists in the United States, Britain and East Germany. Last October, a Soviet newspaper alleged that the AIDS virus may have been the result of Pentagon or CIA experiments.[42]

Service A would continue to push the campaign, at home and abroad, for at least six more months. But the KGB's cameo on CBS Evening News would prove the peak of Operation DENVER.

The Russian government would soon officially disavow the AIDS active measure. On October 23, 1987, U.S. Secretary of State George Shultz met with Mikhail Gorbachev, the Soviet head of state. Shultz reportedly told Gorbachev that Moscow was peddling "bum dope" on AIDS.[43] Three days later, the UN General Assembly passed a resolution, by a margin of 42–8, to unite all countries in the fight against AIDS.[44] The resolution was co-sponsored by the United States and the USSR, and recognized that a naturally occurring virus was the cause of the disease. Four days later, on October 30, 1987, the main Soviet government newspaper, Izvestia, carried an article by two Soviet scientists who officially distanced the Soviet Academy of Sciences from the accusations that AIDS was U.S.-made, and even protested the appearance of Soviet articles claiming the opposite.[45]

DENVER was officially over, but the disinformation work continued in secret. As late as September 1989, just weeks before the fall of the Berlin Wall, Department X argued in an internal meeting that the peak of the AIDS disinformation campaign had not yet been achieved.[46] The X was right. Jakob Segal continued to spread the AIDS-was-made-in-the-USA theory until his death in 1995—the X and Service A had ceased to exist, but the academic remained a committed conspiracy activist. Ten years after that, the hip-hop icon Kanye West rapped, "I know that the government administer AIDS."

The KGB assessed the AIDS campaign as a major success. In 1992, the head of Russian foreign intelligence, Yevgeny Primakov, confirmed the KGB's role in the AIDS disinformation campaign during a talk at MGIMO, an academic institute affiliated with the Ministry of Foreign Affairs in Moscow. Primakov revealed that the AIDS story was "created in the cabinets of the KGB,"[47] and had simply aimed to distract from the Red Army's use of chemical weapons. One prominent defector claimed that DENVER was "probably the most successful active measure in the Third World during the early years of the Gorbachev era."[48]

The success of DENVER must be kept in perspective. Service A did not create the AIDS myth; it did not accurately assess its own role, nor could disinformation specialists stop or effectively contain the story—nevertheless, for a relatively short period, mainly between October 1985 and October 1987, Eastern bloc intelligence agencies amplified and enhanced the myth that AIDS was made in Fort Detrick. But is there a direct line that connects gay community activists, the activities of Service A, and the sentiment expressed in Kanye West's lyrics twenty years later? The answer is, and will remain, uncertain. By the late 1980s, active measures had become highly active and nearly impossible to measure, allowing agencies on the periphery of events to claim credit and get away with it.

The Philosophy of "AM"

B Y THE 1980S, COMMUNISM, LIKE ANY RESILIENT SPIRITUAL system of thought, had long evinced a capacity to tolerate contradiction. Cynicism was widespread, and even intelligence officers were sharing Communist jokes inside Soviet bloc security establishments. This capacity for contradiction might appear to be a weakness at first glance. But contradictions are the raw material of active measures. Cynicism, as opposed to the fiery Marxism of the 1950s, enabled more sophisticated and more active measures, for it removed ideological and ethical limitations.

The Olympic Games in Los Angeles in 1984 offers an extraordinary active measures example. The Soviet Union boycotted the games, and targeted them with special operations instead. Service A, playing both sides, impersonated the KKK and sent vile racist leaflets to African and Asian Olympic

Disinformation operators regularly referred to Lenin's writings.

committees in more than twenty countries in the name of the American militant extremists, threatening bodily harm if they participated in the games. The letters were postmarked in the Washington, D.C., area.[1] At the same time, with help from partner agencies, the KGB's disinformation specialists impersonated a then-fierce Islamic terrorist organization, al-Jihad, and threatened French and Israeli delegations with physical attacks, according to a declassified memo.[2]

By early 1985, active measures had also reached peak bureaucratic performance. Soviet active measures then had an annual budget between $3 billion and $4 billion—an estimate that CIA analysts called "conservative."[3] Service A was making a concerted effort to refine and distribute the philosophy of active measures throughout the Eastern bloc intelligence establishment. The context for this push was probably an attempt by the leadership of Service A to upgrade active measures for the second time, after more than two decades, from a "service" into a full-blown "directorate," on a level with the First Chief Directorate. 1985

In January, Vladimir Ivanov traveled to Sofia to give a lecture, "The Art of Planning, Developing, and Implementing AM"—by then, disinformation was so common that Soviet bloc intelligence services referred to active measures simply as "AM," with no need to spell out the ubiquitous acronym.

"AM are extremely effective, but also a very sharp and delicate weapon of intelligence," Ivanov explained. "Every AM is a sharp political action." Work in this delicate area, he said, "is in itself one of the most acute forms of a secret political struggle, in the full sense of this notion." The KGB general was giving a political talk about a political tool, and he sounded like he was. Ivanov added that active measures would affect the fundamental political, economic, and military interests of all socialist states. He wanted to get the point across to his audience, intelligence officers used to rigidity, rules, order, and hierarchy, that active measures were both "a science and an art." To anchor this important activity in Soviet ideology, the ambitious chief of Service A reached for the very top: Lenin. He referenced a quote from a booklet that Lenin had published in 1920, "Left-Wing Communism, an Infantile Disorder." Rigid rules and recipes would not be helpful, he said.[4] What was required was—and here Ivanov used Lenin's words—"the knowledge, experience and—in addition to knowledge and experience—the political flair [instinct] necessary for the speedy and correct solution of complex political problems."[5]

Then Ivanov delivered the take-home message for the senior intelligence officers and AM operators in the room, again straight from Lenin:

> The more powerful enemy can be vanquished only by exerting the utmost effort, and by the most thorough, careful, attentive, skilful and obligatory use of any, even the smallest, rift between the enemies, any conflict of interests among the bourgeoisie of the various countries and among the various groups or types of bourgeoisie within the various countries, and also by taking advantage of any, even the smallest, opportunity of winning a

mass ally, even though this ally is temporary, vacillating, unstable, unreliable, and conditional.[6]

Ivanov stressed that Lenin's teachings had "retained their power" especially for intelligence operators engaged in active measures. He then went on to outline this delicate art of disinformation.

Based on the analysis of all the material and, if necessary, with the help of scientists and specialists, the officers are obliged to find the overwhelming outbreaks of crises, dissatisfaction, friction, disagreement, rivalry, and struggle in the enemy camp. The discovery of such looming crises, Ivanov explained, and then the identification of the most sensitive vulnerabilities, required scientific knowledge and a scientific approach, knowledge of the objective processes in the world and in the country of residence.[7]

The KGB general spoke as if he were giving a creative-writing class, and, in a way, he was—to a group of forgers. "The process of developing AM is complex, and requires not just intelligence and knowledge, but also great intuition, imagination, ingenuity, and sensibility," he said. Only by keeping all these subtleties in mind would the disinformation specialist be able to achieve the desired effect, which depended on "emotions and psychological sentiments." Local AM operators had to be in touch with political events in their countries, and able to react quickly. "Sometimes, even the 'rumor' of the moment and the knowledge of the subsequent supporting events can prove to be of great influence and effect in solving your tasks," Ivanov explained. He added that solving the task would require carefully maintaining a large circle of trusted ties, with government officials, civil servants, parliamentarians, publishers, and journalists.

The KGB's First Chief Directorate had authorized the HVA and Department X to perform similar outreach with the wider Ministry of State Security in East Berlin. As was recommended by Russian advisors, Rolf Wagenbreth, the head of Department X, embellished his lecture in Belzig with a quote from Lenin: his unit, and the wider Eastern bloc, was engaged in "a war," he said, "a war which is a hundred times more difficult, protracted and complicated than the most stubborn of ordinary wars between states." This war operated under the single objective of driving wedges into preexisting fissures within the adversarial societies.

The West German intelligence community was well aware of the rising threat of active measures, as were many German investigative journalists. Just as the Soviet rollout of their AM philosophy was under way, in early 1985, the German intelligence community finalized a remarkable internal report titled *Active Measures of Eastern Intelligence Services*.[8] It was the first time that the West German government had comprehensively detailed the onslaught of disinformation it had faced for many years. The "offensive role" of disinformation, the West Germans understood, went far beyond the traditional task of collecting information:[9] "The known past and present goal of 'active measures' directed by the Soviet intelligence agency KGB against the Federal Republic of Germany is to degrade the federal government's trust in its U.S. ally."[10]

Across the Berlin Wall, the X immediately took note of the report. The HVA assumed that they were looking at the work of the counterintelligence unit of the BfV, West Germany's domestic intelligence service headquartered in Cologne. "They had analyzed dangerously well," noted the HVA.[11]

West and East Germany, although politically and economically divided, were culturally, geographically, and linguistically one entity. This proximity meant that the East had an overwhelming advantage in active measures—for the West had almost entirely retreated from strategic disinformation operations by then. But a similar dynamic applied in the other direction as well. The West Germans operated in such proximity to the Soviet bloc that they had a superb understanding of the sophistication and intellectual and historical depth of late Cold War active measures. What made the BfV analysis from Cologne so dangerous in the HVA's eyes was that the West German officers understood the *philosophy* of AM. West German counterintelligence had read and understood Lenin, whose ideas formed the basis of *Zersetzung*, or disintegration, and ultimately disinformation.

Lenin's perhaps most influential and visionary pamphlet, written in 1902, is titled *What Is to Be Done?* It sketches out a vision for a revolutionary party. "Have we sufficient forces to be able to direct our propaganda and agitation among *all* classes of the population?" Lenin writes, answering himself, "Of course we have."[12] To mobilize the masses, Lenin suggested, the movement would have to utilize every manifestation of discontent, and seize every grain of even rudimentary protest. One way to whip up and spread agitation was to expose what those in power were trying to hide. "Political exposures are as much a declaration of war against the *government* as economic exposures are a declaration of war against the employers," wrote the young Lenin. Public exposure of government secrets was the political expression of economic class warfare, and the wider and more powerful this campaign of exposure, the larger its mobilization effect on the masses, and the greater its "moral significance." Lenin called for a radical plan not only to expose poor factory conditions and economic inequality for the working class but to reveal the camouflaged "inner workings" of all classes, the true face of tyranny, oppression, violence, and abuse. Exposures, he argued, were an engine for mobilizing the masses against any adversarial government, be it at home or abroad. Lenin foresaw that even in countries with political liberty, there would still be opportunities for exposure. He wrote: "Hence, the political exposures in themselves serve as a powerful instrument for disintegrating the system we oppose, the means of diverting from the enemy his casual or temporary allies, the means for spreading enmity and distrust among those who permanently share power with the autocracy."[13]

Some analysts in West Germany had learned from their East German opponents that understanding active measures required understanding Lenin first.

As West German counterintelligence noted in the 1985 report, Lenin reversed the famous line, by the Prussian military theorist Carl von Clausewitz, that war was a continuation of politics by other means. Politics was a continuation of war by other means, in Lenin's reading, and active measures an "ersatz for (military) warfare."[14]

By this point in the Cold War, the West Germans understood not just Lenin but also the tactics, techniques, and procedures of this form of ersatz war. The analysts in Cologne had "no doubt" that the KGB coordinated the overall planning for offensive political influence operations with the Stasi in Berlin, StB in Prague, and other satellite agencies.

They also highlighted the role of Western journalists as information bearers of active measures throughout the Cold War. "Adversarial services pay attention in particular to journalists in non-Communist states," they noted in the report.[15] "Manipulating the media is the single most commonly used method to realize 'active measures' in the Western world."[16]

But the West was getting better at fighting back. Various congressional committees held several hearings on Soviet active measures in the early 1980s, and both the CIA and the FBI provided a wealth of evidence to Congress in hearings and various highly publicized reports published in the *Congressional Record*. Part of the government's goal was simply to raise awareness among the public and the press. But the State Department would not stop there, and would even apply tradecraft to stop disinformation.

On April 26, 1986, the Chernobyl Nuclear Power Plant's reactor number 4 exploded. The disaster, the worst nuclear accident in history, occurred near Pripyat, a town of nearly fifty thousand then part of the Ukrainian Soviet Socialist Republic of the Soviet Union. Just weeks later, with reactor 4 still smoldering, even before its protective concrete sarcophagus had been built, the KGB decided to take advantage of the catastrophe with an exceptionally cold-blooded yet equally instructive active measure.

The letter was backdated to April 29, 1986, just three days after the Chernobyl disaster. Printed on legitimate U.S. Information Agency (USIA) letterhead, addressed to David Durenberger, the chairman of the Senate Select Committee on Intelligence, it read:

Dear Senator Durenberger:

Now that there is conclusive evidence that the breakdown of a Chernobyl nuclear power plant reactor produced a considerable quantity of radioactive fallout, we have a chance to utilize this fact for propaganda purposes. Furthermore, it is good for us that Moscow has made no official statement on the event.

Therefore we suggest that the following steps should be taken:—
reports should be spread by our associates in European information
media giving the public the details of Chernobyl disaster [sic]:—
number of victims should be alleged to be somewhere between 2,000
and 3,000;—mass evacuation from the 100-mile zone [. . .][17]

The one-page letter was signed by Herbert Romerstein, the senior policy officer on Soviet Active Measures at the USIA, and had been sent to *The
Washington Post* and *U.S. News and World Report* in an attempt to make it
look like the work of a whistle-blower.[18] Neither of the two papers fell for the
letter.[19]

It was a brazen operation on the part of Soviet intelligence, and a big
middle finger to the U.S. government—a Russian active measure camouflaged as an American active measure. In the most cynical way possible, as
if they were trying to deflect some of Chernobyl's nuclear fallout onto the
United States, Eastern operators were trying to take advantage of one of the
great human tragedies of the twentieth century, one that was still playing
out *in the Soviet Union itself.*

The KGB, however, had underestimated Romerstein. The previous year,
he had testified before another high-profile Senate body, the Foreign Relations Committee, on Soviet active measures, his field of expertise. During
his testimony, Romerstein discussed one particular Soviet forgery, a document that purportedly came from Lieutenant General Robert Schweizer,
an influential and hawkish strategic planner. Romerstein had analyzed the
Schweizer forgery and mailed a copy of the analysis to Schweizer himself,
along with a cover letter printed on USIA letterhead. In the 1985 hearing,
Romerstein offered to supply the committee with a copy of the cover letter
and accompanying analysis.

The press attaché of the Czechoslovak embassy, Vaclav Zluva, became
aware of this episode, and inquired with the USIA about whether he could
receive a copy of Romerstein's letter. But Romerstein quickly understood
what was really going on: Czechoslovak intelligence wanted the letterhead
and his signature for future forgeries. So he decided to set a trap. Romerstein

**United States
Information
Agency**

Washington DC 20547

April 29, 1986

COPY

USIA

Senator David Durenberger
375 RSOB
Washington, D.C. 20510

Dear Senator Durenberger:

FORGERY

Now that there is conclusive evidence that the breakdown of a Chernobyl nuclear power plant reactor produced a considerable quantity of radioactive fallout, we have a chance to utilize this fact for propaganda purposes. Furthermore, it is good for us that Moscow has made no official statement on the event.

Therefore we suggest that following steps should be taken:

- Reports should be spread by our associates in European information media giving the public the details of Chernobyl disaster:

  - number of victims should be alleged to be somewhere between 2,000 and 3,000;

  - mass evacuation of population from the 100-mile zone;

  - transport problems, shortage of various goods, chaos, and panic should also be given publicity;

  - appropriate illustrations and textual material should be provided;

  - a campaign should be organized by USIA officials who should also supply the material needed.

- In view of the forthcoming Tokyo summit data should be provided for the statement on the Chernobyl disaster to be issued by the seven leaders.

- Considering the facts about the increased air pollution, our allies should be recommended to stop imports of food and other commodities from Eastern bloc.

- Our allies should be influenced so as to make a request for compensation for contamination of their territory.

We will keep you informed of any future measures.

Best regards,

Herbert Romerstein

Herbert Romerstein,
Senior Policy Officer
on Soviet Active Measures

Forgery of a letter from Herbert Romerstein. The forgery still carries Romerstein's original handwritten markings, especially the "COPY" at the top. (Herbert Romerstein)

drafted a sample letter for Zluva, wrote "COPY" in handwriting at the top, and kept a record of his precise handwritten signature on that particular letter.[20] If a forgery surfaced with those unique features, the USIA would have a clear indication of a forgery—and when the Chernobyl letter emerged, it did.

In retrospect, Ivanov's effort to explain the philosophy of "AM" to his audience in 1985 highlighted a major philosophical and moral asymmetry between Cold War opponents. For a quarter century, the West had deescalated what the CIA once called "political warfare," while the East had escalated. This asymmetry is best illustrated by comparing selected high-end active measures from each side of the Iron Curtain just before the end of the Cold War. On one side is the DENVER campaign and the Romerstein letter, with their representative disregard for the victims of two of the twentieth century's worst humanitarian crises; on the other side is QRPLUMB.

The CIA deescalated, but never ceased, its political influence activities in the Soviet bloc over time. The operation known as QRPLUMB ran for the entire duration of the Cold War, and was the CIA's only covert action program of its kind.[21] It evolved out of an émigré group called the Ukrainian Supreme Liberation Council/Foreign Representation, or ZP/UHVR. The group had emerged during World War II, and supported the Ukrainian Partisan Army in 1944 against the Germans and later the Soviets. The CIA established an "operational relationship" with ZP/UHVR in 1949, initially for the purposes of intelligence collection and counterintelligence, but soon for "covert action."[22]

In 1953, the CIA helped set up the nonprofit Prolog Research Corporation, in New York City, with a publishing affiliate in Munich called the Ukrainian Society for Studies Abroad.[23] In the 1960s, the project "became very closely involved in the national revival in Ukraine," according to the project files.[24] (In the late 1980s, the CIA moved its front organization to Newark, as Manhattan rents had become too expensive.)[25] QRPLUMB's origins may sound adventurous, but by the mid-1980s the project demonstrated the degree of change in the CIA's approach to "political warfare."

The CIA's goal for the Ukrainian front was "to keep alive the Ukrainian nationalist spirit in the U.S.S.R.," according to a 1986 budget renewal request.[26] Another memo described the project's main purpose as encouraging liberalization in Ukraine and "providing intellectual and moral support" to Ukrainians seeking social or economic moderation.[27] By 1986, QRPLUMB had three witting employees, the president, his deputy, and the treasurer. Thirty-three unwitting employees worked full-time or part-time for the front organiza-tion. "All unwitting employees believe they are working for the research/publishing corporation," the CIA noted at the time.[28]

In order to achieve its goal, QRPLUMB published a flagship political and literary magazine called *Suchasnist*, a letter-sized monthly news bulletin on dissident activity in Ukraine, as well as a few books and pamphlets. In one nine-month period in 1972, QRPLUMB smuggled more than fifteen thousand copies of periodicals and books into Ukraine. The project mainly targeted "intellectuals," with essays and poems on a wide range of topics. Texts were either procured from Ukrainian writers, or translated (one was *Waiting for Godot*). Just as *Counterspy* was ramping up its operations against the CIA, in order to prevent George Orwell's *1984* from becoming a reality, the CIA's main remaining European front had *1984* translated into Ukrainian and in-filtrated into the Soviet Union—in the year 1984.[29]

In 1985, QRPLUMB slipped more than twenty-four thousand copies of its publications into the Soviet Union and other Eastern bloc countries. In addi-tion, the CIA lists the infiltration of two video machines, 340 cassette tapes, six cameras, twelve tape recorders, four hundred T-shirts "with appropriate slogans," as well as five thousand stickers with either pro-Ukrainian or anti–Afghan War slogans. QRPLUMB maintained a working relationship with like-minded Polish underground groups and a Czech resistance group in London.

The CIA's curious Ukrainian resistance outfit is noteworthy for what it wasn't, and for what it didn't do. QRPLUMB was a covert research organiza-tion and publishing house that operated as a front, but it appears not to have produced forgeries, nor to have leaked confidential information; instead, it focused on the distribution of genuine Ukrainian and Soviet literature as well as translated Western books. In one 1986 strategic assessment, a CIA analyst laments the "foolhardy" tactical mistakes of the 1960s, namely that the CIA had become too closely involved with activists "involved with liter-ary/political affairs," including using them for intelligence collection.[30] The CIA's tactical restraint in the late Cold War offers a sharp contrast with the KGB's simultaneous strategic escalation.

QRPLUMB is also remarkable for its small size, which it maintained throughout the entire Cold War. It had an annual operating budget of $1.1 million in 1985, which decreased slightly the following year[31]—negligible sums when compared with the resources that the CIA poured into political warfare in the 1950s and early 1960s. Still, in 1985, the Agency considered QRPLUMB an "extensive" operation and treated its New York City front as a "major covert action instrumentality." The contrast in funding is even more striking when compared with Soviet active measures at the same time. QRPLUMB cost around 1 percent of the massive anti-neutron-bomb campaign alone.

The project offers one final lesson: it was one of the first examples of the digitalization of active measures. With video and audio players newly and increasingly available in the Soviet Union, QRPLUMB increased its audio- and videocassette infiltration. In 1988, just before the Soviet Union began to collapse, QRPLUMB slowly began to infiltrate "computer and printing equipment" into Ukraine to support fledging dissident groups and independent publishing initiatives, although the subversive groups struggled with finding software compatible with local equipment to render text in the Cyrillic alphabet.

The end of the Cold War was a temporary setback for the art and craft of disinformation, but it also triggered remarkable conceptual innovation. In late 1997, a curious book on American intelligence activities in the now reunited Germany appeared, titled *Headquarters Germany*. It was a first: the authors were two longtime former HVA officers with a focus on countering U.S. spying, Klaus Eichner and Andreas Dobbert. The two had worked in the IX, HVA's counterintelligence unit, and together had more than forty-four years of Stasi experience under their belts. The book was dripping with details: it included, for example, a list of secret CIA and NSA files now in the archives of the BStU, the German government entity in charge of the Stasi files, and wild stories of the CIA attempting to recruit newly unemployed Stasi officers. Eichner and Dobbert's messaging was not subtle. The 381-page book had a map of unified Germany on the cover, set against a bright red background—and a gigantic tarantula with hairy legs sitting on top of the map. The two veteran counterespionage officers no longer had access to

Headquarters Germany
was a 1997 book
by two former Stasi
counterintelligence
officers. The spider
symbolizes U.S. spying
against the reunited
Germany. The CIA's
assessment was that the
book was sponsored by
Russian intelligence.

HVA documents, they stressed on the book's dust jacket and in the preface—indeed, they described in detail how one of them had helped destroy operational documents by the truckload in January 1990. The authors emphasized that they wrote their tell-all book "mainly" from public sources and "from memory."

The CIA's Directorate of Intelligence immediately studied "this devastating book." The early review called the work of the small group of people in the American section of the HVA's counterintelligence unit "truly impressive," and particularly highlighted the fact that the East Germans were "very successful in identifying CIA employees" in Germany. Langley noted, not without pride, that HVA reportedly developed leads on CIA identities in Germany by gleaning from U.S. military newsletters in Frankfurt that people not listed in telephone directories were winning on-post athletic competitions, thus marking them out. Remarkably, the reviewer at CIA headquarters largely treated the crudely anti-American book as an accurate historical account, and even gave the ex-HVA officers the benefit of the doubt when they "misidentified" State Department personnel as CIA officers because the ex-Stasi men "had to rely on their memories."[32] The CIA station in Germany, it appeared, was less credulous.

In fact, the book included details that were neither public nor preserved in the memory of the two ex-HVA men. Most obvious was the appendix. *Headquarters Germany*—once again—contained supplemental material with hundreds of names of alleged U.S. intelligence personnel, complete with dates of birth, the first names of spouses, and dates of postings abroad.[33] The list was also up-to-date, and in the case of about two dozen alleged CIA officers, the appendix included post-1990 biographical details, all the way to 1997— HVA, of course, no longer existed then. One such entry, for example, read:

Paseman, Floyd Lisle
Bonn (since 1994), COS,
EO: Tokyo 76, Burma 77,
Athens 80–83, Bangkok 86[34]

The information was correct. Paseman indeed became CIA Chief of Station in Germany in 1994, and was still in the post when the book came out. In late 2004, months before his death, Paseman published a memoir in which he revealed that many of the names in *Headquarters Germany* were accurate, and that the CIA judged the book to be "Russian-sponsored."[35] And as with previous red books that revealed alleged CIA short bios, this book also falsely identified—deliberately, not by an accident of memory—a number of Americans as intelligence officers. The project listed, for example, "Brattain, Steven Michael" with a correct date of birth, correct advanced degree, and correct dates of his recent posting in Bonn ("1992–1996"). But Brattain was a diplomat and "never worked for the CIA," he explained later.[36] The successor organization of the KGB's First Chief Directorate, it appeared, had shrewdly worked with their former East German HVA comrades on an effective active measure, a measure that was elevated by the Stasi's reputation for ruthless professionalism. *The Economist* had reviewed the tome with the tarantula on the cover uncritically;[37] *Der Spiegel* later recommended the anti-American Stasi tell-all as one of the best nonfiction spy books of the century.[38] Even serious intelligence historians took the "very informative book" by the ex-HVA counterintelligence officers at face value.[39] Yet the sourcing remained murky despite the many footnotes, and confirming facts was often impossible. The line between activism and operations had been crossed from both sides.

1990–2014: Hack

24.

Digital Measures

THE RUSSIAN STATE TV CHANNEL, RTR, WARNED THAT THE
segment—titled "Three in a Bed"—was not appropriate for
viewers under the age of eighteen. The grainy black-and-
white video showed a man cavorting with two naked younger women. It was
midnight, March 17, 1999, and the man in the video, although difficult to
identify, was rumored to be Yuri Skuratov, Russia's prosecutor general. The
video had been recorded more than a year earlier, at a luxurious flat in Moscow's Polyanka Street.[1]

The midnight broadcast was an escalation of a months-long battle. The
previous fall, Skuratov had opened a criminal investigation into President
Boris Yeltsin's alleged corruption and abuses of power. By early January, Yeltsin's men were waging a counterattack. The president arranged a meeting between his chief of staff and Skuratov; the chief of staff showed the prosecutor

**Prosecutor General Yuri
Skuratov reacts during
a parliament session in
Moscow, Wednesday,
April 21, 1999.**
(Photograph by Ivan Nikitin)

general the video, implied that it could become public, and asked him to resign. Skuratov handed in his resignation, but then decided to fight back. The
video was finally broadcast in mid-March, at the height of the showdown, in
order to influence an upcoming parliamentary vote on the prosecutor general's tenure—but it was unclear whether the naked man really was Skuratov.

Mudslinging was merciless in Moscow then. Vladimir Putin, a career
intelligence officer, was the newly appointed head of the FSB, a successor organization to the KGB. As a young KGB major, Putin had served in the Dresden *rezidentura* that had been opened specifically to run active measures
against West Germany at a time when active measures were at their most
cunning.

Now, ten years later, Putin was leading the FSB, and dirty tricks were
back. Days after RTR aired the "Three in a Bed" video, rumors arose that
Putin himself was linked to the scandal, even that he had been filmed in
intimate situations in the same apartment, and that he, too, would soon step
down.[2]

A screenshot of a video that was engineered to compromise Yuri Skuratov.

The opposite happened. On March 29, Putin was appointed the secretary of the Security Council of the Russian Federation, while retaining his lead role at the FSB. On the night of April 1, a Moscow city prosecutor opened a criminal case against Skuratov. The next morning, Putin held a live press conference. He told reporters that the "person looking like Skuratov" was, in fact, Skuratov:[3] "The initial evaluation of the video tape showing Yuriy Skuratov indicates that it is genuine."[4] Putin then revealed that the prosecutor general's office was opening criminal proceedings against its own leader. The beleaguered Yeltsin had signed a decree suspending Skuratov until the investigation was completed. Skuratov's telephone lines were cut, the office sealed, his guards replaced, and the prosecutor was forbidden from entering his former workplace or any other government building.[5]

Putin's press conference revealed even more dirt on Skuratov. One of the sex workers in the video said that she and her colleague had charged a fee of $500 per romp, and that they had earned $50,000 over the past eighteen months from entertaining Skuratov.[6] The battle among Skuratov, Yeltsin, and Putin would continue for several months. The video was key to the prosecutor general's precipitous fall, and to the equally dizzying rise of a future president.

The video filmed on Polyanka Street was old-school, a compromising video given to the press for political effect—no internet was required. At the time, Russia had just under 1 million internet users, most of them centered in

Moscow (the United States, by contrast, then had about 70 million internet users).[7] Many Russian politicians still did not have websites. Moscow's political elite may not have been early adopters of the internet, but they were quick to see its potential for intrigue and disinformation. It was in the same 1999 presidential campaign, in the same city, and involving some of the same individuals, that internet-driven "kompromat" was pioneered.

Perhaps the first example was lujkov.ru,[8] a website devoted to Yury Luzhkov, Moscow's mayor with an eye on the presidency. The site, which suddenly appeared on the mayor's birthday, September 21, visually cloned the mayor's official site but included jabs at his character on every page.[9] Soon, similar smear sites appeared for other political figures, including Putin; putin-president.da.ru appeared at first glance to endorse Putin, but in fact portrayed him in a very unfavorable light. One 1999 website offering revelations on a wide range of public figures, including politicians, was simply called kompromat.ru. Google was still an obscure start-up at the dawn of the twentieth century, and YouTube, Facebook, and Twitter would not be founded for half a decade. But the rise of the internet as a platform for active measures had begun.

Sergei Tretyakov, the career SVR officer and later defector, ran the New York *rezidentura* from April 1995 to October 2000. The SVR, still housed at Yasenevo, regularly cabled propaganda material to New York to disseminate to the final targets. Russian foreign intelligence officers now took advantage of the internet to spread disinformation. In his memoirs, Tretyakov recalled that SVR officers checked into the New York Public Library to post disinformation material on various websites and send fresh material by email to U.S. press outlets.[10] Right in Manhattan, in the NYPL's sunlit reading room, Russian spies moved among the shadows. Some of the outreach emanating from the library was disguised as educational material or scientific reports, usually credited to respectable-sounding European scholars or research companies.

Russian intelligence exploited the internet just at the right moment: the emerging global network was developed enough to push out disinformation, but not developed enough to uncover disinformation. The SVR targeted the most gullible and innocent victims, just as the KGB had done for decades:

activists and intellectuals who criticized the U.S. government. Environmentalists, anti-globalization activists, and human rights organizations would receive the classic mix of fact and forgery to strengthen existing contradictions. "Our goal was to cause dissension and unrest inside the U.S. and anti-American feelings abroad," Tretyakov recalled.[11]

In the West, meanwhile, networked computers gave rise to utopian and dystopian ideas alike. Twitter made its public debut in mid-July 2006. Two months later, Facebook, originally a platform for college students, opened its gates to everyone thirteen or older. In November, Google purchased YouTube, a highly successful eighteen-month-old start-up. These companies exuded optimism and youthful naïveté. Information wanted to be free, with content created by users and shared often—with ease, with speed, and among as many people as possible. Vetting and fact-checking had little currency on the quickly expanding electronic frontier.

The idea was taking hold in NATO's military establishments that the wars of the future could be won by digital intervention, without firing a shot. Joint warfare of the future would become network-centric and lightning fast, as the Persian Gulf War had demonstrated. Digital shortcuts between sensors and shooters would dispel the fog of war and herald nothing short of a revolution in military affairs. Yet images of military utopia were confronted with dystopian visions of the coming "cyberwar" and an "electronic Pearl Harbor." The country that invented the internet was uniquely vulnerable to remote attacks.

Unbridled optimism predominated in Silicon Valley; pessimism came to dominate the Beltway. Both extremes would benefit active measures operations over the next decade, although for different reasons: utopianism made it easy to run operations undetected; dystopianism made it easy to exaggerate results. A perfect storm system was forming.

A milestone event for the twenty-first-century return of active measures took place in Tallinn, Estonia, where Dzerzhinsky's Operation Trust had taken off in the twentieth century. It began with the planned relocation of a statue of a World War II Red Army soldier. The figure, known as the Bronze Soldier, had been unveiled by Soviet authorities in 1947, as a monument to the "liberators of Tallinn." To ethnic Russians in Estonia, the monument stood for Soviet victory over the Third Reich—but to ethnic Estonians, the monument stood for Soviet occupation during the Cold War, and "liberation" meant getting rid of the monument. In the spring of 2007, the city government planned to move the Bronze Soldier from the city center to a military cemetery in the outskirts. The conflict was perfectly pitched— Tallinn erupted into riots and looting on April 26.

Soon a range of Estonian websites went down, pummeled by denial-of-service attacks, or fake requests for information that overwhelmed servers. The digital equivalent of the street riots reached a peak on May 9, when Russia celebrated the anniversary of its victory over Nazi Germany. Fifty-eight Estonian websites were brought down in what was then one of the largest attacks of its kind. Hansapank, one of the country's largest banks, saw its online services interrupted for ninety minutes on May 9, and for two hours the following day.[12] The network attacks had limited impact on the ground. The psychological and political reaction, however, was disproportionate, both in Estonia and internationally. Estonia's new minister of defense said that "a botnet threatened the national security of an entire nation." The prime minister compared the "blockade of government institutions and newspaper websites" to a "blockade of harbors and airports."

The international press coverage was even more extreme. *Wired* magazine called it "Web War One."[13] *The New York Times* saw "the first war in cyberspace" playing out.[14] It remained unclear whether the denial-of-service attacks were perpetrated by Russian-speaking activists, or by the Russian security establishment, or perhaps by a combination of both.

A new era had begun. To any intelligence analyst watching closely, the episode in Tallinn showed that active measures were becoming more active: the internet now allowed direct attacks on machines, executed through computer code. Subsequent media coverage would then amplify the impact of the remote measures. The novelty of these attacks, combined with the dominant dystopian view of "cyberwar" in NATO's defense establishment, meant that the impact of these newly active measures would be widely exaggerated by politicians, military officers, and journalists. Twenty-first-century active measures appeared to be low-risk, high-impact, and easily deniable. The internet seemed to be custom-designed for disinformation, even before social media had come of age.

Two noteworthy leaks occurred in the summer of 2009. A four-minute video titled "Adventures of Mr. Hudson in Russia" showed up on a small news site called *Informacia*.[15] James Hudson was the UK deputy consul in Ekaterinburg, in the Urals. In the video, Hudson is shown walking into a room, wearing only an open dressing gown and carrying a glass, accompanied by two blond women. He kisses one; the other sits on his lap.

Russian authorities confirmed the event. "There is indeed such a video," a spokesperson for the interior ministry in Ekaterinburg told the *Daily Mail*. "We can't comment on who it is, but you should try the British consulate." Whispers in London said that Hudson may have been an undercover British intelligence officer, and that the Russians had tried to blackmail and turn him. "Russian intelligence has a long history of making sex films and taking compromising photos to control people or further its aims," a British security source told *The Sun*.[16] A few weeks later, a similar leak in the same Russian newspaper targeted thirty-five-year-old Kyle Hatcher, an American diplomat serving in Moscow.[17] This time the sex tape was partly forged, with compromising scenes doctored. A State Department spokesperson explained that Hatcher "was approached by Russians," and that "they tried to blackmail him, but he did everything correctly."[18] The U.S. ambassador backed the officer publicly.

Neither the UK Foreign Office nor the U.S. embassy in Moscow denied (or explicitly confirmed) allegations reported in two Russian newspapers that their diplomats had been working for intelligence services. Intelligence officers in Moscow knew that British tabloids would have a field day with Hudson's story, and boost the operation in an almost retro fashion. *The Sun* did not disappoint: "Our man in Russia pulls out after spy films his Urals sex," the paper reported.[19]

The first decade of the twenty-first century saw an uneasy overlap of two tactics that had not yet been combined: old-school intelligence leaks involving compromising material, and the first attempts at hacking and high-tech internet sabotage. No intelligence agency had yet combined the two.

First Digital Leaks

WHAT WOULD ACTIVE MEASURES BE WITHOUT THE JOURNAL-ist?" asked Rolf Wagenbreth in 1986. Three years later, the Berlin Wall came down. The Russian intelligence community was beset by internal turmoil for a decade or so after the KGB's abrupt end in 1991. When the old spymasters found their footing again, the world around them had drastically changed. Internet utopianism had enveloped the West, and a new crop of internet companies had emerged, transforming the way humans read and wrote, shared images and documents, socialized, consumed news, and spread rumors. The sprawling network, as became progressively clear, was practically optimized for disinformation, at least until the mid-2010s. Active measures operators two decades after Wagenbreth would frame his question differently: What would active measures be without the internet?

U.S. Assistant Secretary of State for European and Eurasian Affairs Victoria Nuland (center) distributes bread to protesters next to U.S. Ambassador Geoffrey Pyatt (left) at Independence Square in Kyiv, on December 11, 2013.
(Reuters / Andrew Kravchenko / Pool)

Journalists were still crucial, but the emerging social media platforms enabled surfacing, amplification, and even testing of active measures without the participation of reporters. Online sharing services, especially those with built-in anonymity, were tailor-made for at-scale deception. Dirty tricksters could now reach their target audiences directly.

Cryptome, a radical transparency site and in effect the world's first leak portal, was created in 1996 by the married couple John Young and Deborah Natsios to call attention to dual-use technology. Young had been active on the cypherpunk list, a loose group of technology utopians with an anti-government, anarchist bent. From West Texas, son of an oil worker, he became an architect in Manhattan and lived on the Upper West Side. Yet for decades, Young operated Cryptome on the tiny budget of less than $2,000 per year.[1] His vision was rather romantic: "Cryptome, aspiring to be a free public library, accepts that libraries are chock full of contaminated material, hoaxes, forgeries, propaganda,"[2] Young told one interviewer in 2013. He attempted to build a submission system that used encryption, and he wanted to allow contributors to be able to remain anonymous, ideally not even revealing their identity to Young or Cryptome itself. "We'll publish anything," Young explained, in what amounted to a philosophy of digital hoarding. "We don't check it out. We don't try to verify it. We don't tell people, 'Believe this because we say it's OK.' We try not to give any authority to what we do. We just serve up the raw data."[3] Indeed, Cryptome had the look of a postmodern antiques shop crammed with valuable-looking items that quickly lost their appeal at closer inspection. Young's collection of oddities included, for instance, the engineering plans of the George Washington Bridge in New York, pictures of George W. Bush's ranch in Texas, details of British undercover activity in Northern Ireland, and high-resolution images of the Fukushima Dai-ichi nuclear plant in Japan. In 2000, Young published a CIA briefing that a former Japanese official had leaked to him.

"We were told very early on that the site could be used to spread disinformation," Young recounted in 2004. "I can't rule out that we are being subjected to a sophisticated disinformation campaign by government agencies."[4] He applied the same sunlight-is-the-best-disinfectant logic to potential abuses: "If it smells, then someone will point it out," he said. "We publish people who object to what's appearing, and then let people decide."[5]

It is unlikely that Cryptome was exploited at scale by foreign governments, but not for the reasons Young cited. The KGB, Stasi, and StB would have loved Cryptome. But in an ironic historical twist, the world's first leak site was at its high point when major active measures were at their lowest since the end of the Cold War.

Yet Cryptome pioneered and precipitated a larger cultural shift that would help reawaken active measures with a vengeance. Young met Julian Assange on the cypherpunk list, and Assange described Cryptome as the "spiritual godfather"[6] of WikiLeaks. In 2006, Assange asked Young to become the public face of WikiLeaks in the United States, and suggested that

Young could register WikiLeaks.org in his name.[7] The cooperation failed; two eccentric personalities clashed, and the radical-libertarian partnership came to an end. Yet WikiLeaks would soon eclipse Cryptome.

In 2010, Chelsea Manning, then a twenty-two-year-old Army private known as Bradley,[8] leaked more than a quarter million State Department and Department of Defense documents to WikiLeaks. The leaked diplomatic cables spanned about a decade, and turned Assange and his website into household names. By 2013, Cryptome had collected and published just 70,000 files, many random and hand-curated. WikiLeaks was pushing out secret information on an industrial scale.

Then, in June 2013, Edward Snowden opened the floodgates. The precise number of files Snowden exfiltrated from the NSA remains unclear, as does the number of files that were passed on to various media outlets and how access to the documents spread from these initial brokers as more and more media organizations reported on the files. One nearly insurmountable problem was that many of the secret files were difficult to read and interpret, and yet the material was irresistible. As a result, several influential media organizations ran incomplete and error-ridden stories, often exaggerating the collection and interception capabilities of the American and British intelligence agencies affected by Snowden's security breach. Snowden fled the United States to Hong Kong, China, and eventually Moscow. Soon speculation mounted that Snowden might have acted as an agent of a hostile power.[9] But in all likelihood, the self-described whistle-blower was acting as a libertarian idealist and genuine transparency activist, not as an agent of a foreign intelligence agency, when he executed the biggest public intelligence leak to date.

Nevertheless, viewed from Russia, the Snowden leaks looked like a spectacularly successful American active measure targeted against America itself. A lowly NSA contractor, under the spell of transparency activism, had done more political and possibly more operational damage to the American intelligence community than most Service A operations during the Cold War. It was impossible to be aware of the history of active measures, while watching the Snowden affair unfold in real time, and not see an opportunity of strategic significance.

Manning and Snowden, meanwhile, had shifted expectations and the terms of the public conversation. Massive government leaks of secret files, it appeared, were not a once-in-a-generation event, as comparisons with the *Pentagon Papers* implied, but something that could occur every few years. This shift was facilitated by the ease with which hundreds of thousands, even millions, of files could be copied and carried digitally on thumbnail-sized chips. Journalists and opinion leaders were now more willing than ever to embrace anonymous leaks without spending too much time on checking their provenance or veracity. By mid-2014, major magazines and newspapers, including *The New Yorker* and *The Guardian*, were competing with activist websites and encouraging anonymous submissions by mail or dedicated end-to-end encrypted submission portals with fortified anonymity.[10]

Yet the leaks could also be a problem for journalists, especially Snowden's material. It was often exceedingly difficult to assess leaked documents on their own merits, and checking secret facts was sometimes impossible. Even the most dogged and well-connected investigative journalist would have a hard time telling whether a specific leak was the outcome of an active measure or of genuine whistle-blowing. Then there was the question of forgeries. By 2013, only a few Cold War historians and veteran intelligence reporters remembered that Eastern bloc intelligence services had once perfected the art of semi-covert active measures enhanced by skillful falsifications, and that Congress had once held hearings on "the forgery offensive."

At the time of the Snowden leaks, Bruce Schneier was a widely respected cryptographer, an authority on information security, and a keen technical observer of NSA operations. In August 2014, Schneier used his popular on-line journal to take a close look at various recent NSA leaks and where they may have originated, concluding that the U.S. intelligence community now had "a third leaker." (The FBI pursued a similar hypothesis.) The stream of stories on U.S. intelligence capabilities and operations, Schneier pointed out, didn't stem from the Snowden cache alone. The types and avenues of leaked documents pointed to two more sources. Schneier discussed various possibilities, but even he did not articulate that an adversarial intelligence agency might have planted particularly damaging leaks. Instead, Schneier spoke for a fast-growing subculture when he closed by recommending some readings to show that leaks were "in general, a good thing."[11]

Schneier wasn't wrong: from the point of view of adversarial intelligence agencies, leaks are even a very good thing. The most aggressive active measures operators were already taking advantage of the new culture of leaking when Schneier wrote these lines. The two-year period after the Snowden disclosures, in fact, was a short, modern golden age of disinformation. That period was characterized by the confluence of several developments that were, ultimately, all temporary afterglow effects of 1990s internet utopianism: the prevailing view, articulated so well by Schneier, that unauthorized releases were a tool to strengthen democracy, not weaken it; the global rise of anonymous internet activism; the widespread notion that it was very hard, if not impossible, to trace hackers on the internet; the absence of publicly available digital forensics and a general understanding of how digital forensic artifacts should be interpreted; and the naïve expectation that sharing news on social media platforms would lead not to abuse but to better-informed users. All of these five features of internet culture in the early 2010s were fleeting, and would change or disappear within half a decade. But in 2013, they formed the perfect techno-cultural cover for active measures, one so good that identifying the first digital leak operations remains a formidable challenge even with the benefit of hindsight.

On October 23, 2013, *Der Spiegel* broke a story that came to define the Snowden affair: that the NSA was spying on Angela Merkel's phone.[12] *Der Spiegel* slipped the story into the frenzied coverage of the Snowden files, yet the magazine never explicitly stated that the information actually came from Snowden.

The story, as first reported by *Der Spiegel*, was odd: the gist was that Merkel had confronted President Obama with allegations that he had spied on her, not that the NSA had been spying on her phone. The difference was subtle but crucial. "Chancellor Cell Phone a U.S. Target?" *Der Spiegel*'s headline asked. Even the lede was cautious: Merkel had "possibly" been targeted by U.S. intelligence. The magazine did not make a claim; it asked a question and reported a claim made by others. Germany's federal government, the

Chancellor Angela Merkel of Germany on her cell phone in the Bundestag in 2013
(Wolfgang Kumm / picture alliance / dpa / AP Images)

magazine explained, was taking the spying allegations seriously enough to confront the president of the United States with the contention that the NSA had been spying on one of America's closest allies.

Der Spiegel was very careful with this particular story, not least because its journalists knew the danger of active measures; the magazine had fallen for Eastern disinformation in the past. Investigative journalists at *Der Spiegel* particularly remembered the humiliating forgery of the CDU strategy paper in Kreuth: "Stasi Also Once Tricked Spiegel," the magazine had announced in 1991. Marcel Rosenbach, one of the journalists who broke the Merkel story, knew the infamous Philip Agee from Hamburg, and once visited Agee's home, where he admired the allegedly bugged typewriter on which the CIA defector had typed *Inside the Company*.[13] Holger Stark, who led the investigation, had, like Rosenbach, done groundbreaking historical reporting on Stasi operations.[14]

The initial tip for the story came before a major general election in late September 2013 that Merkel was expected to win. The sourcing has remained mysterious. *Der Spiegel* has refused to clarify the provenance of the initial tasking order, and curiously claimed they had multiple sources. Glenn Greenwald, one of the few journalists with extensive access to the Snowden archive, later told me that "the source document for the Merkel story certainly did not come from the Snowden files."[15] Greenwald added that his team carefully searched the archive for the NSA tasking order in question. Stark and Rosenbach, however, knew immediately that the story, whatever the source, had extraordinary potential. But there was not enough time for the investigative reporters to thoroughly fact-check the story before the vote. Eventually, a week before they broke the news, two *Spiegel* reporters met with the spokesperson of the chancellor in Berlin, Steffen Seibert. The journalists handed Seibert an A4-sized card that listed the NSA's surveillance order for Merkel, complete with one of her mobile phone numbers, and told Seibert that the NSA order was not an original printout from an NSA database but a copy typed up by one of *Der Spiegel*'s investigative reporters, who was convinced it represented the actual database entry.[16] Seibel informed Merkel, and the chancellery decided it would confront the White House.

Christoph Heusgen, Germany's national security advisor, then spoke with Susan Rice, his U.S. counterpart. Rice at first blocked the request from Berlin. Merkel then took the question up with Obama. The White House press secretary eventually mentioned the sensitive phone call, explaining that "the president assured the chancellor that the United States is not monitoring, and will not monitor the communications of the chancellor."[17] *Der Spiegel*, reportedly along with the German government, then pointed out that the White House denial only mentioned present and future monitoring, not past. German diplomats and reporters subsequently construed this absence as confirmation that the United States had been spying on Merkel.[18]

German-American relations immediately took a very serious hit. "Spying between friends, that's just not done," said Merkel, usually a sober, pro-American voice. The foreign office in Berlin summoned the U.S. ambassador, in a major gesture of frustration. Sixty-two percent of Germans approved of the chancellor's harsh call to Obama, with a quarter of the population saying her reaction was not harsh enough.[19]

The NSA, in a rare step, immediately denied that its director "ever" discussed "alleged operations involving Chancellor Merkel" with Obama. "News reports claiming otherwise are not true," an NSA spokesperson wrote to journalists.[20] Germany's attorney general proceeded to investigate the case for about a year, and eventually concluded that there was no evidence that Merkel's calls had been intercepted. "The document that was publicly perceived as evidence for the actual surveillance of the [Merkel's] mobile phone was not an authentic tasking order by the NSA," the attorney general said at a press conference, adding that the tasking order later published in the German press "did not originate from an NSA database."[21] Still, *Der Spiegel* stuck to its story, and convincingly so.

Some observers in Western intelligence agencies saw more sinister machinations at play. *Der Spiegel*'s sources remained nebulous, thus raising the question of whether the magazine had been played. A close U.S. intelligence ally may have intercepted Merkel's phone, one theory went, and thus made it difficult for the NSA to deny the allegations outright. The timing, framing, and other details of the affair led some senior intelligence officials to one explanation—indeed, to what they believed was the only explanation: that the Merkel story was a professionally executed and highly effective active measure designed to drive a wedge between the United States and one of its closest NATO allies. The story indeed appeared to fit an old pattern. The evidence for this theory, however, remained wafer-thin.

ON THE VERY SAME DAY THE MERKEL STORY BROKE, ANOTHER LESS VISIBLE but no less remarkable event transpired a few hundred kilometers east of Berlin. A mysterious post appeared on one of the main online forums run by members of Anonymous, the then-vibrant online activism movement. The activists were best recognized by their trademark black-and-white Guy Fawkes masks, adopted from the 2005 dystopian movie *V for Vendetta*, and by a whimsical internet dialect characterized by forming plurals with a *z* instead of an *s*. Even participants of the amorphous movement did not know how big Anonymous was or who their fellow activists really were. Anonymity had become a cultlike feature of internet subculture, celebrated and reinforced

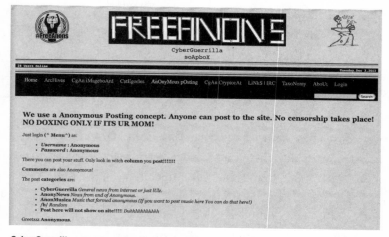

CyberGuerrilla was a genuine Anonymous forum and preferred leak platform of Russian disinformation operators. (Internet Archive)

on forums where no identification was required and true names were covered by a cryptographic veil. Encryption, which for centuries had protected states and spies and armies, suddenly served antigovernment activists. But that fortified anonymity also marked Anonymous out for intelligence agencies— both as a potential threat and as a potential cover for operations.

"Anons," as the activists called one another, ran social media accounts and blogs to foment unrest and advance the fight against tyranny. A late arrival on the scene of Anon sites was http://cyberguerrilla.org. The portal, registered and opened in January 2012, had a simple but appealing retro cyberpunk design, with *Matrix*-like green-on-black code columns in the background. CyberGuerrilla would remain obscure, but quickly gained currency in the amorphous community of nameless online activists. The site had an anonymous posting philosophy. "Anyone can post to the site. No censorship takes place!" the site admins assured users.[22] The Anons simply provided one publicly announced username (Anonymous) and password (Anonymous) for everybody to use. Users could post in columns dedicated to news, music, and general interest. The admins discouraged leaking private information: "NO DOXING ONLY IF ITS UR MOM!" said the tongue-in-cheek how-to guide. A wider network of internet activists monitored the CyberGuerrilla platform, and independently announced or reposted news that emerged there, or reposted news items on CyberGuerrilla that had first appeared elsewhere.

Powerful and secretive agencies were watching the budding Anonymous movement. Intelligence agencies in the West tended to see the leaderless anarchist movement as a diffuse potential threat—and intelligence agencies in the East tended to see the grassroots activist movement as an opportunity. After all, Soviet bloc agencies had been using, steering, and exploiting political activists for about eighty years. CyberGuerrilla, with its idealistic anonymous posting concept, would be an exceptionally attractive vehicle for active measures.

Meanwhile, during the fall of 2013, Vladimir Putin, now the Russian president, increased the pressure on those Eastern European countries flirting with closer trade ties to the European Union and the United States. Russia even threatened renewed sanctions against Ukraine.

Then, on October 23, an unknown individual logged into CyberGuerrilla and posted an unusual message in the site's general section. "Ministry of Foreign Affairs of Ukraine Massive DOCS leak. MFA.GOV.UA hacked," the post was titled.[23] "Greetings fellow lulz!" it began, the salutation betraying a lack of familiarity with Anon-speak. The authors, who referred to themselves in the plural, were agitated by the forces in the Ukrainian government who sought closer ties with the European Union: "Ukraine Government is so fucked up bullshitting Europe about it's intentions to become a member of EU pursuing European Democracy Postulates." The authors then shared a link to a compressed folder.

The folder contained a confusing assortment of letters and documents seemingly sent from German, British, American, and Czech officials to their Ukrainian counterparts. The first document listed in the leak included the diplomatic passport of a U.S. State Department official. The authors signed off with the usual Anonymous formula, "We are Anonymous, We are Legion, We do not forgive, We do not forget," adding "Greetz to our Fellaz in Ukraine, Greetz to all Anons and Lulz."

Five days later, another post from "Anonymous Ukraine" appeared on CyberGuerrilla. This one declared the start of #OpIndependence. The authors emphasized Ukraine's independence from the European Union and Russia, and displayed an especially sharp anti-NATO slant. This post included a video message: "We do not need to be servants of NATO," intoned a person in a white mask and black hoodie.

On November 21, Ukraine halted its plans for a deal with the EU, sparking protests in Kyiv. On November 30, the pro-Russian Ukrainian government deployed a paramilitary police force, the Berkut, to brutally crack down on protesters in Kyiv's Independence Square, which only fueled further protests. On December 11, U.S. Assistant Secretary of State Victoria Nuland visited Kyiv, and met there with the embattled Ukrainian president, Victor Yanukovych—but also, smiling and informally dressed in a blue quilt jacket, with shivering protestors in Independence Square, where she handed out cookies and fresh bread in large plastic bags in subzero temperatures. Nuland told the Ukrainian president that police brutality against protestors was "absolutely impermissible" and expressed "disgust" on behalf of the United States. Russian authorities in turn interpreted American and European attempts at deescalating the crisis as the opposite, as an escalation and as "meddling" in the Russian sphere of influence.[24] American intelligence agencies began to prioritize intelligence collection in Ukraine. A shadow war was on the rise.

Four days later, another highly damaging NSA document appeared. In Hamburg, the annual congress of the Chaos Computer Club was under way. On December 29, the activist Jacob Appelbaum revealed the Advanced Network Technology list, known as the ANT catalog.[25] The ANT catalog outlined custom-designed NSA hardware and software hacking used to penetrate devices produced by U.S. companies, including Apple, Dell, Cisco, Juniper Networks, and others. The document was released alongside a *Spiegel* story on the NSA's elite hacking division, then known as Tailored Access Operations. The document was highly damaging—it drove a double wedge, one between the United States and continental Europe, and another between the NSA and America's technology companies. The story and its timing, like the Merkel report, set off alarm bells in American intelligence circles. *Der Spiegel* had slipped the report into the wider Snowden coverage, but the magazine did not imply that Snowden was its source. No hard evidence for an active measure was available, but the releases sure looked like planned operations. To the public, however, the widely held assumption was that a second whistle-blower had come forward and leaked even more NSA files, just as Schneier and others had intimated. This was how the short, golden age of disinformation worked.

The escalating situation in Kyiv would soon undermine this innocence. As the political and military crisis intensified in Ukraine, so did the flanking active measures campaign. Within about a month, disinformation operations that targeted Western interests became more overtly political in nature, and went beyond the old game of spy agency versus spy agency.

Relations between the EU and the United States were among the first openly political targets of Russian digital active measures. After two months of antigovernment protests in Ukraine, on February 4, two audio clips simultaneously appeared on YouTube, uploaded by the same account. The account, "Re Post," had been created on December 14, 2013, as the Ukraine crisis was deteriorating quickly.

In one of the leaked recordings,[26] Victoria Nuland was speaking with the U.S. ambassador to Ukraine, Geoffrey Pyatt. As a result of her job, Nuland had been eyed by intelligence collectors for some time, and the fact that she had taken sides with demonstrators in Kyiv now made her an especially desirable target for active measures. Nuland and Pyatt were frustrated with the European Union's reluctance to join the United States in threatening sanctions against the Ukrainian government for violently crushing the protests. Nuland told Pyatt that she wanted a UN diplomat to go to Kyiv to seal an accord on the cabinet. "So that would be great, I think, to help glue this thing and have the UN help glue it and, you know, fuck the EU," said Nuland.

"Oh, exactly," Pyatt replied, "and I think we've got to do something to make it stick together, because you can be sure that if it does start to gain altitude the Russians will be working behind the scenes to torpedo it." Though the ambassador didn't know it, the Russians were indeed doing just that.

The other recording, in German, was the European mirror image to the intercepted U.S. phone call.[27] Helga Schmid, a senior foreign service official working for the European Union in Brussels, was surreptitiously recorded as she discussed the Ukraine crisis with Jan Tombinski, the EU ambassador to Ukraine. Schmid complained about what she saw as unfair criticism from the United States. "The Americans are going around telling people we're too weak while they are tougher on sanctions," Schmid said to Tombinski. She relayed some internal discussions from Brussels, and added, "What you should know is that it really bothers us that the Americans are going around naming and shaming us—this is what several journalists have told us. Maybe you can speak to the U.S. ambassador?" That U.S. ambassador was Pyatt, who had just agreed with Nuland to, you know, fuck Schmid and Tombinski.

It was the perfect setup for an active measure. Russian intelligence had intercepted both phone calls: in one, the Americans called the Europeans names, and in the other, the Europeans complained about American name-calling. Releasing both would predictably drive a wedge between Washington and Brussels, and potentially help pro-Russian forces in Ukraine.

When the leak first appeared on YouTube, nothing happened. Nobody of significance seems to have noticed the sudden appearance of the matching audio files for almost two days. One obscure pro-Russian Ukrainian account with an Anonymous avatar linked to the "Fuck the EU" tape on Wednesday;[28] an unnamed pro-Putin blogger wrote about the Nuland recording on a Russian-language platform on Thursday morning.[29] Then, at 2:30 in the afternoon on Thursday, Dmitry Loskutov, an aide to the deputy prime minister of the Russian Federation, Dmitry Rogozin,[30] posted on Twitter: "Sort of controversial judgment from Assistant Secretary of State Victoria Nuland speaking about the EU."[31] The story at once exploded in a flash of publicity across Europe and North America. Reported Reuters, just hours later: "The audio posted on YouTube, along with a second one that captures a reported conversation between senior EU diplomats, reveal apparent rifts between the United States and EU over how to handle Ukraine."

This was the type of press coverage that active measures operators had coveted and counted on for many decades. The incident, thanks to the strong language used by Nuland, quickly dominated the political news cycle in Europe and the United States. And the twin leaks did not fail to act as an effective wedge. Angela Merkel described Nuland's remarks as "totally unacceptable," and sided with Schmid.[32] The State Department had to apologize for the inappropriate remarks. The White House, in an attempt at damage control, pointed to Loskutov, the Kremlin aide, as evidence that the leak was a Russian active measure. "I would say that since the video was first noted and tweeted out by the Russian government, I think it says something about Russia's role," said a U.S. spokesperson.[33]

One American journalist asked Loskutov if his initial post that linked to the Nuland tape was indeed evidence of a Russian operation. Loskutov reacted with an artful nondenial denial: "Disseminating started earlier," he responded truthfully. The fact that he reacted was being used "to hang the blame on RUS," he said, adding a winking emoticon, ;).[34] The U.S. reporter persisted, and asked him to clarify whether his comment meant that the Kremlin had no role in the leak. "How would I know?" the Kremlin aide responded, again playfully not denying official responsibility.

The State Department called the incident "a new low in Russian tradecraft."[35] The opposite was true: the operation was a new high. The leak was the work of professionals. The sound quality of the intercepts was excellent; the leaks were curated and juxtaposed with a certain elegance; the files were no cheap fakes. The surfacing was done at exactly the right moment, as Nuland visited Kyiv to discuss a U.S.-brokered end to the crisis with Yanukovych. The operation was at least partly deniable. The tape was the first high-profile example of a method that represented the future of active measures. The trick was to combine two technical features, one old, one new: technical intelligence collection, in this case, tapping phone lines or possibly tampering with phones used by Western diplomats, and using the internet and social media to surface the leaks. This new technique would make the compromising material public, and amplify it, *before* it would be picked up by traditional middlemen, such as Russian TV stations, outlets in third countries, and ultimately American and European news agencies. This strategy of leaking via the internet would soon redefine how surfacing and amplification worked.

Anonymous

GUY FAWKES–MASKED INTERNET ACTIVISM BEGAN TO COALESCE
in 2007, partly on 4chan, a raucous anonymous image board.
The movement peaked in size and volume in early 2012.[1]
By then an entire news network of collaborative anonymous sources and
accounts had emerged online, on various open platforms and custom-built
websites. Leaking information online, called "doxing" in internet jargon, had
become a common occurrence.

Between October 2013 and the summer of 2016, Anonymous Ukraine or
some of its self-identified offshoots published around one hundred posts on
CyberGuerrilla. These posts comprised at least thirty-seven different leaks,
usually releases of hacked email inboxes. The leaks also contained more than
a dozen forgeries. It was and still is impossible to say how many of the posts
on CyberGuerrilla were made by genuine activists, and how many represent

An anti-American hack-leak-forge operation is camouflaged as coming from the Anonymous movement.

covert Russian intelligence operations interfering in Ukraine. This lack of clarity was a highly desirable feature for covert operators. Many Anons were indeed confused. One leak, for example, exposed Vitali Klitschko, a celebrity heavyweight boxing champion turned pro-European opposition leader.[2] "Guys, you hacked mail of people who support peaceful demonstrations. Klitschko supports students, people, and democracy," one activist wrote in December 2013. "Please delete files," another said. "You're doing it wrong!"[3] Even the founders and administrators of the guerrilla portal could not tell the difference between real and fake activists, and assumed the worst: "These hacker groups on both sides are all State secret service provocateurs," recalled one administrator, who declined to be identified publicly, keeping with the site's anonymous philosophy. "They serve only the state and not the people," she added, noting aptly, "Lenin conquered Russia with the same political warfare."[4]

It is also highly likely that not even the Russian intelligence analysts tasked with analyzing events in Ukraine knew what was real, unless these analysts received internal reporting from the operational unit behind any forgeries. Over time, however, the unmistakable fingerprints of Russian military intelligence operators came into sharper relief. It was likely GRU Unit 74455 that started wearing, at least digitally, the ubiquitous white mask with the black mustache.

As the "Euromaidan" protest movement gained force in Kyiv in early 2014, the Ukrainian government deployed the Berkut riot police to crush the protests. But the revolution was unstoppable. President Yanukovych fled to Moscow in February. Moscow called the pro-European interim government an illegitimate "junta." Russia took advantage of the chaos and moved to annex Crimea, a Ukrainian peninsula protruding into the Black Sea. Early on February 27, masked, unmarked Russian special forces troops stormed Crimea's Parliament building in Simferopol, allegedly to "protect" the Crimean members of Parliament. The Kremlin would admit only a year later that these operations were indeed conducted by Russian personnel.[5]

As the invasion began, it appears that GRU Unit 74455 tried to help shape the operational environment on Crimea. Unit 74455 created around a dozen forged accounts and published a number of posts on Facebook and its Russian counterpart, Vkontakte. One Facebook page was called "Ukrainian Front," with a martial red banner; another fake page was called "Eastern Front."[6] The GRU created "For Crimea's Independence" on the day of the invasion.[7] The GRU's goal for this "active work," according to an internal report, was to stir up negative feelings toward the new government in Kyiv, and to alienate the Crimean population from pro-Western parties and organizations.[8] Four more accounts were focused on Crimean independence.[9] But the officers in 74455 were remarkably inept at social media work: on February 26 and 27, the moment of Russia's invasion of Crimea, the GRU's information operations shop pushed out fifty-four items on social media, not all of them original. The most popular Facebook post on that day received just forty-six likes and fourteen comments. Measuring the success of active measures may be hard—measuring complete failure was straightforward.

The GRU, however, would soon discover a sharper new tool. As Russia's annexation of Crimea was under way, on March 3, a new front organization appeared: CyberBerkut. Perhaps the name was inspired by the surfacing of hacked and forged material on CyberGuerrilla in the preceding weeks and months. The first post smeared the pro-European protesters in Kyiv as "neo-Fascists," and declared a hunt for the criminals. In classic anti-Fascist tradition, the Russian digital fighters depicted all of West-facing Ukraine under a red-and-white swastika against a blood-red background, with only Crimea and part of pro-Russian Eastern Ukraine in bright, liberated blue.[10] The post included a list of sites that the Berkut activists threatened to hack. They signed off Anonymous-style: "We are 'CyberBerkut'! We will not forget and will not forgive!"

On March 12, before 9:00 a.m. in Ukraine, nine days after CyberBerkut burst on the scene, Anonymous Ukraine posted another message on Cyber-Guerrilla, with a special leak to boot. This time, the high-tech Anon packaging belied an old-school active measures tactic. The leak included three forged emails, designed to show that the revolution in Ukraine was a Western plot, masterminded by the CIA. The three phony emails flowed down a conspiratorial chain of command, from the CIA to the U.S. Army, from the U.S. Army to the Ukrainian Army's general staff, and finally to right-wing Ukrainian paramilitaries acting as CIA fronts. Anonymous Ukraine hackers had supposedly discovered the plot by hacking the Gmail inbox of a Ukrainian colonel on the general staff, Igor Protsyk. The three forged emails were slipped in among Protsyk's genuine emails—lies flanked by truth. But this time the truthful content—Protsyk's actual emails—was so uninteresting that the Russian forgers helpfully copied their creative work into a separate folder called "most interesting." The forgery is remarkable in many ways, not least because the operation illustrates the depth of conspiratorial thinking and the layers of deception at play when active measures were reborn in the early 2010s.

The first forgery was an email to Protsyk from Jason P. Gresh, the assistant U.S. Army attaché at the American embassy in Kyiv and a lieutenant colonel. "Ihor [sic]," the Gresh email began, "events are moving fast in the Crimea. Our friends in Washington expect more decisive action from your network[11] . . . I think it's time to implement the plan we discussed." The forgers had the American practically order his Ukrainian contact into action: "Your job is to cause some problems to the transport hubs in the south-east in order to frame-up the neighbor."

Assistant U.S. Army attaché Jason Gresh meeting with Ukrainian military officers
(Ukrainian Armed Forces)

That neighbor's identity was obvious, although the conspiracy carefully avoided mentioning Russia by name. "It will create favorable conditions for Pentagon and the Company to act," the fake Gresh went on, in badly translated English, and using a quaint nickname for the CIA.

The fake conspiracy was elaborate. Two days later, on March 11, in the afternoon, a follow-up message had Protsyk act on U.S. Army orders. The Ukrainian colonel instructed Vasyl Labaychuk, his paramilitary co-conspirator, to strike an airfield in Melitopol and make it look as if Russian troops had attacked Ukraine's 25th Airborne Brigade. "25 brigade is flying combat missions, so do not harm the planes," said Protsyk, stressing that the mock attack should target those planes that were already damaged. "You can do everything with them," the faux colonel wrote. "Remember, everything must look like a real attack by the Russian Spetsnaz."[12] Labaychuk was a young leader of a recently founded far-right Ukrainian nationalist group called Right Sector. The group's street fighters had clashed with riot police at the Euromaidan revolt in early 2014. Now, by early March, Right Sector was just getting ready to set itself up as a party.

Then, three and a half hours later, the third forgery completed the chain: Labaychuk, the Right Sector militant leader, implemented his Ukrainian

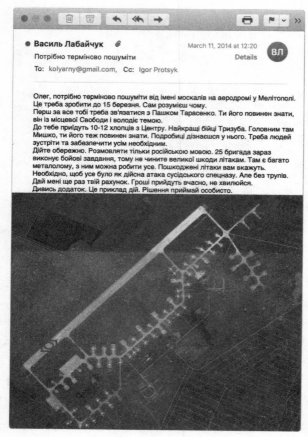

Василь Лабайчук   March 11, 2014 at 12:20

Потрібно терміново пошуміти   Details

To: kolyarny@gmail.com, Cc: Igor Protsyk

Олег, потрібно терміново пошуміти від імені москалів на аеродромі у Мелітополі. Це треба зробити до 15 березня. Сам розумієш чому.

Перш за все тобі треба зв'язатися з Пашком Тарасенко. Ти його повинен знати, він із місцевої Свободи і володіє темою.

До тебе приїдуть 10-12 хлопців з Центру. Найкращі бійці Тризуба. Головним там Мишко, ти його теж повинен знати. Подробиці дізнаєшся у нього. Треба людей зустріти та забезпечити усім необхідним.

Дійте обережно. Розмовляти тільки російською мовою. 25 бригада зараз виконує бойові завдання, тому не чините великої шкоди літакам. Там є багато металолому, з ним можна робити усе. Пошкоджені літаки вам вкажуть.

Необхідно, щоб усе було як дійсна атака сусідського спецназу. Але без трупів.

Дай мені ще раз твій рахунок. Гроші прийдуть вчасно, не хвилюйся.

Дивись додаток. Це приклад дій. Рішення приймай особисто.

Forged email instructing local far-right commanders, on behalf of the CIA, to attack an airfield in eastern Ukraine in order to frame Russia

Army orders and instructed one of his fictional men, Oleg Kolyarny, to carry out the mission in eastern Ukraine, copying Protsyk. Labaychuk told Kolyarny, in coarse language, to "make some noise on behalf of the Muskovites at Melitopol's airbase." The faux email then outlined the logistics of the mission, how to rendezvous with a dozen local fighters ("Speak only in Russian"), and how to mock-attack the damaged planes.[13] To make the combat instruction look real, the active measures operators attached a picture of Melitopol airfield that they had pulled from Google Maps,[14] and marked three locations on the airfield for potential military action, including one for a mock firefight and two damaged Ilyushin Il-76 aircraft for targets of the staged attack. "See the attached file," Kolyarny was told in the email. "It is just a proposal. Decide yourself what to do."

The forgers then slid the folder with the phony messages into the hacked genuine messages of the real Ukrainian colonel, and published the entire package on CyberGuerrilla. They added the following note:

Hello

We are Anonymous Ukraine

We have hacked e-mail correspondence of U.S. Army Attache Assistant in Kiev Jason Gresh and a high ranking official from Ukrainian General Staff Igor Protsyk.

It appears that they are planning to conduct a series of attacks on Ukrainian military bases in order to destabilize the situation in Ukraine.

Particularly, Jason Gresh writes to Igor Protsyk that it's time to implement a plan that implies "causing problems to the transport hubs in the south-east of Ukraine in order to frame-up the neighbor. It will create favorable conditions for Pentagon to act", says Jason Gresh.

In his turn, Protsyk writes to some Vasil and tells him to arrange an attack on an airbase of 25 aviation brigade of Ukrainian air force stationed in Melitopol.

This Vasil is responsible for arranging the details of the attack, gathering of the gunmen and providing them with a map of sites that are chosen to be attacked.

We strongly recommend everyone to look through these documents. There you will find all the details.

http://www.mediafire.com/download/fso0k2ry5yzhr8a/protsyk .7z [. . .]

We will protect Ukraine from Western hirelings and fascists that are trying to hurl Ukraine into chaos! We do not want them to start a war! Expect us

We are Anonymous Ukraine.

We are the Patriots of our country.
We Do Not Forgive.
We Do Not Forget.
Expect Us.[15]

The next day, Voice of Russia carried the story. The leaked emails were accompanied by a rambling nine-minute audio recording and a transcript that the operators apparently had given exclusively to Voice of Russia. In the audio, the robot voice often used by Anonymous vowed to protect Ukraine's freedom against Western interference through NATO; disparaged the regime in Kyiv as Fascists; and likened pro-Western Ukrainian politicians to "Bandera Nazis," a local slur that harkened back to a pro-German Ukrainian World War II nationalist leader, Stepan Bandera, who was assassinated by the KGB in 1959 in West Germany. Voice of Russia explained that Gresh's attack instructions revealed the United States' desperation to consolidate the "overthrow of Ukraine," and that the United States could not tolerate democratic elections. The emails needed explanation, which in principle made them more credible, as most correspondence, when taken out of context, does need explanation. So Voice of Russia explained: The neighbor in this case meant the Russian Federation; the reference to the Company was meant to be insider jargon for the CIA. But the forgery was not particularly professional. The missive contained grammatical errors, and an article was missing in front of "Pentagon"—the forger's Russian accent was practically audible: *it will create favorable conditions for Pentagon.* Even the Voice of Russia reporters felt compelled to comment on the bad English. "One note, for a military attaché Mr. Gresh's English is not that good," the official Russian outlet wrote, "but he could be talking down to his hirelings."

Gresh and others at the U.S. embassy in Kyiv were bemused. The situation was a novel development, a mid-century throwback with a high-tech update. No U.S. government system had been breached, not even a personal email account, yet the State Department and the Army had become the victim of a hack-and-leak. The forgeries were obvious and clumsy, especially the one email so clearly not written by a native speaker, let alone an officer in the

U.S. diplomatic service. "It was comedic," recalled Gresh. "It was serious, but at the same time it was quite funny."[16] For about two months he received a lot of hate mail; he posted some of the best ones in the office. But the story was never covered in the mainstream press. Gresh told me that he considered the operation a "complete and utter failure."

The Ukrainian general staff was not so sure. Ukrainian officers suspected that Russian military intelligence was behind the operation, and they knew their adversary's preference for active measures. In fact, the very email that purported to come from the Ukrainian general staff called for an "active measure."[17] The real Protsyk knew what was going on: the operation specifically targeted the civil-military relations in contested areas in Ukraine, not the State Department. The local population, he knew, was not used to encountering the Ukrainian army in armored vehicles. The novelty of large troop movements presented an opportunity to present the Ukrainian army as invaders, a puppet squadron controlled by dark forces in the United States. "I know what I'm talking about, as I grew up in Soviet system and I'd been trained for things like this in military institute," Protsyk told me later.[18] The Ukrainian police started an investigation, but the war meant that it was never finished.

Ukraine spiraled into civil war. The pro-Russian protest in the Donbass region, in eastern Ukraine, developed in April into a full-blown insurgency against the pro-European government. Presidential elections were to be held on May 25, 2014. On May 16, the Central Election Commission in Kyiv warned that it could not finish preparations in six precincts in the Donetsk and Luhansk regions in the Donbass, "due to unlawful actions of unknown persons."[19] Local members of the election commission received threats against their own safety and that of their families. As political events in Ukraine became more heated, confrontational, and dangerous, so did the digital attacks against the country's fragile democratic institutions.

"The anti-people junta is trying to legalize itself by organizing this show, directed by the West," CyberBerkut said in a statement three days before Ukraine's special presidential election. "We will not allow it!"[20]

Sofacy

THREE DAYS BEFORE THE ELECTION IN UKRAINE, CYBERBERKUT compromised the Central Election Commission's network.[1] Commission staff discovered the damage when they arrived at work the next morning. The attack succeeded in disabling central network nodes and "numerous components of the election system," according to Nikolay Koval, who headed Ukraine's Computer Emergency Response Team during the incident.[2] The election was approaching fast, but the real-time vote-count displays had been knocked out—and stayed that way for nearly twenty hours, as engineers worked frantically to fix the problem. Meanwhile, the digital intruders taunted the Ukrainian officials, leaking photos of the commissioner's bathroom renovation, his passport and that of his wife, and—in an attempt to undermine the election's legitimacy—leaked emails from Western officials to the Ukrainian election commission. Koval

Headquarters of the Russian General Staff's Main Intelligence Department (GRU) in Moscow, December 2016 (Natalia Kolesnikova / AFP / Getty Images)

and his team scrambled to contain the damage. Thankfully, the original network architects had saved a backup of the commission's data, which gave the emergency response crew a head start. At daybreak on Sunday, as Ukrainians started heading out to cast their votes on paper slips, the CEC's systems were back up and running, including the displays. The country eagerly awaited the first counts of the presidential vote at one of the tensest moments in Ukraine's history.

Less than an hour after voting stations had closed, Russia's most popular TV station, Channel One, reported that Dmytro Yarosh, a far-right leader of Right Sector and a combat-experienced commander of the Ukrainian Volunteer Army, was the likely winner of the vote.[3] The Channel One presenter, Irada Zeynalova, showed what she called a "strange chart" which, she alleged, had "appeared on the central website of the CEC of Ukraine a few minutes ago." The chart listed the names of several Ukrainian candidates alongside bars that displayed a number of votes. At the top was Yarosh, with 37.13 percent of the vote, followed by Petro Poroshenko, with 29.63 percent. The graph did appear to be taken from the CEC's website; it had the same dark green logo with a yellow-and-blue wave, a similar layout and fonts. But there was one problem: the image used on Channel One never actually appeared on the public-facing CEC website.[4]

The attack on the displays, it turned out, was a diversion tactic. While the Ukrainian Computer Emergency Response Team scrambled to restore the CEC's display system in the days and hours before the vote, a second, undetected attack was unfolding in secret. The reconnaissance phase for this second attack started more than two months earlier, on March 19. On April 21 the server had been breached.[5] A day before the election, the attackers were busy preparing for their actual mission: placing fake election results on the CEC website, to be ready for prime time at just after eight that evening, when the polls closed and all eyes turned to the CEC in anticipation of the results. The attackers uploaded their bar-chart forgery at 19:52, eight minutes before the end of the election. But in their haste, they failed to fully appreciate how the commission website was set up. To prepare for both the high number of visitors on election night, and to guard against denial-of-service attacks, the commission had "mirrored" its website on several servers. This mirroring made the website more stable under the heavy traffic of election night—and, inadvertently, also slightly harder to hack: the load-bearing mirror sites meant that putting a file on the CEC server, if done incorrectly, would not automatically post the file on the commission's actual, public website. The attackers, it seems, did not grasp the site's complex setup, and placed their carefully prepared forgery in the wrong folder. This meant that the forgery, named "results.jpg," was publicly accessible at the full URL that used the CEC's IP address, but not via the official website.

Immediately after uploading the forged chart, the clandestine attackers forwarded the URL to Russia's Channel One. Twenty-four minutes later, several different journalists and producers at the TV station accessed the obscure, unpublished URL.[6] Shortly thereafter, Russia's prime TV station included the false Yarosh announcement in its 9:00 p.m. news segment.

The Computer Emergency Response Team immediately learned of the Russian breaking news, and started investigating what looked to them like an adversarial operation to interfere in a presidential election. Three days later, the CERT published its technical findings, laying out the errors in tradecraft that the Russian hackers had made and cleverly articulating the suspicion that Channel One may have been complicit in the prime-time election interference. The Ukrainian investigators concluded that Channel One could not have found the forged graph without secret help, and mockingly offered to turn over files to Russian law enforcement in order to get to the bottom of the case.

Instead of Russian authorities, CyberBerkut responded. Just hours after the CERT's analysis was published, the mysterious pseudo-activists posted an explicit note to the press. "We did not hack the CEC website on May 25," the hackers announced, admitting that they, in fact, did hack the CEC's network, adding that they had watched from within the commission's own networks as the CEC attempted to repair the website in real time. "We were inside of the system and were monitoring vain endeavors of the officials to restore it. But they failed."[7] CyberBerkut's claim was incorrect; the Ukrainians had succeeded in restoring the site. Yet CyberBerkut's main purpose was to counter the Ukrainian version of the story, and that meant backing the Yarosh graph and calling into question the Ukrainians' statement that it was not available on the public-facing website. CyberBerkut claimed that the "junta" in Kyiv would understate support for Yarosh, and that the initial graph might in fact be the correct one. "We confirm the table showing that Yarosh and Poroshenko had passed to the second round of the elections appeared on the official CEC site." Then the faux activists even provided the IP address of that official website, and the addresses of six different mirrors.[8] It was an extraordinary admission not just of their own technical error but that the taunting response from the Ukrainian CERT had touched a nerve. As always, CyberBerkut signed off, "We are CyberBerkut! We will not forget! We will not forgive!"

But the wider world would forget and forgive these renewed Russian active measures. CyberBerkut's hacking tools were then brand-new and hard to detect. The Ukrainian responders had found their traces, but at the time only a few intelligence officers and researchers would have been able to do so. Only later would the trail lead to Russian military intelligence.[9]

Less than two months later, on July 17, as passengers settled in for a long flight from Amsterdam to Kuala Lumpur, a Buk anti-aircraft missile ripped into their Boeing 777. All 298 people aboard Malaysia Airlines Flight 17 perished. Debris and body parts fell from the sky above eastern Ukraine, scattered across fields and grassland. Almost immediately, Russian intelligence took advantage of the disaster. Less than two weeks later, online spies started baiting their victims—who later included the Dutch team investigating the shooting down[10]—with a file named MH17.doc. The file contained news on the crash along with a small, well-crafted tool that allowed the attackers remote access to files on their targets' machines.[11] The pace and aggression of operations was picking up.

By September 2014, Russian military intelligence had been hacking for more than a decade. A range of computer security companies had traced Russian hacking sprees for years, and came up with various confusing and meaningless code names for the hacking groups, the first of which was SO-FACY. Others, deliberately vague in order to enable open conversation, were Sednit, Pawn Storm, APT28, Strontium, and FANCY BEAR.[12] Whatever the code name imposed on them, the group's first known digital artifact, a so-called malware sample, dates back to July 15, 2004. But the tool would publicly emerge only more than a decade later.[13] In the early days, until late 2014, analysts weren't quite sure whose activity they were describing with these arcane cryptonyms. Yet three things became increasingly clear: the group was highly prolific and highly capable, and it wasn't particularly stealthy.

The first public hints of high-end hacking behavior started trickling out in late 2012, when the Russian military operators used previously undisclosed software vulnerabilities against their victims.[14] Security companies were tracking the intruders in more detailed, unpublished reports. BAE Systems, a British defense and security firm, distributed a detailed analysis to its clients in late August.[15] By then the Russian spies were going after a growing number of targets. The main public repository and catalog for malicious software, known as VirusTotal, then contained more than six hundred distinct samples of the GRU's favorite digital crowbar, known as "Sofacy," like the group itself.

Google was one of the first companies to call out the perpetrators by name, albeit in an underhanded way. On September 5, 2014, the security team in Mountain View circulated among its malware researchers a report titled "Peering into the Aquarium." The title sounded strange. But those in the intelligence business would understand: "the aquarium" was a reference to the GRU's old headquarters building at the Khodinka airfield near Moscow[16]—one GRU defector even titled his memoirs *Inside the Aquarium*.[17] The Google security team noted that the hackers appeared to have about a week's notice ahead of a Russian military operation in Syria, and had breached online targets accordingly. The GRU seemed to be the obvious perpetrator, but Google wasn't completely sure. The aquarium in the title "was a way to get people to disagree and to let us know if we had got it wrong," one of the authors told me.[18] The actual report only obliquely referred to a "sophisticated state-sponsored group targeting primarily former Soviet republics, NATO members, and other Western European countries." The Republic of Georgia, Google found, was at the top of the target list.

About a month later, the first big public reports came out, beginning on October 8 with ESET, an IT security company headquartered in Bratislava, Slovakia. Based on research enabled by Google's work, the ESET analysts described a customized hacking tool that was used to "relentlessly" attack Eastern European targets.[19] About a week later, one of America's leading advanced computer security companies, FireEye, published a major report, spelling out in public for the first time what many security researchers had long known or suspected in private: that the Russian government was behind the mysterious "APT28," as many outside experts then referred to the entity that they suspected was, in fact, the GRU. "Russia has long been a whispered frontrunner among capable nations for performing sophisticated network operations," the FireEye analysts wrote.[20] They observed that APT28 was skilled, but did not engage in intellectual property theft or economic or financial espionage, only old-school, defense-related spying for geopolitical purposes, with a consistent, eight-year focus on Eastern European governments, the armed forces in Russia's periphery, but also NATO and OSCE, a European security organization, as well as defense attachés and defense events and exhibitions in Europe. Detection rates of Russian hacking tools improved, and breaching high-value targets became harder for the GRU.

A few weeks later, however, on November 12, 2014, NATO's supreme commander in Europe, an American four-star general named Philip Breedlove, publicly announced that he had intelligence that confirmed Russian military equipment was seen entering Ukraine. The GRU now trained its sights on Breedlove, and readied to strike.

The war in Eastern Ukraine continued to churn. By early December, about a thousand people had died in Donbass. On December 16, a senior Russian diplomat accused the West of providing "lethal weapons" to Ukraine.[21] About a week later, the first digital active measures against the United States began. On Christmas Eve 2014, the *Albuquerque Journal* suddenly found that its website had been defaced. A new entity calling itself "CyberCaliphate" had posted a picture of a man with his face covered by a black-and-white keffiyeh scarf against a pitch-black background, with the Islamic State flag and the line "i love you isis" typed in lowercase next to the masked face. The headline was "Christmas Will Never Be Merry Any Longer."[22]

"While the U.S. and its satellites are bombing the Islamic State, we broke into your home networks and personal devices and know everything about you," read the journal's hacked home page.[23] Two weeks later, on January 6, a local Maryland TV station was the target of a similar defacement, using the same moniker and the exact same imagery.[24] The FBI told the station personnel that similar attacks had quietly happened to media companies across the United States. A larger campaign was slowly beginning to take shape, possibly designed to distract the West from the renewed military escalation in Ukraine.

The following day, terror struck in Paris. Between January 7 and 9, several Islamist terrorist attacks killed seventeen people in four shootings, the most infamous of which took place at the offices of the satirical newspaper *Charlie Hebdo*. The massacre was a response to the publication of highly controversial cartoons that lampooned the Prophet Muhammad. Islamic extremism and free speech were among the most divisive issues in Europe

The widely used logo of a Russian military intelligence front, CyberCaliphate, which perpetrated advanced computer network attacks against a range of targets in the name of ISIS

and North America. The West was on edge, expecting the next Islamic State terrorist attack at any moment. The situation was ripe for exploitation.

Three days later, on January 12, U.S. Central Command's social media accounts were compromised.[25] Unknown hackers changed Central Command's profile picture and banner to the same image used in the previous hacks. Then the hackers posted their first note on Twitter from the hijacked U.S. military account: "AMERICAN SOLDIERS, WE ARE COMING, WATCH YOUR BACK. ISIS." Within twenty minutes, the purported Islamic State militants had published seven posts to Central Command's 110,000 followers, who included many journalists. More than two hundred different news stories on the episode appeared that month. Many debunked the claim that ISIS hackers had successfully breached Centcom's sensitive networks, as most of the material that ISIS claimed had been stolen and leaked appeared to be publicly available. But most of the stories repeated the false claim that Islamic State had successfully hacked and attacked U.S. Central Command. "We know everything about you, your wives and children," the faux-Islamic hackers had threatened. "We won't stop!" That part, at least, wasn't a lie.

Ten days later, on January 23, 2015, the GRU penetrated the internal network of the French broadcaster TV5/Monde.[26] The Russian operators installed a specific implant, an updated version of the well-known Sofacy tool, which was configured to call home via two specific command-and-control machines, inside the French broadcaster's network. FireEye intelligence analysts were monitoring one of these command-and-control machines.[27] In February, just days after the full compromise of TV5, FireEye noticed that the implant was communicating with its automated handlers from inside the French TV station. APT28 was researching the TV5 networks from the inside, especially the nature of the machines that controlled the broadcasting operation itself. This was not trivial—rather, the attack was an intriguing engineering challenge for the operators in Moscow. French investigators later suspected that the saboteurs had translated and studied around thirty stolen documents in order to prepare for the next phase.[28]

Three days after the TV5 compromise, on the morning of January 26, 2015, the Malaysia Airlines website was defaced. "404—Plane Not Found," read the text emblazoned over the large picture of a Malaysia Airlines passenger aircraft. Later the image changed to a graphic of a tuxedo-wearing, pipe-smoking lizard with a monocle and top hat, under the text "Hacked by Lizard Squad, Official Cyber Caliphate"—a strange mix of familiar hacker aesthetics, often associated with the Anonymous movement, and Islamic State themes.

On the morning of February 10, at around 10:45 Eastern Time, *Newsweek*'s Twitter account suddenly had its profile picture changed to the keffiyeh-clad ISIS fighter. A series of incendiary posts followed. The first was addressed to the First Lady, and said, "#CyberCaliphate Bloody Valentine's Day #MichelleObama! We're watching you, your girls and your husband!" The hacked *Newsweek* account then proceeded to post allegedly confidential Department of Defense files.

At that time, Angela Ricketts, whose spouse was in the U.S. Army, was taking a bubble bath in her home in Colorado, and had just opened a memoir to read. Suddenly a message appeared on her iPhone. "Dear Angela!" said the

Facebook message. "Bloody Valentine's Day!" Islamic State militants threatened to slaughter her family. Terrorists appeared to have hacked Ricketts's phone and her computer. "We're much closer than you can even imagine."[29] Ricketts was one of at least five military spouses who received such death threats; one was so terrified, she fled her home in fear.[30] The operational pace was fast, and getting faster.

On the same day, a website called cyb3rc.com went live.[31] Registered just hours earlier, the site's URL was a hacker-style shortening of CyberCaliphate.

"Bloody Valentine's Day!" began the first post, yet again. The supposed jihadis vowed to wage holy war on the Pentagon's computers. "We are destroying your national cybersecurity system from inside," they wrote, and then proceeded to use the same text they had already sent to several Army spouses like Ricketts: "We know everything about you and your relatives and we're much closer than you can even imagine."[32]

The self-proclaimed Islamic State website published a mix of documents that were already in the public domain, but hard to find, and documents likely stolen from the Department of Defense. It appeared that the Defense Cyber Investigations Training Academy, shortened to DCITA, had lost a number of documents with personal information on U.S. military personnel. Screenshots of the newly published cyb3rc site also appeared on *Newsweek*'s social media feed.

CyberCaliphate bore all the hallmarks of a coordinated disinformation campaign: these actions were launched simultaneously, with consistent branding and language, and across various fronts and hacked social media sites, both publicly and as silent measures against the military spouses. But it would take years for the forensic evidence to emerge that would allow a high-confidence assessment that the fake Islamic State group was, in fact, the work of Russian military intelligence.

Nonetheless, the similarities between CyberCaliphate and CyberBerkut were uncanny: in both cases the masterminds named their "cyber" front after a known, brutal real-world entity; both opted for medial capitals, FedEx-style, to make their cover names more legible; both assumed the aesthetics of the Anonymous movement, although they were an uneven fit for the fake jihadis. Both combined hacking-and-leaking with crude forgeries; both engaged in data destruction; both had dedicated websites with handcrafted layouts.

The sabotage preparations at TV5 were making good progress. Lurking within the TV station's computer network, the hackers were intercepting the log-ins and passwords for the station's social media feeds, the content management system for TV5's website, and the routers and switches that beamed video into the world. On April 6, the APT28 operators checked whether the stolen log-ins to Facebook, Twitter, and YouTube would work; they did.[33]

Digital D-day was April 8, when TV5, which ran a global broadcasting operation in two hundred countries and territories, with up to 50 million weekly viewers, was set to launch a new channel.[34] French dignitaries were attending the launch at the Paris headquarters. The attackers did a meticulous dry run to check whether their log-in credentials were up to date for the encoders and multiplexers—broadcasting devices that enable the transfer of video and audio simultaneously over one frequency channel.[35] Those passwords were also still good. Finally, at 7:57 p.m., the demolition began. The GRU operators modified the input parameters for the multiplexing machines, laying the groundwork for the programming disruption. One hour later, TV5's social media accounts suddenly displayed the Islamic State flag. Fifty minutes after that came the main strike: the attackers hopped onto some of the station's most critical routers and simply deleted the firmware that kept the broadcasting machines running. All TV5 screens immediately went black.[36]

At that moment, Yves Bigot, TV5's director general, was having a late dinner in a restaurant in Paris. Bigot was out with a fellow broadcaster from Radio Canada, and in a celebratory mood. Suddenly, as the appetizers arrived, Bigot's phone started buzzing. All twelve channels served by TV5, his staff told him, had gone off the air. "It's the worst thing that can happen to you in television," Bigot later recalled.[37] As the TV executives began to panic, the hackers were preparing a flanking attack aimed at TV5's emergency responders. At 10:40 p.m., APT28 managed to bring down TV5's internal messaging system. The situation was dire. Late that night, TV5 called the government for help.

The broadcaster was lucky that night. Because of the launch of the new channel the previous day, many qualified technicians were still close by. Now they scrambled to relaunch the entire station. "One of them was able to locate the very machine where the attack was taking place and he was able to cut out this machine from the internet and it stopped the attack," Bigot later told the BBC. At 5:25 a.m. the next day, the incident responders had managed to restore one channel, and others soon followed.

But the sabotage of TV5 was not over. The hack was accompanied by a shrewd publicity blitz—a small con to support the big con. About twenty-two hours after the attack, the first technical analysis appeared on an obscure blog called Breaking3Zero. The post reproduced several of the supposed ISIS notices posted from the hacked TV5 website and social media accounts; its author claimed that a member of the public had alerted him or her to the TV5 defacement, and that he or she had then "conducted an investigation into cyber jihadism and found the group responsible for the attack." The post claimed, without citing any sources, that TV5 had been breached through a Java flaw in the machine of TV5's social media officer, and that this bridge-head computer was "directly connected to the control room."[38] The post was extraordinarily detailed: the author claimed to have identified the "virus" used to breach TV5, that this malware was named isis.vbs, that the encryption of the virus had been "broken," that the attacker had used a proxy to hide its tracks, and that it had identified the culprit, an Algerian ISIS-affiliated jihadi named "Najaf" who was in reality hiding behind the pseudonym "JoHn.Dz."

At first, government investigators in France and neighboring countries were confused and even led astray by this highly technical and detailed analysis. But after a team of about a dozen investigators spent weeks examining the TV5 network, the French government agency in charge, ANSSI, discovered that Russian military intelligence had hacked the French broadcaster, sabotaged its programming, defaced its digital outreach as CyberCaliphate, and prepared a well-timed and technical incident report to mislead the initial press coverage.[39] The ruse had worked. "TV Monde hacked by Cyber Caliphate group," announced one cartoon in Le Monde the day after the attack.[40] *Le Figaro* saw the hacked TV station as part of a global culture war by Islamic State.[41] Some technology outlets also took the made-up incident report at face value.[42]

Three weeks after the GRU brought down the French broadcaster, it breached the German Parliament. Once in, APT28 installed clandestine backdoors on at least twenty-one workstations and four servers that were used by members of Parliament and their administrators. For their command-and-control communications back to Moscow, the intruders used third-party machines in Eastern Europe. However, these communications did not remain undetected. BAE Systems, the British security firm, soon noticed suspicious connections to the German Parliament emanating from a client connection it had been watching, identified the intruders as APT28, and confidentially informed German domestic intelligence.[43] On May 20, 2015, an investigation later found, spies had exfiltrated sixteen gigabytes of data from the German Parliament.[44] None of the data would be leaked or publicized, but APT28's Bundestag hack would soon provide important forensic artifacts for other investigations.

Also on May 20, 2015, a "Yemen Cyber Army" claimed that it had hacked the website of the Saudi Ministry of Foreign Affairs. The ministry's site now showed the fruits of what the attackers called #OpSaudi. That morning, Saudi diplomats stared at a picture of five men in Anonymous-style Guy Fawkes masks, above a bizarre poem:

> *Beneath this mask*
> *there is more than flesh.*
> *Beneath this mask,*
> *there is an idea,*
> *And ideas are bulletproof.*
> *Yemen Cyber Army is Coming . . .* [45]

The anonymous hackers boasted that they had control over more than three thousand machines, with access to emails and secret files, and that they would destroy all of the ministry's data at noon that Wednesday—less than two hours away. The initial announcement included links to file-sharing sites where the hackers had uploaded samples of the stolen files.[46]

Less than a month later, on June 19, WikiLeaks published more than sixty thousand diplomatic cables from Saudi Arabia. Known as the "Saudi Cables" and widely covered in the international press, the leak was one of the most controversial ever. The Saudi files contained a range of highly sensitive personal data, including more than five hundred passports or identity files and dozens of medical records. The files even exposed several rape victims by name, including Saudi teenagers abused abroad and foreign domestic staff tortured or raped in Saudi Arabia, some of the accounts in haunting detail.[47]

One week later, a new, mysterious, and dedicated leak site appeared. The site took inspiration from WikiLeaks, calling itself WikiSaudiLeaks. The page published more than seven thousand files purportedly stolen from the Saudi foreign ministry, and after a few days claimed that "'WikiLeaks' have been given access to some of these documents."[48]

The Saudi Cables data dump was then one of the most voluminous to date, and bore the hallmarks of an intelligence operation. The identity of the attackers, however, remained undetermined. Western intelligence agencies and private-sector security companies studied the case closely, but could not come to a strong conclusion. Some circumstantial evidence pointed to Russian military intelligence; an investigator with firsthand knowledge of the case told me that the Saudi foreign ministry had been hacked by "APT28" in the spring of 2015.[49] One of the most convincing clues was that some of the technical infrastructure used to host the WikiSaudiLeaks site overlapped with known GRU hacking infrastructure. Such evidence was a bit like finding a similar pair of hand-knitted gloves at two different crime scenes—helpful, but not watertight.[50] Then there was the circumstantial evidence. The purportedly Yemeni site was registered from a Yandex email address—a Russian provider—on a Friday, a day that falls on the weekend in the Middle East. And finally, the leak site's naming convention and tactics followed the similar dedicated sites in Ukraine, including the "Cyber" prefix and the use of Anonymous iconography.[51] Other indicators, however, appeared to point to Iranian authorship—for example, the reuse of a unique name and a mock mathematical equation that had been previously linked to Iranian intelligence operations.

One thing is certain: the world's most powerful intelligence organizations, including Russian spy agencies, carefully studied the Saudi leaks. And to anybody who was watching, the Saudi Cables demonstrated that WikiLeaks, although hard to control, was a highly effective outlet for high-volume data dumps, both credible and implausible, far superior to home-made, specific, stand-alone websites.

2015–2017: Leak

Election Leaks

UNIT 26165 WAS HOUSED IN BUILDINGS OWNED BY THE MIN-
istry of Defense, once part of a vast early nineteenth-century
complex on the grounds of a former linen factory in central
Moscow. An inconspicuous door on Komsomolsky Prospekt passed under a
large yellow arch of stones, with an odd street-facing electrical outlet.[1] During the Cold War, Unit 26165, then known as the 85th Main Center of the
GRU Special Service, specialized in breaking encryption. By the mid-2000s,
the unit had expanded to computer network exploitation—in other words,
hacking.

The commander of 26165 was Viktor Netyksho, a software engineer with
mathematical training. Ambitious and intellectually inclined, Netyksho had
published several articles on probabilistic functions and neural networks.[2]

Aleksey Lukashev, then a twenty-five-year-old senior lieutenant in GRU Unit 26165, targeted the Clinton campaign, including John Podesta. (FBI)

By early 2016, Netyksho's unit had spent more than a decade developing hacking tools, honing their skills, and expanding their targeting. The unit's work was respected inside Russian military intelligence—in early 2009, Sergey Gizunov, the former commander, had even won a prestigious civilian science and technology award for creating and implementing high-performance computing systems with reconfigurable architecture.[3] By 2016, Gizunov had moved up to deputy chief of the GRU.[4]

The work of two of 26165's junior officers would later stand out. One of them was Aleksey Lukashev, a twenty-five-year-old senior lieutenant originally from the Russian part of Lapland in the Arctic. Lukashev was blond and thin, with close-set brown eyes and full lips. For about three years he had been working under the cover of "Den Katenberg," a persona he used for American and Russian social media accounts and a Gmail address. The picture that Lukashev chose for Katenberg showed a more muscular young Russian man of his own age. Lukashev was particularly skilled at crafting and automating email bait that mimicked Google security warnings, but in reality tricked victims into revealing their passwords.

The second noteworthy character was Ivan Yermakov, a twenty-nine-year-old senior lieutenant born in the Urals. Slender, with a prominent nose, dark bangs that spilled down his forehead, and a shy demeanor, he had been hacking since at least 2010. Government hackers like Yermakov and Lukashev commonly use a range of pseudonyms for their online personas. Yermakov preferred female pseudonyms, including Kate S. Milton, which he used for a Twitter profile and a blog, accompanied by a picture of a Canadian actress. "Kate" sometimes privately approached security researchers to seek useful hacking tools and new vulnerabilities, and occasionally claimed to work for the respected Russian computer security firm Kaspersky.

Unit 26165 was sizable, with partly automated exploitation techniques and a ferocious risk appetite. Its target lists had expanded over the years. First they were more focused on the military—navy, army, and air force officers in adversarial and even friendly countries, defense contractors in the private sector, foreign ministries in Riyadh, Brussels, and Rome, but also in Asia, in the Middle East, and especially in Eastern Europe. Later the unit turned to political targets.

Intelligence agencies in the United States and Europe as well as private digital forensics companies had been watching Netyksho's hacking unit for many years under various nicknames: SOFACY, APT28, FANCY BEAR, etc. For years researchers suspected that they were in fact watching the GRU, but the specific unit and its individual officers remained obscure. Then, at the end of January 2016, the German government would take an extraordinary step: anonymous German sources named the GRU as the perpetrator behind the Bundestag hack the previous year, for the first time publicly identifying APT28 and the GRU as one and the same.[5]

Shortly thereafter, on March 10, Unit 26165 started targeting the Brooklyn-based campaign headquarters of Hillary Clinton. That week, the spies sent booby-trapped emails to fifty different addresses every working day. The attacks failed, not just because some of the addresses were obsolete; the Clinton campaign's default email security settings required more than just a password to get in, and therefore protected staff effectively. Then, on Friday, March 18, Lukashev's team changed tactics, and decided to go after private email accounts instead, which were more likely to be vulnerable.

The next day, just before lunch, Lukashev and his team sent another batch of booby-trapped emails to more than seventy targets, including nine Democratic political operatives at their personal accounts. One of these targets was John Podesta, the charismatic and energetic chairman of the Clinton campaign.

"Someone has your password," the rogue message announced, in trademark Google layout. The email continued:[6]

> Hi John
> Someone just used your password to try to sign in to your Google Account john.podesta@gmail.com.
> Details:
> Saturday, 19 March, 8:34:30 UTC
> IP Address: 134.249.139.239
> Location: Ukraine
> Google stopped this sign-in attempt. You should change your password immediately.
> CHANGE PASSWORD
> Best,
> The Gmail Team

The details were all made-up, and the email looked credible at first glance. Podesta's staff had access to his email account. When they read the false security warning, they forwarded it to the Clinton campaign's IT help desk. After a few minutes the help desk responded, acknowledging the threat and recommending that Podesta change his password and activate an advanced security feature.

But Podesta's staff misunderstood the email, and clicked the treacherous GRU link in the response email, instead of the safe Google link provided by the IT help desk. The malicious URL behind "CHANGE PASSWORD" was invisible. It was https://bit.ly/1PibSU0—within fractions of a second, this link took Podesta's staff to a forged Google log-in page. It looked nearly exactly like the real Google page, with John Podesta's actual profile picture against a gray background, his name and email address prefilled. Everything looked right. His staff entered the password. And the GRU was in.

Two days later, on March 21, Lukashev downloaded more than fifty thousand emails, more than five gigabytes of data, from Podesta's inbox. Russian military intelligence had struck gold. Throughout the last week of

March, Lukashev's unit continued to target DNC staffers and the Clinton campaign with more than one hundred bait emails. On April 6, the GRU succeeded in tricking an employee of the Democratic Congressional Campaign Committee, an organization supporting Democrats in the House. Yermakov scanned the DCCC's network connections to identify possible ways to get in.

At that moment, on April 7, President Vladimir Putin convened a gathering of some four hundred journalists, bloggers, and media executives in St. Petersburg. Dressed in a sleek navy suit, Putin looked relaxed, even comfortable, as he took questions. About an hour into the forum, a young blogger in a navy zip-up sweater took the microphone and asked Putin what he thought of the "so-called Panama Papers."[7]

The blogger was referring to a cache of more than 11 million computer files that had been stolen from Mossack Fonseca, a Panamanian law firm. The leak was the largest in history, involving 2.6 terabytes of data. On April 3, four days before the St. Petersburg forum, a group of international news outlets published the first in a series of stories based on the leak, which had taken them more than a year to investigate. The series revealed corruption on a massive scale: Mossack Fonseca's legal maneuverings had been used to hide billions of dollars. A central theme of the group's reporting was a confusing web of shell companies and proxies, worth a reported $2 billion, that belonged to Putin's inner circle and were presumed to shelter some of the Russian president's vast personal wealth. Putin knew that the highly damaging leak was coming. *Süddeutsche Zeitung* had given advance notice to implicated individuals close to Putin on March 1, 2016, and to the Kremlin on March 23.[8]

When Putin heard the blogger's question, his face lit up with a familiar smirk. He nodded slowly and confidently before reciting a litany of humiliations that the United States had inflicted on Russia. Putin reminded his audience about the sidelining of Russia during the 1998 war in Kosovo and, as a more recent example, what he saw as American meddling in Ukraine. Returning to the Panama Papers, Putin insisted that "officials and state agencies in the United States are behind all this." The Americans' aim, he said, was to weaken Russia from within: "to spread distrust for the ruling authorities and the bodies of power within society."

Meanwhile, Unit 26165 officers had "mined" some bitcoin, then a favored cryptocurrency widely, but falsely, believed to enable anonymous payments. This meant that the GRU had earned some of its own cryptographic money by dedicating computing resources to verifying and registering payments on a public ledger.[9] Now, five days after Putin's Q&A, the spies used $37 worth of freshly minted bitcoin to reserve a domain called electionleaks.com with a Romanian web-hosting company called THC Servers, leaving a cryptographic trail of evidence in the process.[10] But the site was never furnished with content.

The same day, April 12, the GRU had breached the Democratic Congressional Campaign Committee. It had taken the Russian hackers three weeks to search for a way in. Six days earlier, a woman working at the DCCC had inadvertently given away her log-in credentials, and now the hackers in Moscow had breached their first major democratic political organization, as opposed to just individual email accounts. The GRU proceeded to install a well-known hacking tool called the X-Agent kit on at least ten computers at the DCCC. The kit would allow them to record and intercept all activity on a workstation, including everything a user typed and saw over an entire workday. The X-Agent implant was customized to communicate with an inconspicuous server in Arizona that had been leased by Netyksho's men. The Arizona machine was running a control panel that allowed the officers to select and activate specific spying functions for their implants in Washington. In the case of one female staffer, for example, the officers in Moscow looked over her shoulder as she handled personal banking and other private matters in the confines of her office. On April 15, the foreign spies logged into one specific DCCC machine and typed "hillary," "cruz," and "trump" into a search box, in an attempt to find opposition research the Democrats had done on Republicans. After about a week of spying on the DCCC, on April 18, the GRU got lucky: they intercepted the log-in and password credentials of another DCCC employee, who was also authorized to log in to the network of the Democratic National Committee.[11] The GRU could now pivot directly from the DCCC network over to the DNC.

The GRU finished the
design of its DCLeaks logo
on April 20, 2016.

Once inside the DNC, the intruders again searched for particularly in-teresting machines that held files related to the hotly contested presidential campaign. Bernie Sanders had just won the Wyoming caucus, and Hillary Clinton was about to prevail in the New York primary. Back in Moscow, the officers were working the DNC from the inside, equipping thirty-three machines with a customized X-Agent tool kit. The attack seriously compro-mised the Democratic Party's internal and external communications.[12] The clandestine intruders also accessed the DNC's telephone systems, giving the military intelligence officers access to phone calls and even voice mail inside the Democratic headquarters, all while an election campaign was in full swing.[13]

Just one day after compromising the DNC, on April 19, the GRU regis-tered yet another website, DCLeaks.com, using the same Romanian hosting company, and paying for the new site out of the same pool of bitcoin. Now the GRU needed to do some web design. The next day, on April 20, the Russian operators finished drawing a sleek logo, with "DC" in blue, the white silhou-ette of the Capitol building perched between the D and the C, and "Leaks" printed in red underneath.[14]

The GRU worked through May on getting the leak portal ready for pub-lication. The first "portfolio" uploaded to DCLeaks betrayed the hidden hand of military intelligence: it consisted of the emails stolen one year earlier from Philip Breedlove, the recently retired supreme commander of NATO forces in Europe.[15] DCLeaks was then supposed to be the GRU's main American document outlet. But the site, so far exclusively focused on military leaks, wasn't yet live.

Three days after registering the leak site, the GRU started preparations to exfiltrate data from the DNC networks.[16] On April 28, IT staff at the DNC detected that unauthorized users had penetrated their network.[17] Clinton had just won four out of five Northeastern primaries. The Russian intruders continued to smuggle out information from the Democratic network until May 25, the latest date of any email in the ultimate WikiLeaks dump. Unit 26165 exfiltrated gigabytes of data from the DNC, this time channeled through a command-and-control machine leased in Illinois. Yermakov and his team half-heartedly attempted to cover their digital traces by deleting logs from the DNC network that showed their surreptitious log-ins and the drainage of data. Meanwhile, 26165 had passed on Podesta's inbox to Unit 74455, which was already busy preparing the next stage of the operation: the active measures.

Unit 74455 had extracted seventy-two mostly random attachments from Podesta's inbox, and now published these attachments on DCLeaks, unmodified, without any reference to Podesta.[18] The unit's work had been crude in Ukraine; it was even cruder in the culturally more distant United States. Despite more than two months of preparation, the GRU officers were unable to recognize and extract politically juicy content from Podesta's inbox.

On June 4, an officer in Unit 74455 logged into a Wordpress account, made sure that DCLeaks was ready, and clicked "publish."[19] The GRU applied the Ukraine playbook to the United States. Unit 74455 wrote that the site had been launched by "American hacktivists" who respected freedom of speech and democracy. DCLeaks was "open for cooperation," ready to publish more leaks submitted by citizen activists, and even added a faux submission portal for would-be whistle-blowers.

The GRU's attempts to surface its first dedicated American leak site were clumsy. The first social media account to mention DCLeaks belonged to an avatar dubbed "Melvin Redick," on Facebook. "These guys show hidden truth about Hillary Clinton, George Soros," Redick posted to a Facebook group about breaking news.[20] "It's really interesting!" A few other Facebook accounts posted similar notes, but nobody noticed. Unit 74455's Facebook game had not noticeably improved, more than two years after its poor showing during the annexation of Crimea.

Meanwhile, the DNC had its networks cleaned up by CrowdStrike, a security firm that specializes in countering advanced network threats. After deploying its tools on the DNC's machines, and after about two hours of work, CrowdStrike found evidence of not one but two "sophisticated adversaries" on the committee's network. On Friday, June 10, the DNC took its machines offline (six days after DCLeaks went live). CrowdStrike called the two groups FANCY BEAR and COZY BEAR, later identified as the GRU and, most likely, the SVR. CrowdStrike found no evidence of collaboration between the two intelligence agencies inside the DNC's networks, "or even an awareness of one by the other."[21]

Senior management told Democratic staffers to hand in their mobile phones and devices before leaving for the weekend. It was an unusual request, and no reason was given. Some staffers were concerned they would get fired. "That Friday night, the plug was pulled," said one DNC staffer later.[22] Repairs and remedies for the security breach and cleanup would cost the DNC more than a million dollars. By the end of the weekend, on June 12, the DNC's networks were cleaned up and back online.[23]

That day, Julian Assange gave an interview to a British news network. He mentioned that a major political leak was forthcoming. "We have upcoming leaks in relation to Hillary Clinton, which are great," Assange said. "WikiLeaks has a very big year ahead."[24] As was often his strategy, Assange was being deliberately cryptic. Later he persistently refused to clarify either from whom or precisely when his organization had received specific leaks.

Two days later, on June 14, the GRU, sensing that DCLeaks was a hard sell and not exactly a success, started to reach out to WikiLeaks directly. The @DCleaks_ Twitter account privately messaged Julian Assange's outfit. "You announced your organization was preparing to publish more Hillary's emails," one GRU officer wrote to @WikiLeaks, referring to Assange's TV interview just two days earlier, adding: "We are ready to support you. We have some sensitive information too, in particular her financial documents. Let's do it together. What do you think about publishing our info at the same moment?"[25] Assange apparently did not respond to this first contact attempt, perhaps because he missed the message on Twitter. The GRU monitored Assange's statements so closely, and then offered their support, because they had likely already passed the archive of John Podesta's inbox to WikiLeaks before June 12, anonymously.[26]

Next, the DNC decided to go public with the story of the Russian double hack. The Democrats knew that this wild claim would have to be backed up by solid evidence. *The Washington Post* was working on a story, but that wouldn't provide enough detail, so CrowdStrike prepared a technical report to post online immediately after the *Post* published its piece. The security firm outlined some of the "superb" tradecraft at play in both intrusions: the Russian software implants were stealthy, they could sense locally installed virus scanners and other defenses, the tools were customizable through encrypted configuration files, they were persistent, and the intruders had used an elaborate command-and-control infrastructure.

In the wee hours of June 14, *The Washington Post* revealed that "Russian government hackers" had penetrated the computer network of the Democratic National Committee. Foreign spies, the *Post* claimed, had gained access to the DNC's entire database of opposition research on the presumptive Republican nominee, Donald Trump, just weeks before the Republican Convention. CrowdStrike went a step further, and exposed Russian tradecraft: the firm published command-and-control nodes and hashes, the unique communication links and secret serial numbers of the Russian break-in tools—the twenty-first-century version of publicly revealing a set of clandestine dead-drop boxes while they were still in use, or of exposing the license plates and secret bugging devices of undercover spies. It meant that the Russian spy agencies would immediately lose visibility into a good number of targets, nixing months and months of hard work, and it meant that they would have to tear down their existing infrastructure and start from scratch. As if to add insult to injury, the American security firm wrote that the two Russian spy agencies had overlapping areas of responsibility, that they occasionally stole sources from each other, and that they even compromised each other's operations. Worse, the driving force behind this costly humiliation was CrowdStrike's Dmitri Alperovitch—a native Russian speaker and the son of a Soviet émigré.

29.

Guccifer Two

THE OFFICERS IN UNIT 74455 WERE FUMING AND READY TO retaliate. They hastily created a new online front to embarrass CrowdStrike. GRU officers decided to name their impromptu online persona "Guccifer 2.0," in reference to an imprisoned Romanian hacker called Guccifer who had implausibly boasted to Fox News, in May and from jail, of hacking Hillary Clinton's server.[1] Unit 74455 registered a blog at https://guccifer2.wordpress.com, and started drafting their first post. The officers in 74455 had only rudimentary English skills, so they searched for several of their own phrases to check spelling and style. They searched for "worldwide known," "some hundred sheets," "think twice about," and "company's competence," among other phrases. The Russian intelligence officers were googling for "dcleaks," probably to check whether anybody had already picked up their clumsily surfaced site from a week earlier.[2] Nobody had.

Agitated by leaked emails, Bernie Sanders supporters protest against the DNC and Hillary Clinton. (John Minchillo / AP)

Late on June 15, just after 7:00 p.m. Moscow time, a post by "Guccifer 2.0" went online. The rambling text dismissed the conclusions reached by the "worldwide known" company CrowdStrike. Instead, Guccifer 2.0 insisted that the DNC had been "hacked by a lone hacker." As proof, the blog would publish eleven documents that the officers claimed came "from the DNC," including an opposition-research file on Donald Trump and a list of major Democratic donors. The blogger claimed to have given "thousands of files and mails" to WikiLeaks, while mocking the firm investigating the case: "I guess CrowdStrike customers should think twice about company's competence," the post said, adding "Fuck CrowdStrike!!!!!!!!!"[3]

Every single detail—except the outrage—was invented, even the claim that the purported lone hacker had given the rest of the DNC files to Wiki-Leaks (that file transfer would happen later).

In reality, almost all of the documents leaked that day were taken from John Podesta's inbox, just like the first alleged Clinton leak published eleven days earlier on DCLeaks. But this time the GRU had tampered with some of

Guccifer 2.0's first post on Wordpress, a blogging platform

the files, as the hidden metadata revealed. Five of the leaked documents were Microsoft Word files, named 1.doc, 2.doc, and so on. All five documents were modified on June 15, just before publication. The GRU used an old active measures trick and upgraded four out of five documents to CONFIDENTIAL, and one of them to SECRET, just to make them appear more interesting. It worked. But in his haste in the aftermath of the first story in the *Post*, the officer who edited the documents forgot to clean the metadata, and left his machine's username visible in Cyrillic: "Феликс Эдмундович." Feliks Edmundovich was the nickname of "Iron" Feliks Dzerzhinsky, the father of active measures and mastermind of the Trust deception ninety years prior.

Document "4.doc," marked SECRET, was of particular interest. The operators posing as Guccifer 2.0 announced this particular document with glee: "They say there were no secret docs! Lies again! Here is a secret document from Hillary's PC she worked with as Secretary of State." Again none of the three claims was accurate: the document wasn't secret; it wasn't from the time when Clinton was secretary of state; and it wasn't even from her machine. The purportedly secret document was titled "Promises and Proposals—National Security & Foreign Policy." In truth the document was headed "CONFIDENTIAL DRAFT FOR REVIEW—9/4/08," which the GRU simply replaced with "SECRET," without changing the font.[4] The document was a first draft of an Obama policy document dated September 2008 (when Condoleezza Rice was secretary of state), and had in actuality come from John Podesta's inbox.

Media pickup of the leaked files was slow at first. The leaked opposition research recycled prerehearsed arguments against the presumptive Republican nominee, that Trump had "no core"; that he was a "bad businessman"; and that he should be branded "misogynist in chief." The *New York Post*, usually adept at finding what it called "hair-raising data," concluded there was none in the released opposition research.[5] Press attention only picked up somewhat when Donald Trump claimed that the DNC itself "did the 'hacking.'"[6] It would take nearly six weeks before the story finally dominated the news cycle.

Next, the GRU recruited the help of WikiLeaks. The Guccifer 2.0 account had claimed, in the first note on the DNC hack, that "the main part of the papers, thousands of files and mails, I gave to WikiLeaks." The GRU had not yet handed over the treasure trove, but the announcement had caught Julian Assange's attention, and WikiLeaks immediately but cryptically reacted on Twitter. "DNC 'hacker' releases 200+ page internal report on Trump, says gave WikiLeaks all the rest," Assange posted hours after the first leaks appeared, carefully not acknowledging receipt, and only repeating what the GRU front had claimed in its ominous blog post.[7]

Events now started to move quickly. Matt Tait, a former GCHQ officer posting anonymously as @pwnallthethings, immediately began examining the leaked files in a long thread. Tait and a group of volunteer sleuths quickly spotted two of the GRU's hasty metadata errors, one that left Cyrillic user-names in the modified files, and one error that revealed the Russian-language settings of the user who had modified the data.[8] "Lol. Russian #opsec fail," Tait posted just a few hours after the Russian leak front appeared.[9]

So far, U.S. intelligence had not come out in support of the claims by the Democrats and their security firm.[10] Nevertheless, the forensic evidence indicating that Russian intelligence was behind both hack and leak was solidifying. Just one day after the first documents became public, Lorenzo Franceschi-Bicchierai, one of the best reporters at the technology-focused website Motherboard, was the first journalist to publish an investigative story calling the DNC hack "a disinformation campaign by Russian spies."[11]

The same day, June 16, a private intelligence firm named Secureworks published a stunning finding. The firm had discovered what would later be recognized as one of the GRU's gravest operational security mistakes, one that became clear only when investigators finally figured out the mechanics of the Russian campaign.

The remarkable discovery began with an email not unlike the one that tricked John Podesta's staffers. The link to the fake log-in page was behind the fake CHANGE PASSWORD button. In Podesta's case, that link was https://bit.ly/1PibSU0, a URL that was shortened with a common link-shortening service. The actual, malicious URL was a clunky six-liner that would likely get picked up by Google's spam filters or antivirus software, but the attackers avoided the detection risk by including the shortened link. The link itself contained a remarkable amount of information: one section of the long link, such as "am9obi5wb2Rlc3RhQGdtYWlsLmNvbQ," would automatically be translated by Podesta's browser as "john.podesta@gmail.com."

These long, information-rich malicious URLs were automatically generated. Each URL, of which there were tens of thousands in total, contained within it details about the targeted account, often the name of the victim, the date of the targeting attempt, and whether the victim had clicked through to the fake log-in page.

Lukashev, however, made a grave error in the process, and it allowed

Secureworks to tie together many thousands of targets. He had used several online accounts with the link-shortening service Bit.ly to generate vast numbers of the desired short URLs. At Bit.ly, Lukashev used the pseudonyms "john356gh" as well as "koyower3."[12] But the young hacker forgot to set the semi-automatic programming interface on "private"—and thus created an intelligence gold mine of the first order. Back in April 2015, one Ukrainian user, also a GRU target, had uploaded information from a bait email to a website that catalogs such hacking attempts, known as Phish Tank.[13] Secureworks, monitoring Phish Tank, checked out the newly submitted link, noted "koyower3," moved over to Bit.ly, queried the other links created by koyower3, and found hundreds of hits. The list immediately looked like a sophisticated hacking campaign. Next, one of the firm's coders wrote a short Python script that would check for new hacking attempts once every day, extract the short links from the GRU's link-shortening accounts, automatically expand them to the information-rich long link, decode the targeting details from those long URLs, and—voilà!—Secureworks analysts had a real-time intelligence feed on GRU targeting, delivered daily by email, for more than a year. "It was exciting to see the Clinton stuff happening in real time," one analyst later recalled.[14] Russia's military spies thus revealed not just an extensive targeting list to investigators but detailed information about the evolution of their targeting attempts over time.

That June, GRU also trained its sights on state-level election infrastructure across the United States. The Russian operators penetrated election-related infrastructure in Illinois that month, and later were in a position to delete and change voter data. Between June and September, Russian military intelligence operators scanned voting-related machines in all fifty states, but only successfully managed to penetrate systems in two states. The Senate Intelligence Committee, however, found no evidence that the foreign intruders attempted to delete or modify any data.[15] That was different on the public-facing side of the attack.

Guccifer 2.0's direct messages on Twitter were open. Anybody could message the undercover GRU unit. On June 22, Assange sent a private message to Guccifer 2.0, asking them to "[s]end any new material here for us to review and it will have a much higher impact than what you are doing."[16] Unit 74455 knew Assange was right. The GRU had not only paid close attention to the Saudi Cables drama a few months earlier; the same unit had likely already provided the Podesta archive to WikiLeaks, and Assange had publicly acknowledged receipt in the British interview, all a few days before Guccifer 2.0 was even created. On July 6, WikiLeaks nudged Guccifer 2.0 again. Assange's typing was sloppy and riddled with typos: "if you have anything hillary related we want it in the next tweo [sic] days prefable [sic] because the DNC is approaching," Assange wrote, referring to the upcoming Democratic Convention in Philadelphia. "She will solidify bernie supporters behind her after." Assange was right again, but this time he moved too quickly for the Russian officers.

"Ok . . . i see," responded the GRU, clearly not following Assange's reasoning.

The WikiLeaks founder slowed down, and explained some of the intricacies of U.S. primary politics. Assange understood that Hillary Clinton would become the nominee in about three weeks, and that she then would have to reach out to intra-party opponents who had supported her main rival, Bernie Sanders, "so conflict between bernie and hillary is interesting," Assange explained.

Some of the first file transfer attempts had failed. Another week later, on July 14, Guccifer 2.0 finally sent an email to WikiLeaks that included an attachment with detailed instructions, titled "wk dnc link1.txt.gpg." On July 18, a Monday, WikiLeaks privately acknowledged the receipt of "the 1 Gb or so archive," and told the intelligence officers that the public release would be ready that week.[17] On Friday, July 22, three days ahead of the convention, Assange delivered on his promise, and released nearly 20,000 emails with more than 8,000 attachments from the Democratic National Committee.

At that moment I was putting the final touches on an investigative piece that would forensically link the operation to the GRU. A few hours later, I contacted the officers posing as Guccifer 2.0 with a direct message, told them I was writing about their work, and asked them for confirmation that they had given the freshly leaked emails to WikiLeaks. "Yeah man," the officer on the other end responded, "i sent them emails."[18]

The story immediately exploded. American political journalists were rummaging through the dump in search of scandal, and they found it in the form of DNC officials taking sides in the political conflict between Bernie Sanders and Hillary Clinton. The DNC was supposed to be neutral, but in several emails, DNC officials took sides. Debbie Wasserman Schultz, the chair, called Bernie's campaign manager an "ass" and a "liar." Pressure on the DNC mounted. Two days later, Wasserman Schultz announced her resignation—the extraordinary hack-and-leak had helped force out the head of one of America's political parties and threatened to disrupt Hillary Clinton's nominating convention.

The GRU operators didn't just rely on WikiLeaks and their homemade front accounts. In old AM tradition, from the start the officers made direct offers to furnish exclusive material to media organizations over the summer of 2016.[19] *Gawker* and *The Smoking Gun* were among the first. One new aspect was that many media organizations soon actively reached out to the intelligence fronts, via their social media accounts, in search of new material. In late August, the GRU provided several emails with exclusive material to one investigative reporter from the Associated Press, Raphael Satter. Satter knew that the operator of the account was not who they claimed to be.

"Why not send this data to WikiLeaks?" asked Satter.

"i don't know when or if they gonna publish them," the Guccifer 2.0 account responded, accurately describing a real problem for the GRU.[20]

Over the summer of 2016, the front accounts regularly corresponded privately with dozens of reporters at major news outlets, in the United States and internationally, including *Politico*, Sky News, and *Der Spiegel*. Over a period of nearly four months, there was ambiguity; only independent experts and a few anonymous U.S. intelligence sources had called out the two strange accounts as a foreign intelligence operation. Yet leaks, to many, were still a legitimate source of news, and it was still assumed the leak accounts were giving out unmodified, original files that sometimes had real news value, so reporters assumed they were ethically on firm ground when they angled for stories. Some high-profile journalists, however, remained usefully ignorant, either wittingly or unwittingly. When Twitter suspended the @DCleaks_ account on August 27, the Fox Business host Lou Dobbs accused the firm of "leftist fascism." Twitter reinstated the Russian front account about a day later.[21]

On October 7, finally, the U.S. intelligence community prominently called out Guccifer 2.0 and DCleaks as Russian intelligence fronts. The U.S. government stated with confidence that "only Russia's senior-most officials could have authorized these activities."[22] About an hour after the U.S. intelligence estimate came out, Assange started to publish the Podesta inbox. The leaks came in thirty-four tranches, about one every day until Election Day. The daily barrage of private emails would put significant public and psychological pressure on the Clinton campaign in a critical period.

The GRU's active measures in 2016 were never meant to be stealthy, only to be effective. In early October, the Russian intelligence officers learned from an official press release of their American counterparts that their two U.S. front accounts had been exposed—which meant, in effect, that they knew the accounts were now under surveillance. Nevertheless, they still continued to use these very accounts to reach out privately to journalists, and to escalate their disinformation game.

On October 18, for example, as the election campaign was white hot and during the daily onslaught of Podesta leaks, both GRU fronts attempted to reach out to Alex Jones, a then-prominent conspiracy theorist who ran a far-right media organization called Infowars. The fronts contacted two reporters at Infowars, offered exclusive material, and asked to be put in touch with the boss directly. One of the reporters was Mikael Thalen, who then covered computer security. First it was DCleaks that contacted Thalen. Then, the following day, Guccifer 2.0 contacted him in a similar fashion. Thalen, however, saw through the ruse and was determined not to "become a pawn" of the Russian disinformation operation; after all, he worked at Infowars. So Thalen waited until his boss was live on a show and distracted, then proceeded to impersonate Jones vis-à-vis the Russian intelligence fronts.[23]

"Hey, Alex here. What can I do for you?" the faux Alex Jones privately messaged to the faux Guccifer 2.0 on Twitter, later on October 18.

"hi," the Guccifer 2.0 account responded, "how r u?"

"Good. Just in between breaks on the show," said the Jones account.

"did u see my last twit about taxes?"

Thalen, pretending to be Jones, said he didn't, and kept responses short. The officers manning the Guccifer 2.0 account, meanwhile, displayed how bad they were at media outreach work, and consequently how much value Julian Assange added to their campaign.

"do u remember story about manafort?" they asked Jones in butchered English, referring to Paul Manafort, Donald Trump's former campaign manager. But Thalen no longer responded. "dems prepared to attack him earlier. I found out it from the docs. is it interesting for u?"[24]

30.

Trolled

I N THE SUMMER AND FALL OF 2013, THE OLD ACTIVE MEASURES mind-set had begun to reassert itself in other, unexpected ways. A new organization emerged in St. Petersburg that would soon become known as the Internet Research Agency—in Russian, the "troll den"; in English, the "troll farm."

The Internet Research Agency was reminiscent of intelligence front organizations from the 1950s, especially the Kampfgruppe and LCCASSOCK in Berlin. The fronts old and new hired a significant number of regular staff, with benefits; sent large volumes of messages, nearly indiscriminately, into adversarial territory; placed ads; tried to obscure the origins of their messaging; impersonated legitimate publications and invented their own; and forged messages. They experimented with different tactics over the years, engaged in administrative harassment, occasionally operated under the thin

Army of Jesus
Sponsored · ⊘

The single most famous Facebook ad purchased by the Internet Research Agency in St. Petersburg was sponsored by a page known as Army of Jesus. The ad received only 71 impressions and 14 clicks on October 19, 2016, the only day it ran. A year later, *The New York Times* opened a front-page story with this ad.

cover of research outfits, and were quickly exposed by local reporters, yet for a long period remained partly deniable. Moreover, both then and now, the front organizations cited metrics to convince their funders to give them more money—in the past, the vast numbers of flyers printed, balloons dispatched, and response letters received; in modern times, the far vaster numbers of posts written, "impressions" earned, images shared, and comments made. All those figures were hard to interpret, but came with the built-in assumption that the organizations' tactics were effective.

Such comparisons can be instructive, but any historical analogy is most instructive when it breaks down, thus revealing new trends. The Internet Research Agency's novel features and the new limitations of its work come into full relief only when viewed against the long history of active measures. The Russian "troll farm" offered a new and surprising answer to Rolf

Wagenbreth's question *What would active measures be without the journalist?* Without inadvertent help from professional news producers, active measures would be more direct, noisier, faster—and less effective.

The Internet Research Agency—commonly and confusingly abbreviated as the IRA—was incorporated in Russia's register of legal entities on July 26, 2013,[1] and bankrolled by Yevgeny Prigozhin, an influential businessman then in his early fifties. Prigozhin held numerous contracts with the government, including with the Ministry of Defense; his company that funded the IRA was known as Concord.[2] The true nature of the IRA was quickly exposed by a woman who applied for an office job there. She revealed that each worker had to write around one hundred fake online comments on contentious Russian domestic issues per day.[3] The first investigative report on the "den of trolls" was published by a St. Petersburg paper just a week later, in early September 2013, after one journalist posed as an applicant for a day and worked a sample shift.[4] The troll den already had several departments, with the titles printed on plain A4 paper and taped to the windowless offices: there was a "creative department," a "rapid response department," a department each for "commentators," "bloggers," and "social media specialists." The organization also had another office in Moscow.

Early on, morale appears to have been low among staff. The first reporter to infiltrate the IRA recounted a conversation with some of the first hired trolls. "You can go crazy," one said, adding that they had to write four posts on a large Russian blogging platform per day, along with comments on internet forums and underneath legitimate news stories. The troll then added, "Nobody upstairs reads our posts, I just copy texts from Wikipedia without thinking."[5] Some played games online when the supervisor left the room.

The low level of professionalism at the supposedly clandestine IRA was illustrated by the appearance of regular and detailed investigative reports on the IRA's work in the Russian press, as well as by the significant number of former employees who openly discussed their surreal experiences. One early reporter recalled how easy it was to get into the strange agency, and mocked the IRA's managers for not immediately discovering—read: googling—that he was a well-known reporter, even though he had let them copy his passport. The troll farm leaked like a sieve.

By 2014, the IRA had set up its headquarters in a drab gray four-story office building on 55 Savushkina Street in St. Petersburg. The GRU's social media operators had discovered that they were rather ineffective in Crimea and eastern Ukraine, which became obvious when even juicy leaked material failed to boost their social media posts. But the crisis in Ukraine, which was ongoing, fueled a period of intense growth at the IRA. The troll farm did not hack or leak, and the trolls lacked advance knowledge of upcoming active measures that, in theory, the organization could have helped to amplify. Instead, the St. Petersburg outfit remained entirely focused on stand-alone social media efforts. The staff had grown to hundreds of individuals, with departments dedicated to graphics, data analysis, and search-engine optimization, and, of course, an IT department dedicated to creating a technical infrastructure with proxy servers to prevent fake accounts from getting blocked.

Around April 2014, weeks after the Victoria Nuland phone leak and the Jason Gresh forgeries in Ukraine, the IRA formed what it called the "translator project," a new department with a regional focus on the United States. The staff working in the "American department" were young, fashionably dressed, with stylish haircuts, beards, horn-rimmed glasses, and iPhones in hand during their smoking breaks—"hipsters," as one former troll-for-hire described his colleagues. The new employees, whose goal as outlined in an internal document was to "spread distrust towards the candidates and the political system in general,"[6] began to follow the U.S. press coverage and social media accounts related to the 2016 presidential election. A reconnaissance team of four IRA troll masters applied for visas to the United States, but only two were granted. Two women working for the Internet Research Agency traveled for three weeks to Nevada, California, New Mexico, Colorado, Illinois, Michigan, Louisiana, Texas, and New York in order to learn more about their target country, and to take pictures to use in their social media posts.[7] They filed an internal report after returning.[8]

The IRA's English-language activity began to pick up, then rose drastically in late 2014. Workers still received their salaries in cash,[9] and most of the activity still focused on Eastern Ukraine.[10] Content was created literally from the top down. Bloggers on the third floor wrote fake firsthand accounts, sometimes pretending to write about Ukraine as if they were in Ukraine, then passed down posts for commenting.

The place had acquired the air of a surreal factory. Building security was strict,[11] and employees were required to hand over their passports. The long corridors were almost completely silent but for the sound of fingers tapping on keys.[12] "I immediately felt like a character in the book *1984*," recalled Marat Mindiyarov, who worked in the troll factory from November 2014 to February 2015 and described it as "a place where you have to write that white is black and black is white." He worked in the commenting department, where staff commented on the news, either directly on the newspapers' websites or on social media. "You were in some kind of factory that turned lying, telling untruths, into an industrial assembly line." The organization indeed ran in factory-like twelve-hour shifts, and had picked up speed—now the "production norms," he said, demanded 135 comments of 200 characters per shift.[13]

The workers on the different floors did not make contact with one another inside the building, and interacted mainly during smoking breaks or over lunch and coffee. "You could have worked there for half a year being on the ground floor and making fake news and you would not have had a single occasion when you could chat with another guy who [wrote comments on it]," recounted another twenty-six-year-old former employee.[14]

The IRA's labor was cheap, and some of the metrics it produced seemed to convince its funders. The troll farm was growing, and quickly.[15] It also experimented with new formats.

In the spring of 2015, several IRA workers gathered excitedly in front of a computer monitor in a second-floor office at the St. Petersburg headquarters. They had a webcam turned on, and the live camera was pointed at a street square in New York City. A few days earlier, the IRA had put out a test balloon, a post on Facebook that announced free hot dogs—no need to bring anything, only come to the right place at the right time in New York City. A few New Yorkers actually showed up, looked around, looked at their phones, looked around again without finding any hot dogs, and finally left.

More than four thousand miles away, the trolls could not hide their joy. The goal of their prank was to test whether they could organize events remotely.

"We were just testing the possibilities, experimenting," one of them later told an investigative journalist. "It was a success."[16] In March, the organization put out a call for "internet operators (night)" who were fluent in English. The IRA was ramping up its American operations, and its arsenal included video production, memes, infographics, its own reporting, interviews, and analytics to drive operations—along with a few fake events.

In a widely read story posted in early June 2015, *The New York Times* exposed "The Agency" to an English-speaking audience. The journalist Adrian Chen opened the piece by describing a fake news item, engineered from St. Petersburg, about a chemical explosion in Louisiana in late 2014: "'A powerful explosion heard from miles away happened at a chemical plant in Centerville, Louisiana #ColumbianChemicals,' a man named Jon Merritt tweeted."[17]

The story in the *Times* harked back, without intending to do so, to the *Times* coverage of that big first American disinformation campaign from April 1930, the Grover Whalen forgeries. Then as now, press coverage of the fakes—and the subsequent congressional investigations—received far more public attention than had the original disinformation items in the first place, thus creating a second-order, post-exposure effect that would ultimately far outweigh the direct, pre-exposure impact.

After the *Times* covered "The Agency," the IRA—probably feeling trolled—dropped the "Agency" from its name, becoming simply "Internet Research." And it continued to grow. By mid-2015, the troll farm boasted a staff of eight or nine hundred.[18] The America Department was headed by the twenty-seven-year-old Dzheykhun Aslanov, an Azerbaijan-born entrepreneur. Aslanov, nicknamed Jay Z, was fit, with short dark hair and full lips; he liked dogs and partying. According to one former co-worker, Aslanov was more popular as a colleague than as a boss; a "great guy," but "frankly speaking, generally incompetent" as a manager.[19] The America Department alone had a budget of approximately $1 million a year. Even the entry-level wage in the department was well above the city's average. The trolls also received bonuses based on audience engagement and reactions in the United States, which created further incentive for creative metrics.[20]

By 2016, the Internet Research Agency had procured computer infrastructure and servers in the United States. To mask its Russian roots, the organization purchased space on U.S. servers and set up dedicated Virtual Private Networks, or VPNs, then routed the disinformation traffic into the United States through these encrypted tunnels. This tactic made it significantly harder for U.S. social media companies to discover Russian disinformation operations on their platforms, even long after the public revelation that a systematic influence campaign was under way. By the fall of 2016, the troll factory's online audience had grown to hundreds of thousands of direct followers.

The platforms and formats were new, but content creation followed a recipe that was half a century old: feigned concern for others; creativity, perhaps demonstrated by a witty slogan; the invocation of familiar and comforting stereotypes; and the appearance of connection to established and credible persons or organizations.

One of the Internet Research Agency's goals was to dissuade black voters from taking part in the election, especially if they were likely to vote on the left. The organization even drafted an internal guidance document, which can safely be called racist: "Colored LGBT are less sophisticated than white; therefore complicated phrases and messages do not work." "Be careful with racial content," one document advised; blacks, Latinos, and Native Americans were "very sensitive to #whiteprivilege and they react to posts and pictures that favor white people."

The young managers of the troll farm's American division based their strategies on their notions of different habits across the U.S. political spectrum. Aslanov and his assistants decided, for instance, that infographics worked better with liberals than with conservatives,[21] and that liberals were more active at night, while conservatives got up earlier in the morning.[22]

The Internet Research Agency created several personas that impersonated activists or organizations on the left, and sometimes boosted them through paid ads to grow their following. There was, for instance, Crystal

Johnson. The Russian workers chose a picture of a young black woman, perhaps in her early twenties, laughing engagingly. By mid-2016 the account had about seven thousand followers. Crystal's bio said, "It is our responsibility to promote the positive things that happen in our communities," and her location was given as Richmond, Virginia. In early June 2016, Crystal posted a picture of Muhammad Ali's star on the Hollywood Walk of Fame, and quipped that Ali's star was the only one "hanging on a wall, not for anyone to step on." The post had more than 22,000 engagements—and no direct impact on the election, as it was one of many posts that were not meant to polarize and influence, but to please and build an audience. But the audience-building was only moderately successful.[23]

By late September 2016, @BlackToLive, one of the IRA's most important fake black activist accounts, had a follower count of 11,200 just before the election, with generally mediocre engagement figures.[24] The account accumulated fewer than 190,000 social interactions in about one year. Only 16 of the account's more than 2,600 posts during the run-up mentioned Hillary Clinton, and most of those mentions were supportive. No posts in the weeks before the election were about voter suppression.

"#AmeriKKKa is killin' us!," tweeted Bleep the Police, another faux–African American account, in February 2016, using a then widely established anti-American hashtag.[25] The account was then one of the IRA's most-followed fake African American accounts, with just under 5,000 followers. The St. Petersburg troll who posted the #AmeriKKKa tweet immediately changed accounts, and sixty seconds later retweeted from 1-800-WOKE-AF, which then had just under 7,000 followers. Despite the attempted boost, the divisive tweet received only fourteen shares and nine likes. None of the IRA's faux-black-activist accounts managed to grow beyond 22,000 followers by early November 2016.[26]

Aslanov's department was somewhat more successful among American conservatives. An example is @Pamela_Moore13, with nearly 15,000 followers by September 2016. Her profile picture looked like something out of a Jean-Luc Godard film: black-and-white, eyes peeking out from under a black hood that was reminiscent of both the KKK and a niqab, two black duct-tape

Pamela Moore was a conservative Texan persona created in St. Petersburg, and she was not subtle. This post received nearly 5,000 retweets.

crosses stuck on her breasts, her back wrapped into an American flag. Pamela's location was given as "Texas, USA." Her highlighted posts said, "I would rather care of TEN homeless US Veterans, more than 50,000 migrants / illegal aliens .. How About You?" (punctuation original). This post alone had nearly 10,000 engagements.

One of Aslanov's most popular conservative sock puppets was John Davis, also in "Texas, USA," posting under the handle @TheFoundingSon. Davis's bio offered a series of clichés meant to appeal to conservatives: *Business owner, proud father, conservative, Christian, patriot, gun rights, politically*

incorrect. Love my country and my family #2A #GOP #tcot #WakeUpAmerica.
His profile image showed a Caucasian man in his thirties, sitting in a car, a
black pit bull on his lap, under a large banner picture of a Smith & Wesson
.45-caliber handgun. An exemplary post from June 12, 2016, featured a photo
of emergency responders after a major shooting incident in Orlando, Flor-
ida, with the hashtag #IslamIsTheProblem. The account's most popular post
before the election, with more than 2,800 engagements, advocated freeing
Julian Assange. The fake patriot often posted content that was pro–Second
Amendment, pro-veterans, anti-Islam, and anti–Hillary Clinton. In total, the
account had 355,000 preelection interactions.

The IRA's most successful English-language social media account by far
was Tennessee GOP, a faux-Republican outfit. By the end of September 2016,
@TEN_GOP had just under 36,000 followers.[27] The account's engagement
was excellent: over almost exactly one year during the run-up to the election, the account generated 3.2 million shares, likes, and comments. It is unknown how many of these interactions were with genuine Americans, but
it was likely the majority. Among the account's top ten preelection posts on
Twitter, five attempted to undermine the legitimacy of the outcome by high-
lighting voter fraud. One post, for example, published just one day before the
election, earned more than 10,000 engagements: "WOW: another proof of
#VoterFraud!! Machine refuses to allow vote for Trump!! RT b/c Media will
never report this!"[28]

It is unlikely that the trolls convinced many, if any, American voters to
change their minds: the overall volume of IRA activity was lower than reported; a lot of the activity was audience-building; only 8.4 percent of IRA
activity was election-related;[29] and the Russian messaging mostly stayed
within echo chambers. The lack of professionalism worthy of a serious intelligence agency at the IRA's American Department is best illustrated by one of
its former employees, who described to an independent Russian news channel what trolling Americans looked like in practice. There was little regional
or cultural specialization, which may explain why messaging never made it
beyond well-worn clichés: "First you gotta be a redneck from Kentucky, then
you need to be a white guy from Minnesota, you've slaved away all your life,

and paid your taxes, and then fifteen minutes later you are from New York, posting in some black slang."[30]

The hectic, superficial roleplay limited the quality of the output and drained morale. "It was a shitty setup," sighed the former troll.[31]

On Twitter, the IRA's impact practically vanished in the staggering number of election-related tweets. Approximately 1 billion tweets related to the campaigns were posted during the fifteen months leading up to the election.[32] The St. Petersburg troll den generated less than 0.05 percent of all election-related posts. The IRA, according to the data released by Twitter, boosted candidate Donald Trump's retweet count with only 860 direct retweets over the entire campaign.[33]

These low figures probably still overstate the effect of the American desk in St. Petersburg. The IRA's most engaged content, perhaps counterintuitively, was not designed to polarize but to build communities. The IRA's overall outreach on Facebook achieved approximately 12 million shares in the United States before Election Day in 2016, just under 15 million "likes," and just over 1 million comments.[34] The majority of these interactions, however, happened with benign crowd-pleasing posts, not with the most polarizing and vile content.

The House Permanent Select Committee on Intelligence added more details. The committee released approximately 2,300 of the Facebook ads that the trolls placed over the two years preceding the November 2016 election. The top ten most popular ads accounted for more than one-quarter of all views—and none of these top ten ads represented sharp, corrosive disinformation. The most popular post simply said "Back The Badge," in support of "our brave" police officers; 73,063 accounts engaged, many of them likely police-supporting Americans. The second-most-viewed item simply said "Blacktivist, *African American Civil Rights Movement!*" The third-most-viewed ad, posted by the account "Being Patriotic," showed a kitschy painted bald eagle in front of stars and stripes, captioned "United We Stand!"

The contrast to the wider press coverage is stark and instructive. The best-known and most widely covered Facebook advertisement depicted Satan in an arm-wrestling match with a white-robed Jesus. The caption said:

SATAN: IF I WIN CLINTON WINS!

JESUS: NOT IF I CAN HELP IT!

The original ad, however, was one of the IRA's least successful; it dis-played just for one day, cost 64 rubles (then $1), had a meager seventy-one impressions, and just fourteen Americans clicked on it.[35] This poor perfor-mance was more representative of the IRA's overall effort than the top ten posts. The median number of so-called impressions for the preelection po-litical ads from St. Petersburg was just 199. Moreover, impressions overstate impact, as this metric counts only what users scroll past on their perpetual feeds, not what they actually read and engage with.

The IRA's overall performance during the 2016 run-up may have been poor, but the House Democrats' release of the Facebook ads turned the ads, and the trolls' wider Facebook outreach, into a spectacular disinformation success story. The next day *The New York Times* ran a front-page piece[36] that described the Satan-vs.-Jesus arm-wrestling image, and scores of news out-lets, national and international, picked up the illustration from there. The ad had become an icon—but not for effective disinformation. The ad epito-mized how mainstream press coverage *generated* the actual effect of a disin-formation operation. This effect was precisely what Wagenbreth, the Stasi's master of dirty tricks, had been talking about in 1986. Social media had ac-tually *increased* the significance of traditional journalism as an amplifier of disinformation operations.

Still, the Internet Research Agency was a major historical novelty. The IRA represented a new division of labor for active measures. By Septem-ber 2016, the monthly budget for the troll factory was approximately $1.25 million.[37] Concord, the trolls' funder, distributed money to the IRA in a semi-clandestine fashion, via more than a dozen bank accounts held by affiliated shell companies with nondescript names such as Internet Research LLC. The payments to the IRA were concealed as software support and development.[38] Nevertheless, a large number of employees were aware of and displeased by Concord's role, according to published interviews. The IRA did not have a cafeteria or canteen, although Prigozhin, known as "Putin's chef," owned a sprawling catering business. "People had to bring food boxes from home," said one former worker to *The Washington Post*. "Prigozhin did not treat the trolls well. He could at least feed them." Such poor discipline and operational security contrasts sharply with proper intelligence fronts, such as the CIA's LCCASSOCK in the 1950s, where only the principal agent and perhaps a treasurer would know about the real source of funding.

Yet a division of labor was emerging. The Russian security establishment effectively kept collection and release within the intelligence community, but outsourced the noisy and cheap business of driving wedges through social media to dedicated third-party service providers. The Internet Research Agency, the best-known and prime example, worked more like a spammy call center than a tight intelligence agency, with limited operational security, very limited presence on the ground in its target area, and no known operational coordination with Russian intelligence. The IRA's social media accounts did not amplify leaks in a meaningful way; the trolls did not mention Cyber-Caliphate, there were no noteworthy mentions of CyberGuerrilla, and they had no advance knowledge of ongoing GRU active measures.[39]

The IRA was the least effective component of the overall Russian disinformation effort in 2016, despite the breathless press coverage and congressional committee hearings with social media executives in 2017 and 2018. It is indeed unlikely that the IRA had any discernible effect on the voting behavior of American citizens.

Aslanov, the head of the American Department, was aware of his most important target audience: Prigozhin and the Russian government. He may not have been a shrewd manager, but he was a shrewd entrepreneur. The money that paid for his bills and his staff didn't come from American social media users, but from Concord. His clients were in Moscow, not in Texas. So, on May 29, 2016, one Russian-controlled social media account asked an unwitting U.S. citizen to stand in front of the White House and hold up a sign that said, "Happy 55th Birthday Dear Boss." The trolls informed the American holder of the sign that it was for someone who "is a leader here and our boss . . . our founder."[40] Prigozhin's fifty-fifth birthday was two days later, on June 1.

The Shadow Brokers

PREPARATIONS FOR THE BIGGEST LEAK OF ALL PICKED UP speed in mid-July 2016. The operators sorted through lists of high-powered hacking tools—in the form of computer code—stolen from the NSA, deciding what to publish and what to keep. One especially brazen operator had the idea of auctioning off a particularly dangerous set of NSA tools for cryptocurrency, a notion more of provocation than potential profit. The operators bundled the stolen NSA tools into two secure virtual packages, encrypted each of them, wrapped both packages into an even bigger digital package, and called it EQGRP-AUCTION-FILE.ZIP.[1] By then U.S. intelligence firms commonly used their own code names to refer to the hacking units of foreign intelligence agencies, such as APT28 or FANCY BEAR for GRU. Russia's foremost computer security firm, Kaspersky, described the NSA hacking operations it had uncovered in 2015 as EQUATION GROUP, abbrevi-

The GRU-engineered NotPetya attack, which reused leaked NSA hacking tools, in the Rost market in Kharkov, Ukraine (Mikhail Golub)

ated as EQGRP.[2] The wider information security community was keenly following high-powered digital espionage operations, and was intimately familiar with this array of code names that appeared so cryptic and confusing to outsiders. EQGRP was a subtle insider reference to Tailored Access Operations, the NSA's elite hacking unit, and thus any messages mentioning the strange file names would immediately get the attention of the world's best security and malware engineers.

The Democratic National Convention began later the same day. U.S. intelligence agencies had informed the White House that they had "high confidence" that the Russian government was behind the DNC hack, and the subsequent leaks.

The NSA and CIA were working hard on a response plan. Behind secure doors in and around Washington, D.C., discussions were held about retaliating against Russian spies for the DNC hack-and-leak. Robert Joyce, the head of Tailored Access Operations, was an electrical engineer by training, and respected as a straight shooter in the wider information-security community.

Three days after the Democratic convention, on July 28, Joyce gave a rare interview on TAO's work to ABC News in New York.[3] Speaking in generalities, he mentioned that his unit had the technical capabilities and legal authorities to "hack back," as ABC reported. "So we will use the NSA's authorities to pursue foreign intelligence to try to get back into that collection," Joyce said, referring vaguely to ongoing attacks against the United States. "That's hard work, but that's one of the responsibilities we have."[4] The timing of the interview was striking—it was nothing less than an open threat against the Russian intelligence establishment.

For a few days nothing happened, at least not in public—in secret, however, the preparations for perhaps the single most damaging intelligence leak in history continued apace. Its operators needed a name. One of the masterminds was a gamer, and a fan of the sci-fi video game Mass Effect, which featured characters known as "shadow brokers," individuals "at the head of an expansive organization which trades in information," selling secrets to the highest bidder.[5] The name was a superb fit, and it stuck.

In the first week of August, the Shadow Brokers prepared the cryptographic key that would unlock their digital container of the NSA's secret hacking gear, practically the crown jewels of a technical intelligence agency in the twenty-first century. Then they created accounts on various websites well known among computer security aficionados, including Pastebin, Reddit, Tumblr, and GitHub, the leading platform for developers to publish open-source computer code. Another week passed.

Not long after midnight Eastern Time on August 13, which would be around nine in the morning in Moscow, the Shadow Brokers got to work. They anticipated, correctly, that the U.S. government would react very quickly and try to unpublish the tools, so the Brokers strengthened their leak by preparing a rollout at a number of international file-sharing sites— Mega, Box, Dropbox, Sync, and Yandex—as well as by including a robust peer-to-peer file-sharing link that would be nearly impossible to tear down. Finally, using proxy machines in different time zones, the operators pushed out links to the NSA's hacking tools on Pastebin, Twitter, and Reddit. The first posts simply linked to the uploaded top-secret files, and tagged some leading media outlets, including CNN, the BBC, Fox News, and Reuters, but also Russia Today, WikiLeaks, and a prominent Anonymous account.

The leak took two days to register. Some former Five Eyes intelligence officers who now worked in the private sector spotted several familiar code names, and started discussing the dump in private channels. One computer-security professional in Australia noted the chatter, tweeted a link to the file dump on GitHub, and attached an animated GIF of the *Daily Show* comedian Jon Stewart, transfixed, gobbling up a box of popcorn.[6]

Thousands of eager hobbyist hackers and professional intelligence analysts across the world immediately started downloading the initial archive, EQGRP-AUCTION-FILE.ZIP—only to discover, when they opened the archive, that the two virtual packages required a cryptographic key to open. The Shadow Brokers had provided one key, which would unlock one package with a few free samples of NSA hacking gear. The key to the other package was for sale to the highest bidder.

This active measure was unprecedented, devastating, and historic. The first result—perhaps even an intended goal—was to distract the NSA and the wider U.S. intelligence community at a critical moment when their political system was already under attack. Whatever plans the NSA had under way to respond to the hack-and-leak attack against Democratic targets, the Shadow Brokers stopped them in their tracks at once. The eerie combination of timing, breathtaking access, and sheer aggressiveness led many close observers to assume they were dealing with Russia's A-team here—although there was, and still is, no solid evidence to back up such a hypothesis.

The predictable, immediate consequence of the Shadow Brokers leak was sending the FBI and NSA into a tailspin of time-consuming and labor-intensive questioning: Did the NSA have a mole? How bad was the breach? Was the compromise ongoing? This type of denial of service was an old tactic in the long history of active measures (a recent example was the diversion hack on the Ukrainian election commission). But there was a novel aspect to uncovering the full compromise in this case. If a technical spy agency loses control of exploits, an adversary and even criminals can take advantage of those tools by, for example, breaking into innocent third-party machines,

potentially at scale. The NSA would have to act immediately and notify affected manufacturers of vulnerable products. These firms would then have
to warn customers, and ideally close and "patch" the holes in its systems as
fast as possible. The Shadow Brokers were aware of this dynamic, and deliberately released their files in an oblique and confusing way—letting the NSA
download an encrypted archive, for example, only to dangle the missing key
in front of them. The goal was to infuriate and to confuse, to keep NSA analysts guessing about the group's identity, about what they wanted, and most
important, about what they had and what they didn't have.

Over almost a year, the Shadow Brokers released many thousands of
pieces of computer code, constantly moving platforms and using obscure
links. The form of the leak itself was designed to maximize confusion and
damage. The substance of the leak was a giant hacking toolbox, packed with
tools to escalate administrator privileges on local machines; tools to break
into remote machines; utilities to commandeer intrusions from afar; back
doors directly into the innermost sanctum of some computers; and even
tools to hide one's traces after break-ins.[7] There were tools to break into
big routers that haul heavy loads in large networks, and crowbars for major
operating systems, such as Windows and Linux, but also for critical niche
products, such as Solaris, a system used often in software development, in
telecommunications, and for critical infrastructure.

The second new feature of the Shadow Brokers episode was the amount
of tactical harm caused to the United States. The operation was the twenty-
first-century equivalent to *Who's Who in CIA,* but far more effective. Releasing
names in the 1960s and 1970s would end the work of officers abroad and damage human intelligence collection; releasing exploits in the 2010s would end the
work of implants abroad and damage signals intelligence collection. The technical harm was achieved faster, at far greater scale, and triggered a cascade of
consequences. The full force of this new dynamic was first felt in January 2017.

On December 29, 2016, the outgoing Obama administration had finally responded to Russia's election interference. The White House expelled
thirty-five Russian intelligence officers from the United States, seized two
Russian-owned waterfront estates, and put five Russian organizations on

```
./specials/etchCore-0.x86.dll
./specials/eteb-2.dll
./specials/etebCore-2.x64.dll
./specials/etebCore-2.x86.dll
./specials/Eternalblue-2.2.0.0.xml
./specials/Eternalblue-2.2.0.0.exe
./specials/Eternalblue-2.2.0.fb
./specials/Eternalchampion-2.0.0.0.xml
./specials/Eternalchampion-2.0.0.exe
./specials/Eternalchampion-2.0.0.fb
./storage
./storage/brdg.dll
./storage/capa_x64.dll
./storage/capa_x86.dll
./storage/danecfg.exe
./storage/dane_x64.dll
./storage/dane_x86.dll
./storage/ESUD.dll
./storage/lipa_x64.dll
./storage/lipa_x86.dll
./storage/pccp.pyc
./storage/rpcproxydll.dll
./storage/rudo_x64.dll
./storage/rudo_x86.dll
./storage/start_dll.mof
./storage/start_exe.mof
./storage/start_pcdll.mof
./storage/wbem.cpl
./touches
./touches/Architouch-1.0.0.0.xml
./touches/Architouch-1.0.0.0.exe
./touches/Architouch-1.0.0.fb
./touches/Domaintouch-1.1.1.0.fb
./touches/Domaintouch-1.1.1.0.xml
./touches/Domaintouch-1.1.1.exe
./touches/Eclipsedwingtouch-1.0.4.0.fb
./touches/Eclipsedwingtouch-1.0.4.0.xml
./touches/Eclipsedwingtouch-1.0.4.exe
./touches/Educatedscholartouch-1.0.0.0.fb
./touches/Educatedscholartouch-1.0.0.0.xml
./touches/Educatedscholartouch-1.0.0.exe
./touches/Emeraldthreadtouch-1.0.0.0.fb
./touches/Emeraldthreadtouch-1.0.0.0.xml
```

The Shadow Brokers published the full list of Windows-related NSA hacking tools in early January 2017, two days after a major U.S. intelligence assessment on the 2016 election interference came out.

a sanctions blacklist, including the FSB. A week later, the U.S. intelligence community came out with a strongly worded assessment—one of the most high-profile intelligence documents published in the United States in living memory—that directly blamed Vladimir Putin for "ordering an influence campaign in 2016."[8]

Two days later, the Shadow Brokers posted a cryptic tweet. It contained screenshots with file names and an unusual temporary link to one particularly curious file, called "WindowsWarez_All_Find." The document was tiny, and contained no computer code, only a long list of odd code names. The list simply enumerated more than 6,400 pieces of computer code under whimsical cryptonyms such as FUZZBUNCH, ETERNALBLUE, and DOUBLEPULSAR. Every one referred to a secret and undisclosed NSA hacking tool or to a resource custom-designed for breaking into Microsoft Windows. It was like a product listing on eBay, with just the names of the items on sale.[9] I remember looking at the list of code names at my desk in London at the time, but it was impossible to make sense of the listing based on publicly available information then.

Not so for the NSA. Alarm bells went off immediately at Fort Meade. Even simply revealing the code names of these NSA collection tools, without publishing the tools themselves, was destroying invaluable capabilities. The Shadow Brokers had already proven their ability to deliver the goods, a bit like an eBay seller with a four-star rating. But now there was a twist that would horrify the intelligence operators who understood what was going on. Some of the code names referred to what computer security experts call zero-days, previously undiscovered cracks and fissures in widespread computer software—in this case, Microsoft Windows, the single most widespread operating system on the planet. The NSA had found and used secret doors into Windows, but had notified no one, not even Microsoft. One former NSA employee told *The Washington Post* later that the intelligence haul of one particular tool, ETERNALBLUE, was "unreal." Another said using the tool was "like fishing with dynamite."[10] Whoever had the zero-days could get in undetected, not into one machine, but any number, and not just to steal things, but to break them.

So far only two parties knew that several zero-days were on the list and likely to come out soon: the Shadow Brokers and the NSA. The mysterious group was sending a secret, terrifying message to America's intelligence community, in plain daylight on public social media platforms. To many in the NSA, the message was clear: a brazen foreign actor had gained access to some of America's most valuable digital spy equipment. One of the NSA's worst nightmares had become reality. Matt Tait, the former GCHQ exploit developer and operator, assessed the damage caused by the Shadow Brokers as "easily the biggest single tactical loss to the NSA in a generation."[11]

The agency knew what to do next: destroy the tools by closing the holes they exploited before anybody could light up the dynamite or, even worse, publish the dynamite recipe. Fort Meade notified Microsoft,[12] where developers began to patch the vulnerabilities that the NSA had been using to such "unreal" effect. On March 14, about two months after the ominous first post that exposed the zero-days had appeared, Microsoft issued a "critical" update for all versions of Windows.[13]

Meanwhile, early on the morning of April 7, the U.S. Navy struck a Syrian airbase with 59 Tomahawk cruise missiles in retaliation against Syria's use of chemical weapons on its own civilians. Russia was a Syrian ally, and later that day a Kremlin spokesperson strongly condemned the American strikes as an "act of aggression against a sovereign country."[14] The next day, after months of silence, the Shadow Brokers reappeared with a long, rambling message expressing disappointment in the Trump administration's decision to strike Syria, denied any links to Russia, and—as "our form of protest"—published the secret key to the encrypted, once-for-sale EQGRP-AUCTION-FILE archive. The drop sparked another frenzied round of analysis and technology press coverage of the newly accessible NSA exploits.[15] To some close observers, the Shadow Brokers more and more looked like a hostile intelligence operation.

One week later came the most significant escalation. On April 14, the mysterious group finally leaked the long-awaited Windows tools— ETERNALROMANCE, ETERNALBLUE, DOUBLEPULSAR, and many others.[16] The recipe for making the proverbial dynamite was now openly available online, although those users who had patched their computers in the meantime were now protected against impact. But many machines were not patched and remained vulnerable. Another phase of the campaign now began.

Next came the third and most harmful new effect: the collateral damage. The Shadow Brokers had predicted and intended such collateral effects, as they stated in carefully crafted Yoda English in their first public appearance, back on August 13, 2016: "We give you some Equation Group files free, you see. This is good proof no? You enjoy!!! You break many things. You find many intrusions. You write many words."[17]

These three lines accurately predicted an entire sequence of events. The samples and lists were indeed "good proof" of a serious NSA compromise, at least to those in the know. Now active measures operators were taking advantage of three groups of unwitting helpers at once: journalists ("you write many words"); the information security research community ("you find many intrusions"); and third-party operators ("you break many things").

Immediately after the first Shadow Brokers leak, some of the world's most competent malware researchers and engineers started feasting on the

released files, many behind closed doors, some sharing their findings publicly. One of them was Mustafa Al-Bassam, a London-based convicted Anonymous activist and hacker turned brilliant PhD student. After two days, he
and other researchers discovered that the NSA was able to break into messages secured by specific Cisco hardware. Several weeks later, going through
another Brokers leak, Al-Bassam found a long list of compromised machines
that the NSA had used as staging grounds for follow-up attacks, many of
them in China and Russia, but also Japan and Germany.[18] Other independent researchers documented more intrusions. Matt Suiche, a French entrepreneur, found the biggest and most contentious case in April 2017. The NSA
had likely gained unauthorized access to the global SWIFT money-transfer
system by breaching service providers in the Middle East and Latin America.
The released files even contained the names of financial institutions targeted
by the NSA, including the Al Quds Bank for Development and Investment in
Ramallah, the Palestinian capital.[19]

These independent researchers in turn enabled journalists to cover this
technically challenging leak. The Shadow Brokers had carefully prepared not
only to weaponize reporters ("you write many words") but also the information security research community ("you find many intrusions").

At last there was the actual collateral damage ("you break many things").
The final dump, the one that included ETERNALBLUE, brought the NSA's
nightmare to life.

On May 12, computer screens in hospitals all over the UK suddenly
went black. Medical personnel were unable to look up patient records or issue
prescriptions. Thirty percent of all machines in the National Health Service
were affected. In some hospitals, medical equipment stopped working.[20] A
vicious computer virus had randomly hit around a quarter million computers, across more than 150 countries, in little more than one day. The virus,
known as WannaCry, caused "hundreds of millions, if not billions" of dollars
of damage, according to the U.S. Department of Justice. An FBI investigation later found that North Korea was responsible. The episode had an unexpected and embarrassing resolution: a developer for Pyongyang had simply
reused two of the NSA's stolen and leaked tools, notably ETERNALBLUE and

DOUBLEPULSAR, to make the virus propagate faster and wider.[21] NSA tools had helped pummel the health-care system of America's closest intelligence ally.

Four more weeks later, an even more potent and devastating attack re-used the same two stolen tools again, with a minor modification, along with a third, ETERNALROMANCE.[22]

The attack started the day before Ukraine's Constitution Day, which commemorates independent Ukraine's constitutional vote in 1996. The digital strike pummeled Ukraine at lightning speed. Supermarkets could not check out customers. The Kyiv metro was brought to a halt. Ukrtelekom, the country's main mobile phone provider, was hit, although mobile phone service was not interrupted. Boryspil, the country's largest airport, in Kyiv, reported delays and damage to its networks; energy utilities were hit. "Our network seems to be down," the deputy prime minister wrote on Facebook, posting the picture of an error message that displayed on all cabinet machines. Even the Chernobyl nuclear power plant had to shut down its Windows computers and transition to manual radiation testing. Approximately 10 percent of all commercial, governmental, and private computers, in a country of more than 42 million people, were locked down by the attack, reported Dmitry Shimkov, the deputy head of the presidential administration and a former Microsoft executive.[23]

After infection, a user's computer displayed a full black screen with a message at the top in red: "If you see this text, then your files are no longer accessible, because they have been encrypted." Such infections, at first glance, appeared to be a widespread, for-profit ransom attack, a common fraud in which users are often encouraged to unlock their files by paying a small ransom. The mysterious Ukraine attack made a similar promise: "We guarantee that you can recover all your files safely and easily. All you need to do is submit the payment and purchase the decryption key." The message then displayed a unique, 60-digit personal installation key. But this, it would soon turn out, was a piece of disinformation. In fact, the entire episode was a new form of an active measure, inspired by techniques that are common in the computer crime underground. The mysterious piece of malicious software soon became known as NotPetya.

More than 70 percent of all affected systems were in Ukraine, but Not-Petya also hit a six-digit number of mostly corporate-owned machines in sixty-five other countries. Most of those international targets were multinational corporations with some business in Ukraine. At Merck, a pharmaceutical giant, the computer virus disrupted manufacturing, research, and sales so severely that the firm had to borrow an important vaccine from the Centers for Disease Control's pediatric vaccine stockpile, with total losses far exceeding $670 million. The Danish shipping giant Møller-Maersk temporarily lost 45,000 computers and 4,000 servers. The firm transported one out of seven containers and was a major part of the world economy's critical infrastructure. NotPetya "made all of our applications and data unavailable for a while," said Jim Hagemann Snabe, Møller-Maersk's chairman, briefly shutting down the largest cargo terminal in the port of Los Angeles.[24] The firm lost up to $300 million. At TNT, a subsidiary of FedEx, the malware ripped through the company's international logistic network within an hour, grinding TNT's global operations to a halt, at a cost of $400 million.[25] At Mondelēz International, an American multinational food company, the worm rendered 1,700 servers and 24,000 laptops dysfunctional, and caused damages in excess of $100 million.[26] At Reckitt Benckiser, a multinational consumer-goods company, NotPetya knocked out 2,000 servers, 15,000 laptops, and slowed down production for weeks, racking up losses of around $120 million.[27] The worldwide digital event had real-life consequences: wholesale deliveries of Oreo cookies started to crumble—Cadbury chocolate production was in meltdown—even Durex condom assembly slipped.

The United States, along with several allies, would eventually attribute the devastating NotPetya attack to Russian military intelligence. The White House called the incident "the most destructive and costly cyber-attack in history," and estimated that it cost billions of dollars of damage worldwide.[28] The driving force behind the White House's decision to call out the Russian military was Rob Joyce, the ex-TAO boss now detailed to work for the president. NotPetya was personal for Joyce. Under his leadership TAO had developed, used, and finally lost many, if not most of the hacking tools that were first leaked by the Shadow Brokers, and then reengineered into NotPetya.

Worse, as if the GRU wanted to add insult to injury, its highly destructive malware actually did not need the NSA exploits to be so highly effective— the tools were something of a backup propagation mechanism in case the simpler default mechanism failed.[29] In the vast majority of victim networks ETERNALBLUE didn't even become active. But it was still there.

The most destructive and costly cyberattack in history had stolen and recycled NSA equipment built-in. Russia, in old active measures tradition, denied any involvement. One day after the United States, Britain, and several allies had publicly called out Russian military intelligence for unleashing NotPetya, in mid-February 2017, I attended a late-night "spy panel" at the Munich Security Conference, in the basement of the Bayerischer Hof. Onstage were current and former officials from major spy agencies, including the CIA, MI6, BND, Mossad, and one official from Moscow without any obvious intelligence link. The Western officials went first, and none mentioned computer network attacks, let alone NotPetya. When it was the turn of the Russian panelist, he eloquently and explicitly brought up ETERNALBLUE, turned toward the ex-CIA man onstage, and observed with a smile that U.S. intelligence, if press reports were to be believed, apparently could no longer keep their most valuable secrets. He was right.

The identity of the Shadow Brokers remains unknown. Several current and former intelligence officials I spoke with confirmed that they have "high confidence" that a Russian intelligence agency was involved in the operation, at least to a degree, although how specifically they could or would not say. Russia was the only foreign power with both means and motive, meaning high-powered spy agencies and a high-risk appetite. Most likely, my sources agreed, the driving force behind the destructively timed and professionally administered series of leaks was not the often sloppy and noisy GRU. No one, however, was able to point me to conclusive evidence, or to go on the record. Still, U.S. intelligence took the theory of Russian involvement in the Shadow Brokers episode so seriously that they attempted to buy access to the stolen material, unsuccessfully, from a shadowy Russian national in Berlin, losing $100,000 in the process.[30]

Indeed, three years later, an alternative theory was gaining ground among close observers of the fantastic Shadow Brokers saga: that a group of former NSA operators could be responsible for the extraordinary theft-and-leak, or, less likely, just one person. The social media behavior of the would-be front was too credible, the in-jokes were too crafty, the Yoda English too smooth, the attacks against ex-NSA staff too personal,[31] the operational security too good to be Russian. Even if the Shadow Brokers leak was an inside job, it wasn't simply would-be whistle-blowing like the Manning or Snowden episodes—it was planned, designed, and executed as an operation, even as a campaign, over many months. And it was brilliantly implemented. The drip-drip of releases and messages was designed to maximize harm to the NSA, to deepen the rift between Fort Meade and Silicon Valley, to cause vast collateral damage, to embarrass the U.S. intelligence community, to seamlessly tie into and enable follow-up attacks by foreign adversaries, and to coincide with Russia-related geopolitical events. This setup appears to have convinced senior officials in America's security establishment that Russia had escalated its active measures game. The mysterious Shadow Brokers may or may not have penetrated the machines of America's top intelligence officers—but they certainly penetrated their minds.

Before the Shadow Brokers, the most harmful active measure that took advantage of an unauthorized release of classified files was probably Operations Plan 10-1 in combination with the Nuclear Yield Requirements, leaked iteratively from the late 1960s to the early 1980s. The KGB had sourced those files from a spy, Robert Lee Johnson. This Cold War leak probably had no meaningful impact on intelligence collection. The Shadow Brokers releases, by contrast, were so harmful to American intelligence collection that comparisons with the Edward Snowden disclosures are not out of place, even without taking the breathtaking collateral damage into account. Never before have active measures been more active.

A Century of Disinformation

WHAT WAS THE STASI'S MOST SUCCESSFUL ACTIVE MEASURE?"
I asked. I was sitting in the small, crammed office of Georg
Herbstritt, a historian in Germany's vast agency in charge
of overseeing the old Stasi files. Herbstritt's employer has an appropriately
unwieldy German name that stretches over three lines, and is therefore
known as the BStU.[1] East Germany's infamous and humongous Ministry of
State Security, MfS, created an unimaginable amount of paper over its forty
years of existence. The BStU's archives hold 111 kilometers of written material in fourteen different locations, serviced by a staff of more than 1,400
people. The Stasi, by 1988, had more than 90,000 full-time employees,[2] with
an additional 175,000 "unofficial collaborators."[3]

The MfS was perhaps the most formidable spying machine the world has
ever seen. The agency even collected samples of its enemies' body odor from

chairs and sofas on which unsuspecting victims had been sitting. At least one analyst was appointed in charge of human "excrements" on an internal organizational chart. Some of the HVA's disinformation work was so well crafted that it even put the KGB's far-bigger First Chief Directorate to shame.

Since Department X represents the acme of Cold War active measures, I was keen to hear what they considered their crowning operation. "Well," said Herbstritt, without having to think very long, "the operation of April 1972." Herbstritt was referring to when the X engineered the outcome of West Germany's first vote of no confidence. In 1991, when some of the former X officers started to speak out publicly, they also pointed to the feat of April 1972 as their showpiece.

As I sat in the BStU office, not far from the TV tower at Alexanderplatz, I was reminded of my student days. I had moved to East Berlin in the mid-1990s, to study at Humboldt University. Whenever I entered the university's main building through its majestic entrance on Unter den Linden, there gleamed Karl Marx's inscription, in brass letters set on a solid red marble wall: "Philosophers have only interpreted the world. The point, however, is to change it."

Ten days before my BStU meeting, I rented a car and drove out to Kyritz, a sleepy town in the beautiful, lake-dotted countryside of Brandenburg, to meet with Horst Kopp. That April of 1972, he had managed to trick a conservative member of Parliament into voting against his own minority whip in a historic vote by luring the MP into the false belief that he was helping the Americans instead of aiding the enemy.

I knew I was a suspicious West German to Kopp (he would immediately place my accent). Worse, he knew that I was coming in from London, that old den of spy intrigue. I needed to break the ice. He offered me coffee in his modest living room. I told him that I had studied at Humboldt, and that I used to live in Prenzlauer Berg in East Berlin, a neighborhood now known as the Brooklyn of Berlin. He wanted to know what street. Immanuelkirchstraße, I told him, and said I remembered carrying up heavy tin buckets full of coal briquettes to make a fire in the morning, and that we showered in a tiny plastic box in the kitchen, warming our cold hands over the gas stove. His eyes lit up.

"Ah, I had a KW on that street," Kopp said. Thankfully, I had learned some Stasi jargon by then: KW was short for *konspirative Wohnung,* or "conspiratorial apartment." The HVA used these secret apartments to conspire with collaborators—perhaps politicians or authors or journalists visiting from West Berlin—and to work on "constructions," as the X called the forgeries used in active measures.[4]

It felt strange. I liked the old man—he was charming and quick and strangely honest. For more than two hours he told me details of his work in the HVA, including personal anecdotes that were surely unpleasant to him, described colleagues and spies he ran in detail, and quickly admitted when he did not know an answer, or could not remember something specific. I reminded myself that he had been one of the most effective handlers of one of the most effective spy agencies, and being witty and likable was a key part of his job.

Kopp's soft Eastern accent, the description of my old neighborhood in Berlin, and talk of "constructions" brought back my student-age fascination with social constructions—with epistemology, with the history of science, with postmodern philosophy and constructivism. An idea flashed across my mind as I drove back through serene Brandenburg. Was it possible that my own apartment had been a "KW" just a few years before I moved in? Was Kopp perhaps designing "operative constructions" in the same building, just a few years before I sat there by the kitchen window reading about philosophical constructions? Was he perhaps changing the world while I only interpreted it?

I started looking at disinformation in a new light. The more I did, the more active measures spooked me.

The postwar decades had exposed a cultural tension within truth itself—or rather, between two common understandings of truth that stand in permanent opposition to each other. One is a given, positive and analytical; something is true when it is accurate and objective, when it lines up with observation, when it is supported by facts, data, or experiments. It orients it-self in the present, not in the distant, mythical past or an unknowable future. Truth, in this classic sense, is inherently apolitical. Truthful observations and facts became the foundation of agreement, not conflict. The analytic truth bridged divides, and brought opposing views together. Professionals such as scientists, investigative journalists, forensic investigators, and intelligence analysts relied upon a set of shared norms designed to value cold, sober evidence over hot, emotional rhetoric. Changing one's position in response to new data was a virtue, not a weakness.

But there has always been another truth, one that corresponds to belief, not facts. Something is true when it is right, when backed up by gospel, or rooted in scripture, anchored in ideology, when it lines up with values. This truth is based in some distant past or future. Truth, in this sense, is relative to a specific community with shared values, and thus inherently political. This truth is preached from a pulpit, not tested in a lab. The style of delivery is hot, passionate, and emotional, not cold, detached, and sober. Changing one's po-sition is a weakness. It tends to confirm and lock in long-held views, and to divide along tribal and communal lines.

These two forms of truth, of course, are exaggerations, ideals, clichés. This distinction is somewhat coarse and simplistic—nevertheless, it helps explain the logic of disinformation. The goal of disinformation is to engineer division by putting emotion over analysis, division over unity, conflict over consensus, the particular over the universal. For, after all, a democracy's approach to the truth is not simply an *epistemic* question, but an *existential* question. Putting objectiv-ity before ideology contributed to opening societies, and to keeping them open. Putting ideology before objectivity, by contrast, contributed to closing socie-ties, and to keeping them closed. It is therefore no coincidence that objectivity was under near-constant assault in the ideologically torn twentieth century.

Ideological certainty and a feeling of epistemic superiority would help rein-terpret the factual in unexpected ways. Already, by the late 1950s, intelligence forgeries served a larger ideological truth—for example, that the United States and its aggressive NATO alliance, armed to the teeth with nuclear missiles, were the imperialist, capitalist oppressors. Forgeries didn't necessarily distort this truth, but articulated it more clearly. "No reporter of any democratic press could have depicted the true backstory of the Eisenhower Doctrine in a more unvarnished way than the oil magnate himself," wrote *Neues Deutschland*, East Germany's state outlet, in its introduction to the 1957 Rockefeller forgery.[5] The publishers of *Neues Deutschland* saw the United States as a capitalist, interest-driven superpower. Another example, from the summer of 1969, is *Peace News* and *Sanity*, the two British peace journals, dismissing the question of whether a leaked American war plan was forged or not, because it was "near enough to the truth." Forgeries were like a novel that spelled out a political utopia with gleaming clarity, or a modernist painting that perfectly articulated an aesthetic form: an artificial vehicle custom-designed to communicate a larger truth.

As I thought about Kopp, I wondered: What was the difference between his operational constructions and my philosophical ones? Was I falling for some active measure myself as I read postmodern philosophy by the window in my very own KW?

The 1960s were a critical moment in this assault on the factual, and not only for intelligence operations. It was a decade of reckoning with the harsh legacy of World War II, of decolonization, the Holocaust, the wars in Algeria and Vietnam, and with the looming destruction of humanity in a global nuclear cataclysm that seemed only hours away at any moment. The 1960s therefore witnessed a major political, cultural, artistic, and intellectual upheaval, at the heart of which was nothing less than the nature of facts themselves. Several different strains of twentieth-century philosophy and art took issue with what they considered to be a naïve "correspondence theory" of truth: facts weren't inalterable, according to the intellectual avant-garde; they were rooted in culture, language, systems of signs, collective perceptions, discourse, not in some inalterable structure of some independent reality. This avant-garde shunned "positivism," "structuralism," and "realism," and instead examined—or "deconstructed"—how facts were created, socially constructed, scientifically built, and put to use. This new approach felt empowering, and it was. By the 1970s, postmodern thought had become more widespread on campuses, although largely confined to the humanities, to art, film, literature, and perhaps architecture. Most academic critical theorists were, however, only studying and deconstructing the "practices" of knowledge production to shape intellectual discourse, to interpret the world. Meanwhile, in the shadows, intelligence agencies were actually producing knowledge, *constructing* new artifacts, shaping discourse in order to serve their tactical or strategic purposes—changing the world as they went.

In 1962, the KGB upgraded Department D to Service A, and ordered intelligence agencies across the Eastern bloc to follow their lead. "A" soon came to stand for active measures. One purpose of this name change, and of this new term of art, was to overcome a counterproductive focus on facts, and indeed on non-facts. What made an active measure active was not whether a construction resonated with reality, but whether it resonated with emotions, with collectively held views in the targeted community, and whether it managed to exacerbate existing tensions—or, in the jargon of Cold War operators, whether it succeeded to strengthen existing contradictions.

Shortly after defecting from Czechoslovak state security, Ladislav Bittman testified on disinformation to the U.S. Senate Committee on the Judiciary. Bittman explained why disinformation worked again and again: "Politicians or journalists wanted to believe in that disinformation message," he told the Senate. "They confirmed their opinion."[6] Just five months earlier, Michel Foucault delivered his landmark inaugural lecture, "The Order of Discourse," at the Collège de France. The iconic French philosopher and social critic considered "the opposition between true and false" as a long-established, power-wielding system of exclusion that he now revealed for what it was: historical, arbitrary, modifiable, and violent.[7] I had been reading Foucault in Prenzlauer Berg in the mid-1990s, and after my conversation with Kopp in Brandenburg, I recalled some of what I'd read. Foucault was breaking down the barrier between analytical truth and ideological truth; so were Agayants and Wagenbreth.

Could this eerie convergence of Eastern spycraft and Western thought really be just a coincidence?

It took a special kind of person to work in disinformation, on both sides of the Iron Curtain. Spotting weakness in adversarial societies, seeing cracks and fissures and political tensions, recognizing exploitable historical traumas, and then writing a forged pamphlet or letter or book—all of this required officers with unusual minds. Intelligence agencies that prized secrecy, military precision, and hierarchy had to find and cultivate individuals with an opposite skill set: free and unconventional thinkers, bookworms, writers, perceptive publicists with an ability to comprehend foreign cultures. Disinformation specialists even needed a certain playful quality of mind, and to enjoy exploring and exploiting contradictions. The best disinformation operators, Kopp told me, were internal rebels. One of the HVA's best men would sometimes "not do any work for two days, or just read or something," but then, all of a sudden, deliver a brilliant forged manuscript.[8] Active measures attracted and required precisely those creative minds who were in touch with the intellectual zeitgeist. As if to illustrate the point, Bittman, after his defection from East to West, became a modernist painter.

The St. Petersburg trolls were a far cry from the professionals of Service A and the X, but even they appeared to sense this convergence. One member of the American Department called the IRA's work "postmodernism in the making," adding that it reminded him of "Dadaism, and surrealism."[9]

So what can postmodernism tell us about the history of operational constructions?

First, that disinformation works, and in unexpected ways. The fine line between fact and forgery may be clear in the moment an operator or an intelligence agency commits the act of falsification—for example, in the moment when a fake paragraph is inserted into an otherwise genuine document, or when an unwitting influence agent is lured into casting a parliamentary vote under false pretenses, or when a bogus online account invites unwitting users to join a street demonstration, or shares extremist posts. But fronts, forgeries, and fakes don't stop there. Active measures will shape what others think, decide, and do—and thus change reality itself. When victims read and react to forged secret documents, their reaction is real. When the cards of an influenced parliamentary vote are counted, the result is real. When social media users gather in the streets following a bogus event invitation, the demonstration is real. When readers start using racial epithets offline, their views are real. These measures are *active*, in the sense that operations actively and immediately change views, decisions, and facts on the ground, in the now.

Second, disinformation works against itself, and again in unexpected ways. Intelligence agencies and other disinformation actors were, again and again, affected by their own constructions. It's not that analysts simply believed their own lies; it's that operators, driven by professional education as well as bureaucratic logic, tended to overstate rather than understate the value of their own disinformation work. Analysts would write after-action reviews and project memos that justified their efforts in terms that were clearer and more convincing than what had happened on the ground, where cause and effect remained entangled by design—exacerbating existing fissures and cracks, or tapping into existing grievances, or enhancing existing activism—all of which meant that engineered effects were very difficult to isolate from organic developments. Yet specialized intelligence units had and will have metrics and data at the ready to support their past projects and future budget authorization requests—balloons launched, protesters counted, forgeries printed, packages mailed, letters received, press stories clipped, or downloads and shares and likes and page views logged. Some disinformers of old had long understood this problem: "I don't think it's possible to measure exactly, realistically, the impact of an active measure," Bittman told me in March 2017, and added that there was always a degree of guessing. "You have no reliable measurement device," he said.[10] Active measures, in short, were impossibly hard to measure by design.

Disinformation about disinformation worsened over time. A one-off disinformation event is unlikely to achieve a given goal. By the early 1960s, some operations had begun to spread out into entire campaigns that could go on for many years, even decades. As more years and decades passed, many subtle lines that once may have demarcated fact from forgery faded until they eventually disappeared entirely. Thus, forged and engineered effects mixed with, and solidified into, actual, observable effects—like a liquid cement mix setting and turning into a firm concrete foundation. With the passing of time, reverse-engineering the delicate construction process became harder and harder.

Then came the internet, with the hacking and dumping of large volumes of data and social media influence campaigns. Higher numbers and refined, real-time online metrics did not make those measurement devices more reliable, but less so. Higher numbers merely translated into higher perceived confidence in assessments, thus creating an even more seductive illusion of metrics. "Measuring the actual impact of trolling and online influence campaigns is probably impossible," said Kate Starbird, one of the world's leading researchers of online disinformation campaigns, who examined the influence of digital disinformation on the Black Lives Matter movement. "But the difficulty of measuring impact doesn't mean that there isn't meaningful impact," she added.[11] Online engagement figures can be staggering, and new bureaucratic politics can make these figures even more staggering. One *New York Times* headline in late 2017 stated, "Russian Influence Reached 126 Million Through Facebook Alone."[12] In reality the preelection reach of the Internet Research Agency was far less, for two reasons: only about 37 percent of Facebook's number of "impressions" were from before November 9, 2016 (the rest was after), and "impressions" are not engagements, only what a user may have scrolled past, perhaps absentmindedly. Facebook was then under intense political pressure, and analysts and executives decided to be as liberal as they could with the data, providing an upper limit of an estimate to Congress, for fear of being accused of lowballing the problem afterward. Many old-school journalists covering what they thought were scandalous social media figures, in turn, were either unable or unwilling to assess the data on their merits, or in the context of a history that had largely been forgotten. Online metrics, in short, created a powerful illusion, an appealing mirage—the metrics created an opportunity for more, and more convincing, disinformation about disinformation. For willfully exaggerating the effects of disinformation means exaggerating the impact of disinformation.

All this is bad news for future historians. Seminars, in-person discussions, and correspondence were always fleeting and rarely archived. Yet the reach of such direct human interactions was limited throughout the twentieth century, and many if not most magazines and published newsletters were archived somewhere. Not so in the early twenty-first century, where secure electronic communications and social media conversations are both more perishable and have a wider reach. Even inside large government bureaucracies more and more memory is lost as screens replace paper, and as files get removed or destroyed. The digital age has upended the way we preserve records, and our collective memory has already begun to corrode more quickly and more thoroughly as a result. It will therefore be even more difficult to study and reconstruct the impact of active measures in the future. The internet, contrary to a popular misconception, forgets every day, especially on ephemeral social media platforms. Suspending accounts for coordinated inauthentic behavior, for example, means hiding the main records of that behavior, and potentially assisting adversaries in hiding their tracks. Accurately gauging impact becomes harder; understating and overstating impact becomes easier. Active measures will thus not only blur the line between fact and fiction in the present, but also in the past, in retrospect.

Active measures, third, crack open divisions by closing distinctions. It is very hard to distinguish—for an activist, for the target of an active measures campaign, even for a large organization running its own active measures—between a cunning influence agent on the one hand, and a genuine activist on the other. In theory, on an individual basis, one person is either a genuine activist or a controlled agitator, but this worldview applies only in the abstract. In practice, one individual can be both genuine and an exploited asset, a witting and unwitting collaborator at the same time. Was Philip Agee, reportedly at one point a witting KGB collaborator, unwitting when he received a forged leak that was camouflaged as coming from a legitimate U.S. government whistle-blower? This postmodern problem gets even more convoluted when applied not to an individual but to a group of people. A 50,000-person demonstration may be a genuine expression of political dissatisfaction, as with the demonstrations against NATO ballistic missiles in Germany. Yet a large demonstration can also be exploited, organized, and even funded by an adversarial power, with, say, an interest in stopping the deployment of NATO ballistic missiles in Europe, all without undermining the legitimate character of the protest. Other examples are activist platforms and leak projects like the Fifth Estate, CyberGuerrilla, or WikiLeaks, which can empower witting participants and genuine activist projects at the same time, even in the same instance. Active measures are therefore difficult to contain conceptually, with no obvious beginning or end. The problem may not be the quality of the data or the design of the research; the problem may be the quality of an operation and the very design of the "construction" in the first place.

This seeming contradiction is no contradiction, but a core feature of active measures over the past century. Active measures are purpose-designed temptations, designed to exaggerate, designed to give in to prejudice, to pre-formed notions—and to erode the capacity of an open society for fact-based, sober debate, and thus wear down the norms and institutions that resolve internal conflict peacefully. This strange postmodern intelligence practice is, confusingly, underdetermined by observable evidence. Saying where an operation ended, and whether it failed or succeeded, requires more than facts; it requires a judgment call, which in practice means a political decision, often a collective decision. Therefore, if a targeted community believes that a disinformation campaign was a major success, then it has made it a major success.

Disinformation, finally, is itself disintegrating. Bureaucratically, this degeneration proceeded with the breakup of the old Soviet security establishment and the dissolution of the once-so-formidable spy agencies of the Eastern bloc. The term "active measures" faded, even in Russia, in the early 1990s as the KGB's First Chief Directorate was transitioned into the SVR. The sweeping official history of Russian foreign intelligence acknowledges that over the past century the designations of the same operational activity— disinformation—came and went, from "operational games" to "active measures" to the blander, more recent "support measures."[13]

Then came the rise of the internet, which upended the old art and science of disinformation in unexpected ways. Cutthroat media competition and distrust in "opinion factories," as the Eastern bloc had recognized by mid-century, still worked to the advantage of disinformation operators in the mid-2010s. But the amount of craftsmanship and work required from disinformation specialists was lower in the twenty-first century than it was in the twentieth. Digital storage made it possible to breach targets remotely and extract vast amounts of compromising material. The internet facilitated acquiring and publishing unprecedented volumes of raw files at a distance and anonymously. Automation helped to create and amplify fake personas and content, to destroy data, and to disrupt. Speed meant that operational adaptation and adjustments could take place not over years, months, or weeks—but in days, hours, even minutes. Activist culture meant existing leak platforms outperformed purpose-created ones. And the darker, more depraved corners of the internet offered teeming petri dishes of vicious, divisive ideas, and guaranteed a permanent supply of fresh conspiracy theories. All this took place while many reporters, worn down by breakneck news cycles, became more receptive to covering leaked, compromising material of questionable provenance, and as publishers recycled unoriginal, repetitive content. The end effect was that a significant and large portion of the disinformation value-creation chain was outsourced to the victim society itself, to journalists, to activists, to freelance conspiracy theorists, and, to a lesser degree, to researchers.

The temptingly obvious conclusion about these trends appears to be that the art and craft of disinformation has become easier—yet such a finding would be misleading. Active measures have become more active and less measured to such a degree that they are themselves disintegrating—and this disintegration creates a new set of challenges. For the offender, campaigns have become harder to control, harder to contain, harder to steer, harder to manage, and harder to assess. For victims, disinformation campaigns have also become more difficult to manage, more difficult to assess in impact, and more difficult to counter. At the beginning of the third decade of the twenty-first century, both open and closed societies, many thrown into self-doubt and outright identity crises by the rise of the internet and its side effects, are both overstating and, more rarely, understating the threat and the potential of disinformation campaigns—and thus helping expand and escalate that very threat and its potential. This constructivist vortex is propelled by an unprecedented confluence of incentives that lead many victims—politicians, journalists, technologists, intelligence analysts, adversary operators, and most researchers—to highlight the potentials of disinformation over its limitations.

Perhaps the most vivid illustration of this trend is the fantastic story of the Shadow Brokers—the devastating NSA leak with its subsequent reuse and integration of U.S. government hacking tools into the Russian Not-Petya computer worm, in the words of the White House the "most destructive and costly" computer network attack in history. That iconic overall campaign was also a disinformation project. The theft, the gradual and meticulously timed release of files, the weaponization of experts and journalists, and the subsequent destructive redeployment of computer code was designed, carefully planned, and executed with skill and discipline as an active measure—yet it has remained unclear for years who was responsible for the different components of this campaign. Whoever initiated the leak, an insider or a foreign intelligence agency, the Shadow Brokers campaign was an artful masterpiece that illustrated, in its cruel uncertainty, the twisted logic of active measures—irreversibly blurring the line between victim and perpetrator, between observation and participation, between reality and representation.

JUST A FEW WEEKS BEFORE I MET HIM, HORST KOPP HAD PRESENTED HIS memoir at the Spy Museum in Berlin. I asked him whether any surviving members of the X were there for his book talk. "Well, you know, the Mutz called me one day ahead of the press conference," Kopp told me. Some Germans have the habit of referring to familiar colleagues by their last names plus the definite article; "the Mutz" was Kopp's former boss, Wagenbreth's longtime deputy and the last head of the X. When the phone rang, Kopp did not even recognize the voice of his former boss, as they had not spoken since 1985. "Wolfgang here," he said. He wanted to know what Kopp was going to reveal about their deception work. Kopp gave him an overview.

"He told me," said Kopp, "that they were going to send two people to my book talk."

NOTES

What Is Disinformation?

1. Sergei Kondrashev, in Tennent Bagley, *Spymaster* (New York: Skyhorse, 2013), pp. 283–84. The other book was a Stasi memoir available only in German, *Auftrag Irreführung*, more on which below.
2. Lawrence (Ladislav) Bittman, former disinformation officer, state security, Prague, interview with Thomas Rid, March 25, 2017, Rockport, MA; audio at https://archive.org/details/bittman-ridt. See Richard Sandomir, "Lawrence Martin-Bittman, 87, Master of Disinformation, Dies," *The New York Times*, September 24, 2018, p. A25.
3. Lorenzo Franceschi-Bicchierai, "'Guccifer 2.0' Is Likely a Russian Government Attempt to Cover Up Its Own Hack," *Motherboard*, June 16, 2016.
4. Gill Bennett, *The Zinoviev Letter* (Oxford: Oxford University Press, 2018).
5. Douglas Selvage and Christopher Nehring, *Die AIDS-Verschwörung*, BF informiert 33, 2014.
6. Less aggressive because the CIA mainly supported existing organizations and publications through covert funding, not by designing and delivering divisive and deceptive

disinformation; see Hugh Wilford, *The Mighty Wurlitzer: How the CIA Played America* (Cambridge, MA: Harvard University Press, 2008); see also Michael Warner's review in *Studies in Intelligence* 52, 2, June 2008, pp. 71–73.

7. This book, like many intelligence agencies, does not see military deception during active military engagements as part of the active measures phenomenon. For a starting point on military deception, see Donald Daniel and Katherine Herbig, *Strategic Military Deception* (New York: Pergamon, 1981). The most pertinent wartime deception campaign was engineered by Sefton Delmer for Britain's Political Warfare Executive during World War II. Stasi's disinformation unit was so impressed by Delmer's 1962 memoir *Black Boomerang* (published in German as *Krieg im Äther* in 1963) that all officers had to read it, and more than twenty years after publication HVA still recommended Delmer's work to partner agencies in the Soviet bloc. See "Разговорите с др. Волфганг Муц—зам.–началник Отдел АМ при разузнавателното управление на МДС–ГДР по време на пребиваването му в България от 16-19.9.1986г," COMDOS-Arch-R, 9, 4, 670, November 22, 1986, pp. 121–28, p. 127, https://archive.org/details/1986-09-19-mutz.

8. Christopher Andrew and Oleg Gordievsky, *KGB: The Inside Story* (London: Faber & Faber, 1990), p. 630.

9. Ladislav Bittman, *The Deception Game* (New York: Ballantine, 1972), p. 22.

1. The Trust

1. Only a very small selection of this material has become available to scholars. See Richard Spence, "Russia's *Operatsiia Trest*: A Reappraisal," *Global Intelligence Monthly*, April 1999, p. 1, https://archive.org/details/1999-operatsiia-trest. A significant amount of historical research on the Trust is available. For an excellent, relatively recent example, see Richard G. Robbins, Jr., "Was Vladimir Dzhunkovskii the Father of 'The Trust'?: A Quest for the Plausible," *Journal of Modern Russian History and Historiography* 1 (2008), pp. 113–43.

2. See the listing of Russian émigré periodicals at Indiana University, https://web .archive.org/web/20181104163933/https://libraries.indiana.edu/periodicals -russian-emigre.

3. John Riddell, *To the Masses: Proceedings of the Third Congress of the Communist International, 1921* (Boston: Brill, 2015), p. 660.

4. "Nicholas of Russia, Grand Duke, Dead," *The New York Times*, January 7, 1929, p. 3.

5. See short description in John Costello and Oleg Tsarev, *Deadly Illusions* (New York: Crown, 1993), p. 31.

6. Jerzy Niezbrzycki (aka Ryszard Wraga), "The 'Trust.' The History of a Soviet Provokation Operation," *Vozrozhdenie* (*Возрождение*), Paris, January–February 1950, translated, CIA-RDP78-03362A002200040004-7, p. 1.

7. Евгений Максимович Примаков, *Очерки истории российской внешней разведки: 1917–1933 годы, Том 2* (Москва: Международные отношения, 1997), p. 112.

8. Ibid.

9. "Оперативной игры," in Примаков, *Очерки истории российской внешней разведки, Том 2*, pp. 90, 93.

10. Walter Pforzheimer, "The Trust," CIA Historical Intelligence Collection, CIA-RDP90G01353R001700020002-4, March 1969, p. 4.

11. The question whether MOTsR already existed or was set up by the Cheka is controversial among historians. The CIA assumed it existed already. The SVR claims it was created after Yakushev's arrest. See Jonathan Haslam, *Near and Distant Neighbors* (New York: Oxford University Press, 2015), p. 19.

12. "Правда, как вы, наверное, догадываетесь, все это будет игрой—нашей с вашим участием—под условным названием 'Трест,'" in Примаков, *Очерки истории российской внешней разведки, Том 2,* p. 114.

13. Pforzheimer, "The Trust," p. 2.

14. Примаков, *Очерки истории российской внешней разведки, Том 2.*

15. The CIA and SVR histories agree on the date and the rough outlines of this trip.

16. Александр Репников, "Дороги Василия Шульгина," *Историк* 3 (March 27, 2017), p. 220.

17. Примаков, *Очерки истории российской внешней разведки, Том 2,* p. 121.

18. Ibid., p. 115.

19. Ibid.

20. David Murphy, Sergei Kondrashev, and George Bailey, *Battleground Berlin* (New Haven: Yale University Press, 1997), p. 447.

21. Haslam, *Near and Distant Neighbors,* p. 31.

22. "Было создано специальное бюро по подготовке дезинформации для военных разведок Запада," in Примаков, *Очерки истории российской внешней разведки, Том 2,* p. 121.

23. Boris Goodze, interview with Oleg Tsarev, quoted in Costello and Tsarev, *Deadly Illusions,* p. 41.

24. See also "Дезинформбюро. 80 лет советской службе дезинформации," *Коммерсантъ* 2 (January 13, 2003), p. 7.

25. Haslam, *Near and Distant Neighbors,* p. 31; Михаил Алексеев, *Советская военная разведка в Китае и хроника "китайской смуты" (1922–1929)* (Moscow: Kuchkovo Pole, 2010), p. 586.

26. "Trust" file 302330, vol. 1, in the KGB's operational counterintelligence archive, Ministry of Security, Moscow, quoted in Boris Goodze, interview with Oleg Tsarev, quoted in Costello and Tsarev, *Deadly Illusions,* p. 32.

27. Both the CIA and the SVR study on the Trust name the same countries in this context. Примаков, *Очерки истории российской внешней разведки, Том 2,* p. 115. Pforzheimer, "The Trust."

28. Wraga, "The 'Trust,'" p. 13.

29. Василий Шульгин, *Три столицы* (Москва: Современник, 1991), p. 6.

30. The details of the Shulgin episode are identical in the CIA and SVR studies.

31. Stephen Harris, *The Trust: The Classic Example of Soviet Manipulation* (Monterey, CA: Naval Postgraduate School, September 1985), p. 54.

32. "Первоначально я категорически отказался описывать свое нелегальное путешествие в Советский Союз, боясь, что подведу своих 'друзей' по Тресту," in Шульгин, *Три столицы,* p. 455.

33. Шульгин, *Три столицы.*

34. Vassili Choulguine, *La résurrection de la Russie: mon voyage secret en Russie soviétique* (Paris: Payot, 1927).

35. Wraga, "The 'Trust,'" p. 1.

36. "кроме подписи автора, т.е. 'В. Шульгин,' под этой книгой можно прочесть невидимую, но неизгладимую ремарку: 'Печатать разрешаю Ф.Дзержинский,'" Шульгин, *Три столицы*, p. 455.

37. Wraga, "The 'Trust,'" p. 12.

38. Ibid., p. 23.

39. Pforzheimer, "The Trust," p. 41.

40. Christopher Andrew and Oleg Gordievsky, *KGB: The Inside Story* (London: Faber & Faber, 1990), p. 384.

41. Ibid., p. 94.

42. Wraga, "The 'Trust,'" p. 3.

43. The best source for this detail is a French historian and chronicler then living in the Soviet Union; see Pierre Pascal, *Mon Journal de Russie, 1927*, vol. 4 (Lausanne: L'Âge d'Homme, 1982), pp. 98 and 124.

44. Mikhail Agursky, "Soviet Disinformation and Forgeries," *International Journal on World Peace* 6, no. 1 (January–March 1989), pp. 13–30.

45. "Операция 'Трест' притягивала, как подслащенная клейкая бумажка— насекомых, наиболее опасную и активную часть белой эмиграции," Евгений Максимович Примаков, Очерки истории российской внешней разведки: 1917– 1933 годы, *Том 2* (Москва: Международные отношения, 1997), p. 120.

2. Japan's *Mein Kampf*

1. The price was likely exaggerated, see 稲生典太郎, "『田中上奏文』をめぐる二三の問題," 国際政治 26 (1964), p. 81.

2. "Premier Tanaka's Memorial: The Document and Dispute," *The New York Times*, May 15, 1932, p. XX3.

3. "惊心动魄之日本满蒙积极政策 (Japan's shocking policy toward Manchuria-Mongolia)" 時事月報 (*Current Affairs Monthly*), Nanking, December 1929, pp. 1–20, https://archive.org/details/1929-Nanking.

4. Hattori Ryūji, "Controversies over the Tanaka Memorial," pp. 121–47 in Daqing Yang, Jie Liu, Hiroshi Mitani, and Andrew Gordon, *Toward a History Beyond Borders* (Cambridge, MA: Harvard University Press, 2012).

5. "The Tanaka Memorial," *China Critic*, Shanghai, 4, no. 8 (September 17, 1931), pp. 1–2.

6. The differences between the Nanking and the Shanghai versions are negligible. The main difference is that the cover sheet was printed as the last paragraph in the Mandarin version, and as the first paragraph in the English version. A few subheadings were also different, and the name of one railway line had been altered. I would like to thank Chenny Zhang for her methodical and meticulous help in comparing the two versions.

7. "Протоколы заседаний американского бюро Тихоокеанского секретариата профсоюзов" (Report of meeting, San Francisco Bureau of the Pan-Pacific Trade Union Secretariat), Minutes no. 4, March 2, 1932, Comintern Archives, Fond 534,

Opis 4, Delo 422, item 1, "Publication of 'P-P Worker.'" See also Minutes no. 7, March 21, 1932, and Minutes no. 12, April 25, 1932, https://archive.org/details /comintern-534-4-422.

8. See the chronological listings on Worldcat.org for author "Tanaka, Giichi," including the various identities in non-Latin scripts, https://web.archive.org/web /20180925183739/http://www.worldcat.org/identities/lccn-n80010393/.

9. *The Tanaka Memorial* (San Francisco: Young China, 1936), cover.

10. Joseph Taussig, "Construction of Certain Naval Vessels," United States Committee on Naval Affairs, H.R. 8026 (Washington, DC: Government Printing office, April 22, 1940), pp. 188–89.

11. Leon Trotsky, "The 'Tanaka Memorial,'" *Fourth International* 2, no. 5 (New York, June 1941), p. 131.

12. Ibid., p. 132.

13. Jefferson Hale, "Japan's Mein Kampf," *Click*, November 1941, p. 10, https://archive .org/details/1941-11-CLICK.

14. NBC Sunday night news roundup, WJZ, Washington, 7 p.m., December 14, 1941.

15. "News Analysis by Jefferson Hale," WQXR, New York, 5 p.m., December 21, 1941.

16. Sally Swift, "Capital Whirl," *The Washington Post*, April 24, 1941, p. 14.

17. Frank Oliver, "Tanaka Memorial," *The Washington Post*, January 10, 1940, p. X9.

18. H. Res. 406, sponsored by Compton Ignatius White (D-ID), 77th Congress, 2nd session, January 13, 1942. Curiously the World Peace Movement edition includes the paragraphs edited out of *Communist International* a decade earlier, see *The Memorial of Premier Tanaka*, New York: World Peace Movement, 108 Park Row, undated, https:// archive.org/details/1941-wpm-tanaka.

19. CIA, "Communism: Exploitation of the International Communist Movement by the Soviet Intelligence Services," 1, CIA-RDP78-00915R000300090002-7, July 1954, p. 55.

20. *The Battle of China*, Frank Capra, produced by the Signal Corps, Army Service Forces, War Department, 1944, https://archive.org/details/BattleOfChina; and *Know Your Enemy—Japan*, Frank Capra, produced by the Army Service Forces, Information and Education Division, Army Service Forces, War Department, 1945, https://archive.org /details/KnowYourEnemyJapan.

21. U.S. National Archives, National Archives Microcopy No. T-82, 198, roll 157, frames 294027–294075, quoted in John J. Stephan "The Tanaka Memorial (1927): Authentic or Spurious?" *Modern Asian Studies* 7, no. 4 (1973), p. 744.

22. Alexander Werth, *The Krushchev Phase* (London: Hale, 1961), p. 234.

23. "الخيار الجرثومي مفتوح أمام الدول الكبرى," القبس (*al-Qabas*), Kuwait, 5286 (January 29, 1987), p. 31, https://archive.org/details/1987-01-29-al-qabas.

24. The first in-depth study on the Tanaka Memorial came out in 1964: 稲生典太郎, "『田中上奏文』をめぐる二三の問題," 国際政治 26 (1964), pp. 72–87.

25. See Stephan, "The Tanaka Memorial (1927)," pp. 733–45.

26. Herbert Romerstein and Stanislav Levchenko, *The KGB Against the "Main Enemy"* (Washington, DC: Lexington Books, 1989), p. 55.

27. Александр Витковский, "А свою фамилию надо забыть," *Парламентская газета* (Москва, August 30, 2003).

28. Виталий Григорьевич Павлов, *Операция "Снег": полвека во внешней разведке КГБ* (Москва: Гея, 1996), pp. 39–40. Also, Виталий Григорьевич Павлов, *Трагедии советской разведки* (Москва: Центрполиграф, 2000), p. 101.

29. See "Очерки истории российской внешней разведки," SVR, 2010, https://web.archive.org/web/20100613050338/http://svr.gov.ru:80/smi/book-ocherki.htm.

30. "Лауреаты премии СВР России," SVR, May 4, 2010, https://web.archive.org/web/20120509075016/http://www.svr.gov.ru/svr_today/premia-2006.htm.

31. Евгений Максимович Примаков, *Очерки истории российской внешней разведки: 1917–1933 годы, Том 2* (Москва: Международные отношения, 1997).

32. "Результатом одной из операций, блестяще проведенных разведчиком, и стало получение секретного документа под названием 'Меморандум Танаки,'" in Примаков, *Очерки истории российской внешней разведки: 1917–1933 годы, Том 2*, p. 257.

33. 彭珊珊, "中日首次共同修史不畏敏感: '侵略战争'上达成重要共识," 澎湃 (*The Paper*), April 3, 2015.

34. Hattori Ryūji, "Controversies over the Tanaka Memorial," pp. 121–47 in Daqing Yang, Jie Liu, Hiroshi Mitani, and Andrew Gordon, *Toward a History Beyond Borders* (Cambridge, MA: Harvard University Press, 2012).

35. "Japanese Imperialism in All Its Insolent Nakedness," *Communist International* (English edition) 8, no. 22 (December 30, 1931), pp. 731–48, https://archive.org/details/1931-12-30-CI.

36. 稲生典太郎, "『田中上奏文』をめぐる二三の問題," 国際政治 26 (1964), p. 81. See also Stephan, "The Tanaka Memorial (1927)," p. 743.

3. The Whalen Forgeries

1. "Socialists Name Thomas for Mayor," *The New York Times*, June 17, 1929, p. 19.

2. "Jobless Revolt Near, Says Green," *The Baltimore Sun*, April 2, 1930, p. 2.

3. "Red Assemblies Abroad," *The Manchester Guardian*, March 7, 1930, p. 17.

4. "A Hundred Heads Clubbed," *Chicago Daily Tribune*, March 7, 1930, p. 3.

5. "Report That Whalen Aims to Quit Promptly Denied," *The Baltimore Sun*, March 22, 1930, p. 1.

6. "Whalen Shows Off Police in Big New York Parade," *The New York Times*, April 27, 1930, p. 12.

7. "Russ Documents Called Forgeries," *The Baltimore Sun*, May 3, 1930, p. 12.

8. John Lyons, "Testimony," in *Investigation of Communist Propaganda*, Special Committee to Investigate Communist Activities in the United States, U.S. House of Representatives (Washington, DC: Government Printing Office, July 18–24, 1930), Part 3, vol. 3, p. 41.

9. "Whalen Discloses Secret Red Orders; Amtorg Implicated," *The New York Times*, May 3, 1930, p. 1.

10. Harriette Flory, "The Arcos Raid and the Rupture of Anglo-Soviet Relations, 1927," *Journal of Contemporary History* 12, no. 4 (October 1, 1977), p. 707.

11. "Whalen Discloses Secret Red Orders; Amtorg Implicated," p. 10.

12. Ibid.

13. Ibid., p. 1.
14. "Soviet Paper Scores Whalen's Activities," *The New York Times*, May 6, 1930, p. 24.
15. The Russian phrase was "Пролетарии всех стран соединяйтесь," see "וההיילען
פארעפנטליכט סענזאציאנעלע געהיימע דאקומענטען צו וויזען ווי מאסקווע פיהרט דורך גאנצע
אמעריקע אין ארבייטשע קאמוניסטישע," in *פֿאָרװערטס* (*Forverts*), May 3, 1930, p. 1, https://
archive.org/details/1930-05-03-forward, as well as Wagner's detailed description
under oath: Max Wagner, "Testimony," in *Investigation of Communist Propaganda*,
Special Committee to Investigate Communist Activities in the United States, U.S.
House of Representatives (Washington, DC: Government Printing Office, July 18–24,
1930), Part 3, vol. 3, p. 308.
16. The line read "Секретариат Американского Отдела." I would like to thank Aleks
Gostev for his help in deciphering the smeared Cyrillic script.
17. "וההיילען פארעפנטליכט סענזאציאנעלע געהיימע דאקומענטען צו וויזען ווי מאסקווע פיהרט
אמעריקע אין ארבייטשע קאמוניסטישע גאנצע דורך," in *פֿאָרװערטס* (*Forverts*), May 3, 1930,
p. 1, the smeared ink was in the fine print that said, "Пролетарии всех стран
соединяйтесь."
18. *Congressional Record*—House, May 12, 1930, p. 8770.
19. "Three Offer Proof Whalen Red Papers Were Forged Here," *The New York Times*,
July 25, 1930, p. 1.
20. The only analysis of the extraordinary episode was co-authored in 1989, by an unusual pair: the U.S. Information Agency's point man on countering disinformation,
Herbert Romerstein, and a prominent KGB defector and active measures operator,
Stanislav Levchenko. Romerstein and Levchenko, *The KGB Against the "Main Enemy"*
(Lexington, MA: Lexington Books, 1989).
21. "Green Says A.F. of L. Is Clear of Reds," *The New York Times*, August 20, 1929, p. 10.
22. "Woll Says Soviet Stirs Trouble Here," *The New York Times*, October 8, 1928, p. 42.
23. "U.S. Labor Leader Tells of Soviets' Spy System Here," *Chicago Tribune*, October 8,
1928, p. 21.
24. "Demands Congress Sift Red Riots Here: Woll Charges," *The New York Times*, March
4, 1930, p. 16.
25. See John Spivak, "Testimony," in *Investigation of Communist Propaganda*, Special Committee to Investigate Communist Activities in the United States, U.S. House of Representatives (Washington, DC: Government Printing Office, July 18–24, 1930), Part 3, vol.
3, p. 283. Also John Spivak, *A Man in His Time* (New York: Horizon, 1967), pp. 149–50.
26. "Whalenovi 'rdeči dokumenti' so ponarejeni," *Prosveta* 199 (Chicago, August 23,
1930), p. 1.
27. "Three Offer Proof Whalen Red Papers Were Forged Here," *The New York Times*,
July 25, 1930, p. 4.
28. Spivak, *A Man in His Time*, p. 164.
29. "Three Offer Proof Whalen Red Papers Were Forged Here."

4. American Disinformation

1. George Kennan, "The Inauguration of Political Warfare," Draft, April, 30, 1948,
NARA release, https://web.archive.org/web/20150123010608/http://digitalarchive
.wilsoncenter.org/document/114320.

2. NARA, RG 273, Records of the National Security Council, NSC 10/2, June 18, 1948. See also Michael Warner, "The CIA's Office of Policy Coordination: From NSC 10/2 to NSC 68," *International Journal of Intelligence and Counterintelligence* 11, no. 2, (Summer, 1998), pp. 211–20.

3. James R. Holbrook, *Potsdam Mission* (Bloomington, IN: AuthorHouse, 2008), p. 20.

4. "Operation GRAVEYARD," DTLINEN-KGU 1-1, CIA CREST Archive, March 18, 1949, p. 1.

5. "250,000 Germans Reported Held," *The New York Times*, February 14, 1949, p. 5.

6. "Proposed Project—EARTHENWARE," MGW-A-102, DTLINEN-KGU VOL. 1_0002, CIA CREST Archive, March 18, 1949, p. 2.

7. Jochen Staadt, "Vergesst sie nicht! Freiheit war ihr Ziel—Die Kampfgruppe gegen Unmenschlichkeit," *ZdF* no. 24 (2008), p. 63.

8. Thomas Boghardt, "The Fighting Group Against Inhumanity," *Studies in Intelligence* 59, no. 4 (2015), pp. 41–42.

9. "Project Outline," CADROIT QKFEARFUL 22, CIA CREST Archive, July 1954 [precise date illegible], p. 2.

10. Ibid., p. 3.

11. Ibid., p. 11.

12. "Your A-529, February 7, 1952 re International Congress of Free Jurists," Department of State, Telegram from Bonn to Secretary of State, no. 1856, March 6, 1952, 6 p.m. CADROIT QKFEARFUL 5, CIA CREST Archive, p. 2.

13. "Dept Pass Bangkok for action as Berlin's 1," Department of State, telegram from Berlin to secretary of state, unnumbered, June 20, 1952, 6 p.m. CADROIT QKFEARFUL 7, CIA CREST Archive, p. 2.

14. The street was renamed Walter-Linse-Straße in 1961. Jörg Rudolph, Frank Drauschke, and Alexander Sachse, "Hingerichtet in Moskau," *Schriftenreihe des Berliner Landesbeauftragten für die Unterlagen des Staatssicherheitsdienstes der ehemaligen DDR* 23 (2007), p. 6.

15. "Ein Agent Ging Verloren," *Der Spiegel* 5 (January 27, 1992), p. 77, see also "How Dr. Linse '... Got Lost,'" *Life* 33, no. 4 (July 28, 1952), p. 37.

16. Benno Kirsch, *Walter Linse: 1903–1953–1996* (Dresden: Stiftung Sächsische Gedenkstätten, 2007).

17. Peter Deriabin, *The Secret World* (New York: Doubleday, 1959), pp. 188–93.

18. The MGB report, in Russian, is reproduced in David Murphy, Sergei Kondrashev, and George Bailey, *Battleground Berlin* (New Haven: Yale University Press, 1997), pp. 118–19.

19. David Martin, "The American James Bond," *Playboy* 27, no. 4 (April 1980), pp. 132, 198, 250, 252, 254, and 258–66.

20. Julius Mader, *Who's Who in CIA* (East Berlin: Julius Mader, 1968), p. 229.

21. "Stanley H. Gaines Attorney, CIA Officer," *The Washington Post*, January 26, 2005, p. B05.

22. Bayard Stockton and Tara Stockton, *Flawed Patriot: The Rise and Fall of CIA Legend Bill Harvey* (Washington, DC: Potomac Books, 2006), p. 62.

23. David Martin, *Wilderness of Mirrors* (New York: HarperCollins, 1980).

24. "HQS Traces on Karlheinz Marbach," MARBACH KARL HEINZ 120, May 26, 1983, CIA CREST Archive, p. 1.
25. CIA report on festival preparations, undated, untitled, CIA-RDP83-00415R009 100080002-0, Secret Control U.S. Officials Only, p. 2.
26. CIA, "Youth Festival in Berlin in August 1951," May 25, 1951, DOC_0000466276, CIA CREST Archive, p. 1.
27. Murphy, Kondrashev, and Bailey, *Battleground Berlin*.
28. Gregory Owen, *The Longest Patrol: A U-Boat Gunner's War* (Lincoln, NB: iUniverse, 2006), p. 209. Herbert Werner, who wrote a bestselling U-Boat memoir, *Iron Coffins*, was Marbach's successor on the ship.
29. "Assessment of Agent Personnel: LCCASSOCK, Monthly Production of a falsified East German Magazine," February 2, 1953, MARBACH, KARL HEINZ 26, CIA CREST Archive, p. 2.
30. Marbach, Karl Heinz 120, CIA CREST Archive, p. 3.
31. "Assessment Agent Personnel," MARBACH, KARL HEINZ 26, CIA CREST Archive, February 2, 1953, p. 1.
32. Marbach, Karl Heinz, 120, CIA CREST Archive, p. 1.
33. "Your request for clearance dated 7 March 1951," CIA Special Collection, MARBACH, KARL HEINZ 20, CIA CREST Archive, July 26, 1951, p. 2.
34. "Assessment Agent Personnel," MARBACH, KARL HEINZ 26, CIA CREST Archive, February 2, 1953, p. 1.
35. The initial grant came out of the budget of the U.S. High Commissioner.
36. "Marbach, Karl Heinz," MARBACH, KARL HEINZ 20, CIA CREST Archive, July 29, 1952, p. 1.
37. "LCCASSOCK," MARBACH, KARL HEINZ 23, CIA CREST Archive, August 23, 1952, p. 1.
38. Chief BOB to Chief EE, "CADORY/Operational," MARBACH, KARL HEINZ 29, CIA CREST Archive, p. 2.
39. "LCCASSOCK Project Review," MARBACH, KARL HEINZ 29, CIA CREST Archive, June 26, 1953, p. 2.
40. Enrico Heitzer, *Die Kampfgruppe gegen Unmenschlichkeit (KgU): Widerstand und Spionage im Kalten Krieg 1948–1959* (Köln: Böhlau Verlag, 2015). Heitzer's book, although favorably reviewed in a CIA journal, is contested among German postwar historians. See Jochen Staadt, "Ein Historikerreinfall. Die Kampfgruppe gegen Unmenschlichkeit—Desinformation macht Geschichte," *Zeitschrift des Forschungsverbandes SED-Staat* 33 (2013), pp. 94–111. Also the 44-page, three-part review, Jochen Staadt, "KgU und früher Widerstand in der DDR—eine Nazi-Verschwörung?" in *Zeitschrift des Forschungsverbandes SED-Staat* 37/38/39 (2015/2016).

5. The Kampfgruppe

1. "Project Outline: Renewal and Redocumentation for Fiscal Year 1957," DTLINEN-KGU 1-94, CIA CREST Archive, August 29, 1956, p. 2.
2. "Boudreau's forced leave from DTLINEN," DTLINEN 35, CIA CREST Archive, 9 November 1951, p. 1.

3. Ibid., p. 2.
4. Gerhard Finn, *Nichtstun ist Mord* (Bad Münstereifel: Westkreuz, 2000), p. 14.
5. "So etwas wie Feme," *Der Spiegel* (November 19, 1952), p. 13.
6. "Recommendations for [redacted]," DTLINEN 55, CIA CREST Archive, September 15, 1952, p. 2.
7. "Satzung der Kampfgruppe gegen Unmenschlichkeit e.V.," Berlin Nikolassee, DTLINEN-KGU, 1–70, p. 1.
8. Finn, *Nichtstun ist Mord*, p. 16.
9. Rainer Hildebrandt, "The Army Stalin Fears Most," *New Leader* 34, no. 38 (September 17, 1951), pp. 9–10.
10. "DTLINEN Project Renewal Request," DTLINEN-KGU 2-7, CIA CREST Archive, June 26, 1957, p. 2.
11. Finn, *Nichtstun ist Mord*, p. 33.
12. "Liquidation of DTLINEN Balloon Team and Termination of [redacted]," DTLINEN-KGU 2-106, CIA CREST Archive, February 9, 1960, p. 1.
13. "Später Werwolf," *Der Spiegel* (July 2, 1958), p. 35.
14. "Transmittal of Revised DTLINEN Project Outline," DTLINEN-KGU 1-66, CIA CREST Archive, January 10, 1955, p. 10.
15. Finn, *Nichtstun ist Mord*, p. 31.
16. "DTLINEN Project Renewal Request," DTLINEN-KGU 2-7, CIA CREST Archive, June 26, 1957, p. 3.
17. Ibid., p. 7.
18. Ibid., p. 4.
19. "Request for LCCASSOCK Termination," LCCASSOCK DEVELOPMENT AND PLANS 3-45, CIA CREST Archive, March 3, 1960, p. 5.
20. "LCCASSOCK/Request for Project Renewal," LCCASSOCK BASIC PAPERS AND FINANCIAL 1-14, CIA CREST Archive, April 8, 1957, p. 32.
21. "Division Project Clearance Sheet," DTLINEN-KGU 1-94, CIA CREST Archive, p. 5.
22. "Recommendations for [redacted]," DTLINEN 55, CIA CREST Archive, September 15, 1952, p. 5. See also DTLINEN 44.
23. "DTLINEN Audit Report, DIR 292211 SFRAN 9117," DTLINEN-KGU 1-46, CIA CREST Archive, December 4, 1952, p. 2.
24. "Recommendations for [redacted]," DTLINEN 55, CIA CREST Archive, September 15, 1952, p. 4.
25. "Dear Michael," DTLINEN 26, CIA CREST Archive, May 10, 1951, p. 2.
26. "DTLINEN 1954 Budget Requirements," DTLINEN-KGU 1–53, CIA CREST Archive, May 15, 1953.
27. "DTLINEN Audit Report," DTLINEN-KGU 1-46, CIA CREST Archive, December 4, 1952, p. 5.
28. "Project Outline," DTLINEN-KGU 1-94, CIA CREST Archive, August 29, 1956, p. 2.
29. See, for example, "CIS Intercept of NEWHAM/BLEY Conversation," BLEY, CURT 40, CIA CREST Archive, from November 23, 1955, 12:45 a.m.
30. "Psychological Asset—Propaganda," DTLINEN-KGU 1-37, CIA CREST Archive, undated, p. 1.

31. "Termination of CA Project DTLINEN," DTLINEN-KGU 1-98, CIA CREST Archive, undated.
32. "Transmittal of Revised DTLINEN Project Outline," DTLINEN-KGU 1-66, CIA CREST Archive, January 10, 1955, p. 8.

6. LC–Cassock, Inc.

1. Memo by the CIA Chief of Station Germany, "LCCASSOCK/Draft Project Outline," CIA CREST Archive, December 26, 1956, p. 2.
2. "LCCASSOCK Project Outline," LCCASSOCK 2-17, January 29, 1954, p. 7.
3. Memo by the CIA Chief of Station Germany, "LCCASSOCK/Draft Project Outline," CIA CREST Archive, December 26, 1956, p. 4.
4. "Project LCCASSOCK Re-Documentation," LCCASSOCK 2-28, CIA CREST Archive, October 16, 1956, p. 24.
5. The correct name of the interim agency was "Cramer Werbung," although the CIA often mistranscribed it. "LCCASSOCK/Request for Project Renewal," LCCASSOCK BASIC PAPERS AND FINANCIAL 1-14, CIA CREST Archive, April 8, 1957, p. 30.
6. "LCCASSOCK Draft Project Outline," LCCASSOCK BASIC PAPERS AND FINANCIAL 1-10, CIA CREST Archive, December 26, 1956, p. 2.
7. "LCCASSOCK 'Request for Project Approval'," MARBACH, KARL HEINZ 30, CIA CREST Archive, July 3, 1953, p. 5.
8. MARBACH, KARL HEINZ 34, CIA CREST Archive, p. 1.
9. MARBACH, KARL HEINZ 39, CIA CREST Archive, p. 5.
10. LCCASSOCK 2-29, CIA CREST Archive, October 16, 1956, p. 24.
11. LCCASSOCK 2-17, CIA CREST Archive, p. 7.
12. LCCASSOCK 2-23, CIA CREST Archive, October 20, 1954, p. 1.
13. MARBACH, KARL HEINZ 39, CIA CREST Archive, p. 3.
14. LCCASSOCK "Request for Project Approval," MARBACH, KARL HEINZ 30, CIA CREST Archive, July 3, 1953.
15. "LCCASSOCK Review," LCCASSOCK BASIC PAPERS AND FINANCIAL, vol. 2-29, CIA CREST Archive, October 19, 1956, p. 3.
16. "Project LCCASSOCK Re-Documentation," LCCASSOCK 2-28, October 16, 1956, CIA CREST Archive, p. 2.
17. LCCASSOCK BASIC PAPERS AND FINANCIAL, vol. 1-11, CIA CREST Archive, p. 18.
18. Ibid.
19. "LCCASSOCK Review," LCCASSOCK BASIC PAPERS AND FINANCIAL 2-29, CIA CREST Archive, October 19, 1956, p. 21.
20. "Project Renewal—LCCASSOCK," LCCASSOCK DEVELOPMENT AND PLANS 3-10, September 18, 1958, p. 1.
21. "RE: EGHA-3300, 2 Jan 1958," LCCASSOCK DEVELOPMENT AND PLANS 3-5, April 7, 1958, p. 3.
22. "LCCASSOCK/FY 1959 Project Renewal," LCCASSOCK DEVELOPMENT AND PLANS 3-10, CIA CREST Archive, September 18, 1958, pp. 2–3.
23. Ibid., p. 3.

24. "KGQW 31230 [et al. illegible]," LCCASSOCK BASIC PAPERS AND FINANCIAL 1-11, CIA CREST Archive, 21 February 21, 1957, p. 21.

25. Ibid.

26. *Schlagzeug* no. 7 (July 1959), p. 23, https://archive.org/details/1959-07-schlagzeug.

27. LCCASSOCK 3-9, CIA CREST Archive, p. 12.

28. Ibid., p. 15.

29. LCCASSOCK 3-49, CIA CREST Archive, p. 1, also LCCASSOCK 2-22, CIA CREST Archive, p. 1.

30. LCCASSOCK 3-25, CIA CREST Archive, p. 2.

31. "Stilvoll und behaglich," *Die Frau* 3, no. 1 (January 1, 1956), p. 12, https://archive.org/details/1956-die-frau.

32. LCCASSOCK BASIC PAPERS AND FINANCIAL 1-11, CIA CREST Archive, p. 13.

33. LCCASSOCK 2-38, CIA CREST Archive, April 18, 1957, p. 2.

34. LCCASSOCK 2-34, CIA CREST Archive, December 27, 1956, p. 2.

35. "HQS Traces on Karlheinz Marbach," MARBACH, KARL HEINZ 120, CIA CREST Archive, May 26, 1983, p. 2.

36. MARBACH, KARL HEINZ 74, CIA CREST Archive, pp. 1–4.

37. "Der Grosse Verrat. Moskau und der Antifaschismus" (Berlin: Äquator Verlag, May 1959), https://archive.org/details/1959-05-der-grosse-verrat.

38. LCCASSOCK 3-50, CIA CREST Archive, p. 1.

7. Faking Back

1. David S. Robarge, "Richard Helms: The Intelligence Professional Personified," Central Intelligence Agency Library, June 27, 2008.

2. Stephen Eric Bronner, *A Rumor About the Jews* (New York: St. Martin's Press, 2000), p. 76; Richard Landes and Steven T. Katz, *The Paranoid Apocalypse: A Hundred-Year Retrospective on the Protocols of the Elders of Zion* (New York: New York University Press, 2012).

3. Richard Helms, "Communist Forgeries," Committee on the Judiciary, U.S. Senate (Washington, DC: Government Printing Office, June 2, 1961), p. 18.

4. It is unlikely that the CIA had briefed the new Kennedy White House on operational details of programs that were in the process of liquidation as the new administration was settling in.

5. "CIA Says Forged Soviet Papers Attribute Many Plots to the U.S.," *The New York Times*, June 18, 1961, p. A8.

6. The original German is "aus einer unbedingt zuverlässigen Quelle," *Neues Deutschland*, February 15, 1957, p. 1; the full letter is on page 3.

7. Edwin Dale, "President Faces Dispute on Scope of Aid Programs," *The New York Times*, December 5, 1955, p. 1.

8. Quoted in CIA, "Sino-Soviet Bloc Propaganda Forgeries. 1 January 1957 to 1 July 1959," CIA-RDP78-02646R000300130001-0, March 1960, p. 19.

9. "Der Feind der arabischen Freiheit," *Neues Deutschland* 12, no. 60 (March 10, 1957), p. 3.

10. "National Security Council Report," NSC 5724, November 7, 1957, in *Foreign Relations of the United States, 1955–1957*, vol. XIX, p. 639.

11. United Nations Security Council, "Urgent Measures . . . ," S/3993, April 21, 1958 (original Russian).

12. The German headline was "Unzurechnungsfähige Piloten am Steuer der USA-Atombomber," *Neues Deutschland*, May 7, 1958, p. 1.

13. "U.S. Flier Crashes in Stolen Bomber," *The Washington Post*, June 14, 1958, p. C14.

14. George Greenfield, *A Smattering of Monsters: A Kind of Memoir* (London: Camden House, 1995), p. 135.

15. The full letter, although not in its original format, is reproduced in Murrey Marder, "Soviet Bares Note from 'U.S. Pilot' Planning to A-Bomb British Coast," *The Washington Post*, July 4, 1958, p. A1.

16. "Russians Reject 'Hoax' Confession," *The New York Times*, July 6, 1958, p. 18.

17. Murrey Marder, "Russians Release 2 More Letters Threatening A-Attack on Britain," *The Washington Post*, July 10, 1958, p. A1.

18. CIA, "Sino-Soviet Bloc Propaganda Forgeries," p. 39.

19. "Resume of OCB Luncheon Meeting," August 20, 1958, CIA-RDP80B01676R00 2700050020-8, p. 2.

20. "Deputies' Meeting," August 22, 1958, DM-657, CIA-RDP80B01676R002300230026-6, p. 1.

21. The full, completed 200-page study was declassified in 1999. CIA (office redacted), "Sino-Soviet Bloc Propaganda Forgeries, 1 January 1957 to 1 July 1959," March 1960, CIA-RDP78-02646R000300130001-0, initially classified as SECRET NOFORN/CONTINUED CONTROL, see pp. 35–37 for some of the details reproduced by Drummond.

22. CIA, "Sino-Soviet Bloc Propaganda Forgeries," p. 69.

23. Helms, "Communist Forgeries," p. 27.

24. In the vast majority of CIA documents, the names and often the offices that authorized plans are redacted. The documents cited here are exceptions and possibly redaction errors, which means that Helms's name is highly likely to be on many more documents. See "LCCASSOCK EE Division Subsidy Project," LCCASSOCK BASIC PAPERS AND FINANCIAL 2-50, CIA CREST Archive, July 12, 1957, p. 3. "Memorandum for Deputy Director (Plans)," DTLINEN-KGU 2-50, CIA CREST Archive, May 20, 1958, p. 1, as well as "Memorandum for Deputy Director (Plans)," DTLINEN-KGU 2-14, CIA CREST Archive, November 8, 1957, p. 1.

25. Thomas Powers, "The Rise and Fall of Richard Helms," *Rolling Stone*, December 16, 1976, p. 46.

8. Kampfverband

1. "Lange genug haben wir zugesehen, wie Ihr Euch in Elsaß-Lothringen frech weit und breit macht, in einem Lande, welches Ihr Euch nur durch ungerechte Verträge angeeignet habt." Reproduction in Miroslav Mares and Jakub Petlák, "Lange Schatten des Attentats in Straßburg im Jahr 1957," *Kriminalistik* 12 (2015), p. 735. For a sample leaflet, likely from 1958, see https://archive.org/details/1958-kampfverband.

2. "Eure schmutzigen Hände, die unsere Leute in Elsaß-Lothringen würgen und durch Erpressungen und Drohungen auf die Knie zwingen wollen, werden wir entzweischlagen." Reproduction in Mares and Petlák, "Lange Schatten des Attentats in Straßburg im Jahr 1957," p. 735.

3. "Streit um das Elsässer Deutsch," *Die Zeit*, April 24, 1958. Reproduction in Mares and Petlák, "Lange Schatten des Attentats in Straßburg im Jahr 1957," p. 737.

4. "Bomb Kills Wife of Frenchman," *The Washington Post*, May 18, 1957, p. A6.

5. The most detailed account of the story is Philippe Broussard, "'Opération Strasbourg,' 1957. Les secrets d'une bombe," *L'Express*, March 9, 2006, p. 76.

6. CIA, Untitled Document, Undated (around 1960), CIA-RDP78-00915R0012000 60034-5, Original Classification SECRET NOFORN/CONTINUED CONTROL, 23 pages, p. 13 in file (p. 62 in original pagination).

7. Bundeskriminalamt, "Kriminaltechnisches Gutachten," KT/U-M-Md 1302/59, September 10, 1959. Quoted in Mares and Petlák, "Lange Schatten des Attentats in Straßburg im Jahr 1957," p. 737.

8. CIA, "Internationally-Distributed Sino-Soviet Bloc Propaganda Forgeries, 1 January 1957 to 1 July 1959," Undated (around 1960), CIA-RDP78-00915R001200060042-6, Original Classification SECRET, 26 pages, p. 12.

9. Ladislav Bittman, *The Deception Game* (New York: Ballantine, 1972), p. 3.

10. CIA, Untitled Document, Undated (around 1960), CIA-RDP78-00915R0012000 60034-5, 23 pages, p. 13 in file (p. 62 in original pagination).

11. CIA, Untitled Document, Undated (around 1960), CIA-RDP78-00915R0012000 60034-5, 23 pages, p. 13 in file (p. 62 in original pagination).

12. "Communist Forgeries," Hearing Before the Subcommittee to Investigate the Administration of the Internal Security Act and Other Internal Security Laws of the Committee on the Judiciary, U.S. Senate, Testimony of Richard Helms, 87th Congress, 1st Session, June 2, 1961, p. 30.

13. "Zigarrenkistenattentat aus dem Kalten Krieg bleibt ungesühnt," *Frankfurter Allgemeine Zeitung*, April 3, 2013, p. 5.

14. Broussard, "'Opération Strasbourg,' 1957. Les secrets d'une bombe," p. 76.

15. Bittman, *The Deception Game*, pp. 3–4.

9. Red Swastikas

1. "Die Schändung der neuen Kölner Synagoge," *Frankfurter Allgemeine Zeitung*, December 28, 1959, p. 1.

2. "Zwischenfälle in Braunschweig und Offenbach," *Süddeutsche Zeitung*, December 31, 1959, p. 2. "In 5 Städten Hakenkreuze," *Neue Rhein Zeitung*, January 1, 1960, p. 1.

3. "'Hetze der besonderer Art' und Schmierereien von Hakenkreuzen," Präsidium der Volkspolizei (Eikemeier), 600229, LAB, C Rep 303, Nr. 41, shared by Jochen Staadt, personal archive.

4. "Hakenkreuze auch in London," *Süddeutsche Zeitung*, January 2–3, 1960, p. 2.

5. "Neue Hakenkreuzschmierereien in England," *Frankfurter Allgemeine Zeitung*, January 7, 1960, p. 4. See also "Schlag gegen Neo-Nazisten," *Kölner Stadtanzeiger*, January 6, 1960, p. 1.

6. "Anti-Jewish Signs, Swastikas Pop Up—Even in Israel," *Chicago Tribune*, January 18, 1960, pp. 1–8.

7. "Anti-Semitic Signs Appear in 8 States," *Chicago Tribune*, January 18, 1960, pp. 1–8; "Zwischenfälle und Gerichtsurteile," *Süddeutsche Zeitung*, January 14, 1960, pp. 1–2.

8. "Third Synagogue in City Is Defaced," *The New York Times*, January 4, 1960, p. 1.

9. "City Police Guard Seats of Worship," *The New York Times*, January 5, 1960, p. 1.

10. "Anti-Semitic Signs Appear in 8 States," *Chicago Tribune*, January 18, 1960, pp. 1–8.

11. Sebastian Haffner, "Bonn Hesitates in Nazi Fight," *The Observer*, January 10, 1960, p. 6.

12. "Note Israels an Bonn," *Süddeutsche Zeitung*, January 12, 1960, p. 1.

13. Irving Spiegel, "Jewish Unit Sees Nazi Resurgence," *The New York Times*, January 6, 1960, p. 3.

14. "Anti-Semitic Signs Appear in 8 States," *Chicago Tribune*, January 18, 1960, pp. 1–8.

15. "Thrash Swastika Thugs, Says Adenauer," *Empire News*, January 17, 1960, p. 1.

16. "50,000 Join in London Protest, March on W. German Embassy," *The Washington Post*, January 18, 1960, p. A7.

17. "Antideutsche Stimmung in England," *Süddeutsche Zeitung*, January 14, 1960, p. 1.

18. "The World: Bonn Reaction," *The New York Times*, January 10, 1960, p. E2.

19. "Antisemitismus beschäftigt die UNO," *Süddeutsche Zeitung*, January 18, 1960, p. 2.

20. "Ursachen der Schmiererei im Dunkel," *Süddeutsche Zeitung*, January 23–24, 1960, p. 2.

21. "Kirkpatrick befürchtet einen Rückfall in Deutschland," *Frankfurter Allgemeine Zeitung*, January 20, 1960, p. 4.

22. "Die antisemitischen und nazistischen Vorfälle. Weißbuch und Erklärung der Bundesregierung," *Bundesregierung* (Bonn: H. Köllen, 1960), https://archive.org/details/1960-weissbuch.

23. Ibid., p. 58. The reference to the BND comes from Franz-Josef Strauss, then the minister of defense. See "Ist die Schmier-Aktion gesteuert?" *Süddeutsche Zeitung*, January 20, 1960, p. 2.

24. "Die antisemitischen und nazistischen Vorfälle," p. 58.

25. Ibid., pp. 56–57.

26. "Germans Nab Red Leader of Nazi Students," *Chicago Tribune*, January 17, 1960, p. 1–8. It is unclear whether Schlottmann was actually involved in daubing swastikas; the German government's Weißbuch does not mention him by name.

27. "Allegedly" because Henry Maule, the journalist who covered this story, likely used Bernard Hutton as one of his sources, and Hutton is not reliable. See also Henry Maule, "Swastika Wave Laid to Reds," *Sunday News* 39, no. 38 (January 17, 1960), pp. 1, 2. The alleged memo is partly reproduced in Bernard Hutton (aka Joseph Heisler), *Danger from Moscow* (London: Spearman, Neville, 1960), pp. 158–60. See also "Caveat Lector," *Studies in Intelligence* 15, no. 3 (1961), pp. A35–37.

28. Henry Maule, "Report Reds Ordered Acts Against Jews," *Chicago Daily Tribune*, January 17, 1960, pp. 1, 3.

29. The seven intelligence professionals (or spies) who mentioned the swastika-daubing operations in various levels of detail are Bittman, Frolik, Rupert Sigl, Kalugin, Deriabin, Kondrashev, and Wolf. An eighth KGB defector, Oleg Gordievski, also described the operation, including Agayants's test run in a Russian village, but his account seems to rely on Barron.

30. Евгений Максимович Примаков, *Очерки истории российской внешней разведки, Том 5*, (Москва: Международные отношения, 1997), pp. 461–70.

31. Tennent Bagley and Sergei Kondrashev, *Spymaster* (New York: Skyhorse, 2013), p. 167.

32. Christopher Andrew and Oleg Gordievsky, *KGB: The Inside Story* (New York: Harper-Collins, 1990), p. 405.

33. "Israel wird ausradiert," *Der Spiegel* 51 (December 18, 1957), p. 35.

34. "Defendant Berates Jews in Key W. German Trial," *The Washington Post*, April 10, 1958, p. A7; and "Jews' Foe Sentenced," *The New York Times*, April 12, 1958, p. 2.

35. John Barron, *KGB* (New York: Readers Digest, 1974), p. 234.

36. Ibid., p. 236. Andrew and Gordievski, a KGB defector and an eminent British chronicler of Russian intelligence, repeat and appear to corroborate Barron's account of this story, but don't seem to add any fresh detail on their own. See *KGB: The Inside Story*, p. 463.

37. Peter Deriabin and Frank Gibney, *The Secret World* (New York: Ballantine, 1959, 1987), p. 340.

38. Bagley and Kondrashev, *Spymaster*, p. 184.

39. Oleg Kalugin, *Spymaster* (New York: Basic Books, 2009), p. 54.

40. Oleg Kalugin, interview with Thomas Rid, June 5, 2017, Washington, DC, audio at https://archive.org/details/kalugin-on-antisemitic-operations.

41. Barron, *KGB*, p. 236.

42. The original quote: "ob gerade ich als Sohne eines jüdischen Vaters der Richtige gewesen wäre, die Schändung jüdischer Friedhöfe oder andere neonazistische Schanddaten zuzulassen oder zu initiieren," Markus Wolf, *Spionagechef im geheimen Krieg* (München: Econ, 1998), p. 354. This quote is missing from the English original of Wolf's memoirs; the German edition of Wolf's memoir appeared after the English original, but is more extensive.

43. Примаков, *Очерки истории российской внешней разведки, Том 5*, p. 461.

44. Ibid.

10. Racial Engineering

1. Oleg Kalugin, *Spymaster* (New York: Basic Books, 2009), p. 54. Kalugin's book was originally published in 1994.

2. Ibid., p. 55.

3. Ibid.

4. Benin was then known as the Republic of Dahomey. "Racist Hate Note Sent to UN Aides," *The New York Times*, November 29, 1960, p. 4.

5. "White America Rejects a Bastardized United Nations," Soviet bloc forgery, reproduced in "Communist Forgeries," Hearing Before the Subcommittee to Investigate the Administration of the Internal Security Act and Other Internal Security Laws of the Committee on the Judiciary, U.S. Senate, Testimony of Richard Helms, 87th Congress, 1st Session, June 2, 1961, p. 32.

6. "FBI Probes Mailed Race Threats at UN," *The Washington Post*, November 28, 1960, p. A6.

7. "Communist Forgeries," Hearing Before the Subcommittee to Investigate the Administration of the Internal Security Act and Other Internal Security Laws of the Committee on the Judiciary, U.S. Senate, Testimony of Richard Helms, 87th Congress, 1st Session, June 2, 1961, p. 30.

8. Ladislav Bittman, *The Deception Game* (New York: Ballantine, 1972), p. 91.

9. "To Our Dear Friends," KGB forgery, p. 3. Reproduced in full in "Communist Forgeries," Hearing Before the Subcommittee to Investigate the Administration of the Internal Security Act and Other Internal Security Laws of the Committee on the Judiciary, U.S. Senate, Testimony of Richard Helms, 87th Congress, 1st Session, June 2, 1961, pp. 46–52.

10. "Klansman Found Guilty in Mutilation," *The Washington Post and Times Herald*, November 1, 1957, p. A3.

11. The KGB did not mention that Aaron was a judge and that he was castrated with a razor blade; nor that Cherry was also accused of beatings along with three other officers. See "No Indictments Found in Georgia Beatings," *The Washington Post and Times Herald*, August 9, 1958, p. A7.

12. Julius Duscha, "School Ousts 9 Negroes; Students Vote to Strike," *The Washington Post*, March 3, 1960, p. D5.

13. Advertisement, *The Washington Post*, January 17, 1960, p. E5.

14. See statement of purpose, *The Minority of One*, December 1961, p. 15.

15. M. S. Arnoni, "A Manifesto of Belief in Man," *The Minority of One*, vol. 7–8, 1965, p. xlix.

16. See, for instance, "Of What I Am Ashamed," *The Minority of One* 4, no. 3 (28) (March 1962), p. 16.

17. Mordecai Chertoff, *The New Left and the Jews*, p. 280.

18. Oleg Kalugin, interview with Thomas Rid, Washington, DC, June 5, 2017.

19. Kalugin, *Spymaster*, pp. 55–56.

20. It is likely, but not certain, that the KGB funded the ad; Arnoni is not explicitly listed as the sponsor, but half a dozen signatories were also on the board of *The Minority of One*. Display ad, *The New York Times*, April 3, 1963, p. 50.

11. *Dezinformatsiya* Rising

1. The Russian designation was *Otdel D* (Отдел Д) for the Department, and *Sluzhba A* (Служба А) for the Service. See Евгений Максимович Примаков, *Очерки истории российской внешней разведки, Том 5, 1945–1965 годы* (Москва: Международные отношения, 1997), p. 13.

2. Ladislav Bittman, *The KGB and Soviet Disinformation: An Insider's View* (Washington, DC: Pergamon-Brassey's, 1985), p. 39.

3. CIA, "The Soviet and Communist Bloc Defamation Campaign," CIA-RDP67B00446 R000500070009-1, September 1965, p. 1.

4. Ibid.

5. Ladislav Bittman, *The Deception Game* (New York: Ballantine, 1972), p. 245.

6. "Testimony of Lawrence Britt" (pseudonym), Hearing, Committee on the Judiciary, U.S. Senate (Washington, DC: Government Printing Office, May 5, 1971).

7. House of Representatives Permanent Select Committee on Intelligence, Subcommittee on Oversight, "Soviet Covert Action (the Forgery Offensive)," February 6, 1980, 96th Congress, 2nd session, p. 34.

8. Richard Sandomir, "Lawrence Martin-Bittman, 87, Cold War Master of 'Dirty Tricks,' Is Dead," *The New York Times*, September 21, 2018, p. A25.

9. Bittman, *The Deception Game*, p. 18.

10. Ibid.

11. CIA, "The Soviet and Communist Bloc Defamation Campaign," CIA-RDP67B00446 R000500070009-1, September 1965, p. 2.

12. "Soviet Defamation Campaign Against DCI, the CIA, and the Intelligence Community," CIA-RDP74-00115R000300020054-2, November 20, 1961, p. 4.

13. CIA, "The Soviet and Communist Bloc Defamation Campaign," CIA-RDP67B00446 R000500070011-8, September 1965, pp. 8–9.

14. Alma Fryxell, "Psywar by Forgery," *Studies in Intelligence* 5 (Winter 1961), p. 25. The study was initially classified secret, but released on September 18, 1995.

15. Ibid.

16. Georg Bönisch and Klaus Wiegrefe, "Ein Abgrund von Lüge," *Der Spiegel* 38 (September 17, 2012), p. 65.

17. Germany never came to terms with the role of disinformation in the affair. *Der Spiegel*, in a fifty-year-anniversary story on the affair, simply ignored the defector accounts, focusing—ironically—on press freedom instead.

18. Graham Turbiville, "Intervention in Yugoslavia," *Strategic Review* 5, no. 1 (Winter 1977), p. 69.

19. Brian Crozier, *The KGB Lawsuits* (London: Claridge Press, 1995), p. 7.

20. The column was widely distributed in the United States and published under different titles. *The Boston Globe* was first, on January 15. The title here is from William Buckley Jr., "The Vindication of Strauss," *National Review*, February 8, 1980, pp. 176–77.

21. Crozier, *The KGB Lawsuits*, p. xiii.

22. "Herbert Wehner 70," *Der Spiegel* 28 (July 5, 1976), p. 49.

23. Crozier, *The KGB Lawsuits*, p. 7. See also Ilya Dzhirkvelov, *Secret Servant* (New York: Harper & Row, 1987), p. 292.

24. Dzhirkvelov, *Secret Servant*, p. 299.

25. Crozier, *The KGB Lawsuits*, p. 44.

26. Ibid.

27. Dzhirkvelov, *Secret Servant*, p. 303.

28. Ibid., p. 301.

29. Ibid., p. 153.

30. Crozier, *The KGB Lawsuits*, p. 7.

31. Oleg Gordievsky, "The Greater Truth" (book review), *The Spectator*, August 26, 1995, p. 25.

32. "Une lettre de l'ambassade de Chine à Berne à l'hebdomadaire 'France Nouvelle,'" *Le Monde*, March 9, 1963.

33. Victor Zorza, "West Plays a Russian Trick," *The Guardian*, March 13, 1963, p. 7.

34. "L'ambassade de Chine a Berne dément avoir adressé une lettre à 'France nouvelle,'" *Le Monde*, March 21, 1963.

35. "More Nazi Printing Gear Is Found in Austrian Lake," *The New York Times*, November 26, 1963, p. 16.

36. "Divers' Search of Austrian Lake Deflates Wild Tales of Nazi Gold," *The New York Times*, December 8, 1963, p. 167.

37. Ladislav Bittman (Brychta) et al, "Návrh na aktivní opatření 'NEPTUN,'" May 5, 1964, V-Neptun, MTH 21998, 90039, 6, pp. 1–9, Ministerstvo vnitra, Archiv bezpečnostních složek, Prague, https://archive.org/details/stb-neptun-90039.

38. Ladislav Bittman (Brychta) et al, "Návrh na aktivní opatřeni 'NEPTUN'," May 5, 1964, V-Neptun, MTH 21998, 90039, 6, pp. 1–9, Ministerstvo vnitra, Archiv bezpečnostních složek, Prague, see also Ladislav Bittman (Brychta), "Věc: Záznam o provedení prvého potapěčskeho průskumu dna Čertova a Černého jezera na Šumavě," May 3, 1964, V-Neptun, MTH 21998, 90039, 8, pp. 53–55.

39. Ladislav Bittman (aka Brychta), "Věc: Záznam z proedení I. etapy akce 'V'," June 22, 1964, V-Neptun, MTH 21998, 90039, 22, pp. 86–87, Ministerstvo vnitra, Archiv bezpečnostních složek, Prague. Stejskal was "Borecký."

40. "Gesundes Volksempfinden," *Der Spiegel* 11 (March 10, 1965), pp. 31–44.

41. Bittman, *The Deception Game*, p. 46.

42. For more details on the counterintelligence ruse, see Klaus Haupt, "Geheimnis des Schwarzen Sees ist gelüftet," *Neues Deutschland* 19, no. 257 (September 17, 1964), p. 7.

43. "Naziarchive im Schwarzen See," *Neue Zeit* 165 (July 17, 1964), p. 2.

44. "Zpráva o otevření čtyř beden a jedné kovové krabice z Černého jezera," July 18, 1964, V-Neptun, MTH 21998, 90039-011, 1, pp. 1–4, Ministerstvo vnitra, Archiv bezpečnostních složek, Prague, https://archive.org/details/stb-neptun-90039-011.

45. Bittman, *The Deception Game*, p. 51.

46. StB's international press clippings of the event are at V-Neptun, MTH 21996, 90039-105, pp. 1–86, Ministerstvo vnitra, Archiv bezpečnostních složek, Prague, https://archive.org/details/stb-neptun-90039-105.

47. "Naziarchive im Schwarzen See."

48. Thomas Rid's automatic page count of the full cache of German documents in StB's NEPTUN case files. The precise number is 30,622. A smaller, unknown number was from Czechoslovak archives. The KGB-StB transfer memorandum is Воробьев (Colonel), "АКТ," September 10, 1964, V-Neptun, MTH 21998, 90039-013, 52, pp. 130–38, Ministerstvo vnitra, Archiv bezpečnostních složek, Prague, https://archive.org/details/stb-neptun-90039-013/page/n143.

49. "Dokumente klagen Nazi-Verbrechen an," *Berliner Zeitung*, August 22, 1965, p. 3.

50. "Découverte d'importants documents du IIIe Reich en Tchécoslovaquie," *Le Monde*, September 17, 1964; and "Les documents allemands trouvés en Tchécoslovaquie apporteraient d'importants éclaircissements sur l'histoire du nazisme," *Le Monde*, September 30, 1964.

51. Josef Houska, "Akce 'NEPTUN'—její průběh a dosavadní výsledky," March 19, 1965, V-Neptun, MTH 21998, 90039, 3, pp. 3–10, Ministerstvo vnitra, Archiv bezpečnostních složek, Prague. See also Stejskal's remarks about sub-measure ANABELA, in Jiří Stejskal (aka Borecký), "Zpráva o činnosti po linii 8. odboru za I. pololetí 1965," June 30, 1965, 8. odbor, I. správy, Čj.: A/1-00 333/80-65, Ministerstvo vnitra, Archiv bezpečnostních složek, Prague, https://archive.org/details/1965-06-30-stb-8-report/page/n13.

52. Josef Houska, "Akce 'NEPTUN'—její průběh a dosavadní výsledky," March 19, 1965, V-Neptun, MTH 21998, 90039, 3, pp. 3–10, Ministerstvo vnitra, Archiv bezpečnostních složek, Prague.

53. Александр Сахаровский, "НАЧАЛЬНИКУ 1 ГЛАВНОГО УПРАВЛЕНИЯ МИНИСТЕРСТВА ВНУТРЕННИХ ДьЛ ЧССР," September 21, 1965, V-Neptun, MTH 21998, 90039-015, 91, pp. 194–95, Ministerstvo vnitra, Archiv

bezpečnostních složek, Prague, https://archive.org/details/stb-neptun-90039-015
/page/n243.

54. "Verjährung? Gesundes Volksempfinden," *Der Spiegel* 11 (March 10, 1965), p. 43.
55. Bittman, *The Deception Game*, p. 69.
56. Ladislav Bittman, interview with Thomas Rid, Rockport, Mass., March 25, 2017.
57. Bittman, *The KGB and Soviet Disinformation*, p. 70.

12. The Book War

1. Leonard McCoy, "The Penkovskiy Case," CIA, CREST DOC_0006183130, classified as SECRET/NOFORN, released on September 10, 2014, p. 4.
2. "Meeting #13," London, May 3, 1961, CIA, CREST DOC_0000012401, p. 1.
3. McCoy, "The Penkovskiy Case," p. 3.
4. Ibid., pp. 1–2.
5. Richard Helms, "Possible Developments in the Trials of Oleg Penkovskiy and Greville Wynne," Memorandum for Director of Central Intelligence, CIA DOC_0000012374, May 3, 1963, attachment, p. 2.
6. Ibid.
7. "İlim adamı olarak gösterilen istihbarat Albayı," *Cumhuriyet* 40, 13923, May 10, 1963, p. 1, 5, https://archive.org/details/1963-05-10-cumhuriyet.
8. Stephen Rosenfeld, "Convicted Penkovsky Had All Earmarks of a Model Spy," *The New York Times*, May 16, 1963, p. C5.
9. Oleg Penkovsky, *The Penkovsky Papers* (New York: Doubleday, 1965), p. 44.
10. Ibid., p. 64.
11. Frank Gibney, "How Russian Agents Communicate with Spies in the U.S.," *The Washington Post*, November 15, 1965, p. A23.
12. Frank Gibney, "Immorality of Russian Elite Disgusted Penkovsky," *The Washington Post*, November 7, 1965, p. A4.
13. Penkovsky, *The Penkovsky Papers*, p. 45.
14. See the review of *The Russia House* by Francis Wheen, "The Traitor Who Saved the World," *Mail on Sunday*, August 18, 2013, p. 44.
15. "Soviet Foreign Ministry Protests Publication of Penkovsky Papers," *The Washington Post*, November 14, 1965, p. A1.
16. "Russians Protest Penkovsky Papers," *The New York Times*, November 15, 1965, p. A3. See *Congressional Record*, Senate, January 14, 1966, p. 260.
17. Victor Zorza, "Soviet Expert Thinks 'Penkovsky Papers' Are a Forgery," *The Washington Post*, November 15, 1965, p. A22.
18. Victor Zorza, "Usage in 'Penkovsky' Said to Prove Forgery," *The Washington Post*, November 16, 1965, highlighted clipping published as CIA-RDP75-00149R000600250029-1, approved for release July 26, 2007.
19. See National Archives and Records Administration, RG 59, Central Files 1964–66, POL 29 U.S.S.R. "Memorandum of Conversation," Confidential, drafted and initialed by Llewellyn E. Thompson, approved in S/AL on November 18, 1965.
20. "Penkovskiy Memoirs," CIA, October 4, 1962, ESDN (CREST): 0000012424, approved for release February 2, 1992.

21. David Robarge, "(U) DCI John McCone and the Assassination of President John F. Kennedy," *Studies in Intelligence* 57, no. 3 (September 2013), p. 3.

22. "Concerning Penkovsiy Memoirs," CIA, May 1, 1963, ESDN (CREST) 0000012426, release date February 2, 1992, p. 1.

23. Gibney told the story in a different way. "In no sense of the word were the papers handed to me as part of some behind-the-scenes CIA publishing project or plot. Quite to the contrary, it was I who got wind of their existence and managed to pry the papers out of the agency for use as a book." See Adam Bernstein, "Frank Gibney, 81," *The Washington Post*, April 13, 2006.

24. United States Senate Select Committee to Study Governmental Operations with respect to Intelligence Activities, "Foreign and Military Intelligence," Book 1 (Washington, DC: Government Printing Office, 1976), p. 453.

25. Stephen Rosenfeld, "An Ex-Moscow Correspondent's CIA Footnote," *The Washington Post*, April 30, 1976, p. A25.

26. David Murphy, "Request for Approval to Publish the Penkovskiy Memoirs," CIA, November 6, 1964, ESDN (CREST): 0000012379, approved for release March 31, 1992.

27. Ibid., p. 2.

28. Julius Mader, *Who's Who in CIA* (East Berlin: Julius Mader, 1968), p. 8 (quoted from the German text).

29. Siegfried Wieczorrek, "'Liebesgrüße' aus Berlin," *Neues Deutschland*, July 10, 1968, p. 6.

30. Peter Worthington, "'Who's Who' in CIA Latest Red Spy Book," *Los Angeles Times*, December 9, 1968, p. 6.

31. "'Who's Who in CIA' Sells Out," *The Washington Post*, November 25, 1968, p. A2.

32. "DIR 554985Y," TPMURILLO, vol. 2, no. 51, CIA CREST Archive, July 5, 1974, p. 2.

33. Anonymous, "Intelligence in Recent Public Literature," CIA Historical Review Program, July 2, 1996.

34. See, for example, Rudolf Rothe, "Who's Who in Dr. Maders CIA?" *Deutschland-Archiv* 3, no. 9 (September 1970), pp. 936–38.

35. House of Representatives Permanent Select Committee on Intelligence, Subcommittee on Oversight, "Soviet Covert Action (the Forgery Offensive)," February 6, 1980, 96th Congress, 2nd session, p. 58.

36. Ladislav Bittman, *The KGB and Soviet Disinformation: An Insider's View* (Washington, DC: Pergamon-Brassey's, 1985), p. 191.

37. MfS-Kaderakte Julius Mader, BStU, MfS, KS 25335/90, quoted in Roger Engelmann, Frank Joestel, *Die Zentrale Auswertungs-und Informationsgruppe* (MfS-Handbuch) (Berlin: BStU, 2009), p. 50.

38. Oberstleutnant Halle, Leiter, Abteilung Agitation, to Minister, April 19, 1961, BStU, ZA, MfS-ZAIG, doc. nr. 16380, 538, quoted in Paul Maddrell, "What We Have Discovered About the Cold War Is What We Already Knew: Julius Mader and the Western Secret Services During the Cold War," *Cold War History* 5, no. 2 (2005), p. 240.

39. "Beurteilung des Genossen Major Julius Mader," June 1989, ZAIG Bereich 6, BStU, ZA, MfS-ZAIG, doc. nr. 16380, 189–90, quoted in Maddrell, "What We Have Discovered About the Cold War Is What We Already Knew," p. 240.

13. Operations Plan 10-1

1. An April 1967 joint Stasi-KGB-memo discusses STORM as "measures" focused on military policy to "sharpen contradictions within NATO," but does not explicitly mention operational details. It is highly likely, but not certain, that the OPLAN 10-1 campaign described here was part of STORM. See "Protokoll über Verhandlungen zwischen Vertretern des MfS der DDR und des KfS beim Ministerrat der UdSSR über gemeinsame aktive Maßnahmen für das Jahr 1967," MfS, BStU, ZA, SdM, 1465 (Moscow, April 14, 1967), 134–47, p. 11, https://archive.org/details/1967-04-mfs-kgb.
2. Richard Helms, "Point of Contact for War Games," CIA Clandestine Services, AE-DEPOT, vol. 4, no. 2 (October 18, 1962).
3. James Stejskal, *Special Forces Berlin* (Philadelphia: Casemate, 2017), pp. 26–27.
4. "Nr. 10–1," *Der Spiegel* 37 (September 8, 1969), pp. 97–99.
5. Ibid.
6. Stejskal, *Special Forces Berlin*, p. 26.
7. "CIA Global War Plan for Clandestine Operations. Tab C to Appendix 1 to Annex A. Concept of CIA Unconventional Warfare Operations in Active Theaters of War," undated, CIA, AEDEPOT, vol. 4, no. 27.
8. "Dette kan skje her!," *Orientering* 15, no. 45 (December 16, 1967), cover and p. 8, https://archive.org/details/1967-12-orientering.
9. On *Paese Sera*'s Soviet sympathies, see Christopher Andrew and Vasili Mitrokhin, *The Sword and the Shield* (New York: Basic Books, 1999), p. 300.
10. "Geheime Notstandshilfe," *Konkret*, March 3, 1968, pp. 48–49, https://archive.org/details/1968-03-03-konkret.
11. "Top Secret: US Occupation Plan," *Peace News* 1656, March 22, 1968, pp. 1, 12, https://archive.org/details/1968-03-22-peace-news.
12. State 127143, R 082247Z Mar 68, CIA-RDP71B00364R000200110044-6.
13. "Trauerfeier für Wendland," *Frankfurter Allgemeine Zeitung*, October 12, 1968, p. 3.
14. "Der Fall Lüdke beschäftigt den Bundestag," *Frankfurter Allgemeine Zeitung*, October 23, 1968, p. 4.
15. Pilippe de Vosjoli, "Scenario of Spies and 'Suicide,'" *Life* 53, no. 24 (December 13, 1968), pp. 26–31.
16. James Angleton, letter to Cecil [unnamed], CIA XAE-06237, 100-2-103, March 22, 1974.
17. Thomas Johnson, "American Cryptology During the Cold War," vol. II (Fort Meade: National Security Agency, Center for Cryptologic History, 1995), p. 412.
18. "Jeden Tag im Knast zahle ich zurück," see "Nr. 10-1," *Der Spiegel* 37 (September 8, 1969), pp. 97–99.
19. Ibid.
20. KGB, *Holocaust Again for Europe* (London: Information Books, 1980), p. 104, https://archive.org/details/1980-kgb-holocaust-again (unpaginated, page starts with "TOP SECRET d. Paragraph 2").
21. Quoted in "Nr. 10-1," p. 97 (translated into German, translated back to English here).
22. "Allies Hunt Mailer of Secret War Plan," *The Washington Post*, August 27, 1969, p. A24.

23. Reproduced with ellipses (. . .). "Allies Hunt Mailer of Secret War Plan," *The Washington Post*, August 27, 1969, p. A24.

24. An additional, partly overlapping section of the letter is quoted in Dan van der Vat, "Alleged-Secret Documents Published: 'U.S. to Hand Out H-bombs,'" *The Times*, July 5, 1969, p. 8.

25. Quoted in "Nr. 10-1," p. 99.

26. "Zweifel and den Bonner Selbstmorden," *Frankfurter Allgemeine Zeitung*, December 12, 1968, p. 6.

27. Quoted in "Nr. 10-1," p. 99.

28. "Seduti sulla polveriera atomica," *ABC* 10, no. 27 (July 4, 1969), pp. 10–12, https://archive.org/details/1969-07-04-abc.

29. Kevin McGrath, "Spain: New Facts of US Military Take-Over Plan," *Peace News* 1721, June 20, 1969, p. 1, https://archive.org/details/1969-06-20-peace-news.

30. Dan van der Vat, "Alleged-Secret Documents Published: 'U.S. to Hand Out H-bombs,'" p. 8.

31. Bob Overy, "Top Secret US Plan," *Peace News* 1723, July 4, 1969, pp. 1, 4, https://archive.org/details/1969-07-04-peace-news.

32. "Nuclear Arms for Guerrillas?—A Frightening Document," *Sanity* 835, July 1969, p. 1, https://archive.org/details/1969-07-sanity.

33. "OPLAN NR 1-10" [*sic*] *Ramparts* 8, no. 4 (October 1969), p. 7.

34. John Barron, *KGB* (New York: Reader's Digest, 1974), p. 214.

35. Ibid., p. 228.

36. *Der Spiegel*'s sources did not know that Igor Agayants had died the previous year, and wrongly identified him as head of Service A. "Nr. 10-1," pp. 97–99.

37. "Im Ernstfall meutern?" *Stern* 4 (January 13, 1970), pp. 116–17.

38. Such targeting details were so highly classified that it is probably still impossible to prove or disprove the veracity of these details. Given the low quality of some of the forgeries added to the Johnson cache, it is likely that the target lists are accurate. The author would like to thank Alex Wellerstein and Martin Pfeiffer for their responses. See @wellerstein, "I checked the target numbers," January 15, 2019, https://web.archive.org/web/20190117230051/https:/twitter.com/wellerstein/status/1085375953339965441.

39. Dan Morgan, "Secret Nuclear Plan Outdated, Germans Say," *The Washington Post*, January 29, 1970, p. A24.

40. The four-part series was "Verrat per Post," *Stern* 35 (August 31, 1969), p. 154; "Partisanenkrieg auf deutschem Boden," *Stern* 37 (September 14, 1969); "Atombomben auf Kiel," *Stern* 6 (January 27, 1970), pp. 170–71; "Rhein und Main in Flammen," *Stern* 7 (February 3, 1970), on OPLAN 10-1.

41. See William E. Knepper, lecture before the Chicago Council on Foreign Relations, May 30, 1984. Printed in *Current Policy*, no. 595 (Washington, DC: Department of State, May 30, 1984).

14. The X

1. Horst Kopp, former officer in Department HVA/X/3, Ministry of State Security, Berlin, interview with Thomas Rid, Kyritz, May 4, 2017.

2. Günter Bohnsack and Herbert Brehmer, *Auftrag Irreführung* (Hamburg: Carlsen, 1992), p. 96.

3. Ibid., p. 26.

4. Ibid., p. 24.

5. Generalbundesanwalt, "Lfd. Nr. 4: Die Abteilung X HVA—Aktive Maßnahmen (Verfahren gegen Wagenbreth u.a.)," p. 497, in Klaus Marxen und Gerhard Werle, *Strajustiz und DDR-Unrecht, Band 4/1 Spionage* (Berlin: De Gruyter, 2004), p. 5 (p. 464), https://archive.org/details/1993-wagenbreth.

6. Ibid., pp. 464, 466.

7. Ibid., p. 54 (p. 476).

8. The source for this dialogue is Günter Bohnsack, who likely had access to some form of meeting protocol that may not have included personal names. Bohnsack wrongly identifies the head of Service A as "Ivanov" (who became head only in 1976) and gets the location and other details wrong. Günter Bohnsack, *Hauptverwaltung Aufklärung. Die Legende stirbt* (Berlin: Edition Ost, 1997), p. 34. See also "АГАЯНЦ Иван Иванович," in Н. В. Петров, *Кто руководил органами госбезопасности 1941–1954* (Moscow: Memorial, 2010), pp. 138–39.

9. See organigram in "Häufig zum Tee," *Der Spiegel* 30 (July 22, 1991), pp. 57–58.

10. Bundesministerium des Innern, *Verfassungsschutzbericht 1981*, Bonn, p. 142.

11. Günter Wernicke, "Zur Genesis der Ostermarschbewegung," *Pax Report* 3 (1997), p. 4.

12. "Protokoll über Verhandlungen zwischen Vertretern des MfS der DDR und des KfS beim Ministerrat der UdSSR über gemeinsame aktive Maßnahmen für das Jahr 1967," MfS, BStU, ZA, SdM, 1465, 134–47, April 14, 1967, Moscow, p. 2.

13. Ibid., p. 4.

14. Ibid., p. 6.

15. Ibid., p. 11.

16. Ibid., p. 7.

17. Ibid.

18. The advisor's name was Rudchenko. No record of this officer appears to exist in public sources. "Protokoll über Verhandlungen zwischen Vertretern des MfS der DDR und des KfS beim Ministerrat der UdSSR über gemeinsame aktive Maßnahmen für das Jahr 1967," p. 8.

19. Markus Wolf, "Schreiben an Genossen Minister Mielke betr. Maßnahmen zur Entlarvung der westdeutschen A-, B-und C-Waffen-Rüstung," August 22, 1968, BStU, ZA, MfS ZAIG 10628, Bl. 7–11, quoted in Erhard Geißler, "Biowaffen für die Bundeswehr?," *Zeitschrift des Forschungsverbundes SED-Staat* (ZdF) 18 (2005), 72–103, pp. 83–86.

20. "German Physicist Goes Back to East," *The New York Times*, October 1, 1968, p. 6.

21. "Aktuelle Kamera," DDR-Fernsehen, November 23, 1968, 7:30 p.m., broadcast not archived.

22. "German Scientist Defects to East," *The New York Times*, November 24, 1968, p. 13.

23. Ibid.

24. Only two, *Bild* and *Frankfurter Allgemeine*, did not credulously report the scientist's accusations; see Otto Köhler, "Anderslautendes Zurückweisen!" *Der Spiegel*, December 2, 1968, p. 216.

25. "Defector Accuses Bonn of Studying Germ Warfare," *The Washington Post*, December 7, 1968, p. A14.

26. Günter Schabowski, "Ich konnte nicht länger schweigen," *Neues Deutschland*, December 28, 1968, p. 6.

27. Ralph Blumenthal, "Three West German Scientists Leave Jobs and Return to East," *The New York Times*, January 5, 1969, p. 2.

28. "West German Says Bonn Works Toward A-Weapons," *Christian Science Monitor*, December 1968, p. 17.

29. "Drei Bonner Wege zu Kernwaffen," *Berliner Zeitung* 25 (January 17, 1969), p. 7.

30. "Bonn bereitet Giftkrieg vor," Berlin: Staatsverlag der Deutschen Demokratischen Republik, 1969; see also "Bonner Griff auch nach B-und C-Waffen," *Neues Deutschland* 24, no. 207 (July 29, 1969), p. 1.

31. "Bericht über die Planungsarbeiten auf dem Gebiet der ABC-Kriegführung," Bundesminister der Verteidigung, Az 31-05-05, August 6, 1964, Bundesarchiv Militärarchiv Freiburg BH2/1584, https://archive.org/details/1964-heer-chemical.

32. Joachim Käppner, "Bundeswehr plante Chemiewaffen-Einsatz," *Süddeutsche Zeitung*, May 3, 2018.

33. Bericht des Leiters der HV A über die Erfüllung der politisch-operativen Verpflichtungen der II. Etappe der Vorbereitung des 20. Jahrestages der Deutschen Demokratischen Republik vom 18. 3. 1969; BStU, ZA, SdM 1474, Bl. 26. Quoted in Hubertus Knabe, *Die unterwanderte Republik* (Berlin: Propyläen, 1999), p. 242.

34. Werner Stiller, *Im Zentrum der Spionage* (Mainz: v. Hase & Koehler Verlag, 1986).

35. Bundesministerium des Innern, *Verfassungsschutzbericht 1981*, Bonn, 1982, p. 142.

36. Christopher Nehring, *Die Zusammenarbeit der DDR-Auslandsaufklärung mit der Aufklärung der Volksrepublik Bulgarien. Regionalfilialen des KGB?* (Heidelberg: University of Heidelberg, 2016), p. 214.

37. "European Neo-Fascist Youth Congress," *Patterns of Prejudice* 65 (1972), pp. 18–24.

38. *Mut*, December 1971, as translated on a flyer distributed by the National Youth Alliance; see "National Youth Alliance," FBI New York, 157-3447, 1972.

39. "Справка относно разговорите, проведени с ръководството на отдела за АМ при Разузнавателното управление на МДС-ГДР, София," June 20, 1972, ДЪРЖАВНА СИГУРНОСТ И ЩАЗИ, КРДОПБГДСРСБНА-Р, f. 9, 2, 914, pp. 28–46, COMDOS Archive, Sofia, 2014, p. 6.

40. Ibid.

41. Ibid.

42. Ibid.

43. Ibid., p. 7.

44. Ibid.

45. Nehring, *Die Zusammenarbeit der DDR-Auslandsaufklärung mit der Aufklärung der Volksrepublik Bulgarien*, pp. 213–14.

46. "Nicht mit Gewalt," *Der Spiegel* 44 (October 26, 1970), p. 30.

47. "Man kann ja nicht in jeden reingucken," *Der Spiegel* 11 (March 6, 1972), pp. 19–24.

48. "Die sind ja alle so mißtrauisch," *Der Spiegel* 23 (June 4, 1973), pp. 24–29.

49. Wagner, quoted in *Deutscher Bundestag*, 7. Wahlperiode, 43. Sitzung, June 15, 1973, p. 2416.

50. Markus Wolf, *Spionagechef im geheimen Krieg* (München: Econ, 1998), p. 261.

51. Andreas Grau, "Auf der Suche nach den fehlenden Stimmen 1972," *Historisch-Politische Mitteilungen*, Archiv für Christlich-Demokratische Politik, Böhlau Verlag Köln, Nr. 16, December 30, 2009, p. 16.

52. "CSU-Spion enttarnt," *Der Spiegel* 48 (November 27, 2000), p. 17.

53. "Name: Wagner," BStU, MfS, HVA, Department X/3, F16 card, XV/6985/75, 8. February 1965, https://archive.org/details/1965-hva-wagner-f16.

54. Horst Kopp, *Der Desinformant* (Berlin: Das Neue Berlin, 2016), pp. 14, 16.

55. Helmut Müller-Enbergs, "Die inoffiziellen Mitarbeiter," in *Anatomie der Staatssicherheit*, MfS-Handbuch IV/2 (Berlin: BStU, 2008), p. 45.

56. Horst Kopp, interview with Thomas Rid, Kyritz, May 4, 2017.

57. Ibid.

58. Georg Herbstritt, *Der Deutsche Bundestag 1949 bis 1989 in den Akten des Ministeriums für Staatssicherheit (MfS) der DDR* (Berlin: BstU, 2013), p. 265.

59. See "Списък на активните мероприятия, чието реализиране е предвидено за юли 1974 г.," София юли 1974 г., *ДЪРЖАВНА СИГУРНОСТ И ЩАЗИ*, КРДОПБГДСРСБНА-Р, COMDOS Archive, Sofia, 2014, f. 9, 2, 540, pp. 137–38.

60. Ibid., pp. 149–51.

61. The flyer is archived in Berlin as well as Sofia. See the foundational work of Nehring, *Die Zusammenarbeit der DDR-Auslandsaufklärung mit der Aufklärung der Volksrepublik Bulgarien*, pp. 171–72.

62. Letter from Mikuszeit to Wagenbreth, dated November 21, 1974, BStU, MfS Teilablage A–593/79, part 2, vol. 7, 375, quoted in Nehring, *Die Zusammenarbeit der DDR-Auslandsaufklärung mit der Aufklärung der Volksrepublik Bulgarien*, p. 173.

63. "Almanya'da Türkiye hakkında hakaretamiz bildiriler dağıtılıyor," *Sabah* 3, 975, November 29, 1974, p. 1, 7, https://archive.org/details/1974-11-29-sabah; in the Bulgarian memo: "ОТНОСНО: ефекта от АМ 'РИГАС,'" София 5.XII.1974 г., *ДЪРЖАВНА СИГУРНОСТ И ЩАЗИ*, КРДОПБГДСРСБНА-Р, COMDOS Archive, Sofia, 2014, f. 9, 2, 540, p. 231, https://archive.org/details/1974-12-05-rigas.

64. Ibid.

65. Nehring, *Die Zusammenarbeit der DDR-Auslandsaufklärung mit der Aufklärung der Volksrepublik Bulgarien*, p. 174.

66. "Справка относно проведените консултации по линия на АМ в Берлин от 3 до 6 май 1976г., София, 10 май 1976 г.," pp. 206–208.

67. "Die Abhör-Affäre," *Stern* 26 (June 19, 1975), cover and pp. 3, 12–20.

68. "Nannen: 'Großer Gott, so what,'" *Der Spiegel* 26 (June 23, 1975), cover, p. 28.

69. "Die Abhör-Affäre."

70. "Nannen: 'Großer Gott, so what,'" p. 21.

71. "Abhör-Affäre: 'Es ist zum Kotzen,'" *Der Spiegel* 25 (June 16, 1975), p. 26.

72. Bohnsack and Brehmer, *Auftrag Irreführung*, p. 146.

73. Generalbundesanwalt, "Lfd. Nr. 4: Die Abteilung X HVA—Aktive Maßnahmen (Verfahren gegen Wagenbreth u.a.)," in Klaus Marxen and Gerhard Werle, *Strafjustiz und DDR-Unrecht, Band 4/1 Spionage* (Berlin: De Gruyter, 2004), p. 70.

74. Helmut Müller-Enbergs, *Hauptverwaltung A. Aufgaben—Strukturen—Quellen (MfS-Handbuch)* (Berlin: BStU, 2011), p. 131.

75. Ibid.; BStU, MfS, Bestand Rosenholz, Reg.-Nr. XV/6004/60.

76. Generalbundesanwalt, "Lfd. Nr. 4: Die Abteilung X HVA—Aktive Maßnahmen (Verfahren gegen Wagenbreth u.a.)," in Marxen and Werle, *Strajustiz und DDR-Unrecht, Band 4/1 Spionage*, p. 70.

77. Friedrich Wilhelm Schlomann, "DDR-Desinformation," *Das Ostpreußenblatt* 46 (November 13, 1993), p. 20. This article, written by a German security establishment figure and former member of the KgU, appears extremely well sourced.

78. Bohnsack and Brehmer, *Auftrag Irreführung*, p. 94.

79. "Fragen für den Monat Juli 1977," *Deutscher Bundestag*, Drucksache 8/793, August 3, 1977, p. 2.

80. Plenarprotokoll 8/207, Bundestag, Bonn, March 19, 1980, p. 16698.

81. "Zuviel Analyse, zuwenig Fakten vom BND," *Die Neue Nachhut* 1 (April 1980), p. 5, https://archive.org/details/1980-neue-nachhut.

82. Bohnsack and Herbert Brehmer, *Auftrag Irreführung*, p. 95.

83. "Fragen für den Monat Juli 1977."

84. "Rückbesinnung auf Kreuth. Zur Strategie der CDU nach dem 5. Oktober," quoted in "Wir mussten vollendete Tatsachen schaffen," *Der Spiegel* 40 (September 29, 1980), p. 20.

85. Generalbundesanwalt, "Lfd. Nr. 4: Die Abteilung X HVA—Aktive Maßnahmen (Verfahren gegen Wagenbreth u.a.)," p. 497, in Marxen and Werle, *Strajustiz und DDR-Unrecht, Band 4/1 Spionage*, p. 7 (p. 465).

86. Ben Fischer, "Books About the Stasi," *Studies in Intelligence* 36, no. 3 (1992), p. 56.

87. Ibid., p. 58.

88. "Prinzip der Zeitbombe," *Der Spiegel* 49 (December 2, 1991), p. 127.

89. "Stasi als Drahtzieher westlicher Polit-Skandale," *Panorama*, ARD, broadcast January 27, 1992, 21:00 CET, first segment, https://youtube.com/watch?v=6p3yrQHYX9Q.

90. Generalbundesanwalt, "Lfd. Nr. 4: Die Abteilung X HVA—Aktive Maßnahmen (Verfahren gegen Wagenbreth u.a.)," p. 497, in Marxen and Werle, *Strajustiz und DDR-Unrecht, Band 4/1 Spionage*, p. 50 (p. 474).

15. The Fifth Estate

1. Richard Fagen, "Death in Uruguay," *The New York Times*, June 28, 1978, p. BR4.

2. The sourcing on the Tupamaros' motivation is not satisfactory, hence "reportedly." See Fletcher Schoen and Christopher Lamb, "Deception, Disinformation, and Strategic Communications: How One Interagency Group Made a Major Difference," *Strategic Perspectives* 11 (Washington, DC: National Defense University, 2012), p. 33.

3. Anna Mudry, "Uruguay: Tummelplatz für CIA-Agenten," *Berliner Zeitung*, August 16, 1970, p. 6.

4. The CIA translation of the article, with an altered headline, is at "Mitrione's Activities, CIA Connections Revealed," CIA-RDP88-01350R000200840011-0, undated.

5. David Blee, "Publication of Reader's Digest Book 'KGB,'" Memorandum to the Director of Central Intelligence, CIA-RDP75-00793R000200110004-2, October 9, 1973.

6. Ibid., p. 2.

7. "Analysis of Sources and Machine Input from John Barron's book, KGB," TPMURILLO, 2, 80, CIA, January 23, 1975, 100-6-139/3.

8. John Crewdson, "The CIA's 3-Decade Effort to Mold the World's Views," *The New York Times*, December 25, 1977, p. 12.

9. "Analysis of Sources and Machine Input from John Barron's book, *KGB*," p. 4.

10. Oleg Kalugin, *Spymaster: My Thirty-two Years in Intelligence and Espionage Against the West* (New York: Basic Books, 2009), p. 170.

11. Ibid.

12. Ilya Dzhirkvelov in "Appendix I," Brian Crozier, *The KGB Lawsuits* (London: Claridge Press, 1995), p. 227.

13. Christopher Andrew, "Russia's Revenge," *The Times*, February 15, 2001, p. 2.

14. Perry Fellwock (aka Winslow Peck), "U.S. Electronic Espionage: A Memoir," *Ramparts* 2, no. 2 (August 1972), pp. 35–50.

15. Ibid., p. 50.

16. Ibid., p. 37.

17. "First Annual Report," *The Organizing Committee for a Fifth Estate*, Washington, DC, January 1974, pp. 15–16. See also Steve Long, "Spying on Big Brother," *The Berkeley Barb*, January 3–9, 1975.

18. *Counterspy* 2, no. 2 (Winter 1975), pagination as archived by the CIA, CIA-RDP88-01315R000200470002-3, pp. 9–10.

19. Walter Pforzheimer, "Counter-Spy: The Bulletin of the Committee for Action/Research on the Intelligence Community," Memorandum for the Deputy Director of Central Intelligence, CIA Historical Intelligence Collection, CIA-RDP75B00380R000600010026-1, May 14, 1973, p. 2.

20. *Counterspy* 2, no. 2, p. 12.

21. Ibid., p. 10.

22. "Request by Senator Lloyd Bentsen (D., Texas) for Unclassified Information on Philip Agee," OLC 78-299/2, CIA, CIA-RDP81M00980R000600300055-3, September 7, 1978, p. 2.

23. John Barron, *KGB Today* (New York: Reader's Digest Press, 1983), p. 228.

24. "Request by Senator Lloyd Bentsen (D., Texas) for Unclassified Information on Philip Agee," p. 3.

25. Julius Mader, *Who's Who in CIA* (Berlin: Mader, 1968), pp. 30–31.

26. Kalugin, *Spymaster*, p. 219.

27. Christopher Andrew and Vasili Mitrokhin, *The Sword and Shield: The Mitrokhin Archive and the Secret History of the KGB* (New York: Basic Books), p. 230.

28. Kalugin, *Spymaster*, p. 220.

29. Andrew and Mitrokhin, *The Sword and Shield*, p. 230.

30. Philip Agee, *Inside the Company: CIA Diary* (London: Stonehill), p. 563.

31. "Subversion of Law Enforcement Intelligence Gathering Operations," Hearings, Part 1: Organizing Committee for a Fifth Estate, Committee on the Judiciary (Washington, DC: Government Printing Office, March 26, 1976), p. 14.

32. Agee, quoted ibid.

33. Andrew and Mitrokhin, *The Sword and Shield*, p. 617.

34. CIA, "Request by Senator Lloyd Bentsen (D., Texas) for Unclassified Information on Philip Agee," Memorandum, OCL 78-2991/2, September 7, 1978, pp. 3–4.

35. Ibid.

36. Philip Agee, Norman Mailer, and Victor Marchetti, "Fifth Estate," undated, "Subversion of Law Enforcement Intelligence Gathering Operations," Hearings, Part 1: Organizing Committee for a Fifth Estate, Committee on the Judiciary, Washington, DC: Government Printing Office, March 26, 1976, pp. 43–44.

37. *Counterspy* 2, no. 2, p. 20.

38. Steven Roberts, "CIA Station Chief Slain Near Athens by Gunmen," *The New York Times*, December 24, 1975, p. 1.

39. Martin Agronsky, Evening Edition, PBS, January 7, 1976, 7:30 p.m.

40. Mark Landler, "Greek Court Convicts 15 in 27-Year-Old Terror Group," *The New York Times*, December 9, 2003.

41. "CIA's Head Man in Greece Slain," *Chicago Tribune*, December 24, 1975, p. 1; "Slain CIA Agent's Cover Exposed by Pamphlet in U.S.," *Chicago Tribune*, December 25, 1975, p. 1.

42. *Counterspy* 2, no. 2, p. 26.

43. CIA, "Re: Fifth Estate," Memo to [redacted], CIA-RDP88-01315R000200470001-4, December 29, 1975, p. 1.

44. Julius Mader, *Who's Who in CIA* (East Berlin: Julius Mader, 1968), p. 537.

45. CIA, "Re: Fifth Estate," p. 1.

46. Laurence Stern, "CIA Agent Welch Buried," *The Washington Post*, January 7, 1976, p. 3.

47. "Britain Orders Deportation of Agee, Ex-Spy Who Brought CIA in from Cold," *The Baltimore Sun*, November 18, 1976, p. A1.

48. Bernard Nossiter, "Writer of Expose on CIA Ordered to Leave Britain," *The Washington Post*, November 17, 1977, p. A1.

49. "Intelligence Analysis," Department of State, Office of Security, Telegram 065438, March 24, 1977.

50. Peter Chippindale, "Agee Takes Freudian Path," *The Guardian*, January 17, 1977, p. A1.

51. Andrew and Mitrokhin, *The Sword and the Shield*, p. 232.

52. Christopher Andrew and Oleg Gordievsky, *KGB: The Inside Story* (London: Faber & Faber, 1990), p. 586.

53. Andrew and Mitrokhin, *The Sword and Shield*, p. 232.

54. Philip Agee, "What Uncle Sam Wants to Know About You: The KIQs," pp. 111–26 in Philip Agee and Louis Wolf, *Dirty Work* (Secaucus, NJ: Lyle Stuart, 1978).

16. Field Manual 30-31B

1. *Covert Action Information Bulletin* 1, no. 1 (July 1978), p. 3.

2. Ibid.

3. The CIA, in congressional testimony, confirmed that "FM 30-31A exists." House of Representatives Permanent Select Committee on Intelligence, Subcommittee on Oversight, "Soviet Covert Action (the Forgery Offensive)," February 6, 1980, 96th Congress, 2nd session, p. 86. Several doctrinal Army publications mention supplement A, including FM 30-31, Department of the Army, January 1972, p. 1-1, https://archive.org/details/1970-fm30-31; also FM 30-17, *Counterintelligence Operations*, Department of the Army, January 1972, pp. 13-5, 13-6.

4. See Army Publications database entry for FM 30-31, October 26, 2018, https://archive.org/details/ARMYPUBS-FM-30-31.

5. FM 30-31B "Stability Operations Intelligence—Special Fields," dated March 10, 1970, as initially surfaced in 1976, U.S. Army Intelligence and Security Command (INSCOM) FOIA release to John Young, May 2001, p. 11 (KGB pagination), p. 27 (U.S. Army pagination), https://archive.org/details/1976-fm30-31b. A curiosity of this FOIA release is that the U.S. Army "declassified" a forged document, with proper strike-throughs and UNCLASSIFIED stamps, that the KGB had simply marked "TOP SECRET."

6. FM 30-31B "Stability Operations Intelligence—Special Fields," dated March 10, 1970, as initially surfaced in 1976, U.S. Army Intelligence and Security Command (INSCOM) FOIA release to John Young, May 2001, p. 11 (KGB pagination), p. 27 (U.S. Army pagination).

7. "Amerika dünyayı nasıl kontrol ediyor?" Barış, March 24–May 9, 1975. The 46-part series was announced on March 23, https://archive.org/details/1975-baris.

8. "Compromise of Top Secret Material," Department of State, Ref: BANGKO 26132, October 21, 1976, FOIA release, https://web.archive.org/web/20060104060835/http://cryptome.org/inscom-foia02.htm.

9. CIA, "Soviet Use of the Media," Appendix R, in "The CIA and the Media," U.S. House of Representatives, Permanent Select Committee on Intelligence, Hearings, December 27, 28, and 29, 1977, January 4 and 5, 1978, and April 20, 1978, p. 535 (4).

10. Robert Meade, Red Brigades (New York: St. Martin's Press, 1990), pp. 166–68.

11. The article was picked up in several European countries, for instance by a left weekly in The Hague, and by Le Monde in Paris; see "U.S. Army Field Manual Forgery, REF: MADRID 11499 (C)," U.S. Department of State, THE HA 05610 080930Z, October 1978. Charles Vanhecke, "Un hebdomadaire fait état de documents secrets américains sur le travail des agents spéciaux dans les 'pays amis,'" Le Monde, September 23, 1978, p. 5.

12. Corrado Incerti, "Dalle carte del Pentagono," L'Europeo 34, no. 43 (October 27, 1978), p. 23.

13. Sandro Ottolenghi, "Gli USA 'aiutano' così," L'Europeo 34, no. 43 (October 27, 1978), pp. 22–24, https://archive.org/details/1978-10-27-l-europeo.

14. Ibid.; see also William Schaap, "The Mysterious Supplement B: Sticking It to the 'Host Country,'" Covert Action Information Bulletin 3 (January 1979), p. 9.

15. Giovanni Valentini, "La riposta degli USA," L'Europeo 34, no. 44 (November 3, 1978), pp. 20–21, https://archive.org/details/1978-11-03-l-europeo.

16. Louis Wolf, interview with Thomas Rid, Washington, DC, August 20, 2018.

17. Schaap, "The Mysterious Supplement B," p. 11.

18. Ibid.

19. Jeff Stein, "The Trenchcoats Retrench," Mother Jones, February/March 1981, p. 55.

20. Louis Wolf, interview with Thomas Rid, Washington, DC, August 20, 2018.

21. John Marks, "How to Spot a Spook," The Washington Monthly, November 1974, pp. 29–39, archived by the CIA at CIA-RDP78-04722A000300030018-3.

22. See also the Covert Action Information Bulletin press release from the same day, "Large CIA Station in Kingston," July 2, 1980.

23. Jo Thomas, "Gunmen in Jamaica Hit Home of U.S. Aide," The New York Times, July 5, 1980, p. A1.

24. N. Richard Kinsman, "Openness and the Future of the Clandestine Service," *Studies in Intelligence* 10, Winter/Spring 2001, pp. 55–61, byline, see also "Staff Meeting Minutes of 7 July 1980," Memorandum for the Record, CIA-RDP84B00130R000600010347-5, July 7, 1980, p. 2.

17. Service A

1. Christopher Andrew and Vasili Mitrokhin, *The Sword and Shield: The Mitrokhin Archive and the Secret History of the KGB* (London: Allen Lane, 1999), p. 7.
2. Oleg Gordievsky, *Next Stop Execution* (London: MacMillan, 1995), p. 189.
3. Stanislav Levchenko and Peter Deriabin, *Counterpoint* 1, no. 1 (April 1985).
4. Vladimir P. Ivanov, "Роля и място на активните мероприятия в разузнаването," April 24, 1979, КГБ И ДС, 9, 3, 209, pp. 45–54, Sofia: COMDOS Archive, 2010, https://archive.org/details/1979-04-24-ivanov.
5. Vladimir P. Ivanov, "Форми и методи на работа. Използването на агентура за влияние" беседа с др. В. П. Иванов на 25.04.1979 г., 5 юни 1979 г., ф. НРС, пф. 9, оп 3, а.е. 209, л. 1–7, Sofia: COMDOS Archive, 2010, https://archive.org/details /1979-04-25-ivanov.   *in Russian*
6. Ivanov, "Роля и място на активните мероприятия в разузнаването."
7. Tennent Bagley and Sergei Kondrashev, *Spymaster* (New York: Skyhorse, 2013), p. 187.
8. Ivanov, "Роля и място на активните мероприятия в разузнаването."
9. Interagency Intelligence Study, "Soviet Active Measures," Washington, DC, 1981, paragraph 19.
10. Carlos Prats González, *Una vida por la legalidad* (México: Fondo de Cultura Económica, 1976).
11. Marlise Simons, "Diary of Murdered Chilean General Surfaces in Mexico," *The Washington Post*, March 8, 1977, p. A.13.
12. Ivanov, "Роля и място на активните мероприятия в разузнаването."
13. Eduardo Labarca, interview with Thomas Rid, September 18, 2018, by phone (Vienna to Miami).
14. Cristóbal Peña, "El hombre que falsificó las memorias del general Carlos Prats," *La Tercera* (Santiago), June 19, 2005.
15. Interagency Intelligence Study, "Soviet Active Measures," Washington, DC, 1981, paragraph 36.
16. See also "Special Report Nr 88" (Washington, DC: State Department, Bureau of Public Affairs, October 1981), p. 1.
17. Carol Honsa, "American Embassy Rebuilds in Islamabad," *Christian Science Monitor*, June 19, 1980, p. 13.
18. Interagency Intelligence Study, "Soviet Active Measures," Washington, DC, 1981, in "CIA Report on Soviet Forgeries," in House of Representatives Permanent Select Committee on Intelligence, "Soviet Active Measures," July 13–14, 1982, 97th Congress, 2nd session (Washington, DC: Government Printing Office), Exhibit I.
19. "Роля и място на активните мероприятия в разузнаването," Vladimir Ivanov, Presentation to PGU-DS, April 24, 1979, ДС И КГБ, f. 9, 3, 209, pp. 45–54, Sofia: COMDOS Archive, 2010, p. 10.

20. "CIA Report on Soviet Forgeries," in: House of Representatives Permanent Select Committee on Intelligence, "Soviet Active Measures," July 13–14, 1982, 97th Congress, 2nd session (Washington, DC: Government Printing Office), Exhibit IX, p. 108.

21. Statement of Edward O'Malley, assistant director, Intelligence Division, FBI, in House of Representatives Permanent Select Committee on Intelligence, "Soviet Active Measures," July 13–14, 1982, 97th Congress, 2nd session (Washington, DC: Government Printing Office), p. 202.

22. House of Representatives Permanent Select Committee on Intelligence, "Soviet Active Measures," July 13–14, 1982, 97th Congress, 2nd session (Washington, DC: Government Printing Office), Exhibit IX, p. 202.

23. Ibid, p. 105.

18. The Neutron Bomb

1. "Moral für Ungeheuer," *Der Spiegel* 38 (September 19, 1961), p. 93.

2. "Neutron Bomb Tested!" *Los Angeles Times*, July 7, 1977, p. 1.

3. "Soviets Plan Neutron Bomb Protest Week," *Chicago Tribune*, August 6, 1977, pp. 1–7.

4. Quoted in Dan Fisher, "Moscow Whips Up Anti-Neutron Drive," *Los Angeles Times*, August 10, 1977, p. 6.

5. For example, *Le Drapeau Rouge*, the outlet of the Belgian Communist Party, *L'Unita* in Italy, the *Volksstimme* in Austria, and *Rhizospastis* in Greece.

6. CIA, *Soviet Covert Action and Propaganda*, February 6, 1980, paragraph 66.

7. CIA, "Soviet Use of the Media," Appendix R, in "The CIA and the Media," U.S. House of Representatives, Permanent Select Committee on Intelligence, Hearings, December 27, 28, and 29, 1977, January 4 and 5, 1978, and April 20, 1978, p. 556 (iv).

8. "Neutron Bomb Opposed by Dutch Parliament," *The New York Times*, March 9, 1978, p. A5.

9. Jonathan Kandell, "Neutron Issue Sparks Wide Dutch Protest," April 16, 1978, p. 3.

10. Walter Alan Levin, *The Efficacy of Propaganda*, Dissertation, Fletcher School of Law and Diplomacy, 1999, p. 417.

11. Jimmy Carter, *Keeping Faith: Memoirs of a President* (Fayetteville: University of Arkansas Press, 1995), pp. 231–34.

12. "NATO Opposition to Neutron Bomb Worries Pentagon," *The Guardian*, March 17, 1978, p. 7.

13. "Dear Mr. Bennett" (forgery), dated February 15, 1978, reproduced in 1980, House of Representatives Permanent Select Committee on Intelligence, Subcommittee on Oversight, "Soviet Covert Action (the Forgery Offensive)," February 6, 1980, 96th Congress, 2nd session.

14. *De Neiuwe*, July 28, 1978, and *De Volkskrant*, August 3, 1978.

15. Anatoly Dobrynin, *In Confidence* (New York: Random House, 1995), p. 436.

16. Ilya Dzhirkvelov, *Secret Servant* (New York: Harper & Row, 1987), p. 306.

17. Interagency Intelligence Study, "Soviet Active Measures," Washington, DC, 1981, paragraph 114.

18. Ibid., paragraph 12.

19. John Vinocur, "KGB Officers Try to Infiltrate Antiwar Groups," *The New York Times*, July 26, 1983, p. A6.

20. CIA, "Soviet Use of the Media," Appendix R, in "The CIA and the Media," U.S. House of Representatives, Permanent Select Committee on Intelligence, Hearings, December 27, 28, and 29, 1977, January 4 and 5, 1978, and April 20, 1978, p. 559 (vii).

21. Department of State, "Soviet Active Measures: The World Peace Council," *Foreign Affairs Note*, April 1985, p. 1.

22. Arkady Shevchenko, *Breaking with Moscow* (New York: Knopf, 1985), p. 225.

23. House of Representatives Permanent Select Committee on Intelligence, Subcommittee on Oversight, "Soviet Covert Action (the Forgery Offensive)," February 6, 1980, 96th Congress, 2nd session, p. 12.

19. Peacewar

1. Christopher Nehring, *Die Zusammenarbeit der DDR-Auslandsaufklärung mit der Aufklärung der Volksrepublik Bulgarien. Regionalfilialen des KGB?* (Heidelberg: University of Heidelberg, 2016), pp. 198–201.

2. Quoted in Hubertus Knabe, *Die unterwanderte Republik* (Berlin: Propyläen, 1999), p. 243.

3. For a discussion of the available files, see Nehring, *Die Zusammenarbeit der DDR*, p. 198.

4. Despite the magnitude of the operation, historical research on this subversive activity is so far limited. Some of the most foundational work has been published in Germany, notably by Hubertus Knabe and Jochen Staadt. This chapter partly relies on their work, especially Knabe, *Die unterwanderte Republik*, and Jochen Staadt, *Die geheime Westpolitik der SED 1960–1970* (Berlin: Akademie Verlag, 1993).

5. "Kommunique der Sondersitzung der Außen-und Verteidigungsminister der NATO in Brüssel," *Bulletin des Presse-und Informationsdienstes der Bundesregierung*, no. 154, (December 18, 1979), pp. 1409–10.

6. Michael White, "Campaign Against Nuclear Arms Opens in Five Capitals," *The Guardian*, April 29, 1980, p. 4.

7. Duncan Campbell, "How to Blow Up the World," *New Statesman*, June 27, 1980, p. 960.

8. [KGB], "Top Secret Documents on U.S. Forces Headquarters in Europe. Holocaust Again for Europe," London, October 1980, p. 15.

9. KGB, *Holocaust Again for Europe* (London: Information Books, 1980), p. 3.

10. Ibid., p. 4.

11. The magazine in question is subtitled *Settimanale politico e di attualita*. "Seduti sulla polveriera atomica," *ABC* 10, no. 27 (July 4, 1969), pp. 10–12.

12. KGB, *Holocaust Again for Europe*, p. 12.

13. Campbell, "How to Blow Up the World," p. 959.

14. See Binnenlandse Veiligheidsdienst, *Een verhulde factor in de kernwapendiscussie*, The Hague, 1981, annex, "Flankerende akties in de campagne tegen N-en TNP-wapens," p. 23.

15. See Bundesministerium des Innern, "'Aktive Maßnahmen' östlicher Dienste" (Bonn, 1985), p. 15, https://archive.org/details/1985-bmi-aktive-massnahmen.

16. "Presseecho," *Konkret*, no. 7 (July 1983), p. 7.

17. Kurt Gailat, "Konzeption für politisch-aktive Maßnahmen zur Förderung der

Friedensbewegung in der BRD," Stasi, Hauptverwaltung A, Abteilung II, Berlin, August 17, 1981, reproduced in Rita Sélitrenny and Thilo Weichert, *Das Unheimliche Erbe* (Leipzig: Forum Verlag, 1991), pp. 196–200, https://archive.org/details/1981-08-gailat.

18. Jens Gieseke, *Wer war wer im Ministerium für Staatssicherheit* (MfS-Handbuch) (Berlin: BStU, 2012), p. 25.

19. Günter Bohnsack, *Hauptverwaltung Aufklärung. Die Legende stirbt* (Berlin: Edition Ost, 1997), p. 35.

20. Hubertus Knabe, "Streit wurde gezielt geschürt," *Frankfurter Allgemeine Zeitung*, September 30, 1999, p. 11.

21. Quoted in Günter Bohnsack and Herbert Brehmer, *Auftrag Irreführung* (Hamburg: Carlsen, 1992), p. 144.

22. See "Generale für den Frieden," *Berliner Zeitung* 117 (May 19, 1981), p. 11. Also "Das Kriegsrisiko erhöht sich," *Neues Deutschland*, May 21, 1981, p. 4.

23. Gerhard Kade, *Generale für den Frieden* (Cologne: Pahl-Rugenstein, 1981), hardcover jacket text.

24. Oleg Kalugin, *Spymaster* (New York: Basic Books, 2009), p. 298.

25. Dirk Banse, "Der Stasi-Maulwurf von Bonn," *Die Welt*, April 28, 2004.

26. Isabel Hilton, "The Green with a Smoking Gun," *The Independent*, April 26, 1994, p. 2.

27. See Knabe, *Der unterwanderte Republik*, p. 254. Also Heike Amos, *Die Westpolitik der SED 1948/49–1961* (Berlin: Akademie Verlag, 1999), pp. 236–41. See Jens Gieseke, *Die Staatssicherheit und die Grünen* (Berlin: Links Verlag, 2016), p. 170.

28. Knabe, *Die unterwanderte Republik*, p. 248.

29. Bohnsack, *Hauptverwaltung Aufklärung*, pp. 111–13.

30. Markus Wolf, *Spionagechef im geheimen Krieg* (München: Econ), p. 343.

31. Banse, "Der Stasi-Maulwurf von Bonn."

32. Wolf, *Spionagechef im geheimen Krieg*, p. 344.

33. Ibid.

34. Staadt, *Die geheime Westpolitik der SED 1960–1970*, p. 272.

35. "Former NATO Generals on Arms Race and U.S. Superiority Plans," *Peace Courier* 12 (October 1981), pp. 6–7.

36. Interagency Intelligence Study, "Soviet Active Measures" (Washington, DC, 1981), p. 40.

37. Wolf, *Spionagechef im geheimen Krieg*, pp. 340–41.

38. "The Arne Herlov Peterson Case," Danish Ministry of Justice, April 17, 1982, translated by the CIA, "Soviet Political Influence Operations," in *Soviet Active Measures*, Permanent Select Committee on Intelligence, House of Representatives, July 13–14, 1982 (Washington, DC: Government Printing Office), pp. 61–63.

39. See also "Arne Herløv Petersen fylder 75 år: Oversætter, forfatter—og spionsigtet," *Århus Stiftstidende*, 13 March 2018.

40. "Schliessung des Berner Novosti-Büros," *Neue Zürcher Zeitung* 100 (April 30, 1983), p. 33.

41. John Vinocur, "KGB Officers Try to Infiltrate Antiwar Groups," *The New York Times*, July 26, 1983, p. A6.

42. Binnenlandse Veiligheidsdienst, *Een verhulde factor in de kernwapendiscussie,* The Hague, April 1981, annex, "Flankerende akties in de campagne tegen N-en TNP-wapens," https://archive.org/details/1981-04-bvd.

43. One example cited by the BVD was the whack-a-mole reappearance of the infamous U.S. military plans from the *Holocaust Again* leak. Johan Olde Kalter, "Sovjet-rol in vredesbeweging brewezen," *De Telegraaf,* November 6, 1982, pp. 1, 9; and Johan Olde Kalter, "Sovjets beïnvloeden onze wapendiscussie," *De Telegraaf,* November 13, 1982, p. 2.

44. See also U.S. Department of State, "Expulsion of Soviet Representatives from Foreign Countries, 1970–81," Foreign Affairs Note, February 1982, CIA-RDP83M00914 R002200160073-5, p. 2.

45. "Waarom kameraad Leonov Nederland moest verlaten," *Reformatorisch Dagblad,* July 15, 1981, p. 7. See also "Communistische infiltratie: Nederland geliefd doelwit," *Reformatorisch Dagblad,* September 12, 1981, p. 14.

46. "Waarom kameraad Leonov Nederland moest verlaten," p. 7.

47. An original "World Peace Council" pin with the slogan is in the possession of the author. See https://archive.org/details/no-missiles.

48. Vinocur, "KGB Officers Try to Infiltrate Antiwar Groups," p. A1.

49. "Auszug aus dem Referat des Genossen Generaloberst Wolf auf der Aktivtagung der Parteiorganisation der HVA," January 13, 1982, BStU, ASt Gera, BV Gera/Abt XV 389, Bl. 10f., quoted in Knabe, *Die unterwanderte Republik,* p. 250.

50. Knabe, *Die unterwanderte Republik,* p. 248.

51. Ibid., p. 259.

52. HVA, Abteilung VII, "Leiterinformation zu aktuellen Aspekten der Entwicklung der Friedensbewegung in der BRD und Westberlin" November 1, 1982, BStU, ZA, ZAIG 6274, Bl. 6–12, p. 8, quoted in Knabe, *Die unterwanderte Republik,* p. 258.

20. Nuclear Freeze

1. J. L. Tierney, "Soviet Active Measures Relating to the U.S. Peace Movement," FBI (Washington, DC, March 9, 1983), p. 5, https://archive.org/details/1983-FBI-active -measures-peace-movement.

2. Ibid., p. 4 (initially classified as secret).

3. Alan Wolfe, "I Was a Cold War Pawn," *The Nation,* January 22, 1983, pp. 1, 79–83.

4. Tierney, "Soviet Active Measures Relating to the U.S. Peace Movement," p. 7.

5. Wolfe, "I Was a Cold War Pawn," p. 82.

6. Tierney, "Soviet Active Measures Relating to the U.S. Peace Movement," p. 9.

7. Ibid., p. 12.

8. Dennis Hevesi, "Randall Forsberg, 64, Nuclear Freeze Advocate, Dies," *The New York Times,* October 26, 2006, p. B6.

9. Ibid.

10. John Barron, "KGB's Magical War for 'Peace,'" *Reader's Digest,* October 1982, p. 238.

11. Robert Levey, "The Arms Race: Amid Rising Nuclear War Fears, a Protest Movement Is Born," *The Boston Globe,* November 15, 1981, p. 1.

12. Tierney, "Soviet Active Measures Relating to the U.S. Peace Movement," p. 32.

13. See "Lehren des zweiten Weltkriegs für unsere Zeit," in Walter Heynowski,

Gerhard Scheumann, and Gerhard Kade, *Die Generale* (Berlin: Verlag der Nation, 1986), pp. 343–49.

14. Jochen Staadt, "Die SED und die 'Generale für den Frieden,'" in Jürgen Maruhn and Manfred Wilke, *Raketenpoker um Europa* (München, 2001), p. 270.

15. "'Generals for Peace' Push Case at UN," *The New York Times*, June 27, 1982, p. 4.

16. "Generals for Peace," *Christian Science Monitor*, June 30, 1982, p. 24.

17. Markus Wolf, *Man Without a Face* (New York: Random House, 1997), p. 244.

18. Ibid., p. 254.

19. Generalbundesanwalt, "Lfd. Nr. 4: Die Abteilung X HVA—Aktive Maßnahmen (Verfahren gegen Wagenbreth u.a.)," p. 497, in Klaus Marxen und Gerhard Werle, *Strajustiz und DDR-Unrecht, Band 4/1 Spionage* (Berlin: De Gruyter, 2004), p. 478.

20. Christopher Nehring, *Die Zusammenarbeit der DDR-Auslandsaufklärung mit der Aufklärung der Volksrepublik Bulgarien. Regionalfilialen des KGB?* (Heidelberg: University of Heidelberg, 2016), p. 200.

21. Писмо с приложени материали, отнасящи се до провеждането на някои от съвместните активни мероприятия, Берлин, 29 юни 1987г., COMDOS-Arch-R, 9, 4, 676, June 29, 1987, pp. 43–45, https://archive.org/details/1987-06-29-am-memo.

22. Markus Wolf, *Spionagechef im geheimen Krieg: Erinnerungen* (Berlin: Ullstein, 2002), pp. 342–45.

23. Anonymous former HVA officer, in conversation with Thomas Rid, by telephone, July 18, 2019.

24. Rüdiger Steinmetz and Tilo Prase, *Dokumentarfilm zwischen Beweis und Pamphlet: Heynowski & Scheumann und Gruppe Katins* (Leipzig: Universitätsverlag, 2002), pp. 128–36.

25. Ronald Reagan, "Remarks in Columbus to Members of Ohio Veterans Organizations," October 4, 1982.

26. "President Says Foes of U.S. Have Duped Arms Freeze Group," *The New York Times*, October 5, 1982, p. A22.

27. Tom Wicker, "Enough Is Enough," *The New York Times*, October 8, 1982, p. A31.

28. "The Freeze, the KGB . . ." *The Washington Post*, November 21, 1982, p. C6.

29. Joanne Omang, "Magazine Articles Cited in KGB-Freeze Link," *The Washington Post*, November 13, 1982, p. A5.

30. "Disarmament Disinformation," *Counterspy* 7, no. 2 (December 1982–February 1983), p. 4.

31. *Covert Action Information Bulletin*, no. 19 (Spring–Summer 1983), p. 7.

32. Tierney, "Soviet Active Measures Relating to the U.S. Peace Movement," p. 17 (headed "III. FBI Assessment").

33. Joanne Omang, "Soviet Effort in Nuclear Freeze Rally Cited," *The Washington Post*, December 10, 1982, p. A4. Also, with a similar thrust, Judith Miller, "U.S. Nuclear Protests Found to Be Affected Very Little by Soviet," *The New York Times*, December 10, 1982, p. A1.

34. No author, "Auf der Grundlage eines gemeinsamen Planes der aktiven Maßnahmen wurden 1981/82 Maßnahmen in folgenden Haptrichtugen durchgeführt," September 3, 1982, BStU, ZA, ZAIG 5171, 111–112, p. 1.

35. Ibid.
36. Vinocur, "KGB Officers Try to Infiltrate Antiwar Groups," p. A6.
37. Barron, "KGB's Magical War for 'Peace,'" p. 207.

21. Nuclear Winter

1. Richard Turco et al., "Nuclear Winter: Global Consequences of Multiple Nuclear Explosions," *Science* 222, no. 4630 (December 23, 1983), pp. 1283–92.
2. Ibid., p. 1284.
3. Philip Shabecoff, "Grimmer View Is Given of Nuclear War Effects," *The New York Times*, October 31, 1983, p. A16.
4. Paul Ehrlich, Carl Sagan, Donald Kennedy, and Walter Roberts, *The Cold and the Dark* (New York: Norton, 1984), p. 27.
5. CIA, "The Soviet Approach to Nuclear Winter," NI IIA 84-10006, SECRET, *Interagency Intelligence Assessment*, December 10, 1984 (Approved for Release July 8, 2010), p. 19.
6. Ibid.
7. Robert Siegel, "Book Details the Defection of 'Comrade J,'" *All Things Considered*, NPR, January 28, 2008.
8. Pete Earley, *Comrade J. The Untold Secrets of Russia's Master Spy in America After the End of the Cold War* (New York: Penguin, 2007), pp. 161–77.
9. T. Rees Shapiro, "Spy Who Defected to U.S. Held 'Keys to a Russian Intelligence Gold Mine,'" *The Washington Post*, July 10, 2010, p. B4.
10. Charles Mohr, "New Vision for Reagan," *The New York Times*, March 23, 1983, p. 21.
11. David K. Willis, "Muddy Visit to NATO's Cruise Site: Britain Allows Rare Look into Base," *Christian Science Monitor*, March 31, 1983, p. 13.
12. "Issue in Europe Shifts to Price in Civil Unrest: U.S. Arms Stance Seen as One-Dimensional," *The Washington Post*, March 27, 1983, p. A1.
13. Lawrence Badash, *A Nuclear Winter's Tale* (Cambridge, MA: MIT Press, 2009), p. 73.
14. "U.S. Soviet Panel Sees No Hope in an Atomic War," *The New York Times*, December 9, 1983, p. A.13.
15. Andrew Revkin, "Missing: The Curious Case of Vladimir Alexandrov," *Science Digest*, July 1986, p. 35.
16. Carl Sagan, "Nuclear War and Climatic Catastrophe: Some Policy Implications," *Foreign Affairs* 62, no. 2 (Winter 1983), p. 259.
17. "The Climatic, Biological, and Strategic Effects of Nuclear War," House of Representatives, Committee on Science and Technology (Washington: Government Printing Office, September 12, 1985), p. 5.
18. R. Jeffrey Smith, "Nuclear Winter Attracts Additional Scrutiny," *Science* 225 (July 6, 1984), p. 31.
19. CIA, "The Soviet Approach to Nuclear Winter," p. 1.
20. Aleksandrov, Soviet Panorama, No. 84, Novosti Press Agency Bulletin, April 27, 1984, quoted in CIA, "The Soviet Approach to Nuclear Winter," p. 2.
21. Caspar Weinberger, "The Potential Effects of Nuclear War on the Climate," Department of Defense (Washington, DC, March 1985), p. 16.
22. "Russian Scientist Vanishes in Spain," *The New York Times*, July 16, 1985, p. A4.
23. I. Andronov, "Where Is Vladimir Aleksandrov?" *Literaturnaya Gazeta* no. 30 (July 23,

1986). (English translation: Lawrence Livermore National Laboratory report UCRL-Trans-12103).

24. William H. Webster, letter to Edward M. Kennedy, June 16, 1987, OCA 87-2458, CIA-RDP90G00152R000901770014-1, p. 1.

25. "Soviets Exploit Nuclear Winter Theory," *Counterpoint* 1, no. 3 (June 1985), p. 6.

22. AIDS Made in the USA

1. "США: бациллы и газы против человечества," *Literaturnaya Gazeta* no. 5 (February 3, 1982), pp. 14–15.

2. "Chemical Warfare in Southeast Asia and Afghanistan," Special Report No. 98, U.S. Department of State, March 22, 1982.

3. The resident's name was Akim. See Vasily Mitrohkin, "KGB Active Measures in Southwest Asia, 1980–82," *Bulletin* (Cold War International History Project), 14/15, Winter 2003–Spring 2004, 193–203, p. 202; also Alexander Thompson, "Pakistan Expels Doctor from Malaria Centre," *The Guardian* (1959–2003), February 12, 1982, p. 6, and "Pakistani Job Decision," *The New York Times*, March 5, 1982, p. A26.

4. Louis Wolf, "The Pentagon's Other Option," *Covert Action Information Bulletin* 17 (Summer 1982); Bill Schaap, "The 1981 Cuba Dengue Epidemic," *Covert Action Information Bulletin* 17 (Summer 1982), p. 28.

5. Milton Leitenberg, "Biological Weapons, Interational Sanctions, and Proliferation," *Asian Perspective* 21, no. 3 (Winter 1997), p. 29.

6. Lawrence Altman, "Rare Cancer Seen in 41 Homosexuals," *The New York Times*, July 3, 1981, p. A20.

7. "A Disease's Spread Provokes Anxiety," *The New York Times*, August 8, 1982, p. 31.

8. Charley Shively, "Speaking Out; The CIA-CDC-AIDS Political Alliance," *Gay Community News* 10, no. 50 (July 9, 1983), p. 5.

9. "A Disease's Spread Provokes Anxiety."

10. "Vor diesem Hintergrund ergab sich das Konzept der Kampagne fast von selbst," *Auftrag Irreführung*, p. 219.

11. "AIDS May Invade India," *Patriot* 21, no. 103 (July 16, 1983), New Delhi, city edition, p. 1, https://archive.org/details/1983-07-16-patriot.

12. "CIA Prolonged Research Germ War, Group Says," *The Washington Post*, March 11, 1980, p. A4; also Gwen McKinney, "Public Should Be Told of Human Experiments," *Philadelphia Tribune*, May 30, 1980, p. 20.

13. Gilbert Lewthwaite, "CIA Mind-Control Tests Used on Public," *The Sun*, July 21, 1977, p. A1.

14. Ilya Dzhirkvelov defected in 1980; see the exceptionally well sourced Robert Gillette, "Soviets Suggest Experiment Leaks in U.S. Created the AIDS Epidemic," *Los Angeles Times*, August 9, 1987, p. D15; and Ilya Dzhirkvelov, *Secret Servant* (New York: Harper & Row, 1987), p. 292.

15. Thomas Boghardt, "Operation INFEKTION," *Studies in Intelligence* 53, no. 4 (December 2009), p. 15.

16. "AIDS May Invade India."

17. "New U.S. Report Names Virus That May Cause AIDS," *The New York Times*, April 24, 1984, p. C1.

18. Charley Shively, "Warning: Reading These Books May Be Hazardous to Your Health," *Gay Community News* 11, no. 47 (June 16, 1984), p. 8.

19. "Science and Weapons Daily Review," CIA, Diretorate of Intelligence, SW SWDR 85-037C, February 28, 1985, CIA-RDP86R00254R000301730001-6-1, p. 1.

20. The memo does not contain the code name. The Soviet-bloc-wide code name was given in various Stasi files; see Douglas Selvage and Christopher Nehring, *Die AIDS-Verschwörung*, BF informier 33 (2014), pp. 35–37.

21. This memo was uncovered in Bulgarian archives by Christoph Nehring. "Справка № 2955," KGB (no unit provided), September 7, 1985, COMDOS-Arch-R, Sofia, 9, 4, 663, p. 208–9, https://archive.org/details/1985-09-07-kgb-2955.

22. Ibid.

23. Валентин Запевалов, "Паника на западе, или что скрывается за сенсацией вокруг AIDS [*sic*]," *Literaturnaya Gazeta* 44, no. 5058 (October 30, 1985), p. 14.

24. Oleg Kalugin, *The First Directorate: My 32 Years in Intelligence and Espionage Against the West* (New York: St. Martin's Press, 1994), p. 158.

25. Запевалов, "Паника на западе, или что скрывается за сенсацией вокруг AIDS."

26. "Soviet Disinformation: Allegations of U.S. Misdeeds," GIM 86-20081, Directorate of Operations, CIA, CIA-RDP86T01017R000100620001-1, March 28, 1986, p. 3.

27. J. Zamgba Browne, "Link AIDS to CIA Warfare," *New York Amsterdam News*, November 30, 1985, p. 12.

28. On December 2, 1985, Segal wrote in a letter about a suspicion raised in *Literaturnaya Gazeta* and "in the Indian newspaper Citizen [*sic*]," quoted in Erhard Geissler, "Disinformation Squared," *Politics and the Life Sciences* 32, no. 2 (Fall 2013), p. 31.

29. Jakob Segal, Lilli Segal, and Ronald Dehmlow, "AIDS—Its Nature And Origin," undated (1986), https://archive.org/details/AIDS-nature-and-origin.

30. *Harare Sunday Mail*, as quoted in Selvage and Nehring, *Die AIDS-Verschwörung*, p. 57.

31. Other code names included PANDEM and, later, DETRICK. "Справка № 2742," KGB (no unit provided), 1987 (November or December), COMDOS-Arch-R, Sofia, 9, 4, 675, pp. 156–59. The folder containing the file is titled "collaboration with KGB 1987," and the memo mentions an event from October 26, 1987, https://archive.org/details/1986-11-kgb-2742.

32. "Разговорите с др. Волфганг Муц—зам.-началник Отдел АМ при разузнавателното управление на МДС–ГДР по време на пребиваването му в България от 16-19.9.1986г," COMDOS-Arch-R, 9, 4, 670, November 22, 1986, pp. 121–128, https://archive.org/details/1986-09-19-mutz.

33. Kunhanandan Nair, *CIA Komplotte gegen die Dritte Welt*, Berlin: Militärverlag der DDR, 1987, p. 127, https://archive.org/details/1987-cia-komplotte.

34. HVA's detailed collaboration with the named, East Berlin-based author, Kunhanandan Nair, remains unclear. HVA referred to the book as "our book" in 1988. See Christopher Nehring, *Die Zusammenarbeit der DDR-Auslandsaufklärung mit der Aufklärung der Volksrepublik Bulgarien. Regionalfilialen des KGB?* (Heidelberg: University of Heidelberg, 2016), p. 236.

35. Selvage and Nehring, *Die AIDS-Verschwörung*, pp. 55–57.

36. Alfred Lee, "Aids Sensation," *Sunday Express*, October 26, 1986, pp. 1–2.

37. Jakob Segal in letter to John Seale, October 26, 1986, quoted in Geissler, "Disinformation Squared," p. 41.

38. "Soviets Accused . . . ," *Toronto Star*, April 28, 1987, p. A14.

39. Figures from "Soviet Influence Activities," U.S. Department of State, Report 9627, August 1987, Appendix E.

40. "Soviet Bulletin Says AIDS Leaked from U.S. Laboratory," Associated Press, March 30, 1987.

41. See Gillette, "Soviets Suggest Experiment Leaks in U.S. Created the AIDS Epidemic."

42. The reference to a "military publication" was incorrect. Reed Irvine, "CBS News Suckered by the Soviets," *Human Events* 47, no. 16 (April 18, 1987), p. 7.

43. David Shipler, "What Happened in Moscow? Shultz Offers Inside Account," *The New York Times*, October 25, 1987, pp. 1, 12.

44. "Prevention and Control of AIDS," United Nations General Assembly, 48/2, October 26, 1987.

45. "Soviet Disavows Charges That U.S. Created AIDS," *The New York Times*, November 5, 1987, p. A31.

46. See Nehring, *Zusammenarbeit*, p. 205.

47. "Внешняя разведка ищет таланты," *Izvestia* 66 (March 19, 1992), p. 3.

48. Christopher Andrew and Oleg Gordievsky, *KGB: The Inside Story* (London: Faber & Faber, 1990), p. 630.

23. The Philosophy of "AM"

1. *Active Measures, A Report on the Substance and Process of Anti-U.S. Disinformation and Propaganda Campaigns*, U.S. Department of State, Washington, DC, August 1986, p. 22, 54.

2. Отчет относно проведени съвместни активни мероприятия с ПГУ КГБ през периода 1981–1985 г., 10 юли 1985 г, ф. НРС, пф. 9, оп 4, а.е. 663, pp. 167–181, Sofia: COMDOS Archive, 2010, https://archive.org/details/1985-07-10-joint-am.

3. House of Representatives Permanent Select Committee on Intelligence, "Soviet Active Measures," July 13–14, 1982, 97th Congress, 2nd session (Washington, DC: Government Printing Office), pp. 15, 221.

4. Vladimir Ivanov, "Изкуството на планирането, разработката и осъществяването на АМ," Presentation to PGU-DS, January 1985, *КГБ И ДС*, COMDOS Archive, Sofia, 2010, https://archive.org/details/1985-01-ivanov.

5. The original quote is in Vladimir I. Lenin, "'Left-Wing' Communism, an Infantile Disorder," in *Collected Works*, vol. 31, April–December 1920 (Moscow: Progress Publishers, 1966), pp. 68–69.

6. Quoted in Vladimir Ivanov "Изкуството на планирането, разработката и осъществяването на АМ," presentation to PGU-DS, January 1985, *КГБ И ДС*, COMDOS Archive, Sofia, 2010. The original quote from Lenin is in "'Left-Wing' Communism, an Infantile Disorder," in *Collected Works*, pp. 70–71.

7. Ivanov, "Изкуството на планирането, разработката и осъществяването на АМ."

8. The text was published with a different title as "Aktivitäten östlicher Nachrichtendienste," *Innere Sicherheit* 1 (March 20, 1985), pp. 6–12.

9. BMI, "'Aktive Maßnahmen' östlicher Dienste," Bonn, 1985, p. 6.

10. Ibid., p. 3.

11. Günter Bohnsack and Herbert Brehmer, *Auftrag Irreführung* (Hamburg: Carlsen, 1992), p. 29.

12. Vladimir Lenin, *What Is to Be Done?* (New York: International Publishers, 1929), p. 84.

13. Ibid., p. 85.

14. "Ersatz für den (militärischen) Krieg," in BMI, "'Aktive Maßnahmen' östlicher Dienste," Bonn, 1985, p. 19.

15. BMI, "'Aktive Maßnahmen' östlicher Dienste," Bonn, 1985, p. 8.

16. Ibid., p. 9.

17. The letter is reproduced in United States Senate Select Committee on Intelligence, "Meeting the Espionage Challenge" (Washington, DC: Government Printing Office, October 3, 1986), p. 142, Appendix F.

18. Federal Bureau of Investigation, "Soviet Active Measures in the United States, 1986–87," *Congressional Record*, December 9, 1987, E4717–24.

19. John Goshko, "For Forgery Specialist, a Case Close to Home," *The Washington Post*, August 19, 1986.

20. Todd Leventhal, in correspondence with Thomas Rid, May 2019.

21. QRPLUMB (Development and Plans, 1970–1978), vol. 2, no. 30, CIA CREST Archive, June 8, 1978, p. 8 (of document).

22. Ibid., p. 1.

23. QRPLUMB (Development and Plans, 1970–1978), vol. 2, no. 18, CIA CREST Archive, April 5, 1973, p. 3 (of document).

24. QRPLUMB (Development and Plans, 1982–1988), vol. 1, no. 3, CIA CREST Archive, July 10, 1986, p. 4.

25. QRPLUMB (Development and Plans, 1982–1988), vol. 4, no. 21, CIA CREST Archive, p. 1.

26. QRPLUMB (Development and Plans, 1982–1988), vol. 4, no. 8, CIA CREST Archive, March 24, 1986, p. 1.

27. "Potential Threat of Exposure to Major Covert Action Instrumentality," QRPLUMB (Development and Plans, 1982–1988), vol. 4, no. 7, CIA CREST Archive, p. 3.

28. QRPLUMB (Development and Plans, 1982–1988), vol. 4, no. 8, CIA CREST Archive, p. 4.

29. "Renewal of Operational Activity PDDYNAMIC," QRPLUMB (Development and Plans, 1982–1988), vol. 4, no. 3, CIA CREST Archive, January 24, 1984, p. 8.

30. QRPLUMB (Development and Plans, 1982–1988), vol. 1, no. 3, CIA CREST Archive, July 10, 1986, p. 4.

31. QRPLUMB (Development and Plans, 1982–1988), vol. 4, no. 21, CIA CREST Archive, p. 8.

32. Thomas M. Troy, "Headquarters Germany," *Studies in Intelligence* 42, 1, 1998, pp. 79–84, https://archive.org/details/1998-troy.

33. Some of the names revealed by Eichner and Dobbert were already public, for instance just months before publication in "Dinner for two," *Der Spiegel* 12, March 17, 1997, p. 34–36; the German press, however, had not revealed dates of birth, spouse names, or place and duration of previous postings.

34. Klaus Eichner and Andreas Dobbert, *Headquarters Germany*, Berlin: Edition Ost, 1997, p. 309, https://archive.org/details/1997-headquarters-germany.

35. Floyd Paseman, *A Spy's Journey* (Grand Rapids, Mich: Zenith, 2005), p. 187.

36. Steven Brattain, "Headquarters Germany," email to Thomas Rid, October 11, 2019, 12:26 EST.

37. "Moreover: Is it really so useful?" *The Economist* 346, 8061, March 28, 1998, p. 82.

38. "Im Spiegel des 20. Jahrhunderts: Literatur zu Geheimdienst und Spionage," *Der Spiegel* 8, February 22, 1999, p. 149.

39. See Paul Maddrell, "Battlefield Germany," *Intelligence and National Security* 13, 2 (Summer 1998), pp.190–212, p. 201. Maddrell did point out that the authors' anti-Americanism "warps their judgment," but does not mention the possibility of an active measure, despite of the suspicious appendix.

24. Digital Measures

1. *Ekho Moskvy*, Moscow, in Russian, March 23, 1999, 0900 GMT.

2. Ibid.

3. Ren TV, Moscow, in Russian, April 2, 1999, 1345 GMT.

4. ITAR-TASS news agency (World Service), Moscow, in English, April 2, 1999, 1205 GMT.

5. Ren TV, Moscow, in Russian, April 2, 1999, 1345 GMT.

6. Ibid.

7. "Analysis: The Russian Presidential Election and the Internet," BBC Monitoring Media, London, February 3, 2000, p. 1.

8. "New Website Collecting Material on Russian Capital's Mayor Opened," BBC Monitoring Former Soviet Union, London, September 21, 1999, p. 1.

9. Paul Quinn-Judge, "Russia's Dick Morris," *Time International* (Canada) 155, no. 14 (April 10, 2000), p. 22. For examples see "Любимый руководитель," http://lujkov.ru and http://web.archive.org/web/20010501212705/http://lujkov.ru/about/.

10. Pete Earley and Sergei Tretyakov, *Comrade J* (New York: Penguin, 2008), p. 194.

11. Pete Earley, *Comrade J: The Untold Secrets of Russia's Master Spy in America after the End of the Cold War* (New York: Penguin, 2007), p. 195.

12. Eneken Tikk, Kadri Kaska, and Liis Vihul, *International Cyber Incidents* (Tallinn: CCDCOE, 2010), p. 17.

13. Joshua Davis, "Hackers Take Down the Most Wired Country in Europe," *Wired*, August 21, 2007.

14. Mark Landler and John Markoff, "In Estonia, What May Be the First War in Cyberspace," *The New York Times*, May 28, 2007.

15. "Adventures of Mr. Hudson in Russia," *Informacia*, July 8, 2009; and "British Diplomat in Russia Resigns after Prostitute Video and Sex Allegations," *Metro*, July 9, 2009.

16. John Bingham, "British Diplomat James Hudson Resigns over Russian 'Brothel' Video," *The Daily Telegraph*, July 10, 2009.

17. Will Stewart, "U.S. Diplomat 'Caught on Video in a New Russian Honeytrap,'" *Daily Mail*, August 7, 2009.

18. Jill Dougherty, "U.S. Calls Purported Sex Tape 'Doctored' and 'Smear Campaign,'" CNN, September 24, 2009.
19. Brian Flynn, "Our Man in Russia Pulls Out after Spy Films His Urals Sex," *The Sun*, July 9, 2009, p. 9.

25. First Digital Leaks

1. David Crary, "Older, Quieter Than WikiLeaks, Cryptome Perseveres," *Sunday Gazette* (Charlston, W.V.), March 10, 2013, p. A12.
2. Ibid.
3. Brian Kladko, "Gadfly Posts Secrets on Web Site," *The Record* (Bergen County, NJ), December 15, 2004, p. A1.
4. Paul T. Colgan, "Spying Game," *Sunday Business Post* (Cork, Ireland), September 5, 2004.
5. Ibid.
6. David Kushner, "Click and Dagger," *Mother Jones*, July/August 2010, p. 64.
7. Jeanne Whalen, "Website Shines Spotlight on Leaks from WikiLeaks," *The Wall Street Journal*, October 27, 2010, p. 12.
8. Manning later changed gender, and took the first name Chelsea.
9. See Charlie Savage, "Was Snowden a Russian Agent?" *New York Review of Books*, February 9, 2017.
10. For implementation dates, see "SecureDrop," Wikipedia, https://web.archive.org/web/20190107195518/https://en.wikipedia.org/wiki/SecureDrop
11. Bruce Schneier, "The U.S. Intelligence Community Has a Third Leaker," *Schneier on Security*, August 7, 2014.
12. Jacob Appelbaum, Holger Stark, Marcel Rosenbach, and Jörg Schindler, "Merkel beschwert sich bei Obama," *Der Spiegel*, October 23, 2013.
13. Marcel Rosenbach, conversation with Thomas Rid, May 8, 2017.
14. Marcel Rosenbach and Holger Stark, "Von Mielke zu Merkel," *Der Spiegel* 39 (September 27, 2010), pp. 30–31.
15. Glenn Greenwald, conversation with Thomas Rid, May 10, 2019.
16. Rüdiger Ditz, "Karriere einer Abschrift," *Der Spiegel*, December 13, 2014.
17. Jay Carney, White House Press Briefing, October 23, 2013, 1:14 p.m. EST.
18. The story predates the press release by ten minutes, but the White House had provided the same talking points to *Der Spiegel* before the briefing. See Appelbaum et al., "Merkel beschwert sich bei Obama."
19. Ibid.
20. Quoted in "German Paper Says Obama Aware of Spying on Merkel Since 2010," Reuters, October 27, 2013.
21. "Range: Kein Beweis für Ausspähung von Merkels Handy," *Frankfurter Allgemeine*, December 11, 2014.
22. "We use a Anonymous Posting concept. Anyone can post to the site. No censorship takes place! NO DOXING ONLY IF ITS UR MOM!," *CyberGuerrilla*, undated, https://web.archive.org/web/20131203114704/https://www.cyberguerrilla.org/blog/?page_id=163.

23. "Ministry of Foreign Affairs of Ukraine Massive DOCS leak. MFA.GOV.UA Hacked," *CyberGuerrilla*, October 23, 2013, https://web.archive.org/web/20131031054428 /http://www.cyberguerrilla.org:80/blog/?p=16121.

24. "'Muddling and Meddling'? U.S., EU Politicians Plunge Deeper into Kiev Protest," Russia Today, December 11, 2013.

25. See James Bamford, "Evidence Points to Another Snowden at the NSA," Reuters, August 21, 2016.

26. Re Post, "Марионетки Майдана" (Puppets of the Maidan), February 4, 2014, 12:33:35 UTC, http://web.archive.org/web/20140206151309/https://www.youtube .com/watch?v=MSxaa-67yGM.

27. Re Post, "Как они делят Украину" (How They Divide Ukraine), February 4, 2014, 12:33:34 UTC, http://web.archive.org/web/20140207063125/http://www.youtube .com/watch?v=kOjrACdTQE8.

28. @SpartakSergiewi, "Марионетки Майдана," February 5, 2014 05:36:11 GMT, https://web.archive.org/web/20140209114828/https://twitter.com/SpartakSergiewi /status/430937877912907776.

29. Putnik1, "НАХОДКА ДЛЯ ШПИОНА," Livejournal, February 6, 2014, 09:53 Moscow time, https://web.archive.org/web/20170714184254/http://putnik1.livejournal .com:80/2694075.html.

30. The YouTube account first posting the video was the pro-Russian "Re Post." "Лев Николаевич Мышкин" (fictional name), 09:41:53 Moscow time, February 6, 2014, http://web.archive.org/web/20140206073624/http://www.youtube.com/watch?v =Q6f3rHZV5JQ.

31. @DLoskutov, "Sort of controversial . . . ," February 5, 2014, 20:35 GMT, https:// web.archive.org/web/20140208234900/https://twitter.com/DLoskutov/status /431330171518345217.

32. "Merkel findet 'Fuck the EU'-Beleidigung inakzeptabel," *Der Spiegel*, February 7, 2014.

33. Ed Pilkington, "U.S. Official Apologises to EU Counterparts for Undiplomatic Language," *The Guardian*, February 6, 2014.

34. @DLoskutov, February 6, 2014, 10:52 GMT https://web.archive.org/web/20140 209235755/https://twitter.com/DLoskutov/status/431545895935811585.

35. Roman Olearchyk and Neil Buckley, "Leaked Ukraine Recording Reveals U.S. Exasperation with EU," *Financial Times*, February 6, 2014.

26. Anonymous

1. This estimate is based on the frequency of the number of archived sites on the Internet Archive (@YourAnonNews, @AnonyOps, @AnonymousPress, and @Anonymous_ UK).

2. "With Love from Anonymous Ukraine—Leak Private Emails of Some Members of the Ukrainian Parliament!" *CyberGuerrilla*, November 19, 2013, https://web .archive.org/web/20131210224312/https://www.cyberguerrilla.org/blog/?p =16476.

3. See comment on a repost, "With Love from Anonymous Ukraine—Leak Private Emails of Some Members of the Ukrainian Parliament!" AnonOps Communications, Decem-

ber 4, 2013, https://web.archive.org/web/20140503125353/http://anonopsofficial.blogspot.com/2013/12/with-love-from-anonymous-ukraine-leak.html.

4. Anonymous administrator, in correspondence with Raphael Satter, December 1, 2018, http://web.archive.org/web/20191022021453/https://medium.com/@rsatter/an-archaeology-of-russian-information-operations-8448fc153525.

5. Courtney Weaver, "Putin Was Ready to Put Nuclear Weapons on Alert in Crimea Crisis," *Financial Times*, March 15, 2015.

6. "Украинский фронт," @UkrainianFront, Facebook, https://archive.org/details/2014-02-22-ukrainianfront.

7. "За независимость Крыма," @ZaNezavisimostkrima, Facebook, https://archive.org/details/2014-02-27-zanezavisimostkrima.

8. "Отчет по размещенным публикациям по украинской тематике 27.02.2014," GRU, Moscow, 2014.

9. Ibid.

10. "Как несгибаемый 'Беркут' стоял до конца, так и 'КиберБеркут' будет охотиться на фашистскую нечисть, пока не истребит её!"; see "Untitled," CyberBerkut, March 3, 2014, http://web.archive.org/web/20140524182153/http://www.cyber-berkut.org/.

11. The URLs pointing to the leaked emails were good for only a few days. The archive, named protsyk.7z, is c8ec1e43796987a210ea27345904ab354f27137c12190b52baaf0c4d94a18dbf; the forged Gresh email (leaked but never sent), titled "Peninsula," WjGDsifeWV4lJ1vNhI.eml, is 623edb07d2931fbbd8246d46fb6653e75b481f46296c503ee063be4e50bf1205. "Operation Independence Continues—Anonymous Exposes U.S. Invasion Plans in Ukraine," *Voice of Russia*, March 14, 2014, http://web.archive.org/web/20140319010821/http://voiceofrussia.com/2014_03_14/Operation-Independence-Continues-Anonymous-exposes-US-invasion-plans-in-Ukraine-7517/.

12. The forged email (leaked but never sent) is titled "Активні дії у Мелітополі," March 11, 2014, WAgW0B5lmceOUxyz.eml, 385f1888416f00ad59dac5e028f99fbcb0a05d809bde8ba185f756f8240bbf56.

13. The forged email (leaked but never sent) is titled: "Потрібно терміново пошуміти," March 11, 2014, edOSJvhrszSQ4BTJX.eml, 7bbaee7c891baa54421b999495489d8bab3d9d880e7c618bce861aaffb2cef83.

14. 46°52'47.4"N 35°18'11.8"E.

15. "Anonymous Ukraine Hack Correspondence of U.S. Army Attache Assistant in Kiev and Discover a Plot Against Ukraine," *CyberGuerrilla*, March 12, 2014, 06:54 BST, https://web.archive.org/web/20140315025403/https://www.cyberguerrilla.org/blog/?p=17628.

16. Jason Gresh, interview with Thomas Rid, April 27, 2018, Tallinn and Washington, DC.

17. The email called for "активні дії," which according to Protsyk is a term of art for active measures in military circles in Ukraine.

18. Igor Protsyk, "Question Pawn Storm," email to Thomas Rid, April 26, 2018, 18:08 EST.

19. "ЦВК: Проведення виборів на Донеччині та Луганщині стає дедалі складнішим," *Українська правда*, May 17, 2014.

20. Margaret Coker and Paul Sonne, "Ukraine: Cyberwar's Hottest Front," *The Wall Street Journal*, November 10, 2015, p. A1.

27. Sofacy

1. Margaret Coker and Paul Sonne, "Ukraine: Cyberwar's Hottest Front," *The Wall Street Journal*, November 10, 2015, p. A1.

2. Nikolay Koval, "Revolution Hacking," in *Cyber War in Perspective* (Tallinn: NATO CCDCOE, 2015), pp. 55–58.

3. Михаил Зеленский, "Первый канал показал 'фейковые' данные о победе Яроша на президентских выборах," *Republic*, May 25, 2014, 23:53 (Moscow time), https://web.archive.org/web/20180302214107/https://republic.ru/fast/russia/pervyy-kanal-pokazal-feykovye-dannye-o-pobede-yarosha-na-prezidentskikh-vyborakh-1103324.xhtml; https://www.youtube.com/watch?v=99cAj-UjcM8.

4. "'Картинка Яроша.' Часть 1," CERT-UA, May 28, 2014, https://web.archive.org/web/20140626215129/http://cert-ua.org/?p=1070.

5. "'Картинка Яроша.' Часть 2," CERT-UA, May 29, 2014, https://web.archive.org/web/20140626215137/http://cert-ua.org/?p=1097.

6. The log files show sixty different requests for the forgery, all from within Channel One's networks. "'Картинка Яроша.' Часть 1," CERT-UA, May 28, 2014, https://web.archive.org/web/20140626215129/http://cert-ua.org/?p=1070, see also "'Картинка Яроша.' Часть 2," CERT-UA, May 29, 2014, and "Взлом ЦИК. Часть 1," CERT-UA, June 6, 2014, https://web.archive.org/web/20150215225135/http://cert-ua.org/?p=1162.

7. "Address to the Press," *КиберБеркут*, May 28, 2014, https://web.archive.org/web/20180313213514/https://cyber-berkut.org/en/olden/index2.php.

8. Ibid.

9. Malware samples found in the network include 55da85d5e2520f0739f6f077dea6d0c8ad5804419df65d5c06dc638b0a36bb35, associated with SOFACY.

10. "Nachrichtendienstlich gesteuerte elektronische Angriffe aus Russland," Beitrag Spionageabwehr, *BfV Newsletter* 1 (2016), p. 2.

11. Two different APT28-linked malware samples used MH17 file name as bait, fff66d856a7c8b6759c1be50bc9a4a553095351fffff04d4560119e2fdff2d6d and adf344f12633ab0738d25e38f40c6adc9199467838ec14428413b1264b1bf540.

12. Chris Dorman, "Phresh Phishing Against Government, Defence and Energy," Price-WaterHouseCoopers, October 9, 2014, https://web.archive.org/web/20141018235007/http://pwc.blogs.com:80/cyber_security_updates/2014/10/phresh-phishing-against-government-defence-and-energy.html.

13. See Nate Beach-Westmoreland's post in response to author's question, @Nate-BeachW, "You may be looking for . . . ," April 26, 2018, https://web.archive.org/web/20180502195232/https://twitter.com/NateBeachW/status/989496118642905089; the first known sample is 1de6d9db409bef73e3585fc08f98b30e2757ec87830e6f84ba85c39210aa962b.

14. "Disclosure of Another φday Malware-Initial Dropper and Downloader (Part 1)," *Malware Reversing*, December 15, 2012, https://web.archive.org/web/20160604005121/http://www.malware-reversing.com:80/2012/12/3-disclosure-of-another-0day-malware.html.

15. "Sofacy Threat Activity," *BAE Systems Applied Intelligence*, August 29, 2014, 15 pages, TLP:AMBER, quoted here with permission.

16. Neel Mehta, Billy Leonard, and Shane Huntley, "Peering into the Aquarium: Analysis of a Sophisticated Multi-Stage Malware Family," Google, September 5, 2014.
17. Viktor Suvorov, *Inside the Aquarium* (New York: Macmillan, 1986).
18. Shane Huntley, correspondence with Thomas Rid, April 29, 2019.
19. "Sednit Espionage Group Now Using Custom Exploit Kit," ESET, October 8, 2014, https://web.archive.org/web/20141011223432/http://www.welivesecurity.com:80/2014/10/08/sednit-espionage-group-now-using-custom-exploit-kit.
20. Dan McWhorter, "APT28: A Window into Russia's Cyber Espionage Operations?," FireEye, October 27, 2014, https://web.archive.org/web/20141111133621/http://www.fireeye.com/blog/technical/2014/10/apt28-a-window-into-russias-cyber-espionage-operations.html.
21. RIA Novosti (MIA Rossiya Segodyna), Moscow, in Russian, December 16, 2014.
22. "Journal Website Attacked," *Albuquerque Journal*, December 24, 2014.
23. Patrick Malone, "'Journal' Site Hacked with Threat to ABQ Residents," *The Santa Fe New Mexican*, December 25, 2014, p. A1.
24. "WBOC Website and Twitter Page Hit by Cyber Attacks," WBOC, January 6, 2015.
25. A dozen forged posts on @CENTCOM's Twitter feed are archived at https://web.archive.org/web/20150112175000/twitter.com/centcom.
26. Gordon Corera, "How France's TV5 Was Almost Destroyed by 'Russian Hackers,'" BBC, October 10, 2016.
27. "Anatomy of Russia's 2016 Influence Operations," FireEye Intelligence, October 2017, p. 58, https://archive.org/details/2017-10-fireeye-anatomy.
28. ANSSI, "TV5 Monde Analyse d'Incident," Rennes, June 7–9, 2017, https://youtube.com/watch?v=9D__deRM7vw, at 23:52.
29. Raphael Satter, "Russians Posed as ISIS Hackers, Threatened U.S. Military Wives," Associated Press, May 8, 2018.
30. Letter from Senators Cory Gardner and Ron Wyden to Attorney General Jeff Sessions, July 9, 2018.
31. See the historical Whois record for cyb3rc.com, https://archive.org/details/whois-cyb3rc.com.
32. "Bloody Valentine's Day," CyberCaliphate, February 10, 2015, https://web.archive.org/web/20150213133616/http://cyb3rc.com/.
33. ANSSI, "TV5 Monde Analyse d'Incident," at 2:32.
34. Martin Untersinger, "Le piratage de TV5 Monde vu de l'intérieur," *Le Monde*, June 10, 2017.
35. ANSSI, "TV5 Monde Analyse d'Incident," at 25:10.
36. Ibid., at 28:30.
37. Corera, "How France's TV5 Was Almost Destroyed by 'Russian Hackers.'"
38. See "Cyber attaque contre TV5 : qui, comment, pourquoi…," Breaking3Zero, April 9, 2015, archived at https://archive.org/details/tv5-isis-vbs.
39. ANSSI regarded the fake incident report as part of the operation. Author interviews with two anonymous sources, December 11, 2018. See also ANSSI, "TV5 Monde Analyse d'Incident," at 1:35.
40. "TV5 Monde piraté par le groupe Cyber Caliphate," *Le Monde*, April 9, 2015.

41. "Cyberattaque contre TV5 monde: la guerre médiatique de Daech décryptée," *Le Figaro*, April 9, 2015.

42. Sylvain Biget, "Cyberattaque de TV5: une méthode classique, par des pirates sans grande compétence?," ZDNet, April 13, 2015.

43. Michael Hange, "Tagesordnungspunkt 1," Kurzprotokoll der 6. Sitzung der IuK-Kommission, Deutscher Bundestag, May 21, 2015, p. 8.

44. Timo Steffens, "Tagesordnungspunkt 1," Kurzprotokoll der 8. Sitzung der IuK-Kommission, Deutscher Bundestag, July 2, 2015.

45. As displayed on services.mofa.gov.sa/mofa.html, May 20, 2015, archived at http://zone-h.com/mirror/id/24345684?zh=1&hz=1.

46. The announcement was posted on a number of sites popular with hackers, for example, "MOFA.GOV.SA Hacked by Yemeni Cy," Pastebin.ro, May 20, 2015, https://web.archive.org/web/20150528083510/http://pastebin.ro/9sAhrWRy.

47. Raphael Satter and Maggie Michael, "Private Lives Are Exposed as WikiLeaks Spills Its Secrets," Associated Press, August 23, 2016.

48. WikiSaudiLeaks, July 20, 2015, https://web.archive.org/web/20150810005744/http://www.wikisaleaks.com/.

49. Thomas Rid, "Disinformation: A Primer in Russian Active Measures and Influence Campaigns," Testimony, United States Senate Select Committee on Intelligence, Washington, DC, March 30, 2017.

50. The leak site was hosted at 87.236.215.129—the IP address was part of a range used by the Lithuanian hosting provider UAB DUOMENU CENTRAS, leased to MonoVM. At least 13 addresses out of a range of 256 were linked to APT28. See "WikiSaudi-Leaks," *BAE Systems Applied Intelligence*, September 21, 2015, p. 6, confidential report quoted with permission.

51. BAE Systems and FireEye both carefully weighed the forensics on WikiSaudiLeaks in internal reports but could not come to a firm assessment. For details on the reuse of "We Are Cutting Sword of Justice [*sic*]" and the use of mock mathematical equations for decryption keys that involved the numbers of killed children and Saudis, I would like to thank Lee Foster and Kelli Vanderlee at FireEye, email from Lee Foster to Thomas Rid, "Various Notes," September 9, 2019.

28. Election Leaks

1. "По следам офицеров ГРУ. Новые детали в 'деле русских хакеров,'" Radio Svoboda (Radio Free Europe/Radio Liberty), July 17, 2018, https://web.archive.org/web/20190103224700/https://www.svoboda.org/a/29372280.html.

2. See, for example, the Google Scholar search results for "Нетыкшо, ВБ," @ridt, "The former commanding officer . . . ," January 3, 2019, https://web.archive.org/web/20190426191420/https://twitter.com/RidT/status/1081012329838534656.

3. "Постановление Правительства Российской Федерации от 10 марта 2009 г. N 221 г. Москва 'О присуждении премий Правительства Российской Федерации 2008 года в области науки и техники'," *Rossiyskaya Gazeta*, Federal Issue 4872, 0, March 20, 2009.

4. "Actions in Response to Russian Malicious Cyber Activity and Harassment," Office of the Press Secretary, White House, December 29, 2016.

5. "Deutsche Beamte beschuldigen russischen Militärgeheimdienst," *Der Spiegel*, January 30, 2016.

6. The original of the email that tricked Podesta is archived at http://web.archive.org /web/20180327125110/https://wikileaks.org/podesta-emails//get/34899.

7. "Медиафорум региональных и местных СМИ 'Правда и справедливость,'" St. Petersburg, Kremlin Press Release, April 7, 2016.

8. The SZ emails to implicated individuals did not mention a direct link to the Kremlin or Putin. The delayed notice to the Kremlin was for security reasons. Frederik Obermaier, in correspondence with Thomas Rid, April 29, 2019.

9. Robert Mueller, *USA v. Viktor Borisovich Netyksho et al.*, case 1:18-cr-00215-ABJ, 1, U.S. District Court for the District of Columbia, July 13, 2018, p. 21; and Lee Foster, FireEye, in conversation with Thomas Rid, November 14, 2019.

10. Raphael Satter, "How Russians Hacked the Democrats' Emails," Associated Press, November 4, 2017.

11. See Robert Mueller, *USA v. Viktor Borisovich Netyksho et al.*," p. 10.

12. Complaint, *Democratic National Committee v. The Russian Federation et al.*, No. 1:18-cv-03501, United States District Court for the Southern District of New York, April 20, 2018, p. 6.

13. Ibid., p. 24.

14. The most recent "modify date" in the exif data of the logo file, "best.png," in the first archived version of DCLeaks.com, is "2016:04:20 11:36:13."

15. The most recent Breedlove email released was written on May 23, 2015.

16. Complaint, *Democratic National Committee v. The Russian Federation et al.*, p. 21.

17. Ibid., p. 22.

18. The MD5 hashes of the Clinton files on DC Leaks and the hashes of the attachments in the Podesta emails (later leaked on WikiLeaks) are identical for all seventy-two files, https://archive.org/details/podesta-dcleaks-hashes.

19. The GRU backdated the first posts on the site to a day that predates its registration. The time stamps on DCLeaks itself are therefore not reliable. The first archived version is from June 13, 2016, https://web.archive.org/web/20160613143949/http://dcleaks.com.

20. Melvin Redick, "These Guys . . . ," Facebook, June 8, 2016, 10:42 EST, https://archive .org/details/20160608-dcleaks.

21. Dmitri Alperovitch, "Bears in the Midst," CrowdStrike Blog, June 14, 2018, https:// web.archive.org/web/20160615025759/https://www.crowdstrike.com/blog/bears -midst-intrusion-democratic-national-committee/.

22. Raffi Khatchadourian, "Man Without a Country," *The New Yorker*, August 21, 2017, p. 52.

23. Ibid.

24. "Assange on Peston on Sunday: 'More Clinton Leaks to Come,'" ITV, June 12, 2016, https://web.archive.org/web/20160614131515/http://www.itv.com/news/update /2016-06-12/assange-on-peston-on-sunday-more-clinton-leaks-to-come/.

25. Robert Mueller, *Report on the Investigation into Russian Interference in the 2016 Presidential Election*, U.S. Department of Justice (Washington, DC, March 2019), p. 45.

26. No intelligence estimate, indictment, or report, not even the Mueller report, includes meaningful evidence on when the GRU transferred the Podesta material to WikiLeaks.

For reasons that I cannot disclose, I have low to moderate confidence that the Podesta transfer happened earlier rather than later.

29. Guccifer Two

1. Catherine Herridge and Pamela K. Browne, "Romanian Hacker Guccifer: I Breached Clinton Server, 'It Was Easy,'" Fox News, May 4, 2016.
2. Robert Mueller, *USA v. Viktor Borisovich Netyksho et al.*, case 1:18-cr-00215-ABJ, 1, U.S. District Court for the District of Columbia, July 13, 2018, p. 15.
3. "DNC's Servers Hacked by a Lone Hacker," *Guccifer 2.0*, June 15, 2016, https://web.archive.org/web/20160615212154/https://guccifer2.wordpress.com/2016/06/15/dnc/.
4. The original draft was sent by email on September 4, 2008, at 20:25 EDT, from Chris Lu from Obama for America, subject line "RE: Draft policy promises," to more than forty-one recipients, including John Podesta. The original email is archived at https://web.archive.org/web/20180326220653/https://wikileaks.org/podesta-emails//get/34007; the leaked version is at http://web.archive.org/web/20160615212639/https://guccifer2.files.wordpress.com/2016/06/4.doc. The forensic overlap between the two documents is beyond reasonable doubt. The two .doc documents have identical text, structure, author, title, print date, revision, and identical numbers of pages, paragraphs, lines, words, characters, and spaces (Word does not count the modified header); original 765028fd d67aeb8b2d8bb8f5b27ec171; modified f79972d72f5304bf1dc4cd2ae6c3a2d4.
5. Daniel Halper, "Election 2016 No Hair-Raising DT Data in Dem Hack," *New York Post*, June 16, 2016, p. 12.
6. Eric Bradner, "Trump: DNC Hacked Itself," CNN Wire Service, June 15, 2016.
7. @Wikileaks, June 16, 2016, 02:37 EST, https://web.archive.org/web/20160617010307/https://twitter.com/wikileaks/status/743377025742798848.
8. Matt Tait, "13) another . . . ," @pwnallthethings, June 15, 2016, 18:29 EST, https://web.archive.org/web/20160922150919/https://twitter.com/pwnallthethings/status/743208737469509632.
9. Matt Tait, "8) Lol . . . ," @pwnallthethings, June 15, 2016, 17:51 EST, https://web.archive.org/web/20161117220229/https://twitter.com/pwnallthethings/status/743197064843104257.
10. Thomas Rid, "Remarkably . . . ," July 8, 2016, 23:03 BST, https://web.archive.org/web/20161117220231/https://twitter.com/RidT/status/751325844002529280.
11. Lorenzo Franceschi-Bicchierai, "'Guccifer 2.0' Is Likely a Russian Government Attempt to Cover Up Its Own Hack," *Motherboard*, June 16, 2016.
12. Secureworks was watching both accounts. Tom Finney, interview with Thomas Rid, January 11, 2019. "Threat Group-4127 Targets Google Accounts," Secureworks, June 26, 2016.
13. Aksana, "Submission #3160712," Phish Tank, April 29, 2015, 20:37 UTC, https://web.archive.org/web/20190111170540/https://www.phishtank.com/phish_detail.php?phish_id=3160712.
14. Tom Finney, interview with Thomas Rid, January 11, 2019. "Threat Group-4127 Targets Google Accounts," Secureworks, June 26, 2016.
15. *Russian Active Measures Campaigns and Interference in the 2016 U.S. Election, Volume 1*, report 116-XX, U.S. Senate Select Committee on Intelligence, Washington, DC, July 25, 2019, p. 15, 22.

16. Mueller, *USA v. Viktor Borisovich Netyksho et al.*, pp. 17–18.

17. Ibid., p. 18.

18. @guccifer_2 to @ridt, Twitter direct message conversation, July 22, 2016, 21:35 Moscow time, archived at https://archive.org/details/ridt-g2.

19. Max Fisher, "Prizing Speed and Scoops, Media Became Ready Bullhorns for Russian Hackers," *The New York Times*, January 9, 2017, p. 7.

20. @GUCCIFER_2 to @razhael, private Twitter message, August 22, 2016.

21. Lou Dobbs, "Leftist Fascism," August 27, 2019, 22:25 EST, https://web.archive.org/web/20190412053329/https://twitter.com/LouDobbs/Status/769722543951536128.

22. Department of Homeland Security and Office of the Director of National Intelligence, Joint Statement on Election Security, DHS Press Office, October 7, 2016.

23. Mikael Thalen, in correspondence with Thomas Rid, December 17, 2016.

24. @guccifer_2 to @alexjones, October 19, 2016, direct message, unpublished.

30. Trolled

1. Александра Гармажапова, "Где живут тролли," *Novaya Gazeta*, September 9, 2013.

2. Robert Mueller, *Report on the Investigation into Russian Interference in the 2016 Presidential Election*, U.S. Department of Justice (Washington, DC, March 2019), p. 14.

3. Natalya Lvova, "Как у нас делается политика," VK, August 29, 2013, 23:56, https://web.archive.org/web/20130915025953/http://vk.com/note458765_11765596.

4. Андрей Сошников, "Под Петербургом обнаружено логово троллей, которые клеймят Навального и хвалят русское кино," *Мой район*, September 4, 2013.

5. Ibid.

6. Robert Mueller, *USA v. Internet Research Agency*: Indictment, Case 1:18-cr-00032-DLF, U.S. District Court for the District of Columbia, February 16, 2018, p. 6.

7. Mueller, *Report on the Investigation into Russian Interference in the 2016 Presidential Election*, p. 14.

8. Mueller, *USA v. Internet Research Agency*: Indictment, p. 13.

9. Naira Davlashyan and Irina Titova, "Ex-Workers at Russian 'Troll Factory' Trust U.S. Indictment," *The Washington Post*, Feburary 19, 2018.

10. Ibid.

11. Ben Popken and Kelly Cobiella, "Russian Troll Describes Work in the Infamous Misinformation Factory" (interview with Vitaly Bespalov), NBC, November 16, 2017.

12. Simon Adler and Annie McEwen, "The Curious Case of the Russian Flash Mob at the West Palm Beach Cheesecake Factory," WNYC, February 20, 2018.

13. Anton Troianovski, "A Former Russian Troll Speaks: 'It Was Like Being in Orwell's World,'" *The Washington Post*, February 17, 2018.

14. Popken and Cobiella, "Russian Troll Describes Work in the Infamous Misinformation Factory.

15. Андрей Сошников, "Столица политического троллинга," *Мой район*, March 11, 2015.

16. Quoted in Russian, "Просто тестирование возможностей, эксперимент. И он удался," in Полина Русяева and Андрей Захаров, "Расследование РБК: как

'фабрика троллей' поработала на выборах в США," *RBC* 11, 135 (November 2017, published online October 17, 2017).

17. Adrian Chen, "The Agency," *The New York Times Magazine*, June 7, 2015, p. 57.

18. Русяева and Захаров, "Расследование РБК: как 'фабрика троллей' поработала на выборах в США."

19. Евгения Котляр, "первое видеоинтервью с экс-сотрудником американского отдела 'фабрики троллей'," *Dozhd*, October 27, 2017.

20. Русяева and Захаров, "Расследование РБК: как 'фабрика троллей' поработала на выборах в США."

21. The quoted guidance is from October 2017. Comparable documents from 2016 or earlier were not available. *USA v. Elena Alekseevna Khusyaynova*: Criminal Complaint, U.S. District Court for the Eastern District of Virginia, Case 1:18-MJ-464, September 28, 2018, p. 14.

22. Ibid.

23. See archived profile of @Crystal1Johnson, version captured on June 9, 2016, https://web.archive.org/web/20160609011222/https://twitter.com/Crystal1Johnson.

24. See archived version of @BlackToLive, captured September 23, 2016, https://web.archive.org/web/20160923220953/https://twitter.com/blacktolive.

25. Data from Twitter's IRA account release.

26. @Crystal1Johnson was the most popular black activist account, with 22.5K followers by November 17, 2016.

27. See the archived @TEN_GOP profile at https://web.archive.org/web/20160929175843/https://twitter.com/TEN_GOP.

28. Posted by @TEN_GOP on November 9, 2016, 21:18, in data released by Twitter.

29. "Update on Twitter's Review of the 2016 US Election," Twitter Blog, January 19, 2018 (updated January 31, 2018).

30. Котляр, "первое видеоинтервью с экс-сотрудником американского отдела 'фабрики троллей.'"

31. Ibid.

32. Bridget Coyne, "How #Election2016 Was Tweeted So far," *Twitter*, November 7, 2016.

33. Twitter, in response to questions from Congress, also cast a wider net and identified all automated accounts with some form of link to Russia, beyond the accounts the firm was able to link directly to the IRA. Twitter identified 50,258 such "Russian-linked" automated accounts. The accounts generated 1 percent of all election-related traffic, but underperformed in generating impressions (only 0.49 percent). The bots generated 4.25 percent of all retweets of the @realDonaldTrump account during the election campaign (0.55 percent for @HillaryClinton). It remains unclear if one agency controlled the majority of these bots, and who that agency was. Sean Edgett, "Update on Results of Retrospective Review of Russian-Related Election Activity," Twitter, published by the U.S. Senate Committee on the Judiciary, 19 January 2019, p. 5.

34. The number of preelection "impressions" was approximately 47 million. Facebook cites 126 million impressions between January 1, 2015, and August 2017. User engagement with IRA content after the election, however, significantly outstriped preelection engagement (37% versus 63%). Author conversations with Facebook; calculations based on data provided to the Senate Select Committee on Intelligence.

35. Data source: "Social Media Advertisements," U.S. House of Representatives, Permanent Select Committee on Intelligence, May 10, 2018; the "Satan v Jesus" ad is at https://archive.org/details/2016-satan-v-jesus.

36. The online headline was "Russia-Financed Ad Linked Clinton and Satan"; the print issue story was headlined, "Congress Scolds Tech Companies over Russia," *The New York Times*, November 2, 2017, p. A1.

37. Mueller, *USA v. Internet Research Agency*: Indictment, p. 7.

38. Ibid.

39. No evidence of coordinated GRU-IRA tasking has emerged, despite press coverage alleging otherwise; see "Study Links Russian Tweets to Release of Hacked Emails," Associated Press, October 11, 2019; also @ridt, "Too many assumptions necessary here that are implausible and not supported by evidence," October 11, 2019, https://web.archive .org/web/20191011182025/https://twitter.com/RidT/status/1182679515094573056.

40. Mueller, *USA v. Internet Research Agency*: Indictment, p. 8.

31. The Shadow Brokers

1. See "EQGRP Auction Files Metadata," Internet Archive, January 22, 2019, https:// archive.org/details/EQGRP-auction-files-metadata.

2. APT28 is GRU with high confidence. The attribution of APT29 to SVR is more difficult to source publicly; I have moderate confidence in this link.

3. Lee Ferran, correspondence with author, January 28, 2019.

4. Lee Ferran, "The NSA Is Likely 'Hacking Back' Russia's Cyber Squads," ABC News, July 30, 2016.

5. Matt Suiche, "Shadow Brokers: NSA Exploits of the Week," *Comae*, August 15, 2016.

6. "github . . . ," @liamosaur, August 15, 2016, 07:03 GMT, https://web.archive.org/web /20190121202843/https://twitter.com/liamosaur/status/765081533535232000.

7. See Matthieu Suiche, *The Shadow Brokers* (Comae Technologies, July 2017), p. 5.

8. "Assessing Russian Activities and Intentions in Recent U.S. Elections," Office of the Director of National Intelligence, January 6, 2017.

9. "#EquationGroup . . . ," @shadowbrokerss, January 8, 2017, 05:05:26 GMT, https:// web.archive.org/web/20170408181603/https://twitter.com/shadowbrokerss/status /817960380815306752.

10. Ellen Nakashima and Craig Timberg, "NSA Officials Worried About the Day Its Potent Hacking Tool Would Get Loose. Then It Did," *The Washington Post*, May 16, 2017.

11. Matt Tait, online conversation with Thomas Rid, January 23, 2019.

12. Nakashima and Timberg, "NSA Officials Worried About the Day Its Potent Hacking Tool Would Get Loose."

13. "MS17-010," Microsoft Support, March 14, 2017.

14. "Putin calls US strikes against Syria 'aggression against sovereign country'," TASS, April 7, 2017.

15. "Don't Forget Your Base," *The Shadow Brokers*, April 8, 2017; https://web.archive.org /web/20170408120807/https://medium.com/@shadowbrokerss/dont-forget-your -base-867d304a94b1.

16. The decrypted archive of Windows tools is 5bb9ddfbcefb75d017a9e745b83729390617 b16f4079356579ef00e5e6b5fbd0.

17. Shadow Brokers, "Equation Group Cyber Weapons Auction—Invitation," GitHub, August 13, 2016, https://web.archive.org/web/20160815124425/https://github.com/theshadowbrokers/EQGRP-AUCTION.

18. "New Shadow Brokers dump contains . . . ," @musalbas, 31 October 31, 2016, 08:06:19 GMT, https://web.archive.org/web/20190124142000/https://twitter.com/musalbas/status/793001139310559232.

19. Matt Suiche, "ShadowBrokers: The NSA Compromised the SWIFT Network," *Comae*, April 14, 2017.

20. "NHS Workers and Patients on How Cyber-attack Has Affected Them," *The Guardian*, May 13, 2017.

21. Fedor Sinitsyn, "Kaspersky Security Bulletin: Story of the Year 2017," *Securelist*, November 28, 2017.

22. Ibid.

23. "Хакерська атака уразила до 10% комп'ютерів в Україні, приватних, урядових і комерційних," Associated Press, July 6, 2017.

24. Jill Leovy, "Cyberattack Cost Maersk as Much as $300 Million," *Los Angeles Times*, August 19, 2017, p. C3.

25. Kim Nash, "One Year After NotPetya Cyberattack, Firms Wrestle with Recovery Costs," *Wall Street Journal*, June 27, 2018.

26. Mondelēz International, Inc., "Complaint," Circuit Court of Cook County, Illinois, October 10, 2018, pp. 2–3.

27. Aaron Ricadela, "Europe's Cyber Victims Are Racking Up Hundreds of Millions in Costs," *Bloomberg*, August 3, 2017.

28. "Statement from the Press Secretary," White House, February 15, 2018.

29. Matthew Olney, @kpyke, "Almost 98% . . . ," July 11, 2019, https://web.archive.org/web/20190809005208/https://twitter.com/kpyke/status/1149350247061229569.

30. Matthew Rosenberg, "U.S. Spies Paid Russian Peddling Trump Secrets," *The New York Times*, February 10, 2018, p. A1.

31. In the wee hours of April 10, 2017, for example, the Shadow Brokers aggressively responded to a blog post by Jake Williams, outing him as a former member of NSA's Tailored Access Operations team. The response included obscure code names like "OddJob" and "CCI"—an insider signal to Williams that the Shadow Brokers were familiar with secret details of his career inside NSA and his public talks since. See @shadowbrokerss, "2/2 leak OddJob? Windows BITS persistence? CCI?," April 10, 2017, 02:56 UTC, post #851267561744289793 not archived at its original URL. For a comprehensive record, see https://web.archive.org/web/20181231215630/https://swithak.github.io/SH20TAATSB18/Archive/Tweets/TSB/TSBTwitterHistory/. For context, see Andy Greenberg, *Sandworm* (New York: Doubleday, 2019), p. 161. Also note the reference by an obscure account, @LexingtonAl, archived at https://web.archive.org/web/20190923140434/https:/twitter.com/Mao_Ware/status/1097891011202875392.

A Century of Disinformation

1. The full name is Bundesbehörde für die Unterlagen des Staatssicherheitsdienstes der ehemaligen Deutschen Demokratischen Republik.

2. Jens Gieseke, *Die Stasi* (Munich: Pantheon, 2011), p. 359.

3. Helmut Müller-Enbergs, "Die inoffiziellen Mitarbeiter," in *Anatomie der Staatssicherheit*, MfS-Handbuch IV/2 (Berlin: BStU, 2008), p. 38.

4. There were, to my knowledge, no female officers in HVA/X. See Günter Bohnsack and Herbert Brehmer, *Auftrag Irreführung* (Hamburg: Carlsen, 1992), p. 81.

5. "Geheimdokument Rockefellers," *Neues Deutschland*, February 15, 1957, p. 1.

6. "Testimony of Lawrence Britt" (pseudonym), Hearing, Committee on the Judiciary, U.S. Senate (Washington, DC: Government Printing Office, May 5, 1971), p. 5.

7. Michel Foucault, *L'ordre du discours* (Paris: Gallimard, 1971), p. 16.

8. Horst Kopp, former officer in HVA X/3, interview with Thomas Rid, Kyritz, May 4, 2017.

9. Евгения Котляр, "первое видеоинтервью с экс-сотрудником американского отдела 'фабрики троллей,'" *Dozhd*, October 27, 2017.

10. Lawrence (Ladislav) Bittman, interview with Thomas Rid, Rockport, Mass., March 25, 2017, https://archive.org/details/bittman-on-measuring-am.

11. Kate Starbird, in correspondence with Thomas Rid, online and offline, Sausalito, CA, April 2019.

12. Mike Isaac and Daisuke Wakabayashi, "Russian Influence Reached 126 Million Through Facebook Alone," *The New York Times*, October 17, 2017.

13. The most recent term, in Russian, is "мероприятия содействия"; see Евгений Максимович Примаков, *Очерки истории российской внешней разведки, Том 2* (Москва: Международные отношения, 1996), p. 14. See also Ivo Juurvee, "The Resurrection of 'Active Measures,'" *Strategic Analysis* (Hybrid CoE), April 2018.

ACKNOWLEDGMENTS

Errors in fact and interpretation that may mar this work are mine and mine alone. A humbling number of individuals shared details and documents with me, or recommended me to their own sources—this book would not be possible without their help, their trust, and their patience. Not all can be named.

Senator Mark Warner, Michael Pevzner, and Andrew Weiss deserve a prominent mention for inviting me to testify on active measures at a crucial moment in front of the U.S. Senate Select Committee on Intelligence, in March 2017. The hearing was a critical impetus for this book. I would particularly like to thank—in alphabetical order—Dmitri Alperovitch, Nathaniel Gleicher, Raffi Khatchadourian, Todd Leventhal, Ellen Nakashima, Raphael Satter, and Matt Tait for their trust and many repeated conversations about arcane details, and for sharing insights as we moved along the story. Tom Finney deserves a special mention for his help in many conversations and for sharing a compelling database with me at a pivotal moment.

A number of individuals helped me in small and big ways, notably David Agranovich, Richard Bach, Bobby Baird, David Balson, Brian Bartholomew, Nate Beach-Westmoreland, Olga Belogolova, Thomas Boghardt, Ben Buchanan, Philip Chertoff, Paul Chichester, Kevin Collier, Paul Ducheine, Nicholas Dujmovic, Gil Elliot, Lee Foster, Lorenzo Franceschi-Bicchierai, Alexander Gabuev, Erhard Geißler, Aleks Gostev, Mark Graham, Jason Gresh, The Grugq, Juan Andrés Guerrero-Saade, Nathaniel Hartley, Georg Herbstritt, Stephen Hilt, John Hultquist, Shane Huntley, Ivo Juurvee, Gary Keeley, Peter Koop (aka Electrospaces), Nikolay Koval, Rob Lee, Adam Meyers, Clint Montgomery, Jerry Mueller, Helmut Müller-Enbergs, Christopher Nehring, Ben Nimmo, Adrian Nish, Nellie Ohr, Dan O'Keefe, Jakub Petlák, Igor Protsyk, Laura Rosenberger, Katerina Sedova, Douglas Selvage, Stephan Somogyi, Valentino De Sousa, Jochen Staadt, Timo Steffens, Mark Stout, Eli Sugarman, David Thomas, Aric Toler, Kelli Vanderlee, and Michael Warner.

For help with translating documents, I would like to thank Mustafa Batuhan Albaş, Marina Dickson, Maria Gershuni, Denitsa Nikolova, and Chenny Zhang. For help with thorny research tasks, my gratitude goes to Batu, Ludovica Barozzi, Joakim Bjørnestad, Mona Damian, Keel Dietz, Lucie Kadlecová, Scott Karo, Jenny Kusmik, Siri Strand, Ingrid Winther, and a good number of my followers on Twitter who responded to my frequent public questions. Danny Moore's wizardry was empowering. I would also like to thank Jan Makovička and Veronika Chromá at the Archiv bezpečnostních složek in Prague, Iris Winkler at the BStU in Berlin, and the COMDOS Archive in Sofia for making their files available.* The Bundesamt für Sicherheit in der Informationstechnik, the Legal Theory Workshop at Yale Law School, Catholic University's Department of History, SANS, CYBERWARCON, FireEye, iDefense, and Facebook hosted valuable discussions of work in progress; the Hewlett Foundation generously supported some of my research. At SAIS I am deeply grateful to my colleagues Eliot Cohen, Mara Karlin, Thayer McKell, John McLaughlin, and Vali Nasr.

None of this would have happened without my invaluable agents George Lucas and Catherine Clarke. Eric Chinski and Julia Ringo's vision, elegance, and sense of style were an inspiration throughout. And of course, thank you, Annette.

---

*BStU stands for the Federal Commissioner for the Records of the State Security Service of the former German Democratic Republic; COMDOS is the colloquial term and website for the Committee for Disclosing the Documents and Announcing the Affiliation of Bulgarian Citizens to the State Security and the Intelligence Services of the Bulgarian National Army (CDDAABCSSISBNA).

INDEX

Page numbers in *italics* refer to illustrations.

A

Aaron, Edward, 138

ABC, *188*, 189

accurate information, 10

Acquired Immune Deficiency
    Syndrome (AIDS), 8, 301–11, *305*

active measures (AM), 6; activism and,
    231–32, 242, 432–33; Agayants's legacy
    with, 132–33, 146; Bittman on, 148–49,
    430; CIA compared to KGB funding of,
    323; contradictions of, 9; covert action
    and, 13–14; cynicism and, 312; digital
    leaks and, 341; effective, 428; features
    of, 9; FM 30-31B and, 240; in Germany,
    316–18; internet reshaping, 7, 12–14,
    336–37, 433–34; Ivanov on, 244–45,
    314–15, 321; journalism and, 318, 336;
    KGB's goals with, 149; measurement
    of, 430–31; origin of, 7; postmodernism
    and, 429–30; recognizing, 9; Service A
    and, 245, 313–14; skill set for, 428–29;
    Soviet budget for, 313; Stasi's history
    with, 121; as support measures, 433;
    the Trust's success inspiring, 31; *see also*
    disinformation

*Active Measures of Eastern Intelligence
    Services* report, 316

activism, 12–13, 226, 231–34, 242,
    302, 339, 344, 351, 432–33; *see also*
    Anonymous; peacewar

Adenauer, Konrad, 123, 126–27, 154–55

"Adventures of Mr. Hudson in Russia," 335

Adzhubei, Alexei, 155

AEDEPOT, 181

Afghanistan, 299–300

AFL (American Federation of Labor), 54

African Friends Association pamphlet, 137–39, *139*

Agayants, Ivan Ivanovich, 130–33, 145–46, *146*, 154, 156, 165, 184–86, 196–97

Agee, Phil, *222*, 222–27, 231–32, 240, 342, 432–33

agent-report forms, of CIA, 208–10

AIDS, *see* Acquired Immune Deficiency Syndrome

Aktionsgruppe B, 70, 72, 87

Albuquerque Journal, 366

Alexander, Keith, 3–4

Alexandrov, Vladimir, *292*, 292–97

Alperovitch, Dmitri, 386

American Communist Party, 280

American Federation of Labor (AFL), 54

American Jewish Committee, 127

Amsterdam News, 308

Amtorg, 49–50, 53, 54, 56

Andronov, Iona, 298–300

Andropov Red Banner Institute, 31

Anonymous, 12, 344–47, *345*, 351–54, *352*, 357–58, 372–74, 484n51

Anonymous Ukraine, 346–47, 351, 354, 357–58

ANT catalog, 347–48

anti-Semitism, 103, 123–26, *124, 125*, 128–33, 451n29

APT28, *see* SOFACY

APT29 (COZY BEAR), 385

Äquator publishing, 70, 87, 91, 98, 99; *see also* LCCASSOCK

Arbeitskreis (Working Group for a Nuclear-Weapons-Free Europe), 277

Arcos Ltd., 49

Armstrong, Louis, 95

Arnoni, Menachem, 139–41

Artuzov, Artur, 20–28, 130

Ashbrook, John, 261–62

Aslanov, Dzheykhun, 402, 404, 409

Assange, Julian, 13, 338–39, 385–86, 390–93

Associated Press, 177

astrology, 90–92

Augstein, Rudolf, 151, 153

Australian, The, 309

B

Bach, Peter, 270

BAE systems, 364, 372, 484n51

Barış, 236

Barron, John, 216–19, *217*, 285

Barzel, Rainer, *152*

Bassam, Mustafa Al-, 418

Bastian, Gert, 271, 284

Baudissin, Wolf Graf von, 271

Bechet, Sidney, 95

Ben-Gurion, David, 141

Bennett, William Tapley, Jr., 259

Berecz, János, 260

Berlin Airlift, 64

Berliner Zeitung, 215

Berlin Operations Base (BOB), 64–66, 69–70, 72

Berlin Tunnel, 70

Bernadsky, Gregory, 55–56

Berry, Frank, 108–109, 112

Bertrand Russell Peace Foundation, 265–66

BfV, 200, 316

Biedenkopf, Kurt, 208–10

Bigot, Yves, 370–71

Biological Weapons Convention of
1972, 306

Bit.ly, 392

Bittman, Ladislav, *102*, 165; on AM,
148–49, 430; defection of, 4, 122,
147; on disinformation, 4–5, 14,
147–48, 428; NEPTUN operation and,
157–58, *159*, 160; as painter, 429; on
Strasbourg cigar box bomb, 122; on
Who's Who in CIA, 178–79

Black Boomerang (Delmer), 438*n*7

Black Lake, 157–62, *159*, *161*

Black Lives Matter movement, 431

BlackToLive (sock puppet), 404

Bleep the Police (sock puppet), 404

Blitz, 308

BND (Bundesnachrichtendienst), 100,
128, 159, 184–91, 211–12

BOB (Berlin Operations Base), 64–66,
69–70, 72

Bogdanov, Peter, 50, 281

Bohnsack, Günter, 271–72, 460*n*8

Boiko, Arkady, 155

Boston Globe, The, 282

Brandt, Willy, 95, 126, 202–204, 269

Brattain, Steven Michael, 325

Bräunig, Werner, 114–15

Breaking3Zero, 371

Breedlove, Philip, 366, 383

Breuer, Klaus, 199

Brezhnev, Leonid, 258

Bronze Soldier conflict, 333–34

BStU, 323, 423–24

Buckley, William F., Jr., 153

Bukharin, Nikolai, 35

Bund, Der, 211

Bundesnachrichtendienst (BND), 100,
128, 159, 184–91, 211–12

Bush, George W., 338

Butz, Timothy, 220, 221

C

CADROIT, 68

Campbell, Duncan, 268

Canaris, Wilhelm, 211

Capra, Frank, 42

CARIC (Committee for Action/
Research on the Intelligence
Community), 220–21

Carter, Jimmy, 257–59

CBS Evening News, 309–10

CEC (Central Election Commission),
360–63

CEDADE, 201

Central Election Commission (CEC),
360–63

Central Intelligence Agency (CIA),
6–7, 449*n*24; Agee exposing, 224;
agent-report forms of, 208–10; AIDS
causes and, 302–306; AM funding
of KGB compared to, 323; Berlin
Tunnel and, 70; BOB of, 64–66,
69–70, 72; Clandestine Services
of, 181; *Covert Action Information
Bulletin* and, 232–33; covert funding
by, 8, 437*n*6; Fifth Estate allegations
of, 225; forgery and, 81, 113, 318–19;
Headquarters Germany and, 323–26,
324; Helms and, 102, 449*n*24;
Kampfverband investigation of,
121–22; *KGB* (Barron) and, 216–19,
217; KgU and, 66–67, 73–75, 81–84;
on nuclear winter, 290; Office of Policy
Coordination of, 64; Penkovsky's
work with, 168–69, 173–74; Phoenix
Program of, 220; QRPLUMB operation
and, 321–23; Red Brigades and, 239;
the Trust study of, 17–18, 21, 23, 24;
UfJ and, 67–70, 72; *see also* LCCASSOCK

CERT (Computer Emergency Response
Team), 362–63

Chandra, Romesh, 280

Channel One, 361–63

Charlie Hebdo massacre, 366

Checkpoint Charlie Museum, 66

Cheka, 19–23, 25–32

chemical weapons, 199–200, 299–308, 417

Chen, Adrian, 402

Chernobyl disaster, 318–20, *320*

Cherry, W. B., 138

Chicago Tribune, 225

Chile, 247–48

China, 33, 37, 39, 43–46, 156–57; *see also* Tanaka Memorial

China Critic, The, 37

Chisholm, Janet Anne, 167

"Christian-Marxist" dialogue workshops, 278–79

Christian Science Monitor, 282

Church Committee, 175

CIA, *see* Central Intelligence Agency

cigar box bomb of Strasbourg, 118–20, 122

Click magazine, 40–41, *41*

Clinton, Hillary, 379–81, 383–85, 387–90, 393–94

Colby, William, 216–17, 226

Cold War, *see specific topics*

Comintern, the, 38, 38–39, 50–52

Committee for Action/Research on the Intelligence Community (CARIC), 220–21

Communist International, 38, *38*, 45, 49

Computer Emergency Response Team (CERT), 362–63

Comrade J. (Tretyakov), 291

Concord, 399, 408, 409

Congressional Record, 318

Congress of Cultural Freedom, 8

Counterspy, 220–21, 224–25, 285, 322

Covert Action Information Bulletin, 231–33, *233*, 239–42, 285, 301

COZY BEAR (APT29), 385

Cramer Advertising Office, *see* LCCASSOCK

Cramer Werbung, *see* LCCASSOCK

Crimea annexation, 353–59

CrowdStrike, 384–88

Cryptome, 337–39

Cuba, 223, 237, 300–301

Cuban Missile Crisis, 169

Cumhuriyet, 170

Curious Camera TV show, 157, *162*

Current Affairs Monthly, 37

cyb3rc.com, 369

CyberBerkut, 353–54, 359, 360, 363, 369

CyberCaliphate, 366–69, *367*

CyberGuerrilla, *345*, 345–47, 351–54, 357

cypherpunks, 12, 337

Czechoslovakia, 122

D

Daily Mail, 335

Davis, John (sock puppet), 405–406

DCCC (Democratic Congressional Campaign Committee), 381–82

DCITA (Defense Cyber Investigations Training Academy), 369

DCLeaks, *383*, 383–85, 394–95

Deception Game, The (Bittman), 4, 122

Defense Cyber Investigations Training Academy (DCITA), 369

Defense Intelligence Agency (DIA), 151–52

Delmer, Sefton, 438*n*7

Democratic Congressional Campaign Committee (DCCC), 381–82

Democratic National Committee (DNC), 4–6, 383–90, 393, 394

dengue fever, 301

DENVER operation, 306–11

Department 8, see Státní bezpečnost

Department D, 130–31, 137, 145–46, 149–50

Department X (the X): *Active Measures of Eastern Intelligence Services* report and, 316; agent-report forms and, 208–10; civil war fought by, 213–14; internal newsletters and, 210–12; legacy of, 424; origins of, 197; professionalism of, 204; RIGAS operation of, 206–208, 207; scientist defectors and, 199–200; secrecy of, 194, 425; Wagner, L., and, 204–206, 205; Wolf, M., and, 196–97, 199; ZEUS operation of, 201–202

Deriabin, Peter, 132, 149–50, 174–75, 297

Dethloff, Walter, 76

DEVASTATION operation, 198–200

Devil and His Dart, 308

Devil's Lake, 157–61

DGI (Dirección General de Inteligencia), 223–24

DIA (Defense Intelligence Agency), 151–52

digital leaks: AM and, 341; Assange on Clinton's emails and, 385, 393; Crimea annexation and, 353–59; Cryptome and, 337–39; CyberBerkut and, 353–54, 359, 360, 363, 369; CyberGuerrilla and, 345, 345–47, 351–54, 357; DCLeaks and, 383, 383–85, 394–95; DNC hack and, 4–6; EU and U.S. exposed in, 348–50; forgery and, 340; Guccifer 2.0 and, 387–96, 389; journalism and, 340; Malaysia Airlines disaster and, 364; Merkel and, 341–44, 342; of NSA hacking tools, 410–13, 417; Panama Papers and, 381–82; Podesta's emails and, 388–90, 395, 485–86n26; Protsyk's forged emails and, 354–59, 356; Schneier on, 340–41; of Shadow Brokers, 412–13, 415–16; Snowden and, 339–40; Ukraine and Russian-orchestrated, 346–50; WikiLeaks and, 10, 338–39; see also Anonymous; hacking operations

Dirección General de Inteligencia (DGI), 223–24

disinformation: accurate information in, 10; Artuzov and, 25–26; Bittman on, 4–5, 14, 147–48, 428; Black Lives Matter movement and, 431; data and, 14; East and West divide on, 11–12; election interference of 2016 and, 6; emotion and, 11, 315, 426; four waves of, 6–7; goals of, 7, 426; HVA's focus on, 121; imperfection of, 9–10; KgU and, 77; learning from past, 8–9; misconceptions about, 9–10; oral, 249–51; passage of time and, 430; postmodernism and, 429–30; self-, 156, 296–97; skill set for, 428–29; targets of, 251; see also active measures

DNC (Democratic National Committee), 4–6, 383–90, 393, 394

Dobbert, Andreas, 323–26, 324

Dobbins, Jim, 268

Dobrynin, Anatoly, 173–74, 260

Dodd, Thomas, 255

Dönitz, Karl, 71

DOUBLEPULSAR, 419

"double-track decision," 265–66

Drummond, Roscoe, 111–12

DTLINEN, 66–67, 77, 81, 83

Dulles, Allen, 64–65, 101–102, 111–12, 149–50

Dulles, John Foster, 106
Dulles Memorandum, 106–107
Dumov, Aleksei, 274
Dunne, Kenneth, 149–50
Durenberger, David, 318–19
Dzerzhinsky, Feliks, *18*, 19–23, 27–36, 46, 389
Dzhirkvelov, Ilya, 154, 260

E
economic inequality, 317
Economist, The, 326
Edwards, Bob, 149–50
Eichner, Klaus, 323–26, *324*
Eisenhower, Dwight D., 104–106, 107, 127
election interference: in Germany, 202–206; of KgU, 81–82; of Russia in Ukraine, 360–63; Stasi and, 10; Wagenbreth and, 212–13
election interference, 2016, 3; DCLeaks and, *383*, 383–85, 394–95; disinformation and, 6; DNC hack and, 4–6, 383–86; GRU and state-level, 392; Guccifer 2.0 and, 387–96, *389*; IRA's effectiveness in, 406; Putin and, 415; U.S. response to, 414–15
electionleaks.com, 382
Ellsberg, Daniel, 219, 258
Elternhaus und Schule, 79
epistemic superiority, 426
EQGRP-AUCTION-FILE.ZIP, 410–13, 417
España Independiente radio station, 112
Estonia, 20, 25, 333–34
ETERNALBLUE, 416, 418–19, 421
ETERNALROMANCE, 419
EU (European Union), 119, 346–50
"Euromaidan" protest movement, in Ukraine, 353
European Union (EU), 119, 346–50

Europeo, L', 238–39
Evening Graphic, 52

F
Facebook, 332, 333, 353, 384, *398*, 401, 407–408, 431, 488*n34*
Fag Rag, 302
FALLEX 62, 150–51, 155
FANCY BEAR, *see* SOFACY
Farmer, Art, 95
FedEx, 420
Fedorov, A., 49
Felfe, Heinz, 185–87, 191
Fellwock, Perry (Winslow Peck), 219–21
Fifth Estate, 220–22, 224–26
Figaro, Le, 372
Finland, 26–27, 30
FireEye, 365, 368, 484*n51*
First Chief Directorate building, 243–44, *244*
Fish, Hamilton, Jr., 52–53
Fish Committee, *48*, 52–53, 55–56
Fitzgerald, Ella, 95
Fleissmann, Georg, 204–206
"Flying Psychoneurosis, The" (Bräunig), 114–15
FM 30-31B, *233*, 465*n3*; AM and, 240; classified information in, 234; *Covert Action Information Bulletin* printing, 230, *230*, 239–42; focus of, 233–34; forgery and, 234–36; in Italy, 238–39; in Philippines, 236–37; Schaap on authenticity of, 241; Service A and, 235; in Spain, 237
Ford, Gerald, 226
Ford Foundation, 83–84
Foreign Affairs (magazine), 290, 294
Foreign Intelligence Service (SVR), 18–19, 23, 30–32, 44–46, 332–33, 410

forgery, 7, 8; CEC attack and, 362–63; CIA and, 81, 113, 318–19; deniability and, 156–57; digital leaks and, 340; distrust spread by, 56; Dulles Memorandum and, 106–107; exposure and spread of, 56–57; FM 30-31B and, 234–36; Helms on, 103, 115; Kampfverband and, 120–21; KGB and, 103, 106, 113–15; of KgU, 80–81; KKK leaflets and, *135*, 135–36; LCCASSOCK and, 70–73, 87–89, 92; Marbach and, 71–72, 92; NEPTUN operation and, 158, 162; neutron bomb and, 259–60; nuclear war threats and, 110–13; OPLAN 10-1 and, *185*, 186–87, 189; *The Penkovsky Papers* and, 172–73; Prats's diary, *247*, 247–48; *Protocols of the Elders of Zion* and, 103; Protsyk's emails and, 354–59, *356*; Rockefeller letter, *104*, 104–106, 111–12; of *Schlagzeug* by KGB, 113–15; spotting, 53; Tanaka Memorial as, 39, 41–42, 45; Whalen documents and, 50–57

Forsberg, Randall, 281
Forward, The, *51*, 52
Foucault, Michel, 428
France Nouvelle, 156
Franceschi-Bicchierai, Lorenzo, 391
Frankfurter Allgemeine Zeitung, 188
Frau, Die, *97*, 98
Frau von Heute, Die, 88
free press, 176
Freie Bauer, Der, 88
Frey, Gerhard, 208
Friedenskampf, *see* peacewar
Fruck, Hans, 91–92
FSB, 330–31, 415
Fuchs, Jürgen, 277

G

Gailat, Kurt, 269–70
Gaines, Stanley, 70
Gates, Robert, 17–18
Gawker, 394
Gay Community News, 302
Gehlen, Reinhard, 185, 211
Geist und Leben, 78–79
Generale, Die (documentary), 283–84
Generals for Peace, *264*, 270–73, 282–83
Genscher, Hans-Dietrich, 270
Germany: AM in, 316–18; Berlin Airlift and, 64; Berlin Tunnel and, 70; BOB in, 64–66, 69–70, 72; election interference in, 202–206; FALLEX 62 and, 150–51; guest worker program in, 206–208, *207*; hate crimes legislation in, 126; special camps in, 61, 63; suicides in security establishment of, 184; UfJ and, 67–70, 72; *see also* Bundesnachrichtendienst; Hauptverwaltung Aufklärung; LCCASSOCK; Stasi
Gevorkyan, Pavel, 155
Gibney, Frank, 175, 457*n23*
Gizunov, Sergey, 378
Glavlit, 32
Global War Plan for Clandestine Operations, of U.S., 182–83
Gold, Stephen, 294
Gonzalez, Fernando, 237
Goodman, Benny, 96
Google, 332, 333, 365, 378, 380, 391
Gorbachev, Mikhail, 310
Gordievsky, Oleg, 155, 451*n29*
GPU (State Political Directorate), 25, 26
graffiti, anti-Semitic, 123–24, *124*

Grapfen, T. G., 49

Great Depression, 6–7, 47–48

Greek guest workers, RIGAS operation
and, 206–208, 207

Greenwald, Glenn, 343

Gresh, Jason P., 354–55, 355, 358–59

GRU: Assange and, 385–86; Clinton
campaign hacked by, 379–81; DCCC
hacked by, 382; DCLeaks and, 383,
383–85, 394–95; Guccifer 2.0 and,
387–96, 389; headquarters of, 361;
IRA and, 489n39; NotPetya attack
and, 411, 419–21; Secureworks
exposing, 391–92; state-level election
interference by, 392; Unit 26165 of,
377–79, 382, 384; Unit 74455 of, 353,
384, 387, 393; WikiLeaks and, 390;
see also Internet Research Agency

Guardian, The, 226, 247, 259, 340

Guccifer 2.0, 387–96, 389

guerrilla units, U.S., 182

guest worker program, 206–208, 207

Guillaume, Günter, 269

H

hacking operations: against Clinton,
379–81; CyberCaliphate and,
366–69, 367; DCCC and, 381–82;
detecting, 366; DNC and, 4–6,
383–86; Google calling out, 365;
Guccifer 2.0 and, 387–96, 389;
NotPetya attack and, 411, 419–21;
#OpSaudi and, 372–74, 484n51;
Podesta's emails and, 379–80,
384; SOFACY, 364, 368; see also
Anonymous; digital leaks

Hahn, Walter, 151–53

Hansapank, 334

Harare Sunday Mail, 308

Harbottle, Michael, 282, 284

Harvey, William King, 69–70, 77, 82,
83, 85, 93, 93–95

Hatcher, Kyle, 335

hate crimes, 123–26, 124, 128, 132,
451n29

Hatfield, Mark, 294

Hauptverwaltung Aufklärung (HVA),
91, 475n34; Active Measures of
Eastern Intelligence Services report
and, 316; Arbeitskreis and, 277;
archival records of, 245; DENVER
operation and, 309; Devil and His
Dart and, 308; disinformation focus
of, 121; effectiveness of, 213–14, 424;
Fleissmann and, 204–206; Generals
for Peace and, 270–73, 282–83;
Headquarters Germany and, 323–26;
Helms's accusations against, 122;
Kampfverband für Unabhängiges
Deutschland and, 121–22; Die Neue
Nachhut project of, 211–12; nuclear
espionage activities of, 200; peacewar
and, 197–98; RACER operation and,
207–208; RIGAS operation and,
206–208; secrecy of, 194, 425; StB
cooperation with, 166; swastika
vandalism absence of, 132; on youth
values shifts, 273; ZEUS operation
and, 201–202; see also Department X

Headquarters Germany (Eichner and
Dobbert), 323–26, 324

Hearst, William Randolph, Jr., 107–108

Hecksher, Henry, 69

Heim, Max, 197

Heitzer, Enrico, 445n40

Helms, Richard, 62, 102–104, 115, 122,
139, 147, 176, 449n24

Herbstritt, Georg, 423–24

Heusgen, Christoph, 343

Hildebrandt, Rainer, 63, 66, 75, 76, 78, 82

HIV, *see* Acquired Immune Deficiency Syndrome
"Holocaust Again for Europe," 266, 471*n*43
Horizont, 91
horoscope harassment letters, 91–92
House Permanent Select Committee on Intelligence, 407–408
Houska, Josef, 158, 164, 165, 166
Hudson, James, 335
Hudson, Rock, 307
Humanité, L', 238
Hutton, Bernard, 451*n*27
HVA, *see* Hauptverwaltung Aufklärung

I

Iklé, Fred, 253
Illustrierte Wochenblatt, Das, 89
Indonesia, 42–43
Informacia, 335
"Information Books No. 1" leak, 266–69
Infowars, 395
Inside the Aquarium, 365
Inside the Company (Agee), 224
International Atomic Energy Agency, 258
International Congress of Free Jurists, 68
International Department, 153–54
International Organization of Journalists, 155
International Week of Action Against the Neutron Bomb, 257
internet: activism and, 12–13, 344, 351; AM reshaped by, 7, 12–14, 336–37, 433–34; anonymity and, 344–45; Bronze Soldier conflict and, 333–34; historians and, 431–32; journalism disempowered by, 13; in Russia, 331–32; SVR targets on, 332–33

Internet Research Agency (IRA): budget and salaries of, 402–403, 408; distrust spread by, 400; effectiveness of, 406–408, 431, 488*n*34; encryption tactics of, 403; Facebook advertisements of, *398*, 401, 407–408, 431, 488*n*34; GRU and, 489*n*39; headquarters of, 400; journalists exposing, 399, 402; morale and professionalism at, 399–400; Prigozhin and, 399, 408–409; racial engineering and, 403–404; sock puppets of, 403–406, *405*; tactics of, 397–98; translator project of, 400; on Twitter, 406, 407; U.S. research by, 400–402
Investigation Committee of Free Jurists (UfJ), 67–70, 72
IRA, *see* Internet Research Agency
Islamic State (ISIS), 366–70
Italy, 237–39
Ivanov, Vladimir Petrovich, 244–49, 247, 251, 252, 314–15, 321
Izvestia, 50, 155, 310

J

Jamaica, 242
Japan, 33–34, 37, 39, 41–42, 63, 338; *see also* Tanaka Memorial
Johnson, Crystal (sock puppet), 403–404
Johnson, Lyndon B., 177
Johnson, Robert Lee, 190–93, 422
Joint State Political Directorate (OGPU), 28, 30, 34–35, 37, 46
Jones, Alex, 395–96
journalism: AM and, 318, 336; digital leaks and, 340; free press and, 176; Guccifer 2.0 and, 394–95; internet disempowering, 13; IRA exposed by,

journalism (*cont.*)
399, 402; leaks and, 195; Shadow
Brokers and, 418; Wagenbreth on
intelligence and, 195–96, 336, 399
Joyce, Robert, 411–12, 420
Junge Generation, 88
Junge Welt, 72, 88

K

Kade, Gerhard, 272
Kaiser, Wolfgang, 79
Kaiser ministry (Ministry for All-
German Affairs), 83–84
Kalugin, Oleg, 132, 134–35, 140–41,
218–19, 223, 307
Kämpfer, Der, 78
Kampfgruppe gegen Unmenschlichkeit
(KgU), 72; administrative harassment
and, 79–81; balloon distribution of,
79, *80*; brochures of, 78–79; CIA and,
66–67, 73–75, 81–84; closure of, 84;
courage of, 65–66; disinformation
and, 77; election interference of, 81–82;
Ford Foundation funding, 83–84;
forgery of, 80–81; founding of, 63;
goals of, 63, 73, 76; graffiti campaign
of, 77; hardware sabotage operations
of, 81; Hildebrandt's removal from, 76;
operating expenses of, 84; registry of,
74–75; size of, 66, 74; success of, 73, 82
Kampfverband für Unabhängiges
Deutschland, 116–18, *118*, 120–22
Kapitsa, Sergei, 294
Kapralov, Yuri, 281–82
Kaspersky, 410
Keitel, Wilhelm von, 65
Kelly, Petra, 271
Kennan, George, 64
Kennedy, Edward, 294, 296
KGB, 43; AIDS and, 304–11, *305*;

AM funding of CIA compared
to, 323; AM goals of, 149; anti-
Semitic campaigns of, *125*, 129–33;
Chernobyl disaster letter forgery
and, 318–19; "Christian-Marxist"
dialogue workshops and, 278–79;
Department D, 130–31, 137, 145–46,
149–50; disinforming itself, 45; end
of, 336; FALLEX 62 and, 150–51;
First Chief Directorate building
of, 243–44, *244*; forgery and, 103,
106, 113–15; *Headquarters Germany*
and, 323–26, *324*; "Information
Books No. 1" leak and, 266–69;
Johnson, R. L., and, 190–93; neutron
bomb campaign of, 257–61; nuclear
winter and, 291–92; Penkovsky and,
169, 174–75; Putin in, 330; racial
engineering and, 134–41, *135*, *139*,
140; *Schlagzeug* forged by, 113–15;
self-disinformation and, 296–97;
silent measures and, 10; *Stern* and,
190; STORM operation of, 180, 198,
458n1; Strauss campaign by, 151–56;
Who's Who in CIA and, 178–79; Wolfe,
A., and, 280; World Peace Council
and, 261–62, 280; *see also* Service A
KGB (Barron), 216–19, *217*
KgU, *see* Kampfgruppe gegen
Unmenschlichkeit
KgU-Archiv, 79
Khrushchev, Nikita, 42–43, 92,
107–109, 130, 136, 171–72
Kiesinger, Kurt Georg, 184
killer mosquitoes story, 298–301
Kinsman, Richard, 242
Kissinger, Henry, 226, 227
KKK (Ku Klux Klan) leaflets, *135*,
135–36
Klatsch, 90

Klitschko, Vitali, 352
KMHITHER-C, 181
Knabe, Hubertus, 469n4
Knaust, Hans, 202
Kohl, Helmut, 208–10
Kolyarny, Oleg, 356–57
kompromat, 332
Kondrashev, Sergei, 43–44, 132, 245
Konkret, 183
Kopp, Horst, 204–206, 424–25, 429, 435
Koucky, Vladimir, 155
Koval, Nikolay, 360–61
Kreuth operation, 212–13
Kruisinga, Roelof, 258
Kryuchkov, Vladimir, 245
Ku Klux Klan (KKK) leaflets, 135, 135–36
Kupin, Ivan, 171

L

Labarca, Eduardo, 247, 247–48
Labaychuk, Vasyl, 355–56
La Guardia, Fiorello, 52
law enforcement, 10–11, 47
LCCASSOCK: administrative harassment operations of, 90; astrology and, 90–92; closure of, 100; costs of, 89, 96–97; cover businesses of, 70, 87; effectiveness of, 88–89, 91, 93–94, 97; forgery and, 70–73, 87–89, 92; Die Frau and, 97, 98; Klatsch and, 90; mail censorship and, 82, 87; Marbach and, 72, 86–87, 97–99; Nazis exposed by, 99, 99–100; objective of, 85–87; risks of, 88, 89; Schlagzeug and, 94, 94–97, 96, 113–15
LCPROWL, 181
le Carré, John, 172
Lenin, Vladimir, 19, 313, 314–17
Leonov, Vadim, 275

Levchenko, Stanislav, 43, 53, 260, 286, 297, 443n20
liberal democracies, 6, 10–11, 176
Liberator, The, 134
Linse, Walter, 68–69, 87
Literaturnaya Gazeta, 223, 298–300, 299, 307
Los Angeles Times, 164, 177, 256
Loskutov, Dmitry, 349–50
Lu, Chris, 486n4
Lüdke, Hermann, 184
lujkov.ru, 332
Lukashev, Aleksey, 378, 378–81, 391–92
Lumumba, Patrice, 308
Luns, Joseph, 259–60
Luzhkov, Yury, 332
Lyons, John, 49

M

Mader, Julius, 176–79
mail censorship, 82, 87
Mailer, Norman, 220, 222, 224
Mailgram operation, 252–54
Malaysia Airlines disaster, 364
Malik, Jacob, 110–11, 113
Manafort, Paul, 396
Manchuria, 33, 37, 39, 46
Mandia, Kevin, 3–4
Manning, Chelsea, 13, 339
Mao Tse Tung, 66
Marbach, Karl-Heinz, 71–72, 86, 86–87, 92, 97–100
Marcos, Ferdinand, 237
Marshall Plan, 64
MARS operation: assessment of, 286–87; Forsberg as target of, 281; Generals for Peace and, 264, 270–73, 282–83; "Information Books No. 1" leak and, 266–69; origins of, 264–65; scale of, 273–75

Maule, Henry, 451*n27*
Mayer, René, 119
McCarthy, Eugene, 177
McElroy, Neil, 108
McMahon, John, 261–62
Meany, George, 177
Meinhof, Ulrike, 183
Meir, Golda, 141
Merck, 420
Merkel, Angela, 341–44, *342*, 350
Merkulov, Vladimir, 274
Meyer, Max, 126
MfS, *see* Stasi
MH17.doc, 364
MI6, 27, 90, 168–69, 174, 184, 296
Mielke, Erich, 198
military deception, 8, 438*n7*
military psychosis theory, 108–109
Mindiyarov, Marat, 401
Ministry for All-German Affairs (Kaiser ministry), 83–84
Ministry of State Security, *see* Stasi
Minority of One, The, 139–41
Mitrione, Daniel A., 215–16
Mitte, Die, 210
MKULTRA experiments, 304
Møller-Maersk, 420
monarchist émigrés (Whites), 19–24, 27–28
Monarchist Organization of Central Russia (MOTsR), 23, 25–31, 439*n11*
Monde, Le, 156–57, 371–72
Mondelēz International, 420
Moonlight Maze, 5
Moore, Pamela (sock puppet), 404–405, *405*
Morgan, Vernon, 109
Moro, Aldo, *232*, 238–39
Mossack Fonseca, 381
Motherboard, 391

MOTsR (Monarchist Organization of Central Russia), 23, 25–31, 439*n11*
Mulligan, Gerry, 95
Murphy, David, 176
Mut, 201
Mutz, Wolfgang, 308–309

N

Nair, Kunhanandan, 475*n34*
Nannen, Henri, 190, 191–93
Nation, The, 279
National-European Youth Congress, 201–202
National Review, 153
National Security Agency (NSA), 177; ANT catalog and, 347–48; ETERNALBLUE and, 416, 418–19, 421; leak of hacking tools from, 410–13, 417; Merkel spied on by, 341–44; NotPetya attack and, *411*, 419–21; Shadow Brokers and, 413–16; Snowden and, 339–41; Tailored Access Operations of, 411, 490*n31*; zero-days and, 416
Nation Europa, 201
Natsios, Deborah, 337
Nazi gold hunts, 157, 164
Nazis, *99*, 99–100, 123–26, *124*, 128, 132, 201–202, 451*n29*; *see also* Kampfverband für Unabhängiges Deutschland
NEPTUN operation: Bittman and, 157–58, *159*, 160; Cyrillic notes and, 162–63, *164*; documents for, 159–60, *161*; forgery and, 158, 162; impact of, 164–65; international press and, 163–64; mock discovery in, 160–61, *161*; myth creation in, 161–62; objectives of, 158–59
Netherlands, the, 274–75

Netyksho, Viktor, 377–79
Neue Nachhut, Die, 211–12
Neuer Weg, 88
Neues Deutschland, 69, *104*, 104–106, 108–109, 112, 128, 177, 199, 427
Neue Zeit, 88
neutron bomb, 255–62, *259*, 274–75
New American, The, 201
Newens, Stan, 266
New Statesman, 268
Newsweek, 368, 369
New Yorker, The, 340
New York Post, 390
New York Times, The, 39, 50, 56, 65, 106, 111, 127, 136, 199, 218, 255, 282, 285, 294, 301–302, 308, 334, 402, 408
Nieuwe, De, 260
Niezbrzycki, Jerzy, 32
1984 (Orwell), 221, 322
Nixon, Richard, 304
Norden, Albert, 265
North Korea, 418–19
NotPetya attacks, *411*, 419–21
Novoe Russkoe Slovo, 55
NSA, *see* National Security Agency
nuclear disarmament, 278, 281–85
nuclear war threats, 108–13, 150–51, 182, 265, *289*; *see also* neutron bomb
Nuclear Weapons Freeze Campaign, 279
nuclear winter: Alexandrov and, 292–97; CIA on, 290; KGB and, 291–92; scenarios of, 288–90, 294; self-disinformation and, 296–97; TTAPS project and, 290–91, 294–95
Nuland, Victoria, *337*, 348–50

O

Obama, Barack, 341, 343–44
Office of Strategic Services, 63–64

OGPU (Joint State Political Directorate), 28, 30, 34–35, 37, 46
Olympic Games, 201–202, 312–13
Operation GRAVEYARD, 65, 66
Operations Plan (OPLAN) 10-1: authenticity of, 183–84; forgery added to, *185*, 186–87, 189; Johnson, R. L., leaking, 190–93; nuclear war and, 182; publication of, 183; STORM operation and, 458n1; target list of, 180–81, 191–92, *193*, 459n38; Wendland's suicide and, 184–90
Opperput, Edward, 30
#OpSaudi, 372–74, 484n51
oral disinformation, 249–51
Organization Gehlen, 73
Orme, Stan, 266
Orwell, George, 221, 322
Osborn, K. Barton, 220, 221
O'Shaughnessy, Elim, 116, 120, 137
Ovchinnikov, Leonid, 274

P

Paese Sera, 183
Pahl-Rugenstein, 272
Pakistan, 249–51, *250*
Panama Papers, 381–82
Pan-Pacific Worker magazine, 38
Parteiarbeiter, Der, 78
Paseman, Floyd Lisle, 325
Pasti, Nino, 270–71
Patriot, 303–304, 307–308
Patzelt, Herbert, 200
Peace Courier, 273
Peace News, 183, 189, 427
peacewar (Friedenskampf): Arbeitskreis and, 277; Bertrand Russell Peace Foundation protests and, 265–66; "Christian-Marxist" dialogue workshops and, 278–79;

peacewar (Friedenskampf) (*cont.*)
Gailat and, 269–70; Generals for
Peace and, *264*, 270–73, 282–83;
"Holocaust Again for Europe" and,
266, 471*n43*; HVA and, 197–98;
"Information Books No. 1" leak and,
266–69; nuclear disarmament and,
278, 281–85; Stasi and, 197–98, 263,
273, 276–77, 286–87; World Peace
Council and, 275–76, *276*; *see also*
MARS operation
Peck, Winslow, *see* Fellwock, Perry
Penkovsky, Oleg, *168*, 168–76
Penkovsky Papers, The, 170–75
Pentagon Papers, 219
Petersen, Arne Herløv, 274
Petras, Ehrenfried, 199
Petrova, Evdokia, 130
Pflimlin, Pierre, 119
Pforzheimer, Walter, 17
Philippines, 236–37
Phish Tank, 392
Phoenix Program, CIA, 220
Pinochet, Augusto, 247–48
Pleven, René, 119
Podesta, John, 379–80, 384, 386,
388–91, 395, 485–86*n26*
Poland, 30–32, 253, 322
political exposures, 317
political warfare, 6–8, 12–14, 62, 64–68,
72, 77, 82–85, 92, 97, 101, 176, 220,
283, 321, 323, 352, 438*n7*, 443*n1*
Ponomarev, Boris, 153–54, 155, 281
Poroshenko, Petro, 361, 363
postmodernism, 427–30
Potapov, Nikolai, 26
Power, Thomas, 112
Prats, Carlos, *247*, 247–48
Pravda, 35
PR Cramer, *see* LCCASSOCK

Prigozhin, Yevgeny, 399, 408–409
Primakov, Yevgeny, 44, 311
Protocols of the Elders of Zion, 103
Protsyk, Igor, 354–59, *356*
Putin, Vladimir, 330–31, 346, 381–82,
415
putin-president.da.ru, 332
Pyatt, Geoffrey, *337*, 348–49
Pym, Francis, 266

Q

Qabas, Al-, 43, 106
QRPLUMB operation, 321–23

R

RACER operation, 207–208
racial engineering, 134–41, *135*, *139*,
140, 403–404
Radio Moscow, 106, 107, 109, 112, 115,
121, 140, 238, 248, 307
Radio Pakistan, 249
Ramparts, 189–90, 220
Rather, Dan, 310
Ray, Ellen, 239–40
Reader's Digest, 280, 285
Reagan, Ronald, 273, 284–86
Reckitt Benckiser, 420
redaction errors, 449*n24*
Red Brigades, 237–39
Redford, Robert, *62*
Reformatorisch Dagblad, 275
Reilly, Sydney, 22, 27–28
Reports from the Soviet Occupied Zone, 79
"Return to Kreuth" paper, 213
Reuter, Ernst, 76
Rice, Condoleezza, 390
Rice, Susan, 343
Ricketts, Angela, 368–69
Rickover, Hyman, 282
RIGAS operation, 206–208, *207*

Rockefeller, Nelson, 104–106
Rockefeller letter, *104*, 104–106, 111–12
Rogozin, Dmitry, 349
Romanov, Nikolai Nikolayevich, 23, 26
Romerstein, Herbert, 319–20, *320*, 443n20
Rosen, Pinhas, 127
Rosenbach, Marcel, 342–43
Rosenfeld, Stephen, 172, 175–76
RTR, 329–30
Rusk, Dean, 183
Russia: Anonymous manipulated by, 351–53, 357–58; Crimea annexation and, 353–59; digital leaks orchestrated by, 346–50, 357–58; election interference in Ukraine, 360–63; internet in, 331–32; Malaysia Airlines disaster and, 364; NotPetya attacks denied by, 421; Protsyk's forged emails and, 354–59, *356*; Twitter accounts linked to, 488n33; U.S. 2016 election interference of, 3; *see also* Soviet Union

S
Sabah, 208
Sagan, Carl, 289–90, 294–95
Sakharovsky, Aleksandr, 164
Sanders, Bernie, 383, 393, 394
Sanity, 189, 427
Satter, Raphael, 394
Saudi Arabia, #OpSaudi hack and, 372–74, 484n51
Schaap, William, 239–41
Schelkmann, Rudolf, 211
Schlagzeug, *94*, 94–97, *96*, 113–15
Schlottmann, Bernhard, 128–29
Schmid, Helga, 348–50
Schmidt, Helmut, 270
Schneier, Bruce, 340–41

Schönen, Paul Josef, 124, 128
Schweizer, Robert, 319
Science magazine, 290, 294
SCIENCE operation, 198
Secureworks, 391–92
Segal, Jakob, 308
Segal, Lilli, 308
Seibert, Steffen, 343
Šejna, Jan, 152–53
Selbmann, Fritz, 92
self-disinformation, 156, 296–97
Service A, 145, 162; Agee and, 223, 226–27; AM and, 245, 313–14; external contractors of, 246–47; FM 30-31B and, 235; Mailgram operation of, 252–54; name change of, 428; offices of, 243–44, *244*; oral disinformation and, 249–51; plan types of, 248–49; Prats's diary forgery and, *247*, 247–48; self-disinformation and, 156; *Stern* and, 191; technology and, 251–52; Wendland's suicide and, 184–90
sex tape operations, 329–31, *331*, 335
Shadow Brokers: digital leaks of, 412–13, 415–16; effectiveness of, 414, 422, 435; EQGRP-AUCTION-FILE .ZIP and, 417; ETERNALBLUE and, 416, 418–19, 421; global impact of, 417–18; identity of, 421–22; journalism and, 418; NotPetya attacks and, 419–21; NSA and, 413–16; Williams and, 490n31; zero-days and, 416
Shelepin, Alexander, 130
Shevchenko, Arkady, 261–62
Shively, Charley, 302
Shulgin, Vasily, 28–30, *29*, 32
Shultz, George, 310
Sigl, Rupert, 132
silent measures, 10

Simonov, F. M., 172
Sitnikov, Vassily, 131–32, 150
Skuratov, Yuri, 329–31, *330*, *331*
Smoking Gun, The, 394
Snabe, Jim Hagemann, 420
Snowden, Edward, 12–13, 339–41, 422
sock puppets, 403–406, *405*
SOFACY (APT28, FANCY BEAR), 364,
    365, 368, 370–73, 379, 385
Soldevillad, Carlos Garcia, 118, 119
SOTFE (Support Operations Task
    Force Europe), 182–83, 186
Soviet Union: Afghanistan invaded by,
    299–300; AM budget in, 313; Berlin
    Tunnel and, 70; Bertrand Russell
    Peace Foundation and, 265–66;
    Cheka, 19–23, 25–32; China goals of,
    43–44; Dulles Memorandum forgery
    of, 106–107; España Independiente
    and, 112; German special camps
    of, 61, 63, 65; Hildebrandt and, 78;
    international recognition of, 54;
    military psychosis theory of, 108–109;
    neutron bomb opposition of, 256–57;
    Protocols of the Elders of Zion and,
    103; Rockefeller letter forgery of, *104*,
    104–106, 111–12; SS-20 Saber and,
    265; *see also* Russia
Spain, 237
SPD Intern, 210
special camps in Germany, 61, 63, 65
Speer, Albert, 65
Speidel, Hans, 126
Spencer, David, 302
Spiegel, Der, 151–56, 190–91, 203,
    209–10, 213, 257, 326, 341–44
Spivak, John, 52
Sputnik satellite, 107
Spy Museum, 435
SS-20 Saber, 265

Staadt, Jochen, 469n4
Stampa, La, 309
Stankov, Dimo, 244–45, 251
Starbird, Kate, 431
Stark, Holger, 342–43
Stasi, 68–69, 75, 77, 91–92, 196, 210,
    438n7; on AIDS fears, 303; AM
    history of, 121; election interference
    and, 10; Generals for Peace and, *264*,
    270–73, 282–83; journalism and leak
    strategy of, 195; legacy of, 423–24;
    Mader and, 179; peacewar and,
    197–98, 263, 273, 276–77, 286–87;
    Stern and, 190; Wagenbreth and, 194,
    408; Wagner, L., and, 204–206, *205*;
    ZEUS operation and, 202; *see also*
    Hauptverwaltung Aufklärung
State Political Directorate (GPU), 25, 26
Státní bezpečnost (StB), 122, 147,
    159–66, 178–79; Department 8,
    147–48, 157–62
Steiner, Julius, 203–204
Stenchikov, G., 295–96
Stern, 190, 191–93, 209, 268
Stiller, Werner, 200
Stoiber, Edmund, 213
STORM operation, 180, 198, 458n1
Strasbourg cigar box bomb, 118–20, 122
Strategic Air Command, U.S., *107*,
    107–109
Strategic Review, 151, 153
Strauss, Franz-Josef, 151–56, *152*, 281
Strunk, Arnold, 124, 128
Study of a Master Spy, A (Edwards and
    Dunne), 149–50
Suchasnist, 322
Süddeutsche Zeitung, 127
Suiche, Matt, 418
Sun, The, 335
Sunday Express, 309

support measures, 433
Support Operations Task Force Europe (SOTFE), 182–83, 186
Supreme Monarchist Council, 23–24
SVR (Foreign Intelligence Service), 18–19, 23, 30–32, 44–46, 332–33, 410
swastika vandalism, 123–26, *124*, 128, 132, 451*n29*
Sweden, 252–53
Syria, 417

T
Tailored Access Operations of NSA, 411, 490*n31*
Tait, Matt, 390–91, 416
Tanaka Giichi, *34*, 36–37
Tanaka Memorial, 33, 440*n6*; authorship of, 43; *The China Critic* publishing of, 37; *Click* magazine on, 40–41, *41*; the Comintern and, 38–39; Dzerzhinsky on, 34–35; emotion and, 44–45; first accounts of, 36–37; as forgery, 39, 41–42, 45; Japan denouncing, 41–42; Manchuria invasion and, 37; Trotsky on, 40
Tarantel newspaper, 71
Taussig, Joseph, 40
technofascism, 221–22
Telegraaf, De, 275
Tennessee GOP (sock puppet), 406
terrorism, 234
Thalen, Mikael, 395
Thatcher, Margaret, 274
THC Servers, 382
Thompson, Llewellyn, 173–74
Three Capitals (Shulgin), *29*, 30, 32
Tillich, Ernst, 76
Times of London, The, 103, 189–90
TNT, 420
Tombinski, Jan, 349

Top Secret Documents on U.S. Forces Headquarters in Europe, 266–69
translator project of IRA, 400
transparency activism, 339
Treaty of Rome, 119
Trémeaud, André, 118–19
Trémeaud, Henriette, *117*, 119, 122
Tretyakov, Sergei, 291–92, 332, 333
TRIBUNAL operation, 198
Tribüne, Die, 88
Triunfo, El, 237–39
troll farm, *see* Internet Research Agency
Trotsky, Leon, 34–36, 40, 46
True Blues (Petersen), 274
Trump, Donald, 386, 388, 390, 407
Trust, the: CIA study on, 17–18, 21, 23, 24; Finland and, 26–27; military goals of, 25; MOTsR and, 23, 25–31; Poland and, 30–31; Reilly's death and, 27–28; Shulgin and, 28–30, *29*, 32; SVR study on, 18–19, 23, 30–32; unraveling of, 30; Yakushev interrogation and, 21–23
TTAPS project, 290–91, 294–95
Turco, Richard, 295
Turkish guest workers, 206–208, *207*
TV5/Monde, 368, 370, 371
Twitter, 332, 333, 367–68, 385, 390, 392–95, 406, 407, 488*n33*

U
UfJ (Untersuchungsausschuss freiheitlicher Juristen), 67–70, 72
Ukraine: Anonymous Ukraine and, 346–47, 351, 354, 357–58; CEC attack in, 360–63; CERT in, 362–63; civil war in, 359, 366; Crimea annexation and, 353–59; EU and, 346–47; "Euromaidan" protest movement in,

Ukraine (*cont.*)
353; NotPetya attack on, 419–20; Protsyk's forged emails and, 354–59, 356; Russian election interference in, 360–63; Russian-orchestrated digital leaks and, 346–50, 357–58
Ukrainian Supreme Liberation Council/Foreign Representation (ZP/UHVR), 321–23
Ulbricht, Walter, 128
UN (United Nations), 63, 135–36, 258, 278–79, 282–83, 291, 299–300, 310
Unemployment Day demonstrations of 1930, 48
Unit 26165, GRU, 377–79, 382, 384
Unit 74455, GRU, 353, 384, 387, 393
United Nations (UN), 63, 135–36, 258, 278–79, 282–83, 291, 299–300, 310
United States (U.S.): American Communist Party in, 280; Berlin Airlift and, 64; CyberCaliphate attack against, 366–69, 367; digital leaks exposing EU and, 348–50; election interference of 2016 response of, 414–15; FSB sanctions from, 415; Global War Plan for Clandestine Operations of, 182–83; guerrilla units of, 182; IRA's research on, 400–402; military psychosis theory and, 108–109; neutron bomb and, 255–59; NotPetya attack against, 420–21; Philippines assistance from, 236–37; Poland monitored by, 253; racial engineering and, 137–39, 139, 140; Russian interference in 2016 election of, 3; Strategic Air Command of, 107, 107–109; Vietnam War and, 140–41, 198, 220, 240; *see also* Central Intelligence Agency
United States Peace Council, 280

Untersuchungsausschuss freiheitlicher Juristen (UfJ), 67–70, 72
U.S., *see* United States

V
Valentini, Giovanni, 239
Vechernyaya Moskva, 257
V for Vendetta, 344
vida por la legalidad, Una (Prats), 247, 247–48
Vietnam War, 140–41, 198, 220, 240
VirusTotal, 364
Voice of Russia, 358
Volkskrant, De, 260
Volkspolizei, Die, 72, 87
Von Herz zu Herz newsletter, 97
Vosjoli, Philippe de, 184
VX, 199

W
Wachtmeister, Wilhelm, 253
Wadsworth, James, 136
Wagenbreth, Rolf, 194–96, 195, 201–206, 212–14, 315, 336, 399, 408, 435
Wagner, Leo, 203–206, 205
Wagner, Max, 50–56
Wahrheit, Die, 78
WannaCry virus, 418–19
Warner, Mark, 4
Washington Post, The, 41, 109, 113, 170, 172–73, 177, 199, 247, 285, 386, 409
Wasserman Schultz, Debbie, 394
Watergate scandal, 219
Wegweiser, Der, 88
Weinberger, Caspar, 295–96
Welch, Richard, 216, 224–26
Wendland, Horst, 184–90
Wessel, Gerhard, 211
West, Kanye, 311
Western Union, 252–54

Whalen, Grover A., 47–49, *48*, 50–57
Whales, William Stanley, 110–11
What Is to Be Done? (Lenin), 316–17
Whites (monarchist émigrés), 19–24, 27–28
Whole Earth Catalog, 221, 232
Whole Spy Catalog, The, 221
Who's Who in CIA, 176–79, 215, 217, 222–23
Why We Fight (1944), 42
Wiesenthal, Simon, 161–62
WikiLeaks, 10, 338–39, 373–74, 386, 388–93, 484*n*51, 485–86*n*26
Williams, Jake, 490*n*31
Wired magazine, 12–13, 334
Wisner, Frank, 64–66, 115
Wochenpost, Die, 88, 89
Wolf, Louis, 239–42
Wolf, Markus, 132, 166, 196–97, 199, 272–73, 276, 283, 452*n*42
Wolfe, Alan, 279–80
Woll, Matthew, 54
Working Group for a Nuclear-Weapons-Free Europe (Arbeitskreis), 277
World Marxist Review, 239
World Peace Council, 258, 261–62, 270, 275–76, *276*, 280
World Peace Movement, 42
World War II, 42, 61, 63, 65, 130–31
Wrangel, Pyotr, 24–25

X
X, the, *see* Department X
X-Agent kit, 382
X-Informationen, 210–11

Y
Yakushev, Alexander, 20–31
Yanukovych, Victor, 347, 350, 353
Yarosh, Dmytro, 361, 363
Yefremov, Alexander, 155
Yeltsin, Boris, 329, 331
Young, John, 337–39
YouTube, 332, 333

Z
Zapevalov, Vitaly, 307
Zavgorodny, Leonid, 155
Zeit, Die, 118
zero-days, 416
ZEUS operation, 201–202
Zeynalova, Irada, 361
Zia-ul-Haq, Muhammad, 249
Zind, Ludwig, 131
Zinoviev letter, 8
Zluva, Vaclav, 319–20
Znamya, 103
Zorza, Victor, 173, 175
ZP/UHVR (Ukrainian Supreme Liberation Council/Foreign Representation), 321–23

A NOTE ABOUT THE AUTHOR

Thomas Rid is an information security professor at Johns Hopkins University. He testified about disinformation before the U.S. Senate Select Committee on Intelligence.